The History of Creighton University
1878–2003

The History of

Creighton University

1878–2003

Dennis N. Mihelich

PRESIDENTIAL SERIES

Creighton University Press

OMAHA, NEBRASKA

Association of Jesuit University Presses

Library of Congress Cataloging-in-Publication Data

Mihelich, Dennis N.
The History of Creighton University, 1878-2003 / by Dennis Mihelich.
p. cm.
Includes bibliographical references and index.
ISBN 1-881871-48-7 (cloth)
ISBN 1-881871-53-3 (paper)
1. Creighton University--History. I. Title.
LD1401.C752M54 2005
378.782'254--dc22
2005022379

EDITORIAL
Creighton University Press
2500 California Plaza
Omaha, Nebraska 68178

MARKETING AND DISTRIBUTION
Fordham University Press
University Box L
Bronx, New York 10458

Presidential Series

Printed in the United States of America

To the Society of Jesus, and

To the dedicated lay faculty, staff, and administrators,
who have aided its educational apostolate, and

To the alumni who have lived the values of the mission.

Contents

Foreword

The History of Creighton University: 1878–2003 was commissioned to celebrate and commemorate the one hundred and twenty fifth anniversary of the founding of this institution and its subsequent development and accomplishments.

In reality, it was only the Creighton College of Arts and Sciences that achieved this historic 125-year landmark in 2003–04. The complex institution of today was probably not what Mary Lucretia Creighton had in mind when her estate, in 1877, provided that a college be established "known as Creighton University."

Her brother-in-law, Count John Creighton, contributed to the enhancement of that original foundation by adding four professional schools and a teaching hospital, all of which have celebrated their centennials: medicine (1991), law (2004), dental (2005), and pharmacy and health professions (2005). Other schools and colleges have been added across the decades.

When I asked Dr. Dennis Mihelich, a Creighton faculty colleague, to undertake the task of writing the *History of Creighton University*, I was confident he would accomplish this request with his traditional thorough and thoughtful professionalism. He notes in the Preface that he "kept the student in the forefront" of his work. I would expect nothing less from a lifelong teacher. His inspiration played to my bias: namely, that Creighton exists for students and for learning, or it does not exist.

As I recalled the Creighton University story, I saw a story of a family, a faith, a commitment to education and care for the sick, and the story of a frontier town. In the pages that follow, the Creighton family is seen as pioneering, visionary, entrepreneurial, and philanthropic. As Irish immigrants, their Roman Catholic faith was the guiding principle that inspired them to support education and health care. The Creighton family was instrumental in transforming Omaha from a post–Civil War river town to a prosperous late-nineteenth-century city. Their benevolence toward Omaha endures today in Creighton University's affection for, service to, and participation in the life of our host community.

When the Jesuits (the Society of Jesus) came to Omaha in 1878 to undertake the nascent Creighton University, they brought with them an essential identity and mission that had survived the vicissitudes and changes of over three centuries. The Jesuits' arrival was the beginning of a love affair between institution and mission, between students and professors, between university and city. Across six score and more years Creighton graduates—from all programs—have worked to make ours a better city, nation, and world. Our graduates have been, and continue to be, generous in intellect and community service, crafters of a more just society, and are women and men for and with others. They continue to serve the Church, their respective communities and the nation in their chosen careers in the arts, education, health care, business, the law, public service, or ministry.

Every Creighton graduate has a special place in her or his heart for a teacher—Jesuit or not—who personified the values of the institution. They also have, I believe, a special place in their hearts for the institution that shaped them to be the women and men they have come to be.

This is the story that unfolds in these pages. To be sure, it is a history, but a history that continues to live and breathe and inspire the next generation. The legacy of the Creighton family, the fidelity of Creighton's institutional commitment to its Catholic and Jesuit heritage, and the response and service of our graduates give great credence to the story that unfolds and the story yet to be told. The Creighton University chronicled in these pages is the bedrock and the inspiration for the Creighton of tomorrow.

AD MAJOREM DEI GLORIAM

John P. Schlegel, S.J.
President
Creighton University

Preface

Universities emerged in the twelfth century as corporations of students that hired scholars to teach them. That model directed my approach in writing this history. I tried to keep the student in the forefront of the story—at any given point in time, what characteristics established the parameters of college life? Then I sought to analyze the evolving nature and role of the faculty, to examine the emergence and development of the administrative bureaucracy, and, finally, to describe the physical development of the campus. The chronology does not follow the artificial scaffolding of administrative tenure (presidents or deans); general reading showed three distinct periods in the University's history, based on cataclysmic events and on social, economic, and pedagogical forces. Moreover, the records revealed a process of assimilation; that is, similar to the generational acculturation and integration of European immigrant families, a foreign institution—the Society of Jesus and its pedagogy, the *Ratio Studiorum*—had to assimilate, first culturally (e.g., speak English), then structurally (equal access to the basic political, social, and economic institutions), into the United States. That process of "becoming American" necessitates the immigrant's desire for inclusion and a willingness on the part of the dominant group to accept the migrant.

I researched and wrote Part 1, 1878–1920 (a scarcity of records), and then followed the same pattern for Part 2, 1920–1950 (the scarcity of records persisted). Having established my thesis, while completing the research for Part 3, 1950–present (a surfeit of records), a new book appeared with a cogent analysis of Catholic (especially Jesuit) education during the late-nineteenth-early-twentieth centuries in the United States. In *Catholic Higher Education in Protestant America*, Kathleen A. Mahoney delineated "the challenges faced by Catholics in the closing decades of the nineteenth century as the age of the university opened: how liberal Protestant leaders of the university movement linked the newly created modern university with the cause of a Protestant America, and how Catholic students and educators variously resisted, accommodated, or embraced Protestant-inspired educational reforms during this revolutionary era in higher education." Moreover, in that struggle, she posited a seminal event: the decision, in 1893, by Harvard University President Charles W. Eliot and the faculty of the Harvard Law School to omit Jesuit universities from its select list of colleges, whose graduates could gain admission without the requirement of taking an entrance examination. Obviously, the policy relegated Jesuit education to an inferior status and it instigated a three-decade conflict, which concluded with the Jesuits accepting American-style education.

Mahoney concentrated her analysis on Jesuit schools located in Atlantic coastal states. My research focused on the historic Missouri Province; at the time, Cincinnati to Denver, Milwaukee to Kansas City. Until the 1950s, the provincials, with the blessing of the superior general, controlled the curriculum of the educational institutions in their provinces. During the late-nineteenth century, Creighton sat on the edge of the "last frontier." Its first graduating class, in 1891, had five students, and the following year, no one received a baccalaureate degree. The Harvard Law School policy had no impact on the University. Nonetheless, Charles Eliot did provide the flashpoint in the pedagogical wars for the schools of the Missouri Province. In an article in the October 1899 issue of *Atlantic Monthly*, he promoted his concept of an elective curriculum (no required classes) and denigrated "unchanging" Jesuit education. The Jesuits of the Missouri Province responded with a thirteen-point argument that attacked "electivism" during the undergraduate years and defended a required "course of study" and the centrality of religion in education. For the following two decades, Creighton published that manifesto in its annual catalogue.

Moreover, while Protestantism provided the vital center to American life, other secular forces influenced the evolution of education at Creighton. For example, before World War I, state regulation of teacher certification brought the first accreditation team to the University and induced it to create the summer school to provide nuns with the education to meet the new standards. Laywomen also flocked to the summer school, producing a revolution—Jesuits teaching women—that began the transformation to American coeducation (a pragmatic money-saving mechanism). Additionally, American pragmatism demanded a job-related education, which resulted in the concept of the "terminal" high-school diploma. The secular American distaste for "useless" classical languages and the independent high school contributed to the demise of the *Ratio Studiorum*. In *Contending with Modernity*, Philip Gleason argued that those secular forces occasioned an "organizational crisis," which resulted in "rationalizing the Catholic System." Among the Jesuits, the Missouri Province rationalized (Americanized) first. Thus, without acceding to Turner's Frontier Thesis, a distinctive environment in the Missouri Province produced a distinctive history for Creighton University as it underwent the process of assimilation—of becoming American.

The Reverend John P. Schlegel, S.J., president of Creighton University, commissioned this book and supported my research with release time and travel expenses. I thank him for his confidence in me and I hope the product meets his expectations. Because no historical monograph existed, Fr. Schlegel asked me to write a history of Creighton University, although only the Creighton College of Arts and Sciences celebrated its 125th anniversary in 2003. I do not possess a personal knowledge of business, legal, or health-sciences education; secondary sources provided the general trends of the various professions and I attempted to blend the histories of the diverse schools into a general narrative. I strove to produce a concise account of the significant elements in the growth of each professional school and placed the emphasis on the arts college—the home of the Jesuits and the *Ratio Studiorum*. In addition, despite the paucity of primary sources, I believe I have written thorough biographical sketches of the Creighton family and of the history of the University up to the 1970s. The last two chapters contain panoramic views of an increasingly complex institution. They coincide with my tenure at Creighton and report on the actions of many living participants in the story. To complete what could have become interminable research, and for the sake of symmetry and succinctness (one volume that fits in one hand), those chapters lack detailed analysis and interpretation. The era awaits the scrutiny of the historian that writes the sesquicentennial or bicentennial volume.

I have an extended list of people to whom I want to express thanks. Reversing the traditional order of acknowledgments, I thank my wife, Joanne, and my daughter, Heidi, for their encouragement and support. Stephen Kline, then director of public relations, and Bryan LeBeau, Ph.D., former chairman of the history department, aided my initial efforts. Julie Fox (history) supplied essential administrative support and Sally Komrofsky (President's office) provided exceptional assistance, coordinated activities, and served as my go-to person (always with her patented smile). General Counsel Greg Jahn imparted significant information and a copy of his father's memoirs. Judge Patrick Lynch shared his memories and his treasure chest of pre–World War I memorabilia. Benjamin Lynch, D.D.S., and Terry Wilwerding, D.D.S., gave insight into the operation of the dental school, and Oliver Pollak, Ph.D., J.D. (1982), and Ronald Volkmer (A.B., 1966; J.D., 1968) did so for the law school. Alumni Office staff, Michelle Cook, Kathy Niedermyer, and Sarah Marie Wootton, graciously fulfilled my frequent telephone requests for information. Hughleen Thorsen (B.A., 1996) perused the Duchesne archives on my behalf. Marsha Botos, formerly of the Office of International Programs, Michael Lawler, Ph.D., theology, and Jayne Schram, development office, read parts of the manuscript and made helpful suggestions. Professor and former dean Rodney Shkolnick reviewed and commented on the law school segments of the chapters of Part III; with his trademark thoroughness and exceptional insight, University professor Robert Heaney (B.S., 1947; M.D., 1951) performed a similar task for the health-sciences sections. Mary Helen "Monnie" Lindsay (B.A., 1977) patiently listened to long monologues pertaining to the research and asked thought-provoking questions, as well as provided sharp-eyed proofreading.

Creighton Reinert Alumni Library staff provided yeomen service: Jennifer Campbell, government documents; Gerry Chase and David Buffington, circulation; Deb Ham, serials; Tom Hassing, PC network technician; Mary Nash, head of reference; Lynn Schneiderman, interlibrary loan; and Debra Sturges, head of access services. Marge Wannarke, who joined the staff of the Medical School Library in 1952, remained its director for thirty-nine years, and since 1991 has served as archivist, directed me through the cramped maze of mysteriously catalogued materials in the "tomb" (i.e., the archives). At the Douglas County Historical Society, Monica Geier, Rita Jerins, and Diedra Routt guided me through its collection. The Reverend Michael Gutgsell shepherded me through the archive of the Catholic Archdiocese of Omaha. Anonymous research staff of the Ohio Historical Society efficiently answered my e-mail requests and delivered materials via "snail mail"; similarly, reference staff at the Cowboy Hall of Fame granted access to the Edward Creighton file. Noah Himes, reference division of the Western Reserve Historical Society (Cleveland, Ohio), aided my research there and Alison L. Oswald, archivist at the Smithsonian Institution, provided materials from the Western Union Telegraph Company records. Archivist Andrea Fahling and her staff at the Nebraska State Historical Society helped me uncover materials related to the Creighton brothers, as did Cynthia Monroe, the former director of the (cattle) brands commission for the State of Nebraska. The Reverend William L. Mugan, S.J., archivist, Nancy Merz, associate archivist, and Mary Struckel, staff, at the Midwest Jesuit Archives supplied invaluable assistance. Two colleagues in the history department assumed particular research assignments pertaining to the ROTC and to intercollegiate athletics at Creighton since 1920:

> Reared in the Pacific Coast states, William A. Sherrard earned a Bachelor of Arts from the University of Washington in anthropology, a Master of Arts from the University of Colorado in political science, and a Doctor of Philosophy from the University of Nebraska in history. His college teaching career began in 1972 at the University of Colorado and progressed through five other academic institutions before coming to Creighton University in 1990. He has received numerous teaching awards from these institutions. Before and during these academic endeavors Dr. Sherrard had a twenty-two year career (1962–1984) in the United States Air Force, which included a tour in Vietnam (1968–1969), reaching the rank of Lieutenant Colonel. This experience proved particularly beneficial to his contribution to this book.

> Born and raised near Bridgeville, Pennsylvania, Angelo J. Louisa earned his Bachelor of Arts degree, magna cum laude, in history from Saint Vincent College, his Master of Arts in early modern European history from Duquesne University, and his Doctor of Philosophy in Tudor-Stuart English history from the University of Minnesota. The recipient of four teaching awards, Dr. Louisa has taught at seven academic institutions, served as assistant to the Minnesota State Director of the National History Day program, and is a member of the Nebraska State Historical Records Advisory Board. He has presented papers and lectures to various academic and public groups, contributed entries to *The Harper Encyclopedia of Military Biography*, published articles in *Deadball Stars of the National League*, the *Oxford Dictionary of National Biography*, and *Sport in American Culture: From Ali to X-Games*, and authored, with Robert Nash, an article for *Nebraska History*. A faculty member at Creighton University since 1999, Dr. Louisa resides in Omaha with his wife, Pamela, a Senior Instructional Designer for First Data Resources, and is currently editing, with David Cicotello, a book on Forbes Field." For their research assistance, he thanks John Anderson, Jennifer Burns, Alexis Janda, Pamela Louisa, John Mitchell, Kathleen Morgan, Mary Nash, Lauren Petit, and Kathy Piere.

With appreciation,
DNM, May 11, 2005

PART ONE

Americanization

Early in the nineteenth century, an Irish mother and her seven children migrated to the United States. By mid-century, all the male children had changed their family name to Creighton and had become successful landowners in Ohio. The oldest sibling, James, had nine offspring, including Edward and John, the founders of Creighton University. The brothers migrated to the frontier town of Omaha and became wealthy businessmen and philanthropists. The family odyssey included assimilation in a new country and the attainment of the American Dream.

Edward's money established Creighton College and John's beneficence enlarged it to a five-school university. The Jesuits administered the institution, following the undergraduate educational method, the *Ratio Studiorum*, a seven-year program stressing classical languages and texts, as well as Thomist theology, anticipated by St. Ignatius of Loyola. While the professional schools immediately adopted the American form of education, like other "immigrants," the European *Ratio* had to "Americanize" to succeed in the United States. American parents and students demanded a "practical" curriculum, states created standalone four-year high schools, and accrediting agencies set standards for collegiate certification. Between 1878 and 1920, Creighton College assimilated culturally; in the latter year, it adopted a curriculum entitled, "The American Plan." The nomenclature broadcast its entrance into the American culture. However, it failed to assimilate structurally; its attempts to present itself as an integral part of the Omaha community, deserving of support from the general populous and the non-Catholic business community, did not elicit a welcoming response.

CHAPTER 1

The Founders

The Progenitors

In 1937, one John B. Creighton, a descendant of the founders of Creighton University, wrote to the institution's president, the Reverend Thomas Bowdern, S.J., and recommended an artist to paint the family coat of arms for the school's President's Room. He identified the crest through genealogy and heraldry, and traced it to a family of Scottish aristocrats who migrated to Ireland in the seventeenth century. Fr. Bowdern commissioned the work; however, the original surname of the founders of the University was not Creighton.[1]

The University bears the name of a family with many branches. Genealogists have discovered several ethnic origins and many root spellings. The various surnames are common throughout the United Kingdom and they may combine Gaelic or Anglo-Saxon words meaning either a bend and a town, or a creek and a farm. During the seventeenth century some Crichtons (Cr-eye-ton) migrated from Scotland to Ireland where they encountered phonetic relatives with different derivative spellings: Creighan, Creaghan (Cr-ay-an), O'Criochan (O-cree-han), Creaton, Creighton (Cr-ay-ton), and similar sounding names starting with G. The aristocratic Scottish Crichtons and the Irish Creightons used the same family crest, a fire-spitting dragon with the motto "God Send Grace," which seemingly indicated a common ancestry.[2]

Yet, despite numerous claims, the University's founders, Edward Charles Creighton and John Andrew Creighton, belonged to none of those clans and were not the scions of noblemen. Actually, the spelling of their bona fide given name evolved in America. Ship manifest records revealed that on July 16, 1805, their father, one James McCrarin, a laborer from Clontibret Parish, County Monaghan, Ireland, sailed from Newry aboard the Roe Buck bound for Philadelphia. Eight weeks later, a clerk in the City of Brotherly Love recorded the disembarkation of a J. McCraland. Six years thereafter, on October 16, 1811, the Rev. W. V. Harold, pastor of St. Mary's Church, joined in matrimony one James McCraren and Bridget Hughes. Eventually, the inscription on that James's tombstone in Holy Trinity Cemetery in Somerset, Perry County, Ohio, reads:

> In memory of James Creighton a native of the County Monaghan, Ireland, Parish of Clentubrit who departed this life March 5th 1848 Aged sixty years. O good reader pray for me / And if God permits I'll pray for thee. May he rest in peace.[3]

To understand the name transformation, first we must assume the role of the nineteenth-century clerks transcribing the name of, possibly, an illiterate Irish peasant rolling his Rs and elongating his As; thus, the various spellings of the name of the young immigrant. The final version, however, apparently resulted from the conscious decision of one sibling, which the rest of the family eventually adopted. The family matriarch, the forty-seven-year-old mother of James, also named Bridget, and her six other children quickly followed her oldest son to America. As early as 1807, one of her sons entered a land claim in Oxford Township, Guernsey County, Ohio, under the name Christopher McCrearen. Two years later, he married Margaret McKiggan, converted to her Methodist faith, and changed his surname to Creighton. The name choice may have related to his religious conversion; family lore did not preserve his reasoning. However, before birth certificates, driver's licenses, and social security cards, the change simply entailed spelling it thereafter in that fashion. Another brother, Francis, followed suit; he died in Guernsey County, Ohio, in 1816, and in his will, he used the Creighton surname. Living nearby in Belmont County, James and his unmarried brother Andrew (with mother Bridget in his household) also assumed the new name, but an 1820 census taker phonetically recorded their last name as Craton. Finally, in the 1840 census, James appeared as a Creighton. Possibly, by that date, the prominent landowner had learned to spell and sign his name on contracts; any of his nine literate children could have taught him the skill. By then, the whole family lived in southeastern and south central Ohio, and used the Creighton surname; only Christopher, however, abandoned the Catholic Church.[4]

Family tradition claimed that a landlord evicted matriarch Bridget from her Irish farmstead, prompting the migration to the United States. Perhaps the death or desertion of her unnamed and unremembered husband resulted in the loss of a land tenure right. James migrated first, probably to establish a foothold in the new country. Regardless, the family was not destitute; members paid for passage to America, they did not come as indentured servants. They obviously possessed a strong work ethic and took advantage of the opportunities presented to them. They moved west seeking employment and land. All six brothers—James, Francis, Andrew, Christopher, John, and Michael—became landowners in Ohio and their one sister, Mary, married a successful farmer, Michael Brady. Mother Bridget died in 1842, at eighty-four years of age, and was buried in the family plot of her son Michael in Duck Creek Cemetery in Guernsey County, Ohio.[5]

James Creighton married a woman also named Bridget—Bridget Hughes—a first cousin of Archbishop John Hughes of New York. James and his bride migrated to Pittsburgh, Pennsylvania, in 1812. The next year he joined brothers Christopher, Francis, and Michael in Ohio, settling a few miles south of them in Belmont County. Subsequently, Andrew moved near James. All the brothers seemingly took advantage of the recently established Jeffersonian land laws, which sold quarter sections for less than $2.00 an acre. They all avoided higher prices by settling just north of the almost two-million-acre Ohio Company land grant, owned by New England speculators. Adding a bit of confusion to the family history, when the brothers arrived in Ohio they entered a new state with an established, but unrelated, prominent politician named William Creighton, Jr., who had been born in Virginia in 1788.[6]

None of the siblings participated in the War of 1812, but some of them did take advantage of the resumption of the construction of the National Road that came with peace. James and John obtained seasonal employment on the project as it moved west through Ohio during the years 1825 to 1833. John used his earnings to purchase eighty acres in Licking County in 1831. The next year he bought additional land and platted the town of Mount Hope. Then, in 1834, he obtained several lots in the town of Etna in Licking County. Likewise, in 1832, James acquired eighty acres just south of John's original farm. Four years later, he purchased his brother's adjoining farm, and then in 1841, also bought all of John's property in Mount Hope, which included twenty-four lots and a quarter section of land north and west of the town. James obviously had obtained the American Dream.[7]

James and wife Bridget, both of whom became American citizens, had nine children. Alice, their first child, was born in Philadelphia and subsequently married Irish immigrant Thomas McShane in 1839. The newlyweds farmed first near Springfield in Clark County, Ohio, and after 1846, in Perry County near the town of New Lexington. They had ten children, eight of whom would make significant contributions to the history of Omaha. Catherine, youngest daughter of James and Bridget, went to live with her sister Alice; however, she died a year later in 1847. Henry, the first-born son of James and Bridget, became a carpenter, but became an invalid due to a fall from a roof while working in Lexington, Kentucky. He lived his remaining fourteen years on the family farm, dying in 1851. The remaining children of James and Bridget Creighton—Francis, Mary, Edward, Joseph, James, and John—all eventually migrated to Omaha.[8]

Edward Charles Creighton

Edward Charles Creighton, James and Bridget's fifth child, came into this world on August 31, 1820, in Belmont County, Ohio, near the present town of Barnesville. He attended public elementary school and shortly after his tenth birthday, the family moved to Licking County, probably following employment opportunities on the construction of the National Road. Shortly thereafter, that turnpike afforded Edward his start as an entrepreneur. At about age fourteen he became a cart boy delivering goods with his friend Philip Sheridan, who went on to become a celebrated Civil War general. Sheridan's father was the superintendent of the road workers who located in Mount Hope, the town developed by Edward's uncle John. Family folklore revealed, "Even at this early date young Sheridan had merited the sobriquet of 'Fighting Phil.' In those days of strong religious antipathies, young Catholics, and especially young Irish Catholics, were frequently forced into quarrels on the score of religion and race. But neither young Sheridan nor his athletic chum [Edward] was disposed to suffer any reflection on either score; and we are told that in their own way they established their titles to respect at the hands of their bigoted acquaintances."[9]

When Edward turned eighteen his father presented him with a wagon and a team of horses. He commenced hauling freight long distance between Cumberland, Maryland, and Cincinnati, Ohio. Within his first decade in business, he also became involved in ancillary teamster activities such as helping to build roads, like the national stage route between Springfield, Ohio, and Wheeling, [West] Virginia. He also secured contracts for grading city streets and preparing roadbeds for the laying of railroad track. His wagon or wagons (no one documented when and how he accumulated multiple teams) could haul dirt and gravel, as well as transport goods. As he finished a job for the Little Miami Railroad in Clark County, Ohio, he made his first acquaintance with a new piece of technology that would set him on the path to riches. At age twenty-seven, Edward witnessed two Irish-American contractors erecting adjacent segments of a telegraph line under construction near Springfield, Ohio. Moreover, the owner of the company with exclusive rights for that section of the United States was Henry O'Rielly, an Irish immigrant, former newspaper editor, and postmaster of Rochester, New York. Edward joined the company and began supplying and hauling poles for a line linking Springfield to Cincinnati and eventually Louisville, Kentucky. Within the year, he acquired the additional responsibilities of superintending the construction of a line from St. Louis to Alton, Illinois. In 1848, he oversaw the construction of lines from Dayton, Ohio, to Cincinnati; Dayton to Evansville, Ohio, and then on to Lafayette, Indiana; and in his first venture outside the confines of the Northeast, from New Orleans to Aberdeen, Mississippi.[10]

Surely, by this point, Edward invested his money in acquiring multiple teams and hiring gangs of laborers to supply poles (fell trees of the correct girth, cut them to length, strip away branches) and transport them to jobs he superintended. Moreover, if reporters used the accurate word and he obtained the "contract" for the grading job, it would mean that he owned much of the equipment and then hired other teamsters with a wagon or two to fill in if extras were needed. Thus, in the next six years, he oversaw the construction of telegraph lines from Cincinnati to Sandusky, Ohio; Buffalo to New York City; Buffalo to Louisville, Kentucky; and Cleveland to Toledo, Ohio, and then to Chicago. When his father died in 1848, he served as the administrator of his estate. After Henry passed away in 1851, Edward sold the family farm and the Mount Hope properties for the handsome price of $3,300. Mother Bridget and sister Mary went to live near relatives in Springfield, Ohio, while youngest brother John Andrew went off to college.[11]

By the mid-1850s, Edward allied himself with the powerbrokers that created the Western Union Telegraph Company, finally incorporated in 1856, as a result of the merger of competing firms. The early strategy of the new corporation aimed at growth and consolidation through acquisition, which shifted Edward's activity briefly. Thus, in 1855–56, while the business grew through aggrandizement, he undertook grading contracts for streets, first in Toledo, Ohio, and then Keokuk, Iowa, and eventually for a railroad right-of-way near Mexico, Missouri. At the same time, he conducted a "lemon Squeezer" at the behest of Hiram Sibley, the president of Western Union. The maneuver consisted of a pseudo survey designed to force the owners of a telegraph line from New Orleans to Cincinnati to offer favorable leases to

Western Union. Edward traversed the existing line; at strategic locations, he sent messages over it to Sibley, quoting prices on poles and other information designed to make the competitors believe that Western Union planned to erect a parallel line. Quickly, the owners of the New Orleans line ended an exclusive arrangement with a competitor, gave Western Union favorable rates for messages it sent over the New Orleans line, and Western Union agreed not to construct the phantom line.[12]

While Edward completed his southern "survey," Keokuk elected a new city council that revoked his grading contract. Illuminating his business stature at that time, he instructed his brother John Andrew (who now worked for him) to sell his equipment "consisting of some forty teams" and to proceed to the recently established town of Omaha, Nebraska. John sold all but three horses, then traded one of them for a harness and carriage, hitched up the remaining pair and headed west. When he arrived in Omaha on June 10, 1856, he rendezvoused with his brothers James and Joseph, and cousins Harry and James "Long Jim" Creighton. All five of them worked for Edward, who paid them a brief visit before returning to Dayton, Ohio, to marry Lucretia Wareham on October 7, 1856. He was thirty-six years of age and decidedly successful. Immediately after the marriage, the newlyweds traveled to Pittsburgh, where Edward purchased lumber, returning with it to Omaha by steamboat via the Ohio, Mississippi, and Missouri rivers. With the sale of the lumber and the funds garnered from the disposal of the teamster stock at Keokuk, Edward initiated his Omaha business career possessing approximately $25,000 in capital. Exaggerating only slightly, a relative boasted, "From the time Mr. Creighton arrived in Omaha he was its leading citizen. Creighton had the greatest visions of any of the early settlers, and he had force behind him. He was the first wealthy man to settle in Omaha."[13]

Edward transferred his operation to Omaha in anticipation of building a telegraph line to the west coast, an idea in circulation since California entered the Union in 1850. In February 1857, the United States Senate passed a bill to subsidize a telegraph line from Washington, D.C., to San Francisco, but the House of Representatives failed to act in deliberate time. The Panic of 1857 ensued, throwing the economy into a tailspin, and the sectional animosity that produced the Civil War prevented passage of another bill. Thus, the Creighton brothers and cousins had to bide their time in a two-year-old village. Luckily, Edward had surplus cash to tide him over the economic downturn and he actually profited by becoming a creditor; for example, in 1857, he loaned $1,400 to J. Sterling Morton, the future United States Secretary of Agriculture and the founder of Arbor Day. The following year, the local economy began to boom after the discovery of gold in Colorado. The ensuing rush offered exceptional opportunities in outfitting, freighting, and financing. Edward formed an association with Augustus and Herman Kountze; the three of them soon extended their banking operation from 12th and Farnam in Omaha to Denver and Central City, Colorado. The return to prosperity also resulted in the construction of new telegraph lines. Although the records are conflicting, Edward may have contributed to the building of the lines from Jefferson, Missouri, to Ft. Smith, Arkansas, and from St. Joseph, Missouri, to Omaha, the latter finished on October 5, 1860.[14]

Simultaneously, however, other projects occupied his time. On the personal side, he took his wife back to her family in Dayton, Ohio, where she gave birth to a son, Charles David, on April 4, 1859. Lucretia and the baby remained with her parents (the 1860 census recorded the Edward Creighton family as part of the David Wareham household in Dayton), while Edward worked on surveys for a transcontinental telegraph line for Western Union promoters. He advised them against routes originating in Memphis, Tennessee, and Ft. Smith, Arkansas. Finally, on June 16, 1860, Congress passed a bill granting a subsidy of $40,000 per annum for ten years for the construction of a transcontinental telegraph. Edward spent the summer reconnoitering between Omaha and Denver. On July 26, 1860, the *Huntsman's Echo* of Buffalo County, Nebraska, reported that he and "a Mr. Kontz of Omaha" (obviously, one of the Kountze brothers) were in the area examining a route for a telegraph line, and when Edward departed for Denver, Kountze remained to make contracts for poles.[15]

A few months later, Edward returned to Omaha only to leave again on a dangerous solo survey through the Rocky Mountains. He left by stagecoach on November 18, 1860, traveled to Ft. Kearney and Ft. Laramie, through the South Pass to Ft. Bridger, and arrived in Salt Lake City in mid December. There he used the carrot-and-stick method to gain the support of Brigham Young, the leader of the Mormon settlement. The *Deseret News* reported:

> Edward Creighton, esq., the agent of the Pacific telegraph line, arrived here by last mail stage, on Saturday, and is still in the city seemingly puzzled whether to carry the line through Salt Lake City or by way of Santa Fe. He has visited Governor Young, but, I think, failed to particularly interest the gentleman in the enterprise. Mr. Creighton already learned that the Mormon chief's example as a shareholder would influence the community, and without it few shares would be taken here. Unless some such encouragement is given, Mr. C. thinks it very doubtful that the telegraph line will pass through this city, for a time at least. He is receiving proposals for supplying poles for 400 east and the same west, but makes no contracts till further informed by his associate agent who went round by the Isthmus to California, as to matters there.

Ultimately, Edward obtained Young's support and he resumed his journey to meet his partner, Jeptha Wade, who had gone to Sacramento to encourage four feuding companies to merge so they could build the line east through the Sierra Nevada Mountains. With the help of the Pony Express stations, Edward made the grueling 600-mile mule ride from Salt Lake City to Carson City, Nevada, and on to San Francisco by stagecoach. Both he and Wade accomplished their tasks; on March 27, 1861, they began their return trip by sea to New York City. Edward picked up his family in Dayton and on May 25, the Omaha *Daily Telegraph* reported that the steamboat *West Wind* had deposited them in Omaha.[16]

On January 11, 1861, the Nebraska Territorial Legislature passed a bill incorporating the Pacific Telegraph Company. Most of the fifteen incorporators, including Edward Creighton, were Western Union executives. They capitalized the company for $1 million, each share costing $100. Edward subscribed for one thousand shares, one-tenth of the company, but only had to pay about ten percent of face value of the stock. By the time all the arrangements were in place, Edward had to superintend the erection of the line from Julesburg, Colorado, to Salt Lake City. The stipulations of the government subsidy turned the construction into a race, but he won, earning more money for his company. He employed many family members and hired Charles Brown, a twenty-seven-year-old graduate of Williams College, as his bookkeeper, paymaster, and secretary. Brown originally came to Omaha to join his brothers, James J. and R. A., who had migrated to open a mercantile store. He now took charge of meeting boats, verifying orders, warehousing materials, and arranging freighting west. He outfitted nearly four hundred men and purchased over one hundred wagons and five hundred oxen, needed to transport supplies west and to do the collecting, hauling, and erecting of poles at the job site.[17]

As the workforce assembled at Julesburg, the Civil War erupted. None of the Creighton family served in the Union Army; they remained busy out on the frontier. The subsequent conscription law did not affect them since the lightly settled Nebraska Territory provided sufficient volunteers. Probably because of the association with the outbreak of the Civil War, many published accounts claimed the first pole of the transcontinental telegraph was set on July 4, 1861. Brown, however, in his journal entry for July 2, wrote that on that day he helped Edward Creighton dig the hole and hoist the first pole. On Independence Day his entry reads, "The 4th day of July! I wonder if there will be many such for this nation as it is now. Can it preserve itself from disintegration? My prayer is that it may." Three months later the crew worked setting the last poles leading into Salt Lake City; one of Brigham Young's sons supplied those poles. On October 17, 1861, Edward sent his wife a telegram reading, "This being the first message over the new line since its completion to Salt Lake, allow me to greet you. In a few days two oceans will be united." Six days later the builders of the western segment reached the city, implementing the first transcontinental telegraph line. Stephen J. Field, Chief Justice of California, sent a message to Abraham Lincoln to announce the achievement of binding the East with the West and "to express their [the people of California] loyalty to the Union and their determination to stand by its Government on this day of trial."[18]

Edward returned to Omaha and became general superintendent of the Pacific Telegraph Company, which entailed managing its operation, and maintaining the existing line, as well as extending it to new areas of settlement. He briefly entertained the idea of promoting a trans-world line by building along the west coast to Alaska, laying a submarine cable under the Bering Strait, and then erecting a land line across Siberia to Europe. The laying of the Atlantic Cable in 1866 rendered the idea moot. One management decision that had a significant long-term impact on Omaha derived from his ability to persuade Edward Rosewater to resign his position in the Army Telegraph Corps and to join the Pacific Telegraph Company. In 1864, Rosewater became manager of the Omaha Office. Subsequently, in 1871, he founded what became one of Omaha's premier newspapers, the *Omaha Bee*.[19]

Creighton's responsibilities demanded frequent travel, especially in response to periodic disruptions of service caused by marauding bands of Indians, meandering buffalo, and prairie fires. He had just returned from a business trip when his four-year-old son died on April 12, 1863. No record of a cause exists; he was first interred at St. Mary's churchyard, but subsequently moved to a family plot at the new Holy Sepulchre Cemetery in 1874, where he lies beneath a simple block headstone inscribed "Charles D." Despite the personal and business problems, Edward continued to direct the construction of branch telegraph lines: from Julesburg to Denver and Central City in 1864; Denver to Salt Lake City in 1866; Salt Lake City to Virginia City, Montana, in 1867; Helena to Ft. Benton, Montana, and Laramie to Promontory Point, Utah, in 1869. In the latter year, Edward also oversaw construction of the railroad-exclusive line for the Union Pacific from North Platte, Nebraska, to Promontory Point. Edward completed the last two projects after he had resigned his superintendent position with Western Union in 1867, although he remained on the company's board of directors for several more years.[20]

Edward profited handsomely from the success of the Pacific Telegraph Company, more handsomely than deserved, according to Congressional testimony. The windfall resulted from the oft-used nineteenth-century business device of watered stock; that is, the value of the stock issued far exceeded the actual value of the company. First, the company received a $400,000 subsidy for a line that cost about $147,000 to build. Then the company issued $1 million in stock, although directors actually paid only pennies on the dollar for their shares. In 1864, when Western Union absorbed Pacific Telegraph, it did so without expending money. It simply issued Pacific Telegraph $2 million of Western Union stock. Shortly thereafter, Western Union tripled the stock issue of the enlarged corporation to a paper value of $6 million. Despite the sleight of hand, the company succeeded, and the actual value of its stock rose, greatly benefiting the insiders who had not paid face value. When the actual market value of the shares climbed from 20 to 85 cents, Edward sold one hundred thousand shares for $85,000; that is, he sold what constituted only one third of his shares for eight times what he had paid for his original holdings three years previously.[21]

Edward used his mounting wealth to finance extremely lucrative freighting expeditions. In 1862, thirty-five laden wagons, accompanied by about five hundred head of cattle, trudged to Salt Lake City. The Mormons paid $20,000 for the cattle, plus $10,000 in gold and another $10,000 in drafts on Ben Holiday's stage line for the goods. The next two years saw similar-sized wagon trains to the gold fields of Montana that netted profits of $33,000 and $52,000, respectively. Those 1,600-mile trips, beginning as early as possible in the spring, entailed stops at Salt Lake City, where some manufactured goods were traded for Mormon agricultural products, which in turn made their way to the mining camps in Montana. Eastbound cargo in the fall consisted mainly of miners returning home for the winter with their gold or other minerals. In 1865, the *Omaha Herald* reported the return of an Edward Creighton wagon train with two-hundred miners aboard.[22]

Fording the Platte River presented a major concern to freighters; thus, in 1864,

Edward helped incorporate the Platte River Bridge Company. However, the plan lost its immediacy with the construction of the transcontinental railroad. By 1866, the Union Pacific had laid track 305 miles west of Omaha. This accomplishment changed the nature of freighting from the Gate City (as contemporary Omahans referred to their town) and led Edward, the Kountze brothers, and others to incorporate the Western Transfer Company. Edward became president of the firm organized to haul goods between gaps in the rail lines. The Chicago and Northwestern Railroad had not reached Council Bluffs, Iowa, so Western Transfer wagons transported goods from its terminus to Omaha, thence onto the Union Pacific, and finally at the latter's terminus, back onto wagons bound for points north and west. The Iowa leg of the business ceased in 1867, when the Chicago and Northwestern reached Council Bluffs, but the western trade continued for many years thereafter. Because the Union Pacific traversed Wyoming, wagon trains to Denver and elsewhere were needed, and it took many years to get the branch railroad lines built. Edward continued to increase his stake in the business: In 1867, he purchased the equipment and stock of Alexander Majors (subsequently a principal in one of the largest western freighting companies, Russell, Majors and Waddell) when he sold his operation headquartered in Nebraska City, Nebraska, and relocated to Salt Lake City. Thus, freighting played a major role in Edward's life and added substantially to the wealth he accumulated from the telegraph.[23]

Furthermore, Edward's freighting activity helped spawn cattle ranching on the northern plains. An oft-repeated myth, with various nuances, proclaimed that Edward, or one of his employees, got trapped around Laramie, Wyoming, in a snow storm and had to abandon teams of oxen to their own devices while he made his way back to Omaha alone. On a return trip the next spring, a work crew found the animals fat and healthy. The serendipity demonstrated the value of the prairie grass and the ability of bovines to survive the harsh winters, thus originating the Great Plains cattle industry. In 1885, a Congressional report gave mistaken imprimatur to the tale and twentieth-century scholarship cannot eradicate it from the popular mind. Actually, fur traders had raised cattle in the area since the 1830s, and road ranches along the Oregon-California-Mormon Trail through Wyoming traded for a profit their fattened grazing stock for the overworked cattle of migrants, grazed them back to a robust state, and repeated the exchange process for years. Still, Edward Creighton was one of the very first modern ranchers in Wyoming and Nebraska.[24]

As the owner of small herds of draft animals used for his freighting, grading, and telegraph-construction businesses, Edward, on a daily and seasonal basis, had to arrange for grazing rights during the 1840s and '50s. When large amounts of pasture became available west of the Missouri River through the Homestead Act of 1862, and by way of the open range on the prairie, ranching presented a natural business extension. Why pay to feed your animals when free grass was available on federally-owned land—get there first, claim thousands of acres as yours, establish a "code of the West," and use vigilante groups to enforce "the law." Moreover, why not graze surplus animals that could be sold at profit? In a letter from 1870, Edward described his decision:

My first grazing in that country was the winter of 1859. Since then for eleven years I have grazed more or less stock, including horses, cattle and sheep in Colorado, Wyoming, Utah and Montana. The first seven winters I grazed work oxen mostly. . . . The last four winters I have been raising stock and have large herds of cows and calves. The present winter I have wintered about eight thousand head. . . . We have had three thousand sheep the past winter and they are in the best of order. . . . I have been interested in stock raising in the [eastern] states for a number of years where we have tame grass pastures and tame grass hay and fenced fields and good shelter for the stock and good American and blooded cattle and an experienced stock raiser to attend to them and after a full trial I have found that with the disadvantage of the vastly inferior Texas cattle and no hay nor grain nor shelter, nothing but the wild grass, there is three times the profit in grazing on the plains, and I have as a consequence determined to transfer my interest in stock raising in the states to the plains. There is no prospective limit to the pasturage west of the Missouri river.[25]

Inexplicably, Edward did not list Nebraska among the states and territories in which he raised stock. Numerous contemporary sources, however, reported that he had cattle along the Elkhorn River in the eastern part of the state as early as 1864, and that three years later, he drove three thousand head of beef cattle from near the town of Schuyler to western Nebraska. By the 1870s, he also had a farm only five miles west of Omaha where he raised Cotswold sheep, a British breed that produced long, coarse wool used to make cashmere coats. Moreover, in the year before he wrote the letter, he organized a longhorn drive from Texas to Ogallala, Nebraska, the site of a new Union Pacific cattle-shipping facility. He soon established ranches near the Horse Creek and the Pumpkin Creek in Cheyenne County, and in the Sandhills area along the Niobrara River in Cherry County. His most prominent brand was an oxbow, although he may also have used his initials in several designs.[26]

Actually, Edward also entered western Nebraska by moving east, since his earliest prairie-grazing experience started in Wyoming in 1859. The venture may have been associated with freighting, or possibly in anticipation of building the transcontinental telegraph. By 1868, with the completion of the first transcontinental railroad, Edward and two associates who worked for him on the telegraph and on a grading contract for the Union Pacific, Thomas Alsop and Charles Hutton, established one of the first ranches in Wyoming dedicated to raising Texas longhorns. They became charter members of the Wyoming Stockgrowers Association, with Alsop elected its first vice president. From their spreads around Laramie, they also moved east and took up public domain land in the Nebraska Panhandle. In these operations Edward capitalized the ventures and gave fifty-percent interest to his partners, who had long been faithful foremen in his other businesses. At the time of his death, he reputedly stood as the wealthiest cattle rancher in the United States. That wealth increased further in Wyoming, because as he graded a section of the Union Pacific rail bed near Rock Creek, he cut through a vein of bituminous coal eight feet thick. He bought up mineral rights from other prospectors in the area and even discovered an anthracite deposit not too far distant. At one point, he had a contract to sell thousands of tons of coal to the Union Pacific for $8.00 a ton that had cost him $2.00 a ton to mine.[27]

Edward also used his wealth to become Omaha's most prominent banker. Following the sale of part of his Western Union stock in 1863, he invested a portion of that money with the Kountze brothers to organize the aptly named First National Bank, the first nationally chartered bank in Nebraska. Those same associates also created the Colorado National Bank in Denver and the Rocky Mountain National Bank in Central City, Colorado. Edward served as president of First National, and during the Panic of 1873, he used his personal fortune to guarantee the deposits of working people, which prevented a run on the bank and actually resulted in increased deposits. Moreover, Edward made scores of personal loans including one for $100,000 to Brigham Young.[28]

Edward also invested a sizeable portion of his wealth in real estate. When the developers of the Grand Central Hotel went over budget, he stepped forward with several other businessmen to underwrite a $100,000 loan to finance the completion, in 1873, of what was supposed to be Omaha's signature lodging establishment. The ill-fated venture never fulfilled its promise, however; a year later, the inventory of Edward's estate placed "no value" on his $5,000 note and in 1878 fire destroyed the structure. As his successes mounted, he built the three-story brick, iron- and glass-fronted Creighton Block (nineteenth-century real estate terminology indicating a large building divided into offices and shops) at Fifteenth and Douglas streets. He also erected the Creighton & Morgan Building (later Morgan & Gallagher, then Paxton & Gallagher) and the Shoaf Building, as well as contributing to the development of the Central Block. In all, in 1874, he owned thirteen lots in Omaha valued at $139,000 and was one of the largest landowners in Nebraska. His estate listed thirty-seven pieces of property totaling just over 900 acres in Douglas County, two pieces at 240 acres in Dodge County, four pieces at 480 acres in Washington County, three pieces at 400 acres in Burt County, eight pieces at 1,600 acres in Pierce County, three pieces at 317 acres in Wayne County, two pieces at 560 acres in Cedar County, and one piece at 160 acres in Knox County. Finally, of course, although he did not own the land, he "possessed" thousands of acres of the open range upon which his various herds grazed.[29]

Additionally, Edward invested in railroads. In 1869, he contributed about $36,000 toward the capitalization of the Omaha and Northwestern Railroad and became president of the company. It received a $200,000 subsidy from the City of Omaha and had plans to lay tracks due north to the mouth of the Niobrara River in the northeastern corner of Nebraska. Edward did not live to witness the bankruptcy of the line, whose tracks only reached Herman, Nebraska, in 1878. New investors reorganized the company and extended its reach to Oakland, Nebraska, but again it failed; the short line eventually became part of the Chicago and Northwestern system. In his other railroading ventures, Edward compiled a four-win, one-loss record in skirmishes with the directors of the Union Pacific Railroad. He played a significant role in determining the route of the Union Pacific through Omaha, carrying on a spirited correspondence with T. C. Durant, the railroad's chief financial promoter, who preferred building west from Bellevue, Nebraska. Further, Edward succeeded in arranging that railroad construction contractors deposit funds at the First National Bank, despite efforts by general superintendent Webster Snyder to steer clients to competitors. Plus, as noted earlier, Edward personally obtained contracts to grade forty miles of track bed near Ft. Bridger, Wyoming, and to construct the Union Pacific telegraph line from North Platte, Nebraska, to Promontory Point, Utah. However, he lost his bid to have Omaha declared the eastern terminus of the Union Pacific. His estate dedicated money to pay the fees of Omaha attorney James M. Woolworth to complete the lawsuit he initiated before his death; ultimately, however, the United States Supreme Court ruled otherwise in 1876. Although the railroad company built its headquarters and a huge engine and railcar manufacture and repair facility in Omaha, the mile-one marker stands in a huge switching yard in Council Bluffs, Iowa.[30]

Edward's career ended abruptly and at a relatively young age. He may have suffered a stroke in 1871, while he and his wife visited her mother in Dayton during the Christmas holiday. He must not have been in the best of health at the time, because the previous summer the *Omaha Weekly Herald* reported that he had gone to Lansing, Michigan, hoping that "magnetic baths" would restore his vigor. Whatever unnamed malady enervated him at that time (another article claimed he suffered from an "inflammation of the bowels—dysentery, perhaps"), he recovered. On November 3, 1874, however, he collapsed in his office and did not regain consciousness, dying two days later at home. His funeral began at St. Philomena's Cathedral; the Mass had to be delayed an hour to accommodate the huge crowd. Virtually all business activity in Omaha ceased that morning. He was laid to rest next to his son at Holy Sepulchre Cemetery on the west side of an obelisk subsequently purchased at the Centennial Exposition in Philadelphia in 1876.[31]

As an Irish-American Catholic who never forgot the workingman, Edward had supported the party of Jefferson and Jackson. In 1858, he served as a delegate to the Douglas County Democratic convention. He also counted himself among the founders of the Near-Vigilance Committee that administered "justice" to wayward debtors and contractors. His charity, however, always tempered his protection of his property. At a time when it was common for those in need to approach the wealthy directly, "he was accustomed every morning to put in his purse a bundle of small bills, which he would distribute during the day to the poor of the city." He directed most of his generosity toward Catholic institutions, contributing the money and lumber to build the house for the first priest in residence in Omaha. He supported St. Mary's Convent and the original Mercy Hospital, as well as providing the largest contribution for the construction of St. Philomena's Cathedral. In 1865, he gave the bishop $2,000 to purchase two lots on the corner of 9th and Harney streets, on which to build the cathedral. Subsequently, he donated $13,000 of the $60,000 total cost, $4,900 of it he put in his wife's name, which she earmarked for the purchase of the marble main alter.[32]

Edward Creighton's life epitomized the American Dream. The son of Irish immigrants, he worked hard and used his skills in an environment of opportunity to succeed at a monumental level and then shared his wealth. The memorials began in his lifetime. In 1871, Joseph A. Bruce organized a colonization society that established a town in Knox County, Nebraska, that he intended to name after himself. His fellow settlers, however, overruled him, "naming it after Edward Creighton, Omaha's leading citizen of that day—to give it the prestige that would guarantee its success as a city." In the 1880s, an Omaha militia unit designated itself the Edward Creighton Guards and the city originated Ed Creighton Boulevard (changed to Avenue after I-480 disrupted its route). In 1958, a gubernatorial committee chose Edward as one of Nebraska's three charter members of the National Cowboy Hall of Fame. In 1965, Aksarben (an Omaha civic organization), and in 1982, the State of Nebraska, added him to their halls of honor. He has been lionized in a comic book and in a Zane Grey novel, as well as gaining citations in the inaugural editions of the prestigious Dictionary of American Biography and the National Cyclopedia of American Biography. Ultimately, of course, the name of Creighton University stands as his most enduring memorial.[33]

John Andrew Creighton

John A. Creighton, the ninth and last child of James and Bridget, arrived on October 15, 1831. He attended public school and related no tales of childhood employment. By the time he became a teenager his father no longer needed working sons bringing in income to help purchase land. Yet surely he had farm chores as a youth and then, after his father's death, he probably helped brother Henry with the operation in a more significant fashion. Following Henry's death, Edward and his mother arranged for the twenty year old John to attend St. Joseph's College, administered by the Dominican order at nearby Somerset, Ohio. He demonstrated admirable scholarship, receiving awards in the second class of arithmetic, first class of English Grammar, Geography, Sacred History, and Christian Doctrine at the end of the 1851–52 academic year. The following year he added awards in the "first division, first class Arithmetic and in Profane History." Note that these mid-nineteenth-century "college" classes equate with contemporary elementary and/or junior-high-school curricula. John's name did not appear on the year-end list of students in July 1854, and his mother died the following November. Thus, the often repeated story that he dropped out of college after his mother died may not be correct. Certainly, finances were not a concern and there was no farm to return to. He may have helped attend to his ailing mother or, perhaps like many his age, with no vocation in mind, he found further higher education superfluous and decided to apply his brains and brawn to his brother Edward's mushrooming businesses.[34]

He began his career by joining Edward's crew constructing a telegraph line between Cleveland and Toledo, Ohio. The next year he went to Mexico, Missouri, to clear a three-mile stretch of timber that obstructed the roadbed of the emerging Northern Missouri Railroad. From there it was on to Keokuk, Iowa, for the street-grading contract that did not materialize. Edward, who had two other brothers and a cousin in the area, demonstrated his confidence in the twenty-five-year-old John by putting him in charge of selling the equipment before continuing on to Omaha. In June 1856, John joined his brothers Joseph and James and his cousin James "Long Jim" Creighton in the frontier settlement where "Farnam street was nothing but a cow pasture and a band of Indians was encamped just over the hill, where the [Central] High School now stands."[35]

For the next four years, while Edward frequently absented himself from Omaha getting married and doing surveys for telegraph routes, John busied himself in various enterprises. First, he served as a clerk to Thomas O'Connor (the ethnic connections again), the register of deeds. He then took a clerical position with J. J. and R. A. Brown, who operated a wholesale and retail general merchandise store. In 1860, he joined them as a partner in a freighting operation, making two excursions to Denver. By that time, he also had become a landowner, purchasing town lots and spending some of his time farming on the Missouri River bottoms. In one instance he filed a claim to land where Courtland Beach stood in the early twentieth century (on the north side of Carter Lake) and grew potatoes on the property. With little demand for potatoes, the venture did not succeed, and he once traded a wagonload of the crop to a shoemaker for a new pair of boots.[36]

When Edward obtained the Pacific Telegraph contract, John headed one of his work crews. Following that short but intense three-month adventure, he and Edward returned to Omaha for the winter. The next spring, John returned to the Ft. Bridger, Wyoming, area to collect the cattle Edward had left there. Edward also advanced him money to purchase a thousand sacks of flour, which John wanted to take to the miners rushing to ore strikes in Montana. Heavy rains that made rivers impossible to ford and rumors of hostile Indian activity combined to lead John to reroute the expedition to Salt Lake City, where he sold the flour and about five hundred head of cattle to Brigham Young for $20,000. Returning home, he spent the winter of 1862 in Iowa and Northern Missouri purchasing cattle for a wagon train Edward would send to Montana come spring. Subsequently, John and cousin Long Jim led a party of thirty-five, four-oxen wagons, and a herd of cattle to Bannock and Virginia City, Montana, in a grueling 117-day trip. They sold the goods for $33,000 in gold, which Long Jim brought back to Omaha.[37]

John stayed behind in Virginia City. While he continued to facilitate Edward's freighting business in Montana, he struck out on his own, opening a wholesale and retail general merchandise store. To stem lawlessness before an effective territorial government emerged, he joined other businessmen to form a vigilante committee. In turn, he and several other local merchants received their own dose of vigilante justice; in response to alleged price gouging, 480 miners confiscated the merchants' supplies of flour. Shortly thereafter, the miners paid the retailers either $27.00 or $30.00 per sack, the standard price in Salt Lake City or St. Louis, respectively. Based on the flour "sale," John operated one of the largest stores in town. He received $270, which would equate to ninety to one hundred sacks. Only two competitors were reimbursed with larger amounts, $459 and $540, respectively. In 1866, working through a contract with Edward and Western Union, John supervised the construction of a telegraph line from Salt Lake City to Virginia City, where grateful hometown people presented him with a watch purchased from Tiffany & Company of New York City. In Virginia City, John formed friendships and business associations with Nelson Story and Patrick A. Largey, the latter from Somerset, Ohio, who migrated to Omaha and then to Montana guiding an Ed Creighton wagon train. They entered ventures in banking and mining, which eventually reaped John ample riches. His sojourn in Montana ended in 1868, after only five years; nonetheless, in 1873, the newly established Montana Historical Society passed a resolution granting him an honorary membership.[38]

Before leaving for his Montana hiatus, John had met and had become enamored of Emma (Sarah Emily) Wareham, a younger sister of Edward's wife, Lucretia. Now established as a successful businessman in his own right, he married her at the devout hour of 6:00 A.M. (probably so they and their guests could partake of Holy Communion) on June 9, 1868, at the newly constructed St. Philomena's Cathedral. Their honeymoon consisted of a tour of the eastern United States, after which they returned to reside with Edward and Lucretia. Just three years prior, Edward had built a two-story, eight-room brick house at 1710 Chicago Street (324 under the nineteenth-century numbering system). Unpretentious, it nonetheless was one of the largest homes in Omaha of that era (it succumbed to a bulldozer in 1941, to make way for a Hinky Dinky grocery store). In May 1869, the newlyweds became the proud parents of a daughter, Lucretia, called Lulu. Tragically, she died eleven months later, on April 9, 1870, and was interred at Holy Sepulchre Cemetery.[39]

The brothers and sisters continued to reside together and carried on an active social life revolving around family gatherings. While Edward concentrated on banking, ranching, and real estate, John continued his interest in the mercantile trade. In 1868, in partnership with Frank C. Morgan, he established J. A. Creighton & Company, which handled groceries, provisions, flour, and liquors, and acted as a commission agent. In 1874, the firm changed its name to Creighton & Morgan; the following year, John exited the business and it became Morgan & Gallagher (ultimately it became the Omaha landmark, Paxton Gallagher Company). In those same years, John acted as a senior partner in a wholesale-freighting concern that transported goods from Corinne, Utah, to Montana. Then his life changed dramatically with Edward's death in 1874. He helped the grief-stricken Lucretia to inventory and administer her husband's estate, a difficult task since Edward died without a will. Then Lucretia became ill and died in 1876; she had prepared for her passing, writing a will and naming John, Long Jim Creighton, and Herman Kountze executors. John received a bequest of $150,000 (because of residuals based on the steep increase in the value of Edward's estate, John ultimately received $300,000).[40]

Instantly wealthy due to a largess he certainly did not want to obtain at that time, John applied it toward charitable enterprises, as well as investments that increased his wealth to astounding proportions. He bought Edward's cattle herd for $75,000, and with partners, he continued to increase it by purchasing Texas longhorns driven to Ogallala. There, by 1877, drafts on well-known banks, "especially the First National of Omaha," were exchanged between Texas drovers and northern buyers. Edward, the First National's founding president, certainly established the prominence of the Omaha financial institution in that area, and John, the current vice president and owner of one fifth of its shares, obviously influenced the firm's continued preeminent status. John grazed the cattle on Edward's open-range ranches in Cheyenne County and along the Niobrara River in north central Nebraska. Those locations provided easy access to the Union Pacific Railroad, as well as "local" sales to nearby United States Army forts and Indian reservations. In 1882, at the peak of the historic "cattle kingdom," the partnership sold the operation to the Bay State Cattle Company, comprised of eastern and British investors, for about $750,000 (John's share was $400,000). A timely sale, by the end of the 1880s, overstocking on the plains and several years of drought followed by severe winters, destroyed many herds. Thereafter, the free-range system of cattle grazing perished and modern ranching began to emerge.[41]

John used the profit from the cattle sale to join Wyoming cattle baron Alexander Hamilton Swan and five other Omaha businessmen to establish the Union Stockyards Company. Other partners included William Paxton (he began his Nebraska career driving a wagon for Edward Creighton) and John's nephew John A. McShane, who had been in other ventures with his uncles. John also became a major investor in the associated business—the South Omaha Land Company, which purchased two thousand acres of land on which grew the stockyards, meatpacking plants, and the "Magic City" of South Omaha (annexed by Omaha in 1915). Furthermore, many of the same principals incorporated the Union Stockyards Railroad Company; its board of directors included John A. Creighton, John A. McShane, William Paxton, and Edward A. Cudahy.[42]

John continued to invest and to diversify. In 1879, he, Long Jim, and John A. McShane purchased the defunct Omaha Nail Company and revived it into a firm with eighty-five employees that produced 350 kegs of nails a day. He also dabbled in a number of street railway schemes, none of which came to fruition. In 1887, he joined William Paxton and other South Omaha businessmen to incorporate the Omaha & South Omaha Street Railway Company capitalized at $1 million. While some speculated it would be a cable line, it was not built. Similarly, in 1890, he joined Andrew Poppleton, James M. Woolworth, and others to form the Interstate Bridge and Street Railway Company, capitalized at $2.5 million, which intended to build a bridge over the Missouri River and run a trolley line on it. The firm obtained a Congressional charter, but competition and the Panic of 1893 forestalled success. Finally, in 1891, John again joined William Paxton, John A. McShane, and others to establish the South Omaha Metropolitan Street Railway. The corporation purchased the franchise rights of a competitor, Dr. Samuel Mercer, to build in South Omaha, but many "interpreted the actions of Metropolitan to indicate that they [*sic*] were planning to build a number of lines in and about South Omaha for the purpose of compelling the Omaha company to buy those lines to avoid annoying competition." The rumors referred to a common business ploy of the nineteenth century; however, the veracity of the allegations cannot be established, since the politics of obtaining franchises through general elections stalled progress, and the owners sold out in 1892. In a related field, in 1889, John Creighton and John A. McShane created the Naphtaline & Natural Soap Company to produce a lubricant for rail systems. They hoped to compete with the Standard Oil Company in providing the product, but failed to carve out a niche in the market.[43]

John continued his interests in banking, maintaining his office in the First National Bank building. In 1886, he helped incorporate and became a director of the Stockyards National Bank, while maintaining his association with the People's Savings Bank of Butte, Montana. When Herman Kountze died in 1906, he accepted the figurehead position of president of First National, but took no salary. He lent the prestige of his name, but did not participate in the active management; he felt he was too old and he wanted to go south for the winter. In his seventies at the time, he went to the office to keep track of his investments and widespread real estate assets, which included his own Creighton Block at Eighth and Howard streets, Courtland Beach (a popular recreation site), and the Creighton Orpheum Theatre (a 2,200 seat complex that featured Orpheum circuit vaudeville). In 1905, he incorporated his vast holdings into the John A. Creighton Real Estate and Trust Company, capitalized at $800,000 (he owned all but two of the shares valued at $100 each).[44]

Despite his wealth, John "delighted in being a common man." To the obvious chagrin of any modern nutritionist, one of his favorite meals remained bacon fried with brown gravy and served with corn bread, oatmeal, and/or mush. He remained a lifelong Democrat and an ardent supporter of his friend William Jennings Bryan. Starting in 1884, he served as a Nebraska delegate at five consecutive national conventions. Illuminating his values, at the 1900 convention, he broadcast his view that the party should not again adopt the 16:1 money plank (unlimited coinage of silver at a value one sixteenth that of gold) that dominated the platform and election of 1896, which Bryan lost. When Bryan's managers collared him and explained the candidate's position, John, out of loyalty to a friend, swayed the Nebraska delegation to pass a resolution in favor of the plank. Besides fealty, he also displayed a feisty demeanor. Newspaper centennial flashback stories printed in the 1960s and 1980s portrayed the freckle-faced young man as having a fiery temper. The articles contained suspect reporting, yet the fact that at the age of sixty-five he resisted robbers who had to knock him unconscious to relieve him of his valuables speaks volumes about his temperament.[45]

Generosity was another ingrained element of his character, and his personal charity was immense. He gave support to strikers short of funds and he donated $300 to the Fireman's Relief Fund in recognition of the good job done extinguishing a fire at his home. He also made weekly visits to St. Joseph Hospital to distribute candy to the patients as "sugar pills," he entertained fifty-sixty children at Christmas and provided them with gifts, and he had the matron of the city jail alert him to incarcerated individuals in need of help. With the help of an elderly neighborhood friend, locomotive engineer John G. Lee, he became a "veritable St. Vincent De Paul Society" before organized Catholic charities existed. Lee researched cases and then presented them to his younger, richer friend to obtain his support. Moreover, John liked to chide a tight-fisted acquaintance that new funeral furnishings no longer had pockets in the shrouds because people were not supposed to take anything with them. He also delighted in telling the story of the miserly Irishman who died and at the pearly gates was asked by St. Peter what he had done for his fellow man. The deceased said he had once given five cents to a widow and five cents to a poor man peddling matches and five cents to a cripple. St. Patrick walked by and St. Peter asked him what he should do about his fellow countryman. St. Patrick replied, "Give him back his fifteen cents and tell him to go to Hell."[46]

Catholicism contributed an essential element to John's character and directed many of his charitable activities. In 1886, he funded the Union Catholic Library in Omaha, and two years later, he and nephews John A. McShane and John B. Fury, Jr., attended the Catholic Centennial celebration in Baltimore. He gave generous support to the founding of the Good Shepard Home for troubled girls, including its new dormitory, chapel, and convent (it closed in 1972). He also built the first American convent for the Sisters of the Poor Clares, constructing a second one for them in 1903, after the original had to be razed. Later chapters will reveal his munificence toward St. Joseph Hospital, St. John's Church, and Creighton University, three closely related institutions. In 1895, in response to his benevolence, Pope Leo XIII made him a Count of the Papal Court, and in 1900, Notre Dame University gave him the Laetare Medal to honor his support of Christian education. The following year, the Very Reverend General Louis Martin, S.J., wrote John:

> So great is your virtue and piety, so great your good will toward our society [the Society of Jesus], that we consider you justly entitled to whatever consideration it is possible for us to show you. Since, however, we can not [*sic*] exhibit our sentiments otherwise than by spiritual gifts, we, in virtue of the authority which our Lord has granted to us, though unworthy, in this our society, hereby make you a sharer in all the Holy Sacrifices, prayers, penances and other good works, as well as in all the pious exercise, both spiritual and corporal, performed by God's grace in our entire society; and with all our heart, in Christ Jesus, we grant you full participation in them, in the name of the Father, Son and Holy Ghost.[47]

On October 15, 1906, John Andrew Creighton celebrated his seventy-fifth birthday. The Creighton University band played in the new uniforms he had just purchased for it and all students enjoyed a holiday from school in his honor. In pictures of the occasion, he stood in front of an entourage of friends and family wearing a wreath of white roses presented to him by his grandniece, the daughter of Mr. and Mrs. John (Clara Creighton) Daugherty, a descendent of his brother Francis. Although he looks robust in the photos, after that day, his health deteriorated rapidly.

Even before the party, he had battled "acute bronchitis" and had spent six weeks at Mt. Clemens, Michigan, taking "treatment at the healing springs." At the end of the year, he contracted pneumonia, lingering for six weeks before succumbing at 1:30 A.M. on February 7, 1907. About four thousand people viewed his body at his home, before a six-block-long cortege of carriages accompanied it to St. John's Church for a Solemn Requiem Mass conducted by the Provincial of the Missouri Province, the Rev. Henry Moeller, S.J. In an ecumenical tribute, the Episcopal Cathedral tolled its bells from 9:00 to 10:00 a.m. When the bells ceased, the streetcars stopped running for five minutes, and for the subsequent hour most factories and stores stopped operating. He was buried in the family plot at Holy Sepulchre Cemetery. On February 28, about three thousand people attended a memorial service at the city auditorium, proclaimed by Mayor James Dahlman. Over 270 "vice presidents of the meeting" sat on the stage; William Jennings Bryan delivered the eulogy and many other prominent citizens spoke. The meeting resolved to undertake a fund drive to erect a monument in John's honor. The effort fizzled, but the city did name a boulevard in his honor. Moreover, in 1904, the Missouri Province had officially proclaimed him a co-founder of Creighton University, and in 1908, the school changed its annual Founders' Day celebration to February 7. For his entry in the Dictionary of American Biography, insufficient research overlooked his business accomplishments; nonetheless, it fittingly described him simply as "philanthropist."[48]

The Omaha Clan

Edward and John Andrew Creighton employed a host of relatives in their business enterprises and several of them succeeded in becoming prominent businessmen in their own right. Brother James may have been the first Creighton to arrive in Omaha in 1856. Four years later, he told the census taker that he was a forty-year-old farm laborer with $5,000 worth of real estate. In 1866, he worked as a freighter, probably for Edward, but died in August and eventually was buried in Holy Sepulchre Cemetery. Another brother, Joseph, also arrived in Omaha in 1856. In 1860, he roomed with brothers James and John Andrew, and listed himself in the census as a thirty-year-old farm laborer with $1,000 in real estate. The next spring, Joseph began work on the transcontinental telegraph as a crew chief, but soon lost that position. The venture's diarist described him thusly:

> To sum up Joe Creighton, his character and his abilities to accomplish anything, in a few words, I must say he was absolutely and largely unqualified to give any results whatever. He was lazy mentally and physically and so destitute of energy that he neither did nor could do anything. He was a human sloth. Yet everybody liked Joe; he was such a good hearted fellow.

Subsequently he worked as a laborer and briefly as a grocer, presumably for brother John Andrew while he maintained the mercantile store. Similarly, when John Andrew owned the Omaha Nail Company for two years, Joseph was listed as its treasurer, but for the last two decades of his life, he claimed no employment. Seemingly, his brothers continued to assist him. He had married Katherine Furlong and they had a daughter, Mary. In 1881, she married John Shelby, a government clerk who became a physician, and they relocated to California in the early twentieth century. Joseph died in 1893, and was interred in Holy Sepulchre Cemetery. Despite his undiagnosed disability, which inhibited his work skills, he left an estate that bequeathed land in Dallas County, Iowa, to the Bishop of Omaha, who in turn gave it to St. James Orphanage.[49]

Edward and John's oldest brother, Francis, migrated to Omaha in the early 1870s. He had farmed and also had become a wealthy quarryman around Springfield, Ohio. In Nebraska, he took no employment and died a relatively young man in 1873. He had married Phoebe Driscoll and they had seven children. Sons Joseph and Edward died at tender ages in Ohio. Another son, James, engaged in the cattle business with his uncle John Andrew and married Maggie Ray, but he died childless in 1878. The following year Francis's unmarried daughter Mary also expired. In Omaha, another daughter, Catherine (Kate), married Mathew McGinn, who had no visible business connection to the extended Creighton family; they had one son, Frank, who married twice but died without an heir. Another of Francis's daughters, Martha, married Hiram Itnyer, a clerk employed at Creighton & Morgan, who became a carpenter in 1880; they also died childless.[50]

More prominently, Francis and Phoebe's first born, John D. Creighton, carried on the family name and made a significant contribution as an Omaha entrepreneur. He attended Omaha (Central) High School, and in 1872, became one of the founders and editors of its school newspaper. In 1880, he joined a group of investors who bought the Omaha Driving Park Association and improved the facility to have it host the state fair, as well as other exhibitions. With his uncle John Andrew, he entered the livestock business and became a director of the First National Bank. He also acquired a number of properties on Farnam Street, as well as about five hundred acres of land on Cole Creek, which he sold to Erastus Benson, who then developed the town bearing his name. At the time of his death in 1922, his secretary revealed that most of his charity consisted of anonymous donations such as a playground for St. John's School and truckloads of toys and food delivered on holidays to Fr. Flanagan, St. James Orphanage, and other children's institutions. He and his wife, Ellen Hennessey, had five children. A son Edward died as a youth, but the others all made successful marriages. Daughter Katherine married Charles Allison; Emma married Frederick Nash, founder of the Omaha Electric Light Company; and Clara married John M. Daugherty, secretary to great-uncle John Andrew, who subsequently became a successful real estate and livestock dealer. Son Charles carried the Creighton name forward through his son Edward, who subsequently produced a son, another Edward, who became the last direct male standard bearer of Edward, John Andrew, and their siblings, possessing the family name in Omaha.[51]

John Creighton, a brother of Edward and John's father James, succeeded as a landowner in Ohio, but resided in Omaha in 1860, with his thirty-year-old daughter, Catherine. Why he joined his nephews is unclear, since the sixty-four-year-old Irish immigrant listed his occupation in the census as "gentleman." He died in 1865, because of a fall from a horse while visiting in Perry County, Ohio. Two of his sons, Harry (who briefly belonged to the Dominican Order) and Long Jim, also came to Omaha to work for cousin Edward. They took a brief hiatus to the Colorado gold fields in 1858; Harry moved on to California (later joined by sister Catherine), while Long Jim returned to Omaha to drive freight for Edward and to supervise work crews on telegraph construction jobs. Subsequently, Long Jim became a general contractor, and in association with John, he superintended the construction of Creighton College, the Convent of the Poor Clares, St. Joseph-Creighton Memorial Hospital, and the John A. Creighton Medical College. Also in partnership with his cousin, he became secretary-treasurer of the Omaha Nail Company. In his own right, he erected a three-story, brick office building at Twelfth and Farnam streets, costing $8,500.

Despite a fiery temper, which erupted into highly publicized public brawls with the likes of critics such as publisher Edward Rosewater, Long Jim had a successful political career. In 1857, he was appointed to the Omaha City council to complete the term of a member who died suddenly. Thereafter, he gained election to the council in 1867 to 1871; the Board of Education, 1872–75; and the Nebraska House of Representatives, 1876–80. He also served as the first chairman of the Omaha Board of Public Works from 1882 to 1885, and as a delegate to the Democratic National Convention in 1896. He married three times; Kate, his one surviving daughter by his first wife, Sarah McCrystal, became Mrs. C. V. Gallagher. He had no children with his second wife, Mary Elizabeth Largey, but produced five daughters and two sons with wife number three, Katherine McCullum. One daughter, Ella, married John O'Connell and moved to Vancouver, Washington. Daughters Mary and Etta remained single, while Clara married Frank Brandle and Anna married Mark Coad. One son, John V., migrated to Portland, Oregon, while son Charles H. Creighton carried the mail in Omaha for forty-four years, dying in 1950. Interestingly, Long Jim's great-granddaughter, Anne Creighton Caldwell Russell, graduated from Creighton University in 1953, and received a prize for winning the Jubilee (75th anniversary) Writing Contest. Twenty-five years later, she earned a master's degree in guidance and became the first winner of the Maurine Hamilton Award for outstanding woman graduate student.[52]

Edward and John Andrew's sister Mary migrated to Omaha and married John McCreary in 1858. McCreary had been born in Morrow County, Ohio, in 1832, and may have worked with Edward in erecting telegraph lines. Before coming to Omaha, he had operated a shingle mill in Page County, Iowa. He subsequently returned to his previous occupation and took employment with Edward in constructing the transcontinental telegraph. He then continued to work for Edward in his freighting business while he began to acquire a significant amount of property in the Omaha area. In the mid-1880s, he exploited Creighton University and John Andrew in a land deal involving property adjacent to the school. The transaction strained family relationships and John Andrew probably felt no sympathy when the Panic of 1893 rendered his brother-in-law virtually property-less. Mary McCreary died in 1898, and subsequently John Andrew did not include his McCreary nephews in his estate.[53]

In comparison, the marriage of Edward and John Andrew's sister Alice to Thomas McShane produced ten cousins, several of whom equaled Long Jim's role in the Omaha clan. Thomas and Alice's youngest daughter, Margaret, died in Omaha at twenty years of age, while the next youngest, Bridget, became Sr. M. Joseph, O.P., and remained in Ohio. Ellen, the second oldest of the four girls, married Martin Cannon and resided in Omaha, but her husband did not associate in business with his in-laws. Oldest daughter Catherine married John B. Furay in 1869, and joined him in Omaha. He had risen to the rank of major in the Eleventh Ohio Volunteer Cavalry during the Civil War and then transplanted to Douglas County, Nebraska, to work as a farm laborer and teach one semester in the county school. Edward Creighton employed thirty men from that military unit to guard the telegraph line in Wyoming, and Furay may have helped recruit them or even served with them. For certain, in 1867, he went into the grocery business in Omaha and became politically active. His connections resulted in patronage jobs with the United States Post Office, but he also became a partner in John A. Creighton and Company, stock dealers, until it sold out to the Bay State Company in 1882. Thereafter, he served a term on the Omaha City Council and two terms on the Board of Public Works. Ultimately, he formed Furay and McCardle, a street-railway advertising firm. A president of Creighton University praised him as a "friend and patron," and all seven of his sons graduated from the institution, including John B. Furay, Jr., who was ordained a Jesuit in 1905, subsequently became president of Loyola University in Chicago, and received an honorary LL.D., from his alma mater as part of its Golden Jubilee celebration in 1928.[54]

Five of Thomas and Alice's six sons grew to adulthood and migrated to Omaha. Edward C. McShane, born in Clark County, Ohio, in 1843, became John Andrew's secretary in 1870, and subsequently entered the cattle business with him. He was active with the Omaha Fire Department, rising to president of Engine Company #3 in 1877; in that same year, he was elected to the Omaha City Council. He married Agnes McGinn and had three daughters, but his blossoming life ended with his premature death in 1880. His brother Thomas Andrew McShane, born in 1848 in Perry County, Ohio, had an equally short life. He first migrated to Wyoming to oversee one of Edward Creighton's herds, subsequently becoming a partner in John A. Creighton and Company. His health deteriorated and he relocated to Omaha in the late 1870s and went into the grocery business. He married Celia Taggart and had four children, but he died in 1883. His son, Thomas J., won an elocution contest at Creighton University in 1899, and for the next seventy years, the champion provided a gold medal for subsequent winners of that oratorical contest; he also received the Alumni Achievement Award in 1956.[55]

The oldest brother, James H. McShane, was born in 1841, in Clark County, Ohio, and came to Omaha in 1862 to work for uncle Edward Creighton in the maintenance department of the Pacific Telegraph Company. In 1864, he took freight to Virginia

City, Montana, for Edward and then worked for his uncle John Andrew in constructing the telegraph line from there to Helena. In 1867, he joined the Union Pacific as a construction contractor and was present at Promontory Point, Utah, for the driving of the golden spike. He spent the remainder of his life in railway construction in the Midwest and the Great Plains, as well as operating a stable in Omaha (a very profitable business in an age of horse and oxen travel and freighting). In 1877, he married Anne Taggart and they had thirteen children. The youngest of Thomas and Alice's sons, Felix (Phil) McShane, was born in Perry County, Ohio, in 1853 and came to Omaha in 1874 to join John A. Creighton and Company as a ranch manager. He also worked for Uncle John at the Omaha Nail Company, before forming a railroad construction firm with his brother James. Carrying on a family tradition, he also became a president of Engine Company #3. He married Agnes O'Connor and they had three children. Although he left Omaha in 1912, when he died in 1937, his body was returned for burial at Holy Sepulchre Cemetery.[56]

The most renowned of the successful McShane brothers was John Albert, born in Perry County, Ohio, in 1850. He went to work on one of Uncle Edward's Wyoming cattle ranches in 1871. He came to Omaha three years later and roomed with his brothers while he attended the Omaha Business School. In 1876, he became the manager of the W. J. Young Company, manufacturers and dealers in shingles and other lumber products. He joined his brothers in moving up the officer ranks of Engine Company #3 and became active with the Board of Trade. He became a partner with Uncle John Andrew in the Omaha Nail Company, and started his own poultry and dairy wholesale distributing firm. In the meantime, he had continued to invest in the cattle industry, merging his interests with the Bay State Company in 1883, and serving as its Nebraska general manager for several years thereafter. He became one of the principals in creating the South Omaha Land Company and the Omaha stockyards. He served as president of the Union Stock Yards Company (1884-1894) and the Union Stock Yards Bank, as well as a director of the First National Bank. Moreover, he owned the Herald Publishing Company for two years before selling it to Gilbert Hitchcock, who created the *Omaha World-Herald* in 1889. At various other times, he was president of the Nebraska Central Railroad, the McShane Building Association, the Columbia Investment Company, the Omaha Cold Storage Company, the McShane Lumber Company (he purchased 60,000 acres of pine forest in Texas), as well as forming the Creighton-McShane Oil Company with John in 1906. At the same time, he maintained an active political career, serving in the Nebraska House of Representatives (1881–83), the Nebraska Senate (1882–86), and the United States House of Representatives (1887–89). He was the first Democrat elected to a national office from Nebraska, but he lost the race for governor in 1888 to the Republican candidate, John Thayer. He had married Mary Lee of Omaha in 1876, and they had a son, Edward, and a daughter, Mary. She married Willard Hosford, a descendent of John Deere, who managed the farm machinery company's Omaha plant. According to the contemporary president of Creighton University, "Among the truest friends of the College, John A. McShane stands conspicuous. . . . He was always close to John A. Creighton, who looked upon him as the natural heir of his own active interest in the college."[57]

The Wareham Family

During 1848, Edward Creighton erected two telegraph lines leading out of Dayton, Ohio. Quite likely, at that time, he became acquainted with David A. Wareham, a carpenter and builder. Wareham served on the Dayton City Council in 1841, and, subsequently, on the Board of Education in 1853 and the Civil War Voluntary Relief Committee in 1861. Wareham was of Dutch Protestant descent, but he married a Catholic from Washington, D.C., and eventually converted to his wife Emily's faith. According to the 1850 census, the family consisted of Lucretia, 16 (born February 3, 1834); George, 11; Emma, 9; Philip, 4; and Mary, 2. Apparently, Wareham and Edward became friends; Edward met the family and became smitten by Lucretia. He married her in Dayton on October 7, 1856; she had reached the age of twenty-two, and he had become a successful thirty-six-year-old businessman. As noted earlier, telegraph work had Edward and Lucretia residing with the Warehams in 1860. When the couple returned to Omaha in the spring of 1861, David Wareham probably accompanied them. Seemingly, he became involved with Edward's businesses and resided in Omaha until his death on June 24, 1864. He was buried at the original Catholic cemetery in Omaha, but then reinterred in the Creighton family plot at Holy Sepulchre Cemetery in 1876.[58]

Little is known about Lucretia Wareham Creighton. Although she had a younger sister with the name, she added Mary to her own after coming to Omaha. Over the years, newspaper reports used both designations, as well as "Lu." All who commented on her demeanor lauded her unpretentiousness and generosity. In memory of her deceased son, she purchased a $5,000 altar for St. Philomena's Cathedral. According to one report, Edward allowed her $25.00 a day for charity. To dispense it,

> In her phaeton, she would ride through the section of the city where dwelt the lowly, . . . Her pony "Billy," was known throughout the city, and in that phaeton one was apt to find almost any article for domestic use—from a spool of thread to a small cook-stove.[59]

She was already in ill health before Edward's death, and as soon as the inventory of his estate was completed, she drafted a will dated September 23, 1875. Still suffering from a "dropsical affection" (edema), she sought treatment in Chicago. Somewhat improved, she proceeded to Dayton to visit her mother and then on to Philadelphia for "special treatment under Professor De Costa." Whatever the regimen, it did not produce healing; she died at the Continental Hotel on January 23, 1876. Her younger sisters Mary and Emma, with her husband John A. Creighton, consoled at her bedside, along with Kate (brother-in-law Francis's daughter) and Long Jim Creighton. They returned the body to Omaha for a funeral at St. Philomena's Cathedral on January 27, and interment next to her son and her husband at Holy Sepulchre Cemetery. Family friend and publisher Dr. George L. Miller eulogized that "although possessed of ample means for the enjoyment of every earthly luxury, she had no taste for fine mansions or for the geegaws that so often turn the heads and corrupt the tastes of the rich."[60]

Mary Lucretia (the name inscribed on the family obelisk and the one she used in her will) named John A. Creighton, Long Jim Creighton, and Herman Kountze executors of her estate, which was attested to by close family friends, attorney James M. Woolworth, and publisher Dr. George L. Miller. She bequeathed $50,000 to her sister Emma, $20,000 to sister Mary, $10,000 to mother Emily, and about $5,000 each to brothers George and Philip. Since Edward had earned the money, she distributed the bulk of the estate to his family, including $150,000 to John Andrew. The other bequests were $75,000 trusts to each of Edward's other brothers and sisters, which would go to their children upon their deaths, except for Joseph, who received $25,000 because he had only one child. Finally, she bequeathed $100,000 to establish Creighton College as a testimony to her late husband's virtues and her affection to his memory. She did so because Edward had expressed a desire to establish an institution of higher learning; an acquaintance argued he wished to do so because his old telegraph colleagues Hiram Sibley and Ezra Cornell had done so.[61]

Lucretia's younger sister Emma also changed her name upon coming to Omaha; her marriage license, issued in Douglas County on June 8, 1868, bears the name Sarah E. (Emily) Wareham. She was born in Dayton on October 17, 1840, and gained an education at a convent school. At age twenty-two, she and her eleven-year-old sister Mary paid an extended visit to their married sister and father in Omaha; where they resided is a matter of conjecture, since Omaha did not have a city directory at the time. Sarah Emily met John Andrew before he departed for Montana; during his absence she kept up an active social schedule. One resident remembered,

> We used to have some pretty good times in those days in spite of primitive methods. There were plenty of pretty girls and they did not want for attention, for there were always a lot of young fellows who were keen for dances. Among some of the young ladies who kept things lively socially I remember Emma [Sarah Emily] and Mary Wareham, . . .[62]

Nonetheless, she waited and married John Andrew after he returned to Omaha following his five-year hiatus in Montana, which established him as a successful businessman in his own right. The newlyweds moved in with Edward and Mary Lucretia, and continued to live in that house until 1884. At that time, John and Sarah Emily built a house at Twentieth and Chicago streets that became the "show place of the city." The three-story structure faced Chicago Street, but had a city directory address of 404 North Twentieth Street. It had a mansard roof and seventeen rooms, and occupied a spacious piece of property on the north slope of Capitol Hill, below Omaha (Central) High School. Stately Corinthian columns supported a porch that traversed the front of the home. Upon John Andrew's death, his nephew John D.

Creighton purchased the house and lived in it until his passing in 1922. Subsequently, the property became an apartment building, and then a rest home for the elderly, before being demolished to make way for I-480. Attempts by preservationists to save the structure, by moving it to the Creighton University campus or the Joslyn Art Museum property, failed because of conflicting views as to whether or not the house could survive relocation, as well as the lack of money to facilitate moving and maintaining the building.[63]

During her twenty-five years in Omaha, Sarah Emily lavished her attention on the Catholic Church. She had a "rich alto voice," which she contributed to the choir of St. Mary's Church. Subsequently, she sang regularly at masses at the Convent of the Poor Clares and at the Creighton University chapel. Money inherited from her sister gave her independent means for charitable activity, and she liberally dispensed money to St. Joseph Hospital, Creighton University, and St. John's Church. Unfortunately, like her older sister, Sarah Emily did not possess good health. She "suffered from a rheumatic complaint" and ultimately "became afflicted with a fatal pulmonary affection," from which she died on September 30, 1888. According to one obituary, she had spent the "last five years of her life . . . in a vain attempt to renew her shattered health." Through special arrangements, the funeral took place at St. John's Collegiate Church: "not being a parochial church, funeral ceremonies are unusual there, but the intimate relations of the deceased to the college and church were grounds for the exception in her case." The choir sang a Gregorian Mass, but other musical features were eliminated at the request of her sister Mary, who had just arranged for the purchase of the church organ back east and now heard the instrument for the first time. Sarah Emily was buried next to her father and infant daughter LuLu in the family plot at Holy Sepulchre Cemetery.[64]

Continuing the name duality, the family inscribed "Sarah Emily" on the cemetery obelisk and "S. E. C." on her individual headstone. However, the Stations of the Cross dedicated in her honor and Mary's Altar in St. John's Church dedicated in the memory of her mother bear the name Emma S. Creighton. On the other hand, she made her will in the name Sarah E. Creighton. The inventory of her estate revealed that she personally owned seven pieces of property in Douglas and Sarpy counties valued at $98,400, as well as several thousands of dollars in stocks, bonds, and personal loans due. Because she possessed wealth independently, her bequests differed from those of Mary Lucretia. She gave her husband the East Store in the Arlington Block at 1511 Dodge Street and conferred on Creighton University a 132' by 44' piece of land adjacent to the Creighton Block. She bestowed on her mother and her younger sister Mary $50,000 each, while $15,000 went to her brother George, but only $5,000 to brother Philip. Mary also received all her "diamonds and jewels," while her personal servant, Ambrose Erland, received $5,000. Finally, she bequeathed $50,000 to the Franciscan Sisterhood of Nebraska to construct a new building for St. Joseph Hospital. She had dictated her will to family friend and attorney James M. Woolworth just nine days before her death, naming John Andrew and John A. Schenk, sister Mary's husband, as executors.[65]

Mary Wareham, born in 1848 and eleven years younger than Sarah Emily, spent her teenage years with her sisters in Omaha, but then at an undetermined time returned to Dayton. She married John A. Schenk, a successful entrepreneur in the piano business. They and their daughter Mary Lucretia Schenk arrived back in Omaha a few days before Sarah Emily's death. John Andrew convinced them to remain in Omaha and live with him. Schenk closed his piano business, but retained his property interests in Dayton. He and John Andrew became close friends, and he remained in Omaha after his wife died in about 1900 (the only Wareham sister to reach fifty years of age). While he kept an office with John Andrew at the First National Bank building, he did not operate any businesses in Omaha. Instead, he engaged his tastes in art and music. A talented musician, he played the organ and directed the choir at St. John's Church. His daughter Mary Lucretia Schenk married Albert Vincent Kinsler (whose brother James was in the first Creighton College graduating class). John Schenk returned to Dayton following John Andrew's death, but died the next year at age fifty-five.[66]

The Jesuits

A popular tale in Montana alleged that John A. Creighton chose the Jesuits to administer Creighton University because of a friendship made in Virginia City. He had suffered a broken leg in a stagecoach accident and, at the time, the Reverend Anthony Ravalli, S.J., happened to visit the boomtown. The priest aided the local physician in treating the patient, who subsequently, in the spirit of gratitude, founded a Jesuit college. The legend was printed as late as 1936, before being corrected in a biography of Fr. Ravalli. Actually, Mary Lucretia founded the University in Edward's name, and the Creighton family in Ohio had a strong attachment to the Dominican order. They had worshiped at their mission churches and John had attended their St. Joseph's College. The original college building (today, the east-west central section of the Administration Building) was built on the Dominican model and records of the order reveal that it received an offer, but refused to accept the administrative assignment.[67]

The Vicariate Apostolic of the Nebraska Territory originated in 1857, but the position was temporarily unoccupied when Mary Lucretia died. The executors began building the college, but then transferred the bequest to the newly appointed Bishop James O'Connor in August 1876. He wanted the school, but had no means to oversee it; therefore, he convinced the Jesuits of the Missouri Province to add the school to their mission. St. Ignatius of Loyola, a Spanish nobleman and military officer (1491–1556) had founded the Company (Society) of Jesus with six followers in 1540. He had attended several schools and had received a master's degree from the University of Paris in 1534. He was not a scholar, however, and his original mission for the order was to imitate the life of Christ. Yet, quickly the necessity of training its own scholastics (college men entering the order) added an educational component that burgeoned as secular students (externs) vied for entrance to the classes. In 1547, the order founded a college at Messina, Italy, exclusively for externs, and three years later Pope Julius III issued a bull confirming the Society, which specifically referred to a teaching mission.[68]

Ignatius embraced the teaching mission, establishing the principles of Jesuit education and opening thirty-three colleges by the time of his death. During the 1540s, he wrote the Spiritual Exercises, an outline of how he saved his soul. It contained valuable lessons in character development and how to achieve unity with Jesus Christ. Thus, it became the bedrock of Jesuit pedagogy, since the goal of education was to train virtuous Christian gentlemen. By the end of the decade, Ignatius had completed the first draft of The Constitutions, a ten-part document that imparted the fundamental law of the order. Part IV, in seventeen short "chapters," dealt specifically with education, but only in terms of statements of principle. For example, applying the "principle of gratuity" ("freely give what we have freely received") meant that Jesuits could not accept pay for their services. When a college education consisted of Jesuits teaching theology and the humanities, the rule also meant that no tuition was charged. In the United States in the nineteenth century, the dictum succumbed to a lack of endowers and to the need for lay faculty to teach vocational subjects, the sciences, and in the professional schools. Furthermore, with these principles, Ignatius understood the need for diversity and flexibility, but he still desired as much uniformity as possible. Like the Catholic Church and the military, he organized the Society in a centralized hierarchical form (a local community subject to a rector, who is in turn subject to a provincial, who is subject to the general in Rome) that also encouraged educational uniformity. The result was the *Ratio Atque Istitutio Studiorum Societatis Iesu;* loosely translated as The Jesuit Code of Liberal Education, but always shortened to the *Ratio Studiorum*.[69]

The drive to uniformity entered its final stage in 1584, when the Very Reverend General Claude Aquaviva, S.J., appointed a committee of six to study the operation of various Jesuit colleges and to prepare a draft document. After fifteen years of haggling along national lines, he instituted the *Ratio Studiorum* in 1599. Ignatius and his colleagues had received training in the philosophy of Scholasticism; thus, the *Ratio Studiorum* emphasized Aristotle and St. Thomas Aquinas. By the sixteenth century, however, Renaissance Humanism significantly modified that late-medieval pedagogy. The *Ratio Studiorum* established guidelines for the administration of Jesuit colleges, as well as for teaching methods. The program was designed to take young boys at the age of puberty (fourteen) and train them until maturity (twenty-one) in order that they might enter the world as moral Christian gentlemen. A single Jesuit instructor taught all subjects to a class of students for the entire year. The principles of "prelection" and "emulation" guided instruction. Prelection consisted of the teacher reading and explaining a text (translation and interpretation), then the students preparing exercises based on that same passage and the lecture just received. If a student studied well, he could recite back what the professor had told the class and possibly add some small personal insight. In writing, the students reproduced a selection they read. The method assumed they would acquire knowledge from the content of the passage and that their Latin grammar and style would improve through imitating the writing of great classical authors. Then, on a regular basis—weekly, monthly, quarterly, semi-annually, annually—students competed as individuals and in groups. Citations and prizes were distributed to the winners, and it was argued that all students benefited from learning how "to emulate" the good student.

Finally, the *Ratio Studiorum* established the content of Jesuit education. It prescribed an emphasis on Greek and Latin (especially the later because it was the language of the educated European of that era), and on Christian and classic texts. It consisted of a three-part division of study: languages (further divided into grammar, humanities, and rhetoric), philosophy, and theology, each of which followed a progression of texts on various subjects suited to each year of study. In its original form the *Ratio Studiorum* lasted until religious-political conflicts led to the suppression of the Society of Jesus in 1773. Following the restoration of the order in 1814, the *Ratio Studiorum* underwent two revisions, in 1832 and 1851, but the system that the Jesuits of the Missouri Province brought to Creighton University in 1878 differed little from the original principles and methods.[70]

The Missouri Province of the Society of Jesus, the second one established in the United States, resulted from a conflict between French-speaking Belgian Jesuits and English-speaking American Jesuits in the Maryland Province. In 1823, two priests, seven scholastics, and three lay brothers were sent to St. Louis, a town recently absorbed with the Louisiana Purchase that had many residents who spoke French. The Missouri Province mushroomed with American westward expansion and, in 1878, the frontier town of Omaha lay within its jurisdiction. It had briefly administered a mission to Indians at a site located in what is now Council Bluffs, Iowa, under the direction of Fr. Peter De Smet, S.J., in 1838–40. It now sent the Reverend Roman Shaffel (originally Vershaffel) to Omaha to create and administer Creighton University. He had been born in Belgium in 1838, had entered the Missouri Province in 1860, had been ordained in 1874, and had celebrated his fortieth birthday two weeks before the school opened. He taught French in St. Louis in the 1860s, finished his theology at Woodstock, Maryland, in the early 1870s, and came to Omaha from the new St. Ignatius College in Chicago, subsequently renamed Loyola University.[71]

With his arrival, the dramatis personae had assembled on stage; the story of Creighton University was ready to begin. A fatherless family of striving Irish immigrants had arrived in Philadelphia at the opening of the nineteenth century. All of the migrating brothers eventually became successful landowners in the then-frontier state of Ohio. One of the brothers, James Creighton, fathered sons—Edward and John—who succeeded brilliantly in business and married Wareham sisters, all of them attaining the status of founders of Creighton University and other Catholic institutions in Omaha. The success of the Creighton brothers also inspired the migration of relatives that established the most prominent clan in Omaha, and most of its members became outstanding benefactors of Creighton University. Moreover, Edward and John's sister Alice contributed three families to the clan. Her marriage to

Thomas McShane produced five eminently successful Omaha businessmen and two of their daughters established other branches of the family tree that flourished in the city. The McShanes and the Furays became intimately associated with the development of Creighton University. Thus, within a century (James migrated in 1805 and John died in 1907), the scions of evicted Irish farm tenants achieved the American Dream—wealth, fame, prestige—and they used their resources benevolently, including the creation of an institution that gives their name immortality.

CHAPTER 2

Getting Started

Hast ever been to Omaha
Where rolls the dark Missouri down,
And four strong horses scarce can draw
An empty wagon through town?
Where sand is blown from every mound
To fill your eyes and ears and throat—
Where all the steamers are aground
And all the shanties are afloat?
Where whiskey shops the livelong night
Are vending poison juice;
Where men are often very tight,
And women deemed a trifle base?
Where taverns have an anxious guest
For every corner shelf and crack;
With half the people going west,
And all the others going back?
Where theaters are all the run,
And bloody scalpers come to trade;
Where everything is overdone
And everybody underpaid?
If not take heed to what I say:
You'll find it just as I have found it;
And if it lies upon your way,
For God's sake, reader, go around it!

Harper's Magazine
SEPTEMBER 1869

Creighton College opened its doors on the first Monday in September of 1878, in a raucous frontier town that possessed an ample number of drinking establishments and houses of prostitution, but lacked paved streets and virtually every other amenity today associated with urban living. Statistically, it became the seventeenth institution of higher learning operated by the Jesuits in the United States, but, actually, it took over a decade to achieve that status. Like most American Catholic colleges, especially in frontier areas, it had to begin with elementary grades and develop those young students to become collegians. Moreover, by the time Creighton College inaugurated its program, the United States had developed a distinctive education system to which the Jesuits had to adapt. Students, for example, had initiated an "extra-curriculum" that included debating clubs, literary societies, and intercollegiate sports. American democracy and pragmatism demanded a more utilitarian curriculum geared toward training the average citizen for productive employment. Furthermore, the explosion in scientific knowledge competed fiercely with the humanities-based *Ratio Studiorum*. Thus, during the gestation period, uncertainty abounded and the Missouri Province almost abandoned the school, but as Omaha became a boomtown, the college also began to succeed. The Jesuits adapted, the Province established a uniform course of study, and the generous support of John Andrew and Sarah Emily Creighton financed the evolution of the institution from a grade school to a college that graduated its first class in 1891.

Harvard College was founded in 1636. By the advent of the American Revolution, eight other colonies boasted their own institutions of higher learning, establish an American tradition. The schools followed the English residency model introduced by Oxford and Cambridge. Thus, American colleges located in small-town, rural settings and became "families" that slept, ate, studied, and worshipped together, requiring dormitories, dining facilities, "parental control," and recreation areas. The American Revolution spawned a movement for a national university, but federalism, sectionalism, and religious pluralism subverted the goal as scores of individual political and religious entities established colleges in the early nineteenth century. The Revolution also sparked a demand for a "modern, practical" curriculum to meet the needs of a new nation, setting in motion an acrimonious debate that lasted well over a century.

The curriculum at the Protestant denominational colleges of the colonial era, minus the Catholic theology, closely resembled the *Ratio Studiorum,* with its emphasis on the classics. The typical college professor had a baccalaureate degree, with perhaps some theological training, and taught a prescribed set of courses to a single class of students (like elementary school teachers do today). Reformers desired new pragmatic courses in modern languages, mathematics, science, and "practical vocationalism," all of which necessitated instructors with specialized knowledge. In 1816, the University of Pennsylvania added a course in the physical science of the rural economy, and the Morrill Act of 1862, gave states land to sell to create agricultural and mechanical colleges. In that same era, students entrenched an "extra-curriculum," which included literary societies that invited controversial speakers to campus and that published their own magazines. Organized athletics erupted with the outdoor gymnasium movement brought to the United States by German immigrants in the 1820s, while Greek-letter fraternities also began to spread during that decade. By the Civil War, about 250 colleges existed in the United States; the postwar era witnessed a further burgeoning of state, Morrill land-grant, and privately endowed colleges in the Midwest and the West. At first, these colleges organized their own "preparatory" departments to ensure a sufficient student body, but by the late nineteenth century they shifted that chore to the new stand-alone public high schools. Thus, Creighton College opened with an inherent clash of traditions, the Jesuit versus the American.[1]

The Jesuit and the Catholic educational traditions overlap markedly in the United States, but are not synonymous. Other orders, dioceses, and female religious communities also established schools at all levels. A very limited population and anti-Catholic colonial statutes prevented the establishment of Catholic colleges until after the American Revolution. John Carroll, the first Bishop of Baltimore, was born in Maryland but largely educated in Europe. He became a Jesuit, but severed his relationship with the Order following its four-decade suppression from 1773 to 1814. He devised the first comprehensive plan for Catholic education in the United States, which included the founding of Georgetown University in 1789, eventually administered by the Jesuits. During the next century and a half, most Catholic immigrants resided in cities; thus, the Catholic Church, unsurprisingly, largely followed the dictum of St. Ignatius to place colleges in urban settings. Forty-two Catholic colleges were founded by 1850, but only twelve succeeded. Similarly, between 1850 and 1900, another 152 Catholic men's colleges arose, but only 30 percent survived. Virtually all of them began as elementary and/or secondary schools that had to evolve to the collegiate level. The hostile Protestant environment and the absence of a large, wealthy consumer base stifled that evolution for a majority of the institutions. Furthermore, compared to some Protestant denominational colleges that prepared their clergy, the Council of Trent (1545–1563) gave seminaries the exclusive right to train Catholic priests, denying Catholic colleges a significant source for students.

For laymen, the Catholic college often stood as the only school of that faith in a wide area; thus, it had to serve students of all ages. Admission standards were low and flexible, and were generally administered through a reading examination used to determine a student's placement in the curriculum. All schools sought to defend the faith and to insulate Catholics from heresy. Thus, well into the twentieth century, Catholic colleges remained marginal in the American educational tradition. Major treatises on higher education categorized them with women's, black, Southern, and conservative Protestant colleges, and ignored analyzing them because they "had little to do with setting the standards that eventually prevailed in American academic life."[2]

Nonetheless, mainstream or not, Catholic colleges had to bow to the prevalent American pressures of interest and utility; parents and students demanded classes in English, business, and science. Extracurricular activities, however, were strictly controlled. Literary, debate, and dramatic clubs found acceptance, while Greek-letter fraternities remained prohibited. Similarly, religious associations and military drill groups burgeoned, while sports received a chilly response. Intramural games gained acceptance, but intercollegiate competition did not emerge until the late nineteenth century because of transportation problems between isolated Catholic colleges and fear of contact with non-Catholic schools. Moreover, the American situation—too few Jesuits to fulfill the necessary assignments on a subsistence-pay basis, the need to pay salaries to lay faculty, and a meager endowment—led St. Louis University to obtain operating capital by seeking an exemption from St. Ignatius' no-tuition rule, which the Very Reverend General Jan Roothan, S.J., granted in 1833.[3]

Located on the frontier, the American experience affected Creighton College to the maximum. As late as 1880, Nebraska was a sparsely populated state with only about 450,000 inhabitants, and fewer than 40,000 residents called Douglas County (Omaha) home. Catholics, largely Irish and German, numbered around 12,000 for the multi-state Diocese of Nebraska, headquartered in Omaha thanks to the city council, which had donated twenty-four lots to the Church to entice the bishop to take up residence there. A significant portion of the Catholic population migrated to Nebraska because of ethnic Catholic colonization societies. The Rev. James C. O'Connor, vicar apostolic of Nebraska (1876–1885) and Bishop of Omaha (1885–1890) after the diocese was divided, eagerly supported the Catholic colonization efforts of Civil War general John O'Neill, which produced the towns of O'Neill and Atkinson in Holt County. After the general's premature death at the age of forty-three, Bishop O'Connor participated in founding the Irish Catholic Colonization Association incorporated in Illinois in 1879. Providing long-term, low-interest loans, it enticed 2,000 Catholics to migrate to Greely County, Nebraska, by 1884. Similarly, the Polish Roman Catholic Union organized in 1873, and three years later, with the bishop's blessing, it began to direct settlement to Howard, Sherman, and Valley counties in central Nebraska. A significant settlement of Poles also occurred in "Sheelytown" in Omaha, a neighborhood radiating out from the intersection of 24th and Vinton streets. The immigrants obtained employment at the Joseph Sheely & Company meatpacking plant. Bohemian Catholics also migrated in groups, settling in Butler, Colfax, Saline, and Saunders counties. German Catholics contributed significant numbers, but did not come in colonization groups. Finally, because of the employment opportunities, a significant number of Catholics from all those ethnic groups migrated as individuals and families (e.g., the Creightons) and settled in Omaha.[4]

The relatively sparse population and the substantial geographic size of Nebraska presented problems in terms of creating and maintaining extensive public and parochial school systems. The Nebraska Territorial Legislature passed the Free Public School Act in 1855, but during the 1870s less than half the school-age cohort attended classes. The revised Nebraska Constitution of 1875 provided for a complete public school system from elementary to university, but attendance in the lower grades remained problematic until the state legislature passed a compulsory education act in 1891. Omaha operated three one-room schools in 1859, but the system closed during the Civil War. Public and private schools reopened and expanded during the late 1860s and the 1870s, although barely two thirds of the age cohort five to twenty-one years old actually attended classes by 1880. By that date, the Omaha Public School system consisted of a high school with two teachers and nine elementary schools consisting of grades one through eight. Five of those schools had only one or two teachers, and system-wide, attendance remained erratic—in 1885, the district had 11,202 school-aged children, but daily attendance averaged only 4,253. Older students in lower grades (in 1885, eighteen boys aged seventeen entered elementary school), tardiness, absences, and expulsions plagued the system; and in 1878, only four students graduated from the high school.[5]

The same concerns beleaguered the nascent Catholic system. Before the twentieth century, only a few Catholic elementary schools existed outside of Omaha; interestingly, in some areas of concentrated Catholic settlement, the residents constituted the public school district, hired Catholic teachers, and virtually ran a parochial school financed by a tax levy. In Omaha, the Creighton name was also associated with elementary education; reputedly, Long Jim's sister, Kate, held the first Catholic school classes in her brother's home in 1858, but the sessions did not last long, as she married and moved to California. That year or the next, St. Mary's Church, at 8th and Howard streets, opened a school in its sacristy taught by Miss Johanna O'Brien. Subsequently, in 1862, Bishop James Myles O'Gorman built the first Catholic school building adjacent to St. Mary's and named it Holy Angels. The Sisters of Mercy inherited the school in 1864, and operated it coed for a few years until the bishop hired male instructors to teach the boys, as was Church principle (girls in the church basement, boys in the new school). Shortly thereafter, the Sisters opened Mount Saint Mary Academy at their convent at 24th Street and St. Mary's Avenue; despite the terminology ("academy" designated high school and two years of college-level course work), for many years the school also contained primary grades for its female students. Both schools remained poor, but timely donations of food, money, and furnishings for the convent from the families of the Creighton clan eased the burdens and saved the institutions during economic downturns. The second exclusively elementary Catholic school, operated by the Sisters of the Precious Blood, opened in the basement of the German national parish, St. Mary Magdalene, at 17th and Douglas streets in 1869; most German migrants insisted on establishing separate German-language parishes and schools. The previous year, Omaha Catholics had successfully petitioned the state legislature for $1,000 of public-school funds. At first the Omaha School Board refused to dispense the money, but then compromised by renting the class space at St. Mary Magdalene for $1,000 for the year (the pact revealed the political clout of Catholics in early Nebraska history, but the arrangement did not persist). Finally, in 1877, Bishop James O'Connor sponsored St. Catherine's Academy, a three-story structure with a capacity of one hundred students, also entrusted to the Sisters of Mercy, which enrolled boys in the primary grades. Thus, when Creighton College began teaching boys as young as six years old in 1878, it helped alleviate a shortage in Catholic elementary education.[6]

Clearly, operating a college on the frontier presented a daunting challenge. By the end of territorial days in 1867, the Nebraska Legislature had chartered twenty-three colleges, only one of which survived; the new state government purchased the Methodist seminary and college at Peru, Nebraska, and reorganized it as the Nebraska State Normal School. In 1869, the legislature approved a charter to take advantage of the Morrill Act and located the combined state university and agriculture college in the capital city of Lincoln. It followed the example of Wisconsin and Minnesota, instead of neighboring Iowa and Kansas; both of the latter established two schools, e.g., University of Iowa and Iowa State University. The University of Nebraska did, however, establish a two-year "Latin School" as part of the arts college to prepare students for the prescribed, "rigorously classical" curriculum. The first year, 130 students enrolled tuition-free, but 110 of them entered the preparatory school. Ordained ministers from various Protestant denominations composed the vast majority of the faculty, which taught by the recitation method. Thus, for many years, few distinctions existed between the University of Nebraska and its denominational competitors: Doane College, Congregationalists, 1872, in Crete; Creighton College, Catholics, 1878, in Omaha; Hastings College, Presbyterians, 1882, in Hastings; Luther College, Lutherans, 1883, in Wahoo (later absorbed into Midland Lutheran College in Fremont); Dana College, Danish Lutherans, 1884, in Blair (originally Trinity Seminary); Wesleyan College, Methodists, 1887, in Lincoln; Union College, Seventh Day Adventists, 1891, in Lincoln; and Concordia College, Lutheran Church-Missouri Synod, 1894, in Seward.[7]

Thus, in the educational context, as Creighton College opened, strong revolutionary pedagogical forces stood poised to challenge the Jesuit model. On the frontier in Nebraska, the school came into existence as one of many examples of American religious pluralism, each denomination creating institutions seeking to preserve its faith. Located in a region with a sparse population that included a small minority of Catholics, Creighton College's greatest immediate test came in the form of attracting sufficient students. Since nationally less than 2 percent of the eighteen- to twenty-one-year-olds attended the 311 extant colleges, little likelihood existed that Creighton could begin as an actual college.[8] Moreover, because the majority of the Catholic parents simply wanted their sons to obtain a few years of training in vocationally related subjects, retaining the student population until it reached college age posed an equally daunting task.

With Mary Lucretia's bequest in hand, in March 1877 Bishop O'Connor announced the imminent construction of Creighton College on a seven-acre site composed of five pieces of property purchased from five different parties for the total cost of $12,000. Its position on a crest northwest of Capitol Hill would give it a "grand view of the surrounding country" and, when completed, the building would be "the largest in the city, and its architecture the most artistic." Bishop O'Connor also explained that the college would not be "a boarding institution, but a day school, and at first the instruction [would] be of a primary character until pupils shall have reached a college grade, when the higher branches will be taught." One month later, the bishop began recruiting the Jesuits of the Missouri Province. His initial letter stated that his intention "from the first" had been to invite the Society to administer the school, but he had deferred because he understood that a rejection loomed likely "owing to a want of members." Therefore, he resolved to have one of his priests operate the facility until it prepared sufficient students able to enter college-level classes. "But a careful examination of my surroundings," he revealed, "has satisfied me, that it will be exceedingly difficult for me to conduct the establishment on the proposed plan, and I have, accordingly concluded to ask you if it would not be possible for you to take charge of it, from the start." He asked for only one or two priests, who could hire lay faculty until the Society gained more members, and he promised "all possible security against being disturbed by myself, or my successors, in the possession and administration of the institution."[9]

The Reverend Provincial Thomas O'Neil, S.J., hesitated making a decision until he could visit the site and analyze the bequest. Furthermore, he argued he could not reach a conclusion until he knew the consequences of having accepted the offer to operate Detroit College, set to open in September 1877. The bishop responded by sweetening the pot, pointing out that with the inventory of property completed, it became clear that with residuals due to the increase in the value of Mary Lucretia's estate the total bequest rose to about $200,000. While no correspondences exist in the Midwest Jesuit Archives to verify the machinations, several Jesuit scholars later recorded that Bishop O'Connor had to appeal directly to the Very Reverend General Pieter Beckx, S.J., in Rome to finally convince Fr. Provincial O'Neil to accept the assignment. Construction began in early May, workers laid the cornerstone on August 27, and Fr. Roman A. Shaffel, S.J., arrived on December 6, 1877, in anticipation of welcoming the first students to class in early January. Watching the progress, the Omaha Ministerial Association met but failed to agree upon a motion to build a competing Protestant college in Omaha.[10]

While several decades elapsed before a Protestant college opened its doors in Omaha, the delay in starting classes at Creighton College was anguishing but tolerably short. Fr. Shaffel spent his first night in Omaha with the bishop and the next day assumed his collateral duty as chaplain of the houses of the Sisters of Mercy, residing temporarily in a cottage adjacent to their convent at 18th and Cass streets. Long Jim Creighton bought furniture for the residence, while Sarah Emily and her sister Mary Schenk arranged it and decorated the abode appropriately. On December 10, 1877, Fr. Shaffel and Long Jim visited classrooms at the two Omaha Catholic academies and the public high school, before selecting furniture for the College. The following Sunday, a hastily arranged meeting, not "sufficiently announced," garnered the parents of only twenty-four potential students at St. Philomena's Cathedral. Subsequently, on December 20, Fr. Shaffel placed an advertisement in three Omaha newspapers:

> As the Preparatory Department of the Creighton College will open on the first Monday of January, 1878, the parents who desire to send their sons to this institution will please apply before Christmas to the President, Rev. R. A. Shaffel, at his residence on Eighteenth street, between Cass and California streets.[11]

Bishop O'Connor complained of being "greatly annoyed, and embarrassed by the delay in finishing the College," caused by the lack of "reliable contractors," especially those in charge of delivering the exterior stone, those doing the interior plastering, and those constructing the roof. Unwilling to lose six months of class time, he broached the idea of commencing instruction in January on the first floor of the unfinished building. Father Provincial O'Neil accepted the idea, thinking that three furnished rooms would suffice, and had thus sent Fr. Shaffel to Omaha, who had immediately placed the advertisement. At some point, for unstated reasons probably

associated with the weather and the actual status of the building, Bishop O'Connor
and/or Fr. Provincial O'Neill, possibly in consultation with John A. Creighton,
decided against beginning classes amidst the hazards of a construction site. Father
Shaffel spent the Christmas holiday in Chicago and returned on January 8, one day
after the miss-scheduled opening day, to meet with John, who laid "most of the blame
[for the delay] on James [Long Jim] Creighton." "Some difficulty" (the rooms still
had not been plastered), he reported, had occurred during his absence that necessitated postponing the opening. Shaffel found John Andrew "exceedingly kind" and
said he "repeatedly" stated his willingness "to do anything for the success of the college." As work on the building continued, Fr. Shaffel spent his time making himself
"useful to the Catholics of Omaha," even serving as assistant pastor at the cathedral
for a month and a half. Long Jim left Omaha "to establish ranches on the Niobrara
[River]." The building's architect, a Mr. Dunfrene, now oversaw the completion of
the project and Fr. Shaffel finally moved into his room in Creighton College on July
10, 1878. The first use of the building occurred July 23 through 31, as the Reverend
Walter Hill of St. Louis University conducted a retreat for the bishop and twenty-
seven local clergymen, who used the second floor classrooms as a dormitory.[12]

Creighton College occupied the center of a crest, graded to create level ground
for a few hundred yards on all sides of the school. The excess dirt became two prominent terraces west and north of the structure. In modified form, they are still visible
today: from the Anderson Plaza in front of the Hixson-Lied Science Building, the
first terrace rises to the level of Reinert Alumni Library, and then the second continues up to the level of the Creighton College, that is, the Administration Building.
The land west of the terraces was "low and sloping, and not devoted to any use,
except perhaps as pasturage for the college cow. A small piece was cultivated as a
vegetable garden for a while." Workers dug a well for drinking water sixty-six feet
north of the building and it remained in use until the building became part of the
city water system in 1882. Thirty-five feet west of the building lay a large cistern that
captured rainwater used for the steam-heat boiler, bathing, clothes washing, and
other non-potable purposes.[13]

For the first decade, California Street existed as the only road that abutted the
school. The city possessed no paved streets until 1880; thus, at times "the town could
not be seen from the college on account of dust." Directly east of the building lay a
farm with its smelly stable only yards away from the walkway to the entrance. Radiating away from the school in opposite directions, Jefferson Street ran south from
Cass Street and Saunders Street headed north from Cuming Street, bisecting an
established neighborhood of scores of houses. Only a few houses, however, existed
northwest of Cuming Street, and nothing stood directly west of the building, except
a brickyard on the next hill (where the Creighton University Medical Center sits
today). In the valley between, the North Omaha Creek flowed northeasterly toward
the Missouri River (modern buildings such as Rigge Science constructed in the old
creek bed sit on concrete pilings needed to stabilize the ground). Students erected
dams across the creek and swam in the pools they created during noon recess and

after school. Houses crowded the area southeast of the College and due east along California Street, as that was a thoroughfare leading to the center of town. The nearest trolley lines ran as far west as 20th and California streets, and Saunders (today's 24th) and Cuming streets; faculty and students avoided the latter because the hill from Cuming to the College was too steep to walk up regularly. Finally, the school demarcated its property on three sides with a high wooden fence—on the west, the north, and partly on the east, south to Webster Street.[14]

Creighton College originally consisted of a three-story building with a basement. The upper floors were framed with red St. Louis pressed brick and the basement, which stood partially above ground, was trimmed with Kansas limestone. The structure measured 54 feet across the front, 124 feet deep, and rose 110 feet high to the top of its tower. John A. Creighton intimated that he wanted an impressive 3,000-pound bell for the tower, but he did not follow through on that idea. The east entrance (on level with today's second floor) was for visitors only, and it had several steps leading up to a porch that could accommodate chairs to seat six or eight people. Similar steps and a porch formed the student entrance to the building on the west side.[15] A contemporary journalist provided a guided tour of the structure:

> Within the college, the exterior indications of simplicity and durability are everywhere, and in everything visible. The main entrance opens upon a hall furnished in hard pine and black walnut. On either side of this hall is the office and parlor, the latter tastefully furnished, and containing beautifully executed life-size portraits of Mr. and Mrs. Edward Creighton. . . . The hall from which this parlor opens leads to another running at right angles, from which stairs, on either side lead to the upper floors, as also to the basement, and from which entrance is also had to lavatories and wardrobes, which in turn, open upon classrooms. On the first floor there are four class-rooms in daily use. They are separated by glass partitions, the lower windows of which are stained, while the upper panes permit the light fromc both sides of the building to pass for the benefit of all classes. These partitions are so constructed as to be raised and lowered at will, thus making it possible when desired to throw two rooms into one, which is done when lectures are given to more than one class. The rooms are furnished in the same woods as the hall, in keeping with which is furniture in ash and walnut. In the floor below [the basement] are the engine and boiler room and playrooms, which are used in stormy weather. On the second floor there are four more class rooms, furnished like those on the first floor. In these rooms are the two advanced classes of the college. On the third floor is the main hall of the college as also the rooms of most of the faculty. The hall is used on Fridays and Sundays for religious exercises. Near the main entrance is an altar of walnut and ash, chastely designed and richly ornamented, the gift of Mr. John A. Creighton.[16]

Thus, the interior of the building was a large square formed by solid walls, with the first and second floors quartered into adjoining classrooms. In comparison to the above description, the Reverend Provincial E. A. Higgins, S.J., wrote that the partitions were solid on the lower five feet and doors at the four-corners led from room to room. The Reverend William Rigge, S.J., explained further that the upper glass portions of the partitions were like wide windows so that the lower half opened up and the upper half opened down. When needed, the lower window panel(s) could be raised allowing a single faculty member to oversee two, three, or four classes during study periods or in case of the illness of a faculty member (substitute teachers did not exist). All accounts agreed that blackboards hung on the east and west exterior wall of each classroom, respectively. The lower grades of "rudiments" and "first grammar" held classes on the first floor, while the upper two grades of "second grammar" and "third humanities" occupied the second floor. The third floor contained the auditorium-chapel and the quarters for the Jesuits. The basement housed the utilities and a recreation room. Staircases to all floors existed outside the interior square on the east (front) and west (rear) sides of the building. Inconveniently, if a person wished to go from the west to the east side of the first or second floor without disturbing classes in session, he had to go up to the third floor, through the auditorium and down the stairs on the other side, or down to the basement, across the utility room and up the stairs. Good exercise, perhaps, but not a jaunt one relished undertaking routinely.[17]

Fr. Shaffel, "undersized in stature" and "parsimonious," whose actions seemed "somewhat nervous," nonetheless recruited two lay teachers in Chicago during the week of August 6, 1878. Two weeks later, four Jesuits, one priest and three scholastics, arrived in Omaha from St. Louis. Father Shaffel, the president and prefect of studies (duties of a contemporary dean), and his staff were unknown to each other, which probably added to the anxiety associated with their inaugural enterprise. The Reverend Hubert Peters, S.J., ordained in 1874, assumed the duties of vice president and prefect of discipline, as well as replacing Fr. Shaffel as chaplain to the Sisters of Mercy. A "loveable man" with "a shock of white hair worn rather long," he spoke English "badly." He definitely was "not a college man," but "everyone liked him" and called him "George Washington or Quaker Oats," because he resembled pictures of the first American president or the character on the cereal container.[18]

Michael Eicher entered the order in 1874, and was the only scholastic with teaching experience—one year. He was a "good teacher and liked by everyone" and stayed for three years. Augustus Beile had only became a scholastic in 1876, but taught the highest class (third humanities) despite being the youngest faculty member. He contracted consumption, taught little, and tried to oversee the bookstore. "Ambitious, he took his fate very hard"; the day he left Creighton College he wrote on the blackboard, "Life is but an empty dream." He died Easter Sunday, April 17, 1880, at the age of twenty-two. The third scholastic, Gulielmus (William) F. Rigge, came to Omaha to rest the eyes he "overstrained" during his noviceship. Thus, during the first year, he took charge of the boiler room, cleaned the private rooms, and generally did the manual work of a "lay brother." He also served as sacristan, but admitted to possessing no artistic flare, so Eicher actually decorated the altar on feast days. Rigge's sight recovered and he began teaching a full schedule the second year.[19]

Students "idolized" layman Edward A. O'Brien as "a remarkably fine teacher"; he taught a rudiments section, at first called "second English," but left after one year to become a reporter for the *Omaha Bee* newspaper. The widow Mary E. (Mrs. Marcus

L.) Hall assumed the duties for the youngest group, "third English." Her husband had operated a second-hand furniture store in Omaha, but had died in 1874. She migrated to Chicago about 1876, and returned to Omaha to teach at Creighton College for one year. In print she was described as a "competent teacher." Neither of the original secular teachers returned for a second year and turnover in those positions remained high for the rest of the century.[20]

Creighton College commenced on Monday, September 2, 1878. The following day the *Omaha Daily Herald*, the only one of the three daily newspapers to report the event, wrote:

> Creighton College was on yesterday morning thrown open for the reception of students, of whom, up to noon, about 180 [actually 120] had been enrolled. After the assignments to classes had been made the students were dismissed till this morning, when the regular studies of the classes, of which there are four, will be commenced.[21]

Students had applied for admission all during the month of August. The entrance reading examination consisted of a completion exercise. For example, the tester gave an applicant a sheet of paper with "the boy" and "top" written on it, and the youngster had to recite a complete sentence using the words. "The boy spins the top" would garner a "you pass" response. Except at elite universities, this type of admissions test was quite common, and by the 1870s, sparked the movement demanding higher uniform standards that led to the creation of the College Entrance Examination Board at the turn of the century. The reply above equated to a level called "second reader"; Fr. William Rigge asserted, "The Class of Rudiments of the Year One deserved its name. It was what we would now [1920s] call almost kindergarten. Some of the children in it—they surely were not students—were barely six years old [John B. Furay, Jr., a future president of Loyola University, Chicago, entered Creighton at the start of the second semester, seven weeks shy of his sixth birthday]. The reader need not, therefore, be told what they did in the classroom." At the other end of the spectrum, "the most advanced class, Third Humanities, was in many respects on a level only with the higher grades of the present-day grammar school." Students paid no tuition but did have to purchase their books from the college bookstore. The enrollment increased for most of the year, reaching 155 in mid-November and peaking at 170 in January 1879. During the year, the proportion of Protestants increased; a Jesuit chronicler avowed, "They seem to have kept aloof for a time; but now are anxious to come to college."[22]

The course of study followed the modified *Ratio Studiorum* established at St. Louis University. Theoretically, Creighton College offered the standard six-year classical course "designed to impart a thorough knowledge of the English, Latin and Greek languages; of Mental and Moral Philosophy; of Pure and Mixed Mathematics, and of the Physical Sciences, besides all the usual branches of a polite education." Actually, as noted above, no one "imparted" college-level instruction in the first decade. The school also offered a four-year commercial course, which embraced "all branches of a good English education . . . [to prepare] students chiefly for business and commercial pursuits," but few students were ready for that level of instruction.

The preparatory department for those who could read and write, and who were "not under ten years of age," attracted the vast majority of students, and did so only by lowering the age requirement.[23]

Thus, Creighton College opened as an elementary school beset by all the attendant problems. Regular attendance interfered with other more important pursuits for many students. Warm weather, and the fall and spring horseracing seasons, produced many absences, as did the preview of a new fire engine for the city ("Fr. Peters went to the spot…and caught about a dozen at fault"; they were "severely punished"). Many students started classes late because of fall employment opportunities and left as early as March to return to work again. In November, afternoon dismissal changed from 4:00 to 3:30 because "evenings [were] getting short," but returned to the original time as the days lengthened in April (this was based on natural time; daylight savings time was not introduced until World War I).[24]

Numerous holidays also interrupted the schedule. Five days after school began, the mayor declared a day of mourning for the victims of the tragic Grand Central Hotel fire, in which five firemen lost their lives; to show respect, Fr. Shaffel dismissed afternoon classes. A common practice at Jesuit schools included celebrating the feast day of the college president; thus, on Fr. Shaffel's name day, February 28 (St. Romanus), instead of classes, students attended mass and then played games in the yard. Contest winners chose prizes in a competitive fashion: "About a dozen small paper bags were hung on nails on a board and filled with candies, nuts, and the like, but one or two among them with small stones. The winner of the game then designated the number of the bag he wanted. An unfortunate choice on his part then added to the general merriment." The College also happily included May Day and St. Patrick's Day as annual celebrations; yet, the unassimilated Jesuits (many of the early teachers and administrators were immigrants or had received their education in Europe) stressed the fact that while May 30, 1879, was also the American holiday Decoration Day (now Memorial Day), the "recreation was not given on that account." Similarly, Fr. Shaffel complained that he had to dismiss classes on the Friday following Thanksgiving because the public high school did so, and Creighton students would just play hooky. He vowed not to do it again and did not do so the next two years. His successor, however, began to Americanize the College's holiday schedule. On the other hand, Fr. Shaffel benefited immediately from a newly established Nebraska holiday, Arbor Day, created by a friend of the Creighton clan, J. Sterling Morton, in 1872. Morton intended that his birthday, April 22, be celebrated by planting trees and in 1879, John's nephew, John D. Creighton, purchased four hundred trees and had them planted on the campus.[25]

The first-year schedule also introduced many religious practices that became custom. On Sunday, September 8, 1878, at 9:00 A.M., the Jesuits held their first Mass for students in the third-floor chapel; they admitted the public because some of them were parents bringing their young children and others were prominent individuals like members of the Creighton clan, who took a proprietary interest in the College. A portable altar on casters stored in the hallway was rolled into the room and stationed near the large doors on the east side of the room. Fr. Shaffel had to do the homilies because Fr. Peters, who spoke English poorly and was the only other Jesuit priest, refused to preach. Weekly collections averaged $1.40, which included a silver dollar from John A. Creighton. Obviously, weekly revenue suffered greatly when John Andrew was out of town on business or vacation. The Sunday morning service included an "instruction" for the young students in attendance. On September 21, the two priests initiated Saturday confessions at the chapel for adults, and students who had made their First Communion. The following year, the Sunday Mass at the College became mandatory for all Catholic students, unless they acted as servers at a neighborhood church.[26]

The first annual three-day retreat began Tuesday, September 24, 1878. Then, in mid-October, Fr. Peters became the director of the newly initiated Sodality of the Blessed Virgin Mary. Reputedly, white and blue immediately became the school colors because the "Jesuit Administration of the School" chose them "primarily because they place the University under the patronage of the Blessed Virgin Mary, Mother of God, whose colors these traditionally are." In subsequent months, special masses celebrated on the day of death of Edward (November 5) and Mary Lucretia Creighton (January 23) became part of the annual schedule. In 1881, Fr. Provincial Higgins named St. Edward the patron saint of the College, adding the feast day of October 13 to the list of special Masses. Finally, on February 10, 1879, Fr. Shaffel instituted catechism lessons for forty boys that resulted in twenty-eight of them making their First Communion on May 4.[27]

The first year also witnessed the introduction of a limited "extra-curriculum." On Friday night, February 21, 1879, the College held its first public entertainment in the third-floor auditorium-chapel. A temporary stage was erected on the west end of the room. Poor Catholics in Omaha received the proceeds from an overflow crowd that heard songs sung by the week-old choir and "declamations" from other students. Lay teacher Edward O'Brien managed the extravaganza and played the lead in the evening's finale, a "costumed reenactment" of *The Trial of Robert Emmet*, a play about the Irish nationalist who was tried and hanged for instigating an uprising in 1803. Because of the young age of the students, athletics merely consisted of intramural games during the "recreation" period. The "big boys" played on the 120-by-240-foot field south of the building, while the "little boys" used the 190-by-210-foot north lawn. "Football according to the old style [pre-rugby, soccer-style game of trying to kick or punt a ball to score a goal at the opponents end of the field] was the favorite game of the students in the yard. The small boys especially enjoyed it." The one "interscholastic sport" that existed the Jesuits frowned upon because it came in the form of fisticuffs. According to Fr. John B. Furay, Jr., S.J., "Most of the boys came from the south and southeast sectors [of Omaha]. As they passed the [Omaha Central] High School on Capitol Avenue there were occasional scrimmages and fights between the two high schools." "Scrimmages" probably was a euphemism for group fights, although it may have referred to brief games of rugby football, which was emerging at the time.[28]

The first year ended with examinations and Commencement (promotion to the next grade). On Monday, June 16, 1879, the faculty formed two boards to test the students (instructors did not prepare exams for their own class). On Wednesday, June 25, Mmes. Edward C. and Felix McShane decorated the auditorium and hung a picture of Edward and Mary Lucretia Creighton, commissioned by John in Dayton, above the temporary stage. Although a rainstorm erupted that evening, "few of the 700 chairs [sat] empty." Some students gave speeches or sang songs, and the affair ended before 10:00 P.M. After the exhibition, refreshments (wine, cakes, and cigars) were served to the clergy and reporters. Subsequently, as the College embarked on year two, a journalist offered an evaluation:

> The college has now entered upon its second year, with the prestige of success of an unequivocal kind, which attended the first year of its existence. It has seemingly established itself in the community, as is evidenced by its increased attendance and the uniform kindliness of expression with which it is spoken of in our midst. A new institution, established under novel circumstances, gathering together strange students and placing them under professors in many respects unknown to them, it has achieved a success which, to say the least, is gratifying and commendable. With the advance of time this success will become more and more pronounced, especially when the graduates, trained to think, to speak, to write, to live lives of purity and honesty before God and man, come forth to fight the battle of life in all its stern reality. For such is the aim of Creighton College. Let it be hoped it may be eminently successful in its laudable undertaking for the sake of our city, our State, and for humanity; and that it may convey to posterity the name of its generous founder, of whose energy and liability it is, indeed, a befitting memorial.[29]

Father Shaffel probably sent the editor a thank-you note. Year two did get off to a rousing start: 140 students enrolled on the first Monday in September and the maximum reached 200 by Thanksgiving. Attendance, of course, remained a different story. Six weeks before the end of the academic year, the number of students began diminishing rapidly: "A good many . . . gone to work." On numerous occasions, rain also took a heavy toll; muddy unpaved roads invariably produced high absentee rates, as well as frequent complaints about the dirtying of the hallways by the students that did arrive. New policies that affected those in attendance included dismissing Protestants from the mass schedule and initiating monthly deportment reports to the parents. Father Shaffel had 1,500 cards printed at the *Omaha Bee* for $10. Besides trying to elevate learning through improved behavior, the creation of libraries also aimed at improving the intellectual life of the school. In 1879, John donated two thirds of the $3,000 used to purchase about 3,000 volumes from the library of the recently defunct Jesuit Bardstown College (Kentucky). The collection, which reached about 7,200 volumes in 1894, was intended for the exclusive use of the faculty and included works in theology, philosophy, history, literature, law, medicine, mathematics, natural science, and some ancient classics. In April 1880, a group of students formed an association that charged dues (fifteen cents per month), sought donations, and held entertainments to raise funds that they invested in a library of their own. Housed in glass cases in the southeast classroom on the second floor, it grew rapidly and held about 11,000 volumes in 1894. Five years later, the student library moved to the northwest room of the first floor, and with the additional space, gained a comfortable reading room. In a non-academic pursuit, the older boys initiated the first "intercollegiate" sporting event. On Saturday, May 22, 1880, a team of Creighton students lost a baseball game to "a club of town"; the names of the players and the score went unreported.[30]

The second year also produced two closely related monumental changes in the legal status of Creighton College: It incorporated under Nebraska law as a university and the new entity assumed ownership of the Mary Lucretia Creighton Trust. Father Shaffel and Fr. Provincial Higgins feared that in the future a successor to Bishop O'Connor might find cause to alter the agreement between the Nebraska Diocese and the Missouri Province. On his part, Bishop O'Connor worried that the vast expanse of his see would divert his attention from overseeing the Creighton trust and that the future might entail frequent turnovers with extended vacancies in the position of Bishop of Nebraska. To insure the uninterrupted operation of Creighton College, he proposed transferring the Creighton trust to the Missouri Province. Therefore, the Society, with Bishop O'Connor's blessing, engaged the services of James M. Woolworth, John A. Creighton's attorney, to study the issue. All parties agreed to follow his recommendation to incorporate Creighton College under the new Nebraska statute authorizing the creation of universities, and then to have the bishop transfer the Creighton Trust to that new legal entity.[31]

The idea of a comprehensive university on the German model, composed of a liberal arts college and several professional schools, developed in the United States in the mid-nineteenth century. By that time, medical and legal education began to shift from apprenticeship arrangements to proprietary vocational schools administered by a member of the profession. Liberal arts colleges could then acquire a professional school by starting one of their own or by affiliating with, or purchasing, an existing operation. The State of Nebraska decided to encourage such development. On February 27, 1879, the Nebraska Legislature passed an act providing for the incorporation of universities. It required the institution to have a minimum of $100,000 in properties and securities, to submit to a verification inspection by commissioner(s) appointed by a judge of the district court, and to create, at minimum, a five-member board of trustees that had to register with the county clerk. Following some discussion, Fr. General Beckx and Fr. Provincial Higgins agreed to Woolworth's plan. On July 26, 1879, Bishop O'Connor informed the district court of the arrangement and the judge appointed Edward C. McShane as commissioner. He reported favorably, the bishop appointed five Jesuits as trustees, and on August 14, 1879, The Creighton University officially incorporated (in 1968, the University reincorporated and eliminated "The" from its name).[32]

Bishop O'Connor then provided a draft agreement that transferred the trust to the Missouri Province, which promised to abide by the stipulations of the will of Mary Lucretia Creighton. The contract also renewed an earlier promise from the bishop that the university could build a church that would not have the rights and obligations of a parish, and that when the Omaha Diocese had sufficient population to warrant the building of a third church, it would be entrusted to the Jesuits. Father Provincial Higgins insisted on only one amendment, which eventually became exceedingly significant. In 1879, the trust endowment stood at $147,500, which seemed sufficient to operate the university at that time. However, in interpreting Mary Lucretia's will, the court specified that the trustees could invest the money only in mortgages in the state of Nebraska, and in United States, Nebraska, and county bonds. The additional clause in the accord addressed the eventuality that, if in the future, income from the endowment did not meet expenses, the trustees could charge tuition. John A. Creighton accepted the provision, but stated that such a situation would not occur, implying that he would see to it that tuition never became necessary. All parties signed the document and the trust became the property of The Creighton University on December 4, 1879.

Subsequently, all five parts of the settlement—university status, control of the endowment, the right to charge tuition, the right to erect a college church, and the right to administer the next parish established in Omaha—would have dramatic impacts on the institution. Creighton University ended its second year with a new legal status, which established a new fiduciary responsibility and granted significant independence from the Nebraska Diocese. At the time, of course, except by quirk of name and law, the school was neither a college nor a university. Actually, the functioning grammar school concluded its second year initiating written examinations for all but the lowest grades (Harvard had instituted written testing in 1857, and most other colleges quickly followed the example). Creighton University also finished year two with an annual budget balance of $1,174.73 and held its commencement in the auditorium-chapel, which Sarah Emily Creighton, Mary Wareham Schenk, and Miss M. Burkley decorated with flags obtained at Ft. Omaha. Optimism abounded, but the new decade held many surprises in store.[33]

During much of the 1880s, the Missouri Province struggled to operate Creighton University, even as an elementary school. At one point, the Provincial sought to abandon the effort completely; instead, the school temporarily eliminated the *Ratio Studiorum*. Yet while the situation looked discouraging, the institution continued to evolve in the necessary direction. It developed new programs and a wider array of extracurricular activities. At the same time, Omaha entered a boomtown stage that finally provided the essential population base required to support a college in the city.

Finances posed no problem during the decade of the 1880s. Much of the endowment, invested in county bonds, drew 7 to 10 percent interest; even daily balances in a bank account of over $2,000 accrued 4 percent interest. Thus, the endowment produced about $13,000 per annum, easily covering the average annual operating cost of about $11,000. The Jesuits worked for room, board, and clothing; the few lay teachers "were seldom paid more than $60 a month." Moreover, each member of the Society "turned into the common fund whatever came to him from any source," bringing in another "couple of thousands of dollars came in annually" from giving public lectures, conducting missions and retreats, and assisting the secular clergy in nearby parishes.

Supporters left small bequests and members of the Creighton clan regularly donated artifacts, equipment, and supplies, as well as sponsoring the annual premiums and prizes given to the top students. Jesuit frugality also contributed to financial stability. According to a College chronicler, "Weather [in January] turned quite cold toward noon—therm 20; no steam turned on in the chapel, for boys devotions, hence it was somewhat uncomfortable, say some of the scholastics." Seeing your breath while saying your prayers built character and saved money. Thus, by 1887, the University accumulated an "interest fund" beyond the endowment of over $25,000 that it could expend as it saw fit.[34]

The so-called Jesuit checkerboard, frequent changes in assignments and/or locale, did not affect finances, but it did result in six different presidents of Creighton University by the end of the decade. On August 25, 1880, the Fr. General Beckx raised the house (i.e., the Jesuit community) in Omaha to the rank of a college and appointed its first Rector-President, the Rev. Thomas Miles, S.J., a "Southern gentleman" from Kentucky. The rector headed the Jesuit community and the president administered the college; until after World War II, the Society believed that efficient administration necessitated one person hold both positions simultaneously. Since Jesuits held a majority of the faculty and all of the administrative positions, logic dictated that one person direct the community's spiritual and professional lives. As part of the checkerboard Jesuits also frequently moved up and down the chain of command. Thus, for the 1880–81 academic year, Fr. Shaffel remained at the school as vice president (a new position), prefect of studies (formerly the purview of the president), and director of the Sodality of the Blessed Virgin Mary.[35]

On May 9, 1881, however, Fr. Shaffel became pastor of Holy Family Church. As per the Mary Lucretia Creighton trust-transfer agreement, the Jesuit community had the right to administer the new parish and Fr. Provincial Higgins signed the papers deeding the church to the Missouri Province on November 4, 1881. The added responsibility reduced the number of Jesuits at the College, causing staffing problems. Creighton College began the year with ten Jesuits and four secular teachers. According to Fr. Miles, however, obtaining "reliable help from the outside was one of our greatest difficulties. We had to take what we could get to make the most of the disagreeable circumstances." On occasion, the conduct of a lay teacher was not "edifying" and it "brought some discredit on the Institution in the minds of those who were only too glad to see us in trouble." Just after the community received Holy Family parish, one lay teacher went "on a spree," and the new semester opened in January with the termination of the contracts of two other secular faculty members. The Creighton clan found one lay replacement in Perry County, Ohio, but frequent turnover affected morale negatively. In the words of the College chronicler, students seemed "demoralized," the Creighton family "disaffected," and the bishop "displeased."[36]

The dearth of qualified secular teachers exacerbated the historic bane of the Missouri Province—a shortage of Jesuits. The new parish responsibility added a further strain and in 1882, the Reverend Provincial Leopold Bushart, S.J., considered closing a college in Omaha or Chicago. He offered to return the Creighton Trust to the bishop, "but he would not listen to it." Father Provincial Bushart then offered the University and jurisdiction over Nebraska to a newly established group of German Jesuits located at Buffalo, New York, who also conducted a college at Prairie du Chien, Wisconsin. The Missouri Province would gain Jesuits for other tasks through recalling those in Nebraska and improve its overall situation by lessening the number of its missions. Representatives of the German Jesuits visited Omaha in 1883, but declined the tender because they considered the endowment too meager. Father Provincial Bushart responded by taking a step back, abandoning the *Ratio Studiorum,* and restructuring the curriculum at the "college" to "a few lower classes until it be possible after some years with an increase of personnel to equip and maintain higher grades." Unfortunately, as late as 1885, "in a firm tone," Fr. Provincial Bushart turned down a request from Creighton University for a scholastic because none was available; he suggested hiring secular teachers and having the Jesuits stop giving public lectures.[37]

Thus, a reduced staff contributed to a reduced curriculum in 1884. The process began to unfold with Commencement on June 28, 1882, at which the Creighton clan received sixty reserved seats, three full rows on each side of the center aisle. For the first time, the Jesuits distributed a *Catalogue of Creighton College,* which contained a prospectus, a list of the faculty, the names of the students, and the prizewinners in each course in each of the classes. The next year, it also included the students' grades. In 1877, Harvard, the American educational innovator, under the leadership of Charles Eliot, adopted a grading system based on 100 points; Creighton initiated a similar method in 1881. The *Catalogue* also described two distinct courses of study noted previously—the classical and the commercial. The latter revealed the impact on Jesuit education of the public demand for utilitarian classes; by this date, over twenty colleges and universities, most in the Midwest, competed with proprietary business schools by offering commercial courses, and the University of Pennsylvania had established the Wharton School, which became the model for undergraduate business schools. The Creighton commercial course consisted of four years of study that included classes in English, arithmetic, history, geography, penmanship, bookkeeping, mathematics, natural sciences, Christian doctrine, and catechism. Religion, of course, was central to all courses of study; obviously, Jesuits only taught Catholicism, but the "religious opinions of non-Catholics" were "studiously respected." The *Catechism of Catholic Doctrine* was "a text-book in every class, and lectures on it [were] given twice a week. In all the classes the day's [*sic*] work [began] and [ended] with prayer."[38]

In 1883, Fr. Provincial Bushart allowed the school to drop the Greek language from the classical program; the move had the blessing of Bishop O'Connor, "for he had often heard the best people of Omaha find fault with the College because it devoted too much time to the classics, and especially Greek." Creighton did not act alone; for example, a decade earlier Kansas State Agricultural College had ceased instruction of Greek and many more schools eliminated it as an entrance requirement. Then, beginning in the fall of 1884, the Missouri Province allowed the temporary abolition of the *Ratio Studiorum*, replacing it with a four-year program, which combined two years from the commercial course with two years of the classical course. The school retained a "class of rudiments" and added the elective study of the German language. Without mentioning the shortage of Jesuits, the *Catalogue* explained the change as a response to parental pressure:

> Although the College is fully prepared to give a thorough education in the Classical Course and in the higher departments of science, yet, as experience has taught the faculty the parents do not leave their sons long enough at College to be fully educated in the more advanced studies, we have endeavored to accommodate ourselves to the present wants of the public, and have selected a course of instruction, which, completed in four years, will fit the student for a practical business life, whether in literary or scientific pursuits. We shall however hold ourselves ready to advance the standard, whenever a sufficient number of students, fit for still higher studies, will present themselves.[39]

For the moment, the Jesuit tradition succumbed to the American environment. The administration's explanation above actually fit the pattern for Jesuit colleges in the United States, which enrolled almost six thousand students in 1884, but less than 2 percent of that number graduated with an A.B. (Arts Baccalaureate; Creighton retained the terminology until 1971, then shifted to the B.A. designation). The vast majority of Americans, Catholics included, in the late nineteenth century found college irrelevant. Yet, while the course of study at Creighton College diminished in one fashion, it increased in another. Modern science began to make its impact. The reduced four-year program now included a "Scientific Department," a gift from John A. Creighton who supplied "a complete and perfect, chemical, physical, and astronomical outfit." During the third year, students studied physics (primary properties of matter, electricity, and magnetism) and chemistry (inorganic, laboratory practice); the fourth year included astronomy (application of trigonometry, observations), physics (mechanics of solids, liquids, and gasses; outlines of optics and acoustics), and chemistry (organic, laboratory practice).[40]

At mid-century, Abbott Lawrence had endowed a science department at Harvard, ten years later Joseph Sheffield underwrote one at Yale, and John A. Creighton added Creighton College to the increasing number of schools that would augment the classics with a parallel course of study in the sciences. The Jesuits approached John Andrew in the fall of 1883, and he readily agreed to their proposition. His first donation consisted of a wide array of instruments and resources, including a five-inch telescope, a chronometer, and a transit theodolite for astronomy. For physics, apparatus included a Malden triple lantern (with Chadwick-Steward dissolving system), a microscope, a polariscope, a kaleidoscope, electrical apparatus, batteries, Geissler tubes, and cabinets to house the paraphernalia (which obviously emphasized the study of light, motion, and electricity). Chemicals, glassware, "many valuable specimens of gold and silver ore," photography equipment and dark room, and a new building to house a chemical laboratory completed the scientific contribution.[41]

Vice President, the Reverend A. A. Lambert, S.J., received the enviable task of
selecting the instruments and resources, overseeing the design of the chemical building and delivering the first science lecture on the evening of November 14, 1883,
which was well attended, including the bishop and many local clergy. The 30-by-60-
foot, one-story, frame Chemical Building, costing $10,000, was constructed west of
the College and completed by early 1884; the chemicals arrived in March and special
evening classes entailing a $6 fee began in November. The night classes ran intermit-
tently for several years. The 30-by-30-foot laboratory and lecture room for chemistry
dominated the new building, but it also housed the photography rooms and a
mechanical workshop. Unfortunately, poor heating stoves meant that during the winter all chemicals had to be transported to the College Building each evening to prevent freezing. In 1885, the institution secured the services of the Reverend Joseph
Rigge, S.J., to teach chemistry. He also gave numerous public lectures, did public-
service research for the City of Omaha, and became one of the few Jesuits at
Creighton to publish. After a decade, he left Creighton University to do missionary
work; his brother Fr. William Rigge, S.J., fifteen years younger, also pursuing a career
in science, lamented his decision:

> [Joseph] shifted his affections from science to the ministry. The latter is of vastly
> greater importance, I grant, but then there are more workers in its field than that of
> science. . . . But the number of scientific men, Catholic, clerical, and Jesuit, especially
> of his ability is even now lamentably small.[42]

The physics department evolved in the College Building. It began as a "Museum
of Natural History"; i.e., "a varied collection of minerals, coins, petrifications, gold
and silver ores," which included gifts from Bishop O'Connor, and John and other
Creighton clan members. The first equipment included "a lathe, with wood working
apparatus; a set of steam-fitting tools; and many odds and ends of implements," obviously suited more to industrial arts classes. On Ash Wednesday 1883, however, the
first shipment of truly scientific instruments arrived from London. Periodic ship-
ments from London and Boston continued to arrive for the next three years. Thereafter, John Andrew made virtually annual donations. By the time of his death, he had
outfitted a 35-by-54-foot room lined on three sides with tall cabinets filled with
instruments, while the center of the room contained low showcases displaying minerals (a 33-by-26-foot lecture room adjoined). In 1886, the Interstate Exposition
opened in Omaha at the Exposition Hall on 15th and Douglas streets. Creighton
College exhibited many of its museum items and scientific equipment, and students
acted as docents "to explain the utility of the apparatus, and to illustrate by experiment when necessary."[43]

The Creighton exhibit at the Exposition did not include the telescope, purchased
as a physical instrument and housed in a specially built room in the Chemical Building. At first, astronomical observation remained impractical, because it was too cum-
bersome to wheel the telescope and its driving clock to a point some distance from
the tall College Building. Moreover, the detailed calibration of the instruments on a

nightly basis would have left little time for actual observations. The Reverend Michael P. Dowling, S.J., serving his first term as rector-president, secured the support of John Andrew, in 1885, to build "a plain but substantial," fifteen-foot-diameter round house, 250 feet north of the College at a cost of $2,500. John A. McShane donated $1,000 for an astronomical clock, chronograph, and "the necessary electrical outfit." Observatory director, Fr. Joseph Rigge, wanted to provide precise time to Omaha residents, but to do so he needed a sidereal clock and an accurate transit. Again, John provided the money for the instruments and the College built a small square addition on the east side of the observatory to house them. Because Fr. Joseph Rigge was unavailable during the summer of 1888, scholastic William Rigge returned from a temporary post in Chicago to oversee the installation of the equipment. Subsequently, while he studied theology at Woodstock, Maryland, he spent his summer vacations at the Observatory at Creighton; the administration reprinted three articles he wrote for the *Omaha Herald*, concerning plotting the latitude and longitude of the city, in the 1886–87 *Catalogue*. He considered them the first of his approximately five hundred scholarly publications. In 1895, he replaced his brother as director of the Observatory and began a prominent thirty-year career as a Creighton physics teacher and an internationally esteemed astronomer.[44]

Western Union ran a telegraph line to the Observatory that allowed the daily interchange of time signals for longitude with the National Observatory in Washington, D.C. Moreover, the Observatory at Creighton assembled its own library and created an associated "meteorology department" equipped with "barometer, hygrometer, maximum and minimum thermometers [*sic*], and government weather reports." The creation of a "Scientific Department'" consisting of four areas—physics, chemistry, astronomy, and meteorology—precipitated the introduction of public evening science lectures in 1885. The series sought to enlighten "young men of literary and scientific tastes who are engaged in commercial pursuits, students and graduates of law and medicine, [and] gentlemen of maturer years who desire to renew the memory of earlier studies." Oddly, the administration advertised the lectures "for *gentlemen* only," but then stated that "both *ladies* and *gentlemen*" could attend [bold and italics in announcement]. During the Jesuit shortage of the 1880s, these were among the lectures that Fr. Provincial Bushart suggested canceling.[45]

The science department also offered new opportunities to some of the students. In 1885, Fr. Joseph Rigge organized the Chemical Circle, composed of students who attended bi-monthly meetings, which consisted of sophisticated lectures and experiments designed to instill "a facility in lecturing on chemical subjects." The next year, he created the Scientific Circle for physics students; subsequently, he combined them under the rubric Scientific Academy, which annually, in May, presented a program of lectures by the best students. At first, the number of participants remained quite small because the upper grades attracted few students. A large majority of Creighton students enrolled in the lower classes despite their age (e.g., a twelve-, a sixteen-, and a twenty-year-old gained admission to rudiments in 1882), and although a student could earn promotion at any time during the year, few wished to progress to the higher classes. On September 4, 1882, for example, 165 boys registered, 61 for the first time, perpetuating the grade-school atmosphere for another year. Furthermore, a goodly number maintained a part-time relationship with scholarship. As late as 1886, a Jesuit complained, "Brickyard boys, alias 'snow-birds' begin to apply," referring to the students who annually began school in October or November and left in March or April, depending on the weather and employment opportunities.[46]

In 1884, St. Philomena's Cathedral opened its parish school, allowing Creighton College to initiate stricter entrance requirements. On September 7, 1885, "Black Monday, [a] rainy, muddy & disagreeable" day, 110 students registered, while 30 were rejected. Parents who inquired as to why, received the unwelcome reply, "Creighton College is not a Reformatory [or] Accommodation school for winter-birds." The administration explained that it wished to operate the school minus the boys who "in past years, have brought discredit to the College, and by want of manners and of cleanliness have alienated good families, besides causing trouble by negligent attendance & insubordination." It argued, "weeding was necessary," but "done moderately & gently." The above private journal entries conflict significantly with many of the nostalgic reminiscences shared with the University on its twenty-fifth anniversary. For example, Fr. Eicher, who taught the inaugural year as a scholastic, recalled,

> Many of them [student's parents] lived in the poorer quarters of the town and not a few of them were poor. They were, however, good pious, religious people and their children, increasing daily in inherited piety and virtue, were not slow in making earnest endeavors to put on that politeness and refinement of manner, which one looks for with education.

Another former faculty member opined:

> The average Creighton student is good material to work upon; . . . they were keenly alive to the value of an education and determined to have it. Hence, earnestness was their most predominant trait. They were not distracted by the frivolities of the world nor weakened by its vices. Work did not deter nor frighten them.[47]

Such selective memory distorted the magnitude of the attendance problems. Understandable schedule interruptions occurred; for example, the national day of mourning on September 26, 1881, due to the death of President James Garfield or the frequent outbreaks of measles, diphtheria, and/or small pox. The Jesuits, however, chaffed at having to grant another day off in 1885, because the high school initiated a three-day celebration of Thanksgiving and they bristled over the high absence rates (sometimes over 50 percent) when the circus, or a touring baseball team or thespian troop came to town. Succumbing to the realities of the situation, however, the administration not only granted an extra "recreation" day so the students could attend the state fair, it procured free tickets for them. Yet, for un-absolved infractions, the prefect of discipline, dubbed "a true knight of the strap," could "apply the birch with no tender hand."[48]

In 1885, in order to combat the attendance problems, the school issued a new set of stringent regulations for student behavior, aimed at gaining parental support. The *Catalogue* now included a long paragraph stressing "the important duty of *home study*," explaining, "Since recitations in the various branches fill up almost all the school hours, it is very difficult to advance, and utterly impossible to accomplish the work laid out for each year, unless the student devotes at least *two hours daily* to class study at home." In February 1886, the administration followed up by distributing a circular to parents, which they had to sign and return to the president: "The Officers of the College take this occasion of insisting upon the necessity of regular and prompt attendance at class as well as private study at home." It also explained the deportment evaluations and encouraged the parents to contact the president "to inquire why their sons have failed to receive monthly merit-cards."

The administrators continued to lecture the parents, proclaiming their responsibility for "punctuality," which meant "attendance from the *first day* of the session, attendance *every day*,[and] attendance the *whole day* is strictly required [all italics in the *Catalogue*]." Furthermore, "a student not prepared to recite is considered morally absent." Finally, the parents had to understand "politeness" because "the faculty lays great stress on the development of the manners of perfect gentlemen." Thus, boisterous conduct, rough play, disrespect, or insubordination would receive "severe punishment," while "profane language or anything bordering on immorality" would result in "immediate expulsion."[49]

Despite the menacing problems that elicited such stern warnings from the administration, the school did attract a core group that made progress and initiated an increasing number of extracurricular activities. The Mass of the Holy Ghost (changed to Holy Spirit in the 1960s) became an annual celebration in early September, quickly followed by the feast of St. Edward. The Sodality of the Blessed Virgin Mary gained renewed vigor under the direction of the Reverend Peter Leeson, S.J. At first it met on Sunday afternoon at 2:30 for a "sermonette" (a story about Mary with a moral), followed by baseball games until about 5:00. Games also ensued after the Mass on special feast days. According to the "general custom" at Jesuit colleges, Thursdays became the weekly recreation day at Creighton in 1880, while students attended classes on Saturday mornings. Almost "everybody played marbles in those days," especially a game called "Boston," where shooters engaged one another in a ring 8 to 10 feet in diameter. In 1881, a one-wall handball alley was built just north of the west entrance to the College Building. Old style football ("soccer") among the younger students entailed frequent retrieval of the ball kicked over the perimeter fence. New style football (rugby) also got some early play, although in late October 1881, play ceased for a few days because the boys "burst their 'Rugby'." Faculty complaints about rough play surfaced immediately and found their way into the new student regulations discussed above. In 1882, Creighton obtained "an outdoor gymnasium, consisting of a ring-swing, horizon bar, parallel bars, and a large grasshopper (probably, a teeter-totter)." The following year, a water hydrant in the yard marked the inauguration of city water and allowed a portion of the yard to be flooded, producing an outdoor ice rink on cold winter days. Baseball, however, emerged as the most popular team sport and the first played on an interscholastic basis, with the young Jesuit scholastics participating. On May 23, 1885, jubilation descended upon Creighton College as it beat the [Omaha Central] High School team for the first time, 17–8.[50]

Non-sport activity also proliferated. By 1882, the Sodality of the Immaculate Conception (alternate name for the Sodality of the Blessed Virgin Mary) had 110 members, nearly 50 percent of the student body. That same year, the fledgling choir (eventually renamed the College Glee Club) expanded to include the thirty-five-member St. Caecilla (Cecilia) Society, which provided "music for all solemn Religious services, the Monthly Exhibitions, Annual Commencements, and other public exercises of the College." The College Sanctuary Society, first organized in 1879 and renamed the Acolythical Society in 1883, trained altar boys. In 1884, sufficient fourth-year scholars existed to organize the Debating Society to train "ready speakers and fluent writers." The next year, students created a game room supported "by the voluntary contributions of its members" possessing "a large collection of interesting and instructive games, and a suitable apartment [a fourth-year classroom] for indoor amusements during severe or inclement weather." Equipment included "boxing gloves, a shuffle-table, a few pairs of Indian clubs, and several games, principally checkers, chess and back-gammon." The fact that Omaha recorded a temperature of minus 34 degrees Fahrenheit on January 3, 1884, probably spurred the desire for the indoor recreation facility.[51]

Ultimately, Omaha entered a boomtown phase during the 1880s, and at mid-decade the Reverend Provincial Rudolph J. Meyer, S.J., organized a committee on studies to standardize the educational program at the province's colleges. These two developments set Creighton on the path of finally becoming an institution of higher learning. In 1886, the administration introduced the "Supplementary Course," whereby a student could earn an S.B. (Supplementary Bachelors degree) "by devoting one or two years more [beyond the four-year program] to the study of the higher branches." Five students availed themselves of the opportunity and it signaled the imminent return to the *Ratio Studiorum*. The change in the course of study came at a propitious time, as the population of Omaha probably tripled during the 1880s, although most scholars view the figure of 140,000, reported in the 1890 census, as inflated. The sizeable population finally provided an adequate cohort from which to attract college-level students. The percentage of students attending an institution of higher learning remained a single digit, but 3 percent of several thousand young men produced a viable class.[52]

As the population skyrocketed, Omaha grew around the College and modern amenities became available. In 1884, the city extended Jefferson Street north to California and redesignated it 24th Street. That summer work began on grading California Street down twelve feet where it passed the College, which, in turn, created terraces with stone steps to descend to the lower street level. Despite the activity, a bear disrupted the composure of the campus in October, reminding city folk of Omaha's continuing proximity to the frontier. Manufactured gas, distilled from coal and piped west from a riverside plant, became standard for lighting, except for one month in

1886, when the grading of California left the gas lines well above the recently lowered ground level and reburial interrupted service. The following year the Dodge Street horse trolley laid track north on 25th Street to California and thence west (the line was electrified in 1890).[53]

The College Building also received some modern conveniences; with the arrival of city water in 1882, the faculty obtained indoor "water closets," (the large water tank for flushing went in the attic). In 1885, the College acquired an electric doorbell, electric bells for the confessional, and a telephone in the parlor. The Jesuits negotiated a reduced rate for the phone; the standard cost stood at $5 per month for a one-mile radius of operation, but Creighton signed a contract for $50 per year. The College's first phone number was 330; its first outbound call went to number 365; Mary Lucretia informed the caller, "John A. not in." That same year, the administration constructed an east-west corridor down the axis of the four rooms on the first floor, but only half way on the second floor (necessitating an extension several years later). Moreover, in 1886, The Creighton University began to carry on its correspondence on letterhead stationary.[54]

Finally, the College dressed up its front door, although it entailed a family feud and an exorbitant amount of money. A Mr. Reilly, who owned the farm immediately east of the entrance to the College Building, with its odiferous barnyard, had originally offered the property to Bishop O'Connor for $8,000. The bishop thought the price too high and gave a counter offer of $6,000. John McCreary, Mary Creighton's husband and John's brother-in-law, paid Reilly his price and devised a get-rich scheme. He purposely allowed animal manure to accumulate along the common property line, to the great annoyance of the Jesuits. In 1885, they tried to entice him to donate or to sell the acreage inexpensively by offering to place his name on the Observatory. He declined the honor, clutching "his money-bag, and [asked] for his pound of flesh," suggesting they persuade John Andrew to purchase the property in their behalf. John became quite angry, but eventually relented, though his mood did not improve when McCreary refused to trade his property for two lots west of the city. Ultimately, in an exchange in 1887, John Andrew gave McCreary a $15,000 piece of property in downtown Omaha and the College paid him a $2,000 "bonus" to acquire the cow-pie littered property. Immediately, the barn was removed, the yard cleaned, and the residence remodeled to house a few Jesuits.[55]

That same year, the College changed its curriculum. An academic truism states, "changing a curriculum is harder than moving a graveyard." Yet Creighton now did it for the second time in three years. More precisely, the Missouri Province continued to adapt the *Ratio Studiorum* to conditions in the United States. When Fr. General Roothaan issued the updated *Ratio Studiorum* in 1832, he advised its implementation "as far as conditions in America would allow." The revised program maintained the "class system," whereby one teacher taught all subjects to a class; but, as early as 1849, St. Louis University introduced an ancillary "branch system" in which specialized teachers taught a particular subject to some classes. Creighton College began with the mixed system, some specialized laymen teaching courses like bookkeeping and, following John Andrew's endowment of the science department, other specialized Jesuits teaching science classes. Other colleges in the Missouri Province also had distinctions in their course of study. In 1886, in order to eliminate disparities and unnecessary deviations from the *Ratio Studiorum*, the Provincial Congregation, representing St. Louis, Milwaukee (Marquette), Cincinnati (Xavier), Detroit, Omaha, and St. Mary, Kansas, voted unanimously to establish a uniform course of study. To implement the recommendation, Fr. Provincial Meyer mandated that each college establish a local committee to discuss issues "freely and thoroughly." He appointed a central committee to coordinate the activity of the local groups and to write a final report. The work proceeded expeditiously and he promulgated the new uniform course of study on June 2, 1887.[56]

The 1887 Course of Instruction established a seven-year program—three years of high school (Third through First Academic) and four collegiate, Humanities (freshman), Poetry (sophomore), Rhetoric (junior), and Philosophy (senior). It eliminated the "commercial course," but maintained bookkeeping as a freshman subject. The next year the Central Committee issued a "supplement to the report," which made only cosmetic changes (e.g., a specific textbook for a class); therefore, the course of instruction for schools of the Missouri Province endured for the next twenty years with only minor changes. The standard program maintained a "preparatory" level, but it increased the minimum age to twelve (a guideline easily ignored). Humanities initiated college-level study, aiming "to train the students in minor species of Composition, as Narration, Description, Dialogue, Letter-writing. Comparative Grammar is made a special feature. Versification is begun." In terms of subjects, the first year entailed the study of Latin, Greek, English, Christian Doctrine, and Geometry. The so-called Accessory Branches, included ancient history, bookkeeping, and elocution. The second year sought "the cultivation, in special manner, of taste, sentiment and style, which is to be affected chiefly by the study of Poetry in its best models." Cicero, Virgil, Horace, Xenophon, and an array of Christian and English poets provided the models. "Evidences of religion" and plane and spherical trigonometry completed the core courses; ancient history, elocution, physics and chemistry composed the accessory branches. The third year (Rhetoric) provided "the study of Oratory, Historical Composition and Dramatic poetry." It involved more Cicero, with the addition of Demosthenes, Sophocles, Aeschylus, and a select group of Christian and English writers. Mathematics encompassed algebra and analytic geometry, while the United States Constitution and government, elocution, physics, and chemistry provided the accessories. Capping the program, "Philosophy" sought "to form the mind to habits of correct reasoning, and, as the crowning perfection of the whole Course of Instruction, to impart sound principles of mental and moral philosophy." Religion, logic and metaphysics, and ethics provided the core elements. Astronomy, elocution, special courses in literature and science, and "circles and specimens" (special study groups and experiments) completed the class load for the final year.[57]

The adoption of the revised *Ratio Studiorum*, with its seven-year program of prescribed courses, set the Jesuit colleges of the Missouri Province on a collision course with two unrelenting American pedagogical forces—the elective system and the high school movement. Charles Eliot, the first non-clergyman to hold the position, began his forty-year tenure as president at Harvard University in 1869 and immediately initiated a series of educational reforms that had immediate national influence. The most controversial change eliminated required classes and allowed students to choose from a wide array of courses based on individual interest, which soon swept aside the traditional classical course of study at most leading universities in the United States. In 1870, Harvard employed thirty-two professors to teach seventy-three courses; in 1910, the faculty comprised 169 professors who taught 401 courses. Similarly, the expansion of the public school system led to the rapid increase in the number of high schools, allowing state and prestigious private colleges to remove their preparatory departments. In 1870 in the United States, only 72,156 students attended 1,026 high schools; by 1900, the number jumped to 519,251 students in 6,005 high schools. That advance permitted most American colleges to disassociate themselves from adolescent education and to become separate four-year institutions of higher learning. Jesuit educators in the United States had adapted the *Ratio Studiorum* to the American environment during the nineteenth century, but these two pedagogical forces threatened its very existence. The losing struggle was long and agonizing, and lasted well into the twentieth century.[58]

Creighton College returned to the *Ratio Studiorum* with six students in the fifth year (Poetry); five were new and one was repeating the "supplementary class" (fifth-year extension of the previous four-year program) he had not passed the previous year. The four other students from the 1886–87 "supplementary class" did not return to begin their sixth year (Rhetoric), reinforcing the established pattern of students seeking only a few years of utilitarian schooling. The pattern persisted for a few more years, as none of the fifth-year students advanced to Philosophy by 1889. Nonetheless, the administration dropped Rudiments B, the lowest level of the preparatory course, in 1888. The number of college-level students remained a single digit, but the increase of students in the preparatory and academic courses of study pushed the total enrollment toward two hundred.[59]

Now that a trolley ran to the College's doorstep, daily Mass became a requirement for all Catholic students (they could attend their parish church on Sunday). Singing became one of the few elective classes and it brought the employment of the second woman faculty member, a Mrs. C. Burkhart. As a sign of the times, in 1888, a Fr. McGinnis (not on the faculty roster) established the League of the Cross temperance society, which asked Catholic students to "stand up and swear off." Considering the age of the vast majority of the students, the organization at the College seemed unnecessary; apparently, it did not survive summer vacation. That same year, a militia unit appeared on campus. The Civil War-era Morrill Act of 1862 had required land-grant colleges to establish student military companies, but it did not mandate participation by all students. Although not required at private schools, Creighton students had an example at the state university and Jesuits generally supported military organizations. Moreover, the social unrest of the late nineteenth century (strikes, riots) made militia groups popular among the general population, but the oblique references to the Creighton Guards that drilled on the campus did not clarify the unit's nature. Alumni provided the officer corps and, seemingly, students contributed to the rank-and-file of the short-lived troop. The *Catalogue* did not list the unit as one of the College's extracurricular groups, however, a Jesuit chronicler noted that on October 12, 1888, the "boys drilled" at 10:00 A.M. and then marched to 22nd and California streets to greet President Grover Cleveland as he toured Omaha. The rector declared the afternoon a holiday and the baseball team played two games against the high school (i.e., Omaha Central, no scores reported). Reputedly, Creighton won a mythical city baseball championship at about that time. A local sporting-goods firm offered a silver ball to the champion of a playoff among the teams of Omaha. Creighton defeated all comers except the high school, which refused to play. The sponsor tried to withdraw the prize, but John intervened and secured it and it went on display in the College museum.[60]

The Americanization of the holiday schedule continued as it responded favorably to a circular from Bishop O'Connor and agreed participate in a national celebration on April 20, 1889, in honor of the centennial of the inauguration of George Washington as the first president of the United States. Two weeks after those festivities, President Benjamin Harrison visited the institution and delivered a few words to the students. The College decorated in his honor, draping bunting across the building and displaying flags in the windows. The chief executive probably enjoyed the ride up recently paved California Street (on June 14, 1887, a horse had sunk up to its tail in the mud at 23rd and California, following five days of rain). With California Street now a major thoroughfare, Creighton redesigned its approach to the road; it built a new driveway entrance and beautified it with landscaping. It also sold a run-down house it owned on the corner of 25th and California streets; when the new owner moved it to a different lot, the administration graded the property down to street level, removing a steep embankment that had resulted from the original lowering of California Street. On the west, Creighton had to cede twenty-nine yards of property to the city, which constructed a new north-south road, 25th Avenue. It did not pave the street nor grade down its steep slope, so it received little traffic but did tempt "the mountain-climbing proclivities of the students."[61]

While Creighton continued to experience problems attracting college-level students, finances remained robust. During the 1880s, investments produced increasingly healthy returns; for example, the annual surplus amounted to approximately $1,400 in 1880, and about $6,500 in 1885, creating a discretionary fund of around $50,000 by the end of the decade. The Jesuit community survived a scare in 1889, when Platte County, Nebraska, announced it would default on bonds it claimed previous commissioners issued illegally. The administration put the matter in the hands of Judge James M. Woolworth (acting as the school's attorney) and commended "this matter to the prayers of the League of the Sacred Heart." The efforts succeeded; the Supreme Court of Nebraska ruled in favor of the bondholders on May 1, 1890, and "a few days later [Creighton] received a check for $6,000.00 of accrued interest."

Jesuit frugality also continued to contribute to the hearty bottom line. For example, the College depleted its coal supply of 180 tons (to produce steam heat) on April 27, 1888. A chronicle entry for May 1 read, "very rainy morning—chilly and cold all day—no steam because no coal." While the administration refused to order more coal, it did increase the efficiency of the faculty by purchasing a mimeograph machine (recently invented by Thomas Edison) and by providing the students with a welcome creature comfort, indoor toilets in the basement of the school building.[62]

The continued beneficence of the Creighton family spurred further monumental development. Sarah Emily acted as the prime mover in two significant projects. First, she encouraged the Society to build a college church. The Jesuits responded with alacrity, "because of the impropriety and disturbance to the religious piety of the students arising from the fact that in the same hall which was used as the chapel were also held numerous and daily secular events." The Very Reverend General Anton Anderledy, S.J., and Fr. Provincial Meyer agreed, but the former warned the Omaha house not to allow the new responsibility to "distract the fathers from College work." Omaha Architect P. J. Creedon designed a $50,000 sandstone, English Gothic church to seat five hundred, which actually cost less because it was built without the planned transept and apse. The Society acquired the church debt-free. In part, it financed the construction through the sale of a plot of land called Park Place, then on the western edge of town. Father Shaffel had purchased the property for $1,200; due to the boom of the 1880s, it sold for $35,000. John supplied the remaining needed funds, donating $10,000 on the day he helped lay the church's cornerstone. To clear the church site, the remaining student outhouses and the Chemical Building shifted to the northwest. At its new location, the southeast corner of the Chemical Building touched the northwest corner of the College Building, allowing the former to retain its south entrance and east porch. Graders charged ten cents per cubic yard to remove the hilltop that dominated the church site and to deposit it along the creek to the west. On several occasions, when the spring wind gusted, laborers could not shovel the plowed earth into wagons, because the loose clods became dust clouds. Economically, the Administration subsequently sold the excess dirt for eight cents a cubic yard to developers looking to fill ravines.[63]

Long Jim Creighton wanted the church towering atop the crest of the hill above the terminus of Webster Street, north of the Observatory. Father President Dowling, however, "felt the church was intended for use, rather than a monument" and rejected the suggestion, which "resulted in coolness and alienation on the part of a man who had always taken a deep interest in the College." Nonetheless, the Society laid the cornerstone on June 26, 1887. The governor, mayor, congressman, bishop, four bands, and over six hundred members of Catholic societies participated, and about four thousand spectators witnessed the event. It began at 3:00 P.M., with the societies marching from St. Philomena's Cathedral to the site, and concluded by sealing a copper box filled with parchment documents within the cornerstone. That evening, ne'r-do-wells chipped the stone in a failed attempt to steal the box, which a young Jesuit had removed for safekeeping.[64]

Eleven months later, on May 6, 1888, a huge crowd reassembled to dedicate the new collegiate church; that is, it had no parish responsibilities and it could only perform routine church functions such as weddings with the bishop's prior approval. Bishop O'Connor mistakenly dedicated the church in honor of the saint whose name day was celebrated on that date, St. John-before-the-Latin-Gate, instead of the intended St. John the Baptist, the patron saint of John Andrew Creighton, but the error did not affect the church's name. The rest of the ceremony went according to plans, the crowd toured the church, and a choir composed of "the best singers" of Omaha and Council Bluffs serenaded the assembled. The throng viewed a house of worship beautifully appointed through donations, most by members of the Creighton clan. Sarah Emily purchased two side altars (each cost $2,500), one of the stained-glass windows, the sanctuary carpet, upholstered chairs, and other church furniture. Her sister Mary Schenk contributed a $2,500 organ, John A. McShane donated the $5,600 marble main altar, and Agnes McShane and Catherine Furay purchased the other stained-glass windows. Other prominent Catholics supplied the remaining accouterments.[65]

St. John's posed a threat "to become a serious burden" because it "lacked ordinary sources of revenue." To help raise funds, the rector instructed the pastor to "invite a number of ladies of the congregation to form" an altar society, as well as to establish a men's sodality. The financial threat, however, did not delay Sarah Emily's other major building project. With the increase in the size of the Jesuit community, she viewed its personal quarters as cramped and lacking in privacy; therefore, she proposed the immediate construction of a south wing to the College to serve as a residence. She convinced John Andrew to donate the necessary $13,000, but did not live to see the project come to fruition. Shortly after her funeral at St. John's, John donated in her memory a $1,400 artistic set of statues depicting the Stations of the Cross. The Jesuits began to move into their new quarters on February 25, 1889. They sold the former McCreary house, which the new owner relocated. The Creighton University now consisted of a four-building campus—an L-shaped building, housing the College, with an attached Jesuit residence radiating to the south, the wood-framed Chemical Building, the impressive Observatory, and a stunning stone church.[66]

The College had the necessary physical structure, but it had to surmount one more hurdle before achieving its goal. In 1889, Edward, Charles, and John B. Furay, Jr., wished to begin their seventh year (Philosophy) and become the school's first college graduates in June 1890. The Reverend Provincial John P. Frieden, S.J., however, ruled that a graduating class must consist of a minimum of six students. The rector-president, the Reverend Thomas S. Fitzgerald, S.J., protested vehemently, to no avail. Father Provincial Frieden traveled to Omaha to meet with Father Fitzgerald (who succeeded to the office of provincial in 1894), Major John B. Furay, father of the students, and John. The Provincial threatened to pull the Jesuits out of Creighton University if they did not follow his injunction. John Andrew did not retaliate or abandon the institution; "he recovered quickly and completely from the shock, so much so that frequently afterward he would delight to mimic 'John P.' shaking his big right index finger with authority and vehemence while laying down his law, and then laugh at the occurrence [*sic*]." The Furay children transferred to St. Mary's, Kansas, and, unfortunately, in a significantly symbolic manner, the subsequent first graduating class at Creighton College did not include the three Creighton nephews.[67]

Finally, on June 24, 1891, Creighton College granted A.B. degrees to five students (so much for the obduracy of the Provincial): William P. Flynn, James C. Kinsler, Michael P. O'Connor, Francis J. Otis, and Patrick A. McGovern, who entered the priesthood and eventually became rector of St. Philomena's Cathedral. The administration added splendor to Commencement by holding it at Boyd's Opera House, Omaha's premier public venue. The large audience included many non-Catholics "who came to see what 'the Irish High School' (as the college has been dubbed) could accomplish." Subsequently, during the summer, the new Creighton rector-president, the Reverend James F. X. Hoeffer, S.J., announced the elimination of grammar-school education at Creighton. In 1884, the Council of Baltimore encouraged each Catholic parish in the United States that had the resources to establish an elementary school with grades one through eight. While it did not threaten to excommunicate Catholics who did not send their children to a parish school, congregants supported the request wholeheartedly. The boom in Omaha during the 1880s facilitated the rapid development of public and parochial grammar schools. By 1889, the Omaha public system consisted of forty schools and produced fifty high-school graduates. Similarly, nine new parish elementary schools appeared in Omaha alone. Thus, Fr. Hoeffer was actually responding to the complaints of pastors who wanted to retain boys in their parish schools. He ceased accepting elementary students from Omaha, but retained the one hundred previous enrollees. He assigned the forty best students to Third Academic (alleged 10th grade) and created a new division, Third Academic B (those not ready for high school level studies), for the remainder. Rural recruits from Nebraska and Iowa kept the rudiments division operating into the mid-1890s.[68]

Thus Creighton College came of age. In despair, the Missouri Province had tried to abandon the school and the state of Nebraska; instead, it merely eliminated the *Ratio Studiorum* temporarily. Through the continued generosity of the Creighton family, especially Sarah Emily and John Andrew, the school added a science department, which included the Observatory and the Chemical Building, a residence wing to the College Building, and a spectacular college church. The new 1887 Course of Instruction revealed the adaptation of the Jesuits to the conditions of the American environment, but also extended the clash between the Jesuit model and the evolving American model of education. While it continued to furnish elementary education for a few more years, as of 1891, Creighton College achieved its goal. Although the number of students enrolled in the college-level course of study remained small, Creighton College had become an institution of higher learning based on the seven-year Jesuit program of the *Ratio Studiorum*.

CHAPTER 3

Starting Over

There are those who say that there should be no election of studies in secondary schools. . . . This is precisely the method followed in Moslem countries, where the Koran prescribes the perfect education to be administered to all children alike. . . . Another instance of uniform prescribed education may be found in the curriculum of the Jesuit colleges, which has remained unchanged for four hundred years, disregarding some trifling concessions to natural sciences.

Charles W. Eliot
Atlantic Monthly
OCTOBER 1899

The sense of achievement gained from producing the first graduating class at Creighton University evaporated quickly. The Panic of 1893 ushered in a national depression that ravaged the institution's finances. Once again, the College entered the doldrums and the Missouri Province considered shuttering the school. Moreover, the depredations of the anti-Catholic American Protective Association contributed to a siege mentality and further disheartened spirits. The boom of the 1880s ended with the bust of the 1890s and forced Creighton University to start over again at the dawn of the new century. Yet, similar to the previous decade, the University did not merely survive the downturn, it actually nurtured new initiatives that would thrive when the environment improved. John A. Creighton not only underwrote the continued existence of the school, he established two new affiliates—a medical school and a hospital, creating a university in deed, not simply in name. Then, in 1898, Fr. Michael P. Dowling, S.J., reassumed the duties of rector-president and provided energetic leadership for the next decade. John and Fr. Dowling established a vibrant partnership that transformed the university into a dynamo. When John Andrew departed this world in February 1907, and Fr. Dowling moved on to a new assignment one year later, they bequeathed a thriving institution to their successors. The burgeoning University boasted a large liberal arts college (which maintained a high-school division), professional schools for medicine, law, dentistry, and pharmacy, and programs in post-baccalaureate studies. Symbolically, Creighton University reached maturity (twenty-one years of age) in 1899; it had endured a tempestuous childhood, but during early adulthood, historical trade winds began to blow. Subsequently, it celebrated its thirtieth birthday as a financially secure, stable, proud Jesuit American university, but one constantly on guard, defending the *Ratio Studiorum* against the onslaught of American educational reformers led by Charles Eliot.

The poor economic climate of the mid-1890s fertilized the reincarnated anti-Catholic movement in the Midwest. On March 13, 1887, at Clinton, Iowa, Henry F. Bowers, a transplanted Maryland lawyer, organized the American Protective Association (APA). He fanned the flames of "hereditary Protestant antagonism and suspicion of the Catholic Church," and repackaged the nostrums of the mid-century "Know Nothing" American Party, which had questioned Catholic citizenship (one could not be devoted to the pope and be loyal to the United States). Bowers reacted against the late-nineteenth-century increase in Catholic immigration from southern and eastern Europe, and the accentuated power of Irish politicians, especially in urban political machines. He claimed that the installation of the Reverend Richard Scannell as Bishop of Omaha brought him many local adherents. Supposedly, in making the appointment, Pope Leo XIII had ignored the recommendation of the Omaha consulting priests, and Bishop Thomas Bonacum of the new Lincoln Diocese publicly took the side of the hometown clergy. Moreover, at Bishop Scannell's installation Mass, Bishop John Hennessey of Wichita delivered a sermon that strongly chastised critics of the Catholic Church. Reputedly, those actions energized the local APA and precipitated its takeover of the Omaha Republican party, which used anti-Catholic issues to gain control of the local government between 1891 and 1895. The alleged controversy also fostered the creation of an APA weekly newspaper, *The American*, edited by John C. Thompson. A former deputy United States revenue collector and railroad clerk turned printer-publisher, Thompson's one-person operation (indicating limited distribution) appeared between 1892 and 1899.[1]

The local tabloid spewed out vitriolic articles claiming that Catholics fortified their churches and convents, and stockpiled arms for the imminent Armageddon with Protestants. Meanwhile, the national organization circulated spurious documents defaming the pope and warning about looming treachery. One such instrument, "Instructions to Catholics," claimed that the pontiff warned the faithful not to associate with heretics, which "proved" that they could not be loyal Americans. A second publication masqueraded as an encyclical ordering Catholics to massacre Protestants on the feast of St. Ignatius, July 31, 1893. Gullible bigots searched St. Philomena's Cathedral; finding no weapons, they tried to create a scandal concerning empty altar-wine bottles discovered in the basement. Another rumor asserted that a Catholic militia unit drilled nightly on the Creighton College campus. According to Fr. Dowling, several "emissaries from one of the lodges lay on their faces in the grass, one or two nights, watching the College, but had to report 'Nothing doing' in the line of drilling."[2]

The American printed any vicious gossip as gospel, including the far-fetched tale that the Sisters of the Sacred Heart intended to kidnap the daughter of George and Sarah Joslyn, a wealthy Omaha couple (later benefactors of the Joslyn Art Museum). The paper also kept up a steady drumbeat against parochial schools. In most areas of the United States, Protestants controlled the public schools; Catholics complained that the curriculum did not truly meet the standard of nondenominationally Christian. A Protestant perspective dominated history courses and Bible reading posed a two-pronged threat—public schools used the King James Version and discussion denied the position of the Catholic Church as the sole interpreter of scripture. The APA demanded the abolition of Catholic schools and a local supportive politician maneuvered to bankrupt them. Seemingly, the Douglas County treasurer was "infected with the viciousness" and he attempted to tax the property of the Sisters of the Sacred Heart. They sued in district court and the judge ruled in their favor; the treasurer appealed to the Nebraska Supreme Court, but it also upheld the tax-exempt status of the Order and its schools.[3]

The local politicians and their supporters called themselves the White Caps and they proudly thumped their chests as true American patriots. Father Dowling, however, asserted, "Strangely enough, the A.P.A. was largely in the hands of Scandinavians who could hardly speak or write the English language, whose citizenship was of yesterday, and of Orangemen [Irish Protestants] who had crossed the borders of Canada to the United States within the preceding decade." Another local Irish politician concurred, claiming, "Their recruits came principally from naturalized former British subjects, such as Canadians, Scotch and English, with a scattering of Swedes." Nonetheless, Fr. Dowling claimed they conducted a religious war against Catholic institutions and property holders "by opening streets, changing grades, ordering paving, curbing, guttering and other expensive municipal improvements, which piled up special taxes beyond measure and endurance at a time of great financial distress." In 1893, one such attempt included a plan to connect North and South 24th streets by cutting the missing middle segment through college property east of the main building. Creighton College would have lost 526 feet of property and gained "a ridiculously trifling compensation," but Fr. Dowling argued that "vigorous protest" thwarted the plan.[4]

Father Dowling's analysis revealed a siege mentality, whereby an embattled minority attributed virtually every action to bigotry. He overlooked the explosive growth Omaha had experienced the previous decade and the obvious need for street improvements. In fact, the plan to lengthen 24th Street originated in 1889, and the College had supported the proposal. Moreover, the House Consultors contradicted Fr. Dowling's assertion of forceful resistance to the reconstituted project. (House Consultors served as advisors to the rector, and in 1892, some had not become United States citizens. Lawyers informed the rector that citizenship was not a prerequisite to serve as a University trustee, an advisor to the president. Thenceforth, the same five Jesuits who served as Consultors also served as trustees.) Actually, they had reached a consensus that "opposition would not be the wisest course, and [*sic*] that an effort should be made to get all the compensation possible." Despite the fact that sixty thousand Catholics resided in the Omaha Diocese in the early 1890s, Church leaders did not confront their tormentors; they adopted a passive response, which "won increasing respect and eventually helped arouse public indignation against their enemies." The administration had a flag painted on the outdoor handball court and on the dome of the Observatory, "the sections being alternately red and white and the shutter blue with white stars." Father William Rigge claimed to have prevented "further caricaturing of a scientific building" by vigorously arguing against the proposal to paint the walls in a similar patriotic fashion.[5]

Gauging the tangible impact of the APA in Omaha remains problematic. Father Dowling, who returned to the city in 1898 after a ten-year hiatus, proclaimed that the organization "raged with special violence," but that was hyperbole. The organization seemingly influenced the outcome of a few elections for a few offices, but did not establish political dominance in the city or county. Fortunately, no violence occurred, the movement consisting of literary and verbal bigotry. The vicious stories, however, certainly intimidated and annoyed the Jesuit community at Creighton University; in 1893, the House Consultors recommended that the *litterae annuae*, the annual letters from individual Jesuits to the provincial, "contain some account of the petty persecutions" suffered at the hands of the APA. At that time, the organization disgorged its venom through about seventy publications in the United States, but all of them had a "very limited circulation." Moreover, in Omaha, open-minded non-Catholics provided an effective antidote to the fulminations of *The American*. The daily newspapers "held aloof" and kept the malicious diatribes out of their columns. More directly, the Rev. John Williams, Pastor of St. Barnabas Episcopalian Church, "carried on a vigorous defense of the Catholics" in 1893–1894 through articles in the "Parish Messenger." The following year, the *Omaha Bee*, which supported the Republican Party, nevertheless "came out flat-footed against the bigots and for an entire year offered uncompromising opposition to the party of proscription."[6]

Furthermore, The APA had no success in ending the public subsidy to Catholic schools where it existed in Nebraska and, in Omaha, Frank Burkley, prefect of the Gentleman's Sodality of St. John's College Church, gained election to the city council in 1895. According to Fr. Dowling, "At the peak of the excitement Father Hoeffer [President of Creighton University], always a popular preacher and lecturer, delivered a masterly lecture on 'The Jesuits,' which appeared in the *Bee*, while Father Thomas E. Sherman spoke on 'True Americanism' in Exposition Hall before as large and representative an audience as ever gathered in Omaha, the reception committee comprising seventy-five of the most prominent non-Catholic citizens of the town." In comparison, in 1897, the Dark Lantern Society sponsored a "slimly attended" lecture by Margaret Shepard, an English woman in the "ex-nun business." In truth, her mother had confined her to a Catholic home for wayward girls; sometime thereafter, she fleetingly established a lucrative career as an anti-Catholic lecturer in the United States. Later that same year, "a certain Kostelo" lectured "on Romanism &c." to a "meagre [*sic*] and apathetic" audience, "most of them having gone out of curiosity." The Catholic chief of police made sure no mayhem accompanied either performance and none of the daily newspapers accepted advertisements promoting the speeches or reported about the events. Thus, fortuitously, the APA episode in Omaha consisted of a lot of huff, but little puff. It caused consternation, but cosmopolitan citizens such as business partners Irish-Catholic John A. Creighton and German-Lutheran Herman Kountze held a minority of bigots in check.[7]

Despite its limited influence, Fr. Dowling attributed the College's financial problems to the "inequity of the A.P.A.," since "no Catholic Institution had a shadow of a show for fair play even in the courts, and certainly not at the hands of sheriffs, deputies, appraisers, or any one else beholden to these fanatics for his position." He cited the "Sweezy case" as proof. Following the regulations governing the investment of the Mary Lucretia Creighton trust, the trustees lent Sweezy $10,000 and took "a mortgage on property which amply secured its claims." Sweezy experienced financial losses and sold the property to a person named Clark, who obtained loans to build houses on the property. Clark could not sell the homes during the economic downturn and the holders of the second mortgage sued to foreclose on the property, which would have rendered Creighton's lien valueless. The case resided in the courts for several years until the Nebraska Supreme Court finally ruled in favor of Creighton University (contradicting Fr. Dowling's analysis, above). The case involved land speculators and wealthy creditors seeking to recoup losses, not APA members attacking Jesuits (although a speculator or a lawyer or a judge may have held enmity toward Catholics).[8]

The Sweezy case exemplified the impact of the Panic of 1893, which depressed property values. Actually, by 1890, a drought already had a disastrous impact on the regional economy. The boom of the 1880s went bust; borrowers who used property as collateral defaulted, creditors foreclosed and put huge amounts of land up for sale, few buyers existed and prices declined sharply. Because of the restrictions on investing the trust, Creighton University had become a major mortgage holder in Nebraska. Unfortunately, it had to foreclose on mortgages worth $48,000 at face value. The market value of those properties, when or if, they could be sold, dropped by about one half, and in some instances borrowers had not maintained the property or paid the taxes, and Creighton had to absorb the attorney fees and court costs associated with foreclosure. In other cases, the trustees granted extensions or arranged barter situations—for example, a leaseholder papered the College's parlors in lieu of $900 rent on a Douglas Street store. Thus, it was "not astonishing that in light of these reverses the superiors of the Society should more than once have deliberated about surrendering their trust to the Bishop and quitting Omaha."[9]

The bursting economic bubble had immediate effects, felt by the start of the academic year of 1893. According to one diarist, "The financial crisis has struck the Procurator's pocket. No dime can be obtained for Courtland Beach." The lack of recreation contributed to the gloom: "All teachers are in. A spirit of doubt hangs over them. Some are sadly over-burdened with work. The financial crisis makes it necessary for them to do the work of two men." The deficient funds forestalled hiring lay teachers. Furthermore, an optimistic decision in 1892 threatened calamity. The Reverend Francis G. Hillman, S.J., pastor of Holy Family Church (former vice president of the University), purchased eight lots on the east side of 21st Street between Paul and Charles streets for $37,000 to build a new church. The Omaha Jesuit House administered the parish, which it had not incorporated separately. Therefore, Creighton University Rector-President, Fr. James Hoeffer, S.J., signed the contract.

However, the parishioners refused to accept what they saw as excessive debt, leaving the University responsible and vulnerable. Eventually, to prevent the bankruptcy of the Omaha Jesuit House, the Missouri Province assumed the debt and ownership of the property (no new church was built).[10]

While the hardship continued, the University only undertook minor improvements. In 1894, it constructed a "permanent sidewalk" (to replace wood) for California Street, considering brick and flagstone, but inexplicably deciding on the "somewhat expensive Grantiod." When Fr. William Rigge returned to teach physics in 1896, he had to rely on student donations to purchase needed electrical equipment; many students contributed indirectly by not reclaiming their "breakage fee" at year's end. He complained that he had to rely "absolutely on the goodwill of Fr. Dowling who was by no means liberal in the cause of science even after his means had increased." Yet in 1896, the House Consultors granted Fr. Rigge's petition for electricity for the physics room cabinet and lecture hall, and the following year the entire College Building received electric light fixtures.[11]

The chronicler did not divulge the source of the funds to pay for the improvements. They seem an anomaly, considering the ominous picture painted by Fr. Dowling upon his arrival in November 1898. He revealed that $74,850 of the trust fund lay inoperative, yielding no revenue. That sum included $48,850 in foreclosed mortgages, $10,000 tied up in the Sweezy case, $5,000 in an unforeclosed mortgage that had not produced an interest payment in four years, and $11,000 that the former president the Reverend John F. Pahls, S.J., had used from the trust "to keep the college afloat." Thus, only one half of the trust garnered revenue and it did not equal the $7,500 per annum necessary to meet expenses. Given the circumstances, Fr. Dowling proposed five options: repay the trust and return it to the bishop, start charging tuition, suspend either the high-school or collegiate course of study, or "suspend all classes until we have had time to recover somewhat."[12] Fortunately, the economy improved at the turn of the century and the dire alternatives became moot.

The Panic of 1893 had also affected enrollment and student activities. At first, the number of students dropped because of a significant decline in the academic (high-school) department, from 127 in 1892 to 98 in 1893. The collegiate level only lost three students, decreasing to forty. Although no one graduated in 1892, an average of six per year did so thereafter. Subsequently, the lack of jobs actually contributed to a steady increase in the number of academic (145 in 1900) and college students (56 in 1900) during the remainder of the decade (no tuition and minimal fees, and school would occupy idle hands and minds). Students came mostly from the towns in Nebraska, although their number included "not a few from neighboring States, notably from Iowa." Although enrollment increased, approximately two thirds of all Catholics attending college in the 1890s matriculated at secular schools (no figures exist for the Omaha Diocese). Paradoxically, because of the inability to hire lay faculty, Creighton instituted competitive exams in the mid-1890s in order to restrict the third academic (first year of high school) to a class of forty, which one Jesuit could handle. Yet despite the encouraging enrollment, a second attempt to create a seminary at

Creighton University failed. In 1886, Bishop O'Connor had outlined plans for a "preparatory seminary" (high school), but the scheme languished. In 1896, Bishop Scannell revived the proposal; it opened with "only nine aspirants to the priesthood" in a brick house at 24th and Cass streets, but support lagged due to the weak economy and "on account of a paucity of applicants" the seminary did not open for a second year.[13]

The sharp drop in the number of students in the academic department in 1893 also resulted from the promulgation of a revised course of study, which eliminated the preparatory department. In response, Fr. President Hoeffer "raised the standard of requirements"—he wanted all entrants to have the minimum of a sixth-grade education, which prepared them to pass entrance exams in English grammar, spelling, arithmetic, and geography. The decision forced some Catholic students to go to public school first, because they could not do "decimal fractions." Another new admission standard required "satisfactory testimonials of good conduct" in behalf of students transferring from other institutions. Yet most Catholic schools, Creighton included, phrased and applied these general statements "in such a way that any boy they chose to admit could qualify." They did so because they sought to produce productive Catholics, not Catholic scholars.[14]

The 1893 course of study for schools in the Missouri Province emphasized the need for strict grading; that is, assigning "a certain definite amount of [subject] matter to each class, thus preventing one class from trespassing on another." Furthermore, at a time when the lecture system rapidly eclipsed the recitation system at secular colleges, the revised course of study demanded that, "Prelection [the Jesuit method of classroom discourse] should be strictly carried out by the professors of all classes." It also specified the number of annual competitions and the nature of the premiums awarded, as well as mandating that each college operate a free student library (Creighton's "Select Library," for the use of "the students, all of whom can enjoy the privileges of membership," dated from 1881). Surprisingly, the chroniclers did not discuss, and the course of study contained no reference to, the major religious controversy of the era, Darwinian evolution. In the 1870s, American Catholic scholars "only occasionally" discussed the issue, but when they did "it was to wield the shillelah with vengeance." During the following decade, some Catholics followed Liberal Protestants in abandoning their opposition to the theory, and in 1896, the Reverend John Zahm, CSC, of the University of Notre Dame, wrote *Evolution and Dogma*, which argued that no conflict existed between religion and science. In 1899, however, Pope Leo XIII issued *Testem Benevolentiae*, warning against erroneous ideas of faith in the United States. Although the encyclical did not specifically address evolution as an error, Fr. Zahm withdrew his book from print. At the time, Creighton College did not teach specific science classes in biology or geology (the fossil record), and Fr. William Rigge's research in astronomy did not deal with the origins of the universe; thus, the controversy seemingly had no impact on Creighton's curriculum.[15]

While the curriculum remained largely unchanged during the 1890s, student activities witnessed some innovation and there were attempts to organize the alumni:

The Alumni took advantage of the Columbian festivities [400-year anniversary of Columbus's discovery of America] to give their first banquet, to which they invited the bishop, the mayor, and prominent Catholic laymen of the city. The dining hall of the Millard hotel was elegantly decorated for the occasion. Intellectually and socially the banquet proved a great event for the Catholics of Omaha.

Some of the attendees established an Alumni Association "to perpetuate the work of the University by preserving and strengthening a feeling of fellowship among old students." At the time, "the University" had only produced five college graduates, as few students completed the seven-year curriculum; locally, the organizers thought in terms of anyone who had attended, not graduated from, the school since its inception. Actually, any student or graduate of any Jesuit college could apply for membership. The Panic of 1893, however, doomed the group.[16]

Another group, the University Cadets, also succumbed quickly. Its ephemeral existence during 1893 may have sparked the APA rumor of a Catholic militia, especially among residents who remembered the short-lived Creighton Guard of the mid-1880s. According to a contemporary Jesuit, Vice President and Prefect of Studies, the Reverend John B. De Shryver, S.J., had a military background and pushed for its establishment. In his words,

> Well the students did not take to the idea with enthusiasm and so the cadets just about dragged along. Whatever enthusiasm was alive was manifested by the most unsoldierly set in the Institution. These worthy sons of Mars [Roman god of war] were always on hand for the drill and always out of step and order. The Reverend Commandant could not retire them, and they declined a generous furlough.[17]

While soldiering faltered, the College continued to field a baseball team, but "positive and vigorous opposition from the faculty" suppressed rugby-style football. On the other hand, intercollegiate academic competition blossomed. In 1895, the Missouri Province introduced contests in Latin and English composition among its colleges—St. Louis University, Xavier (Cincinnati), Ignatius (Chicago), Marquette (Milwaukee) and Creighton. In the second year of competition, Creighton students won first and fourth places in Latin, and the following year, first, third, and fourth in English composition, while managing only a seventh place in Latin. Despite the success, many students commented on "the absence of interest, enthusiasm and unity among the boys"; apparently, the old college spirit had not developed, inhibited by a young student body of local day students that resided at home.[18]

While the faculty and the students seemed dispirited, several developments boded well for the future. In 1892, St. John's Collegiate Church, the largest Catholic church in Omaha, put a financial strain on the Jesuit community. Father President Hoeffer created a men's sodality among influential Catholics; John A. McShane chaired the board, which also include meatpacking magnate Edward Cudahy and Creighton clan members John F. Coad, John A. Schenk, and Mathew McGinn. Even with the high-powered sodality, "a discussion concerning methods of improving the revenue developed an unanimous sentiment among the Fathers present that the present plan of having two churches in the same territory—within the same parish limits—is ill-advised and hurtful to both." The second church in this case was Holy Family, administered by Jesuits. Railroad construction necessitated relocating the church, and the Jesuit pastor, without consulting the Creighton community, had purchased expensive land, which Creighton College had to hold in its name. The Creighton Jesuit House decided it did not want or need two communities and two churches in Omaha. On November 4, 1892, Fr. Hoeffer broached the topic with Bishop Scannell, who responded favorably to "doing away with the H. Family Church, and of redistricting the city in such a way as to make St. John's Church central in a new parish." All concerned also hoped the plan would silence the other local parish priests who found St. John's "unwelcome" because it attracted "certain people" (the wealthy Creighton clan and their friends), who did not support their parish of residence.[19]

The Panic of 1893 exacerbated the financial problems related to the churches and legal problems precluded their quick resolution. Father Hoeffer and Fr. Provincial Frieden hoped that the University could sell or lease St. John's to the bishop, who would establish parish boundaries. Attorney James M. Woolworth, however, concluded that the church stood on property that was part of the bequest from Mary Lucretia, and as such, the trustees could not sell or lease it without obtaining permission from the district court. He thought the court unlikely to grant such a change, but he believed the trustees could, "by resolution, superadd to the uses of the Collegiate Church, the uses and duties of a parish church." The seemingly simple procedure, for unknown reasons, took five years to secure papal approval. Finally, on January 9, 1897, the trustees passed the necessary resolution and one week later, passed a second one, which transferred Holy Family Church back to the bishop. Bishop Scannell, still somewhat "cool" toward the Jesuits, established the parish boundaries for St. John's Church—20th Street on the east, 30th Street on the west, Dodge Street on the South and Grace and Parker streets on the north. The Reverend Joseph Meuffels, S.J., became the first pastor and with St. John's as a parish, the Jesuits hoped its members would become more generous.[20]

Father Hoeffer proposed to take Creighton's share of the Holy Family settlement and use it to erect a school with a chapel so the elementary school children could attend Sunday Mass there. At the time, Holy Family Church already operated two schools, St. Aloysius in the church itself at 918 N. 18th Street and St. Stanislaus (1888), two frame buildings also called "the barracks," at 27th and Decatur streets in the northwest segment of the parish. The barracks now stood within St. John's Parish, so instead of absorbing construction costs, the pastor had the buildings moved close to the church, to a lot owned by the University at the southwest corner of 25th and California streets (directly across the mall from the current front entrance to the Administration Building). St. John's School, consisting of four elementary grades, opened on September 6, 1897, with forty-five students (jumped to seventy-five the next day) under the supervision of two Sisters of Mercy. The Jesuit House of Omaha now owned and operated a university, a parish church and a grade school.[21]

Actually, Creighton University had become even more complex in 1892, granting its first graduate degrees, adding an off-campus medical college, and establishing an affiliation with a hospital. The idea of post-baccalaureate study originated in Europe at the turn to the nineteenth century. American educators looked especially to the German model of advanced study; the Doctor of Philosophy degree (Ph.D.) became the crowning achievement of graduate study. Among Catholic universities, Georgetown, St. Louis University, and Notre Dame all contend to have created the first graduate program. Catholic or not, early graduate study did not entail the creation of a separate school, it merely consisted of one more year of general study or successful completion of a specified length of employment in any number of accepted professions. In fact, the first Creighton *Catalogue* of 1882 provided that "the degree of A.M. can be obtained by devoting two years more to any of the learned professions." The option had no candidates during the grade-school years and disappeared with the *Ratio Studiorum*, 1884–87. With the first graduating class in 1891, the College reinstituted the A.M. degree, with the choice of garnering it by on-the-job training or one year of additional study. It also created the category of honorary degree, conferred "at the discretion of the board of trustees, upon those who unite proficiency in the Classics with eminence in Literature and Science." In June 1893, Creighton granted five A.B. and five A.M. degrees, but only one of the recipients completed the extra year of study. The following year, the University established the strangely titled Bachelor of Doctor of Philosophy, "granted only to Masters of Arts after successful Post-Graduate Courses in Philosophy and Science." Contemporary style Ph.D. programs proliferated in the 1890s (in 1884, only 19 of 189 Harvard faculty held the Ph.D. degree), but no records demonstrate that during that era Creighton University joined the ranks of those elite graduate-school programs. Finally, in terms of post-baccalaureate study, the catalogues of the late 1890s also listed the availability of one-year scholarships offered by Georgetown University to its law, medical and graduate departments. The Creighton faculty could chose one student for each area, but no records of student applications exist.[22]

"The Creighton College," the "Free School of Arts and Sciences," continued to grant A.B. and A.M. degrees annually after 1892. It adopted the new lengthy descriptive designation because, in that year, the University established a medical college. Actually, the Creighton trustees first gained control of the new St. Joseph's Hospital (original spelling used possessive form). The House Consultors believed the "hospital department" contributed the crucial element to the success of a "medical department" of a university. To assure that Catholic physicians controlled the hospital department, the Consultors convinced John that physicians from the medical department must constitute a majority of the governing board of the hospital. They considered the superioress of the order of nuns who administered the hospital too weak to control a large group of visiting physicians. With Catholic Creighton-associated physicians in control, the University could then develop the medical department slowly and systematically, with the assurance of an affiliated professional training facility.[23]

By the late nineteenth century, medical science, especially surgery, had transformed hospitals from a place associated with paupers into their modern relationship
with professional medicine. In 1866, Dr. Samuel Mercer established the first hospital in Omaha, the American Surgical Institute, but fire soon consumed it. The Sisters
of Mercy came to Omaha in 1864 to teach, but in 1870, at the invitation of Bishop
O'Gorman, the Order agreed to operate St. Joseph's Mercy Hospital upon its completion that fall. Then, in 1878, Mother Teresa Bonzel, founder of the Order of the
Poor Sisters of St. Francis Seraph of Perpetual Adoration of Lafayette, Indiana,
undertook fundraising with the intention of establishing a hospital in Columbus,
Nebraska. The sisters went door to door in Omaha and obtained a $1,000 donation
from John Andrew. However, he and the bishop advised them to purchase St.
Joseph's Hospital, which had financial problems associated with a shortage of Mercy
nuns to fulfill their dual missions to nurse and to teach. Thus, in 1880, the Sisters of
Mercy sold St. Joseph's Hospital to the Poor Sisters of St. Francis. Eight years later,
Sarah Emily bequeathed $50,000 to the sisters to construct a new hospital; she and
John Andrew had already given them a $15,000 lot at the northeast corner of 10th and
Castelar streets for its location. Following his wife's death, John Andrew donated an
additional $150,000. Construction began in 1890, and in Sarah Emily's honor, the
new Creighton Memorial St. Joseph's Hospital opened June 13, 1892.[24]

Like hospitals, medical education also evolved during the nineteenth century:
from apprenticeship relations to proprietary schools, where a physician taught several
students simultaneously, to modern medical colleges. About one hundred medical
schools came into existence between 1875–1890. Concurrently, physicians organized
to standardize fees and practices. In 1869, the American Medical Association petitioned in behalf of national legislation to regulate medical education, and the American Medical College Association, the forerunner of the Association of American
Medical Colleges (AAMC), organized to raise educational standards. In 1866, the
Omaha Medical Society organized "for the advancement and promotion of medical
science, as well as for the mutual protection and welfare of its members" and three
years later, a group of proprietary physicians incorporated the Omaha Medical College. In 1881, the Nebraska Legislature passed the state's first medical licensing law.
Two years later, it funded the creation of the University of Nebraska Medical College
in Lincoln, but it disbanded four years later (in 1909, a state medical school began to
develop at 42nd and Dewey streets in Omaha).[25]

During most of the nineteenth century, professional schools such as medical and
normal (teacher training) colleges existed separately from liberal arts colleges and
universities. In the last decades of the century, however, medical-education reformers
demanded that medical schools have a three-year curriculum and an affiliation with
a hospital and a university. When John stepped forward to fund a medical department for Creighton University, he followed the reformers' guidelines. In 1977, a University self-study stated the "popular belief " that he "founded a medical college to
help poor young Catholics gain a medical education." On the other hand, DeWitt
Clinton Bryant, M.D., a contemporary physician who helped plan the medical

school and joined the original faculty, opined that John Andrew memorialized his wife with the hospital and wanted the new facility "as a monument to himself." In another view, William J. Galbraith, M.D., another project planner, charter faculty member, and friend, had recently resigned from the Omaha Medical College and may have encouraged John to fund a rival school. Most likely, however, the Jesuit community, interested in instilling Catholic values in professional training, also broached the topic with its benefactor and assembled the supporters. Patrick Keogh, M.D., who became the first dean, also contributed to the planning. John Andrew guaranteed the funding and on May 30, 1892, the University trustees resolved to establish the John A. Creighton Medical College of Creighton University.[26]

John Andrew arranged for the medical school to use the recently abandoned St. Joseph's Hospital at 12th and Mason; from that location the faculty also provided an "outdoor dispensary for the gratuitous treatment of the poor." The clinic operated six days per week for two hours each day and senior medical students completed various rotations at the facility. That fall, thirty-six students from six states became the first class of the medical department of Creighton University (by 1900, total enrollment reached 143). The charter class included Kate Drake, probably the first female to attend a Jesuit university in the United States, another concession to the American model of education. The Women's Emancipation Movement made great strides in the field of education during the Progressive Era of the late nineteenth to early twentieth centuries. Jesuits did not teach in the professional schools and could not operate them maintaining the Catholic principle of gender-segregated education. Thus, they appointed a Jesuit regent to monitor the administration of the lay deans recruited from the various professions, who oversaw coeducational programs. Drake did not graduate; Miss A.M. Griffith garnered the honor as the first Creighton-educated physician in 1898. Three more women received diplomas with the twelve-person class of 1899, and another two followed the next year. In 1901, William M. Gordon, probably the first African American to attend the University, received his medical degree. The school began with a three-year program; attendance required students to have a high-school diploma or hold a teacher's certificate or pass an entrance exam. Students paid a $5 matriculation fee, $65 for tuition and fees, and $25 to graduate. The length of the term increased from six months in 1892, to seven months in 1894, to seven and one-half months in 1900. Previously, in 1896, the medical school had become the first in the American West to institute a four-year program. In doing so, the school adopted the standards of the AAMC, which it had joined in 1895.[27]

The Panic of 1893 forestalled the construction of a modern teaching facility; seemingly, John suffered some short-term reversals of fortune. However, in 1895 he provided $80,000 to build and furnish a medical-school building on the northwest corner of 14th and Davenport streets. That gift, as well as many others to Catholic institutions over the years, prompted Pope Leo XIII to knight John Andrew a Count of the Holy Roman Empire. The Count, as many publicly addressed him, chose his cousin Long Jim Creighton to supervise the medical-building project, despite the

earlier controversies over delays associated with construction of the College and over
the location of St. John's Church. The Italian Renaissance, brick-and-stone structure
had a basement and three stories, which contained lecture halls, laboratories, recreation rooms, a 350-seat amphitheater, and "out-door" clinics and a drug store. The
center of the building, which rose over the three-arch entrance, had a fourth floor
containing the dissecting room, which could accommodate four hundred students.
The *Creighton Medical Bulletin* began publication in February 1898, and ballyhooed
the opening of the new facility the following October. At the same time, John
Andrew funded the construction of a two-story, $10,000 operating building with an
amphitheater, the only one in Omaha, between the wings of the new Creighton
Memorial St. Joseph's Hospital. The next year, he built a $22,000 chapel attached to
the north side of the hospital. St. Joseph's remained the primary teaching hospital,
but the medical school also established clinical affiliations with Presbyterian Hospital in 1894 (another indication of the limits of APA influence), St. Bernard's Hospital in Council Bluffs, Iowa, for psychiatry in 1895, and Douglas County Hospital in
Omaha in 1899. The affiliation with secular institutions demonstrated that despite
the concern about University and Catholic control of St. Joseph's Hospital, medical
education could not exist as an exclusively Catholic function.[28]

The flood of construction announced the onset of an improving economy. Generally, nationwide, the Spanish-American War (1898) signaled the end of the depression of the 1890s; simultaneously, new gold discoveries helped alleviate the deflation-
ary spiral. In Nebraska, in support of the war, towns organized high-school student
militias, which participated in "mafficking [extravagant public celebration] demonstrations as the news media released information about the deeds of the 3rd Nebraska
Regiment fighting in Cuba and the Nebraskans stationed in the Philippines. The
cadet groups in military uniforms and armed with government-issued weapons,
drilled regularly during school time, frequently under supervision of army officers."
On January 4, 1895, the *Fremont Daily Herald* "credited Omaha with being the first
city in the United States to take advantage of the high school cadet law." Strangely,
for all the commotion, the Creighton chroniclers made no mention of the war or of
student participation in the patriotic outpouring. Similarly, the Trans-Mississippi
and International Exposition (a "world's fair" that attracted over 2.6 million visitors
to Omaha between June 1 and October 31, 1898), the local event that signified the end
of the depression, seemingly garnered no Creighton support. It was the "most important extra-curricular school event of the decade," to which "schools across the state
devoted unnumbered hours of effort on displays." If the academic and/or collegiate
departments participated, they did not publicize their efforts in the normal fashion.
However, they did record the size and nature of the exhibit the school submitted to
the St. Louis World's Fair of 1904 (located in the headquarters city of the Missouri
Province). Father Dowling stated that the Trans-Mississippi Expo encouraged John
Andrew to resume construction of the medical-school building, but John gave no
donation to the fair's organizing committee (his banking partner Herman Kountze
served as treasurer and contributed $10,000). The event was closely associated with

the Knights of Ak-Sar-Ben and John Andrew had no association with that business-men's philanthropic organization, although subsequently his grandniece Clare Daugh-erty was crowned queen during its annual coronation of 1921.[29]

Father Dowling arrived at Creighton as the Trans-Mississippi Expo closed its doors. While the general economy started to turn around, he found the University finances in desperate condition and issued his chilling memorandum, which included the suggestion to shutter the school temporarily. He claimed that the memo, for the first time, alerted John Andrew "of the extraordinary straits to which [the University] was reduced, for the responsible officials of the College had tried to keep from him these sources of uneasiness, both because at the time he had enough troubles of his own and because he had hardly yet recovered from the tax put upon his resources by the erection of the Creighton Medical College during a period of financial depres-sion unequalled in the West." Once made aware, he "came to the rescue and lifted the College out of its embarrassment."[30]

John began to solidify the endowment, to add schools to the University, and to expand Creighton College. From 1899 to 1902, he underwrote the construction of an east-west residential addition to the south wing and a new L-shaped mirror-image north wing to the College, which transformed the building into a "W" shape. The north wing contained many recitation rooms and its third floor became the new home of the physics department. The expansion prompted the development of a room-numbering system. At the same time, a new library arose between the south wing and the original College Building, filling in the south "U" of the "W." It con-tained 46,000 volumes, as well as pamphlets and government reports and publica-tions. The Reverend Michael I. Stritch, S.J., became the first librarian, securing book-purchasing donations from Mr. and Mrs. Edward Cudahy ($1,000), Mr. and Mrs. Edward Hayden ($1,000), and James M. Woolworth ($250). Students obtained a reading room—dubbed "Assembly Hall"—on the first floor of the original College and the student Library Association continued to support acquisitions through fundraising efforts.[31]

Simultaneously, a gift of $100,000 from John funded the erection of University Hall, a 700-seat auditorium on the north side of California Street, west of St. John's Church, as well as a new heating plant north of the auditorium. The new construc-tion rendered the Chemistry Building superfluous; the administration sold it and the new owner moved it to Burt Street, remodeling it into a residence. Students had to do without chemistry classes during the 1901–02 school year while the second floor of the original College building underwent renovation—removal of one of the glass partitions and installation of laboratory tables and a tiered lecture hall. St. John's Church also received upgrading, completing much deferred maintenance, but it also included frescoing the interior, installing electric lights, and building a stone walk and retaining wall with four large built-in flowerpots. Furthermore, the "barracks" (St. John's School) moved again, west across 25th Street, directly south of the church across California Street. To hold that property, the Jesuit House created a new cor-poration, which included the bishop, the vicar general of the diocese, and two laymen as ex officio trustees. The barracks sat to the rear of the property and a new two-story brick school, with attic, was built with the entrance facing California Street. It opened on January 22, 1901, with 196 students.[32]

The flurry of activity resulted from Fr. Dowling's suggestion that John Andrew complete his plan for the University while alive, "since whatever provision he might make for this purpose in his will might be frustrated by efforts that would no doubt be made to break the will [by disappointed relatives]." In 1901, John Andrew transferred the deed to the Creighton Block to the University, but archived it at the First National Bank with instructions to have it delivered to the president of Creighton University upon his death. The previous year, while construction boomed, the president of Notre Dame University came to Omaha to present John Andrew with the *Laetare* Medal to recognize his support for Catholic institutions. Recognizing the competition from another order, which administered a different college, the Missouri Province now moved to honor John A. Creighton appropriately. The Reverend Provincial Joseph Grimmelsman, S.J., traveled to Omaha to present him with a diploma of "Participation in all the Spiritual Works of the Society."[33]

Realizing the endowment had become insufficient to maintain the enlarged University, John's munificence continued unabated. Despite the economic recovery, interest rates remained well below the level of the explosive 1880s; thus, he had contributed about $7,000 annually to balance the budget. Now, in 1904, he revised his "upon death" plan and gave the trustees the Creighton Block, as well as the Arlington Block, developed by Sarah Emily and located on Dodge Street between 15th and 16th. Both properties produced good revenue and had a combined value of $200,000. On June 18, the trustees voted to open a law school and to finance it in part by selling the Arlington Block, using the proceeds to purchase a lot on 18th Street between Farnam and Douglas streets, opposite the City Hall and one-half block from the County Courthouse. John Andrew promised to fund construction of a $40,000 structure and to make another "liberal contribution" in the fall.[34]

At the time, no law school existed in Omaha. In 1888, proprietors had established the Central College of Law in Lincoln, which the University of Nebraska acquired in 1893, retaining its two-year program well into the pre–World War I era. According to legend, in 1903, Fr. Dowling formulated plans for a law department and approached John Andrew for financing. The Count purportedly replied, "Why should I lend my support to such a project when it is common knowledge that all lawyers are scoundrels?" Father Dowling replied, "That is one of the best reasons why Creighton University should undertake the education of young men for the legal profession." A witty tale for attorney baiters. However, John had committed to the concept of a law school in 1892, when he funded the medical school. Father Dowling may have played a role, but so did influential Democratic Party politicians and members of the Omaha Bar Association Timothy J. Mahoney and Constantine J. Smyth. The law department opened on October 3, 1904, with twenty-three students temporarily housed in the Medical College. Mahoney, a former superintendent of schools of Guthrie County, Iowa (1882–84), graduate of the State University of Iowa Law

School (1885), and successful Omaha attorney, became the first dean. Smyth, a native of Ireland, early student at Creighton College, Nebraska legislator (1887), chairman of the Democratic State Committee, Nebraska Attorney General (1897–1901), and unsuccessful gubernatorial candidate (1898, 1902), became associate dean. Thus, as with the medical department, the subsequent administrators contributed to the initial planning of the institution.[35]

Thirty-one members of the bar, including nine judges, donated their time as the first faculty of the law department, each teaching a class while maintaining their professional positions. The school admitted "Graduates of accredited Normal Schools, High Schools, Academies, Academic and High School departments of Colleges, or their equivalents." Other applicants had to have attained the age of eighteen and to have passed an examination "on the entire subject matter required for admission" (at the time, the "median level of education required for admission" to the eighty-six American law schools was "the equivalent of eighth grade"). The law department charged $45 tuition, plus fees of $5 for matriculation, $1 for library use, $10 for examinations, and ultimately $10 for a diploma. The three-year program consisted of weekday classes held from 8:00 A.M. to noon, with special lectures on Friday evenings and a mandatory three-hour Moot Court on Saturday afternoons. First-year students served as witnesses and jurors, while second and third-year students conducted trials before a county judge. Litigants appealed to an Appellate Moot Court; each senior had to serve as an appellate judge twice and write at least one opinion. The American Association of Law Schools accredited the Creighton program in 1907; also in that year, the Nebraska Supreme Court ordered that Creighton law graduates "be admitted to the bar without examination." Students established a dance club and a debating society as their first extracurricular institutions. In 1908, however the "Alabama Club" stood as the most exclusive organization, its membership consisting of the lone African-American student, freshman Noah W. Ware from Selma, Alabama (he attended Creighton intermittently into his junior year, but did not graduate).[36]

The development of the law department capped a five-year period of gift giving that led to a signal honor. On March 25, 1904, the Very Reverend General Louis Martin, S.J., named John A. Creighton a founder of the University, because by "the erection of large buildings and by princely donations, [he] so enlarged and enriched our college in Omaha." Apparently pleased by the tribute, John Andrew continued to found. That fall, the trustees opened negotiations to purchase the Omaha Dental College, but soon rejected a proffered contract because management of the facility would have remained in the hands of the original proprietors. The following spring, with "several donations of $10,000.00 each, made by our generous benefactor," the administration decided to create an independent dental school. It opened in the fall of 1905 with 113 students; entrance to the three-year program required at least two years of high-school education. One could also enter by examination, although "a slight deficiency in these requirements may be made up during the first year." Students paid a $5 matriculation fee, $100 tuition, and $10 dissection fee each year, and a $20 examination and diploma fee. The school also offered postgraduate courses for practicing dentists and a thirty-week dental assistant program, the first in Nebraska. In July 1906, the new department absorbed the Omaha Dental College. Ellen Kelley and Mazzie McGlaughlin became the first women to complete the curriculum in 1908; Loretta M. White followed in 1914, but only one other woman graduated before World War II.[37]

In comparison to dentistry, pharmacy attracted and accepted a significant number of women students. In 1905, the trustees also purchased the Omaha School of Pharmacy (founded in 1901) by granting the proprietor "40% of the gross receipts for five years. This would be his salary for teaching and would also be payment for his fixtures, stock, goodwill, etc." By its third year of existence, the new school began to offer two courses of study. The "Ph. G. Course" (graduate in pharmacy) consisted of two terms of twenty-four weeks each, the "Junior Course" and the "Senior Course." The classes started in September and January, but ran simultaneously, and a student could complete them in a calendar year. Subjects included chemistry, physics, pharmaceutical Latin and arithmetic, physiology, toxicology, drug assaying, and commercial training, among others. The "Ph. C. Course" (Pharmaceutical Chemist) consisted of "lectures and much laboratory work" in advanced science classes designed to prepare students "for such positions as public analysts, pure food examiners, and practical chemists in commercial industries" (the Pure Food and Drug Act passed in 1906). To gain admission, the administration advised, "No one should undertake the study of pharmacy who has not, at least, a good common school education, or such qualifications as would enable him to enter a high school." However, "Those entering for the degree of Pharmaceutical Chemist must be graduates of a twelve-grade high school and must have completed the Ph. G. course." Tuition stood at $60 for each six-month course, plus a $10 fee for graduation. Women composed about 10 percent of each class before World War I.[38]

The "liberal contribution" from John Andrew in the fall of 1904 consisted of an additional $100,000 that funded the construction of the Edward Creighton Institute (ECI) at 210 South 18th Street. The medical school had grown rapidly, enrolling over one hundred students on its tenth anniversary, and it received a highly favorable evaluation from the United States Bureau of Education. It also added clinical affiliations with the new Mercy Hospital in Council Bluffs, Iowa (1903), and the Omaha General Hospital at 14th and Capitol streets (1906). The medical school had become too large to share its facility with the law school. To provide adequate space for all the professional programs, John commissioned the new building to house the law, dental, and pharmacy schools. Pharmacy occupied the first floor, but shared laboratories for botany, chemistry, and physics with dentistry on the third floor, which also had a "large and elegantly carpeted and furnished hall intended for the use of the Knights of Columbus and other Catholic organizations." Law made its home on the second floor, which included the ten-thousand-volume library, jointly owned with the Bar Association of Omaha and Douglas County. The University provided the rooms, utilities, and janitor and subscribed for one fourth of the stock in the library corporation (John Andrew donated $10,000 earmarked for that purpose). Finally, part of the basement and first floor contained "a fair sized assembly hall . . . suitable for scientific conventions and entertainments." For two decades, the ECI served as a multi-purpose professional facility for the University and the city.[39]

Students must have marveled—another year, another building—as in 1906 the first dormitory opened. Directly across from the College on the southwest corner of 25th and California streets sat the Schaller house. A deteriorating dwelling occupied by two sisters, it perched atop a twelve-foot embankment left from a grading project. After two years of negotiation, Fr. Dowling purchased the property, which did not possess indoor plumbing or a gas hookup, for $7,000 and relocated it to 26th and Cass streets. The administration graded the lot, using the dirt to fill the creek ravine west of campus, and erected St. John's Hall on the Schaller site. Quickly, one month before the city began to remove the old wood paving blocks and to narrow California Street from forty to thirty feet wide and repave it with bricks, the University tunneled steam pipes from the powerhouse west of St. John's Church under the road to provide heat for the dormitory.[40]

John donated $25,000 to construct St. John's Hall, which wrapped around the corner of 25th and California streets. It contained sixty-six single rooms, five double rooms, and a first-floor cafeteria soon dubbed "the Beanery," allegedly because beans appeared on the breakfast, lunch, and dinner menus. The difficulty for out-of-town students to find "accommodations favorable to serious study had long caused much concern to the University authorities." Yet the administration stated that it had "no intention to inaugurate any new system, or to assume the responsibilities of a boarding-school," having operated as a day school for twenty-eight years.

The trustees, after some debate, rented the building to the Sisters of Mercy, who then oversaw its operation. The dorm opened for occupancy on September 6, 1906, with every room filled and seven students on a waiting list (the University renamed the building Wareham Hall in 1934).[41]

On October 15, 1906, John A. Creighton celebrated his seventy-fifth birthday; since June 8, he and brother-in-law John Schenk had lived in rooms 111 and 115 at the College or at St. Joseph's Hospital, because a fire had caused substantial damage to his house. Although not completely renovated, he held a brief reception at his home to announce that he intended to act as his "own executor, as far as possible," and that since he had only "one child, and that is Creighton University," he would secure it "against any financial reverse that might threaten its welfare." Following a brief address to friends, family, and reporters who gathered for the occasion, John Andrew presented Fr. Dowling with the deeds to two large real estate blocks he had recently constructed. The eight-story Byrne-Hammer Dry Goods building at 9th and Howard streets and a six-story warehouse on Jones Street between 10th and 11th streets, occupied by the John Deere Company, had a combined value of about $400,000 and produced about $2,000 a month in rents. In 1920, the University went to district court to gain the right to sell one of the buildings, and in 1966, it returned to the court to obtain the power to invest the proceeds from the second building in stocks, which, at the time, brought a higher rate of return than bonds.[42]

With renewed financial security, the University began further remodeling of the College Building. The new 700-seat University Hall rendered the original third-floor auditorium-chapel superfluous; tradesmen divided it into four classrooms and constructed additional rooms on the end of the corridors on all three floors (rooms 119 and 169, 219 and 269, and 319 and probably 369). Then, in September 1907, the pharmacy department occupied its new quarters, a three-story building adjoining the medical school on the west, at 14th and Davenport streets. The first floor contained a large lobby, steel student lockers, the administrative office, a library, a museum, and a "ladies' rest room . . . furnished with every convenience for their comfort." The second floor housed the faculty room, two large lecture halls, a "model prescription room, and a private laboratory for the use of the members of the faculty." The top story consisted of the "general stock room and main pharmaceutical and chemical laboratories," which provided "space for one hundred and forty students to work at one time." Significantly, by 1907, in the terminology of the day, the Department of Medicine—medical school with 157 students, dental school with 100, and pharmacy school with 96—established the health science domination at Creighton University. The Creighton College consisted of a mere 61 students, while the high-school department had 295.[43]

Although the undergraduates studying the *Ratio Studiorum* probably remained unaware of the pedagogical turmoil, a thoughtless, prejudiced, off-hand statement by Charles Eliot caused distress among Jesuit educators and intensified the controversy concerning baccalaureate education. Actually, at least four distinct groups argued over the nature and purpose of the curriculum at the turn of the twentieth century. Historian Herbert Kliebard categorized the contending parties as (1) the "humanists," who defended the "ancient tradition"; (2) the devotees of the "child-study movement," who wanted to reform the curriculum to match "the natural order of development in the child"; (3) the "social-efficiency educators," who wished to use science to create a "coolly efficient, smoothly running society"; and (4) the "social meliorists," who wanted to use the schools to affect social change. Eliot made the distinctive element of "electivism" central to the multifaceted debate; at Harvard, he had abolished required classes for seniors in 1872, for juniors in 1879, for sophomores in 1884, for freshmen in 1885, and proposed their elimination down to the high-school level. In 1893, he chaired the National Education Association's Committee of Ten, which distributed a report that compromised the issue, advocating the creation of a choice of four different courses of study for high schools. Then, in 1899, in the *Atlantic Monthly*, Eliot published an article describing the application and expansion of the elective system. He concluded the scholarly analysis with a flippant remark about required courses of study:

> This is precisely the method followed in Moslem countries, where the Koran prescribes the perfect education to be administered to all children alike. . . . Another instance of uniform prescribed education may be found in the curriculum of the Jesuit colleges, which has remained almost unchanged for four hundred years, disregarding some trifling concessions to natural sciences.[44]

Creighton University founder Edward Charles Creighton (1820–1871)

Mary Lucretia Wareham Creighton, wife of Edward Creighton (1834–1876)

Creighton University founder John Andrew Creighton (1831–1907)

Sarah Emily Wareham Creighton, wife of John Andrew Creighton (1840–1888)

Top: Signs of the Creightons appear in Virginia City, Montana, where John Andrew lived during the 1860s in order to oversee Edward's freighting business and to run a general store. Photo courtesy of the Montana Historical Society.

Bottom: This view from the Omaha High School tower shows the original Creighton College overlooking the scattered houses and farms of Omaha in 1878. The house in front of the College was sold by John and Mary (Creighton) McCreary for use as a Jesuit residence in 1887.

Top: This 1882 view of the original St. Joseph's Hospital, built in 1870 by the Sisters of Mercy, shows the addition (far left) that J. A. Creighton funded in 1880.

Bottom: Creighton Memorial St. Joseph's Hospital opens its doors in 1892, thanks, in large part, to the gifts of Sarah Emily and John Andrew Creighton.

The grandeur of St. John's Church, constructed in 1888, serves as a lasting reminder of the faith and generosity of Creighton University's founders.

Top: A display of skulls and stuffed and mounted animals stands at the center of a room in the J. A. Creighton Medical College, circa 1900.

Bottom: Students stand in front of their new two-story brick building, replacing the "barracks" that formerly housed St. John's School. The building opened on January 22, 1901, to 196 students.

Top: The seven-hundred-seat University Hall, seen here in the year of its construction (1902), stands next to St. John's Church, which was built in 1888.

Bottom: St. John's Hall, Creighton's first dormitory, opens its doors in 1906, making it easier for out-of-town students to find accommodations in Omaha. The building, which stood on the corner of 25th and California Streets, contained seventy-one rooms and a cafeteria known as the Beanery.

Father Michael Dowling joins John Andrew Creighton, bedecked in a rosary of white roses, to celebrate the Creighton University founder's seventy-fifth birthday on October 15, 1906.

Top: Built in 1904 at 210 South 18th Street, the Edward Creighton Institute housed the Law, Dental, and Pharmacy school throughout the early twentieth century.

Bottom: The Administration Building, seen here circa 1906, stands as a marker to Creighton's growth. The original College Building was expanded with the south wing in 1889. Additions to the north and west were constructed in 1901 and 1902.

Sunday October 6 1918.

Father McNeive says Mass at the observatory on Sunday, October 6, 1918. Parishoners celebrated Mass outside because an outbreak of Spanish Influenza had prevented people from being able to safely congregate indoors.

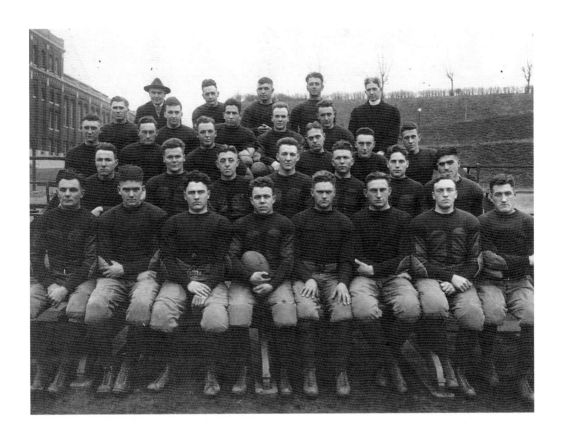

The 1918 football team gathers in the glory days of Creighton football.

Top: Rows of the latest equipment await Dental students and their patients in the Dental Clinic in 1921. The Clinic was part of a new Dental Building constructed in 1920 on the corner of 26th and California Streets.

Bottom: The reading room of the newly-constructed Law School (later Hitchcock) building awaits students and faculty in 1921.

Construction of the Creighton Stadium in 1924 requires the power of men and mules.

Top: The football team practices in 1925.

Bottom: Members of the 1925 women's intramural basketball team stand as the exception to the rule in the early history of male-dominated college athletics. The start of "girl's gymnasium class" in 1933 finally made the basketball court, indoor track, and swimming pool accessible to all female students, and it would be decades later before women's sports took their place alongside men's athletics.

The insult provoked an instant response from the "humanists" and other defenders of the classical tradition. Ruth Everett, a Catholic educator, chastised the "unchanged for four hundred years" comment, arguing that, "professors of the Jesuit colleges keep up with the times." She claimed, "To-day forty-seven per cent. [*sic*] of the students time is given to modern studies—proportioned during four years to the study of English, mathematics, modern languages, and natural sciences." For her, the disagreement hinged "on the age at which the student is deemed competent to elect for himself." Jesuits believed that undergraduates lacked the maturity to choose courses wisely and that they had devised a program that developed the student as "a thinker and a reasoner," before he would specialize in professional school. Although one Catholic historian stated, "The 1905 catalogue at [the Jesuit College of the] Holy Cross resembled Yale's catalogue for 1828," the Reverend Timothy Brosnahan, S.J., the former president of Boston College, complained that Eliot ignored the evolution of the *Ratio Studiorum* and provided a vivid metaphor to explain the Jesuit rejection of his "extreme electivism":

> The man whose whole education has been special or elective is as pitiable an object as a hollow-chested acrobat who can toss barrels with his feet. Both have undergone "training for power," both have made a thorough study of a few things, but both will remain to the end of their days educational curiosities.[45]

Creighton University joined the fray immediately. The 1899-1900 *Catalogue* included a thirteen-point defense of the *Ratio Studiorum*, which asserted "that the aim of a truly liberal education is the harmonious development of all the faculties, the careful training of mind and heart, the formation of character, rather than the actual imparting of knowledge and the specific equipment for a limited sphere of action." Moreover, it stipulated "that there are some branches of study absolutely necessary in any scheme of liberal education," and "that young students are not the proper judges of the studies essential for a systematic and thorough development of their faculties." The statement also proclaimed "that religion should not be divorced from education; that morality is impossible without religion and that is far more important than knowledge for the welfare of the individual and the safety of society. The commonwealth needs good men more than it needs clever men." Subsequently, at the June 19, 1903 Commencement, which celebrated the University's silver jubilee, Fr. Dowling announced the publication of his history of the school, available for $1.25. To obtain data for *Reminiscences*, he had sent a twenty-one-question circular to former students and faculty. He edited the responses and added his personal analysis. Chapter XVI consisted of a nine-page, point-by-point examination of the existing thirteen-point *Catalogue* argument. That same year, the Reverend Robert Schwickerath, S.J., reserved almost four hundred pages of his book on Jesuit education for a critique of Eliot's comment, his elective pedagogy, and German-style university training, which stressed research.[46]

While the controversy swirled, a conference of Catholic colleges met in Chicago in 1899, which resulted in the creation of the Association of the Catholic Colleges of the United States (ACC), as of 1904, the Catholic Education Association (CEA). In part, the Association coalesced as part of the movement toward the national organization of institutions during the Progressive Era, in an attempt to standardize operations and increase efficiency (e.g., National Association of State Universities, 1896; Association of American Universities, 1900). It also resulted from the desire of small Catholic colleges to address the problems posed by competition from large private and state universities. However, localism inhibited its effectiveness and its ability to enforce standards. Despite erroneous newspaper reports, at the 1899 meeting, "No resolutions however were adopted either in favor of widening the scope of our scientific studies, or of increasing the number of optional studies." The conference did pass a resolution "with the purpose of sounding a note of warning to apathetic college men in some states [who] are allowing their educational rights to be filched from them by unscrupulous and secularizing educators."[47]

The resolution referred to the early stages of accreditation. The profusion of colleges, curriculums, and standards created a demand from elite schools for ways to certify programs, which then related to their entrance requirements for undergraduate and graduate education. In 1884, for example, the University of Nebraska established entrance requirements and began accrediting high schools that met its standards. In 1889, only twelve high schools in the state could send their graduates to the University of Nebraska without examination. At the university level, at the turn of the century, Harvard University dropped all Catholic schools except Georgetown and Notre Dame from its list of schools whose students could enroll in its law school without examination. The United States Bureau of Education, national education organizations, and state governments joined the accreditation crusade. Fr. William Rigge revealed the legitimacy of the situation, writing, "Indeed, it was a notorious fact that sometimes degrees were given in branches the student had not studied at all; and degrees could even be bought." Nonetheless, the ACC feared state requirements could signal the demise of Catholic colleges.[48]

Jesuits played a prominent role in the meetings of the ACC, delivering about one fourth of the papers at the first conference, including one by Fr. Dowling. One commenter proudly noted, "Every suggestion of a Jesuit seemed to carry great weight with the conference. A big-hearted Lazarist father warmly grasping the hand of one of Ours [a Jesuit] said to him, 'The Jesuits present at this meeting are an honor to the Catholic Church.' Another delegate remarked jocosely that 'the conference was gotten up for the glorification of the Jesuits'." The author noted "these manifestations of cordiality and goodwill toward the Society" because he believed they demonstrated an appreciation for the Order. The fact that he felt obliged to mention them also reveals the competition and tension that exist between the various orders, as well as between the orders and the secular clergy, that could limit the effectiveness of Catholic organizations. At the second conference of the ACC, Fr. Dowling again presented a paper, "Development of Character in College Students," but Fr. Brosnahan's paper on "The Relative Merits of Courses in Catholic and Non-Catholic Colleges for the Baccalaureate," generated the greatest interest because of the recent publication of his rebuttal to Eliot.[49]

Most likely, the students of Creighton College continued unaware of the Eliot controversy. Probably, watching the eight graduates at Commencement, seated on the stage of the College Hall (the third-floor auditorium) in ceremonial caps and gowns for the first time, provided the highlight of 1899. The number of graduates fell to five the following year, then climbed to ten in 1902, fifteen in 1903, reached a record high of twenty-two in 1904, but dropped to sixteen the following year and averaged only thirteen for the remainder of the decade (ceremonies were held at the Creighton Orpheum Theatre 1900–1912). During that era, total enrollment increased; in 1904 the administration created four divisions of Third Academic and hired two Sisters of Mercy (Sr. M. Bonaventure and Sr. M. Camillus) to teach two of the sections in the "barracks." The arrangement continued into the 1909–10 academic year, when they taught syntax and Greek rudiments, Latin, English, and Mathematics. (By that time, Creighton College also employed a Mrs. C. Burkhard as a vocal music teacher and the medical school had hired Mary Strong, M.D., as "Demonstrator in Obstetrics"). Despite increasing total enrollment, the problem of students not finishing the seven-year program persisted well into the twentieth century; the phenomenon plagued all Jesuit colleges. In 1907, about four out of five students attending Creighton College enrolled in the high-school department. However, if students attempted the final three years of the *Ratio Studiorum*, they usually succeeded. Thus, to produce thirteen graduates from an entering class of approximately eighteen, one third of a three-year college department of fifty-three students, computes to a relative equivalent of contemporary graduation rates.[50]

Part of the increase in the total enrollment resulted from the creation the "Special Classes" category, which attracted twenty-six students by 1906. Individuals in that group usually possessed sufficient skills in English and mathematics, but not in Greek or Latin. Some of them were older than average students, had little formal education, and needed special tutoring; for example, a twenty-nine-year-old evangelist who wanted formal training in "sacred oratory." At the other end of the spectrum, in 1899, the College introduced an honors program, consisting of special study beyond the ordinary work of a class, for the Poetry (sophomore) and the Rhetoric (junior) years. At the same time, the American model of education continued to affect the *Ratio Studiorum*. In 1902, Creighton College divided itself into departments and began to abandon Jesuit terminology. The "High School or Academic Department" consisted of four years of study; "Humanities," previously the first year, college-level class, became the last year of high school and included the bookkeeping and business-writing classes of the old "Commercial Course.") In 1906, the terminology, "University High School, the College Preparatory Department," appeared in the *Catalogue*; immediately, faculty and students began to use the shorthand designation "Prep." The following year, the Reverend John F. Weir, S.J., acquired the title "principal," but for another decade, the same University officer administered the high school and the college, and the schools continued to issue a joint catalogue. For a brief interval, the three years of college became the freshman, the sophomore, and the combined junior-senior year. Overall, the seven-year plan called for a student to enter high school at fourteen years of age and graduate from college at twenty-one.[51]

Vocal music provided one of the few electives in the program. In 1899, the University could have expanded the offerings, as the Omaha College of Music proposed affiliation, but for unexplained reasons, Fr. Provincial Grimmelsman did not approve the tender. Two years later, however, the administration provided elective "courses of instruction in typewriting with Remington and Smith Premier Machines" for students inclined to obtain the skill. Unfortunately, in 1902 the College received a lukewarm review from the United States Bureau of Education; the assessment did not denigrate the program, but it alluded more to weaknesses than to strengths. It asserted, "The standard in the classics and mathematics [was] . . . fully equal to that of any school in the state." However, while the "people of Omaha have been remarkably generous in gifts for the scientific departments," the collection was not "extensive" and the school gave "less attention . . . to scientific studies by the faculty than is the case in the State University or other secular schools." Similarly, the faculty library's seven thousand volumes seemed adequate, but funds for acquisitions ($200 per year) remained "too limited." Moreover, although the curriculum paid "about the usual amount of attention" to philosophy, logic, and ethics, "a marked contrast" existed in comparison "with the best universities of the time," the "course is almost wholly prescribed."[52]

On the other hand, Creighton College received a personal, glowing review from the home of the elective revolution. Paul L. Martin obtained his A.B. at Creighton in 1902, and entered Harvard Law School that fall. Over the next three years, he wrote eight letters to Fr. Dowling extolling his undergraduate experience. His opening epistle evaluated his class of 250 students from all over the United States:

> . . . [F]rom what I have thus far seen of them in and out of class I have not the slightest hesitation in saying that Creighton men who take advantage of their opportunities need have no fear in competing with these fellows whom President Eliot would have us believe vastly superior in training to the students of Jesuit colleges.

His concluding letter maintained the same tone, arguing that although Harvard may have better facilities and a greater variety of classes, his years there "only served to convince me the more firmly that for the undergraduate Creighton is much to be preferred to Harvard."[53]

While the controversy over the prescribed curriculum continued unabated, the curriculum of Creighton College did not remain stagnant. In 1905, it introduced a combined six-year course in literature, science, and medicine: Student studied at Creighton College the first year; the next three years included combined undergraduate and medical-school classes; at the end of the fourth year the student earned his A.B., followed by two more years at the medical school to gain the M.D. degree. During this era, colleges adopted many new programs to overcome what reformers referred to as the "four-year fetish." Another innovation Creighton instituted in 1905 consisted of a five-year all-medical course; the extra year of study produced the equivalent of an honors degree in medicine. The College also introduced two new teacher-training programs in response to new certification standards. The State of Nebraska followed national trends in trying to improve the quality of teachers by increasing the requirements for certification. A 1907 statute raised "the standard of certification of teachers by private and denominational schools by providing for rigid inspection by the state board of examiners of life certificate candidates." That summer, the College provided rooms to the Sisters of Mercy for a four-week summer school, and they hired three secular women teachers to teach the classes. That fall, for its own students, the administration created the School of Pedagogy. It presented "the special studies required by law for teachers; such as the theory and art of teaching, the history of education, methods of instruction, school supervision, etc." A "University Teachers' Certificate" accompanied the A.B. degree if a student completed the additional eighteen-hour course of study (twelve in education, six in philosophy). The expanded curriculum, which included the separation of the four-year high school, ultimately resulted in a four-year college course of study, as directed by the Missouri Province in 1907. Two years later, the "Department of Arts" no longer included a high-school division, and in 1912, the Reverend Francis X. McMenamy, S.J., became the first administrator to hold the title of Dean of the College of Arts and Sciences.[54]

Despite being the smallest school in the University, the Creighton College not only experienced physical growth and curriculum expansion after 1898, it also finally began to develop "the old college spirit." An unidentified former student contributed his early assessment to *Reminiscences*:

> Certain individual students would strive to instill a college spirit, but would give up in despair. Interest in Creighton's welfare, if felt, was not in evidence; and such a thing as college songs, college yells, the display of colors, class and social organizations, were as foreign to us as the quadrangles of Oxford or Cambridge.

Another former student agreed:

> When I first arrived at Creighton in 1898, there was a notable absence of anything like a college spirit. [As soon as classes, ended students] decamped like workmen glad to get away from the scene of hard toil.

That same student also recalled that later,

> The most striking proof of this spirit was manifested when Creighton sent its first representative to the annual contest of the Nebraska Oratorical Association. . . . The idea of competing with other Institutions was like a call to arms.[55]

The College taught elocution and held annual intramural contests open to the public from the year it opened its doors. The competitions did not necessarily follow the debate model, as sometimes groups of students presented dialogues or a scene from a play. In 1898, a nascent debate club changed its name to the Creighton Oratorical Association and joined the Nebraska Collegiate Oratorical Association, whose other members included Cotner University and Wesleyan University in Lincoln, Doane College in Crete, and Bellevue College, Grand Island College, and Hastings College, all located in the towns of those names. The Creighton University club, which included alumni members, held weekly meetings, consisting of "readings, recitations and literary essays," and bi-weekly debates. That year, the college participated in its first intercollegiate debate, but "returned a sadder but a much wiser crowd then when they went forth. It was their first experience and it afforded more practical education than months in the class-room. They declared that they never dreamed that people were so narrow and bigoted, so ignorant of the truth." Displaying their siege mentality, the "victims" vowed to withdraw from the organization, but Fr. Dowling convinced them it "would be a wiser, as well as a more manly policy, to stay in." Miraculously, the bigotry evaporated and Creighton College won first place the next four years in a row. By 1902, the debaters also began to participate in an interstate competition, with representatives from Colorado, Indiana, Illinois, Kansas, Minnesota, Nebraska, Iowa, Missouri, Wisconsin, and Ohio, as well as competing in public dual meets against such opponents as the Delian League of Lincoln (admission 25 cents).[56]

A college spirit also burgeoned from the organization of other cultural organizations. A play, acted solely by students, originated in 1894: *Elma*, "a tragedy of Druid days." Then, in 1898, students presented a play about Rip Van Winkle that attracted almost five hundred patrons who paid 50 cents each; the revenue procured electric lights for the stage and a chandelier for the third-floor auditorium. The productions became a regular occurrence with the creation of the Creighton Dramatic Circle in 1899. That same year the Creighton Literary Society organized to extend to lower classmen the activities of the Oratorical Association, and the Mandolin Club formed to gain their first instrumental music lessons (twelve guitar and forty mandolin players). By 1906, the latter group evolved into the Creighton University Orchestra and Band. Finally, with the advent of the new library in 1900, the Creighton Catalogue Society assembled to "acquire the theoretical and practical knowledge for library cataloguing according to the methods at present, most in use"; the group adopted the recently established Dewey decimal system and C. A. Cutter's Alphabetical Order Table of Authors.[57]

The growth in physical plant and student spirit impressed a group of former students who reunited in Omaha in the summer of 1902. They decided to promote a fundraising scheme and an alumni association. Alumni organizations dated from the early nineteenth century, but mushroomed in size and influence as it reached its conclusion. The small number of graduates, and the fact that most graduates had just begun their careers, hindered the development at Creighton University. After a decade of conferring A.B. degrees, Creighton College had issued only sixty-one, and the medical school had produced eighty-five physicians in the previous six years. The Reverend Charles Coppens, S.J., a faculty member, and the author of an English composition textbook used at many Catholic colleges, surveyed the college graduates and found that,

Of them [the 61 A.B. degrees] 4 entered our society, and 2 the ranks of the secular clergy,—not counting, of course, the several others who left from Rhetoric or Poetry for our novitiate or the seminary, 12 have entered on the practice or study of law, 9 on that of Medicine, 2 on that of Pharmacy, 1 is an electrician, 1 a student of mining engineering, 2 are engaged in editorial work on newspapers, 1 in post-graduate studies of literature, 2 became principals of high schools, 1 has died, 1 is a real estate agent, 8 are engaged in commerce, and 15 are still clerking, though of these several will probably later on enter on more important careers.[58]

Obviously, the alumni did not consist of well-established or well-heeled professionals. Nonetheless, C. J. Smyth, Thomas J. McShane (A.B., 1899), William J. Coad (A.B., 1899), J. T. Smith (A.B., 1899) and E. V. Krug (A.B., 1900) sent a letter to the other graduates asking them to adopt the Princeton University model, whereby each class organized itself before graduation and pledged to donate a specified sum to their alma mater. They revealed that the Omaha gathering had given them the opportunity to thank Count John A. Creighton for his unending generosity, then they queried, "why should so much of the burden rest upon him?" They beseeched their former classmates, "If Princetonians and others, after paying for everything in course, feel that there is a major debt owing, why should not the men who have received benefit from Creighton, do something for her in turn?" The rhetorical question went unanswered. The University established an Alumni Association on October 26, 1903, which held annual banquets in 1904 and 1905, but the organization struggled as an essentially Omaha group and the fundraising scheme did not materialize.[59]

Despite the failure to organize nationally, the attempt itself manifested the escalating college spirit at Creighton University. Among students and with alumni, sport probably provided the major impetus. Father Dowling's paper presented at the 1900 ACC meeting on character development "was a strong appeal for the development of manliness and honor in the building up of true character, and asserted that no small element in character building was to be found in athletics, since character is developed on the campus as well as in the classroom." Administrators, who recognized athletics as a public relations tool and as a means to raise funds from alumni, began to take over the domain established by students as part of an "extracurriculum." Many clergy abandoned previously negative attitudes toward athletics and began to view sports as a positive contribution to "strenuous life" and "muscular Christianity." Many late-nineteenth-century commentators feared that the new urban lifestyle made educated middle-class men effeminate and advocated the virtues of rugged outdoor activity. Bully-Bully President Theodore Roosevelt became the movement's symbol and a prime spokesman. Similarly, some clergymen dreaded what they perceived as a feminization of their churches (women provided a majority of those attending services and volunteering for church activities) and began to preach a Christian version of the strenuous life. Athletic contests provided an outlet for building and displaying "manly" values (recall Fr. Dowling's use of the terminology in counseling the debate team and in extolling athletics).[60]

In 1903, Fr. Dowling reiterated his support for the concept, claiming, "The splendid college spirit that now exists is due to athletics perhaps more than to any other influence." He justified athletics as a means "to meet the wants of the living age, which requires a sound mind in a sound body." He complained that the critics "of systematic physical culture are those who would be content to see boys Hatchet-faced, thin-blooded, scrawny, with spindle shanks, flat chests, narrow shoulders, soft muscles, weak arms and a lack of physical courage." How could such a man compete in Darwin's age of "struggle for survival" and sociologist Herbert Spencer's "survival of the fittest"? Thus, according to Fr. Dowling, "If people want an education which includes physical culture, give them what they want and they will send their children to you." The argument provided another compromise with the American educational model and demonstrated one more stage in the evolution and Americanization of the Jesuit Creighton University (European Jesuit schools did not sponsor athletic teams).[61]

After his return in 1898, Fr. Dowling oversaw the organization of the Athletic Association, composed of students and alumni and created "for the double purpose of fostering a college spirit and encouraging healthful exercise among students." Intercollegiate sports at Creighton University burgeoned; by 1901, accounts of fall rugby-style football and baseball, as well as spring baseball games, began to appear in local newspapers. Schedules included games against high schools, military teams such as at Ft. Omaha, and other colleges, and, on one occasion, it included travel to another town in the proximate region. On October 19, the Creighton Medics called off a game against Creighton College "because they had bargained to play a practice-game not a scheduled pay game." From its inception, intercollegiate sport immediately became a commercial venture and the custom had developed fully by the time Creighton entered the playing field. Seemingly, the above intramural contest entailed competing for, or splitting, gate receipts. The next week, the College football team traveled to College Springs, Iowa, to defeat the Amity College club 10-0 (rugby rules and scoring).[62]

The team quickly became part of the local spectator-sport culture. During the afternoon of Thanksgiving Day, November 28, 1901, following the noon meal, the College participated in a double-header at the Ames Avenue Park that attracted a crowd estimated at between four and six thousand. In the first game, the Omaha High School defeated the Genoa (Nebraska) Indian School team 11–6; then Creighton beat the Lincoln Medics. Dan Butler ran forty yards for the only score and Edward Creighton (grandson of John D. Creighton) kicked the goal in the 6–0 victory (the five-point "touchdown" and the one-point goal did not conform to rugby or contemporary American football scoring). Someone had enticed great-uncle John Andrew to attend; the thrill of victory produced an instant fan who declared a holiday for the students (no classes Saturday, November 30) and gave $100 to the Athletic Association. In 1943, Omaha Mayor Dan Butler remembered the game as occurring in 1902, his run consisting of sixty yards, that John gave him the $100 personally, and told him to treat the team, which enjoyed "a royal banquet." Significantly, Butler was one of three players on the team who were not listed in the

Catalogue as registered students that year (he had been a Special Course student previously). Otherwise, the team consisted of two Specials, three high-school students, and two collegians.[63]

In comparison, the football team's 5–11 loss to the [Omaha Central] High School, provided few thrills, but "a good deal of soreness." The previous spring, however, the Creighton baseball team had drubbed the high school by a score of 30-3. Overall, the administration felt it had had a good year and touted its accomplishments in a Jesuit magazine, the *Woodstock Letters*. Credit for success went to the fact that the College included a number of older students, especially those enrolled in the Special Course, such as "an M.D., another an LL.B., and one a Protestant Evangelist," (whom we know was twenty-nine years of age). According to the author of the article, "As a consequence of their age, we have had this year a stronger football team than usual, and confidence in their baseball abilities is evidenced by the fact that games have been secured with the University teams of Minnesota and Nebraska." Creighton University stood poised to enter major college athletics.[64]

The following year the schedule of games expanded and a coach appeared. The desire to win promoted professionalism in college sport; as early as 1864, Yale had hired a gymnasium instructor to coach its crew team to victory over Harvard. By the dawn of the twentieth century, the paid coach became a standard figure, especially in football. While a student manager still played a role with teams at Creighton University, a Jesuit chronicler noted that in the game against Amity College, "by order of the coach," the Creighton eleven left the field before the end of the first half, "claiming unfair treatment." In 1902, the coach at Creighton may have been a volunteer, a Jesuit and/or alum, or an older student, but other amenities for athletes appeared. A new description of the Athletic Association proclaimed:

> The association has been in existence a number of years, but only during the last two years has it made its presence felt in intercollegiate contests on the gridiron and the diamond. During the past year particularly a new impetus was given to outdoor sports by the laying out of the new athletic field near the University buildings, and by providing larger and more convenient apartments with baths and lockers for the exclusive use of the players. It is the hope and purpose of the athletic association to further indoor athletics to a like extent by fitting up in the near future a modern gymnasium with all necessary appurtenances.[65]

Obviously, the Athletic Association adopted the attitude that it had to provide benefits to attract "student" athletes. It sponsored plays as fundraisers and John "was a great help to the athletic managers who could always rely upon his assistance in making up a deficit in finances or in arranging some coveted trip in the interest of the student body." By 1905, early dismissal of Saturday classes for football games became standard, but faculty began to insist on "conditioning" a student; that is, not allowing him to play unless he made an average of sixty notes." At that time, one hundred notes equaled a perfect grade in a class (e.g., freshman year, all subjects combined, in a cumulative grade as the year progressed), thus athletes had to maintain a sixty-note average in their class (raised to seventy in 1908). No one established a correlation between grades and players, but on September 30, 1905, Ft. Crook beat the Creighton football team 0-10, then on October 28, the University of Nebraska triumphed by a score of 0-102, and on November 6, despite the first appearance of the new brass band, the winless team disbanded.[66]

If a correlation existed between players and grades, it did not have a lengthy impact. The school experienced its "greatest victory" on May 12, 1906, defeating the University of Nebraska baseball team 4-2. "The band and many 'rooters' went in two street cars all over town for two hours before the game in order to advertise it. After the game the band and a big crowd marched along some of the neighboring streets. At night the band & a big crowd played and yelled before the newspaper offices and Mr. Creighton's home." The following Tuesday, the students gained a recreation day "on account of the great victory" and the mushrooming college spirit carried over to the fall. On September 28, 1906, a "mass meeting" took place at the Creighton Auditorium "for the purpose of arousing a good college spirit with regard to athletics." J. V. Dwyer, manager of the football team, presided and Frank Furay, president of the Alumni Association, "gave a short, witty and happy speech urging all to do their utmost for Creighton sports." Coach George Cavanaugh, the first identifiable professional coach at Creighton, asked "students to help him get up a winning team" and Fr. President Dowling "added that while he encouraged athletics every way, he thought it beneath the dignity of a university to pay any student or anybody else for playing." The National Collegiate Athletic Association (NCAA) organized that year to establish standards for intercollegiate athletics and to enforce new rules for the sport of football. Besides concerns for player eligibility and amateurism, the new organization addressed the problem of brutality in the game. In 1905, eighteen players had died in the mass formations of the rugby-style game, and President Theodore Roosevelt arranged a White House conference that sparked reforms in the nature of the game and the formation of the NCAA. Creighton's rejuvenated team gained some victories that year, but lost again to Nebraska, although by a more respectable score (0–17) before 2,500 fans.[67]

In 1907, at a cost of $18,500, Creighton University purchased the land between 25th Avenue and 26th Street, California to Burt streets. The city vacated 25th Avenue and gave it to the University; the acquisition doubled the size of the campus to just over eleven acres. On March 2, 1908, at the first meeting of the House Consultors with the new rector-president, the Reverend Eugene A. Magevney, S.J., they voted to grade the property to create a level athletic field nearly three hundred yards square. They hired Clearance Kenney, a "phenomenal half-back" and the 1907 captain of the St. Louis University football team, as coach. Moreover, they added another new statement on athletics in the *Catalogue*:

> The attitude of Creighton University toward athletics is that they should be encouraged, since they tend to a proper physical and mental development of the students. As their only purpose is to afford healthful exercise and permit gentlemanly rivalry and

competition, care is taken to keep them within limits, so that they may aid and not detract from study. A creditable standing in class is the necessary condition of eligibility to any of the University teams.

While the statement voiced faculty concerns that intercollegiate athletics could distract students from study, it also promised that by September 1, 1908, for the "opportunity to enjoy the pleasure of a home-ground," the campus would include a gridiron, a ball field, tennis courts, and handball alleys. The 420-by-400-foot field would have bleachers to "accommodate about 4,000 spectators," who could easily reach it since "the Harney and Cuming street [trolley] cars pass within a block of its main entrance." At the same time, the University created an athletic board consisting of Fr. President Magevney, the Reverend Chancellor Michael J. O'Connor, S.J., and Athletic Director the Reverend Albert Wise, S.J. An advisory board, with a representative from the Alumni Association, and one each from the medical, dental, and law schools, would assist the athletic board and the "physical directors," C. J. Kenny, M.D., W. J. Schneider, and student manager J. F. Mullen, Creighton College class of 1909.[68]

Thus by the time of the death of Count John A. Creighton and the departure of Fr. Michael P. Dowling, Creighton University had rebounded to become a robust institution. A third person added luster to the institution, Fr. William Rigge, who had arrived as a scholastic in 1878, completed his studies elsewhere, but returned in 1896 and began an illustrious career as a science teacher and internationally acclaimed astronomer. In 1908, he gained election to the British Royal Astronomical Society, a signal honor for a Jesuit of the era, since few at that time entered scientific fields or published scholarly works in any discipline outside theology. Fr. Rigge also served the history of the University well; he compiled a personal chronicle and wrote his memoirs, which detailed activities two decades subsequent to Fr. Dowling's *Reminiscences*.[69]

Father Dowling served as rector-president of Creighton University twice, from 1885 to 1889 and again from 1898 to 1908, the only person to serve more than two three-year terms until after World War II. Ex-President of the United States Rutherford B. Hayes, who served on the Board of Directors of Ohio State University in the early 1890s, argued that a university president had to have a fine appearance and a commanding presence. He also had to be a good speaker, preacher, and a great scholar and teacher, have tact to govern a faculty, be popular with students, and be a man of business training and a great administrator. He knew such a person did not exist. Father Michael P. Dowling's eulogizers, however, described that person. According to Fr. Rigge, "When he laid down the keys of office on March 12, 1889, and departed for Detroit to erect a college building there also, enterprise and success departed with him. . . . It was only upon Fr. Dowling's resumption of the reins on November 12, 1898 for his second term, that the University began again vigorously to lift its head and awaken to new life."[70]

Father Dowling was born in Cincinnati on June 14, 1851; in 1869, he followed his older brother James into the Society of Jesus, entering the priesthood in 1882. After serving as rector-president of Creighton College, he filled the same position at Detroit College from 1889 to 1893. Fortuitously, being a rector-president during the depression of the 1890s escaped him, as he served as pastor at Holy Family Parish in Chicago from 1894 to 1898. Then, after a decade at Creighton University, he accepted the fact that a gratified public in Omaha "recognized the value of his services [*sic*] to the city, even though they overvalue them very much." He knew that he had arrived "at an opportune time." Father Rigge's evaluation underestimated the strain of the depression, while Fr. Dowling's self-assessment undervalued his own talents. Father Dowling, a handsome man and a powerful orator, had vision and charisma; most importantly, he had established a special bond with John Andrew. According to an eulogizer, "Their friendship was genuine, deep-seated, inspiring, the spontaneous outburst of kindred natures which naturally attracted each other." Therefore, although no records document the decision, Fr. Provincial Thomas Fitzgerald may have selected Fr. Dowling for a second tenure at Creighton University, and extended that tenure to coincide with the life of John Andrew, based on the dire straights of the situation in 1898 and on the recognized bond of the existing friendship.[71]

John Andrew and some members of the Creighton family clan had always attended school functions and dined regularly with the faculty; after Dowling's return this camaraderie intensified. For example, "In Father Dowling's [*sic*] days vehicles could be used [at one point a previous rector had prohibited riding in carriages] and at times the whole faculty joined Mr. Creighton and his friends on private picnics at Courtland Beach and at Priess Lake." Besides initiating a less puritanical regime and gaining recognition as "the savior of Creighton University," Fr. Dowling contributed to "a rebellion of the clergy." He led a revolt that wrested control of the *True Voice*, a purported Catholic weekly, from the Western Publishing Company and its lay editor, Charles Curtz Hahn. After only a few weekly issues appearing in 1903, the Reverend Peter C. Gannon replaced Hahn, and a new corporation emerged, directed by an all-priest board chaired by Fr. Dowling. An article written by Fr. Stritch of Creighton University claimed that only "competent editorship and the sanction and active cooperation of ecclesiastical authorities" could fill the need for a Catholic paper in Omaha.[72]

Before Fr. Dowling left Omaha, the city and the University feted him with a royal banquet. In his farewell address he stated, "As for myself, I have given to the university my best years, I have devoted to it the best that was in me, and now after fourteen years, out of 'the Creighton millions' to which someone alluded a moment ago, I take with me six dollars—just enough to pay my fare to Kansas City." He spent his last years in that city as pastor at St. Aloysius Church and in purchasing a site for Rockhurst College. He lived long enough to see that new institution open its doors, but died a few months later, at age sixty-four, on February 13, 1915. After a Mass in Kansas City, his body was returned to Omaha to lie in state at St. John's Church, before burial at Holy Sepulchre Cemetery at a spot near the Creighton family obelisk.[73]

Previously, Dowling had spent his last year in Omaha writing a biography of John A. Creighton, which he did not publish because of disagreements with censors.

He argued, "I do not see how justice can be done to the subject of the sketch, without telling the terms of his will; and that cannot be done without saying why his intentions were not carried out." He claimed he would only have written what newspapers published and used no names. Settling John's estate taxed Fr. Dowling's health and made his last year in Omaha a trying one. The Count had signed his will on January 6, 1904, but the value of his estate increased almost 400 percent by the time of his death. "Like nearly every other wealthy man in Omaha he had a large block of worthless mining stock," such as 58,000 shares of the Wabash Mining Company that had cost him $150,000. On the other hand, in 1905, he and partner Patrick Largey of Butte, Montana, after reaping several years of hefty dividends, sold the Speculator Mine for $5,000,000. Father Dowling fretted as newspapers printed rumors of lawsuits, "There is too much money there and too dazzling an invitation to the lawyers to work in some big fees to let the will have smooth sailing." Ultimately, two prominent business associates, William Paxton, Sr., and Milton T. Barlow, appraised John Andrew's estate at $3,847,464.24, bequeathed to twenty-eight heirs and beneficiaries. However, he left nothing to his estranged nieces, Mary Shelby (daughter of brother Joseph) and Mary (McCreary) Daxon, and nephews James, Charles, John, William, and Emmet McCreary (children of sister Mary). They sued the estate and a year-long three-cornered struggle ensued between them, the extended-family heirs, and the institutional beneficiaries: Creighton University, the Franciscan Sisterhood for the maintenance of St. Joseph's Hospital, the Little Sisters of the Poor for a charity house, the Sisters of the Good Shepherd for charity work, and a proposed home for poor working girls.[74]

The University stood to receive about 40 percent of the estate and, therefore, it acted as the primary negotiator for the institutions. Father Provincial Meyer empowered the rector "to spend if necessary one third of the bequest left to Creighton University [approximately $400,000] rather than have a lawsuit." Father Dowling, however, instructed the lawyers "that they were not to exceed $320,000.00" in settling with the litigious relatives, who also sued to vacate the grant for a working-girls home. Ultimately, in an out-of-court agreement each plaintiff received $52,666.66, while the Nebraska Supreme Court ruled in favor of the working-girls home, which eventually received $177,453.80. The Little Sisters of the Poor no longer maintained a presence in Omaha and waived their bequest. Sixteen extended-family heirs obtained between $15,500 and $132,666.67 each, while housekeeper Mary Cotter received $21,000. Four institutions divided the remainder: the House of the Good Shepherd, $119,000; the Franciscan Monastery of St. Clare, $125,000; the Franciscan Sisterhood for St. Joseph's Hospital, $476,000; and Creighton University, $1,250,000. Reporters asked Fr. Dowling what the University would do with the money, but he refused specific answers, except to allude to a separate building for the pharmacy school, because the rapid expansion of the dental school caused crowding at the ECI. Privately, he revealed that John "was anxious to establish a first-class divinity school" and "was very much taken with the idea" of a pedagogical school. The new administrators brought neither to fruition.[75]

Problems remained after the "final" agreement on the estate. As part of its bequest, Creighton University received one third of the shares in the John A. Creighton Real Estate and Trust Company. Father Dowling argued that the University should acquire a controlling interest in the firm by using inherited bonds to purchase the shares of the Franciscan Sisterhood. However, John Andrew had stipulated that his bequest go to the endowment, preventing such use of the bonds. The trustees devised a paper-shuffling scheme to obtain the desired results. They used $35,000 in non-endowment cash and a $105,000 "loan" to purchase the real estate company shares, which gave them majority control of the firm. In a paper transaction, Creighton University sold the Society of Jesus of Omaha its inherited bonds on a promissory note bearing 5 percent interest, a legal use of trust assets. The Society (not the University trustees) used the bonds to purchase the sisterhood's stock; thus, the University and the Society (actually the same group of Jesuits) each owned about one third of the stock. To complete the paper shuffle, the University and the Missouri Province exchanged notes for $114,975, as if they had loaned each other money (the mortgage the University held was a legal investment under trust regulation). The signatories decided to keep the notes in vaults "until such time as we may deem it safe to make the re-exchange." In legalese, the transaction consisted in a "circle of checks," in which all participants received full value.[76]

While they gained control of a real estate company, the trustees lost $100,000 to a late claim against John Andrew's estate. A Jesuit chronicler gave credence to the demand by reporting that on January 9, 1908, the *Omaha Daily News*, "a sensational paper, is the first to mention Creighton's 'daughter' as getting $100,000.00, which the heirs agreed to give her to save litigation. No more appeared in this or any other paper." The newspaper piece stated that Mabel Eaton, "educated largely at the expense of Count Creighton," claimed to be his daughter and originally demanded $1 million. She had left Omaha fifteen years earlier and pursued a career on the stage; subsequently, her alleged parents, Mr. and Mrs. E. L. Eaton, joined her in Chicago. A Mr. Ednik L. Eaton had married Emma Salveter in Omaha on May 30, 1866, but no birth record exists for Mabel. The estate managers compromised to save litigation, but "incorporated in the settlement papers a statement that absolutely repudiated the [paternal] claim." While the Jesuit chronicler validated the agreement, a reporter's quote from one of Eaton's lawyers clouded the issue of paternity: "Judge Baxter [acting as an attorney in this case] refuses to discuss the case, although he practically admitted its truth when the direct question was put to him." But what was the question: Is she just acting? Is she really his daughter?[77]

On a less soap opera-like note, one year to the date after John Andrew's death, all heirs and beneficiaries signed the "final" final agreement, which allowed the distribution of the estate (actually received at the end of March). That same day, February 7, 1908, became the first Founders' Day at Creighton University, celebrated with a memorial service to Edward and John Creighton, and an evening banquet extolling their virtues. Edward's fortune endowed the original school; John's expanded it to a university consisting of five "departments" and positioned it to thrive because of his generous bequest. The University struggled through the doldrums caused by the Panic of 1893, and survived the depredations of the American Protective Association, which had largely consisted of vicious rumormongering. John Andrew rescued the financially ailing institution and created a new campus for the Creighton College, which included new wings on the original building, and a library, auditorium, heating plant and dormitory. He also built impressive homes for the medical, dental, law, and pharmacy schools. Moreover, he contributed to the growing college spirit by subsidizing the cultural clubs and athletic programs. Thus, upon the death of Count John A. Creighton and with the departure of his friend and colleague Fr. Rector-President Michael P. Dowling, who had provided him with vision and advice, the University stood primed to enter an era of stable and satisfying maturity.

CHAPTER 4

The Mature University

War and assimilation dominated the decade after the death of John A. Creighton and the departure of Fr. Michael Dowling. The professional schools flourished and developed new programs. Creighton College evolved into the College of Arts and Sciences, as the high school became a stand-alone institution. The University, no longer supported by a single benefactor who underwrote every project, began a booster campaign to marshal the support of its alumni and the populace of Omaha. It directed its fundraising efforts especially toward the expansion of athletics, including the construction of a state-of-the-art gymnasium. Just as Creighton University accomplished its goals, World War I erupted; the conflagration immediately affected the lives of the faculty and students in all the various departments. In 1917, after the United States became a belligerent, the University reoriented the schedules and programs of all its schools in behalf of the war effort. Briefly, the patriotic effort transformed the University into a military training camp. Subsequently, peacetime demanded another restructuring, which came in the form of a reluctant, but virtually obligatory, assimilation with the American model of education. During the second decade of the twentieth century, the Missouri Province made significant changes to its course of study, enabling its colleges and universities to meet accreditation standards for their professional schools and undergraduate colleges. Ultimately, in 1920, Creighton abandoned the *Ratio Studiorum*, in its place adopting a course of study dubbed the "American Plan," which created the assimilated Creighton University. The University retained distinctive Catholic features and it maintained a Jesuit faculty and administration, but its curriculum and the "extra-curriculum" had Americanized.

Early in the twentieth century, many Catholic colleges introduced the rank system for its faculty. On numerous occasions, conflict ensued because clerical faculty members gained tenure and promotion without fulfilling the requirements demanded of lay teachers. Creighton University escaped the controversy because the faculty of the professional schools consisted entirely of lay practitioners, and few laymen held full-time positions in Creighton College until after World War I. As late as 1912, only one layman, teaching "physical culture," served on the College faculty. The 1914–15 academic year experienced a significant increase of part-time lay instructors for voice and instrumental music, as well as a person with a B.S. teaching biology, another with an A.M. serving as registrar and teaching history, and one without a degree teaching elocution. The war years reoriented the lay faculty; only three laymen remained on the academic staff, while the United States Army provided six military instructors. Significantly, women again appeared among the lay faculty: Florence Lacy served as "Instructress in Arts" in 1915, and Lillian Fitch became "Professor of Elocution and Dramatic Art" in 1917. The previous year, the College offered no class in art, probably because it could not hire an instructor.[1]

The University touted its faculty, claiming, "Many of the Creighton professors have done work of unusual excellence in the field of research and have received fitting recognition from learned societies both at home and abroad." The boast, however, exaggerated the situation. In 1912, J. S. Foote, A.M., M.D., professor of physiology, histology, and pathology in the medical school, became the first person from Creighton University elected as a fellow of the American Association for the Advancement of Science. The following year the organization added its first Jesuit, Fr. William Rigge, the only faculty member of Creighton College who did scholarly research. Much of his research educated the public; in 1910, for example, Halley's comet became visible in the northern hemisphere and he drew "enormous" crowds to the Observatory for lectures and viewings. That same year, he became a national celebrity by solving a local crime. Omaha's political boss, Tom Dennison, discovered an unexploded bomb on his porch and subsequently had a political rival arrested for the crime. The only evidence came from two young girls who claimed to have witnessed the accused place the device on the porch. The girls had attended church, had their picture taken on the church steps, and then allegedly saw the crime unfold as they passed Dennison's house on their way home. The defense attorney knew of Fr. Rigge's work and asked him to view the photograph and determine the time of day. From the shadows visible in the picture, Fr. Rigge concluded that the photographer snapped the shot at 3:20 P.M., one half hour after the discovery of the bomb. Because of the partisan machine politics involved in the case, it took three trials before the Nebraska Supreme Court freed the defendant. Father Rigge published an article about how he determined the time of day in the July 20, 1912, *Scientific American*. For over a decade he also contributed articles on science to the Creighton alumni magazine, and in 1917, for his body of work, Georgetown University awarded him an honorary Ph.D.[2]

In comparison to the accessible and loquacious Fr. Rigge, Creighton University's new president, Fr. Eugene Magevney, S.J., displayed "a retiring nature and disliked publicity." While he also differed markedly from his predecessor Fr. Michael Dowling, he oversaw the continued expansion of the University. In one of his first acts, he tried to rescind Dowling's donation to the building fund for a new cathedral in Omaha; he claimed the proffer by the University to memorialize the name of John A. Creighton in the archdiocese violated the rules of the Creighton trust. The Very Reverend General Franz Wernz, S.J., and Fr. Provincial Meyer overruled his decision, ordering payment of the gift from discretionary funds. On a less controversial note, in 1909, Fr. Magevney remodeled the college building, including new frescoed murals for the main vestibule, and in 1913, he separated the House Consultors and the Board of Trustees into distinct entities with different personnel.[3]

A fire necessitated further major renovations (in 1887, fire had damaged a scholastic's room, and in 1905, another had consumed the contents of the kitchen storage room in the basement). The third fire, on May 8, 1911, however, became a major conflagration. It started at 2:00 A.M., in the electric elevator on the third floor of the north wing, spread to the attic and eventually to the roof of the north and center segments of the College Building. Seven fire companies responded and sprayed fourteen streams of water that put out the blaze, but caused significant damage to the historic main section, as the plaster ceilings of all stories collapsed. Before carpenters could repair the roof, several drenching rains added to the water damage. Since the north wing had steel ceilings that remained in tact, students lost only one of the few days remaining in the semester. Insurance paid for only part of the repairs and equipment replacement, but work proceeded rapidly and classes resumed on schedule the following September.[4]

Father President Magevney also oversaw another major reconfiguration of the campus, this one in response to the long-awaited construction of 24th Street. Discussion of the project had begun in 1889 and arose periodically thereafter. In 1906, the Omaha Bee newspaper reported that the University opposed the latest plan for the road's construction, but then-president Dowling "entered a prompt denial." In 1908, the Trustees authorized transferring a thirty-foot-wide swath of University property to the city in order to escape owner liability associated with the cost of street construction (grading, paving, and improvements such as sewers and curbs). Subsequently, the University claimed $22,800 in damages associated with the project. The city denied the claim (submitted after the 30-day deadline) and paid $7,000 for the strip of property, but charged $6,000 for improvements.[5]

Cutting 24th Street through from Cass to Cuming threatened the Observatory, because it sheared the hill on the east side of the campus in order to create a relatively level roadbed for the street railway that would extend northward along the new thoroughfare (the dirt was dumped in the gully at 30th and Cuming streets). Before he left, Fr. Dowling had proposed moving the Observatory to the roof of the College Building and grading the campus down to street level to the east and the north. The plan proved impractical, as did suggestions to relocate the Observatory to a new location outside the city. Thus, at a cost of $17,500, the administration decided to erect a 426-foot-long concrete retaining wall, which rose in height from four feet on the south to twenty-nine feet on the north. Just south of the Observatory, a concrete stairway ($3,500 additional expense), which ascended from street level to the north lawn, divided the retaining wall. The steps, however, invited "dubious characters" to campus, so in 1917 Fr. Magevney demanded the addition of an iron gate that he could lock at night (shortly thereafter the lock became permanent and in 1993 the litter-collecting stairwell was eliminated). The University once again graded the campus (dumping the soil west of the north wing and north of St. John's, all the way to Burt Street), lowering the north lawn ten feet and crafting a twenty-degree grade terrace, which slanted eastward down to the top of the retaining wall. The grading left the Observatory perched atop a ten-foot mound; a ladder provided the means to reach it until a wall with steps came to encircle the structure.[6]

Immediately, for some, the retaining wall became an "eyesore"; others welcomed it as a privacy fence (the college sat well above street level) and a sound barrier (trolley traffic commenced October 16, 1910, and with paving, the street opened to all traffic on August 7, 1911). For decades, the wall defined the eastern boundary of the campus, but growth continued to the west and north. Between 1910 and 1915, the University purchased eight lots on the south side of Burt Street between 24th and 26th streets, relocating the houses to the north side of Burt or to Cass Street, west of 26th. The purchases increased the area of the campus to 12.6 acres; the University now owned the entire rectangle, from California to Burt between 24th and 26th, except for a couple of small pieces on California Street. Actually, University Treasurer the Reverend Thomas J. Livingstone, S.J., explained that the Society of Jesus owned some of the properties in Omaha separately from the Creighton trust and that he carefully distinguished between the two accounts.[7]

In 1913, from the John A. Creighton estate, the administration (the majority stockholder) sold "a large corn field, forty-five acres, southwest of the Poor Clares, between 30 & 33rd and Cuming and Hamilton" for $85,000, from which it realized more than one half. Subsequently, in 1916, worried by rumors about the development of apartment houses, the University acquired the two blocks west of the Auditorium, bounded by California and Burt, 26th to 27th streets, for $52,200. That same year, John D. Creighton donated two lots on Cass Street, west of 25th. For the next half century, 27th Street, which ran only between California and Burt and did not align with the other north-south streets of the neighborhood, stood as the west boundary of the campus, which consisted of 16.6 acres of land.[8]

Serendipitously, in 1917 the University gained the use of another structure. Archbishop Jeremiah Harty revived the preparatory seminary plan for a third time and purchased the "elegant Henry T. Clark home a block from the arts college." Previously, the administration had rejected a plan to construct a second dormitory, but when the seminary once again failed to attract sufficient applicants, Bishop Harty allowed seventeen Creighton students to reside in the house, named Bishop O'Connor Hall. The arrangement persisted until dissolved in 1937, when the building became the diocesan chancery. Finally, in 1917, the Omaha & Council Bluffs Street Railway Company sealed the University's growth to the north for several decades by building a huge car barn on land between 26th and 27th, Burt to Cumming streets.[9]

While the campus assumed its historical proportions, the professional schools remained located in Omaha's central business district. The University proudly proclaimed the quality of those departments: "One of the most reliable methods of determining, within reasonable limits, the relative standing of the professional schools of the country is afforded by the rank conferred by the New York Board of Regents"—all the Creighton professional schools received the highest ranking. Generally, each school maintained good ratings by conforming to the increasingly stringent educational requirements demanded by the respective professional associations and their accrediting organizations. Thus, the dental college increased its entrance requirement to a high-school diploma in 1914, and initiated a four-year course of study in 1917; Dean A. Hugh Hipple, D.D.S., had built a program with a credible national reputation. In 1909, enrollment had dropped to seventy, from eighty-one the previous year. This fluctuation, however, resulted from an extraordinary enrollment spike produced by the closure of the Omaha Dental College and the Drake University Dental College. Despite the increased standards, matriculation steadily increased to a record high of 119 in 1918. The following year, scandal besmirched the school's enviable reputation: the administration presented no degrees at Commencement because it learned that a thief had stolen and sold copies of the final examination. However, a retest solved the problem and the episode did not produce any long-term repercussions.[10]

The Pharmacy College also continued to follow professional guidelines, but with different results. During the early twentieth century, pharmaceutical organizations failed to standardize educational programs as thoroughly as other professions. A vast array of one, two, and three-year programs continued to issue a variety of degrees during the pre–World War I era. In 1908, the American Conference of Pharmaceutical Faculties mandated one year of high school as an entrance requirement for its members and the Pharmaceutical Syllabus Committee (founded 1906) published its first Pharmaceutical Syllabus in 1910. Creighton instituted the new entrance requirement in 1914 and matriculation plummeted over the next several years. From a high of 138 students in 1913 (with 72 "juniors," actually first-year students in a two-year program instituted in 1910), enrollment dipped to a mere 48 in 1918, before it began to climb upward again. By the latter date, the demands of war enticed more students to the field, even though the entrance requirement increased to two years of high school in 1919. Women continued to play a significant role in the program: In 1913, graduate Virginia Bryan scored the highest grade on the State Pharmacy Board exam (of seventy-one candidates, sixty-nine were male). Moreover, women composed 15 percent of the "freshman" class of 1918. Students enrolled either in the redesigned two-year "graduate in pharmacy" course or the three-year "pharmaceutical chemist" course. Subsequently, in 1920, the school added a four-year B.S. in Pharmacy degree to its program.[11]

The Creighton College of Law also molded its program to meet national professional standards. On September 1, 1909, the school initiated a four-year night course, which utilized the same "professors, books, method of instruction, entrance, attendance and graduation requirements," as the three-year day course. A temporary (1908 to 1914) graduation requirement included a three-thousand-word thesis on "some legal topic" of the student's "own selection, approved by faculty." Following the recommendation of the American Bar Association, the night course consisted of four years of study of thirty-four weeks each; Creighton became only the eleventh law school in the country to offer day and night programs. That same academic year it awarded its first scholarships and a book prize. The person with the highest grade average from the first- and second-year classes received $50, the equivalent of a year's tuition and fees. The person ranked number one in the graduating class garnered a $12 book prize underwritten by Callaghan & Co. of Chicago, Illinois. The law college also began to favor a method of instruction that emphasized the "case system" over the "largely discredited" lecture and textbook systems. Paul L. Martin, who had received his A.B. at Creighton College in 1902 and his LL.B. at the Harvard Law School in 1905, returned to teach at the Creighton College of Law and probably influenced the verbiage above, as well as the evolving curriculum. In 1910, he succeeded Timothy Mahoney, becoming the second dean of the school.[12]

Martin introduced upper-class electives and Model House, a device mirroring the operation of the Nebraska House of Representatives (Nebraska instituted the unicameral legislature in 1937), which stressed public speaking and the intricacies of the legislative process. Model House also emphasized networking. According to the faculty director,

> The necessities of making acquaintances among the men who count in a community, as a means of getting legal business, demand a more or less active part in community affairs. This requires an ability to take an active part in formal and informal public meetings. The route to acquaintance through fraternal societies is also made more smooth by such a practical knowledge as will enable the young lawyer to participate in lodge affairs. Early professional opportunities often lead to business before a town council, board of county commissioners, board of education or the board of directors of a corporation and sometimes acquaintance and prestige are sought through legislative experiences.[13]

To gain those practical skills, the entire student body of the law college participated in Model House, which met every Wednesday evening for seven weeks each semester. Students elected their own House officers, who selected topics and assigned students to represent a Nebraska legislative district. Each student group studied its specific topic, prepared a bill or joint resolution, and guided it through the legislative process, including pro and con floor debate.

The process entailed six aims:

1. "A practical knowledge of the elements of proper legislative procedure,"
2. "training in the preparation of proposed bills or joint resolutions with the end in view of securing clear, concise and effective laws,"
3. "arousing interest in the more important curent problems of professional and political life,"
4. "actual practice in the improvement, from desirable legal and legislative standpoints, of bills and resolutions presented,"
5. "training in both the theory and practice of parliamentary law and procedure," and
6. "practical experience in affirmative and rebuttal debate."[14]

In 1912, the law school also acquired its own library. The House Consultors agreed to sell the University's one-third interest in the existing law library to the county commissioners, who arranged to house it in their building. The administration provided $9,000 to purchase necessary books, reports, and periodicals to create an independent 10,000-volume Creighton Law Library for students and faculty. That same year, Douglas County razed its old court house and sold Creighton the contents of Criminal Court Room #1, which included an ornate cherry-wood bench that came to adorn the moot-court room of the law college.[15]

The number of students at the Creighton College of Law continued to increase until World War I, when a new entrance requirement halted the growth temporarily. The school enrolled 98 students in 1910, and the figure rose to 177 in 1916, despite mandating graduation from a four-year high school for entrance after 1914. The increase included few women and only two earned their degree during the pre–World War I era. In 1911, Florence W. Driscoll, from Wichita, Kansas, became the first female to graduate. Subsequently, of note, Geneva Marsh became the first woman "to win a place on any of Creighton's teams," when she gained a place on the law school forensic team that debated against its counterpart from the University of South Dakota in 1913. She worked as a stenographer for a law firm and attended night classes, but did not complete the course. The second distaff pioneer, Bertha Schick, a graduate of Peru State Normal College, came to Omaha to teach and subsequently graduated from the night course in 1916. That year also witnessed the initiation of the one-year-of-college requirement for entrance to the law school and a sharp drop in enrollment to only 54 in the war year of 1918. The following year, with peace and time to adjust to the new entrance requirements, matriculation rebounded to 112, and the profession remained largely a male preserve.[16]

For the law school, the decade ended on a cheerless note, as Paul Martin resigned as dean, effective December 10, 1919. He had also served as dean of the fledgling summer school and as the editor of an alumni magazine. A distressed Jesuit chronicler mused, "He certainly was an able and hard-working man, a staunch Catholic, and much devoted to the interests of Creighton University. What may the real cause be?" Subsequently Martin disclosed that, in part, a salary dispute precipitated the move. He had a verbal agreement with then-president Fr. McMenamy that increased his salary "about $60 each year," but when the Reverend John F. McCormick, S.J., became president on July 2, 1919, he "brusquely swept the agreement aside." More important, however, Martin felt McCormick lacked administrative skills and failed to support his efforts with the summer school. Frustrated, but with "no animosity toward the university," Martin "accosted Fr. McCormick as he walked in the garden" in October and informed him he would leave at the end of the semester.[17]

In comparison, the medical school suffered through a distinct set of tribulations. Following the death of John A. Creighton, the school eliminated its benefactor's name from its official designation, although the old name remained on the building and continued to appear in print frequently for many years thereafter. In 1908, it became the Creighton University Department of Medicine and Surgery, but the following year it changed to the Creighton University College of Medicine. In 1909, the administration paid $12,000 for a lot adjacent to the medical school, north on 14th Street, and erected a new building. The facility included four stories of laboratories and lecture rooms; the first floor housed the free clinic, while the basement included a gym and locker rooms. On another positive note, in 1913, M. J. Scott, M.D., donated $5,000 for a medical library, which the administration named in his honor. The University deemed the gift "significant not only because it emphasizes the success attained by a Creighton man, but it marks the beginning of what may reasonably be expected to ripen into a fixed policy of alumni aid for various colleges of the university."[18]

Despite the new laboratory facility, accreditation problems plagued the College of Medicine. In 1909, the Carnegie Foundation for the Advancement of Teaching commissioned Abraham Flexner to study medical education in the United States and Canada. In April, he visited Creighton, en route to evaluating 155 medical schools. He gave the institution a passing mark and found the labs adequate, but the faculty-student ratio (only one full-time teacher), the small library and museum, and the limited hospital associations failed to impress him. The low entrance requirements troubled him most, especially the common practice of admitting students deficient in a subject(s), sending that person to Creighton College for remedial work, and his return to the medical school with a certificate "presumably of questionable merit." The school responded by adding three new hospital affiliations—City Emergency Hospital for Infectious Disease in 1916, and St. Catherine's and the Salvation Army Rescue Home in 1917. Moreover, in 1914 it mandated high-school graduation plus one year of college credit in biology, chemistry, physics, and French or German as its entrance requirements. In 1918, it increased the demand to two years of college credit.[19]

The University continued to strive to improve the ratings for the College of Medicine. The American Medical Association Council on Medical Education began inspecting and rating programs. A 1913 evaluation produced a low rating and a second visit in 1915 resulted in a "B"—"acceptable, with certain improvements needed." Finally, by 1918, the school completed the necessary reforms and renovations, which resulted in an "A"—"acceptable." However, as with the other professional schools, the more stringent entrance requirements resulted in a steep drop in enrollment (a goal of the reformers concerned with the number and quality of physicians graduated). In 1916, the College of Medicine lost its position as the largest professional school of Creighton University, as enrollment fell from a high of 194 in 1912 to 128. It bottomed out at 84 students in 1917, and then began a steady ascent, finishing the decade with 102.[20]

The relationship between the professional schools, their relationship with Creighton College, and the relationship of Creighton University with its alumni and the Omaha community promoted a desire for unity and fostered a booster campaign. The University had considered establishing a magazine as early as 1906, but the venture failed because the Reverend Provincial Henry Moeller, S.J., could not supply an editor. Three years later, however, Paul Martin, dean of the law school, accepted the added responsibility and volume I, number 1 of the *Chronicle* appeared. Published monthly, October through May, the magazine contained advertisements, University news, and articles written by professors; it sold for 20 cents per copy or $1.25 for an annual subscription. Within two years, it added an editorial page and a student segment, and it became free to all students of all five schools. Martin suggested "that the various numbers be carefully preserved and bound together in lieu of a university year-book." In his forward of the inaugural issue, he emphasized the unity theme:

> The Chronicle seems to its founders well fitted to fill a real need, for, with the multiplication and ever-widening scope of the University's activities, and the scattering of its graduates, the time has been deemed particularly appropriate for the foundation of a monthly magazine which would catch up the tangled strands of University life, weaving them into a fabric depicting the story of student life at Creighton, and perpetuating, at least in a measure, the added charm imparted to college days, whether by pen or spoken word, of faculty, invited guests, alumni or students.[21]

Subsequently, in one of his first editorials, Martin addressed individuals who criticized the scattered nature of the University, with Creighton College on a hilltop on California Street and the professional schools in various locations in the central business district. The commentators "suggested that a deeper impression would be made upon the city, and 'college spirit' more easily fostered if all the Colleges were grouped on the same campus." Martin defended the existing situation, arguing that a contiguous campus "would detract decidedly from the effectiveness of the training given in the professional colleges" because it would interfere with the operation of the medical and dental clinics, and would make it more difficult for "successful practitioners" to participate as faculty. By the time he wrote the justification, the administration had responded to the unity issue by organizing the first combined professional school commencement. The April 30, 1910, ceremony at the Brandeis Theater included the schools of law, medicine, and dentistry. Pharmacy joined the ceremony in 1914, and then, on April 29, 1915, the first all-University Commencement occurred at the same venue. However, Creighton College students received blank diplomas, returned to classes, took final exams and received actual diplomas at a separate Commencement held on June 16.[22]

The critics of the scattered campus won a quick victory. By 1912, Martin editorialized (obviously on behalf of the Administration) that the five years before the death of John A. Creighton had witnessed tremendous expansion and that the next five years would realize consolidation. The administrators recognized the "danger that the university would develop into a group of disconnected colleges without a semblance of university organization." Martin pointed to unity devices such as the *Chronicle*, the combined commencement, and the reorganized Founders' Day Banquet, which included alumni and faculty from all departments. The coup de grace came in 1919, when the administration announced the sale of the Edward Creighton Institute to the Equitable Trust Company for $250,000 (Dowling had paid $15,000 for the lot and $70,000 to build the structure, which housed the law and dental departments). Creighton University had two years to vacate and made plans to locate the schools adjacent to Creighton College.[23]

The drive for unity overlapped and interacted with the booster campaign. In

December 1911, Martin titled a *Chronicle* editorial, "Dollars and Cents," in which he complained, "Perhaps Omaha has not reflected upon Creighton University's importance financially." He pointed out the tens of thousands of dollars expended annually by Creighton students, alumni, and the University itself. Moreover, Creighton contributed to Omaha's prestige (it could advertise itself as a university city) and supplied it with many of its professionals. Martin concluded, "It must be evident, therefore, that Omaha has every reason to take an interest in Creighton University." The private Catholic institution now strove to eliminate its parochial and minority status in the Protestant-majority city of Omaha. The *Omaha World-Herald* accepted the logic and within the year published a laudatory full-page article filled with pictures of the buildings of the various schools (headline: CREIGHTON UNIVERSITY THIRTY-FOUR YEARS OLD. ONE OF OMAHA'S BEST ASSETS. STUDENTS SPEND HALF-MILLION IN CITY YEARLY).[24]

The campaign quickly expanded to include students and alumni who should become boosters because of their "free education." To provide examples of booster activity, the *Chronicle* added a new feature titled, "The Educational World," which contained brief stories in reference to events at other universities. Invariably, the reports pertained to prestigious eastern schools—pronouncements from their presidents, references to their sizeable endowments, and announcements of major contributions. The public relations effort entered a new dimension on June 1, 1912, with the publication of the *Creighton Courier,* a twice-monthly publication "sent gratuitous to a select list of nearly sixteen thousand names." A *Chronicle* editorial explained, "Some wise man has said that 'Nothing succeeds like success.' This should be modified by adding, 'if properly advertised.'" Thus, "after exhaustive investigation and careful deliberation," the University embarked "upon a policy of publicity designed to make the institution and its facilities better known." The *Creighton Courier* began as a summer supplement to the *Creighton Chronicle,* but soon became a year-round publication.[25]

Both magazines undertook a campaign to organize the alumni and their giving. A *Chronicle* editorial in May, 1912, asked each alumnus to donate $10 annually, which would supplement University revenue by $20,000. The administration provided a wish list the money could satisfy, including "a suitable gymnasium, a commodious stadium, additional dormitories for both undergraduate and professional students, new educational buildings and equipment, endowment of professional chairs in the various colleges [and] the putting of athletics and all other student activities on a firm basis." The aspirations, with their emphasis on athletics, revealed the depth of the Americanization of the Jesuit institution by the second decade of the twentieth century, and some of the alumni accepted the mission. A group "proposed in the future to have each outgoing class organize before graduation, arrange for yearly contributions for a fund which in ten years [would] be presented to the university for the purpose to be designated by the donors." The plan for existing graduates included the creation of a trust to receive donations and make proper investments; C. J. Smyth, former associate dean of the College of Law, and Thomas J. McShane (Arts, 1899), of the Creighton family clan, "kindly consented to act as trustees."[26]

Neither format succeeded, but revenue problems pushed the administration to continue the effort. It needed to supplement the tuition in the professional schools that did not cover the actual costs of education, as well as to support the larger Jesuit community needed to staff the tuition-free high school and college. Funds generated from the endowment covered operating expenses, but could not satisfy the wish list. M. J. Scott, donor to the College of Medicine library, provided new impetus. In 1913, he called for the creation of an all-University alumni association that would incorporate, elect officers, and raise money; individual schools could continue to maintain separate groups "for closer companionship and special helps." The administration jumped on the bandwagon, developing an Alumni Directory, but had trouble locating individuals who attended before 1891, since they did not graduate from college. At the time, Creighton University had about 2,000 alumni (the eventual directory listed 1,409 individuals) and the organizers emphasized the funding of a gymnasium. On December 21, 1913, at a banquet of alumni from the five departments, which included the entire football team as guests, the assembled accepted the constitution and bylaws of the Creighton University Alumni Association. They also elected its officers—E. J. McVann ("arts," 1885) president, and a vice president from each school, M. F. Donegan (A.B., '95), A. P. Schnell (LL.B., 1906), M. J. Scott (M.D., 1903), G. M. Boehler (D.D.S., 1908), and C. B. Fricke (Pharm.D., 1903).[27]

The Alumni Association organized the first Homecoming for the week of Commencement, each school arranging events to entertain its specific alumni. For example, the medical and dental schools offered special clinics for their graduates. Festivities concluded with a "pan-alumni banquet" held in the Commercial Club dinning room on the eighteenth floor of the original Woodman of the World Building. The Alumni Association also spurred the concept of class gifts. In 1914, the high school graduates presented a flag and a fifty-foot-high pole placed near the Observatory (subsequently moved to the new Creighton Prep campus). Simultaneously, the exiting College students donated a three-tiered circular fountain, with gold fish, erected in front of the building's east entrance (removed to create a delivery area for the post-1930 Jesuit refectory). Two years later, the senior classes of the five schools joined together to establish the Creighton University Endowment Association; the "class of 1916" pledged $25,000, hoping that in twenty years the endowment would grow to $500,000. The generous donation came in the form of life insurance (a plan inspired by the alumni of the University of California); that is, with all graduates contributing, five students from each of the five colleges purchased $1,000 life insurance policies, fully paid in twenty years, at which time they would donate the money to the University. The classes of 1917 and 1918 followed suit, but World War I interrupted the program and postwar attempts to revive it fizzled.[28]

Extracurricular activities contributed mightily toward energizing the alumni and promoting unity, and also served as an effective public-relations promotional tool. The administration heralded the Glee Club, organized in 1909, for building spirit and cohesion, because it consisted of students from all schools and its public concerts attracted faculty and students from the entire University, as well as the public. Operated by an eight-member board of directors consisting of alumni from the various colleges, the Glee Club gave its first public performance at the Brandeis Theater in 1911. The Omaha concerts became an annual event and included guest professional artists of national renown; out-of-town concerts soon became part of the schedule.[29]

Music spurred other activities: The Creighton University Band continued to thrive (it projected seventy members in 1909) and John D. Creighton donated $425 toward the purchase of new instruments. The recently established instrumental music program began to pay dividends through the development of the Creighton University Orchestra, which held its first annual concert in April of 1914. Music also generated a mild controversy. Students of all the schools loved dancing and held regularly scheduled events; the creation of the Creighton University Alumni Association led to the establishment of the Mixer Club to host all-University dances. Father General Wernz, however, opposed dancing by undergraduates and requested that Fr. President Magevney discontinue "the annual senior hop . . . if not at once, at least in the near future." The previous year, about one hundred couples (obviously others than seniors participated) had attended the annual dance held at the Rome Hotel. The administration avoided a hullabaloo as World War I distracted all parties and rearranged priorities. Actually, Fr. General Wernz did not stand alone on this issue; some Progressive reformers of the era, alarmed by the rapid increase in unsupervised urban adolescents and the growth of dance halls, campaigned for the regulation or abolition of public dancing venues.[30]

Among other well-established extracurricular activities, debate continued to engage significant support. At the College, several intramural oratorical contests flourished; the winners of specific events received medals and qualified to represent the school at inter-collegiate contests. In 1911, William Jennings Bryan, Nebraska's most famous politician and anti-imperialist, created a new competition by offering a $75 prize for the best oration on "International Peace and Arbitration." Two anonymous women supporters from Massachusetts donated another $50 for second place. Creighton hosted the first event, open to all Nebraska colleges. The second year, ten schools participated; Bellevue College served as the host, but the debates occurred at the Creighton Auditorium. Moreover, with the unity drive, a reconstituted University forensic team, consisting of one medical and seven law students, participated in the annual debate against the University of South Dakota.[31]

Other established activities persisted; the memorial Masses for Edward, John, Mary Lucretia, and Sarah Emily Creighton remained scheduled events, and Founders' Day became a University holiday—memorial Mass and exercises in the morning, suspension of classes for the remainder of the day, and the all-University faculty banquet in the evening. The annual name-day holiday, in honor of the president of the University, became a Saturday-morning occasion at the Auditorium, consisting of performances by the glee club and orchestra, student speeches, and a "thank you" from the celebrant. In 1914, religious and leisure activities switched schedules—Saturdays became the recreation day and confessions and religious instruction moved to Thursdays. Attendance and motivation problems may have prompted the change; the year featured extended discussions by the Jesuits concerning a lack of piety among the students. Some critics suggested that moving the annual retreat to the beginning of the school year would establish a spiritual starting point. However, the annual three-day retreat for high-school and college students, arranged by class level and including four lectures each day, remained a spring event associated with the Easter obligation. One new institution did appear to promote piety, the "Jeanne D'Arc Club," which sought "to make known the lives of God's heroes and heroines—the Saints." Student members presented lectures "illustrated with stereopticon views"; the club survived for several years, but no records exist to reveal its membership or its impact on student piety.[32]

New activities joined the old. Father Mageveny's renovation of the College building included a dark room on the third floor, allowing the development of the Camera Club in 1909. In an act of unfortunate timing, a Creighton German Literary Society organized in October 1913; it encouraged advanced study among those who took the elective modern language course, but disbanded a year later with the onset of World War I. A student council appeared in 1915, but the first attempt at student government did not survive the wartime disruptions. A special treat of the prewar era came from a visit by presidential candidate Woodrow Wilson. On the morning of October 5, 1912, in the packed auditorium, he delivered a short, rambling campaign speech filled with platitudes (a month later, the nation elected him its chief executive).[33]

An unscheduled and unwelcome extracurricular activity followed the Easter tornado of March 23, 1913. The University suffered no damage as a funnel cloud traversed a northwesterly trajectory west of the campus; many faculty and students, however, lost their homes, relatives, and/or spouses. Duchesne Academy lay in the storm's path and was hit as the Sacred Heart nuns went to mass at 5:30 A.M., but none perished (the tornado did kill 174 people in Omaha). The Reverend Archibald Tallmadge, S.J., professor of French and Classics, led a team of Creighton student volunteers that helped clean the severely damaged building and salvage useable equipment. The *Chronicle* made special note of the efforts of two law students, Carl C. Katleman and African American Noah W. Ware, the latter "confining his attention to the colored sufferers and Mr. Katleman being busy with the Jewish people." Furthermore, upper-class medical, dental, and pharmacy students helped staff emergency-relief stations for several days after the disaster.[34]

Mayor James Dahlman proclaimed Saturday, April 5, general clean-up day; approximately 700 Creighton students volunteered to work from 7:00 A.M. to 2:00 P.M., in the area around 48th and Leavenworth streets. The Omaha & Council Bluffs Street Railway donated free transportation and the city provided lunch. The students organized into teams, with seniors and members of the football and baseball squads appointed captains. They piled debris into mounds so other crews could remove it to dump sites and they also salvaged items, including heirlooms, family papers, business records and "a considerable amount of money." In one ballyhooed event, "Fifty or sixty [students] got underneath a house that had been toppled over on its side. 'B-

4-73-14-16!' yelled 'Wild Bill' Brennan, quarterback on the varsity, and the house slowly rose until, with a little lurch, it settled back in its upright position on its foundation." Most of the damaged areas of the city did not resettle that quickly and even undamaged Creighton University suspended classes for several days because of commuting problems and the outpouring of student volunteer efforts in its severely damaged adjacent neighborhood.[35]

The positions of leadership doled out to the athletes in the tornado clean-up operation bespoke the elevated status that sports had achieved at Creighton University. Some of the Jesuits, however, struggled with the American educational model, which allotted increasing prominence to athletics. In 1909, the administration issued a revised and extended description of the Creighton University Athletic Association that, on the one hand, clearly promoted sports. The acknowledged purpose of the organization included the addition of indoor sports through the acquisition of "a modern gymnasium with all necessary appurtenances," as well as providing the athletes with the "opportunity to enjoy the pleasure of a home ground," by constructing a field consisting of a gridiron, a ball diamond, tennis courts, and handball alleys. Moreover, the policy statement accepted athletics as "a source of recreation and healthful exercise and help toward implanting in the character habits of gentlemanly self-repression, which cannot be disregarded in any system of education." On the other hand, to accomplish those goals, the administration remained "keenly alive to the fact that athletic sports will not be productive of good, when they become a separate and recognized department of the University, with a corps of managers, coaches and trainers, having the sole objective of winning in inter-collegiate contests at any cost, by clean methods or foul." Thus, "To keep an influence so deteriorating from exerting an effect upon our students, Athletics are under the immediate control of the faculty, which uniformly adheres to well-defined regulations in their management. A creditable standing in class is a requisite of eligibility to any university teams. Long schedules and trips which necessitate absence from class are discouraged." Those Jesuits trying to limit the influence of athletics received their due in the statement, but within five years, the declaration rang hollow.[36]

While they drafted the athletic-policy statement, the Trustees simultaneously strained the proclamation against the professionalization of college sport by authorizing the hiring of a salaried football coach ($800) for the 1909 season. However, they rejected a proposal to allow the alumni to finance and direct the intercollegiate teams; control would remain with a faculty director and a student manager, although the latter would no longer come from the ranks of the undergraduates. The "older" student manager became possible because the Trustees also decided in the name of unity (but also to have the ability to field competitive teams) that students from all the departments could participate on all-University teams. The law school provided student managers and a number of players in several sports during the pre–World War I era. The medical school contributed the first minority athletes at Creighton—African Americans R. S. Taylor in football and baseball in 1911 and 1912 and a misidentified "C." Wilson in baseball in 1915. As noted earlier, at the turn of the century, administrators had struggled with the idea of admitting a student of Japanese ancestry. In 1906, however, they admitted John A. "Jap" Tamisea to Creighton College, and in 1911 (his fifth year into the seven-year program), he became a star running back on the football team (at the time, ethnic nicknames were common and did not necessarily indicate racism; e.g., two other players of the era were "Swede" and "Dutch").[37]

The University demonstrated its commitment to sports with the construction of a new athletic field. As originally designed, it would have cost $25,000, which included a perimeter fence and a 5,000-seat grandstand (the site would have necessitated sinking ninety concrete pillars into the loose soil that had been dumped into the creek bed below the terraces west of the College Building). Father Provincial Meyer and his Consultors found the project too expensive and mandated cutting the cost in half by "reversing the position of the field," placing the grandstand on the east side, eliminating the need for the pillars. Thus, athletics did not receive a carte blanche. Subsequently, a 2,000-seat grandstand debuted for the first home football game of the season on October 12, 1912. The new structure served as a reserve-seat area, while the automobiles of spectators, parked abreast, lined the remainder of the fenceless rectangle. Mayor Dahlman "kicked the first ball," a la President William Howard Taft's inaugural "first pitch" to open the 1909 professional baseball season. The field generated some extra revenue, as the Omaha [Central] High School used it for track and baseball practice in the early afternoon, before the Creighton teams occupied the area.[38]

The University also raised funds through the booster effort and by initiating a student activity fee. The administration argued that Creighton athletics gave Omaha "the complexion of a varsity town" (the pre–World War I equivalent of the late twentieth century "major-league" city) and that the city had "to realize what a prize" it possessed. It asked the community to "hasten the day of a better appreciation of what Creighton means to Omaha and the West" by playing "Santa Clause" in helping to provide "suitable facilities for athletics." No notice of sizeable donations came forth. Thus, the Trustees decided that the students had to undertake some of the burden. First, in 1910, they voted to apply the profit from the bookstore to the "general athletic fund." Simultaneously, they raised the rent on dorm rooms by $1, using the extra revenue for the same purpose. Then, in 1912, they instituted a student activity fee "to ensure the maximum of pleasure to the student body at the least cost consistent with security." They did not illuminate the "security" issue, but claimed that many students could not afford the ticket costs for extracurricular activities. Therefore, the annual $5 fee included entrance to the college play, glee club concert, varsity debate, all athletic contests, and a subscription to the *Creighton Chronicle*. Within a month of its inception, the administration argued it worked well because attendance at football games went up (the only point mentioned, revealing the athletic priority). A year later, administrators adopted the term of economic reformer Henry George, referring to the fee as a "Single Tax" and asserting that, "No single act in the history of the institution has contributed so much to its solidarity or marked such a decided advance toward a proper varsity spirit."[39]

The creation of the all-University alumni organization in 1913 signaled another change of direction in athletic policy and a concerted fund drive to build a gymnasium. The new group pledged to raise $25,000 to build the structure; in turn, the administration created an athletic board, composed of Omaha-area businessmen alumni, which would "take the burden of handling athletics from the shoulders" of Faculty Director Fr. Albert Wise. The alteration eliminated another major principle (faculty control) of the Jesuits who attempted to manage athletics as an acceptable component of higher education. For the gymnasium, the administration first planned to enclose the existing Auditorium within the new facility and to add an upper floor that would serve as a dormitory. Father President McMenamy toured gyms in Chicago and discussed operations with their managers; he also received elaborate suggestions from the Alumni Association. He desired a modest $80,000 structure, since the renovations to the College Building from the 1911 fire exceeded insurance payments by $45,000. He also had to contend with the fact that the growth of high-school-aged students created a desire for a separate building for their instruction. Subsequently, bids for the gym-auditorium-dormitory ranged from $170,000 to $190,000. Father General Wernz balked at the cost and gave permission to erect a less expensive stand-alone gymnasium.[40]

The choice of a site "presented some puzzling difficulties." The administration abandoned the idea to build on the tennis-court segment of the athletic field and decided to place the structure on the northeast corner of the campus because the area served "no purpose" and would "never be suitable for any other building." Ultimately, the facility sat on a plateau (twenty-three feet above street level) carved out of the hill that descended steeply northward from the Observatory to Burt Street. The 94-foot frontage faced west and stretched 254 feet east toward 24th Street. Architect J. M. Nachtigall designed, and the Selden-Breck Construction Company erected, the $140,000 gymnasium, which opened on September 30, 1916. It contained all the amenities the alumni desired, although they had not raised their pledge by dedication day. The ground-floor lobby separated a varsity room for the exclusive use of team players (violating another principle of the 1909 policy statement by providing special benefits to a select student group—athletes) and a billiard room. The central segment of the first floor contained a six-lane bowling alley, general and team locker rooms, a storage room, a machinery room, a physical examination room, and a steam room. The entire eastern section of the first floor consisted of a swimming pool and shower and toilet facilities. The second level contained the varsity basketball court, running east to west (in the same space, three intramural basketball courts running north to south), flanked on the east by handball and squash courts and on the west by club rooms and the director's office. A third floor, on the west side of the building only, held three more handball courts; level with it, a banked, overhead running track encircled the basketball court.[41]

The new outdoor facilities and the gymnasium contributed significantly to expansion of athletics at Creighton. To the benefit of the entire student body, the variety of intramural contests increased and virtually all of them now took place on campus, rather than at city parks. In 1911, the first intramural track meet was held, with separate divisions for high-school and college students. An interclass baseball league played on the school diamond, the annual tennis tournament took place on home courts, and the juniors contested the seniors in an annual football game on the Creighton gridiron. The gymnasium brought the handball games indoors year-round, as well as introducing swim meets. The Friday-Saturday student bowling leagues abandoned the Farnam Bowl for the new on-campus alleys, and the outdoor fall basketball league (formed in 1911, with two groups of six teams, based on height) became an indoor winter sporting diversion.[42]

Obviously, the new facilities also promoted an expansion of varsity athletics. Creighton, however, struggled to maintain viable teams in non-revenue-producing sports (athletes on those teams reject the frequently used term "minor sports"). In 1911, in the first meet on the new courts, the Creighton tennis team volleyed against the University of Nebraska before a crowd of approximately two hundred, hardly enough spectators to defray the cost of a coach, uniforms, and travel expenses. Two years later, the varsity tennis team temporarily disbanded because only three players from the previous year's team returned to school (thereafter, students organized tennis as a club sport and arranged a short schedule).[43]

Baseball suffered under similar circumstances. Creighton did not field a team in 1910, while the new field was under construction. Instead, St. John's Hall organized a club that played in a city league. The following year, the University team played a twelve-game "inter-collegiate" schedule, which actually included games against Ft. Crook, Ft. Omaha, and a semi-pro Omaha nine. Subsequently, because it lacked high caliber battery mates and because the team did not generate sufficient revenue, the administration decided not to field a baseball team in 1913. It explained that the arts college had "no pitchers or catchers of varsity caliber" and that baseball was "not a paying proposition." It argued, "Even in small towns, where practically the entire population attends the college games, it does not pay. Consequently, the school authorities do not believe university baseball in a city the size of Omaha where a professional team is established, would prove remunerative." The new alumni-controlled athletic board begged to differ; it provided coaches and organized a schedule. However, the enthusiastic alumni businessmen immediately encountered the same bottom line and baseball ceased as a varsity sport for three years. Eventually, with the gymnasium providing an indoor practice venue and the University a paid coach, baseball resumed its varsity status in 1917.[44]

In comparison, basketball sputtered briefly, but then became an instant success following the completion of the gymnasium. James Naismith invented the game in 1891, and early in the twentieth century, Creighton listed adoption of the sport as a primary reason it needed a gym. The University fielded its first team in 1912, playing a four-game schedule against Tabor College, Dana College, the University of Omaha, and the Pirates, a city team. At the end of the undefeated season, the eight-man squad received sweaters and letters, recognition "as the first basketball team to represent the university." That same year, a team of College seniors won the Omaha city championship, beating the YMCA team. Following the auspicious beginning, varsity basketball faltered, possibly because of a lack of a home court. In 1915, a team from the law school finished second in the Omaha Commercial League, with an overall record of 15-5, although it split its games with the Omaha [Central] High School, 15-12 and 3-6. Obviously, the original rules did not encourage a fast pace of play, and, of course, remembering the law school entrance requirements, some members of the team may have been of high-school age.[45]

The gymnasium brought rapid growth in the popularity of varsity basketball and the abandonment of another principle of the 1909 athletic policy statement. The 1916–17 team played twenty-three games, finishing the regular season 18–2, and winning both the Nebraska Collegiate Conference and the Western Catholic Conference championships. However, it lost the Omaha city tournament to "the fast professional team representing the Brandeis Store in a three game series that brought overflow crowds to the spacious gymnasium." Creighton won the first game 22-14, but then lost 20-22 and 23-25. Then, in December, the second-year schedule included "a road trip" through Iowa, Missouri, Arkansas, and Kansas to play small-college teams; given the travel conditions of the era (most likely the team went from town to town via the railroad) and the fact that the short Christmas recess began on Friday, December 21, 1917, and ended on Wednesday, January 2, 1918 (with the holidays in between), classes likely had to give way in favor of the basketball junket.[46]

American style football, of course, evolved during the era and quickly became the king of collegiate sports. It happened at Creighton, but not without a struggle. In 1909, Fr. General Wernz replied to a letter from Fr. Provincial Meyer, asking the latter to "write to me candidly whether you think that 'Rugby Football' should be prohibited in our colleges. I am speaking, however, about all of America, not only about the Missouri Province." Obviously, those trying to control sports in American Jesuit universities had filtered their concerns through channels to the highest authorities. The issue remained under discussion "extensively" in "all the provinces of the United States" for several years. Then, in 1914, based on "a certain unanimity of thought," Fr. General Wernz issued a three-point statement:

1. The game itself, in view of the violent force with which it is often played, must be moderated and within reasonable limits must be contained and must not be played with those external colleges that employ a violent format.
2. The frequency of play with external colleges must be moderated.
3. Refrain also with appropriate precautions from allowing the game to be played with other colleges when this necessitates absence from the college overnight.[47]

In 1911, during the debate, the then Creighton University Faculty Director of Athletics, the Reverend Terence H. Devlin, S.J., wrote an article titled "The Status of Athletics in a College Course." He argued that football benefited only a select group of students and that its status needed diminishing. Before football mania buried his ideas, he may have tried to institute "Association Football," that is, European-style soccer. The University fielded a team only in 1913, and its only reported game came against the Omaha [Central] High School on the home field (no score given).[48]

Seemingly, the professional coaches and the athletic board created in 1913 swept the critics of rugby-football from the field. Creighton's team stood 3-1 in October 1909, but no University scribe bothered to report the scores of the remaining four games. Harry Miller, star running back from Notre Dame, whom legendary coach Walter Camp described as "brilliant," became the football coach of record following his 1910 playing season. In February 1912, the administration agreed to extend his contract to become Creighton's first year-round coach, handling tennis, basketball, and football; in return, he received a $1,000 salary and waiver of his tuition to the Creighton law school. Coach Miller's slogan, "Clean football, win or lose," dovetailed with the university motto, "Success fairly won." Miles Greenleaf, a sports editor for the *Omaha World-Herald,* argued that Creighton played "the cleanest, wholesomest, and most honorable football ever seen in the city."[49]

In conjunction with the first meeting that led to the creation of the Creighton University Alumni Association, the participants organized a parade before the football game with St. Louis University, a line of fifty autos driving from the downtown law school to the field. On campus, seven hundred students marched across the gridiron before the game and during half time, they "stepped off" the "time-honored snake dance," as well as parading Mayor Dahlman and his political opponent in the upcoming election, John Moore, around the field. The largest crowd in Creighton history watched the home team lose 3-28, although it became the first team to score any points against Saint Louis that year. Purportedly, the competition and the level of play witnessed "marked progress," and in 1913, the University began talk of joining the Missouri Valley Conference (not actually attained until 1928). In order to maintain the momentum, in 1914, because "the work [was] too heavy for any one coach," the athletic board hired Chester Dudley, former fullback at Dartmouth and an assistant at the University of Nebraska the previous year, as associate football coach.[50]

In 1915, Thomas Mills, who had coached at the Omaha [Central] High School for the three years, became Creighton's new football coach, with the promise of full-time status and the added responsibility of coaching basketball once the gymnasium opened. By the time he arrived, an annual Thanksgiving Day football game on the Creighton gridiron had become tradition and cheerleaders had made their appearance with the parades. In 1916, a new record crowd of about eight thousand fans watched the Blue and White (still no mascot) defeat the University of South Dakota 20-13. The next year the University organized a new Creighton Athletic Association "to boost the games . . . and the spirit of the student body." The Association began to organize pep rallies that fall, the final one of the season including speeches by the University president, various deans, members of the athletic board, Coach Mills, players, and alumni. Spectator sports had become a major component in the American educational model. Fans had muffled the critics. At Creighton, Jesuit supporters, spurred on by a vocal, local alumni group, promoted the University's integration of the entire American athletic package.[51]

During the era, Creighton College also integrated the organization and the curriculum of the American educational model. In 1909, the Provincial Committee on Studies established the principle of an eight-year program—four years of high school and four years of college. The committee issued a new course of study in 1911 and the set-aside high school became the rule in the province in 1912. Three years later, with a revised high-school curriculum, "the number, character and distribution of studies in the present-day schedules of Midwestern Jesuit high schools became the same general type as those obtaining in the public high schools." The 1915 program established four distinct courses of study for Jesuit high schools in the Missouri Province—the classical and three that avoided many of the classes prescribed by the *Ratio Studiorum*, the English, the commercial, and the scientific. The Reverend Provincial Alexander Burrowes, S.J., and the committee members understood that state regulation and the secular schools set the standards in the United States, and that for Jesuit schools isolation equaled "suicide." A majority of Catholics attended public schools and, in Creighton's case, curriculum not tuition drove some of them there. Moreover, a low percentage of students completed the seven-year program and, when they left, they left empty handed. By World War I, American reformers defined secondary education "not as a repository of liberal values, but as a school in citizenship, job skills, and homemaking." Thus, for most students, a high-school degree became an end product, while a minority viewed it as preparation for college.[52]

Therefore, in 1914, Trustees voted to construct a $125,000 stand-alone high school. Two years later, the administration purchased two pieces of property west of the auditorium for the building. However, World War I intervened and exacerbated the fear of depleting cash reserves; subsequent concerns delayed the construction for four decades. In 1916, however, Creighton University High School, a separate administrative entity but still housed in the north wing of College Building, began to hold separate commencements and issue diplomas, as well as to maintain its own faculty, administrators, coaches, and athletic teams (football began in 1911 and baseball in 1913).[53]

For many years, as the first boy's Catholic high school in the Omaha Diocese, Creighton University High School avoided competition with parish or diocesan high schools, because few of notable size came into existence before the 1950s. The Creighton Jesuits, however, in 1912 established a parish high school for girls at St. John's School, operated by the Sisters of Mercy. Two spaces in the basement of St. John's Church served as extra classrooms for the high school. The Catholic Church, the Jesuits in particular, remained adamant against coeducation above the primary grades. Their arguments claimed that coeducation produced "feminized" men and "hoydenish" women, and that pubescent children would lose their scholarly focus. The public schools fostered coeducation as a cost-saving device. In comparison, one Jesuit claimed, "From every point of view it is undesirable to have the problems of love and marriage presented for decision to a young girl during the four years when she ought to devote her energies to profiting by the only systematic intellectual training she is likely to receive during her life."[54]

The indirect involvement with educating women through owning a parish grade school and girl's high school (the House Consultors frequently discussed the policy and finances of the schools) became more direct with the creation of the Creighton Summer School in 1913. Marquette University had opened the first such program in 1909, which brought women to campus after the men left for vacation. Teacher training for nuns motivated both schools. The mass migration of Catholics from southern and eastern Europe spurred the development of parish school systems, and the various women's orders could not keep up with the demand for teachers and/or meet increasingly stringent state teacher-certification standards. In 1910, the Sisters of Mercy convinced Fr. President McMenemy to help alleviate the situation in the Omaha area. He appointed law dean Paul Martin to study the situation. Martin acquired catalogues of normal colleges, consulted state superintendents of education, and reported in favor of the venture (Martin had two sisters who became Sisters of Mercy). The administration advertised the program thusly,

> The purpose is to afford teachers and advanced students a chance to perfect themselves, and to give undergraduates an opportunity to remove entrance conditions. In addition to the regular work of the school there will be a series of popular lectures given by persons of note, and ample provision will be made for the entertainment of the students. The entire plant of the university will be available for the school and the regular staff will be supplemented by educators of note from other institutions.[55]

The six-week session, June 23 through August 2, 1913, which suffered through several days of temperatures that reached 100 degrees, cost $15. Fifty-minute classes ran between 8:00 and noon, Monday through Saturday and students could take a maximum of three classes, which translated to eighteen hours per week. The State Superintendent of Education agreed to count the six-week, six-periods-a-week course the equivalent of eight weeks with five meetings per week; thus, two Creighton summer sessions would equal one traditional college semester. Students did not finish their classes during the summer session; they continued to study at home for the remainder of the year and took exams upon their return the succeeding summer. While the rector-president supported the endeavor, Martin found that all the Creighton Jesuits had other plans for the summer. He had to hire two secular women and thirteen men, as well as eight Jesuits from other houses. The program became an instant success, attracting ninety-nine nuns from thirteen different orders and twenty-two lay people the first year. Besides the lectures, their afternoons included sixteen "educational moving picture exhibitions."[56]

Teachers accounted for eighty-nine of the first-year attendees and they immediately secured a commitment for degree work. They printed a resolution thanking Creighton University, which "has opened the doors of its College of Arts to women, including religious, and will hereafter confer upon them the degrees equal to those heretofore granted exclusively to men." In 1916, eighteen nuns from Nebraska, Kansas, Texas, Colorado, Oklahoma, Wyoming, Indiana, and Massachusetts received A.B. degrees, while two obtained a B.S., and another four the Bachelors in Literature degree. By 1919, the degree-granting summer school enrolled 626 students, still mostly nuns, and granted 10 of them A.M. degrees. Despite the program's success, the new president, Fr. McCormick, gave it little support. When Martin asked him to address the opening gathering in 1919, he "growled: Well I don't see why we should try to educate all the nuns in the United States." At that point, Martin decided to resign from the University.[57]

The popularity of the summer sessions spawned the creation of extension classes, which brought women to campus during the regular school year. Each class met for one hour on Tuesday evening and a second hour on Saturday morning. They began on October 8, 1919, and the first session drew sixty-six nuns, twenty-seven laywomen (mostly teachers), and four men. All but four of those registered resided in the Omaha-Council Bluffs area. They had their choice of four classes taught by Creighton Jesuits: The Principles of Literary Criticism Applied to Fiction, General Physics, Constitutional History of the United States, and Practical Psychology of the Will. Thus, despite the known objections of the Very Reverend General Wlodimir Ledochowski, S.J., (1915–42) to coeducation, the Creighton House responded to the demands of Catholic education in the United States, and through the summer school and the extension classes obliquely integrated another feature of the American educational model.[58]

Competition from the secular schools and the need for accreditation also continued to shape the curriculum of Creighton College. In 1909, the University abandoned the historic practice of publishing a Catalogue for the June Commencement, which recapped the events of the academic year. Each school of the University began to publish an Announcement, which explained the requirements and schedule for the ensuing year. The Announcement listed the degrees granted, awards won (a one-page list because it only included gold medals and not all the premiums for individual courses), and a copy of the Commencement program for the previous year. Annually, the Administration bound them into a volume labeled *The Creighton University Bulletin*. In response to the Missouri Province's decision to create the stand-alone high school, Creighton College renamed itself "The Creighton College of Arts and Sciences" (CCAS), and its first Announcement stated that it was composed of "three distinct departments, viz.: The Graduate and Undergraduate Schools, The School of Pedagogy, and Natural Sciences."[59]

The School of Pedagogy, which began in 1906, consisted of a set of classes designed to allow a student to obtain a teacher's certificate along with the CCAS diploma (the Jesuits also used the designations College of Liberal Arts, as well as arts college, interchangeably). In 1909, all eleven graduates followed that course of study; until World War I, the vast majority of undergraduates followed suit. The program, which acquired the peculiar name "First Grade City State Teacher's Certificate," involved the CCAS in the secular accreditation process. Like the professional schools previously, an undergraduate program now came within the purview of a secular authority. On March 18, 1910, the deputy state superintendent of schools and the president of the board of examiners for state certificates, "paid an official visit of inspection . . . [and] they expressed themselves highly pleased with the standard of efficiency set in the High School and College."[60]

In comparison, without citing any particular college, Fr. Provincial Meyer complained about lax standards in the core of the *Ratio Studiorum*. In 1911, he rued, "There is no denying the fact that with few exceptions our students, after five or six years of study of Latin, know very little Latin." The American student's disdain for "dead, impractical" languages continued to affect the Jesuit educational model and Fr. Meyer believed that members of the faculty exacerbated the problem. He chastised "[u]nlimited tolerance . . . of student's neglect of work, poorly supervised examinations, carelessly marked papers, unmerited promotions, indefinite standards . . . [and] want of ready obedience and submission on the part of faculty to the Prefect of Studies." Despite his concern about the deteriorating quality of the preeminent classes in the course of study, enrollment in the arts college began to rise sharply during the second decade of the twentieth century. Partly in response to the changing curriculum, the number of undergraduates rose from 79 in 1910, to 106 in 1913 (the first year to top the century mark), to 244 in 1919. The last figure finally surpassed the numbers posted by the various professional schools, establishing the CCAS as the largest college, but it remained 131 students fewer than the high school (total enrollment for the University exceeded the then magical number of 1,000 in 1912). During the era, the University also attracted students from a dozen foreign countries, and in the CCAS, out-of-town students outnumbered Omaha students 3 to 1; thus, the demographics continued to erode the historic concept of the day school).[61]

In 1911, as part of the curricular enticement, the administration undertook a feasibility study concerning the initiation of an engineering program. It came in conjunction with the opening of a physics lab for the high school. The program did not come to fruition; instead, two years later, the CCAS introduced an enhanced science course, which entailed "a deeper study of physics, a more advanced and mathematical treatment of theorems, and a use of a more expensive and elaborate apparatus" in laboratory work. In the meantime, with the introduction of the autonomous high school, the Missouri Province introduced the new four-year college course of study. It included new degree programs and the possibility of eight hours of electives in each of the junior and senior years.[62]

With the dean's approval, upper-classmen could register for an elective class in mathematics, one of the sciences or languages, public speaking, or mechanical drawing, among others not listed in the Announcement. The Bachelor of Arts degree (A.B., the standard classical course) required two half-hour classes in religion per week during all four years. As freshmen, students also took three forty-five-minute classes of English and history or mathematics, five fifty-minute classes of Greek and physics, and five one-hour classes of Latin. Sophomore year, chemistry replaced physics, which in turn was replaced by semester-long courses in logic, general metaphysics, cosmology, and psychology in the junior year, and theodicy, English, and ethics senior year. The new Bachelor of Science (B.S.), Bachelor of Literature (Litt.B.), and Bachelor of Philosophy (Ph.B.) degrees all retained the four-year religion requirement, but modern languages replaced Greek and Latin. The new degree programs also retained most of the other prerequisites of the A.B., but allowed a student to emphasize the study of science, literature, or philosophy, respectively. Obviously, with the elimination of Greek and Latin, the new degrees eviscerated the *Ratio Studiorum* by eliminating the study of the classical languages and texts that had served as the bedrock of traditional education since the Middle Ages and of Jesuit education since the Renaissance.[63]

The curriculum changes continued at a rapid pace. In 1915, the Creighton University Bulletin eliminated the thirteen-point defense of the *Ratio Studiorum*, which had first appeared in response to the Eliot controversy in 1899. It did so because the Jesuit model of education had evolved into an American hybrid. Father Provincial Burrowes wrote, "The day is not far distant when our College diplomas and High School certificates will be of little value to the owners unless our institutions have the standing recognized by the State. As we cannot set the standard, we shall have to follow." In 1915, his Committee on Studies rearranged the "overcrowded curriculum"; that is, a Jesuit college in the Missouri Province included twenty-six hours of study per week during the freshman year, while Yale College only demanded fifteen. This had resulted from the fact that the colleges retained the classical course and added "a variety of other subjects that have forced their way into our schools owing partly to the advance of modern education, partly to the demands of local circumstances." The committee argued that it had integrated the curriculum of the autonomous high school and the time had come to do the same for the college. Realistically, it concluded,

> A second reason for rearranging the schedule was felt to be the fact that state governments are ever more and more taking in hand the work of regulating and supervising educational matters. The sooner we forestall this by bringing our schools up to required standards and putting our work into such shape as is intelligible to those outside of the Society [of Jesus], the easier will it be for our schools to receive due recognition. Even now standard entrance-requirements exist for Law and Medicine; and our students may reasonably expect us to equip them for these requirements. Again, the unavoidable interchange of students between our colleges and high schools and the state high schools, make it expedient to have a common ground of uniformity, as far as possible.[64]

The new course of study reduced the schedule to an eighteen- to twenty-hour course load per year, mandated a maximum of four different classes per day and allowed electives as early as the sophomore year. It also made the branch system obligatory, necessitating discipline-specific professors to teach specific subjects. For example, it required a minimum of one year's study of history and encouraged Jesuits to pursue the discipline in order to write history from a Catholic perspective (obviously, at that time, virtually all history written in English displayed a Protestant interpretation of events). Moreover, the new program included a pre-medical course, which rearranged the freshman schedule to meet the new one-year of college credits demanded for medical school enrollment in the United States. It allowed the student to study chemistry, physics, and biology in one year and move on to medical school without receiving an undergraduate degree. In 1915, almost one-half of the freshmen (forty-two of ninety), enrolled in the pre-medical course, extending the health science dominance of the University directly to the CCAS. Actually, the program became the engine that drove the rapid increase in undergraduate enrollment during the second decade of the twentieth century (although those students remained in the arts college for only one year). The CCAS also offered the "six year combined medical course"; students studied a two-year undergraduate curriculum, attended Creighton University Medical School for four years, and upon graduation, received B.S. and M.D. degrees.[65]

Because the 1915 Course of Studies mandated the branch system for all classes, it also inaugurated a new examination procedure, whereby each professor, for the first time, tested the students in his class. Course descriptions and course numbers began to appear in the Bulletin. Finally, the new program also redefined graduate education. The Master of Arts degree entailed study in one or two departments and "ordinarily" embraced "one major and two minor subjects." Possible areas of "concentrated work" included philosophy, history, economics, sociology, foreign languages, English, education, mathematics, physics, chemistry, and biology. The candidate had to pass examinations in all subjects studied, as well as to present a thesis in the major subject. The new Master of Science degree had the same requirements, except that the major subject had to be science. Since, at that time, graduate study remained a function of the CCAS, students did not pay tuition and obtained their degree for a $10 fee. Significantly, the inclusion of sociology in the curriculum put Creighton in a select realm of Catholic education, which had shunned the discipline because of its reliance on positivist philosophy and evolutionary theory. William Graham Sumner had taught the first course in the United States using that disciplinary designation at Yale in 1873; the Catholic University of America became the only institution of the faith to introduce the subject before 1900.[66]

The new course of study allowed the arts college to attain accreditation. Private foundations and professional associations had joined state governments in establishing educational standards. Foundation requirements to receive grants served as bludgeons or enticements, depending upon the eye of the beholder. The Carnegie Foundation for the Advancement of Teaching, for example, demanded that department chairs hold a Ph.D. in the appropriate field. In the early-twentieth century, however, Jesuits eschewed the degree as unnecessary or as too difficult to earn. Regardless of the requirement, Carnegie specifically barred gifts from his foundation to Catholic universities. In 1911, the Catholic Education Association condemned the Carnegie Foundation for aiming to "dechristianize American education." Father Timothy Brosnahan, S.J., specifically charged that its director, Henry S. Pritchett, sought to eliminate religious schools in the United States. Father Brosnahan feared the foundation would "exercise monopolistic control" of education, and in doing so, it narrowly defined "non-sectarian" only to include "certain prominent universities like Princeton, Yale and Harvard," while excluding all Catholic colleges. He called the organization "The Carnegie Foundation for the Secularization of Education," and the Creighton University Bulletin of the era inserted a statement explaining the importance of religion in education.[67]

Similarly, in 1913, the Association of American Universities accredited 119 schools, only two of which were Catholic—Fordham (Jesuit) and the Catholic University. That same year, the North Central Association (NCA), a regional group formed five years earlier to promote standardization, published its first directory and included only one Catholic college, Notre Dame. In response, in 1915, the Catholic Educational Association (CEA) printed criteria for its members modeled on the NCA guidelines. At first, Jesuits ignored both the NCA and the CEA; they viewed standardization as a threat to their "historic mission, governances structure, *Ratio Studiorum*, and faculty preparation of the Society's educational apostolate." Moreover, the Constitutions of the Society of Jesus forbad regulation from outside the Order. However, in 1916, Creighton administrators announced that the CCAS had become a member of the NCA and that friends of the University were "pleased" to receive "the stamp of approval." Membership, among other things, meant that the arts college possessed necessary admission standards, graduation requirements, library and laboratory facilities, and a sufficiently degreed faculty (majority held the M.A.) who taught a maximum of eighteen hours per week. Moreover, it had to maintain an endowment not less than $200,000 and a minimum of "eight distinct departments in liberal arts, each with at least one professor giving full time to the college work in that department."[68]

Membership in the NCA pushed the CCAS to the forefront of curricular change in the Missouri Province. The demands of the professional schools also prompted continued innovation. In 1917, for example, the arts college created the Pre-Legal Courses. The new one-year-of-college entrance requirement for admission to American law schools precipitated the creation of one and two-year courses of studies tailored to prepare students to enter the study of law absent an undergraduate degree. After the first year of the new pre-professional plans, the CCAS did not identify students by program; thus, the number of non-degree pre-med and pre-law students remains indeterminate. In 1918, however, 92 freshmen enrolled in the College (over half its total of 160), while it graduated a mere 4 students that year. Obviously, the non-degree pre-professional courses generated the rapid increase in enrollment during the pre–World War I decade. The arts college also offered two other pre-law degree programs—a three-year course in which the student completed all undergraduate course requirements, but satisfied all electives with law classes to obtain the undergraduate diploma with the LL.B., and an indistinct four-year program that simply mirrored a standard degree from the CCAS. Few, if any students availed themselves of the latter options.[69]

Other changes came at the behest of meeting NCA standards. As early as the 1880s, David Starr Jordan, president of Indiana University, promoted the idea of a "major," whereby a student could gain some advanced knowledge in an area of choice, instead of indiscriminately careening all over the elective system. The NCA adopted the idea and the CCAS instituted it in 1918. The College actually began to require students to complete a major and two minors—a major consisted of six upper-division courses in one department, and four upper-division courses in a department equaled a minor. That same year, it also abandoned the premium system and began "grading" diplomas as "rite, cum laude, magna cum laude, summa cum laude." Harvard ("undemocratically," according to critics) had initiated the system in 1889 in order to encourage students to seek academic excellence. Rite indicated a standard diploma, while the cum laude designations rewarded increasingly superior cumulative grade-point averages.[70]

Those changes anticipated the imprimatur of the Provincial, but Creighton Jesuits played a key role in their acceptance. Father Burrowes understood the necessity of accreditation and had his various committees on studies working on the problems of stagnant (or shrinking) enrollments and graduations at Jesuit colleges. In 1919 a committee, chaired by former Creighton student Fr. John B. Furay, S.J., and which included Fr. John F. McCormick, the new president of Creighton University, devised the "American Plan," which met NCA guidelines. As the plan unfolded, Fr. Burrowes became acting president of Creighton University for three months (replaced by Fr. McCormick) and Creighton's Fr. President McMenamy moved to St. Louis to become the Provincial who approved the plan. The new course of study eliminated 58 required course hours, including the Greek requirement for the A.B. degree. It retained a total of 90 required hours, but lowered the Latin requirement from 22 to 16, and philosophy from 20 to 10, establishing the total hours for graduation at 128. It mandated the major-minor system, eliminated the Litt.B. degree, sanctioned a letter-percentage grading scheme, changed the titles of administrators (prefect of studies became dean, although Fr. McMenamy had served as the first "dean" of CCAS from 1911 to 1914), and abolished class medals and premiums because "the yearly average of excellence would have to be computed from results in subjects so widely different." The new program asked the Province's colleges to assign students advisors and it established an attendance policy—the maximum number of unexcused absences "without a deduction of grade" equaled the number of class meetings per week and students "not present at recitations during the twenty-four hours preceding or following Christmas or summer recess" received three absent marks. Finally, the program prescribed monthly 2,000-word papers in philosophy and two 1,800-word papers per semester in history and sociology, one of which "should give unmistakable signs of original research, preferably in some local Catholic subject." The *Ratio Studiorum* in terms of content and teaching method ceased to exist; Creighton College became an assimilated Jesuit-American institution (the professional schools had all begun according to the American model, with an overlay of Catholic theology). As part of the metamorphosis, however, the arts college faculty and administration remained Jesuit, and the Latin and philosophy core stressed the teachings of St. Thomas Aquinas; these two features becoming the new essence of Jesuit education in the United States. The evolution of the curriculum manifested the historic characteristics of American pluralism, whereby an immigrant or a foreign institution Americanizes while retaining distinctive features of the old-world culture.[71]

While the need for accreditation induced Creighton's Americanization, World War I further disrupted standard University procedures, although it also provided a vehicle whereby the school's profoundly patriotic response illuminated the depth of its assimilation. A variety of events demonstrated some of the immediate effects of the war, even on non-belligerents. Within months of the outbreak of hostilities in August 1914, Creighton felt the impact of wartime inflation: "Owing to the war, the prices of drugs and chemicals used in the Colleges of Medicine, Dentistry and Pharmacy, [have] advanced many times beyond the figures prevailing a year ago." Individual professional students began to volunteer to serve with the Allies in the French war zone. August M. Borglum ("Arts," 1885), professor of piano and music critic for the *Omaha World-Herald* (older brother of Gutzon, the sculptor that carved the monument at Mt. Rushmore), bemoaned the immediate negative effect on American music due to the fact that approximately fifty thousand students from the United States now lost the opportunity to study at the music centers in Paris, Vienna, and Berlin. Creighton students showed their concern, petitioning President Woodrow Wilson to "immediately invite other nations of Europe to send delegates to unite with delegates appointed by you to demand the nations now at war that they declare immediate cessation of hostilities for the purpose of considering terms of peace." Wilson's subsequent petitions to the belligerents failed to generate interest, and one year later, a Creighton student garnered first place at the Nebraska Intercollegiate Oratorical Contest with a stirring defense of the Preparedness Movement (military and economic mobilization in case the United States entered the conflict). The University also demonstrated its support of preparedness, initiating "temporary" military drills for undergraduates in March 1917.[72]

The American declaration of war, on Good Friday, April 6, 1917, further affected the University in a myriad of ways. On the same day, in order to prevent fifth column activities, President Wilson ordered the cessation of all amateur wireless communication; Fr. Rigge had to dismantle the apparatus atop the College Building that had received time signals from Arlington, Virginia, for three years. Additionally, at the behest of the Bureau of Education, Department of the Interior, the University conducted an inventory of resources that could be "immediately mobilized for the public defense," including people with special skills that could fill non-combat roles. In May, officers of the Bryan's peace oratory contest cancelled the event and Fr. Provincial Burrows urged economy because of inflation (it also affected the Jesuits at mealtime, "fewer first feasts, fewer drinks, meat three times a week at breakfast, one kind of meat only at a meal, plainer first-class breakfasts, etc."). That year, the CCAS conducted final examinations two weeks early to give the students a chance to help "relieve the farm labor situation." Actually, a "large number" of undergraduates had already left to help plant the rapidly increasing number of acres under the plow in the Midwest (the yield of European agriculture had plummeted drastically during three years of war). The arts college promised to give students full semester credits if they had established an 80 average in February and presented a statement from the farmer attesting to their satisfactory work as a cultivator. The University conducted a rearranged Commencement from under a big-top tent erected on the north lawn and the Alumni Association cancelled Homecoming. Following President Wilson's directive to avoid "unnecessary expenditures," it substituted a luncheon in the gymnasium for the annual Pan-Alumni Banquet.[73]

The University's patriotic response demonstrated the unwarranted nature of the Protestant fear of Catholic disloyalty. Actually, as early as 1884, the Third Plenary Council of the Catholic Church in the United States had issued the "Baltimore Pledge." It promised that if anyone imperiled American freedom, "our Catholic citizens will be found to stand forward as one man, ready to pledge anew their lives, their fortunes and their sacred honor." The Pledge reiterated the phraseology of the Founding Fathers, and twelve days after the American declaration of war in 1917, the United States Catholic bishops sent President Wilson a letter reaffirming the Pledge. The Church leaders also established the National Catholic War Council to coordinate the "patriotic effort of all Catholic organizations"; subsequently, it published a book to document the myriad activities.[74]

The summer of 1917 brought further disruption; Fr. Provincial Burrows cancelled vacations for the scholastics and distributed the student teachers among the various colleges for extra study. The six at Creighton remained in place; fourteen others joined them and unused classrooms became their dorm. The United States Congress passed conscription legislation, and on June 5, 1917, males between twenty-one and thirty-one registered for the draft, including three of the Creighton scholastics. On July 20, the United States Army conducted the first conscription drawing; only three of those registered at the University had their name called. Also in June, the United States conducted its first Liberty Loan drive. Margaret B. Cuming, wife of a former governor of Nebraska, had recently bequeathed $40,000 "for the purpose of enlarging and completing" St. John's Church; however, not ready to undertake the project, the Jesuits subscribed the sum in Liberty Bonds. Health sciences students demonstrated the same patriotic spirit when eighteen medical school seniors volunteered for the Navy medical corps (only five were accepted, as the government limited the number of volunteers from an individual college). The College of Medicine operated through the summer to speed seniors toward graduation and entry into the military; by the fall, Creighton graduates in significant numbers served in the Medical Reserve Corps and the Dental Reserve Corps in army stateside training camps.[75]

The fall of 1917 brought more of the same. The Jesuit community donated $1,000 to the Knights of Columbus War Camp Fund, voted to follow the wheatless and meatless days of the government's voluntary rationing plan, and the Reverend William J. Corboy, S.J., became the first Creighton Jesuit called to service as a chaplain. Furthermore, the Administration responded to a government appeal and made military training "obligatory in the Undergraduate Department." A lieutenant from Ft. Crook received the appointment to direct "military affairs on the 'Hill'," but the three companies went most of the year without rifles because the government could not supply the burgeoning cadet militias. After the embarrassment of marching in a patriotic parade in downtown Omaha in uniform, but without arms, the administration agreed to purchase one hundred imitation Springfield rifles, enough to "arm" two companies. They arrived during the winter, as the units did calisthenics and drilled in the warmth of the gymnasium. By that time, the cadet corps had subsumed the college band, which played during drill, and it had organized indoor inter-company athletic contests in boxing, wrestling, and track.[76]

Despite the loss of underclassmen that volunteered for active service, enrollment in the CCAS continued to rise during the war years, keeping in mind the pre-professional caveat. Nationally, General Leonard Wood advised students to remain in school; he did not want to repeat the errors of France and Great Britain, which had lost a large number of potential officers by rushing college men to the front as privates. Locally, the Administration editorialized that in a war of science, young men should serve their country by "enlisting" in college to receive the training that would make them leaders in war and the reconstruction that would follow. The *Chronicle* also regularly published materials at the request of the Patriotic News Service of the National Committee of Patriotic Societies, many of which reiterated the stay-in-school-and-become-a-leader theme. Unwittingly, however, since it may have whetted the appetite for enlistment, the journal also published frequent articles about enlisted men from Creighton and a segment titled "A Sheaf of Letters," which contained epistles from former students in the service.[77]

The belligerent status of the United States also had an immediate impact on intercollegiate athletics. On August 4, 1917, the National Collegiate Athletic Association (NCAA) voted to retain athletic competition, following an address by Secretary of War Newton D. Baker that stressed the fact that sports prepared men for military training. Locally, law dean Paul Martin, editorializing on behalf of those seeking to reign in intercollegiate athletics, hoped the war would "mark the return of sanity in the college athletics of the country." He hoped the new spirit would cleanse the extravagance, the professionalism, and the "excessive training of a few men who were all too often called 'students' only through courtesy." The war produced no such long-term effects. In the short run, it shifted many activities to cadet intramurals and disrupted the schedules of varsity teams. In the 1917–18 academic year, while the Creighton University basketball team enjoyed a 14–0 season that included three victories against military teams, intercollegiate baseball took a three-year hiatus, and the running track constructed at the field in 1916 had to postpone hosting its first varsity event until peacetime. Similarly, the football team played only three games in the fall of 1918 because of cancellations due to the Spanish Flu pandemic and "certain rulings" by the military.[78]

The war effort also affected other extracurricular activities. For example, two spring-1918 intercollegiate debates covered the topics "Should the United States have a Navy Inferior to None?" and "Resolved, that in the United States all railroads be owned and operated by the Federal Government—Constitutionality Waived" (President Wilson established a board to coordinate the operation of the railroads for the duration of the war). On April 6, the one-year anniversary of the U.S. declaration of war and the newly designated Flag Day, the University participated in "The Great Parade." It lasted for three hours in downtown Omaha and included marchers only (no floats or automobiles), each carrying an American flag. "Every organization" participated, including a contingent composed of seventeen of the twenty-four Creighton Jesuits. By that date, the administration again decided to terminate the academic year early, to allow undergraduates and high-school students to relieve the farm-labor shortage. The concluding ceremonies began with three-days of patriotic exercises, which culminated with the unfurling of a Creighton Service Flag (eight hundred stars representing Creighton men serving their country, arranged to form the letter "C") and held Commencement on June 1 in the gymnasium. The *Chronicle* continued to tout the record of Creighton men by publishing the "Sheaf of Letters" from servicemen well into 1920, a year and a half after the armistice.[79]

America's belligerency continued to intensify the burdens placed upon the University. Because of shortages and the priorities established for the use of metals, the administration could not make necessary repairs to the fence "surrounding the campus." Then, under the new stipulations for conscription, on September 12, 1918, the day before classes resumed for the CCAS, all males eighteen to forty-six had to register for the draft. Father President McMenamy escaped the requirement by ten days, but nine other Creighton Jesuits filled out papers. Worried that conscription would deplete the schools, and advised by the army that it would need ninety thousand officers by summer, the United States created the Student Army Training Corps (SATC), which inducted all draft-aged students and commandeered colleges with enrollments of over one hundred males of draft age. The new organization scrapped the voluntary military-training program described in the 1918 Bulletin. On October 1, in the Auditorium, all eligible Creighton students took their oath of allegiance and became the wards of Commandant Lt. Denver B. Braun. The health-professions schools undertook a year-round schedule to speed graduations, incorporated military topics into their curriculums and instituted military conditioning, drill, and courses in tactics and logistics.[80]

The SATC organized students in the arts college and the law school by age, not class standing. Twenty-year-olds received preparation for a call to active service in three months, those nineteen in six months, and those eighteen in nine months. Individuals demonstrating desirable military qualities would receive an early call and a transfer to officer-training school; those lacking the qualities would report to army-vocational or non-commissioned-officer schools. While a member of the SATC, the government provided the students with uniforms, housing, food, and pay at the infantry private level. St. John's Hall and the gymnasium, outfitted with about 270 bunks, served as barracks. The new curriculum for the CCAS included theoretical military study and physical training for eleven hours a week, plus classes in tactics and theory, hygiene and sanitation, military law and practice, and surveying and map reading. The law school added courses in international law, military law, and war issues. The Creighton SATC unit immediately participated in the fourth Liberty

Loan drive; it received a quota of $21,500, but actually subscribed for $35,000 (the Jesuits subscribed for an additional $10,000).[81]

The SATC existed long enough to disrupt one academic semester. On November 7, 1918, a Jesuit chronicler ecstatically wrote, "PEACE! The Great War is Over! The whistles were tooting for an hour or two beginning at noon." Actually, the celebration proved premature, but on November 11, 1918, the belligerents signed the armistice (the scribe entered "THE WAR IS OVER NOW, SURE!"). SATC classes ceased for a week, then resumed on November 18 and continued until the unit demobilized between December 8 and 11. For the remainder of the semester, class selection became optional, but two thirds of the students disappeared. "It was an open secret," Fr. Rigge lamented, "that the only reason that our classes were so large was that life in a college appeared more agreeable than life in an ordinary camp or cantonment."[82]

With the new semester, the University began to make the transition to peacetime and from the SATC to the Reserve Officer Training Corps (ROTC). The National Defense Act of 1916 established the ROTC and in 1917, the University sought affiliation for its militia group. The SATC preempted its establishment at Creighton, but the National Defense Act of 1920 reauthorized the ROTC during peacetime. Father President McCormick decided to make the program mandatory for undergraduates at Creighton, consisting of three drills per week. Lieutenant Braun, and then Capt. Robert Hardin, served short stints as commandant during the conversion; eventually, in September 1919, Lt. Col. Corbit S. Hoffman obtained the appointment as commandant and professor of military science. The medical school held its last quarterly graduation in April 1919, and the University proudly proclaimed its service record— a total of 1,285 faculty, students, and alumni had served their country, 27 died. Ralph T. Wilson, arts college student-athlete in tennis, basketball, and handball, who had won the class gold medal six consecutive years and had served in the Balloon Corps at Camp Wise, Texas, won a Rhodes Scholarship and departed for Oxford University in December 1919.[83]

The "reconversion" (institutions had converted to wartime purposes, now they had to convert back to peacetime pursuits) also entailed dealing with a too-popular summer school and rebuilding the athletic program. In 1919, the summer school attracted over six hundred applicants, which produced a housing crisis. Dean Paul Martin obtained the use of the vacated Episcopalian school, Brownell Hall. It lacked cooking facilities, so he had to arrange for catered meals. It also lacked furniture, so through the ROTC commandant he arranged for Ft. Omaha to provide the beds and accessories as if it were a summer encampment. When it came time to move the furnishing, the teamsters had gone on strike, so he had to recruit students and rent trucks to accomplish the transfer. With few complaints, the nuns endured the six-week session. Then that fall the University resumed active promotion of intercollegiate athletics. It organized a booster club with representatives from each class and school. It reorganized the dormant Alumni Athletic Board and all-sports coach Tommy Mills applied for membership in the Missouri Valley Conference. Baseball resumed in the spring, but the failed conference bid delayed the creation of a varsity track team.[84]

Finally, World War I also contributed to tangential issues of great magnitude. Wartime censorship heated up the academic-freedom controversy that had arisen around the turn of the century, as wealthy patrons forced universities to dismiss faculty who expressed ideas they did not like. Considering the temperament of John A. Creighton, the communal organization of the Society of Jesus, and the unity of the *Ratio Studiorum*, Creighton University avoided that storm. Shortly after the United States declaration of war, the Nebraska Legislature created the state Council of Defense to monitor the loyalty of Nebraskans. It hassled several professors at the University of Nebraska and Paul Martin wrote an editorial concerning the issue that had "the educational world . . . agog." He inferred that the situation called for some restraint: "Freedom there must be in colleges and universities, . . . but freedom well regulated—not freedom running riot and quickly degenerating in license." On another issue, the Jesuits showed little respect for regulation. Wartime antipathy toward beer-drinking, beer-distilling German Americans gave the state legislature the final impetus to pass a Nebraska prohibition law. For several years thereafter, however, Jesuit chroniclers reported the frequent discrete consumption of beer and wine at meals (but not in front of certain guests or the lay staff). Seemingly, the community received its spirits from out-of-state deliveries and by home brewing, disregarding a law it viewed as a misdirected regulation advocated by teetotaling Protestants.[85]

The war contributed to the spread of a far more dangerous plague than alcohol consumption—the Spanish Influenza. It erupted among combatants on the Western Front, and by the fall of 1918 had become a pandemic in Europe and the United States, eventually killing millions. In October, Omaha public health officials closed the schools, theaters, churches, and other public venues that brought large numbers of people together. For the next four Sundays, the Jesuits held Mass outdoors on the north lawn. The CCAS closed on October 7, the downtown professional schools on October 21; the University reopened on November 4, closed for a week to celebrate the armistice, and when classes resumed on November 18, about fifty students remained hospitalized. Robert H. Loree, a freshman in the law school, seems to have been the only Creighton student or faculty member to succumb to the disease. The arts college made a promise "on behalf of the students of erecting a statue to the Sacred Heart in case the student body were protected." The plan escalated to include statues of a sailor and soldier, and the construction of a war memorial building. Fundraising drives by other groups quickly deflated the plans and the administration reverted to the original idea of a statue of the Sacred Heart. It took an Italian sculptor two years to complete the piece, carved from Carrara marble; Fr. President McCormick dedicated it the day before the Feast of the Sacred Heart (June 21, 1921) and it assumed its place at the north end of the north lawn, near the Observatory.[86]

Furthermore, World War I sparked the Great Migration, a significant milestone in African-American history. The booming economy and the conscription of millions of white males created a labor shortage in northern and western industrial cities. Middle-class white women and southern black migrants filled the vacuum; the African-American population of Omaha doubled to about ten thousand during the war years.

A 1917 photograph of the Creighton University Cadet Regiment revealed that it included an African American, probably the first student of his race to attend the arts college. Two years later, Omaha suffered one of the scores of race riots that stained the wartime record of respect for civil liberties and civil rights in the United States. For several weeks, the CCAS entertained several uninvited guests as "about nine soldiers guarded our student rifles and ammunition in the southwest room of the basement in the main building." In those troubled times, possibly at the behest of an African-American student at Creighton, the Reverend Francis B. Cassilly, S.J., professor of pedagogy and Christian Doctrine, initiated a "mission to Negroes," which became the Community House of St. Benedict the Moor. A Jesuit chronicler revealed that he "had been talking up Catholic Action to the Jesuit community; [challenged, he] put on his coat and hat, and sallied forth in the highways and byways to look for the colored people." The impulse did not sprout out of anger, civil rights had been a lifelong passion. Shortly after entering the Society of Jesus in St. Louis in 1878, he had taught catichism to a "Negro family," and about 1890, he had published an article in the *Sacred Heart Messenger*, entitled, "Solving the Race Problem."[87]

In addition to racial strife, the super patriotism of World War I produced other unfortunate attempts to deny some American citizens their civil liberties. To ensure loyalty to the United States war effort, "native" Americans (assimilated Protestants who had migrated from allied European countries during the eighteenth and nineteenth centuries), with the help of state and the national governments, undertook a program to "Americanize" recent immigrants, mostly Catholics and Jews who had migrated from southern and eastern Europe in the late-nineteenth or early-twentieth centuries. For example, Adlai Rhodes, arts college sophomore, won first place in the 1919 Intercollegiate English Contest with an essay entitled "Americanization," which argued that prewar labor unrest and problems of dissent during the war necessitated educating immigrants in "a common language, a common citizenship, and an understanding of the ideals and principles" of the United States. The Nebraska Americanization program easily distorted those sentiments by forbidding aliens to teach and by demanding that all classes be taught in English. Nebraska's new teacher-certification rules led to a gigantic summer school enrollment at Creighton that year; the state also sponsored the first law in the nation to make English the official language of a state and pushed an attempt to legislate parochial schools out of existence. Law dean Paul Martin and his successor, Louis J. TePoel, led the Catholic opposition. They received a document proponents had circulated privately and publicized it to assail its bigoted message and to appeal to fair-minded non-Catholics. They orchestrated a compromise in the legislature. The subsequent measure mandated that principals be American citizens, teachers be certified, secular classes be taught in English, and that parochial and public curriculums be similar.[88]

World War I also ignited the Irish Revolution and the attempt to create an independent republic. Eamon de Valera, the president of the self-proclaimed new government, spent two days on the Creighton campus lecturing in behalf of his cause. On Monday, October 27, 1919, he regaled a crowd of approximately four thousand well-wishers in the gymnasium; the next afternoon, he addressed the assembled high school and College, which, at his behest, received a holiday on Wednesday. A month to the day later, students garnered another unscheduled recess due to the coal strike. Wartime government controls had ceased and millions of workers in dozens of industries walked off their jobs in labor-management disputes during an era of rampant inflation. In response to the United Mine Workers stoppage, the Omaha city government ordered all schools, churches, and similar public institutions to close for a week and to establish rationing programs. Bitter cold produced hardships for many and officials extended the closures; the strike ended December 10, a day that registered a low temperature of –15 degrees Fahrenheit. Fuel restrictions ended three days later, but coal shortages led the administration to keep the CCAS idle until after the Christmas holiday, with classes resuming in January 1920. Thus, a variety of war-related events continued to prevent rapid "reconversion," well after the signing of the armistice. Eventually, a new decade would open a new chapter in the history of Creighton University.[89]

World War I had disrupted the University and made the immediate "return to normalcy" difficult. For a time, the professional and undergraduates schools became virtual army camps. Generally, however, the wartime distortions remained temporary and they actually aided and abetted the on-going assimilation process. During the post–John A. Creighton-Michael Dowling era, all the schools received accreditation from their particular professional organizations and the booster campaign promoted the institution's contributions. But, while the administration proclaimed Creighton a beacon of Omaha, few non-Catholics in the environs included it in their philanthropic endeavors. The new Creighton University Alumni Association made its presence felt, especially in athletics, pushing the construction of the gymnasium and gaining a voice in management through the athletic board. Women became a regular, although tangential part of the College of Arts and Sciences. The terminology, CCAS, appeared because the American model of education forced the Jesuits to create stand-alone high schools and to abandon the seven-year *Ratio Studiorum*. Subsequently, the Missouri Province adopted a course of study dubbed the "American Plan," which assimilated the curriculum of the secular colleges of the United States. It became the model for post–World War I Jesuit education and Fr. Alexander Burrowes, a former provincial and former interim president of Creighton University, published an appeal to Catholics to take better advantage of a college education. World War I, he argued, had demonstrated the shortage of college-educated individuals to fill leadership roles. Therefore, he felt the clergy should "foster a desire for higher education among the parish schools and high schools" because the Church needed "an educated laity," not just for itself, but one that could "take part in the organization and management of great social movements." Moreover, this new attitude toward higher education included women, since they provided much of the personnel involved with state charities and social boards. Catholics in general, and Jesuits in particular, now thought in assimilated American terms. In forty years, Creighton University had evolved from a grade school for the poor Catholic boys of Omaha into a viable regional Catholic Jesuit American University.[90]

PART TWO

Marking Time

Usually, historians construe the era between 1920 and 1950 as a story of contrasting decades—the roaring twenties versus the depressed thirties versus the war-torn forties. For Creighton University, however, the distinction between the decades was not quite as stark. The twenties "purred" briefly, but a regional economic slump produced stagnation. The Great Depression intensified the existing downturn, but never threatened to bankrupt the institution. World War II militarized the campus and the postwar G.I. Bill generated record enrollments. Yet, the common theme of the entire three-decade era revolved around unfulfilled dreams.

In his column in the November 1938 issue of the *Creighton Alumnus,* Fr. President Joseph Zuercher, S.J., complained, "With the present income from endowment and tuition Creighton can mark time but cannot advance." The observation succinctly described the situation during the era. In the May 1978 issue of *Alumnews,* a centennial history article authored by Dr. Arthur Umscheid, Ph.D., who came to the history department in 1937, attributed the predicament to failed leadership. He stated: "The administrators of the 1930s, most notably the Rev. Patrick J. Mahan, S.J., [1931–1937] and Rev. Joseph P. Zuercher, S.J., [1937–1943] seemed comfortable with a low level of advancement."

Doctor Umscheid's analysis downplayed the promotion of grandiose building plans, the repeated fund drives that generated a significant amount of hoopla but raised little additional revenue, the debilitating effect of a depressed economy, and the military disruption associated with World War II. During the era, Creighton continued to evolve in a positive direction; the undergraduate experience became thoroughly coed, new colleges joined the system, and students devised additional activities and institutions that continue to define the essence of University life. However, the anemic economy, alumni with little wealth, and the inability of the administration to cultivate the desired structural assimilation doomed the fundraising efforts and stunted institutional growth. That is, a fifty-year effort to establish a symbiotic relationship with the people of Omaha failed—the University remained "in" Omaha, but did not become part "of" Omaha. The leaders did not feel "comfortable with a low level of advancement"; they developed pie-in-the-sky models, but they lacked a healthy economic environment and the public relations skills necessary to raise the money that would fulfill their dreams. Thus, relative to its stated goals, between 1920 and 1950, Creighton advanced minimally, while it "marked time."

CHAPTER 5

Undergrad, 1920–41

To administrators, the years between the world wars proved disappointing. They envisioned a "New Creighton University," consisting of a unified campus filled with new buildings serving the needs of the arts college, staffed by a highly trained faculty, teaching a large, sophisticated student body. They believed that the alumni and the Omaha community would view the new Creighton as their jewel and would support it accordingly. However, successive fundraising drives failed, dashing the dream and producing disillusionment. Yet, although the ultimate aspiration failed to materialize, a new stadium, a second dormitory, and an enlarged and renovated administration Building appeared. Moreover, the administration evolved into a modern bureaucracy, lay faculty became a majority in the arts college, and its curriculum adopted virtually all the elements recognizable to students of the early twenty-first century. Thus, as with past eras, while the perception of stagnation presented itself, significant evolution ensued. While administrators stressed the failed emergence of the new Creighton University during the interwar era, they actually fashioned many of the basic characteristics of the contemporary Creighton College of Arts and Sciences.

The 1920–21 academic year marked the opening of a new decade and the completion of the "reconversion" back to a traditional peacetime university. Father John F. McCormick, S.J., continued as rector-president, and during his tenure he oversaw substantial changes in administrative form and function. In October 1921, in the south wing to the College Building, close to St. John's Church, a "'storm door' was put on the old pastors' entrance on California Street and marked 'Administration Building,'" inaugurating the contemporary name for the historic structure. Four years later, Fr. McCormick moved his office close to that door, just east of the treasurer's office. Among other duties, the treasurer supervised the operation of the university bookstore located in the basement of the Administration Building, which now advertised the sale of all sorts of memorabilia emblazoned with the official school seal. The promotions continued to proclaim, "All Profits Are Turned Over to Student Activities." By the end of the decade, the increased functions of the treasurer's office necessitated the addition of a bursar and Miss M. Isabel Keyser began a twenty-year career in that position. All Creighton students came to know her well, as they paid her their registration fees and for their bookstore purchases.[1]

Keyser had female administrative companionship from Clare McDermott, whose forty-year career began as assistant director of the summer school in 1919. In 1928, she began a twenty-year stint as registrar, but completed the last dozen years of her service as an assistant in that office. Women also soon filled the new positions in the library. Father McCormick lamented the fact that CCAS students had "inadequate library facilities" and "no common study-room." Thus, he opened the Jesuit library to collegians, which necessitated hiring a librarian. Those students received borrower cards to the "varsity library," accessible to them 8:00 A.M. to 5:00 P.M. weekdays and 8:00 A.M. to noon on Saturdays. Jesuit oversight of library functions must have become an issue, because in 1925, the rector-president appointed the Reverend James McCabe, S.J., "regent" of the facility. That same year, the administration divided the first floor assembly hall, which housed the wall cabinets containing the old student-library collection (located on the west end of the original College Building abutting the new library), into a reading room for college students and a study hall for high-school students. The additional space allowed the staff to institute a closed-stack system to eliminate "all misplacing of books and their handling by inexperienced persons." Yet the library remained a novelty for many students. The student newspaper claimed "it is astonishing how little is known about it" and urged students of all the schools to use it: "So when the Frat. house is noisy, or your room is cold, come up to the library and read or study, thus showing your appreciation of the opportunities it offers." It offered about 32,000 books, "especially strong in History and Religion," and about 80 periodicals. In 1926, Miss Alberta Brown initiated a long era of women librarians; she immediately hired a female reference librarian and another as assistant cataloger. In 1928, Mary Hunt succeeded to the position of librarian for both the college and the high school libraries, retiring forty-five years later.[2]

Father McCormick also completed the metamorphosis of the traditional Jesuit position of the prefect of discipline. In 1923, he appointed the Reverend Charles Schuetz, S.J., to fill an enlarged role as the first dean of men. The newly titled position now emphasized student counseling; Fr. Schuetz obtained an office and students received an invitation to visit with him to discuss their problems, 8:00 A.M. to 9:00 P.M., daily. Thirteen years later, two lay faculty members, Laurence H. Brown (A.B., 1923) and Leo R. Kennedy, Ph.D. (A.B., 1924), became the first assistant deans, assigned to "act jointly in supervising student social affairs." The rector-president also began to seek advice beyond his all-Jesuit House Consultors and Board of Trustees. In 1923, Fr. McCormick instituted a faculty-administrator committee system, in which University activities came under the "control of Faculty Committees composed of deans and heads of various departments." The president chaired the committee on affairs of the University; Fr. Corboy chaired the committee on athletics, which replaced alumni control of the reinstituted sports program; Fr. Schuetz chaired the committee on social activities; and lay Public Relations Director P. H. Bogardus headed the committee on commencement and public ceremonies.[3]

That same year, the *Courier* incorrectly touted the creation of a lay board of regents as the first named by a Jesuit university in the United States. Actually, about 1903, the Reverend President William Banks Rogers, S.J., of Saint Louis University established a lay board of advisors to help with the financial planning for a medical school for his institution. Then, in 1921, Jesuit provincials created the Inter-Province

Committee on Studies (IPCS) to deal with contemporary education problems with a national and unified perspective. Jealously guarded provincial prerogatives, and the fear of promoting animosity from other Catholic educators by creating an exclusive Jesuit association, limited the committee's effectiveness. However, the IPCS did issue reports regularly. An early recommendation promoted the idea of lay advisory boards. Thus, in 1923, Fr. McCormick appointed four prominent local businessmen: Walter W. Head, president of the Omaha National Bank; Charles Kountze, vice president and chairman of the board of the First National Bank; Frank J. Burkley, president of the Burkley Printing Company and the Burkley Envelope Company; and Fred Hamilton, president of the Merchants National Bank. Lay Regent activity, until after World War II, seems minimal. Meeting minutes exist for 1925, and then ceased until 1946 (indicating no official meetings). In the 1930s, publications only listed three members and the administration reorganized and enlarged the group in 1939. Seemingly, the administration sought the help of prominent lay businessmen for fundraising, but following the experience of other Jesuit universities, it limited the effectiveness of the group by severely restricting its access to information, especially the budget. Thus, in the pre–World War II era, the venture failed; ostensibly, the board existed in name only.[4]

Father McCormick's tenure produced important administrative changes, but his talents as an administrator seem questionable. His disdain for the summer school and his unwillingness to recognize a verbal contract of his predecessor prompted the resignation of its dean, Paul Martin, also dean of the law school. Furthermore, between 1920–1923, Fr. McCormick used the $40,000 bequest of Mrs. Thomas Cuming to double the size of St. John's Church and to erect a pastor's residence adjacent to the new sacristy. The residence stretched east to within a few feet of the north wing of the College Building, necessitating the elimination of the bridge that connected the two structures and of the student handball courts. Seemingly he undertook the project without consultation; the site of the parsonage, according to a Jesuit chronicler, was "condemned by all Ours [the Jesuit community]," because of its proximity to the College, and without the bridge the "community must now go to church through all weathers [*sic*] in the open." The pastors' relocation to their new building, however, made their apartments in the south wing of the College available for an enlargement of the treasurer's office and the addition of other administrative space for the procurator, the publicity bureau, and the new telephone exchange.[5]

On November 28, 1921, the University inaugurated a new telephone system, which employed a full-time switchboard operator, who doubled as the institution's information bureau. The new private exchange, DO(uglas)-2873, connected the various buildings on campus, although the gymnasium and the medical and pharmacy schools downtown remained outside the system. Technology, however, did not necessarily mean progress for many of the Jesuits. As a chronicler explained, "There is a phone on each floor in our residence section [the south wing]. When a man is wanted, his signal is rung. But as many have never educated themselves to listen to the call bell to see if they are wanted, and as the calling bells are weak and there is much reflection of sound, many of ours pronounced the new venture a failure." The following year, to aid out-going calls, the telephones became the dial variety already in use in the city for many years, and in 1925, the original thirty-extension callboard exited, replaced by an exchange board, AT(lantic)-0191, capable of handling eighty extensions.[6]

Besides acquiring technology, Fr. McCormick continued to acquire property contiguous to the campus. In 1923, the University purchased three "little frame houses" on California Street, west of the Auditorium. The owner of a fourth dwelling on the northeast corner of 26th Street demanded three times the appraised value, and threatened to raze the structure and build a rental duplex on the lot if the administration refused his offer. The antagonists failed to compromise and a two-story brick duplex arose on the site (the University subsequently acquired the complex in the post–World War II era; for two decades, it provided office space for various administrators, then the philosophy department, before being razed in 1995). Moreover, Fr. McCormick bought another house on the south side of California Street, west of 26th Street, completing the university's ownership of that three-lot city block. In 1925, he acquired a "row of ten brick houses extending on the North side of Cass St. from 24th to 25th streets"; the sale of property on Webster Street and the leasing of a lot at 20th and Farnam streets to build a theater (currently, "The Rose"), paid for the row house purchase. Two other real-estate deals during his tenure resulted in the disappearance of the Creighton name from downtown Omaha. The University leased the Creighton Block at 15th and Dodge streets to the Brandeis Company, which razed it in 1921 to construct a new building. In a similar situation, in 1926, the Creighton Orpheum Theater came down; the Creighton Glee Club participated in the closing ceremony and the University received the large portrait of John that had hung over the vaudeville stage. Within a year, a larger Orpheum Theater, minus the Creighton name, appeared.[7]

The timing of those property purchases helped determine the configuration of "The New Creighton University." In 1920, with revenue from the sale of the Edward Creighton Institute, the University undertook construction of new law and dental schools on campus. The new dental building stood on the northwest corner of 26th Street, its main entrance facing California Street. Bearing the same exterior design, the law school occupied a lot on the northeast side of 26th Street, with its entrance facing north (the un-purchase-able "little frame houses" sat to its south on California Street). That same year, the administration revealed a campus-expansion plan, which foresaw the construction of physics and chemistry buildings (mirror images of the new professional schools, situated to their north), two dormitories, a liberal arts building, an administration-library building, a new auditorium, and a football stadium. John Latenser & Sons drew the plans for the $1.2 million scheme, which would have created a unified campus enclosed by 24th to 27th streets, Burt to California streets. The ultimate proposal also included the enlargement of St. John's Church, a cafeteria on the ground floor of the gymnasium and a new medical school adjacent to St. Joseph's Hospital on 10th Street.[8]

Existing University capital covered construction costs of only the church expansion and the on-campus professional schools. Therefore, "aware that Creighton University has borne the reputation of being endowed with large resources," the administration renewed its war-interrupted booster campaign in Omaha. First, it published a treasurer's report, which sought to demonstrate that the University struggled to balance its annual budget. The document asserted that although the University owned a majority of the John A. Creighton Real Estate Company, the asset was "at present mostly unproductive," its "small income" used to pay "office expenses and taxes." Its annual budget revealed

	INCOME		EXPENSES
From endowment	$156,094.26	Coll.-H. S.	$95,618.09
From tuition, fees, etc.		(no tuition charged)	
Medical School	$18,220.75		$52,116.09
Law School	$12,911.84		$24,181.82
Dental School	$34,269.75		$34,427.44
Pharmacy	$ 9,058.75		$14,575.22
Summer School	$24,003.94		$23,998.85
		Advertising	$1,335.38
TOTAL	$254,513.67	TOTAL	$246,252.89
SURPLUS	$ 8,260.78[9]		

The ledger revealed a small annual surplus, that the tuition-free college and high school accounted for 60 percent of the annual expenditures, and that the medical and law schools consumed two to three times the funds they generated. For expansion to occur, the University had to establish new sources of income. Thus, the administration rejuvenated its pre–World War I campaign to convince the residents of Omaha to consider the University a city institution. It confidently asserted, "Omaha is fast realizing that it is a college center as well as an industrial and manufacturing center. The Creighton University is distinctly an Omaha institution. It prides itself in this fact, and whatever fame and glory it may achieve it tenders humbly to the city, happy in the thought that it may raise the standards of the community." In one attempt to demonstrate the connection, the University began to film Creighton football games and to distribute highlight reels to local theaters for public viewing. It also held a banquet, which sought to "strengthen the union between the University and the city of Omaha." The City Council demonstrated its willingness to cooperate by vacating 26th Street, California to Burt, eliminating the possible annoyance of a transportation artery bisecting the proposed campus (today, the short alley between the Humanities and Hitchcock buildings is all that remains of the former city street).[10]

After a year of preparation, on September 2, 1922, Fr. President McCormick, through newspaper articles and a radio broadcast, announced plans to undertake a $2 million fund drive in February 1923, $1 million for endowment and $1 million for four buildings and a stadium. He proclaimed that the Administration Building (home to the high school and the arts college) had become "increasingly inadequate"; thus, he established "a new class-room building for the Liberal Arts College" as the "first and most immediate need." The chemistry facility was priority number two, followed by the dormitory, since one half to two thirds of the undergraduates now came from outside Omaha. He emphasized that the Creighton endowment stood at $2,885,000 and barely provided sufficient revenue to cover annual operating costs. Subsequently, he wrote an editorial illuminating the need for increasing the endowment. The previously published budget had provided aggregate data; this time he presented individual costs. He explained that the annual cost to educate one undergraduate amounted to $156.53, but that the student paid only a laboratory fee of $13.03. For the other schools the costs versus tuition-fees ratios were

	COSTS	TUITION AND FEES
Medicine	$412.11	$152.82
Law	$187.34	$108.30
Dentistry	$381.33	$152.72
Pharmacy	$228.21	$121.17
Commerce	$123.03	$ 78.11
High School	$ 62.76	$ .60
Summer	$ 12.56	$ 12.43[11]

To prime the pump, the newly established Creighton University Building and Endowment Association sponsored a series of twelve radio lectures, delivered weekly on Thursday evenings from the Omaha Grain Exchange (Fr. Rigge initiated the series with an address entitled, "Is Mars Inhabited?"). The administration also used the 1922 Homecoming as another promotional device. It touted Creighton football as a tourist lure that should garner the support of the entire business community. It explained that the bleachers of the existing field needed repair and that the new chemistry and liberal arts buildings would preempt part of the gridiron, thus the need for a new stadium. Moreover, the popularity of the sport demanded a larger venue. The Omaha Chamber of Commerce responded by fashioning 2,500 keys to the city to distribute to returning alumni. Father McCormick presented a pre-campaign message that opened with a paragraph that tied spirit to sports, and then explained that the additional $1 million in endowment, invested at a 5 percent rate of return, would generate $250,000 annually, which would cover the expenses of the expanded University. The final preparation for the drive consisted of organizing the 3,200 alumni. The administration divided Nebraska into seventeen sections, Iowa into eight, South Dakota and Kansas into three, the other states of the region into one each, and the rest of the country, with few alumni, into inter-state districts.[12]

In January 1923, the *Creighton Courier*, the alumni magazine, changed its letterhead motto from "Devoted to the Interests of the Creighton University" to "Devoted to the Interests of the Creighton Building and Endowment Campaign" and published pictures of a revised plan. The new scaled-down scheme eliminated the separate physics and high-school buildings, and one of the dorms. Ward Burgess, president of M. E. Smith & Co., the Burgess-Nash Company, and the Nebraska Power Company, chairman of the board of the Omaha National Bank, and the former director of the War Savings Stamp campaign in Nebraska, agreed to chair the executive committee of the Creighton Building and Endowment Campaign. Ominously, four vice presidents to aid his efforts did not materialize in a timely fashion. However, Mrs. Arthur F. Mullen accepted the chair of the women's division and secured the aid of Miss Margaret McShane, Mrs. L. F. Crofoot, Miss Mary Kennedy, Mrs. John M. Glavin, Mrs. William Jamison, and Mrs. John Mullin. John L. Kennedy, a prominent attorney and president of the United States Bank, served as treasurer. They planned a two-week blitz that would raise $1 million in Omaha and $1 million in the rest of the country.[13]

Confidently on Founders' Day, February 7, 1923, one month before the official campaign kickoff, the committee held a groundbreaking ceremony for Dowling Memorial, the proposed liberal arts college building, planting United States flags on the four corners of the site north of the law school. Fundraising finally began on March 5, and the results immediately quashed expectations. A Jesuit chronicler revealed, "The Great Two-Million Dollar Drive, which began on the 5th, according to today's paper has so far brought in $250,000 mostly from small sums. It is to continue for 30 days, instead of finishing today, as planned." In April, the *Courier* lamented that "the campaign is not going as well as was expected" and that subscriptions totaled a mere $200,000. Nonetheless, since it remained "absolutely necessary," the administration planned to construct Dowling Memorial "at once" and during the summer to erect the new stadium, but with only the south grandstand. It also revised the fundraising schedule, establishing a $500,000 quota for the remainder of the year, with a similar goal for 1924, thus allowing construction of all the buildings. Thereafter, the campaign would seek the endowment funds.[14]

By June 1923, as donations barely trickled in, the Administration pondered, "What's the Matter with Omaha?" It complained that at "no time since the high water mark of the World War production, has our commercial machinery been so busily engaged as now. . . . And yet the merchants of Omaha are crying 'hard times' and 'no money.'" Recriminations abounded, but administrators refused "to attribute the lack of returns to mismanagement." Even students received blame "for being too easily satisfied," and for lacking "punch." Student leaders told their cohorts to strive to excel so that "in the achievement of a better Creighton, people cannot fail to see the need of a better one." On May 31, 1924, Fr. McCormick announced the failure of the campaign, which had subscribed a "little over $310,000" (less than one-fourth received), only $52,000 from outside Omaha. Naiveté on the part of the administration, in terms of the rudiments of solicitation, in terms of the amount of wealth it assumed the alumni possessed, and in terms of the stature it perceived the Catholic institution held in Protestant Omaha and Nebraska, contributed to the failure of the campaign. In perspective, however, fund drives at Boston College, Santa Clara, Fordham, and St. Louis University all foundered during the 1920s. Moreover, concerning the financial problems hindering the expansion of Catholic universities of the era,

Creighton's $2.3 million endowment stood second only to the $2.9 million of Catholic University (yet, both paled before the $98 million of Columbia or the $76 million of Harvard).[15]

The unproductive campaign, which failed to enlarge the endowment, capped a three-year discussion concerning undergraduate tuition. To generate some funds for the endowment-supported free undergraduate education, the College had long charged certain fees—the most notable covered science laboratory costs, and the activity fee helped offset expenses for athletics and other extracurricular events. The increasing number of undergraduate students, which necessitated an enlarged Jesuit community and the employment of lay teachers, sparked the addition of a $5 matriculation fee in 1921 ($10 for the pre-medical and pre-law students, who did not spend four years at the CCAS, but who made up a majority of its enrollment). Furthermore, as the budget announcements had revealed, tuition for the professional schools did not cover the actual costs of education, thus the endowment had to subsidize their expenses. The additional demands on the largely stagnant endowment, coupled with the failed drive, culminated in a three-tiered arts college tuition structure in 1924. Special students paid $3 per hour, those enrolled in the regular undergraduate course paid $25 per semester, and those in the pre-professional courses paid $37.50 per semester.[16]

Undaunted by the recent failure and mistakenly relying on promises, Fr. McCormick undertook a second fundraising drive in 1925. During the doldrums of the previous campaign, Fr. Corboy, chairman of the athletic committee, had attended the state convention of the Nebraska Knights of Columbus and had secured the organization's pledge to raise $250,000 to support building a $400,000 stadium that would seat thirty thousand. Forgetting the "absolute necessity" for the arts college building, in mid-March, Fr. McCormick orchestrated a "mass meeting" in the gymnasium, initiating a $160,000 campaign to secure the remaining un-pledged funds to construct a stadium. He encouraged students to buttress the endeavor by selling as many bags of cement, at a dollar each, as possible. The student newspaper "confidently predicted the sale of 10,000 bags; the result was $1011 in cash and $4,320 in pledges." Arbor Day, April 22, 1925, became a recreation day for the entire University in order to allow students to canvass the city to sell cement, with an equally dismal outcome. Not discouraged, the administration gave permission to proceed with construction on May 8. Unfortunately, the Knights of Columbus actually raised only $4,400 and the administration's fund drive fizzled. Subsequently, the Trustees had to issue $200,000 worth of bonds, bearing 6 percent interest, and $75,000 in second-mortgage bonds accepted by the contractors, to finance the construction.[17]

Sadly, the fundraising ventures ended with a scandal. In January 1926, the administration forced the resignation of P. H. Bogardus, the director of the Building and Endowment Association, and the director of publicity and advertising. He had collected $90,000 in the endowment drive and claimed as much as his expenses; he claimed ownership of a University camera and automobile, and allegedly falsely added a sentence to his contract which entitled him to 5 percent of the income of the drive. The results of the failed campaign became significantly worse. Some Jesuits grumbled, "Many of our men think it is a great defect in the Constitution of our Society to give a superior [rector-president] such absolute power. Our debt on the stadium is one-third million dollars." Apparently, reminiscent of the pastor-residence decision, Fr. McCormick initiated the construction of the stadium without seeking (or ignoring) the advice of his consultors. His decision realigned the priorities of the original building plan from academics to athletics and saddled the University with debilitating debt. Father McCormick's six-year presidency ended in 1925, and while overseeing noteworthy changes, his legacy remained contentious. A Jesuit chronicling his farewell dinner briefly related his accomplishments, but the thirty lines of narrative in the journal following the mention of the precipitating event of the financial scandal are unreadable; someone blackened them out with ink. Although assumptions can be dangerous, one may assume the editor did not conceal flattery.[18]

The Reverend William J. Grace, S.J., dean of the CCAS for the previous five years, succeeded to the presidency of the University in July 1925. The House Consultors, still seeking to position Creighton as an Omaha institution that the entire business community should support, encouraged a gala multiday inauguration, in order to promote the status of the school. The appointed committee mailed invitations to "5,000 universities, colleges, bishops, governors, etc. etc.[,] sixty-one institutions promised to send delegates." The committee filmed the entire event, subsequently showing the movie of the inaugural at alumni gatherings around the country. The first day (Thursday, November 19) began with a procession of about sixty priests and two bishops from the main entrance of the College Building to St. John's Church for a Pontifical Mass. It ended with a banquet at the Fontenelle Hotel, attended by about six hundred businessmen and politicians, which included a speech by the governor of Nebraska and a response by Fr. Grace. The second day included "a grand procession of all students, the ROTC in uniform, the sixty-five delegates from various institutions, the professors, etc.," for academic exercises in the gymnasium, at which time Fr. McCormick passed the keys to the University to Fr. Grace. That evening, the Dramatic Club presented *Charlie's Aunt* at the Creighton Auditorium. The third day of the event coincided with Homecoming, but it disappointed, as few alumni attended and the football team lost to the Haskell Indians, 7-16. Mayor James Dahlman's proclamation encouraging Omahans to attend the contest produced a disheartening crowd of only six thousand, less than half the seating capacity of the recently completed Creighton Stadium.[19]

Denied an outpouring of support, Fr. Grace confronted the problem immediately. He professionalized the publicity bureau, hiring an agent to "work on publicity in the city & state newspapers; also to arrange & list in [a] uniform way the large amount of cuts on hand [*sic*] for publicity; to act as financial secretary to our alumni after trying to get them to be more active." The first agent did not earn his keep, but alumnus Francis P. "Frank" Fogarty (A.B., 1926) soon brought vigor to the position, as well as serving as editor of the alumni magazine, debate coach, and a member of the summer school faculty. In 1929, Fogarty moved on to the Omaha Chamber of Commerce, but remained a staunch supporter of the University. Frank E. Pellegrin, editor of the school newspaper, replaced him (today, Pellegrin's name adorns the wall of the journalism department's laboratory).[20]

Subsequently, Fr. Grace also pushed the reorganization of the alumni. World War I had disrupted the all-University group and the individual school associations floundered during the early postwar years. In 1926, a Jesuit chronicler complained:

> The spirit of our alumni is well shown in this incident. For home-coming day on the 30th the medical alumni invited a doctor from Kansas City to come and give them a lecture. As they could not raise the honorarium among themselves, the two on the committee came to Rev. Fr. Rector to get Creighton University to foot the bill of $160. Fr. Rector declined. It then turned out that the doctor had said he would be satisfied with $100. The question now is, what about the $60? Yes, 'Creighton University is rich.' This is supposed to be a smart way of saying 'Please, excuse me from contributing.' The alumni as a class have never done anything. Even the life-insurance of five students in each department soon turned out to be a failure.

The classes of 1920 and 1922 reinstituted the prewar program of 25 students each subscribing to a $1,000, twenty-year life insurance policy, with the university named the beneficiary. Seemingly, the students did not continue to pay their premiums.[21]

On November 16, 1926, the administration prompted a meeting hosted by arts college alumni to discuss reviving the pan-alumni association. A second meeting on December 14 produced a new constitution, as well as a recommendation that the *Creighton Courier* become a magazine "devoted entirely to the interests of the Alumni and be placed on a subscription basis." The new year witnessed the journal's demise and the birth of a new publication for alumni, the *Creighton Alumnus,* which cost $2 per year, but circulation remained "small" for years to come. The new constitution maintained the Alumni Council elected at Homecoming, but established a new electoral system. The council acted as the nominating committee for officers and mailed ballots to all alumni. To avoid rivalry, the system established a rotation of officers by schools, based on seniority of the college. Thus, for the first election in 1927, candidates for president came from the oldest school, the arts college; candidates for vice president from the medical school, and in subsequent years the other schools, in order of their founding, would provide the candidates. Frank McDermott (A.B., 1914; LL.B., 1916) became the first president and Dr. J. Frederick Langdon (M.D., 1904) gained the vice presidency. They established a budget of $5,000 for the 1927–28 academic year and solicited fifty "key men" to canvass Omaha to secure pledges. This drive, too, fell woefully short.[22]

While the new Alumni Council struggled to become effective, Fr. Grace instituted another unity device, the all-University convocation, held in the gymnasium, at which he addressed the students. Quickly, the "general assemblies" became semiannual, attendance became mandatory, and prominent speakers addressed the students. As a sign of the times (the era of prohibition), at the fall convocation of 1927, Fr. Grace "issued a vigorous manifesto against the evil of drinking." Moreover, Fr. Grace expanded the scope of control over student activities. The recently created student newspaper, the *Creightonian*, included an editorial critical of a presidential action. Father Grace expelled the editor, law freshman Milton Abrahams (today, his name graces the Law School Legal Clinic). Eventually, the two reached a compromise, by which Fr. Grace reinstated Abrahams, who in turn agreed to allow the president to review his editorials before publication (later in life, he chuckled at his acquiescence in the abridgment of the First Amendment). While the episode unfolded, the Reverend Provincial Mathew Germing, S.J., ordered faculty oversight of student publications. Father Grace replaced the ad hoc arrangement with the appointment of Jesuit censors for the newspaper, the yearbook, and the literary magazine, *Shadows*. Within months, the Administration also issued "dance rules," which mandated faculty sanction for all student-sponsored mixers, as well as creating a University certification system for off-campus student housing.[23]

In 1928, Fr. Grace undertook another disappointing publicity event, the celebration of Creighton University's fiftieth anniversary. An ad hoc executive committee conferred with the Reverend Daniel A. Lord, S.J. (subsequently, the nationally known director of the Legion of Decency, which pressured Hollywood to eliminate sex and violence from feature films), to write a pageant to be staged for five nights during the second week of December, which would serve as the "heart of the celebration." The spectacle did not materialize; instead, the occasion became a Homecoming-Jubilee celebrated in October. Again, the "attendance of the alumni" failed to meet expectations, although fifty institutions sent representatives to the three-day event, which included the conferring of three honorary Doctor of Law degrees to Nebraska literary lights John Neihardt and Willa Cather, and to Creighton alumnus Fr. John B. Furay, S.J., former president of Loyola University, Chicago, and John Carroll University. Homecoming Day included a barbeque lunch at the gymnasium, a football defeat at the hands of the University of Oklahoma (0–7), and a banquet and ball attended by a substandard crowd of only 450 people.[24]

Despite a second less-than-satisfactory publicity, fundraising, alumni-activating event, Fr. Grace proceeded with a major construction project, something new and not associated with the failed development program. While planning the golden jubilee, he and the House Consultors discussed erecting a building as a memorial to the event. They identified wealthy Catholics who could finance the structure—a faculty building, or a commerce college, or a high school at a non-campus location. Father Grace appealed to prospective donors to no avail. He also appealed to Fr. Provincial Germing for funds; the latter suggested, but did not mandate, closing the high school and using the savings to finance a new building. Father Grace and the consultors disregarded the suggestion. They decided on a new faculty building "located somewhere on campus probably west of the Observatory" and on converting the Jesuit residences (the south wing) into classroom space; they hired architect Leo Daly, Sr. (A.B., 1911), to do a feasibility study. Despite lamenting the contradiction that the lack "of financial means alone prevents the University from making further and rapid advances in the scope and variety of courses offered," Fr. Grace decided on a major renovation and expansion of the Administration Building.[25]

Father Grace and Leo Daly, Sr., traveled to Chicago and Detroit to inspect buildings to get ideas. With the approval of Fr. Provincial Germing and Fr. General Ledochowski, the administration let bids for two projects, subsequently awarding the contracts to A. Borchman & Sons. At that point, in 1928, the Reverend William Agnew, S.J., president of St. Ignatius College (subsequently Loyola University) in Chicago, became the fifteenth rector-president of Creighton University (Fr. Grace left for Marquette University to become dean of its arts college). Soon a new heating plant began to rise on the north edge of campus, just west of the gymnasium, with its entrance facing Burt Street (today's Markoe Building). Constructed at a cost of $130,000 the facility housed two three-hundred-horsepower boilers with overhead hoppers that automatically fed coal to the fires to produce the steam that heated all the buildings on campus. The power plant also contained a carpenter shop, living quarters for the engineer and his workmen, and additional locker rooms and showers for the athletic teams. Steam began pumping the first week of October 1930, and the plant's 160-foot tall, concrete, smoke-belching chimney stood as the tallest such spire in the downtown area.[26]

Simultaneously, workmen reconfigured the Administration Building and added a 78-foot eastward extension to the south wing. A five-story central tower connected the old and new segments of the Jesuit residences and it became the new California Street entrance to the College (the cupola above the old east entrance was removed, an unstylish beacon of yore). The tower contained a central lobby with three first-floor corridors—one leading west to the existing administrative offices, one leading east to new offices, parlors, refectory, and kitchen, and one ushering students north into the college and the high school. The second floor of the new addition included a common room, a Jesuit library, and a chapel; Jesuit residences occupied the remaining floors. On the exterior, the entire 190-foot sweep of the new California front of the Administration Building became an elegant seamless art deco façade. The new building was constructed with Bedford stone, ornamental terra cotta, and aluminum spandrels between the windows, carved with emblems of Creighton University, Catholic symbolisms, and scenes of Nebraska agricultural activity. The existing red brick west extension of the south wing received a veneer of the same materials, tying the old and new structures together and giving them an architectural symmetry.[27]

The original College Building and the north wing underwent renovation. The basement, with steam pipes removed and relocated to underground tunnels, became the new first floor with appropriate stone flooring, new lighting, and new offices and classrooms. The walls separating the college and high school sections of the library came down, doubling the size of the college library, while the old student chapel in the north wing became the high school library. Moreover, two new classrooms were reconfigured from other existing space in the north wing and the old lavatory in the basement disappeared, replaced by four new facilities, one on each floor. Finally, the steps to the old east entrance came down, replaced by a ground-level door (old basement level, today's first floor; that is why you see the Loyola family crest in the terrazzo floor outside the dean's office on today's second floor). The renovation, the eastward south-wing extension, and the power plant (plus new lights for the stadium) cost $375,000. The new Administration Building looked stylish, but it did little to ameliorate the space needs of the high school and CCAS. It made a significant statement in terms of the burgeoning number of administrators and the need for office and meeting space, but the expanded Jesuit residences housed fewer members of the Society than a decade earlier. The House chroniclers did not record the decision-making process, which for a second time in a handful of years ignored the number one publicly stated priority—a new building for the arts college. Moreover, in 1928, the year of the decision, Bishop Joseph Rummel converted O'Connor Hall (used as a Creighton dorm since 1916) into the Omaha Archdiocese Chancery, rendering "the dormitory congestion even more acute." Finally, the principle of unintended consequences ensued—the edifice may have made a counter-productive statement. The administration had campaigned to convince the public and the alumni that the University's endowment barely covered expenses. Yet without a capital campaign, it erected a facility with one of the most elegant art deco exteriors in the city. The new Administration Building may have reinforced the "wealthy Creighton" myth the administrators wished to dispel and contributed to the failure of subsequent fundraising appeals.[28]

The inaugural of the new Administration Building coincided with Creighton's hosting the sixth National Eucharistic Congress, which sought to strengthen congregants' commitment to the Catholic Church through lectures, seminars, discussion groups, processions, and benedictions. The administration set up altars in classrooms so visiting clergy could celebrate daily Mass, and American flags and the papal colors adorned the campus. The Priests' Eucharistic League held its business meetings in the auditorium and received lunch daily in the gymnasium, medical students staffed first-aid tents on campus and at the Aksarben race track, and classes were suspended at all Catholic schools, including Creighton University, so students could participate in the three-day event. On September 24, seating at the stadium tripled with the installation of temporary bleachers and ten thousand folding chairs donated by businessmen. Crews erected a 50-x-90-foot platform at the fifty-yard line and an estimated forty to sixty thousand people packed the facility to participate in the Holy Name Society rally and to receive the benediction from George Cardinal Mundelein.[29]

Unfortunately, Fr. Agnew lived to enjoy the new Administration Building and the success of the Congress for only a few months, succumbing at the age of forty-nine to cancer, on February 13, 1931. During his presidency, Fr. Agnew did not maintain the House Consultors Minute Book, last entry dated July 23, 1928, and during his illness, compilation of the *Historia Domas* ceased on May 1, 1930. Thus, within three years of the death of Fr. Rigge, all three primary accounts of the history of Creighton University ceased. Windows to the past closed, and historians lost the forthright discussions of the operation of the Jesuit community and the institution. The Reverend Eugene P. Mullaney, S.J., the superintendent of buildings and grounds, became the acting president. His month-long tenure ended with the appointment of the Reverend Patrick J. Mahan, S.J., for the past thirteen years regent to the schools of medicine and nursing at Loyola University, Chicago. Father Mahan immediately complained that the low tuition "barely pays the salaries of the lay faculty" and that "he could mention no bequests or sizeable gifts to Creighton during the past year." Regrettably, his poor health made the transition disconcerting. During 1932, he successfully hosted the National Conference of Catholic Charities; its fifteen hundred delegates held their general session in the gymnasium, as well as two public pep rallies that filled the building. Thereafter, however, he suffered several months of debilitating illness, forcing him to spend "some weeks" in St. Joseph's Hospital. The Reverend Thomas J. Smith, S.J., a native of Omaha and 1896 Creighton College graduate, previous president of John Carroll University, and a member of the Creighton faculty since 1928, became acting president. Father Mahan returned to his position in February 1933, to deal with the depth of the Great Depression.[30]

The monetary reforms of Franklin Roosevelt's New Deal deflated the value of the dollar 40 percent, and a stagnant enrollment meant a huge loss of revenue. Furthermore, the endowment suffered heavy losses due to suspended mortgage payments or foreclosures. At the 1934 Commencement, Fr. Mahan "denied again the unfounded belief that Creighton is a wealthy institution" and he revived the campaign to convince Omaha of the value of the University to the city. Besides the standard arguments that stressed the economic and athletic impacts, he emphasized that Creighton educated students to resist "the numerous 'isms' that plague our world [fascism and communism]," that its clinics provided $250,000 in charity per annum, and that it gave "relief and assistance to taxpayers." The last point referred to the fact that the formerly private Omaha University had recently become a municipal entity.[31]

To provide another source for support, Fr. Mahan encouraged the formation of the Creighton Women's Club in 1933, "to assist in the activities of the university students, to promote social programs, to draw attention to the university as an educational, cultural and charitable center, and to raise funds for the support of its numerous charities." Mrs. Adolph Sachs, wife of a 1907 medical school graduate, became the first president and appealed to the mothers, wives, sisters, and daughters of alumni, faculty, and non-sectarian friends of the University to join and pay the $1 per year dues. By the end of the academic year, the group sponsored its first fundraiser, the May Musicale, the first all-University concert (orchestra, band, glee club), held at the recently renamed Omaha Central High School Auditorium (bespeaking the deteriorating condition of the Creighton Auditorium).[32]

Father Mahan also oversaw yet another reorganization of the Alumni Association. In 1931, the Alumni Council employed a full-time secretary (heretofore the publicity director had handled that chore) and began to appoint a secretary for each graduating class, who assumed the task of recruiting dues-paying members. They sought to enlist two thousand members from the six thousand alumni. The next year, the Council abandoned the $2-per-year dues (subscription cost of the *Creighton Alumnus*); Fr. Mahan supported the creation of the Alumni Loyalty Fund with an editorial entitled, "Alumni—cast aside this lack of interest in Creighton." The rector-president wished no longer to be "compelled to assume the annual deficit incurred by the alumni office."

The new annual drive, however, also failed to generate meaningful contributions, as few alumni gave few dollars. The alumni rejected the idea of returning to dues, but as of September 30, 1936, the aggregate totals consisted of 1,095 donors who pledged $9,895.50 (an average of $9.04 per person). The following year, the council advertised, "the money is raised by the alumni, controlled by the alumni and spent by the alumni." The records reveal no specific disagreement(s) with the administration, but the verbiage seemingly indicated that the Alumni Council perceived the need to establish autonomy—to no avail, the fundraising results remained dismal.[33]

Despite the financial problems, Fr. Mahan completed three significant capital projects during his tenure. In 1933, St. John's Dormitory received a $40,000 remodeling and a new name, Wareham Hall, in honor of the sisters who had married Edward and John Creighton. The L-shaped building, now reserved for freshmen, had its entry moved to California Street and obtained a new cafeteria and lounges, as well as having its rooms updated. The next year, the University converted two brick apartment houses it owned on the southeast corner of 25th and California streets into Dowling Hall, a dormitory for upperclassmen. For $37,500, Leo Daly, Sr., designed, and Philip McCardle constructed, a new building that connected the two existing flats and remodeled the old structures into twenty-nine single and twelve double rooms, plus lounges and recreation areas. They also built a softball field and two tennis courts on the adjacent land. Finally, in 1935, Fr. Mahan had the Creighton Auditorium renovated. The employment of existing Creighton maintenance staff and student laborers kept the costs to a minimum. They moved the back wall of the building fifteen feet north to abut against a service facility. The addition allowed for a larger backstage area and more dressing rooms.[34]

Father Mahan's six-year tenure ended unceremoniously at dinner on May 18, 1937. After the first course in the refectory, a reader revealed the contents of a letter from Fr. General Ledochowski appointing the Reverend Joseph P. Zuercher, S.J., the new rector-president of Creighton University. Father Mahan and Fr. Zuercher exchanged places at the table. At age thirty-nine, Fr. Zuercher became the youngest president in the school's history. He had taught at the St. Francis Mission High School on the Rosebud Indian Reservation in South Dakota and had helped organize Camp de Smet, "a western camp for eastern boys," on the reservation in 1925. He came to Creighton in 1932 as "dean of residence halls" and became dean of the CCAS the following year. In a state-of-the-University address in January 1938, Fr. Zuercher stated that the medical and pharmacy schools needed to be separated and that both needed new facilities. Moreover, the high school, the arts college, and the library needed more space, the Auditorium was "outmoded and inadequate," and since two thirds of the students came from outside Omaha another dormitory became a prime concern. Unfortunately, he proclaimed, the endowment produced "an income so slender as to be no help at all in this situation." He had guided the arts college during the depths of the Great Depression; he understood the gravity of the economic situation. Realistically, he stated, "These troubles, however, even if they give a new president gray hairs are 'cheerful troubles.' They are not a death agony. They are growing pains."[35]

With inadequate dormitory space, Fr. Zuercher went beyond simply generating a roster of approved rental units; he listed rules of conduct enforceable by the landlords. The guidelines issued in 1938 included no visitors of the opposite sex in private rooms, opposite-sex visitations in parlors must end at 11:30 P.M., same-sex visitations must end by 1:30 A.M., and "students may not be absent from their rooms overnight without consent of the dean of men." Moreover, without special permission, no student could reside east of 24th Street (considered "blighted") and all freshmen had to room in Wareham Hall.[36]

Father Zuercher also attacked the financial exigency. In 1939, he reorganized the board of regents. Two of the three members of the dormant board resigned and he appointed seven new members: W. J. Coad, president of Omar Inc., the lone holdover; W. M. Jeffers, president of the Union Pacific Railroad; D. B. Woodyard, Omaha manager of the J. C. Penney store; William Diesing, vice president of Cudahy Packing Company; Francis P. Matthews, an attorney; Dr. Adolph Sachs, head of the Creighton Medical School; W. D. Hosford, vice president of the John Deere Company; and A. A. Lowman, president of Northwestern Bell Telephone Company. He divided the board into four committees—finance, public relations, athletics, and medicine—but no records exist to reveal how well they functioned. Furthermore, Fr. Zuercher appropriated the failed Loyalty Fund from the Alumni Council. In 1940, he initiated the first annual Loyalty Appeal, but it suffered the same dreary result. A dejected rector-president revealed, "An undeniable and distressing fact . . . is that the alumni are not responding to the Annual Loyalty Appeal in sufficient numbers to insure its success." By the end of the year, about five hundred alumni out of sixty-five hundred or 13 percent, donated only $5,100.[37] Shortly thereafter, World War II erupted, loyalty appeals came in the form of government war bonds, and two decades of University fundraising came to an inglorious end. Although the administration made significant strides in professionalization and added the stadium, a dormitory, and the power plant, as well as an impressive new wing to the thoroughly renovated Administration Building, compared to the 1922 plan for "The New Creighton University," it had merely "marked time."[37]

The faculty of the arts college experienced a similar evolution. During the interwar years, the distinctiveness of the American situation and the American educational model continued their agonizing pressure for change; reluctantly, the Jesuit system continued to adapt. In 1921, a "Memorial of the Visitation of the Missouri Province" declared, "the primary end of our [Jesuit] colleges is to imbue the minds of boys and young men with solid and manly piety." Catholic seminaries reinforced the approach by isolating their students from American social and academic attitudes. The Reverend Charles Carroll, S.J., a reform activist, who favored molding the American model of education to Jesuit values, blamed the slow pace of change on "our ultra-conservative scholastics." Ultimately, Jesuit education continued to face the dilemma of all ethnic and religious minorities in the United States—how much acculturation can they absorb, how much can they assimilate and remain themselves? Ethnic endogamy succumbed relatively easily and produced the mythical American

Melting Pot; interracial and interfaith marriages, however, remain problematic—what will the progeny become? Thus, how could the American and Jesuit educational models merge—would the outcome still be Jesuit and Catholic? In terms of undergraduate faculty, the questions manifested themselves in issues such as the nature of academic training for Jesuits and the employment of laymen as faculty, especially non-Catholic laymen. Because of the necessary credentials, the dilemma presented itself differently in the professional schools. Laymen had always staffed them and non-Catholics played a small but significant role.[38]

In 1921, in comparison to the religion-oriented "Memorial" above, the newly organized IPCS recommended that Jesuits seek the Ph.D. degree in order to enhance the status of their universities and to create doctoral-granting graduate schools in order to produce Ph.D. lay Catholics who could teach at Catholic universities. Between 1900–1919, only eleven members of the Missouri Province had earned Ph.D. degrees, only one from a secular university. In 1932, the editor of the Jesuit journal *America* grumbled that he could not publish articles by his coreligious, because they "generally speaking, show a great lack of acquaintance with recent books in the fields of literature and philosophy, and for this reason their contributions often fail to meet present needs." During the 1920s, few Jesuits outside the Missouri Province sought the Ph.D. degree, while twenty-three from that province obtained one, thirteen from secular universities. In 1931, the Jesuit Commission on Higher Studies "urgently recommended" a program of study whereby the Ph.D. became "their normal goal." That same year, the Reverend George A. Deglman, S.J. (Ph.D., Marquette, 1916), came to Creighton as professor of philosophy and dean of the CCAS, becoming the first member of the Society in the College holding the terminal degree. The following year, the Reverend Leo H. Mullany, S.J. (Ph.D., Fordham, 1931), joined the staff as professor of English and director of the department, and in 1933, the Reverend Louis F. Doyle, S.J. (Ph.D., Fordham, 1932), assistant professor of English, who had taught at Creighton since 1927, finished his degree work. The Reverend Thomas Bowdern, S.J., associate professor of education, took a leave of absence and finished his Ph.D. at St. Louis University in 1936, becoming the final Jesuit at Creighton during the interwar years to possess the elite degree.[39]

Ph.D. or not, Jesuits could not fulfill staffing needs as college enrollment mushroomed during the 1920s. Therefore, the number of lay teachers in their arts colleges burgeoned during the interwar years. The vast majority of the laymen were Catholics; as late as 1940, only about 7 percent of the lay faculty members at American Jesuit colleges did not profess the faith. While they maintained the correct beliefs, few of them held the Ph.D. degree, since few congregants of the era sought it. Nonetheless, the employment of laymen, especially non-Catholics, produced controversy. In 1927, a group of American Catholics protested that American Jesuit universities in the United States had strayed from the faith by hiring Protestants, Jews, and atheists, and that "Jesuits exercised practically no influence on the spiritual and religious welfare of the students." Father General Ledochowski investigated, and the following year issued directives to minimize the number of non-Catholic students and teachers and to forbid the employment of non-Catholic deans. Nevertheless, the shortage of Jesuits required hiring increasing numbers of lay teachers (limiting enrollment to a level at which only Jesuits taught classes would have forced even more Catholics to attend secular schools), but their role remained problematic. As late as 1948, Jesuit administrators barred lay faculty from participating in a national conference to discuss curriculum at their institutions.[40] Although Jesuits needed laymen to teach, they obviously did not believe that even Catholic laymen possessed sufficient understanding of the mission to help them determine the course of study.

Lay Catholics had taught at the arts college from its founding, but until after World War I, their numbers had remained few and most had taught ancillary courses part time. In 1921, an article in the *Creighton Alumnus* incorrectly asserted that only Jesuits taught in the arts college. Actually, the author of that story slighted nine laymen, probably part-time, but carrying the titles of instructor, assistant professor, or professor, teaching modern foreign languages, music, public speaking, chemistry, and physical training during the 1920–21 academic year. Due to increasing enrollment, in 1926, the school employed ten full-time and six part-time laymen, with plans to hire three more the following year. The 1926 lay faculty included the first Ph.Ds on the College's staff: Dr. Charles Felix Crowley (who also held the degrees of Pharmaceutical Chemist and M.D.), professor of chemistry, and Dr. Aloysius A. Klammer, professor of modern languages. From that date, the number of lay faculty, including those with a Ph.D., increased significantly. A 1928 diary entry revealed, "Fr. Rector went in quest of Ph. D professors to Lafayette, Ind.— Detroit—&c.," seemingly the search included secular state universities. Despite the prominence of laymen, under the title of "Arts Professors," the 1926 yearbook only printed the picture of Jesuits (the editors corrected the omission the following year, picturing eleven Jesuits and ten laymen).[41]

In 1925, the College received its first endowed chair, a position in theology funded through a bequest from James Murphy, "the biggest hog speculator in the country & world, & a resident for years of So. Omaha." Properly invested, the administration expected "the income at 5% being $1,250.00[,] enough to pay the salary of such a professor." Moreover, during the era, two laywomen, who possessed master's degrees, spent a year each at the College—Kathleen Cecilia Fields, instructor of elementary education (1931), and Dorothy Abts, lecturer in social work (1933). The Commission on Higher Studies, in 1931, had recommended "that the choice of lay professors for our faculties in any rank above that of instructor fall hereafter only on Doctors recognized for their scholarship." The shortage of Catholics with the doctorate, the low salary scale, and the financial exigencies produced by the Great Depression doomed that goal during the interwar era. However, during the 1930s, as a step in the right direction, the presidents of St. Louis and Creighton universities subsidized the graduate education of a few Catholic laymen, and then hired them. By 1940, the number of arts college faculty nearly doubled and the number of lay faculty (twenty-nine total, ten with the Ph.D.) far outstripped the number of Jesuits (seventeen total, four with the Ph.D.).[42]

With or without the terminal degree, in the interest of maintaining accreditation and building status for the colleges, the Commission on Higher Studies also encouraged all faculty members to pursue scholarship and to participate in the national associations of their various disciplines. Minus a sophisticated research library, extensive science laboratories, and a travel budget, few faculty members could heed the call. Moreover, the degree and/or research and publication did not seen to correlate with faculty title. Before 1920, all Jesuit teachers carried the title of professor; subsequently, without explanation or printed guidelines, the administration instituted a rank system, using the designations instructor, assistant professor, associate professor and professor. During the interwar era, no pattern of degree held, publications, or length of service seems to relate to the title granted (seemingly by the rector-president, possibly with advice from the Trustees). In 1925, Fr. President McCormick undertook the first faculty evaluation, a one-time event. He distributed a questionnaire to students who complained that some Jesuits criticized each other in classes, and that some were "overbearing, others aloof and distant," while many would not "tolerate an opposite opinion." His motive for the survey remains a mystery; his successor did not repeat the experiment, but in 1931, the Commission on Higher Studies recommended establishing "definite norms for appointment, tenure and promotion." At the time, the administration did not publish standards. Finally, in 1939, without printed guidelines, it created a rank and tenure committee for the undergraduate schools, consisting of three Jesuit administrators. At that time, however, it was unclear that the term tenure meant a granting of lasting employment. The American Association of University Professors, formed in 1915, promoted the idea of tenure as related to "professional security of faculty members." In 1940, it chose Creighton as one of two representatives of Catholic universities with enrollment between one and two thousand for its study of tenure. The report, however, presented only aggregate data, and the author used the term "tenure" in the connotation of years of service, not as a granted status of secure employment. Thus, the nature of rank and tenure at Creighton before World War II remains inexplicable. On the other hand, the stature of some existing lay faculty in the arts college rose in 1932, as six of them gained the title of department director—Alvin Bettinger, mathematics; Leo V. Jacks, Ph.D., classical languages; Aloysius Klammer, Ph.D., modern languages; Christopher L. Kenny, Ph.D., chemistry; William A. Kelly, Ph.D., education; and Gregor Pirsch, biology.[43]

While few arts college faculty established national renown, locally many contributed their expertise to two outreach ventures. The Speakers' Bureau established in 1932, provided lecturers to civic groups. Also, use of the new medium of radio had exploded during the 1920s. As early as 1922, it provided entertainment for the Jesuits: "The fathers sitting on the front lawn during recreation after dinner (7 P.M.) were regaled by radio music and speeches coming from the Daily News, Mr. Perk [a scholastic] having put the Magnavox in the window of the physical cabinet. These radio concerts are quite common now and ever so many antennae may be seen on the roofs of houses." By the standards of Fr. Provincial McMenamy, the Creighton

Jesuits abused another of the modern entertainments, watching a movie per week. Also in 1922, the administration purchased "a moveable moving picture machine to be used in the various buildings and departments for educational purposes." Obviously, Fr. McMenamy believed his flock received too much "education" during their recreation time and dictated that Hollywood movies become *admodum rarum*, "this interpreted as only once a month." However, as the administration had used film to promote the University, it also immediately adopted radio as a public-relations tool. In 1922, it sponsored a series of twelve faculty lectures broadcast over WAAW, the station of the Omaha Grain Exchange, at 8:00 P.M. on Thursdays. In 1925, the schedule expanded as station KOIL, then located in Council Bluffs, Iowa, became "the air voice of Creighton University," broadcasting its football and basketball games, musicals, plays, and "other contests or exhibitions." The following year, station WOW (Woodman of the World) in Omaha, received the broadcast rights, but in 1931, KOIL re-obtained them for the remainder of the era. The administration created a studio on the fifth floor of the tower of the Administration Building and began transmitting daily fifteen-minute programs for rebroadcast. In 1935, the "Creighton University of the Air" appointed five student announcers, including Mary Ellen Martin, the first coed radio personality. Moreover, the American Assistancy of the Society of Jesus chose March 23, 1941 (the anniversary of the planting of the colony of Maryland), as a day of celebration marking the four hundredth anniversary of the founding of the Order. The ceremonies included a national radio broadcast that included speeches by three Creighton graduates—Francis P. Mathews, Omaha attorney and Supreme Knight of the Knights of Columbus; Thomas Smith, general counsel for the General Motors Corporation; and James H. Furay, vice president of the United Press.[44]

While the Speakers' Bureau and "the Creighton University of the Air" integrated the arts college faculty into the larger institution and into the Omaha community, the administration also continued to promote faculty unity by hosting all-University informal "faculty smokers" (an extension of the nineteenth-century Jesuit "jollifications"), as well as adding six formal all-University faculty meetings per semester. Moreover, an all-University faculty banquet remained the hallmark of Founders' Day, moved to November 5 in 1929 (the anniversary of Edward Creighton's death). Subsequently, the administration switched the celebration to the first week of December (the anniversary of the transfer of the property of Creighton College and the Creighton Trust from the Bishop of Omaha to the Missouri Province) in 1937, at which time it began honoring faculty for twenty-five years of service. Four of the twenty charter honorees came from the arts college—Fr. Corboy, assistant professor of classics; the Reverend Alfred Kaufmann, S.J., professor of history; the Reverend William Leahy, S.J., associate professor of philosophy; and the Reverend Francis S. Reilly, S.J., professor of English, actually in his thirty-fifth year. Father Kaufmann, who died in 1941, had coauthored *The Modern World From Charlemagne to Present Time* (1919), a text used in a majority of Catholic high schools in the United States, and had written *Modern Europe* (1930); at alumni meetings, he continually garnered the "most remembered teacher" declarations, and in 1928, the students had dedicated the yearbook to him.[45]

An equally popular colleague, Fr. William Rigge, S.J., had celebrated his anniversary of twenty-five years of consecutive service in 1921. He was the first person with that many years of service, actually his twenty-eighth at Creighton, since he had taught as a scholastic from 1878 to 1881. He died at age sixty-nine, "just after sundown" on March 30, 1927, in "a bare little room in St. Joseph's hospital," felled by a lung disorder that had plagued him for a decade. His prominence brought him an entry in the prestigious Dictionary of American Biography, published eight years after his passing. In 1928, another pioneer, who replaced Fr. Rigge as the longest-serving Jesuit, the Reverend William Whelan, S.J., left Creighton after twenty-seven years of teaching elocution and holding several administrative positions. One other standout Jesuit of the era inexplicably did not receive a twenty-five-year plaque. Father Francis Cassilly came to Creighton University in 1913, and five years later founded St. Benedict's Mission to the Negroes of Omaha serving as its pastor for fourteen years. In 1923, he purchased an old Methodist Episcopal church for the mission and started a school in it. In 1925, the bishop "commended to the Jesuits the welfare of the Negroes"; three years later, Fr. Cassilly held a bazaar and fundraiser at the Creighton gymnasium, which raised $3,800 toward building a mission school. He taught education in the arts college until 1926, religion in the high school until 1928, and from 1929 until his death, he served as a University Trustee. Father Cassilly died of heart disease on October 1, 1938; his passing marked the end of an era of transformation for the faculty of the arts college. Jesuits had become a minority in the institution they created, and henceforth the vast majority of twenty-five-year honorees would be laymen.[46]

Obviously during the interwar years, as the administration and the faculty evolved into their contemporary forms, changes in the nature of the CCAS also affected students. Under the new "American Plan," the College continued to offer the A.B., B.S., Ph.B., and B.S. Med. degrees, plus the pre-legal plan, which did not confer an undergraduate degree. In 1922, the College introduced the B.S. Dent. degree that consisted of the same requirements followed by students in the pre-medical program. Three years later, it initiated a 3-3 arts-law plan in which undergraduates completed the required core of arts classes and used law school classes as their electives to receive an A.B. and LL.B. In 1926, a similar joint-degree program appeared in conjunction with the medical school, but the registrar did not indicate the conferring of any such degrees. Probably the administration invented the degrees to entice students to study the "sadly neglected" liberal arts. As one Creighton commentator lamented, "From this neglect it is evident that the A.B. course is not considered of very much importance by the American student of today. He is not willing to spend his valuable time in an unprofitable pursuit. He must rush through some professional course, rent an office, and become rich." The actual degrees conferred during the era highlight the disenchantment:

	1920	1940
A.B.	9	10
Ph.B.	2	11
B.S. Med.	18	29
B.S. Dent.		1
B.S.		9[47]

The course of study for the various degrees differed slightly, but each contained a sizeable prescribed core. For the A.B., students had to take a minimum of sixteen hours each in Latin, philosophy, and a modern language, twelve hours in English, eight hours each in science and evidence of religion (Catholic students only), and six hours each in mathematics and history. While Greek was no longer mandatory, students could substitute it for hours in mathematics or history. Actually, the "outline of courses" for the Bachelor of Arts listed ninety-seven hours of prescribed classes, leaving only thirty-one hours of electives permissible during the junior and senior years combined (throughout the era some Jesuits continued to argue for the reintroduction of the *Ratio Studiorum*). The B.S. program allowed for more electives because it eliminated the Latin requirement, but necessitated sixteen hours in science. The Ph.B. degree permitted the greatest flexibility, because it maintained only six hours of required science, while excusing the student from Latin. Finally, as of 1923, regardless of the degree sought, all undergraduate males had to join the Reserve Officers Training Corps (ROTC) during their freshman and sophomore years (thus, it included all the two-year pre-professionals), which added four hours to the core (one hour of credit per semester).[48]

The "American Plan" also introduced the concept of majors and minors, as mechanisms that allowed a semblance of specialization in undergraduate study. The program established three groups of related disciplines:

GROUP I	GROUP II	GROUP III
English	Economics	Astronomy
French	Education	Biology
German	History	Chemistry
Greek	Philosophy	Mathematics
Latin	Political Science	Physics
Public Speaking	Sociology	
Spanish		

In 1926, Fr., Rigge's illness and subsequent death eliminated astronomy from the major-minor grouping; the following year, the economics faculty moved to the commerce college, but the discipline remained open to arts students; and in 1934, religion joined Group II. A candidate for the A.B. had to complete one major by taking eighteen hours in one of the departments listed in Group I or II, the Ph.B. candidate selected from Group II and the B.S. candidate from Group III. All degree candidates had to chose two minors, consisting of twelve semester hours: a "correlated minor" in a department listed in the same group as his major and a "free or unrestricted minor" from another group. Moreover, students had to select all electives from classes offered in their major and minors.[49]

The "American Plan" eliminated the traditional Jesuit pedagogy whereby one instructor taught all subjects to a class. During the nineteenth century, demands for courses in areas such as business methods, the fine arts and the sciences had necessitated specialists, lay professionals or specially trained Jesuits, to teach in those areas (e.g, Fr. William Rigge only taught physics and astronomy to the various grade levels). The new course of study, however, demanded specialization throughout and precipitated the organization of the faculty by departments. The arts college became one of the first Jesuit institutions in the United States to implement such an organization, creating departments of

Astronomy	Geology	Philosophy
Biology	German	Physical Education
Chemistry	Greek	Physics
Economics	History	Political Science
Education	Latin	Public Speaking
English	Mathematics	Sociology
Evidences of Religion	Military Science & Tactics	Spanish
French		

In 1922, a new department of expression appeared, which taught "expressive movement" and the "philosophy of expression" ("significance of voice and body; relationship of voice and body to health"). The next year, it became part of the department of public speaking, shortly thereafter renamed the speech department, administered as part of the English department. Similarly, the history department administered the political science program. In 1925, the department of library methods (changed to department of bibliography) and the Czech (Bohemian) department began. The latter highlighted the increasing significance of students whose parents had recently migrated from southern and eastern Europe. The following year, the Administration reorganized the language structure, creating Classics (Greek, Latin, Czech) and Modern Languages (French, German, Spanish, and subsequently Czech).[50]

Moreover, in 1921, the "ever-increasing number of students desiring courses in biology [impact of the B.S. Med. degree] necessitated the removal of the department to quarters in the New College of Dentistry." Students and faculty obtained adjoining laboratories on the first floor and located the aquarium (fish, frogs, etc. needed for dissection) in the basement, although the "animal house" remained on the first floor of the Administration Building. In 1931, at the behest of Fr. President Agnew, a physicist, the physics department, still located on the third floor of the north wing of the Administration Building, received "about $15,000 worth of equipment and general scientific facilities for the students." In comparison, psychology did not exist as a separate department during the interwar years, though the philosophy department taught a few related classes (e.g., in 1935, it offered four classes titled Sense, Rational, Dynamic, and Social Psychology). Finally, in 1938, the Catholic interest in social service and social justice led to the creation of a social-science major, consisting of forty-eight hours distributed among the departments of economics, history and political science, and sociology.[51]

Another area of burgeoning interest, physical education, also restructured itself to meet contemporary demands. By the 1930s, most states had passed laws requiring the teaching of physical education at all levels in the public schools. Thus, the arts college reorganized its department to prepare students "to become directors of School Athletics and Physical Education." Moreover, the popularity of the extracurricular music ensembles prompted a call for the establishment of a college of music. The dream did not become reality, but in 1929, the administration did create a department of fine arts by arranging for art appreciation classes through the Art Institute of Omaha. The onset of the Great Depression terminated that modest program and thereafter stifled all attempts to add programs in the fine and performing arts. Despite those setbacks, in comparison to the attrition in the number of classes taught at many of the premier private and public universities in the United States during the 1930s, the CCAS maintained a steady growth in its course offerings. A sampling of the number of classes listed reveals

	1922–23	1938–39
Biology	4	21
Chemistry	7	20
English	16	59
History	10	47
Mathematics	11	23
Sociology	4	22

Obviously, the departments did not offer all the classes every semester. The list, however, demonstrated an interesting phenomenon. Many institutions employing the elective system, which spawned a profusion of specialized courses necessitating a huge faculty, subsequently downsized because of the exigencies of the Great Depression. In comparison, the CCAS, with a highly structured undergraduate course of study, increased the number of its faculty, who in turn expanded the number of classes they taught in their disciplines.[52]

The complexity of the new course of study precipitated an advising system. Johns Hopkins University had introduced the concept of faculty advisors in 1877, and by World War I the concept had become widespread. The traditional prescribed seven-year Jesuit course of study in which a class had one instructor for virtually all subjects had required little academic advising. The "American Plan," on the other hand, with its options for major, minors, and electives, necessitated helping students make correct choices. Thus, in 1921 each second semester freshman received a "general advisor" who oversaw his two- or four-year program. Juniors and seniors also had to have their schedules approved by the chairman of their major. In 1929, the administration

introduced the "freshman lecture," a one-hour credit consisting of "a series of conferences aiming to acquaint the freshman student with the fundamentals of the educational process, the evaluation of each field of study, and the correlation of the curricula." Similarly, for upperclassmen the flexibility of an honors program required
faculty oversight. Ivy League schools had experimented with the concept early in the
twentieth century and then in 1922 Swarthmore College systematized the first honors program. In 1939, Creighton followed suit, establishing an honors independent
study program (no attendance or tests, but a comprehensive final in a discipline) for
high-achieving juniors and seniors (2.5 grade point average in a 3.0 system). A faculty
committee directed the program; participating departments included classics, English, mathematics, modern languages, philosophy, and those of the physical and social
sciences.[53]

By the end of the interwar period, freshman registration itself had become an
involved process requiring several days. Beginning in 1924, incoming freshman had to
undergo a health exam administered by staff members of the Creighton medical and
dental schools (all student health services, including a two-week stay at St. Joseph's
Hospital, if necessary, remained free). The physical sought "to determine the state of
health of the student body and give each student the benefit of advice regarding the
maintenance of health and personal efficiency, and to call his attention to remedial
physical defects, errors in personal hygiene and habits that handicap." Arts freshmen
also took "a rigid psychological test" to determine their "exact mental capacity." Senior
education majors "scored" the "papers" and published the results, although the ranking
"in no way affected [*sic*] the scholastic standing of those examined." Moreover, by
1930, freshman placement exams for English, mathematics, and the sciences became
standard. With the accumulation of matriculation activities by the mid-1930s, in order
to "whittle down" the "rough edges" of the introduction to college life, the administration initiated "freshman week," a series of "smokers, luncheons, theatre parties, site-
seeing [*sic*] tours and entertainments" to complement the rigors of the examination
schedule, and each arts freshman received a "big brother" to guide him through the
first year. Finally, Fr. President Grace had made a "student pledge" a part of his all-
University convocation in 1926, but the practice did not survive his tenure. However,
starting in 1932, freshmen in all undergraduate schools culminated their initiation to
the University by reciting the Creighton Pledge at the Mass of the Holy Ghost:

> I pledge myself:
> To regard my education as a sacred trust.
> To keep my honor without stain.
> To be loyal to my country and flag.
> To serve God and my fellow man.
> To be true until death to the Creighton ideal.

While the pledge remained a part of the freshman initiation, in 1940 it also became part
of the graduation ceremony. At the all-University Commencement, all graduates rose,
removed their academic caps, and recited the oath administered by Fr. President.[54]

In addition to the new curriculum, advising structure, and oath, arts college students received a new academic calendar, daily order, and building entrance. The revised thirty-six-week academic year began the second week of September and included a Christmas recess, first semester final exams the third week of January, an inter-session retreat, a second semester start the first week of February, a week recess at Easter, and Commencement the first week of June. In 1934, Commencement began to include an "honors night," an all-University affair (seniors mandatory, all other students welcome) at the Auditorium, in which each school awarded its special prizes. The adjusted daily schedule began an hour earlier at 8:00 A.M., but provided numerous study periods between classes and most students had at least one afternoon off per week. Moreover, as "a privilege and a means for 'college men' to distinguish themselves from 'high school kids,'" the formal east entrance to the historic building was "thrown open for their daily use." The perquisite and the American "men versus kids" terminology demonstrated a further distancing from the undifferentiated student cohort of the *Ratio Studiorum*.[55]

Tuition, however, loomed as one of the most significant new student requirements of the interwar years. Predictably, the two-tiered tuition system rose steadily during the 1920s. In 1925–26, it cost $35 per semester to enroll in the baccalaureate program and $50 for the pre-med, pre-dent, and pre-law plans. In 1929–30, tuition became a uniform $80 per semester for all undergraduate study. It remained stable until increasing to $100 in 1935–36, and then continued unchanged for the remainder of the pre–World War II era. Expectedly, scholarships appeared simultaneously with tuition. The administration decided "proper boys i.e. poor & deserving boys" could attend the high school and the CCAS gratuitously. Until 1935, need provided the criterion for scholarships, and the Creighton Endowment and the Jesuit contributions financed the program (recipients continued to pay all student fees). With the rate increase in 1935, only juniors and seniors could vie for the aid; the administration hoped to entice more students to complete the baccalaureate program. The next year, administrators issued new grade-based guidelines for the upper-class awards—"A" students received $40, "B" students $30, and "C" students $20. In 1936, the arts college awarded forty-eight scholarships, which equaled almost one half of the seventy-nine juniors and twenty-two seniors enrolled. At the same time, a new freshman-only award began; the President's Scholarship of $150 became available to the honor graduate of each public and parochial high school in Nebraska (subsequently expanded to the high schools of contiguous states). In 1940, the College awarded thirty such grants, out of the approximate 120 incoming freshmen. Finally, in 1941, only seniors with "A" or "B" averages, who had spent three years at Creighton, became eligible for the upper-class scholarships, but the onset of World War II rendered the offers moot.[56]

Besides scholarships, student loans helped offset the burden of tuition. In 1924, John R. and John Potter Webster, successful Omaha father and son real estate and mortgage brokers, donated $1,000 to create a student loan fund. One half of the money became the endowment, while the other half was loaned to students at "current interest rates." The interest collected went into the Webster Loan Fund to increase the loan pool. In 1931, while Fr. President Agnew lay ill at the Rochester Clinic, a former CCAS student teaching history at Creighton Prep, Alphonse T. Fiore, organized the Agnew Loan Fund. Fiore subsequently obtained an M.A. from his alma mater and joined its history department, eventually leaving in 1938, to pursue a Ph.D. at the University of California. The Agnew Loan Fund became an all-University account administered by Creighton's treasurer. The first year, students raised $2,060 and interest collected went into the following year's pot. In 1933, student leaders began holding dances and other fundraisers to augment the annual fund drive. The following year, Fiore stepped down as director of the fund and the Pep Council (a student athletic spirit booster group) and the dean of men assumed the fundraising and loan-distribution responsibilities. They published new rules, including loans to needy students only, loans for tuition only, and a maximum loan of $50 per semester (significantly less than tuition in all schools). By 1940, the maximum loan increased to $75 and books became an allowable expense, but underclassmen became ineligible for loans—"scholastic mortality in the first two years didn't warrant the risk involved." Students paid no interest the first year, but 6 percent thereafter. To that date, the Agnew Fund granted 417 loans for $15,916.34 (in 1940, 21 loans for $1,320.15). Not surprisingly, medical students borrowed most vigorously (one sixth of the money disbursed), but arts college undergraduates also benefited.[57]

To supplement scholarships and loans for many students, employment played a major role in meeting expenses. For some, the administration provided jobs in lieu of tuition and it included statements about job opportunities in Omaha in the bulletins of the various colleges before undergraduate tuition became a factor. By the end of the 1920s, a student organization began to operate an employment bureau and the Creighton University Bulletin included the statement, "No student, however, should rely on outside work to pay all expenses. One should have means sufficient for the first year." In 1931, with the impact of the Great Depression mushrooming, the administration "estimated that more than 60 percent of the student body now at the university are engaged in some sort of full or part time employment." Obviously, the demands of job and school sometimes clashed. Thus, despite the economic downturn, that same year the administration changed its statement on employment to include, "Students are strongly urged to avoid work requiring more than two hours a day."[58]

As the depression deepened, the New Deal established programs to keep the young in school and out of the job market. Despite its misgivings about employment, the University accepted work-study grants in order to maintain enrollment. In 1934, the Federal Emergency Relief Act made money available for part-time work for needy students. Creighton University received $1,800 per month to hire clerical, library, research, and janitorial assistants at $.30 per hour. The following year, a new agency, the National Youth Administration, assumed the duties of funding student employment. Gladys J. Shamp (Law, 1918) became the state director in Nebraska, and until the end of the decade, the University received sufficient funds to employ between 150 to 200 students annually. The government-sponsored jobs, as well as the few available in the private sector, became a mainstay. According to the administration, "At Creighton it is estimated that about ninety percent of the students pay all or part of their tuition themselves, and fifty percent of them support themselves entirely." The professional students probably made up a majority of the latter category. In 1940, the administration claimed the most popular form of work at Creighton consisted of a job entailing two hours of work a day, at $.35 per hour, in order to earn $4.50 to $5.00 to cover the cost of three meals per day for the week. No complete statistics on student employment exist; therefore, one cannot evaluate if the administrator had simply stated the University's goal as a fact.[59]

Tuition and the Great Depression affected enrollment temporarily, but did not stifle overall growth. As the children of the New Immigrant (late nineteenth to early twentieth century migrants from southern and eastern Europe) came of age during the interwar era, they swelled the ranks of collegiate Catholics, although a slight majority of congregants attended secular colleges and universities. That distribution of Catholic college students led many Jesuits and other coreligionists to criticize the Newman Movement (Catholic missions at secular colleges) for luring Catholics from religious schools. Nonetheless, during the interwar period, the total enrollment at Jesuit institutions of higher learning tripled. Creighton contributed to the increase. With the introduction of tuition in 1924, enrollment in the arts college fell slightly from 483 to 452, but two years later, it rebounded to 524. The high school number, however, immediately plummeted from 443 to 339, bottomed out at 294 in 1926, recovered to 321 in 1930, then slipped well below 300 until 1936, before ending the era slightly above 300 (figures reported at different times during the year differed by a score or more). According to the House Consultors, the principal of the high school "thinks that about 85% of the decrease is owing to this tuition & other expenses." Only about 10 percent of the high-school students received scholarships; thus, the lure of the free public high schools and, especially, the opening of the new Omaha Technical High School a few blocks from the Creighton campus, contributed to the instantaneous downturn, while the Great Depression blunted the recovery.[60]

In comparison, the arts college did not suffer competition from a free alternative. The University of Nebraska started charging tuition in 1923, and at $1 per credit hour ($2 for science and special classes), it approximated the arts college cost. Yet, as arts and sciences enrollment approached 600 at the end of the 1920s, the administration proclaimed, "MAN-POWER is Creighton's sorest need." The statement emphasized the significance of tuition in the annual budget. Subsequently, the situation became nerve wracking as the Great Depression and the Dust Bowl blew onto the Great Plains. The number of arts students shrank from 581 in 1930 to 373 in 1934 before the scholarship, loan, and New Deal work-study programs stemmed the slide. At the same time, the University established a student-recruiting program. Father President Mahan explained:

> Within the past 20 years, among Midwestern colleges and universities, the practice has grown of circularizing all senior students in high school and of sending out paid field agents to the homes of prospective students to canvas them. In addition to this, state

universities have made available hundreds of scholarships by which they bid for the best students, athletes, debaters, musicians, etc. The natural result of these practices is a 'freeze-out' for the institutions that rely upon their educational prestige to attract students. Hence two years ago [1932] Creighton decided to adopt the policy that competition forced upon her of campaigning for students.[61]

During the first "campaign," the University concentrated on Nebraska and the contiguous states of Iowa, Minnesota, South Dakota, Kansas, and Missouri; its third mailing consisted of "20,000 pieces of promotional literature." The registrar received over 1,000 inquiries and followed them up through personal contact by field representatives. The Alumni Association complemented the effort by inaugurating the "Talk Creighton" program, whereby it urged each alumnus to talk to 1,500 prospective students during the year. The *Creighton Alumnus* also began to include a form that alums could send to the dean of the arts college to notify him of jobs for graduates. Moreover, during the summer faculty and coaches traveled adjacent states recruiting students, and in 1938 the University adopted Nebraska's White Spot Campaign. That is, in an attempt to attract businesses and industries, the state advertised with a map of the United States in which the entire country lay in black, except for the white spot of Nebraska, signifying that it had no luxury, income, or sales taxes, and no bonded indebtedness, which gave enterprises freedom to grow and prosper. As "the only good-sized, private university in this section of the United States," Creighton promoted itself as the "white spot for education." With the combination of aid and recruiting, the College ended the decade with an enrollment of 470.[62]

While the arts college recovered from the enrollment decline, Fr. President Mahan remained unimpressed by the quality of the students. He decried the predominance of the two-year pre-professionals and claimed that "this mistake" would correct itself only when the professional schools established the A.B or B.S. as an entrance requirement. Even more egregious, he argued that he and the council of deans and regents came to the "unanimous verdict" that the "majority" of incoming freshmen entered Creighton "seriously lacking the proper preparation for college." He asserted that if the Omaha Chamber of Commerce established a committee of fifty-year-olds to compare their education with that of contemporary students, they would find their eighth-grade studies equivalent to 1930s twelfth grade in "neatness of handwriting, spelling, punctuation, sentence structure, arithmetic, working of problems, knowledge of American history and general geography." The lament speaks to the generational divide that burgeoned in the twentieth-century urban-industrial world, and all back-to-basics educators, who criticize the nature of curricular change in secondary education, probably resonate with Fr. Mahan's grievance.[63]

Finally, in terms of the characteristics of the student body, non-Catholics continued to enroll in small, yet significant numbers. In 1925, the dean of men distributed a questionnaire on religion; 71 percent of the arts and 63 percent of the professional students returned the forms. The study revealed that "ninety-two percent were of Catholic parents, the others having one parent non-Catholic. Eighty percent had attended Catholic grade schools; fifty-one percent came from Catholic high schools."

The odd categories make it impossible to ascertain the ratio of non-Catholic students. Obviously, the professional schools attracted more non-Catholics than the undergraduate schools. Given the enrollment problems engendered by tuition and the Great Depression, Fr. General Ledochowski's directive to limit the number of non-Catholics probably had a limited impact. If the arts college maintained its historic open-enrollment policy, the ratio of non-Catholics probably continued to hover between 10 and 15 percent. The nondiscriminatory policy also continued to attract exceptional African Americans. In 1931, an all-University Creighton Colored Cooperative Club began with twelve members. Two years later, James Bernard Baker, a member of the Math Club, French Club, Debate, and Orchestra, received a B.S., probably attaining the distinction of being the first African-American graduate of the College of Arts and Sciences. Moreover, in 1925 the arts college made its first direct reference to foreign students, demanding they "present original and complete educational credentials for entrance." Few foreigners, however, enrolled during the interwar era; overall, in 1925, the group consisted of five Canadians, three Filipinos, two Germans and Japanese, and one each from China, Ireland, and Mexico.[64]

Thus, the College of Arts and Sciences survived the financial woes of the 1920s and the Great Depression. While administrators perceived stagnation and complained about "marking time," the arts college evolved into its modern form. During the interwar era, the administration became a professional bureaucracy and stamped its name on the enlarged and renovated original College Building. Moreover, during the interwar era, laymen became a majority of the faculty and a significant number of Jesuits and laymen sought the distinguished Ph.D. degree. The curriculum also evolved into its contemporary form, with majors and minors, separation by subject areas organized into departments, and a proliferation of specialized classes in each of the disciplines. Tuition became a burden for students, but loans, scholarships, and New Deal subsidies prevented a bankrupting decline in enrollment. The era did not end with a robust arts college, but it had evolved, it had survived the worst economic downturn in American history, and it maintained sufficient stability to absorb yet another potentially devastating blow—World War II.

CHAPTER 6

The Coed University

In 1928, in his response to criticism of American Jesuit education, Fr. General Ledochowski mandated minimizing the role of non-Catholic students and faculty. In that same communiqué, once again he forbade the coeducation of males and females in Jesuit high schools and colleges. His directive did not include the professional schools, which at Creighton had allowed women to matriculate from their inception. He also made an exception for women religious during summer school, but admonished rectors to end other coeducation programs as soon as possible. By that time, however, Creighton University had established an array of coeducational venues to supplement the summer school (established in 1913, to provide teacher training for nuns). First, the Teachers' Course presented lay and religious women with a night-school option. Then affiliations with Duchesne College and the College of Saint Mary created the "women's colleges of Creighton University." Other affiliations with the St. Joseph and St. Catherine's schools of nursing allowed women to take daytime classes in the College of Arts and Sciences. Finally, the founding of the College of Commerce and of University College established the full-time daily presence of women on campus. The failed fund drives of the 1920s, the debt from the stadium, the downturn in enrollment due to tuition, and the financial exigencies of the Great Depression combined to render Fr. General's anti-coeducation edict unenforceable at Creighton. As the number of women graduates increased, the Alumni Council recognized the fait accompli in 1934; its meetings ceased being "stag affairs," as it granted representation to women's schools. Once again, the American situation contradicted Catholic doctrine and European standards, and by the end of the inter-war era, undergraduate education at Creighton became significantly coeducational.[1]

Following the resignation of Paul Martin as dean of the law school and the summer school in 1919, Jesuit faculty-administrators oversaw the summer program. First, the Reverend William P. Whelan, S.J., secretary of the Board of Trustees, regent of the medical school, and professor of Latin, assumed the duties of "director" of the summer session. In 1922, the Reverend Thomas A. Egan, S.J., regent of the law school and professor of economics and sociology, succeeded to the post. In 1928, the summer school became the responsibility of the Reverend Joseph C. Flynn, S.J., dean of the College of Arts and Sciences, assisted by a new four-person administrative board. Finally, in 1932, because its schedule lay outside the regular academic year, because its student body consisted mostly of women and because many of those students pursued post-baccalaureate study, the summer school became part of the purview of the Reverend Thomas Bowdern, S.J., dean of the graduate school and University College, a new night school for women. For the remainder of the interwar era, the three schools issued a combined bulletin.[2]

The makeup of the summer school faculty followed the evolution of the arts college, from which it drew most of its teachers. After 1921, most classes convened in the new on-campus law and dental buildings, except for those offered by the physics department located in the Administration Building. That same year, the faculty totaled thirteen, which included nine Jesuits. By 1938, the number of faculty climbed to forty-one, but included only eight Jesuits. During the 1920s, women contributed significantly to the summer-session faculty, peaking with nine staff members in 1928 and teaching classes in education, music, and library science. The Great Depression, however, eliminated those adjunct positions as full-time arts faculty members accepted summer assignments in order to supplement their income. In 1940, instructors from the departments of biology, chemistry, classical languages, education, English, history, mathematics, modern languages, philosophy, political science, physics, religion, speech, and sociology, as well as faculty from the College of Commerce, offered seventy-three different courses.[3]

During the 1920s, the summer school remained a female preserve while establishing itself as the largest division of the University. In 1921, enrollment reached 581, which included 471 nuns from twenty-four states and Canada, representing forty-six religious communities. The numbers continued in that range until the onset of the Great Depression. Seemingly, costs during hard times affected members of religious communities and lay women similarly. However, nuns received a concession. In 1930, the matriculation fee (a one-time charge instituted four years earlier) increased to $10 and tuition became $5 per hour or six hours for $25 ($20 for sisters). Enrollment dropped below 500 for the summer session of 1930, slid down to 349 for 1932, and bottomed out at 269 in 1938; thereafter it made slight gains. Religious women continued to constitute a sizeable majority of the students. Therefore, in 1933 Wareham Hall became the "Sisters' Dormitory" for the summer school and the new Dowling Hall joined it the following year. The religious tuition deduction ended in 1940 when the maximum summer-session load became eight hours in a new eight-week session, which cost all students $5 per hour or eight hours for $30.[4]

Teacher training continued as the primary mission of the summer school, as states revamped their certification laws. In 1919, for example, Nebraska "materially changed" the law covering teachers' certificates, creating categories for city, for county, and for state-issued certificates. They differed in terms of grade level, their years of validity, and the subjects required for certification examinations. Moreover, during the interwar era, the number of students seeking graduate classes also increased, including many nuns needing an advanced degree to satisfy accreditation requirements for their Catholic women's academies or colleges. In 1939, graduate students contributed 44 of the 289 enrolled in the summer school. During the 1920s, the number of students earning degrees from the summer school steadily increased before declining in relation to the drop in enrollment during the Great Depression. Temporarily, between

1923 and 1925, the office of the Nebraska State Superintendent of Schools challenged Creighton's right to grant degrees to women, except in the medical school. Eventually, however, "Mr. Matson State Superintendent of Schools [*sic*] wrote a letter to Rev. Fr. Rector stating that it was settled that Cr. U. could give degrees to women His former 1st assistant and secretary Miss Lulu Wolford had denied this & fought against it." The superintendent did not explain his secretary's motives or argument, but her objections had not caused the University to cease issuing degrees through the summer school. In 1923, for example, the summer school issued one B.Lit., two B.S., seven Ph.B, twenty-two A.B., and forty-nine M.A. degrees, all to nuns, except for three lay women. By the end of the interwar era, a few men graduated from the summer school and, more commonly, students from other schools of the University took classes during the summer, some finishing their degree at that time. By the 1930s, the summer Commencement regularly included graduates from all the various schools of the University. Thus, the nature of the summer school had begun to change, but the vast majority of students enrolled exclusively in it remained women, especially nuns.[5]

In addition to summers, the evenings and weekends presented other times when undergraduate males did not occupy classrooms. Thus, during the 1919–20 academic year, the University offered weekday evening and Saturday-morning extension courses open to women. For unexplained reasons, that experiment lasted only one year. Other groups, however, temporarily filled the void. In 1920–21, the Knights of Columbus sponsored a program for discharged service men and women, consisting of seventeen vocational courses such as bookkeeping, auto mechanics, radio telegraphy, shorthand, and typewriting. With money left from its war-activities fund, the Knights provided tuition and books and paid the University a fee to cover utilities and janitorial services. Similarly, on several occasions the Boy Scouts and the Girl Scouts subsidized scout-leadership training courses at night on campus. In 1922, the Catholic Daughters of America promoted an evening series of six lectures by Creighton Jesuit and lay faculty on citizenship. Obviously inspired by the recently ratified Nineteenth Amendment to the United States Constitution, the series aimed at "the political education of women."[6]

Ancillary learning opportunities for women continued, but the demand for educators and social workers (a burgeoning profession promoted by Progressive-era reformers) necessitated a structured program. In 1923, the University responded by creating the Teachers' Course, a curriculum designed "for teachers and those interested in Social Problems." One module, costing $5 and consisting of thirty-six lectures by a member of the Creighton faculty, earned two semester hours' credit. Classes met in the College of Law weekdays after 4:00 P.M. and Saturday mornings. The first year's offering of ten classes from the departments of education, sociology and history attracted 207 students (91 single lay women, 73 nuns, 38 men, 5 married women). Within three years, enrollment climbed to 343 before dropping back to 148 in 1927. The administration did not explain the sudden downturn, but local summer school students, given the opportunity to take classes year round, may have rushed to complete degrees, temporarily swelling the client base for the Teachers' Course. By 1930, however, despite the addition of a $10 matriculation fee and a tuition increase to $5 per hour, 239 registered for classes. By that time, students could earn graduate credit and could choose from twenty-two classes offered by the departments of astronomy, classics, Czech, education, English, history, public health, philosophy, and sociology.[7]

On December 1, 1931 (the same year as Pope Pius XI's Doctrina Catholica discouraging coeducation), the Teachers' Course became "an independent college organization under the style of University College." The original aim of teacher training "expanded to include the intellectual and cultural interests of mature students who wish to improve themselves in their leisure time, of professional men and women who wish to complete college studies required for a college degree, and professional students who wish to increase their cultural development or complete requirements for study in professional schools." University College absorbed all classes taught outside regular hours in the arts college and the College of Commerce. Because of the time schedule and the faculty involved, Fr. Bowdern, dean of the graduate school, assumed administrative responsibilities (years later, he related in an interview that he received the appointment because he had seven sisters and was told, "I'd know what to do"). Tuition remained $5 per hour for undergraduates and $7 per hour for graduate students, who had to do extra assignments in the classes they took. Until the end of the interwar era, enrollment maintained itself in the mid-200s, with full-time students accounting for about one third of the total. Women continued to contribute the vast majority of those students. In 1936, for example, the student body consisted of 151 laywomen, 60 nuns, and 52 men. Many of the full-time students made steady progress in their studies and graduated; in 1938, University College granted five Ph.B., four A.B., and three B.S. degrees, all to women, who had the right to register for daytime classes in the CCAS (seven of those graduates also earned teacher certification).[8]

Certification and accreditation also played a key role in the invention of the concept of corporate colleges, another device that made women a part of Creighton University. The contrivance originated from the fact that most nuns teaching at Catholic women's colleges lacked advanced degrees and the schools could not afford to hire properly credentialed lay people. Thus, in order to get accreditation, strategically placed Catholic women's colleges sought help from nearby Catholic men's universities. In July 1925, Duchesne College, operated by the Sisters of the Sacred Heart of Jesus and located at 36th and Burt streets, signed an agreement that transformed it into "the College for Women of the Creighton University." In a similar arrangement, later that year, on December 16, 1925, nine Catholic women's colleges "merged" under the "leadership" of St. Louis University. Actually, neither of the arrangements affected "in any way the articles of incorporation of any colleges or of the university"; it left "all parties legally and corporately exactly where they were before the agreement was signed." The contracts received the sanction of the North Central Association and both universities saw themselves "rendering a service to Catholic education."[9]

The Sisters of the Sacred Heart had founded a girl's academy in Omaha in 1881, added a junior college to it in 1915, and in 1920 expanded it to become the only four-year Catholic women's college in Nebraska. Using the model established by the understanding between Barnard College of New York and Columbia University, the Sisters pursued an affiliation with Creighton, which maintained their autonomy while obtaining the resources necessary to gain accreditation. Thus, Duchesne retained "its identity as a corporation and its financial independence," as well as the responsibility for "student discipline and government." Creighton University, on the other hand, assumed control of "the administration of the requirements for admission and graduation," and opened its "Library and other facilities" to Duchesne students "as far as the faculties of both institutions deem advisable." According to a vaguely worded official pronunciation, it now became "possible for women to obtain full-time residential work in Arts and Science at Creighton University by matriculating in Duchesne College." In 1927, graduates from Duchesne participated in the all-University Commencement for the first time and received Creighton diplomas.[10]

Duchesne students paid a substantially higher tuition to their college than did undergraduate Creighton men, $75 per semester in 1926, which increased to $100 per semester in 1930, the year in which the $450,000 addition to the Duchesne College building opened. Nonetheless, between 1925 and 1929, enrollment spurted from 52 to 112, and remained in that vicinity during the Great Depression. The addition of Creighton faculty gave the ability to handle more students and the sanction of the North Central Association made the degree more credible. Thus, for example, in 1929, six Duchesne seniors did their student teaching in public high schools in Omaha, the first time the Board of Education granted the opportunity to the college. Obviously, the presence of five Jesuit and six lay faculty members from the arts college, teaching history, philosophy, sociology, chemistry, Spanish, German, education, mathematics, and speech at Duchesne College, added the necessary stature. No records indicate that Duchesne women attended day classes in the arts college, but they (and later College of Saint Mary students) participated in Creighton theater productions and elected representatives to the editorial boards of Creighton student publications.[11]

Duchesne College adopted the CCAS course of study and degree programs. While the former's bulletins advertised the two-year pre-law and B.S. Med programs, no records indicate that any of the women availed themselves of the opportunity. Most career-minded women opted for the teacher-certification program. Then in 1930 the institution initiated two distinct courses of study: secretarial and home economics. The former, a two-year program, combined history, English, economics, and a modern language with commercial law, office methods, shorthand, and typing. The "science" of home economics required the standard four-year arts college course of study, with a major in the new department that sought "to train Home-Makers, Teachers, Dieticians and Social Workers." The discipline consisted of courses in textiles and clothing, design (house and clothing), food and nutrition, and housing and home management. While home economics remained a popular major for women into the 1960s, the affiliation of the women's college with Creighton University ceased at the behest of the North Central Association in 1936. By that time, a sufficient number of sisters had obtained graduate degrees and Duchesne had hired qualified laywomen to fill staff requirements. Subsequently, the North Central Association accredited Duchesne independently as a junior college in 1936 and as a four-year college in 1937.[12]

The North Central Association dissolution of the corporate college arrangement also ended Creighton's affiliation with the College of Saint Mary (CSM). In 1923, the Sisters of Mercy had established a junior college at 14th and Castelar streets, and as of May 1, 1929, it became the second women's college of Creighton University. The Reverend Joseph C. Flynn, S.J., dean of the CCAS, also became the dean of the CSM, and six arts college faculty members began teaching classes in biology, chemistry, English, modern languages, philosophy, and religion. Students paid $100 tuition per semester to take classes in their choice of seven two-year programs: freshman and sophomore years of the baccalaureate, teacher certification, fine arts, pre-nursing, pre-law, pre-medical, or pre-dental. No records exist to reveal which plans students followed or if they transferred to complete four-year or professional degrees (in 1940, the CSM expanded to a four-year college, and in 1955, it moved to its new campus at 72nd and Mercy streets).[13]

The demise of the corporate colleges still left two women's nursing programs affiliated with the University in a distinct arrangement. In 1897, physicians at St. Joseph Hospital organized voluntary instruction for nuns in some basic medical techniques such as bandaging. Two years later, at the urging of Bishop Richard Scannell, they organized the service into a school of nursing for nuns. The two-year program attracted fourteen students who graduated in 1901 at a ceremony presided over by Fr. Michael Dowling. A dramatic transformation occurred in 1917, as the Sisters of St. Francis opened a central school of nursing for the Order at St. Elizabeth's Hospital in Lafayette, Indiana. In response, the St. Joseph's program began admitting laywomen and established a three-year course of study, which followed the education guidelines of the Nebraska State Board of Nurse Examiners (formulated in 1914). The Reverend William Whelan, S.J., regent to the Creighton Medical School, assisted in establishing the new program, served as an advisor, taught a class in religion, and designed the pin worn by the graduates and subsequently adopted by all schools administered by the Sisters of St. Francis.[14]

The school admitted women 18 to 30 years of age who possessed good health, good character, United States citizenship and two years of high-school study (raised to four years in 1922, but not rigorously enforced). They paid an "admission fee" of $75 to cover books, uniforms and other expenses, but received an allowance of $8 per month as compensation for their work with patients. Students began their day with Mass at 6:30 A.M., and had ward duty from 7:30 A.M. to 7:30 P.M., with four hours off in the afternoon. They provided most of the patient care and took classes during their "free" time in the afternoon or after coming off ward duty. Enrollment jumped to ninety in 1922; thus, for student convenience and safety, housing became a priority.

In 1923, construction began on a $300,000 six-story residence for 150 students that also contained a library, parlors, and a gymnasium. Administrators dedicated the building, adjacent to the hospital, on the feast of St. Joseph, March 19, 1924.[15]

Moreover, in 1923, under the auspices of the National Organization of Public Health Nursing, the Rockefeller Foundation funded the publication of *Nursing and Nursing Education in the United States,* written by Josephine Goldmark, which emphasized the development of university schools of nursing. As part of the professionalization of the field, practitioners believed that a bachelor of science in nursing (BSN) should become the standard for administrators, teachers, and public health nurses (actually implemented sixty years later). Based on that belief, the sisters administering the St. Joseph's program approached Fr. President Grace to inquire "how they could arrange to get degrees for themselves & the lay nurses. Nothing much was done till Fr. Sellmeyer came & received his appointment as Regent." While Fr. President Grace ignored the request, an affiliation of sorts already existed because of the Jesuit ownership of Creighton University and the Creighton Medical School, and because of the medical school's affiliation with St. Joseph's Hospital. Thus, in 1920, the first lay graduating class of the St. Joseph's School of Nursing participated in Creighton's all-University Commencement. Moreover, in 1924, the publication of the first Creighton yearbook incorporated pictures of three staff members from the St. Joseph's program, and the photos of the "Class of '24" included the graduates of "Nurses Training" (in subsequent years, alternately referred to as "St. Joseph's Training School" or "Creighton Memorial Training School"). Thus, the student editors perceived the nursing students as part of the University before official affiliation.[16]

In 1927, Fr. President Grace asked the Reverend Bernard L. Sellmeyer, S.J., who had become a physician before joining the Order and had come to Creighton to teach biology, to gather information and lead the deliberations with the Sisters of St. Francis. He consulted with the Rockefeller Foundation, the University of Minnesota (it had established the first BSN program in the United States in 1909), and Michigan, Northwestern, Yale, and Marquette universities. In February 1928, his work resulted in an agreement whereby the hospital school became "St. Joseph's Hospital Unit of the School of Nursing of the Creighton University." The union did not affect the finances of either school; the University jurisdiction extended "only to the academic activities of the training school." An administrative board with members from the hospital, the medical school, and the University oversaw the program. Father Sellmeyer became regent; the office integrated the traditional functions of a dean. Sister M. Livina, director of the St. Joseph's Unit of the School of Nursing, 1919–48, and the other nuns on the faculty did not possess a college degree. Therefore, she and Sr. Henrica took thirty-two hours of credit in one year at Duchesne and the Creighton Summer School to obtain degrees in 1928. With the proper credentials and with the addition of science, religion, and philosophy classes taught in the arts college, the hospital program qualified as a pre-BSN program.[17]

In January 1929, the Sisters of Mercy, who operated St. Catherine's Hospital and its nursing school, signed a letter of affiliation with Creighton University containing "virtually identical" provisions as the one with the Sisters of St. Francis. Mrs. E. W. (Catherine) Nash, wife of a prominent Omaha department store magnate, had donated funds to the archdiocese that secured the purchase of the Herman Kountze residence and additional grounds at 811 Forrest Street. In 1910, Bishop Scannell had secured the services of the Sisters of Mercy to operate a women's hospital in the home, which contained 40 beds and 10 bassinets (a novel feature, as no Omaha hospital to that date had admitted maternity patients). Saint Catherine's Hospital (named after the benefactor and Catherine McAuley, founder of the Order) completed a three-story addition in 1916, which increased its capacity to 75 beds and prompted its shift to a "general" hospital. Subsequently, in 1925, it added a fourth floor and another wing to the earlier addition, expanding the number of beds to about 170.[18]

To help with patient care, St. Catherine's Hospital established a nursing school in 1911. Fourteen women paid a $20 admission fee to enter the three-year program and worked sixty-five hours per week in the wards. Students received an $8 per month stipend, but also had to attend night classes taught by physicians, upon availability. For the first fifteen years, the school purchased neighborhood homes and renovated them into miniature dormitories; in 1926, at 8th and Williams streets, on the grounds of the hospital, it erected a frame building large enough to house all students. By that time, students also began to provide well-child care at St. James Orphanage, another institution administered by the Sisters of Mercy (originally attached to its convent at 24th Street and St. Mary's Avenue; after 1891, located in a new building in the suburb of Benson). The Creighton Medical School entered affiliations with St. James and St. Catherine's to obtain more clinical placements for its students; the associations prompted the Sisters of Mercy to seek an arrangement for its nursing school similar to the recently established St. Joseph's accord (that same year, the Order obtained affiliation for its College of Saint Mary).[19]

In 1930, with two affiliated hospital-nursing programs, administration of the associations changed. Saint Joseph's and St. Catherine's each became "hospital units," with separate administrative boards, of the Creighton University School of Nursing, directed by the University Board of Nursing Education. The Reverend T. H. Ahern, S.J., became regent to all the health-professions schools, chairman of the nursing board and dean of the Nursing School. In 1932, the Reverend John McInerny, S.J., succeeded to the positions and held them until 1948. Each unit began with a small number of faculty members consisting of hospital-associated physicians and practicing nurses giving instruction on the premises. While the number of on-site nurse-teachers increased dramatically during the interwar era, their stature did not. Few women instructors, religious or lay, possessed a BSN or a master's degree. Nationwide, Catholic nursing programs rated low, although the Creighton units ranked above the average of the more than four hundred Catholic schools of nursing in existence in the 1930s.[20]

While the hospital units remained autonomous and distinct, a standardized curriculum emerged. Creighton University established the admissions and graduation requirements, and the hospital units adopted the semester schedule and coordinated their calendars with the University. Each program consisted of a three-year course of study, leading to a diploma of Graduate Nurse. While course names and the schedule of classes differed slightly between the units, the basic curriculum consisted of on-site nursing classes and science, liberal arts, and religion classes on the Creighton campus. Courses in nursing methods, the basic sciences, English, and religion remained standard during the interwar era, while clinical rotations in psychiatric nursing at St. Bernard's Hospital in Council Bluffs and a month in the outpatient clinic of the Creighton Medical School offered new experiences. Three-year diploma graduates could complete the BSN with full-time study for two more years in University College. In 1932, the St. Joseph's Alumnae Association established a $100 scholarship, given to the nurse with the highest three-year grade average, for use toward post-diploma study within a year of graduation. The curriculum for the BSN demanded sixty-four credit hours and equated to the core lower-division requirements in the CCAS. Few nursing students of the interwar era, however, perceived any value in baccalaureate study. In May 1940, for example, St. Joseph's granted forty-two diplomas, St. Catherine's twenty, and University College awarded a single BSN.[21]

Nursing students paid no tuition, but an admission fee "of $75.00 covers the cost of registration, uniforms and books for the preliminary period. Room and board and plain laundry are furnished the student during the entire three years. No monthly allowance is given, the services of the student in the hospital being regarded as a working scholarship for training received by her." The admission fee increased to $150 in 1935, then held steady for the remainder of the decade. Students received a half-day holiday weekly and a two-week vacation each year from their year-round eight-hour-day workload. Students had to observe a strict dress code: "Uniforms and aprons are made at the hospital. Candidates should bring with them: Sufficient plain substantial underwear for frequent changes. Two pairs of plain black oxfords with broad rubber heels, for wear on duty. One pair white oxfords with rubber heels for wear on Sundays and holidays." If ill, students received "hospital and medical attention free in cases not exceeding three months."[22]

The hospital units admitted women between the ages of eighteen and thirty, who possessed a high-school diploma and who could provide references from a clergyman and "two other persons not relatives." Saint Joseph's, the second "largest institution of its kind west of the Mississippi River . . . [and in 1935] the twelfth largest Catholic general hospital in the United States," maintained the larger enrollment. Both schools suffered enrollment declines during the Great Depression, but the economic downturn allowed the hospitals to hire unemployed nurses at low wages who often took night duty, thus lessening student workloads. Saint Joseph's had 114 students in 1930, dropped down to 87 in 1935, but rebounded at the end of the interwar era to 134 in 1940. For the same dates, St. Catherine's started with 80, dipped to 48, and finished with 78. Most of those students came from Omaha, with a significant number from Nebraska and a few from surrounding states. Since many orders of religious women operated centralized nursing schools for their members, few nuns attended the Creighton University School of Nursing during the interwar era.[23]

Like nurse training, education for careers in business expanded during the late-nineteenth and early-twentieth centuries. The Industrial Revolution and the "big businesses" it spawned, with their expanding white-collar bureaucracies, produced a seemingly insatiable demand for individuals trained in various business methods. Apprenticeships in small firms atrophied as formal education paid for by the prospective employee replaced business compensated on-the-job training. As with the other professions, universities challenged or absorbed the proprietary schools that had entered the field. In 1913, the University of Nebraska established its School of Commerce, and in December 1919, Creighton began its process as a "Fr. Davis came from St. Louis to see about starting a course here on Commerce and Finance." Discussions moved rapidly, and in September 1920, the College of Commerce, Accounts, and Finance opened. The University's announcement of its new college revealed its acceptance of the emergent professional business philosophy:

> The scientific spirit, so much in evidence in every field of activity during the past half-century, has subjected modern commercial and industrial activities to careful analysis and has shown that the successful conduct of any form of business is dependent upon a close adherence to well-defined, fundamental principles which can readily be grasped by those who are willing to devote sufficient and earnest attention to their study. . . . Modern business is a science and success in it demands special education and training just as in medicine and law.[24]

Thus, the administration created another undergraduate professional school. As with the similarly positioned Nursing School, the role of the liberal arts in the curriculum would pose a contentious issue for the College of Commerce. Moreover, as a professional school, it admitted women. At first, their presence had little impact on the arts college, because classes (three per night) were held from 7:00 to 9:30 P.M., Monday, Tuesday, Thursday, and Friday. A shortage of campus classroom space precluded day classes, but the evening schedule helped to recruit employed workers seeking credentials to further their careers. Classes met in the historic Creighton College (the central section of the Administration Building) and its north wing. The Reverend William P. Quinlan, S.J., administered a part-time faculty, consisting of Edwin Puls (arts college, public speaking), Hugh Gillespie (law, economics), the Reverend Gabriel Salinas, A.R., (rector of Holy Ghost Church, Spanish), and four local businessmen. In 1923, Fr. President McCormack replaced Fr. Quinlan (who led "the life of an outlaw . . . he rarely came to community exercise . . . [and stayed] out most of the time, even late at night") with the soon-to-be-disgraced P. H. Bogardus.[25]

The College of Commerce would admit high-school graduate as a "regular student" and those over the age of twenty-one who did not possess a high-school diploma, but the faculty deemed capable "of pursuing with profit the work offered," as a "special student." All who registered paid a $5 matriculation fee; part-time students paid $15 per hour, while full-timers paid $55 tuition per semester. The school offered a Bachelor of Commercial Science degree (BCS, subsequently, Bachelor of Science in Commerce, BSC) that emphasized accounting and arranged its course of study to prepare students to pass the Nebraska examination for certification as a public accountant. Full-time students took "nine hours of work a week" in a four-year program, which would equate to a seventy-two-hour degree program. The course of study consisted of prescribed lower-division classes in accounting, advertising, economics, business English, law and mathematics, public speaking, salesmanship, commercial Spanish ("owing to the constantly increasing volume of trade between Omaha and the Latin American countries"), and commercial French, followed by upper-division classes in accounting. Graduates also had to present a thesis "on some economic question" and "submit evidence of at least two years of successful experience in business." The school also offered a Bachelor of Arts in Commerce that necessitated fulfilling all requirements in both the arts and the commerce colleges, but no one pursued that degree. Finally, special students who completed the program earned a "Certificate of Proficiency," while regular diploma graduates could study another year to obtain a Masters in Commercial Science.[26]

The inaugural class drew thirty-eight special students and seventy-four regular students (sixty-five men and nine women), all but nineteen from Omaha. None of the women and only one of the men (John P. Begley, who soon became the luminary of the commerce faculty) graduated in 1924. Extremely low graduation rates indicate that the vast majority of the students studied part time and a substantial number (e.g., fourteen in 1920–21) of the special students withdrew without completing a single class. Total numbers held steady for three years, then dropped in half inexplicably for the 1923–24 academic year; thereafter, enrollment rebounded.[27]

The College of Commerce changed dramatically in 1924, with the purchase the three-story Greystone Apartments on the southeast corner of 25th and Cass streets and "a simple residence to the east of the building known as 'the cottage,' [which] served as a lounge for women students until 1950." Grace Ringer and Margaret Tolbert graduated in 1929, followed by an average of five women per annum during the 1930s. Night classes remained in a "special division" alternately referred to as the "Extension Division" or "Evening Division." It offered credit and non-credit classes on campus and in locations around Omaha, "arranged in two sections; specialized courses for people who are employed in the daytime and who wish to take work that will advance them immediately in their employment; and, advanced, courses for teachers and others who want the work for graduate or employment credit." Thus, the Evening Division of the Commerce College, first billing itself as "Spare-Time University Training for Business Success" and subsequently as "University Training for Community Leadership," joined the Teachers' Course of the arts college in providing night classes for non-traditional students.[28]

The renovated Greystone flats provided classroom space for a full-time day school reorganized as the College of Commerce, Finance, and Journalism. P. H. Bogardus became the director of the new school, with D. B. Harmon, Ph.D., as assistant director in charge of the journalism program. With the increase in women in the professional schools and a new coed undergraduate day college, Mrs. Margaret Curran, head of the secretarial science department, also assumed the "necessary" position of dean of women. Seemingly, the title caused problems, and Curran lost it after two years, but remained an administrative mainstay for over three decades, retiring in 1960. Following the dismissal of Bogardus in 1926, Floyd Edward Walsh (M.A., 1920; Ph.D., 1932) became dean of the College of Commerce for the next thirty-six years. Starting with Fr. Thomas Egan, successive regents also played a significant role in administering the school. Then, beginning with Fr. George Deglman in 1934, for the next quarter-century, the dean of the arts college served as the regent of the commerce college. The arrangement testified to the Jesuit desire to maintain a liberal arts core in the business curriculum. At times, the regent vis-à-vis the secular dean may have caused conflicts, but Dean Walsh supported the liberal arts component, and his long tenure attested to an overall amicable relationship.[29]

The College of Commerce Bulletin listed twenty-five faculty members, but most came from the arts college, including five members of the military science department. Ten may have taught exclusively in the College of Commerce, but five of them held the title of instructor, indicating part-time status (the 1925 yearbook pictured five commerce faculty members: Rose McAleer, instructor of stenography and typewriting, plus four men). John P. Begley, who taught accounting, business mathematics, and English, joined Dean Walsh, who also taught accounting, as the celebrity faculty members of the school. Begley was a native of Omaha, who graduated from South Omaha High School and worked in the accounting department at the Swift packing plant before obtaining his BCS in 1924 and joining the staff of his alma mater. To enhance camaraderie, Walsh instituted informal commerce-faculty luncheons and Fr. Regent Egan developed a Faculty Study Club. The number of exclusively commerce college faculty remained small, finishing the interwar era with eight, three of whom had a Ph.D., and one woman, Lucille Kendall, long-serving instructor of shorthand and typing, and the secretary to the department.[30]

When the daytime College of Commerce began, the nine-year-old American Association of Collegiate Schools of Business had not yet established a core curriculum. In 1925, it did state that, "at least 40 percent of the 120 credit hours or its equivalent required for the Bachelors degree must be taken in commercial and economic subjects" (accounting, business law, and economics composed three classes required by virtually all programs). That year, the Creighton commerce curriculum began with a two-year "Pre-Commerce Course," consisting of sixty-five hours of study in English (six hours), a modern language (eight hours), economics, accounting, business law, and the two-year ROTC obligation. Additionally, sophomores had to produce a two-thousand-word thesis on a topic assigned by the director. The administration advertised that the Pre-Commerce Course met the sixty-hour requirement to enter the Creighton law school, but it encouraged pursuing the "Commerce-Law Course." The latter consisted of three years study in commerce and three years in law school, resulting in the awarding of the BCS and LL.B. The upper-division "General Business Course," leading to the four-year BCS, listed sixty-eight hours of classes in specific areas such as insurance, real estate, and labor problems. Students arranged the courses according to their program department: sales management, advertising management, retail management, business administration, banking and finance, accounting, secretarial science, or journalism. Upper classmen had to spend the summers between years two and three, and three and four, "in the employ of some business concern." They used these summers to gain work experience and "for making investigations and accumulating data for [a] thesis," a three-thousand-word paper on a topic related to his or her department of specialization. The school awarded a gold medal for the best sophomore thesis and a $50 prize to the outstanding senior thesis. Graduation also required accumulating 1,080 points for attendance. A student received 10 points for perfect attendance for each semester hour, for a possible total of 1,200 points.[31]

The new leadership team of Dean Walsh and Fr. Regent Egan restructured the program, increasing its liberal arts component in an attempt to increase its stature. According to Walsh, "[I]n 1926, the College of Commerce was looked upon as being, more or less . . . a dumping ground for the athletes and general incompetents. Business students weren't supposed to have the intellect to comprehend any philosophy, hence there was no philosophy in the curriculum." Walsh believed a business education should rest on the pillars of accounting, the basic liberal arts, and business ethics; he strove for higher academic standards to rebuff the perceived "snobbery of the liberal arts faculty." In 1927, the new "Prescribed Commerce Course" debuted. It maintained the foreign-language and English-composition classes, and added six hours of literature, five or six hours of mathematics (college algebra and trigonometry), four hours of religion and three hours of psychology, as well as allowing juniors and seniors twelve hours of commerce electives and eighteen hours of general electives. The new curriculum also instituted field trips to acquire a sense of business operations, and because of the increased demand for high-school teachers of commercial subjects, it created a teacher-training program, whereby students used their electives in the education department to qualify for state certification. The "Prescribed Journalism Course" resembled the commerce course closely, except it substituted history or politic science for freshman accounting and upper-division journalism classes for some business classes (in June 1930, Gene Mari Vani became "the first girl student" to complete the four-year course in journalism). Finally, to combat the delinquency problem, especially associated with athletes (which had necessitated the attendance point system), and to mirror the system of the CCAS, the commerce college established an advisor system. Dean Walsh advised commerce students and C. L. Sanders, a journalism professor, advised students in that program. By 1935, arts faculty teaching in the commerce college also served as advisors to commerce freshmen.[32]

In 1929, the commerce college received accreditation from the New York State Department of Education, which placed "the Creighton business course on a par with those of the ranking eastern schools." The program continued to evolve; by 1931, the school joined the arts college in mandating freshman placement exams and a one-hour religion class for non-Catholics. It added a year-long, six-hour statistics-

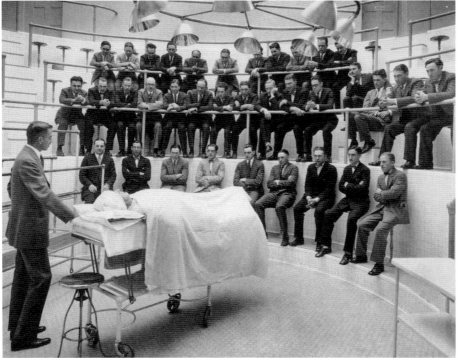

Top: A poster celebrating the fiftieth anniversary of the Medical School charts the changes in how and where students studied during the first five decades of Creighton's history. Photo courtesy of KMTV.

Bottom: Medical students learn by example in the amphitheatre of St. Joseph's Hospital in 1926.

Top: A night view of the refurbished façade of the Administration Building facing the California Street Mall. Photo courtesy of Jay Langhurst.

Bottom: The California Street Mall looking west past the Reinert Alumni Library, Hitchcock Communication Arts Building, Humanities Center, and Criss Buildings (on right). The Spanish Colonial spires of St. Cecilia's Cathedral are seen in the sunset just beyond the Creighton University Medical Center. Photo Courtesy of Jay Langhurst.

Players from Creighton and Texas A & M struggle for the ball in a 1940 game.

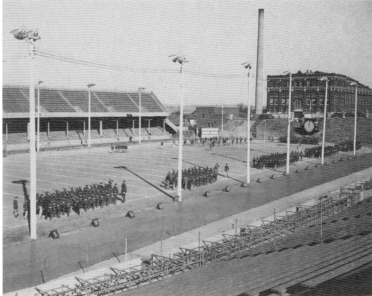

Top: One of the college's last football teams plays a home game at Creighton Stadium in 1940. The team was disbanded in 1942.

Bottom: ROTC members march in formation across the football field in 1942. The number of men able to attend Creighton dropped drastically in November of that year, when Congress lowered the draft age from twenty-one to eighteen.

ROTC members dash over, under, around, and through their college-campus-turned-military-training-ground in 1942. That year, about 85 percent of the male student body were enlisted in the military reserves.

Workers begin construction of barracks to be used as temporary classrooms in 1946.

Mass is celebrated at St. John's Church.

Top: Cars drive past St. John's Church and the Administration Building in the early 1940s. At the time of Creighton's founding, California Street was simply a muddy road. Throughout the years, the street was paved and had a street car line running along it before eventually being closed to traffic.

Bottom: Members of the Women's Society carry their candles in a Marian Night procession during the mid-1940s.

Rev. Francis Deglman, S.J., spiritual advisor from 1933 until 1955

Members of the 1950 Creightonian staff prepare for their next publication.

Working in conjunction with Creighton's KOCU, WOW-TV cameras film the "Doors of Knowledge" television program in 1952. During the 1950s, Creighton offered pioneering opportunities for students interested in the fields of radio and television. KOCU radio station was shut down in 1989.

BASEBALL COACH SUBBY SALERNO TALKS OVER A
FEW HITTING POINTERS WITH OUTFIELDERS JACK

Top: A tennis player practices his serve in 1952. Sports like tennis often struggled to receive recognition alongside the more highly regarded men's basketball program.

Bottom: Coach Sebastian "Subby" Salerno examines the team's equipment with outfielders Jack McGraw, Jerry Mancuso, and Jim Knowles in 1952. Salerno had been a star basketball player while a student at Creighton and later moved back to that sport as head basketball coach.

Top: J. V. "Duce" Belford poses here as a basketball coach but was known to history as "Mr. Everything" to Creighton athletics. He began as a student manager in 1922 and later worked his way up through the program as an athlete, a coach, and, from 1934 to 1961, athletic director.

Bottom: Members of the 1952 golf team discuss strategy. "Minor sports" such as golf, track, and swimming struggled to recruit players and receive funding during early days of Creighton athletics.

The newly-organized Pep Club of 1952 hopes to boister excitement for college sports. After the demise of the football program in the 1940s and the loss of male athletes during World War II, Creighton athletics struggled to garner the popularity they had achieved during the interwar years.

The cheer squad serves as the backbone of Creighton's school spirit. This team from 1953 was one of the last to include men for the next decade.

College co-eds make their rooms comfortable. During the 1950s, Creighton purchased several houses in order to gain much-needed space for its growing population of female students.

Creighton women find a place in their rooms to take a break from studying. Co-eds suffered from a general lack of space during the 1950s, when housing for female students was limited and the ladies' lounge, the Commerce Cottage, was demolished to make room for a parking lot.

class requirement, but dropped the mandatory all-school Thursday assemblies, because of the unreliability of scheduled speakers, as well as the difficulty of picking topics interesting to the diversified student body—freshmen through seniors, and the various business and journalism majors. In 1935, commerce matched arts by requiring 128 hours for graduation, and the next year, acting on the recommendations of a national report, the school substantially revamped its curriculum. The revised "Prescribed Freshman-Sophomore Commerce Program" dropped the foreign-language requirement and substituted six hours of philosophy, as well as six hours of political science and four hours of speech ("or other lower-division non-commerce electives approved by the Dean"). The "Prescribed Junior-Senior Program for the Bachelor of Science in Commerce Degree" added nine hours of philosophy (a total of fifteen, putting it on par with the four-year CCAS requirement) and reintroduced the concept of majors: accounting, finance, industrial management, business organization, marketing, merchandising, and business law. It also revamped the 3-3 commerce-law Program, specifying the junior-year classes in mathematics, economics, marketing, and philosophy, and requiring a commerce elective, the thesis, and thirteen freshman law hours for senior commerce credit and the awarding of the BSC.[33]

The tuition structure changed with the founding of the commerce day school to match the arts college. Part-timers began paying $5 per hour, while full-time students initially paid $75 per semester, raised to $80 in 1927, then $100 in 1929, and it remained at that level for the rest of the interwar era. In 1925, the Warfield Advertising Company began to award a scholarship to the junior with the highest rank in the advertising department to cover tuition for their senior year. That stipend ended in 1927, however, with the decade-long elimination of majors from the course of study. Subsequently in 1940, an article by Dr. John Begley, in the *Creighton Alumnus,* spurred Mrs. Agnes Leahy Sutherland (Pharmacy, 1907), a high-school math teacher in San Diego and sister of the Reverend William Leahy, S.J., former professor of philosophy at Creighton, to donate $1,000 to establish a loan fund for commerce students.[34]

Despite the lack of scholarships and loans, the commerce college maintained healthy enrollment figures. In 1924, the daytime program opened with 170 students, which included 27 special students and 21 women. The part-time night division registered 124 students, 27 on the distaff side. By 1930, the total enrollment reached 397, including 45 registered as journalism students and over 60 women. The administration recognized that the commerce college "should prove a drawing card to young women, and it will no doubt mark a large change in Creighton as a co-educational institution." The amount of change may have surprised many Jesuits, as a significant number of women enrolled in the commerce college only in order to take classes in the arts college, in which they could not matriculate. The subsequent creation of University College ended the ruse in 1931, and contributed to a decline in the number of students who registered in the commerce college. Obviously, the impact of the Great Depression also affected a rapid downturn to only 284 students for 1933. As with the arts college, a rebound, based on federal government assistance, pushed the number up to 406 in 1938, before a significant waning to end the interwar era at 284 in 1940. The job opportunities in the rebounding economy may have provided stiff competition to business education.[35]

In addition, the creation of a separate College of Journalism contributed to the drop in commerce enrollment in 1933. At first, administrators at Creighton obviously perceived journalism in relationship to nineteenth-century entrepreneurial publishers and to the myriad of small-business, small-town newspapers in the Midwest and the Great Plains states. Thus, when they devised a program in 1924, they placed it in the College of Commerce, and Publicity Director James A. Shanahan administered the program from 1925 to 1927. Their perceptions, however, changed quickly; Dean Walsh toured eastern colleges to analyze their forms of administration. He returned to encourage the University to capitalize on the increasing popularity of journalism education in its modern form, preparing news gatherers and reporters, not small businessmen. He recommended a program whereby freshmen and sophomores completed the lower-division requirements in either the arts or commerce colleges, and then specialized in their junior and senior year to receive the appropriate degree and a certificate in journalism analogous to the teacher-certification program available in both colleges. Charles L. Sanders, formerly of the University of Missouri, came to direct the revised program that attracted thirty students. He left for the University of Iowa in 1930, and John N. McCabe (1930–33) succeeded as overseer of the program, which remained part of the commerce college because of the matriculation of women (although they registered in University College after 1932). That same year, McCabe established an internship project, in which each journalism student worked six weeks in the Creighton Publicity Office writing stories for distribution to newspapers published in the hometowns of Creighton students (the publicity project anticipated the student-recruitment program). Ultimately, between 1924 and 1932, the program produced fourteen graduates; all received a BSC.[36]

The move from a business to a liberal-arts preparation took another step in 1933, with the creation of the College of Journalism. The Reverend John Danihy, S.J., founder and dean of the Marquette College of Journalism (1915–28), first dean elected to the National Editorial Association (1928), regent to the Creighton colleges of commerce and law, organized the new entity. The new college and its print shop occupied the first floor of the law school, and it assumed responsibility for publication of the yearbook, the student newspaper, the alumni magazine, and the student literary journal. It also inherited the responsibility for the classes in advertising and continued to offer classes in the evening. It listed seven faculty members, but four held part-time positions, one from the Creighton law school.[37]

The Journalism College offered three types of degrees: the A.B. (required fifteen hours of Latin), the B.S. (required sixteen hours of science and six of mathematics), and the Ph.B. (no Latin and only six to eight hours of math and science). Regardless of degree program, all students had to take twenty-four hours of journalism, fifteen hours of philosophy, twelve to sixteen hours of a modern language or Greek (four hours credit awarded for high-school study), twelve hours of English, six hours of history, and two hours of speech, and write a senior thesis. All men had to participate in the ROTC and all Catholics had to take eight hours of religion. Each student majored in journalism and chose two minors, one each from Group 2 and Group 3 of the CCAS major-minor groups. Father Danihy secured accreditation from the North Central Association before his death in 1936; Stuart A. Mahuran succeeded to his position. As "a gesture toward closer professional relations between Nebraska editors and newspapermen and the Creighton College of Journalism," he supervised undergraduates in the publication of the twenty-eight-page *Nebraska Style Book*, distributed to high schools and colleges in the state.[38]

In 1934, the program undertook another reorientation, allowing students to major in journalism or a foreign language; the following year, it acknowledged a "more direct relationship with the Liberal Arts Colleges and became the School of Journalism." Subsequently, in 1948, the migration reached fruition, as journalism ceased its brief sojourn with independence and became a department in the College of Arts and Sciences. The College of Journalism began with thirty-five students, peaked at sixty-four in 1937, but declined to forty-five in 1940 (it provided no register of students after 1941). Throughout the interwar era, women contributed twenty to thirty percent of the total enrollment (for many years Creighton University enrollment figures included a "duplication" category; women contributed to it substantially, because the College of Journalism counted its female students and University College counted all undergraduate women outside the nursing units). During its independence, the program granted sixty-seven degrees; sixty-one students chose the Ph.B., while only six garnered an A.B. in Journalism.[39]

Like journalism, commerce, and nursing, administrators viewed pharmacy as professional education and, like nursing, part of the "health sciences," but also at the undergraduate level. Moreover, like the other professional schools, the College of Pharmacy began as a coeducational institution. Yet, pharmacy began the interwar era as a two-year program that only required two years of high-school preparation. Pharmacy education began its transformation into a full-fledged undergraduate professional-degree program in 1923, when the American Conference of Pharmaceutical Faculties (ACPF) mandated that its members require candidates for entrance to their schools possess a high-school diploma. The following year, the Creighton College of Pharmacy adopted a three-year curriculum (one hundred hours) and began to phase out the two-year Graduate in Pharmacy degree. A fourth ("graduate") year of study in economics, logic, psychology, physics, and a foreign language would result in a bachelor of science in pharmacy, but virtually no students pursued that option. To meet the desires of the students of the three-year Pharmaceutical Chemist degree, the school inserted a business element into the curriculum in 1926. Administrators realized that the "chief causes of so many failures in the drug business have been due to the lack of commercial training." According to an ACPF report, "Pharmacy education is veering toward commerce and law and the nations druggists of the future will be men and women of sound business training." Thus, Dean Howard Newton arranged with commerce dean Walsh to offer an accounting and business-administration course to pharmacy students.[40]

Father President Agnew, however, debated "the educational value of the College of Pharmacy and for a time [1931] was contemplating the closing of that department and assigning its space to the ever-growing and crowded medical school." Advisors, however, convinced him of its value and it remained open as the only pharmacy school in Omaha. In 1932, the program became a four-year course of study leading to a Bachelor of Science degree (the three-year pharmaceutical chemist degree phased out). The curriculum consisted of thirty-four hours of pharmacy classes, thirty-two in chemistry, sixteen in biology, six in English, four in arithmetic, two each in Latin and ethics, with no classes in business, but with twenty-two hours of "approved electives." The evolution from a two-year to a four-year course of study did not result in a significant increase in faculty. Faculty from the colleges of arts, commerce, law, and medicine supplemented the pharmacy classes taught by Dean Newton and three full-time staff members. The interwar era ended with five faculty members, one with a Ph.D. In 1934, emulating his medical counterpart, and recognizing the burgeoning stress on research by health-science faculty, Dean Newton created the Creighton Council of Pharmaceutical Research. The following year, after nineteen in the position, he retired; William A. Jarrett (Massachusetts College of Pharmacy, 1913) succeeded to the position.[41]

Tuition in the College of Pharmacy rose steadily during the interwar era, from $62.50 to $97 per semester. It developed two short-lived scholarships (1932–37) and several prizes for outstanding students (e.g., a gold medal to the sophomore who prepared the best case of specimens or a one-year membership to the American Pharmaceutical Association to the top freshman). It also acquired two exclusive loan funds donated by the Nebraska Pharmaceutical Association (1929, $500) and the Retail Druggists of Omaha (1932, $600). Enrollment peaked in 1924 at 143, but fell thereafter, because of the introduction of the three-year, then four-year curriculum, plus the subsequent impact of the Great Depression. It slid below one hundred and remained there for the remainder of the interwar era, standing at eighty-four in 1940. Women maintained a significant presence. Their numbers fluctuated (the yearbook identified Thelma Carmichael as "the only coed in the '26 graduating class" of Creighton University), but females consistently provided 5 to 10 percent of the total College of Pharmacy registrants and most of them finished their degrees. By the outbreak of World War II, pharmacy far outdistanced the other professional schools in the number of women graduates, well over one hundred in the school's thirty-five-year history. That number included a significant number of nuns, who then worked in pharmacies located in hospitals run by their orders (in 1934, for example, five sisters graduated).[42]

As with pharmacy and the other professional schools, medical education continued to demand higher standards and a more homogeneous curriculum. During the post-World War I era, state licensing laws for physicians eliminated the historic proprietary schools and helped standardize the course of study at accredited medical schools. The Creighton Medical School had already instituted national guidelines; therefore, during the interwar era administrators only had to adjust the hours dedicated to the study of certain disciplines. The adjustments reflected current emphasis and knowledge, as well as the trend away from the general practitioner toward the medical specialist (e.g., between 1920 and 1930, the number of hours allotted for the study of diagnosis increased from twenty-four to sixty-four). Furthermore, beginning with the May 1920 graduates, seniors had to produce a three-thousand-word thesis on a topic assigned by a professor of medicine and surgery. The assignment required a larger library; thus the medical school petitioned and received an annual $1,000 donation from University funds for the purchase of library materials. By the 1920s, however, medical reformers realized that the four-year education could only provide the "fundamentals of medical knowledge," and internships increasingly became a necessary part of medical training. "During World War I, the average physician took one and one-half years of internship and entered practice at the age of twenty-eight years." By 1932, at Creighton the assignment had become so ingrained, the medical school bulletin began to list "Interne Appointments" along with the list of graduates.[43]

Pre-graduation clinical clerkships also continued to expand. During the 1920s, each fourth-year student participated for twenty-two weeks and was "required during this period of service to fulfill all the duties of a junior interne." During the 1930s, fourth-year students received assignments "to dispensary service in the specialties for one-third of the year" and spent the other two thirds of the year in one of the affiliated hospitals, one third in medicine, one third in surgery. They served their clerkships at St. Joseph's, St. Catherine's, Douglas County, and City Emergency hospitals in Omaha, Mercy and St. Bernard's hospitals in Council Bluffs, and at St. James Orphanage and the Salvation Army Rescue Home in Omaha. In 1920, the local medical alumni group (115 practitioners in the Omaha–Council Bluffs area) reestablished the war-interrupted business committee, which advised on the operation of the clinics. Moreover, in 1926, the medical school established a social-service office to act as "intermediary between the physician, the patient, the home, the [social service] agency and the hospital." The duties of the medical social worker were "arduous and varied"; visiting "homes, looking after follow-up cases, attending to free hospitalization, [and] checking over the charities' work to prevent duplication." In 1925, the St. Joseph's Hospital clinic served 2,562 nonpaying patients and another 1,451 who only paid part of their bill, as well as dispensing thousands of free meals. By 1936, the administration estimated that in its forty-four-year history, the medical school's charity included 30,000 patients treated free at its clinic and over 100,000 free prescriptions issued by students of the College of Pharmacy.[44]

The medical faculty had to evolve to meet the new demands. Nationally, the interwar era witnessed an increase in full-time faculty holding the Ph.D. degree to teach the pre-clinical classes (basic sciences such as anatomy), as well as an attempt to expand the number of full-time clinical faculty. "Very few schools adopted the strict version of full time" for their clinical faculty, they could not afford it. Most clinical professors fell within the category of "geographic full time," which meant that they maintained a limited private practice while they devoted some or most of their time to teaching. The Creighton Medical School could not keep pace. The number of full-time faculty increased slowly, few of the faculty possessed the Ph.D. (two in 1920, none in 1930 and in 1940), and about two thirds had obtained their M.D. at Creighton. The number of part-time clinical faculty exploded so that the total number of staff members soared impressively to well above 125, but most had very limited responsibilities. In 1929, the Administration bragged that its minimal cost to educate a physician (University of Nebraska Medical School $2,000, Creighton University Medical School $1,000) resulted, in part, from "a plethora of efficient but low-salaried instructors."[45]

By the 1920s, research had also become an important element of medical education. Opening the following decade, Fr. President Agnew provided extra incentive: his "greatest contribution" to "the scientific life of Omaha was his intense interest in the affairs of the medical school. A short visit of inspection after his arrival elicited the characteristic order: 'Clean it up'." Immediately, the administration expended $10,000 renovating virtually every room in the aging facility (the "New Creighton University" plan of 1922, had included a new medical-school building adjacent to St. Joseph's Hospital). Father Agnew also believed that "an insensibility to the research possibilities of his own field [physics] made a man unfitted to teach young men in the medical schools of today [1930s]." He put his values into practice through "the compilation of the research work of the school, with a view to determining who, in his opinion, were teachers and who were not." He also approved the creation of the rank of clinical professor to reward faculty members in those departments who "distinguished themselves for scholarship, publications of merit, or professional service of note." Furthermore, the administration created the degree of Master of Science in pre-clinical subject areas (available through the graduate school) and supported the degree by granting medical students tuition remission in the summer school for "doing extra research for the benefit of the school." Starting in 1934, the University began awarding one or two M.S. Med. Degrees per year.[46]

Subsequent presidents of the interwar era did not possess Fr. Agnew's preoccupation with science and medicine, but they gave the medical school its due attention. As the fall session opened in 1932, Dean Herman W. von Schulte died suddenly at his residence from a heart attack at age fifty-five. He had led the medical school since 1918, and had participated in numerous civic activities, including serving on the boards of the Omaha Public Library and the Omaha Chamber of Commerce, and as president of the Council of Social Work and the Omaha Art Institute. Von Schulte had also served as a Lt. Col. in the Army Medical Reserve; in 1922, he had established the Creighton Medical Unit of the Organized Reserves, designated the 55th General Hospital. It consisted of two score of medical school faculty and students and functioned throughout the interwar era; in 1935, for example, twenty-four graduating physicians received ROTC reserve commissions as first lieutenants. Father Regent McInerny served as acting dean until the appointment of Bryan M. Riley (Creighton M.D., 1900) in 1933. Riley served six years, succeeded by Charles M. Wilhelmj (M.D., Saint Louis University, 1922). In 1939, unable to build a new medical school, the University constructed a $20,000 air-conditioned, 60-by-48 foot, two-story addition attached to the rear of the south building of the medical complex. The first floor held the dispensary, double its previous size, and the second floor housed the anatomy department. Moreover, the emphasis on research did not die with Fr. Agnew; in 1940, the medical school published a twelve-page booklet citing research done by its faculty. The accomplishments did not push the school to the forefront of medical institutions, but it did contribute to maintaining the overall status of the University. In 1941, the American Association of Universities added Creighton to its "approved" list, stating that the "committee on classification of universities and colleges was favorably impressed by the number of Creighton University graduates who have gone on to further study, and by the fact that several professional schools have merited approval by their respective accrediting agencies."[47]

The improved medical school complex actually served fewer students, as tuition increases, more stringent entrance requirements, and the exigencies of the Great Depression burst the bubble of escalating enrollments. Between 1920 and 1932, tuition rose from $160 to $300 per year. Yet enrollment skyrocketed from 117 to over 300; the 1929 St. Catherine's Hospital affiliation and a remodeling at St. Joseph's Hospital, which increased the number of beds and clinical opportunities, allowed the medical school to increase the size of its freshman class from fifty-four to one hundred. During that period, one or two women graduated annually from classes that also displayed increasing geographic diversity. In 1920, virtually all Creighton medical students came from Nebraska and adjacent states (in 1923, the student newspaper reported the unusual distinction that sixteen of fifty-six medical freshmen had not attended a Creighton undergraduate college). By the mid-twenties, a trickle of students from the west coast and New York appeared, and by 1932, Nebraska provided eighty students, California fifty, New York thirty-seven and Iowa twenty-one. By that time, medicine had become a much more lucrative and desired profession, and the Creighton Medical School received up to nine applicants for each student position available. Obviously, in the competitive situation, students from the populous coastal states had to seek opportunities outside their home states.[48]

After 1932, however, medical enrollment began to tumble. That year, for the first time, the medical school required candidates to take the Scholastic Aptitude Test for Medical Students and to supply two letters of reference from "instructors in science testifying to the character of the applicant and his apparent fitness for the profession of medicine." The number of applicants remained high, but the new requirements may have shrunk the pool of qualified candidates. More importantly, new guidelines on attendance and work probably affected some students already having a difficult time paying the tuition and the additional estimated costs of $240 for equipment and supplies. Medical students received the highest proportion of University loan funds, top students could win small cash prizes ($25 to $50) for performing well in particular classes or writing exceptional papers, and a few scholarships existed. In 1923, Mrs. Kathryn O'Keefe Murphy donated $2,000 to create an endowment, with interest funding two annual scholarships in the name of her husband (Henry C.). The administration offered two annual tuition-remission scholarships to students interested in becoming medical missionaries, but they languished. Moreover, in 1932 it created a "limited number" of teaching fellowships, which carried a $500 stipend, for medical master's degree candidates for aiding in laboratory exercises (no records reveal the number granted). In 1939, regent and acting dean Fr. McInerny "bent the rules and allowed full time faculty appointees to conduct classes and attend medical school at the same time." Creighton had always hired its graduates to teach in its medical school; with the dislocations of the Great Depression, it seems as though a few assumed their positions before graduating.[49]

With few opportunities for financial aid, many students worked to pay their educational bills, and it must have affected their classroom performance. Thus, in 1932, the medical school issued a new directive on attendance, instructing "absences to the extent of 15 percent or more from any course debar from examination of the course." That policy supplemented a new statement on student employment, which, on the one hand, offered the services of the University in finding a job, but, on the other hand, warned that new students should have sufficient funds "to meet the expenses of the first year." The school also offered third-year students the opportunity to become a "junior interne" at a local hospital, but then warned all working students that, "The Faculty reserves the right to order discontinued any work which interferes with satisfactory prosecution of the prescribed course. In no case can the exigencies of employment serve to excuse unsatisfactory performance of school duties." Thus, 102 freshmen enrolled in 1932, but only 78 seniors remained in 1936. Despite the surfeit of applicants, the school admitted just 75 freshmen in 1936, and the senior class that year consisted of only 59. The next year, total medical enrollment slipped to 268, as the school published a new tuition rate of $400 per year for all students not from Nebraska or contiguous states. The following year, it revised the policy to apply the new rate to all students who had not attended the CCAS. Finally, in 1940, the medical school demanded three years of undergraduate preparation for entrance and finished the pre–World War II era with only 227 students (women continued to number one to three per class). Obviously, the admissions committee must have felt that many of the applicants did not possess the skills or the finances to warrant acceptance. Moreover, for scholastic and/or financial reasons, a significant attrition rate persisted during the 1930s. Thus, the Great Depression, rising costs, and more stringent entrance requirements reversed the pattern of burgeoning enrollment of the previous decade.[50]

The dental school experienced a similar roller-coaster ride during the interwar era. It began the post–World War I decade with a ground breaking ceremony for a new on-campus facility on May 28, 1920. The lot on the northwest corner of 26th and California streets had once belonged to "Omaha's leading brick yard" and a creek ran adjacent to it to the west. Thus, construction crews drove over two hundred piles into the ground to stabilize the area and the administration had them move four frame homes, which stood on the north side of California Street in front of the emerging building, across to the south side of the street on University-owned property. The volatile postwar economy forced a temporary halt to construction on April 4, 1921, as workers went on strike to protest a 20 percent wage reduction (union membership and wages had risen dramatically during World War I). They resumed work three days later, having agreed to an immediate 10 percent decrease, followed by a second 10 percent reduction in July. Thereafter, construction proceeded smoothly, students attended their first classes in the new structure on September 23, 1921, and an official dedication on January 15, 1922, opened it for public inspection. In 1926, the administration gave the dental school a special $1,000 appropriation for book purchases, which swelled its library collection to over three thousand volumes and prompted the hiring of its first full-time librarian. However, despite the newness of the facility, the dental clinic continued to operate with "obsolete equipment." Thus, in 1929, the school installed modern electrical equipment at all chairs at a cost of $15,000. While current dentists might cringe, to demonstrate the prowess of the new clinic, three students and their faculty demonstrator established a local record of note by extracting 108 teeth in a two-hour period (usual production numbered 30 to 35).[51]

The facilities, the students and the faculty enhanced the stature of the Creighton Dental School during the interwar era. A survey published in 1921, revealed that only 8 of 251 graduates (3.1 percent) between 1910 and 1919 did not pass certification examinations in the various states. The national average for failure stood at 15 percent; only five of sixty dental schools in the United States produced a lower rate than Creighton. In 1922, the Carnegie Foundation for the Advancement of Teaching and the National Dental Education Council established a committee to study dental education. Doctor W. J. Gies of Columbia University chaired the four-person commission, which visited Creighton on May 9 (the fiftieth of fifty-two schools on its schedule). Creighton impressed the group; the Council's classification of dental schools the following year listed it as one of twenty "Class A" schools in the United States. The faculty, led by Dean A. Hugh Hipple, D.D.S., elected president of the American Institute of Dental Teachers in 1922, contributed to the premier status. The number of full-time faculty hovered around ten, supported by several dozen part-time clinical adjuncts and faculty from other colleges of the University. The vast majority of the teachers held a Creighton D.D.S. degree. Several achieved national prominence, including J. S. Foote, M.D., professor of pathology and histology, whom the university honored with a Doctor of Law degree in 1924, for his thirty-year association with the dental school; E. J. La Porte (Creighton D.D.S., 1923), inventor of a commercially successful gold-inlay casting machine; and Dr. Charles E. Woodbury, D.D.S., inventor of several dental instruments, prolific author, founder of the nationally significant Woodbury Study Club, a founding fellow of the American College of Dentistry, and the "world's leading authority on gold foil manipulation."[52]

The faculty taught a curriculum that remained basic to dental education, but responded to changes in entrance requirements and to advances in science and technology. Thus, as of September 1926, the dental school, following national guidelines, required one year (thirty semester hours) of college preparation for matriculation. The mandate included six hours each of biology, chemistry, and English, allowing dentistry to eliminate those hours from its freshman schedule. Moreover, in 1925, the

Creighton Dental School became one of three in the United States to make ortho-dontia a major part of the curriculum. While most dental schools prescribed "only a short series of lectures supplemented with a few demonstrations and clinics," admin-istrators and faculty at Creighton believed that "since 70% of this human family of ours have irregular teeth and the greater percentage of these people could be mate-rially benefited by orthodontic treatment," it would emphasize more practice in the field. Another distinctive element of Creighton dental education began in 1921, with the organization of a dental ROTC unit. The following year, it became "obligatory" for all freshman and sophomore male dental students. At the time of its initiation, first and second-year dental students were usually the same age as their arts, com-merce and pharmacy cohorts; thus, in one sense the University simply standardized its mandatory-ROTC policy. Dean Hipple, however, maintained a special relation-ship with the unit, which did not survive his death. Hipple, who had served as dean since 1908, drowned on July 29, 1933, while fishing near his summer home near Brockville, Ontario, Canada. Frank J. Viner (Creighton DDS, 1918) became acting dean for two years, and dean in his own right in 1935; with a two-year college-prepa-ration entrance requirement looming, he immediately eliminated the ROTC require-ment. At the same time, with the new status conferred by the two-year undergrad-uate requirement, the dental school now mirrored the medical school and demanded a thesis for graduation.[53]

The students attending the Creighton Dental School during the interwar era faced the same tribulations as their counterparts in the other colleges. Tuition rose steadily during the twenties. In 1920, it stood at $175 per year, plus books and instru-ments. In 1925, the school introduced a two-tiered structure: $200 per year for fresh-men and $175 for upper classmen. In 1927, the administrators added a third tier and began charging by semester—freshmen $125, sophomores $112.50, juniors and seniors $100. In 1929, they jettisoned the tiers and began charging a uniform $140 per semes-ter. In the face of the Great Depression and decreased enrollment, they lowered tuition to $125 and maintained that rate for fourteen years. During the era, the den-tal school adhered to the same employment policies as the other colleges, but it failed to garner any scholarships. However, in 1928, when a "serious need for additional loan funds existed," Dr. Charles Woodbury donated $1,000 to establish the Woodbury Loan Fund for dental students. That same year, he also began to offer a prize of $25 each to the sophomore and junior who performed the best gold-foil operations. Sub-sequently, other colleagues followed his example: V. T. Joseph offered $25 to the per-son with the highest four-year grade average, George A. Hollenbach presented $10 to the student who showed the "best aptitude toward clinical practice during [his] jun-ior and senior years," and Henry A. Merchant awarded $10 to the senior who wrote the best paper on the history of dentistry.[54]

Financial concerns and enhanced entrance requirements negatively affected enrollment in the dental school. During the prosperous twenties, the student popu-lation jumped dramatically, from 145 in 1920 to 230 in 1925. The one-year-of-college entrance requirement of 1926 reversed the trend nationwide and Creighton dental students dwindled to 92 in 1930. It remained close to that number until the 1936 two-years-of-college entrance requirement, which pushed enrollment down to 77 the following year. While the school ended the interwar era on a numerical downslide, the student body gained a distinctive element of diversity. After a decade's hiatus, two women became freshman in 1921, and at least one woman studied annually in the dental school until Lillian White completed the program and graduated in 1929. Thereafter, no women entered until 1936, and subsequently only a total of three graced the halls of the dental school until World War II. Similarly, few African Americans chose to study dentistry at Creighton. The yearbook, however, did picture a black underclassman in 1927, and a second in 1928. In comparison to the few women and African Americans, the dental school inaugurated the distinguishing Hawaiian connection at Creighton. In 1923, D. L. Chang of Honolulu enrolled, and in 1927, that city provided five more freshmen. By the end of the thirties, Dr. W. S. Char (Creighton D.D.S., 1926) had organized a Hawaii Creighton Alumni Club and his wife operated the "Blue-Jay Beauty Shop next to her husband's dental office."[55]

The new law school facility rose simultaneously with the dental school building, their exteriors mirroring each other, except that the law school entrance sat on the north side of the structure because of the University's inability to purchase one of the houses that abutted the northeast corner of 26th and California streets. "Designed for 150 students and eight full-time professors, the first floor contained a smoker, locker room, offices and a moot court. The second floor housed the two-story [*sic*] library reading room, a large classroom, women's lounge, administrative offices and access to the multi-level library stacks designed to hold 50,000 volumes. The third floor had three classrooms, a faculty lounge and four faculty offices." Since law students did not occupy the building in the afternoon, the arts college partially solved its lack-of-space problem by scheduling "many" of its classes in the facility during those hours. The law library included a special vault to house a priceless collection of rare books and manuscripts, most "collected during the recent war when their owners anxious to sell, forgot the real value and parted with them for a fraction of their intrinsic value." Professor Hugh Gillespie administered the law library during the interwar period; with adequate appropriations, he built the collection to over 40,000 volumes by 1938, which helped secure a favorable rating by the Association of American Law Schools.[56]

During the interwar era, the law school did not reach its full complement of full-time faculty. Louis J. TePoel became dean in 1919, and held the position for twenty-nine years. He had graduated from Columbia University with an M.A. in political Science and an LL.B., and began teaching at the Creighton law school in 1907. According to those who knew him, he maintained a "judicious and sever address," and "a posture somewhat removed from the students both as professor and dean." He served on a Nebraska Constitutional Convention committee and "was of sufficient caliber to be seriously considered for a seat on the United States Supreme Court but his dogged conservatism may have destroyed his chances" (he opposed Roosevelt's New Deal). As dean, he administered a long-serving full-time faculty that merely expanded from four to five. The group included William P. Sternberg and Charles Bongardt, World War I recipient of the Distinguished Service Cross and two Croix de Guerre. It also claimed Hugh F. Gillespie (Creighton A.B., 1909; LL.B., 1915), who had become the Creighton librarian and instructor of mathematics and economics in 1911, then registrar and professor of history in 1913, law librarian and professor of law in 1917, and finally, in 1939, after twenty-eight years of service, "Secretary of the Law School." Over the years, many part-time instructors gave the school added breadth.[57]

The faculty taught a traditional legal curriculum that incorporated the pedagogical innovations of the interwar era and responded to its social, economic, and political trends. Thus, the seminar became a popular manner of expanding electives and at the Creighton law school their number doubled from five to ten between 1920 and 1940. The call for on-the-job "clinical training" resulted in encouraging internships. The classes followed national trends, expanding in the areas of business law and public administration, especially in response to the rapid expansion of government programs and regulation fostered by the New Deal. The school maintained its "Class A" ranking from the Association of American Law Schools, but to do so it had to return to the semester system and phase out the night school (in 1923, it accepted no new registrants, and the last class graduated June 1926). It also eliminated the feature that allowed law students to take classes for credit in the arts college and established a minimum of seventy-eight hours for graduation (twenty more hours possible with electives). In 1931, the school also eliminated its distinctive requirement of participation in Model House, and in 1937, the State of Nebraska terminated the waiver that, since 1907, had exempted Creighton law school graduates from taking the Nebraska bar exam.[58]

Tuition to the law school rose moderately during the 1920s to $100 per semester, which included the use of required books. The school maintained that rate during the subsequent decade; thus, tuition remained minimal and did not constrain enrollment. In 1938, Mrs. Margaret P. Hynes, mother of the late William J. Hynes, Jr. (Law 1932, deceased December 31, 1936), established an annual $500 scholarship exclusive to the law school in honor of her son. The demise of the night school and more demanding entrance requirements, however, affected enrollment significantly. By 1924, combined day and night classes attracted 231 students. Apparently, the two-years-of-college entrance requirement pushed by the Nebraska Bar Association, which went into effect in January 1922, did not stifle enrollment. However, as night-school students finished the program, the total number of students quickly fell by 100, and temporarily stabilized at approximately 150 (all full-time day students). Women remained a rarity and no African Americans graduated during the interwar era. The vast majority of students came from Omaha and Nebraska, with a small contingent from surrounding states. Enrollment rose as high as 197 in 1936, but at the behest of the American Bar Association, Creighton raised its entrance requirement to three years of college in 1937, and the total number of law students plummeted to only 61 in 1941, three months before the bombing of Pearl Harbor.[59]

Finally, in 1926, the interwar period witnessed the creation of yet another coeducational college—the graduate school. The University had granted the A.M. degree as early as 1893 to students who applied for it after two years employment in any profession. In 1903, it had supplemented that program with graduate classes presented at the Edward Creighton Institute, intended primarily for physicians and attorneys, but open to all professionals. In 1915, the arts college had begun to promote graduate study as an extension of its program and its dean administered graduate education for the next decade. In 1919, ten nuns obtained masters degrees through the summer school. The latter program continued to flourish and students enrolled in the evening Teachers' Course could take graduate classes and received A.M. degrees, although between 1919 and 1926, the Creighton University Bulletin did not delineate a specific graduate-level course of study. Between 1893 and 1926, the University awarded 726 graduate degrees, 383 of them to nuns.[60]

In 1925, as part of the on-going struggle to obtain and to maintain accreditation, the Missouri Province established guidelines for graduate study; the following year, the Inter-Province Committee added its imprimatur, stating, "No university is considered complete without a graduate school, which should be organized and conducted according to approved standards." Creighton University responded by printing requirements for graduate work in the College of Arts and Sciences Bulletin in 1926, as well as publishing a "Bulletin of Graduate Courses." It issued no separate bulletin for the next two years, but in 1929, the graduate school Bulletin became an independent publication. The University organized a committee on graduate instruction and appointed Fr. Thomas Egan its chairman. In 1927, Edwin J. Bashe, Ph.D., formerly professor of English at the University of Iowa, became acting dean of the graduate school, followed by two other short-term appointees. Finally, in 1931, Fr. Thomas Bowdern assumed the position and guided the development of the graduate school for the next dozen years. The graduate committee became the graduate council; in 1933, the arts college dean ceased to hold membership on the council and all reference to graduate study disappeared from the bulletin of the arts college—the graduate school stood as an independent entity in the University.[61]

According to Fr. Bowdern, "the Jesuit universities clung to the cultural ideals of the English-type university and were slow to accept the research ideals of the German-type university." He predicted, "As this feature of university work, the graduate school, evolves in the Jesuit university, it will probably be a compromise between the cultural and research types. This compromise or combination may result in a new or American type of university. The Jesuit universities of the Middle West are now pushing toward this goal as fast as their limited resources in men and money permit." The "limited resources" at Creighton dictated a graduate school that offered work only in the departments of chemistry, education, English, and history, because, according to Fr. President Grace, "These departments have been strengthened during the past year [1925] by the acquisition of additional faculty members, qualified with the highest degrees obtainable." That graduate faculty consisted of nine members of the arts college, three of whom possessed the Ph.D. Despite the negative impact of the Great Depression, the school expanded, adding "research work in medicine" in 1929, the departments of classical languages and mathematics in 1930, and modern languages in 1932. During the early 1930s, the medical school graduate research program expanded to include anatomy, biochemistry, nutrition, pathology, bacteriology, preventative medicine, and physiology. Graduate students could also take classes, but not earn degrees, in economics, philosophy, and sociology. In 1934, the "graduate school of Commerce and University College" issued a separate bulletin, which listed classes in commerce, finance, and journalism, as well as classes from other graduate school departments, but did not describe an MBA program. By 1940, the increase in course offerings enlarged the graduate faculty to include members from the colleges of commerce, medicine, and pharmacy (a total of forty, twenty-four of whom held the Ph.D. degree).[62]

The graduate program of study mandated thirty hours, with one major and two minors (subsequently changed several times, ending the interwar era with a preference for all hours in one department, but allowing one elective minor of eight to twelve hours). Students took oral and written exams in their major and minors, wrote a thesis in their major department and defended it by oral examination. In 1929, the school added a foreign-language requirement, and the next year stipulated a preference for French or German. In 1931, Fr. President Agnew reorganized the school to promote "graduate and research work in all departments," and added funds "for securing an adequate faculty." In conjunction with the remodeling of the Administration Building, he doubled the size of the University library, increased the annual appropriation for book acquisitions, and added one thousand volumes per year "for research purposes alone." Obviously, considering his simultaneous demand for research from the medical school faculty, the German model of a university influenced Fr. Agnew more than it did Fr. Bowdern. During the 1930s, concerns about graduate education contributed to the creation of the Jesuit Education Association (JEA) in the United States. In 1937, it established "norms" for "Appraising Graduate Work," which had little significance for Creighton. For masters-level work, the graduate school stood well ahead of the curve, but it lacked the finances to initiate doctoral programs. Nonetheless, the deans of the graduate schools of the University of Nebraska and the University of Kansas reported favorably on the quality of the Creighton graduate program in 1933 and 1934, and professors of the University of Nebraska continued to serve on oral-comprehensive-examination committees of the graduate school throughout the interwar era.[63]

During the interwar era, despite the expansion of participating departments, the number of faculty members, and of the course offerings, graduate enrollment remained stagnant at about 130. Tuition rose moderately from $60 per semester in 1926, to $75 in 1931 ($5 per hour part-time), then shifted to $7 per hour for all students in 1934 ($84 per semester for a full-time student taking twelve hours). The school began offering fellowships in 1929, but finances limited their number; 1931 stood as an exceptional year with three in chemistry and one each in mathematics and English. Most graduate students studied part-time; the 1940 graduate school Bulletin listed

only thirty full-time students, while University enrollment figures posted 139 registered in the school. Women, lay and religious, remained a significant majority of the
graduate students. For example, in the 1934–35 academic year, those registered
included thirty-seven men, but forty lay women, and forty-nine nuns. Obviously,
teaching continued as the primary profession of graduate students and all but 10 of
those 126 graduate students (5 in chemistry, 3 in medical research, 2 in classics)
majored in education, English, or history. While women dominated the graduate
school, an African-American presence remained extremely rare. Yet, the Reverend
Joseph H. Jackson (M.A. 1933), subsequent head of the National Baptist Convention,
stands out as one of the graduate school's most distinguished alumni.[64]

By the time the United States entered World War II, Creighton University had
evolved into a coeducational institution. The summer school and the Teachers'
Course offered women venues at times when undergraduate males traditionally had
completed their schedule. The corporate-college experiment maintained separate
campuses, but integrated women into theatrical productions and student publications. Technically, the arts college remained a male preserve, but starting in the 1920s,
its classrooms increasingly experienced the presence of females. Nursing, commerce,
journalism, and University College students all had to fulfill liberal-arts requirements
offered by CCAS faculty in regularly scheduled day classes. Moreover, a few undergraduate men began to take summer and or evening classes to finish their degrees.
The attitudes of the undergraduate men remained mixed. In 1920, one observer
revealed that College of Commerce students considered themselves "objects of envy . .
. for falling in with the equal-suffrage and other advanced ideas of the present age."
The reporter found women "very welcome"; yet, at the same time, another student
lamented the "invasion" that disrupted the delightful "Eveless Paradise" that had
existed since 1878. As late as 1936, a coed-authored editorial in the student newspaper,
entitled "Give Us a Break," complained about a "sense of superiority" that some men
"carried too far in many cases."[65]

The gender conflict probably also reflected the situation in the professional
schools, except that they had matriculated women from their inception. Each continued their individual traditions during the interwar era. The medical, dental, and law
schools attracted a few brave women willing to endure the isolation, while the pharmacy school drew more females than the other three combined. In comparison, the
newest professional school, the graduate school, became a haven for women. Most
female graduate students attended part-time and most of them sought further credentials for their teaching jobs. Thus, despite papal bulls and admonitions against coeducation at the collegiate level by Fr. General Ledochowski, the American environment, the exigencies of the Great Depression, and the torpid financial situation of
Creighton University combined to direct its evolution into a coeducational institution.

CHAPTER 7

Student Life

Sandwiched between world wars that converted the campus to military use, the "roaring twenties" and the "depressed thirties" each gave student life at Creighton University a distinctive flavor. During both conflagrations student organizations dissolved and most extracurricular activities ceased. Thus, when World War I ended and the boot camp at Creighton folded its tents, administrators and students had to reestablish traditional groups and activities. Debate, drama, and music clubs, as well as the various intramural and intercollegiate scholastic competitions, reemerged. Religious sodalities and annual spiritual ceremonies expanded. Intercollegiate athletics reasserted its leading role, with "king" football maintaining its dominant position. With tradition reenergized, campus life burgeoned with novel institutions. The administration chose to make the ROTC mandatory for male undergraduates during their freshmen and sophomore years. Moreover, while students of each school and college developed distinguishing behaviors, the entire student body formed a corporation—the Creighton Student Union—to foster a program for unity. It sponsored all-University events and assumed control of existing publications, as well as creating a student newspaper and yearbook. Fraternities and sororities mushroomed and, of course, the presence of women on campus altered the nature of virtually every extracurricular activity. During the roaring twenties, students thought in grandiose terms and accomplished noteworthy feats. The budget woes of the University, however, hampered many efforts even during the good times; the vibrancy of extracurricular activities began to wither well before the Great Depression contributed significant additional constraints, which resulted in further unfulfilled wishes.

Toward the end of the 1920–21 academic year, Fr. President McCormick encouraged the students to form a union. He did not envision students organizing for strikes; he foresaw a organization assuming the responsibility for many of the extracurricular activities. The concept of student government originated with Progressive reformers, but World War I delayed its emergence at Creighton. The rapid postwar response demonstrated the currency of the idea. Law senior Charles B. Morearty spearheaded the movement and chaired the organizing committee, which published a draft constitution in January 1922. The document sought to unify the University (with the law and dental schools now on campus) with a union administered by a student board of governors (SBG), consisting of one elected upper-class representative from each school, plus two alumni and a faculty member appointed by the administration. All male students paid a mandatory $5 fee to become "active members of the union," while "all other members of the University shall be eligible to the active membership." The union would aim "to further the best interests of the University; to promote good fellowship among the members; to provide and maintain a suitable clubhouse for members and to centralize the student activities in the University." The organizing committee held a smoker in the gymnasium on March 16, 1922, to discuss the constitution, while providing entertainment plus "smoke enough to make the place look like Pittsburgh." Nearly one thousand students and alumni attended; "honorary alum" Omaha Mayor James Dahlman spoke and the participants adopted the constitution. In the elections in April, only 117 of 270 arts college students voted (a "trifle weak" according to editorialists), but dental, medical, and law students participated at a "gratifyingly heavy" rate. The elected representatives then chose one of their members, Albert K. Stevens (D.D.S., 1923), as the first president of the SBG and hired Morearty as business manager. Shortly thereafter, Stevens attended the second annual meeting of the Mid-West Student Conference of Colleges in Lexington, Kentucky, to discuss governance and the management of extracurricular activities and student publications. The SBG accomplished a major step in that direction by legally incorporating in 1925.[1]

During the fall semester of 1923, the SBG sponsored a freshman dance, a parade before the football game with Marquette, a three-day carnival, and an outing to Krug Park (a local amusement park). The administration also gave the SBG the right to convene all-University assemblies to consider "campus problems that might arise from time to time." Despite "an exceptionally fine program" for Columbus Day and successful pep rallies for football games, "one of the discouraging features [*sic*] of these assemblies was a poor attendance on the part of the students." Because of the unity goal, Fr. President McCormick maintained the devise, but appointed a faculty committee on public functions, with only one SBG representative, to plan and administer the events. Similarly, the fledgling organization failed to procure "a permanent union house, containing smoker rooms, study rooms, rooms for visiting alumni, a cafeteria, and all those things which tend to knit the bonds of friendship existing among university men. Such a home should be built along the [Lincoln] boulevard within sight of the university [to the west]." The planners knew students could not undertake a fundraising effort while the University initiated its $2 million campaign. They hoped a savings and loan company would build it and lease it to the SBG, which would earmark $3 of its $5 fee for rent and use part of the remaining funds to furnish the building. Projected increases in the number of students promised growing revenue; however, the University's fund drive failed and the advent of undergraduate tuition in 1924 stifled enrollment. Actually, the SBG entered the 1924–25 academic year with a deficit and had to begin to charge "a nominal fee for admission at union dances."[2]

The SBG scaled back its dream and gained control of a portion of the gymnasium. It leased the north half of the first floor, and remodeled and refurnished the area. The new quarters included a union office, clubroom, billiard and bowling room (reduced to three alleys), a candy store (originally operated by the arts college in the

Administration Building and moved to the gymnasium in 1920), and a lunch counter. The SBG also maintained control of "a private ballroom on the second floor and the use of the main floor [basketball court] for the regular calendar of union dances." The "new furnishings completely surpass[ed] all expectations" and club-room amenities included "the latest magazines, Victrola [a record player] and a brand new expensive radio." In 1927, the SBG hired Edward D. Murphy (BSC 1927) as manager of the student union at a salary of $175 per annum. Despite financial con-straints, Murphy expanded union services and activities; he and the board organized a student employment bureau, a book exchange, and a housing service, as well as sponsoring four plays and five all-University dances per year. In 1933, Murphy was elected president of the Alumni Association and accepted the position of assistant treasurer of the university. Thereafter, in succession, he became bursar, business man-ager, personnel director, and the affirmative action administrator during a sixty-nine-year career at Creighton.[3]

During the interwar years, the SBG struggled to build student interest and spirit, as well as to reform its political structure and to encourage unity among the schools of the University. In 1926, it introduced staggered elections in an attempt to provide experienced leadership; each year one of two representatives of a school would stand for election to a two-year term (thus, the board doubled in size and one-half its membership would always possess one year's experience). In 1928, it introduced pri-mary elections, hoping to generate wider student interest. Originally, the sitting board chose the candidates, producing cronyism. Interested students could get on the ballot by petition, but the wearisome effort discouraged the mass of scarcely inter-ested students. That same year, the SBG developed a student-leadership program, asking each representative to create a bond with the president of each class in his school. In turn, each member would form "a subcommittee of three or four influen-tial members of his class" (women students could not join the union), which could form a "reliable body to fill the gap existing between the Board of Governors and the students." The scheme failed and a 1932 editorial in the student newspaper called for the abolition of "unneeded" and "duty-less" class officers. Seemingly, most students remained satisfied with an arrangement whereby they paid their dues and allowed a cadre of involved students to provide them with services and activities that they may or may not have supported.[4]

One activity, however, agitated a significant segment of the student body, thus convulsing the board—the election of royalty for the annual junior-senior prom. The event began as a "Pan-Arts Dance" in 1922, with the underclassmen sponsoring it for the seniors. The following year, it became an all-University dance, with a committee of juniors from all the schools hosting the event. Persistent deficits led the union to assume management duties. The system of representation (two representatives per school) gave the professional colleges a majority on the SBG and they allegedly col-luded to select the king, queen, and princes. In February 1934, following one such election, the six representatives from the arts, commerce, and journalism colleges announced their resignation from the SBG. The dramatic protest had legal ramifications threatening the existence of a Nebraska corporation. Quickly, the remaining SBG members established a committee to review reform proposals submitted by "individuals, clubs and fraternities." The committee decided that the union had failed "to function in the manner in which it was calculated to work," but student apathy smothered speedy progress. The editor of the student newspaper lamented, "The report of that committee's activities during the last 10 days is almost unbelievable even for a Creighton student group. Out of three committee meetings called, one was held. Five of nine members appeared. Nothing was accomplished."[5]

Subsequently, a revised committee accepted a plan "submitted by Michael Brown, formerly junior arts representative on the board who resigned at the prom." In early April, Fr. President Mahan approved the proposed restructuring and sanctioned a special assembly for April 19, 1934, to vote on the amendments to the union constitution. Despite a membership of nearly one thousand, the committee scheduled the assembly for the clubroom in the gymnasium, which held only one hundred. Three SBG representatives sought signatures giving them proxy votes; a total of ninety-seven students (with 224 proxies), voted unanimously to accept the revisions:

1. Proportional representation, which increased the SBG from fourteen to nineteen members—two representatives per school with 100 students or less, with an additional representative for each 100 additional students in a school.
2. Popular nomination and election for SBG members and prom princes.
3. A nine-year rotation system whereby each school "must have a prom king and queen and president of the board" during that period.
4. SBG meetings opened to students and reporters.
5. One vote per school on matters of finance.
6. Three-fourths vote of SBG to elect the king, queen and board officers.
7. Established a recall procedure for SBG members.[6]

The new rules survived one prom and underwent a second revision in January 1936. The three-fourths rule resulted in too many delays caused by "organized minorities"; the system shifted to a two-thirds vote, which still demanded a "hearty majority" acceptable to the "persistent minorities." At the same time, the union codified and standardized election procedures by mandating that all schools follow the regulations for candidate registration, election dates, polling-place guidelines, and the validating and counting of ballots developed by professor Hugh Gillespie of the law school. The mechanics of the vote, however, plagued the SBG for another year. Finally, in May 1938, members of the union approved the addition of preferential balloting for all representatives, officers and royalty. Each voter chose a number 1 (three points), number 2 (two points) and number 3 (one point) candidate; the person receiving the highest total points gained election. Union members also approved an amendment that limited candidacy for royalty to students in the upper one third of their class who would graduate in June following the prom. Moreover, an undergraduate prince could win reelection in one of the professional schools if his cohorts chose him. Finally, in that same election, members endorsed the concept of dividing the

SBG into six standing committees: rules, student services, social activities, Agnew Loan Fund, cultural activities, and athletics and school spirit.[7]

However, during the interwar era, one amendment the all-male SBG continually refused to submit to the members related to union membership for women. Thus, as early as October 1924, "Not to be outdone by their big brothers in the University, the coeds of all departments [colleges] . . . organized a union of their own." Over twenty-five women (all but two from commerce and pharmacy) met at the YWCA to form a coed student union (subsequently named Chi Chi Chi or the Tri Chi sorority) and to elect Dorothy Horn (commerce) president, Lucille Winkler (pharmacy), vice president, and Romaine Flaherty (medicine) secretary-treasurer. Subsequently, the original 1934 reorganization plan had included the addition of a woman's council on the SBG, but the suggestion did not make the ballot. That year, while the SBG again refused female representation, it did acquiesce to the proposal that it appoint princesses from each school to the prom royalty court. As late as 1940, women still petitioned for SBG representation, complaining, "It's about time that somebody realize that this is now a co-educational school." The one distaff victory that year resulted in their ability to use the union clubroom in the gymnasium on Monday evenings, 7:00 to 9:00 P.M., in exchange for a fifty cent per woman assessment.[8]

While the SBG ignored accountability to the coeds, it assumed responsibility for existing student publications and created new ones. Students had edited the *Creighton Chronicle* since 1919, when law dean Paul Martin resigned. Ralph E. Svoboda (arts) became the first student editor-in-chief, with Charles F. Bongardt (law, future law professor), Lawrence Custer (law), and Carroll R. Mullen (arts) as associate editors, but the journal appeared sporadically until its last issue in November 1922. The following month *Shadows: The Activities and Literary Magazine of Creighton University* appeared. The staff altered the journal to a smaller catalogue size, issued it quarterly, and explained that it was not a new journal, but rather was "hotly in pursuit of the magazine ideal which has existed in the minds of a majority of Creighton men." Thus, they decided to sequence it with the *Chronicle* (i.e., first issue numbered vol. 14, no. 3). The name they gleaned from the fact that, "The humor of life is drawn from watching shadows. But a shadow may represent a true picture. . . . The nature of the shadow depends on the angle from which the light is thrown. It is by casting gleams from many angles on current phases of university activity that we aim to evolve, in successive months."[9]

The shade of insufficient funds and lack of alumni support immediately cast a pall over the staff's youthful idealism. It entertained suggestions to make the magazine a monthly publication, but attempts to increase circulation by one thousand subscriptions ($1 per annum), which also would have enticed more advertising revenue, failed and the administration stated it could not afford to subsidize the venture. By 1928, the magazine dropped editorials and feature stories, printing only literary pieces written by students, but it remained an all-University publication with editors, staff, and submissions coming from all schools, including Duchesne, the College of Saint Mary, and the hospital nursing units. The Student Union assumed responsibility for the journal in October 1929, briefly published six issues per year, and initiated prizes to entice submissions of poetry, short stories, and works of art ($15 first prize, $5 second prize). In 1932, the SBG relinquished control of the magazine, renamed the *Creighton Quarterly*. The numbering sequence continued uninterrupted, and by the fourth issue *Shadows* returned as a subtitle. The new run began as an eighty-eight-page publication modeled on the *Atlantic Monthly,* but by April 1932, it shrank to only sixteen pages, before switching back to the smaller size, printed on cheaper paper, with an average of sixty-four pages, for the remainder of the decade. Finally, in May 1941, with prosperity returning, the staff published a new thirty-two-page magazine on glossy paper as "an experiment designed to improve the readability and increase the popularity of the Hilltop's literary publication." The experiment failed; no fall issue followed and World War II curtailed its publication for the duration ("a further defense economy measure").[10]

The student union created a second unity publication, the *Creightonian,* a weekly student newspaper. Law student Thomas J. McGovern emerged as the first editor-in-chief, with Milton Abrahams (LL.B., 1926) and Stephen Spitznagle (arts junior) as associate editors, and the inaugural issue arrived on Wednesday, October 4, 1922. During the interwar era, it sold for five cents a copy, usually consisted of four pages (five columns wide), had several special eight-page issues during the 1920s, but had as few as two pages for some editions in 1934. During various years, it alternately came out on Wednesdays, Thursdays, Fridays, or Saturdays (until 1970, all schools scheduled Saturday morning classes). The coed staff continued to come from all schools of the University, and in 1924, the journalism program began to require its students to work as reporters. The "merger" provided journalism majors on-the-job training and it gave the SBG-selected editors a means to "groom [*sic*] promising members of the class for executive positions." Student leaders believed that the "paper, acting as the official mouthpiece of the Creighton Student body and the Student Union, has exerted an incalculable influence in linking the various departments which were once segregated units, but now unified into a great university." The administration agreed and discontinued publication of the *Courier,* choosing instead to mail every fourth issue of the *Creightonian* to alumni (the venture quickly proved misguided; students did not have the resources to produce alumni news features).[11]

The students, however, did have the wherewithal to produce an award-winning university newspaper. Creighton became a member of the North Central Press Association, composed of schools in Nebraska, Iowa, and North and South Dakota. In 1925, it won first prize for all-round paper in the Association; in 1930, it garnered second best all-round and top front page, and the following year captured firsts in both of those categories. During the thirties, the staff entered national competitions, and for five consecutive years (1933–37), it received all-American honors from the National Scholastic Press Association (47 university papers gained all-American status, while 293 filled three lower rankings in 1937). Subsequently, in 1940 and 1941, the paper acquired an all-Catholic rating from the Catholic School and Press Association. Meanwhile, on campus an annual battle of the sexes emerged during the 1930s.

The Journalism School hosted, judged, and awarded prizes in an annual contest, which evaluated all-women vs. all-men editions of the *Creightonian*. The women provided worthy competition and swept all categories (editorials, headlines, etc.) in the last pre–World War II confrontation.[12]

While the staff collected accolades, it paid scant attention to pressing national or world issues. The short-lived term of student publication of the *Chronicle* had witnessed editorials against the Smith-Towner Act (federal aid to education, opposed by the Catholic Church) and the Volstead Act (established the parameters of prohibition), and *Shadows* frequently published satirical anti-prohibition stories. The *Creightonian* staff believed that the *Chronicle* reported "generally obsolete" news because of its monthly publication. The *Creightonian* promised to provide "timely" coverage; yet, in turn, its weekly schedule dulled the timeliness of coverage of "breaking stories." The editors probably decided against competing with the daily professional newspapers and the host of radio news broadcasts, concentrating instead on internal University issues and events. However, in conjunction with reporting campus news the paper did produce stories reviewing faculty speeches and activities that related to contemporary issues, events, and concerns. Occasionally, the paper also conducted a few student polls; for example, in 1930, it participated in a national survey on student attitudes toward prohibition. By a 25-1 margin, Creighton students favored repeal, but only 464 students bothered to register an opinion, demonstrating widespread apathy. The paper briefly reported that the American Student Union (a federation of politically active student groups) adopted the Oxford Pledge (an oath not to fight in a foreign war), but it did not conduct a campus survey and it did not cover the widespread student antiwar activity in the United States. Its most consistent polling sought information on presidential preference in 1932, 1936, and 1940—FDR swept the campus in landslides on the first two occasions and won handily on the last (student participation in the polls neared 50 percent in 1932, but dropped to less than one third in 1940).[13]

As the Creighton Student Union initiated the creation of a student newspaper, it simultaneously began to publish student handbooks ("little blue covered book contains information about faculty, student organizations, publications, sports, rules and regulations, and all other dates concerning Creighton University life in general") and a student directory. Moreover, it spearheaded the movement for a yearbook, which culminated with an all-University assembly in the Creighton Auditorium on Thursday morning, November 23, 1923. Student leaders explained the concept of an annual and presented a scheme whereby officers of each class in all schools would distribute pledge cards to students who would give a $3 deposit and promise to complete the purchase in June with another $2 or $3 payment. Although it failed to meet the financial break-even goal of an 80 percent subscription rate, in December the SBG appointed Brendan F. Brown (law) editor-in-chief, and designated each of its representatives as editors for their various schools. Subsequently, the board chose "Blue-Jay" as the title, but quickly opted for the alternate spelling, "Bluejay." Ultimately, 650 students purchased a yearbook; the union had published 700 and unsuccessfully tried to sell the extras to the public for $6 (the brief history of the University included in the first edition contained several factual errors).[14]

The annual began with a deficit and continued to operate in the red for the next two years. Facing a shortfall of approximately $1,200 for the 1926 issue, the SBG conducted a plebiscite to allow it to assess every student $5 per year to meet yearbook expenses. With seniors not included in the balloting (they would not return to pay the new fee), a whopping majority (509 yeas out of 621 votes cast) approved the resolution. The all-University coed staff now enjoyed some financial security, but could not afford extravagant features. In 1928, in order "to get out a book that would be a credit to the Jubilee year, they asked the University to supply the extra money needed for this." The administration denied the request; subsequently, working within its limited budget, the staff produced yearbooks of admirable quality. In 1931, the editors entered the National Scholastic Press Association competition for the first time and received a "second class honor" rating, a status above average for its cohort. The following year, the *Bluejay* competed in the senior division (schools with an enrollment of 2,500 and over) and received a "first class honor," the second highest ranking awarded. It repeated that performance in 1938. Three years later, however, Fr. President Zuercher announced that his advisors voted to cease publication of the annual: "In this year of emergency, scarcity and rising prices, the deans feel it is fitting and proper to discontinue publication of the yearbooks as one of our contributions to national defense." It became another of the many sacrifices demanded by another war.[15]

Two decades earlier, World War I had curtailed the activity of virtually all student extracurricular clubs, including the regionally acclaimed music groups. All had to regroup. Quickly, a male Glee Club reorganized and began giving public concerts and making radio broadcasts. Similarly, in 1922, an all-University band separated from the ROTC unit and performed its first public concert in the Creighton Auditorium. In addition, a sixteen-piece, all-male, all-string orchestra also appeared. By mid decade, however, the University lost its energetic music director and its financial problems began to affect the music program. In 1925, a *Creightonian* editorial asked, "Why is our band so small? With a student body such as Creighton boasts of surely a band that can at least be heard above the cheering at a football game should be organized." Temporarily, designated fundraising efforts tried to solve the problem. Before his ignominious departure, P. H. Bogardus arranged five fundraising concerts at the City Auditorium, with earnings earmarked for support of the music groups. Seemingly, only two performances came to fruition, one by the noted humorist Will Rogers and the other by the Ballet Russe, after "precautions regarding sufficient dress for the female actors has been insisted on & agreed to."[16]

Apparently, the cajoling editorial and the fundraising provided a quick fix, as a twenty-four-member band, with new uniforms and instruments (clarinets, saxes, trombones, trumpets, and tuba), played at football and basketball games in 1926. However, the 1927 yearbook pictured no bands, the 1928 edition displayed only the ROTC band and the 1929 edition explained that the "civilian student band" lacked instruments (students did not own one or did not bring it to college, while the

ROTC needed a band for military purposes and the army furnished the instruments to the cadets). The orchestra also went dormant in 1929, but reorganized as a coed entity in 1932, and performed at lectures, plays, and convocations. Furthermore, in 1929, the thirty-voice, all-University coed Creighton Choral Club supplanted the Glee Club and participated in a vocal contest in Kansas City, Missouri. It proved a last hurrah, however, and the voices went silent for over two years. In 1934, the administration hired the choir director of St. John's Church to revive the all-University coed Glee Club, which, on certain occasions, separated into a Male Chorus and a "Girls Chorus." Overall, the music program did not regain its early-twentieth-century grandeur and limped its way through the 1930s, concluding with a deficit incurred by the 1940 annual spring concert (competition from radio and the movies diminished public support for these forms of amateur entertainment). Moreover, the University did not have the resources to pay an experienced energetic musical director, to fund travel expenses for its musical groups, or purchase new instruments and uniforms. Thus, the historically vibrant music program atrophied during the interwar era.[17]

The theater program suffered a similar trauma. As early as March 1920, arts and high school students presented a play, although a drama club, the "Mask and Wig," did not reemerge until 1922. Two years later, it reorganized as the self-supporting (box-office receipts had to cover expenses) Drama Club, which staged the first coed drama in Creighton history, ironically titled "The Man of the Hour," which cast Katherine Cushing and Josephine Newton from the College of Commerce (pre–World War I plays had featured women from the community to act necessary female parts). In 1928, the club reorganized as an all-University stock company, which won prestigious awards for its presentation of "A Night in an Inn." At a play contest sponsored by Northwestern University, the troupe won $150 and the first-place Eva LaGallien Cup, and the Reverend Louis F. Doyle, S.J., assistant professor of English, garnered the Samuel French Cup for best direction. While Fr. Doyle remained director of dramatics during the interwar era, in 1929, Mrs. Anita Mae Marsh became a director for the company, now controlled by the Student Union, which effectively made each male student a stock holder. The company survived the Great Depression, but the financial woes and the competition from inexpensive mass entertainment demonstrated itself in the form of the "Little Theater" movement. While the company continued to perform professional dramas for the public, in 1934 it introduced a new policy:

> In the Little Theater, the Creighton Players are inaugurating a new policy, an experimental and self educational policy. In the past, they have catered more or less to the public in the choice and mounting of plays. Their present aim is to find and develop the creative and dramatic talent of the campus without consulting the taste of the general theater-goer. This seems more in keeping with the nature and purpose of a school.

Clearly, Creighton's participation in the national little-theater movement suited the situation, which necessitated a scaled-back program. To induce participation, it offered cash awards to student playwrights ($25 for best long play, two-and-a-quarter hours with intermissions; $10 for best short drama, 20-30 minutes with "no curtain drops").[18]

In comparison to diminished music and theater programs, debate flourished during the interwar era. It resembled the role puzzle making fulfilled for the frugal depression-era family for inexpensive entertainment—debate required no expensive uniforms, instruments, costumes, props, large-group travel expenses, or salaries for extra professional directors. Existing faculty served as coaches to the teams (two to eight members each); for example, law regent Fr. Thomas Egan reorganized that school's debate team in 1921. Two years later, the University became a charter member of the Missouri Province Debate League, organized into four districts of three schools each, which combined into six-team eastern and western districts. The inaugural year witnessed Creighton defeat St. Louis University for the district championship and Saint Mary's (Kansas) for the western crown, only to lose the province honor to Saint Ignatius College of Cleveland, Ohio. In 1927, Creighton won its first province title. In 1924, the league and the ongoing drive for unity led to the creation of the Oratorical Society, an all-University debate club, and the awarding of varsity letters to forensic team members (for the first time, on May 22, 1924, they lined up with varsity athletes to receive their letters at the annual sports banquet). Edwin M. Puls, professor of public speaking (a required class for all arts students) served as the head coach of the University team, while the Oratorical Society (the second largest group on campus with ninety members) sponsored intramural debate in which individual classes and clubs of the various colleges entered teams. In 1925, the junior law team, composed of Walter Traynor and Milton Abrahams, won the all-University contest, deemed a brilliant success by "the fact that even the busy medics found time for debating."[19]

While intramural debate competitions for individuals and teams remained commonplace during the interwar era, the decade of the thirties incorporated two dramatic elements. First, in 1929 while two thousand spectators watched and listened at the Technical High School Auditorium, the three-man all-University team defeated its opponent from Harvard University, debating the controversial question, "Resolved, that modern woman is a curse" (remember the Flapper). The victory capped an undefeated season (11-0-3) for coach Frank P. Fogarty. The following fall, his team initiated a six-year run of international debates, as a large crowd paid 25 cents for general admission or 50 cents for reserved seating (high-school and college students, 15 cents and 25 cents, respectively) to view Creighton debate Oxford University. Subsequently, Cambridge University also included Creighton on their United States tours. Creighton won all the events, although the audience usually chose the winner; the "home-court" advantage and the scoring system produced landslide victories (e.g., Creighton 1,119, Harvard 316; Creighton 1,007, Oxford 468), although three local judges award Creighton its triumph over Cambridge in 1933. While some would label the system biased, it should not reflect badly on a program that obtained a chapter of Delta Sigma Rho, the national honorary debate fraternity, in 1934 and garnered many victories in traditionally scored contests, including first place at a national forensic tournament at Madison, Wisconsin, in 1937. Law professor Charles F. Bongardt coached the all-University team, which became coed again. In 1931, the University had fielded two women's teams that met gender-based opponents from Iowa State University, and in 1935, the first coed in the post–World War I era, joined the all-University team. After a three-year hiatus, coeds annually became team members.[20]

Like debate, intramural and regional essay contests reappeared after World War I and remained popular because of their inexpensive nature and the prize money involved. The Missouri Province reinstituted its Latin and English essay contests for undergraduates; for the later, it revamped the procedure, allowing students to compose their entry "privately anytime within a space of four weeks in place of during a period of several hours under supervision," as was formerly the case. Moreover, the University resumed awarding the Bishop McGovern medal for the best paper on "evidences of religion." In 1926, Omaha attorney Arthur F. Mullen donated $1,000 to fund the Jefferson-Mullen Prize (all-University, $50 first prize), given for the best essay on "the Life or Works of Thomas Jefferson." The administration followed suit, sponsoring annual contests with monetary rewards on other special topics. Combined with the *Shadows* literary contests, students could choose to compete in a variety of writing forms; coeds regularly submitted to the all-University venues and fared well.[21]

Following the First World War, undergraduate students also reorganized their academic clubs. In the arts college, the languages led the way, with Spanish, French, German, Czech (in 1925, Roman Hruska, law freshman and future United States Senator, became its charter vice president), Italian, and Polish groups forming in chronological order from 1921 to 1931. During the thirties, other departments joined the list, organizing the Press Club (journalism), the Pasteur Club (biology), and the more obviously named Math Club and Chemistry Club. In 1925, the Commerce Club, "composed of male students and members of the faculty . . . organized for the purpose of encouraging good fellowship and the discussion of economic and business subjects." However, it failed for lack of interest; in 1928, the Creighton Chamber of Commerce supplanted it. A commerce college committee, composed of the dean, the regent, and the faculty, annually selected twenty-four members for this honorary group, which served as the "parent organization to several subsidiaries which function along more specialized lines and in which membership is open to any student in the College of Commerce." In 1933, commerce students also organized the Economics Club, "prompted by a desire on the part of students interested in the numerous economic problems associated with the National Recovery Program." Thus, while student apathy prevailed in one sense, in a general manner, for large numbers of students who felt no connection to contemporary national issues or organizations, discipline-based companionship groups attracted viable memberships.[22]

Most of the academic, music, and drama clubs and the University publications, welcomed coed members. Nonetheless, undergraduate women created satellite gender-exclusive organizations. Although women contributed eight of the seventeen charter members of the Press Club, in 1935, those same women established the independent Coed Press Club. The following year witnessed the creation of the Commerce Coed Club to foster spirit among women in that college. Seemingly, some coeds desired an intimate support group, as well as the right to participate in mixed-gender organizations. The University maintained "the cottage" adjacent to the commerce college as their "home of jollification," while the Student Union ignored their entreaties for membership. The Administration did not pressure the SBG to change its policy, probably because in comparison to faculty-monitored clubs and chaperoned public events, it did not relish the idea of unsupervised daily coed interaction in the union clubrooms. The affiliated women's colleges added to the mixture of gender inclusion and exclusion. Each maintained separate organizations, while participating in many all-University groups. Thus, for example, Duchesne, Saint Mary, and hospital-nursing-unit women served on the staffs of the various publications and acted in Creighton plays, but each school possessed its own newspaper and/or literary magazine, drama club, orchestra, and/or chorus.[23]

Maintaining the same pattern of inclusion/exclusion, the coeds also began to participate in a variety of religious groups and activities. Immediately after World War I, the various sodalities reorganized. In 1921, the Senior Sodality established a "truth society" for "the purpose of combating statements appearing in the press hostile or derogatory to the Catholic Church." The national resurgence of the KKK, with a limited local reawakening, prompted that response. In 1925, an unfulfilled threat of some type of demonstration at a Creighton football game had administrators thinking about seeking an injunction against the group, but the bigoted bravado proved to be empty rhetoric. Spirituality, however, played an increasingly important role in student life during the interwar era. Catholic students continued to take classes on doctrine, attend chapel, make an annual retreat, and go to confession and communion once a month. In 1922, the three-day retreat shifted from being an Easter exercise during Holy Week, to late January during the recess between semesters. In 1924, it became an all-University event, as the professional schools scheduled one for the first time. Subsequently, the professional schools shifted their combined retreat (except for the pharmacy school, which remained part of the undergraduate event) to early December to coincide with the Feast of the Immaculate Conception; only the graduate school, because of its predominantly part-time evening student body, did not require a retreat. The events, held at St. John's Church, directed by prominent non-Creighton clergy, and including outside speakers, acquired increasing participation (a required event, but daily attendance not taken) according to student publications.[24]

In 1922, sodality members sponsored a short-lived perpetual adoration group; more significantly, they converted the American Mother's Day celebration (established in 1908) into a day to honor the Blessed Virgin Mary as the "patroness of all motherhood." In 1924, students and delegations representing Omaha parishes attended Mass at St. John's Church. Afterward, they rejoiced together on the north lawn with singing and music by the Creighton band, and dedicated a Marian shrine

erected on the terrace adjacent to the Observatory. It became an annual event during the interwar era, supplemented by other large ad hoc outdoor services held at the
stadium—e.g., in 1927, approximately five hundred students and Omaha parishioners
attended a Mass of the Feast of Christ the King on Sunday, October 30. Students
also manifested their spiritual concern through charitable endeavors. In 1921, arts and
high school students met in the Auditorium to view a program presented by residents
of Fr. Edward Flanagan's Boys Home and pledged over $2,200 to its fund drive (the
Jesuit community contributed an additional $500). The following year the Student
Union initiated a Christmas project, in conjunction with local charities, which distributed 120 baskets valued at $250. The union raised the money through raffles and
donations. Moreover, starting in 1926, sociology students from the arts college and
Duchesne began to volunteer at the Christ Child Society; thirty-six volunteer hours
gained them a year's credit in the department. The agency's staff valued the annual
student contribution to the services of the social settlement at $5,000.[25]

Furthermore, spiritual activities increased during the thirties in response to Fr.
General Ledochowski's directives to emphasize Catholicism. In 1932, Creighton
appointed its first full-time Spiritual Life Director to coordinate events and to serve
as a spiritual counselor. The next year, the Reverend Francis G. Deglman, S.J.,
assumed the position and soon established an enviable record of achievement and a
revered status among the students. In 1933, the Sodality of the Blessed Virgin Mary
inducted 298 candidates, bringing its membership to 650, by far the largest student
organization on campus (coeds established a separate Sodality of the BVM and
attended separate retreats). The Creighton Knights of Columbus offered another all-
male venue, while the Xavier Forum, organized to discuss mission topics, and the
Catholic Action Club, established "to develop leadership in solving socio-economic
problems," both accepted women members. Conferences for non-Catholics, held
simultaneously with the annual retreat, became a mandatory part of the curriculum
(1933) and the administration devised an attendance-taking system (1935, each school
assigned a section of the church, each student signed a card collected at time of seating). By the mid-thirties, the "spiritual life" section of the yearbook consisted of
eleven pages of pictures of groups and events.[26]

The ROTC, a large, mostly involuntary group, also commanded significant attention from the yearbook staff. In 1919, Maj. Corbet S. Hoffman, without staff assistance, organized a high school "junior unit" and a CCAS "senior unit." The following
year, he had to teach military theory and tactics to 174 "senior" cadets (Basic ROTC)
and 86 "junior" cadets, as well as to assemble a military band and organize a signal
corps for interested students. Instruction and drill changed to reflect the "open order"
based on the experiences of the American Expeditionary Force in World War I, and
basic courses included map-making and automatic weapons mechanics. For some
time, military equipment remained in short supply and the ill-fitting uniforms the
cadets wore for drills elicited a mildly mocking *Courier* editorial titled, "All Slicked
Out." The first cadet officers received their appointments in December 1920, and
actual practice with small arms began the following month, as Fr. President

McCormick ordered the conversion of one of the rooms in the gymnasium into a rifle range. Subsequently, the range moved to the stadium, but in 1931, a new, fully equipped range opened on the fourth floor of the gymnasium (staff offices moved from "a red brick building on 25th & Cass" to the second floor). Some cadets (only seventeen volunteered) completed their first full year with a summer camp at Ft. Snelling, Minnesota (Ft. Crook, Bellevue, Nebraska, after 1926). Subsequent years included "camping out at Plattsmouth" to learn bivouacking in tents.[27]

The military staff increased during the twenties to include two captains and two sergeants, while Hoffman and subsequent commanding officers served a three-year rotation. The staff recruited qualified cadets from the "senior unit" (all male freshmen and sophomores in the arts, commerce, and pharmacy schools) to join Advanced ROTC for their junior and senior years. The Creighton battalion usually consisted of three to four companies organized into four to six platoons. Freshmen ranked as privates, outstanding sophomores rose to the rank of corporal, superior juniors became non-commissioned student officers, and stellar seniors achieved the elite positions of cadet officers. In 1921, Harold Leo Downing (arts) became the first graduate of the advanced course and received his commission as a second lieutenant of the infantry of the United States Army Reserve Officer Corps; he had begun the program as an advanced cadet. The next commissions came in 1923, and the army granted 20 or more annually thereafter (a total of 435 during the interwar era). In the twenties, up to 20 percent of the individual sophomore classes opted for advanced training; because it included some pay and benefits, the percentage jumped toward 30 percent for many of the Depression years. Distinctively, over a score of Creighton ROTC graduates received commissions as executive officers in the Civilian Conservation Corps, a New Deal relief agency that operated on a quasi-military basis. Moreover, in 1936, the United States Congress passed a law allowing for the appointment of distinguished ROTC graduates directly to the United States Army, as opposed to the Reserves.[28]

The Creighton battalion attained exceptional status under the command of Maj. Hardin C. Sweeney, appointed in September 1930. By 1933, it received the army's highest rating—the Blue Star—and maintained it for the next six years. In 1935, the *Bluejay* editors accorded Sweeney extraordinary recognition, dedicating the yearbook in his honor. When the army transferred him in 1937, the University awarded him a Master of Science in Military Science for having served as commandant for seven years, including three one-year extensions "at the urgent request" of Creighton's president. He served during the onset of the student antiwar activity in the United States; the Creighton response included a couple of isolated anti-ROTC editorials in the *Creightonian*, but anti-pacifism declarations more than balanced the ledger. Ultimately, while students nationally expressed "overwhelming sentiment against compulsory drill in any institution of learning except purely military schools," Creighton students voted in favor of the ROTC in 1938; two years later, they decisively supported peacetime conscription (men, 354-77; coeds, 44-28; although, again, the numbers reveal minimal student partition in the referendum).[29]

Military participation also had a social side. In 1923, cadet officers organized a Greek-letter fraternity, Chi Delta Chi, which began sponsoring a military ball in 1928. Five years later, it reorganized as the Delta Morae chapter of a national organization known as Phalanx, an exclusive ROTC group founded at the University of Illinois in 1925, and open only to units receiving the army's highest rating (only six chapters in 1936). In 1929, Maj. George Hicks created a fraternal society for basic cadets, the "Commandant's Hundred," which grew rapidly and adopted the Greek letters Alpha Phi Delta. Its raison d'etre included recruiting for Advanced ROTC and providing an honor guard for the "Honorary Colonel" at the military ball. Annually, the cadets chose a coed to serve as the battalion's combination prom queen and Miss America; in 1936, mirroring the turmoil associated with selection of junior-senior prom royalty, each company secured the right to chose a coed to serve in a "court" for the honorary colonel.[30]

Chi Delta Chi joined a flourishing Greek-letter community that created an interfraternity council in 1921. Father Neil Cahill, S.J., in his history of the Creighton College of Business Administration, wrote,

> For some inexplicable reason, social fraternities and sororities did not appear on the campus of any Catholic educational institution in the United States. It is difficult to explain this phenomenon. Possibly it was due to the fact that for ages authorities of the Catholic Church had forbidden its members to join "secret organizations," whose constitutions were not open to scrutiny by the American bishops. Whatever the cause, the Creighton campus was the first of any Catholic educational institution to allow a Greek social fraternity in its midst. This was the Phi Alpha Psi fraternity, established at Creighton in 1965.[31]

Father Cahill's interpretation resulted from faulty data and from an extremely narrow definition of "social fraternity." Actually, during the interwar era, all schools of the University created a vibrant system of Greek-letter groups. In 1925, the *Creightonian* published a "Fraternity Directory":

LAW:	Gamma Eta Gamma 3504 Harney St.	MEDICAL:	Phi Beta Pi 121 South 33rd St.
	Delta Theta Phi No House		Phi Chi 3514 Burt St.
DENTAL:	Delta Sigma Delta No House		Phi Rho Sigma 3501 Harney St.
	Xi Psi Phi 404 North 20th St.	PHARMACY:	Kappa Psi 2023 Cass St.
	Psi Omega No House		Lamba Kappa Sigma No House
SOCIAL:	Delta Kappa Delta 404 North 22nd St.		Phi Delta Chi No House
	Kappa Pi Delta No House[32]		

Two years earlier, an article in *Shadows* had stated that twelve professional and two "general" fraternities existed at Creighton, and that those without houses produced a post-graduation giving plan, which initiated building funds (subsequently, several frats listed as "homeless" in 1925 acquired houses). The *Shadows* total, one more than listed in the *Creightonian* directory, may have included the Crustacea Club, a social organization that held dances and a banquet, formed in the arts college in 1921, that had become an all-University group as graduates moved on to the Creighton professional schools. Significantly, while the professional fraternities had a relationship to a particular college, they acted like social fraternities not honorary societies, holding rushes, smokers, dances, and banquets. Moreover, both social fraternities listed in the *Creightonian* directory applied for national membership in 1922, although neither received a charter at that time. Actually, Pi Delta Sigma, a local all-University social fraternity established in 1925 for Jewish students, became the "first national social frat on campus" in 1928, re-lettered Pi Lamba Phi with twenty-five members. The following year, Kappa Pi Delta, a local Creighton social fraternity, became a chapter of Delta Sigma Pi, "one of the strongest national commerce fraternities."[33]

In 1925, the faculty committee on discipline and social affairs suspended two law and two medical fraternities, and one social fraternity, meaning they could not hold meetings, host parties or dances, nor pledge or initiate candidates. The committee revealed no charges, but "much speculation" surfaced and it had "been rumored for some time that the axe was to fall." Most likely, the suspended frats violated one or more of the social regulations promulgated by the committee the previous year. Generally, the rules insisted that only sanctioned student groups could hold functions on campus, they had to petition the committee for approval at least two weeks prior to an event, they could hold social functions only on Tuesday and Friday nights, the activity had to end at midnight and two committee-approved chaperones had to oversee the event. Furthermore, no organization could charge admission without committee authorization, hold subscription dances (pay for more than one at a time), sponsor more than two dances per semester, or schedule them during Lent or the week before semester exams. Obviously, the committee sought to control the number, the nature, and the cost of the burgeoning extracurricular events, especially dances. Regarding fraternities specifically, the committee banned rushing and pledging before the second week of classes, and initiating until after the candidate passed quarterly exams. It also prescribed that initiations take place indoors and "be of such a nature as not to attract public attention," that all social events prohibit "drinking of intoxicants," and that no frat "entertain women in its house or rooms after six o'clock in the evening, except on an evening when a reception, dance or party is being held." Surely the committee outlawed existing activities and behavior it found unacceptable, and if rumors buzzed the campus, the suspended fraternities blatantly failed to amend their practices (which ones, the committee did not make public).[34]

The new social-policy statement and the suspensions prompted the dean of men to require "all fraternities desiring to remain active factors on the Creighton campus" to join the newly established Pan-Hellenic Council composed of the presidents of each fraternity. Obviously, the administration viewed the fraternities—some specific to a professional school, some all-University in nature—as "social" groups needing oversight, regardless of any official affiliation with the national undergraduate Greek-letter social system. Subsequently, the council forbade the rushing of first-semester freshmen, and "to forestall the usual mid-winter storm of criticism" of Greek-letter organizations, Psi Omega (Dentistry) "voluntarily eliminated all hazing, paddling and public ordeals from its initiation ceremony." No records indicate that other frats followed its lead, and despite the suspensions and annual "criticism," the number of fraternities grew to nineteen by 1931, and then held steady for the remainder of the interwar era. That number did not include the academic honor society, Alpha Sigma Tau, created at Marquette University in 1915. Creighton administrators viewed it as another unity device and established the second chapter in 1922. The deans of each school annually chose two candidates for membership. In 1928, the honorary fraternity held its four-chapter national convention in Omaha; four years later, at its national conference at St. Louis, the organization changed its name to Alpha Sigma Nu, after becoming aware of an existing west-coast fraternity that used the former Greek letters. Moreover, in 1926, Albert Van Hee (Ph.B., 1926) and David Cavanaugh (A.B., 1926) founded the Order of the Gold Caldron for alumni of Jesuit universities. Within three years, the local group gained seventy-five members and seven companion chapters, and transformed itself into the Greek-letter fraternity Alpha Chi Kappa. In 1931, Hee returned as national secretary and moved the frat's headquarters to Kansas City, Kansas.[35]

The coeds also jumped on the Greek bandwagon. In 1920, the eight women attending the pharmacy school organized the Theta Chapter of Lamba Kappa Sigma sorority. At the end of the decade, the commerce coeds established Chi Mu Kappa and the Journalism women organized Tau Delta Gamma, re-lettered Pi Delta Chi. As the thirties began, other coeds created Kappa Zeta Kappa, a local social and education sorority. The women then campaigned for membership on the Pan-Hellenic Council, arguing that, "if girls are to be encouraged to come to Creighton" they should receive "equal consideration on campus." Despite the conjecture that a majority of the frat members in the arts college supported their admission and an editorial of support from the *Creightonian,* the council denied the request, taking "refuge behind a supposedly iron-clad constitution forbidding participation in the affairs of the group by coeds." Subsequently, in the fall of 1935, at the suggestion of faculty advisor the Reverend J. A. Herbers, S.J., the Inter-Sorority Council organized, consisting of the presidents of the four existing chapters. In 1940, Pi Phi Epsilon, a local social sorority with eleven charter members, became the last women's Greek-letter group to form during the interwar era.[36]

The frenzy of fraternity, sorority, and club extracurricular activities led the *Creightonian* staff to join the national debate regarding, "What is modern youth? Is this a reckless age, where the words of 'flask-toting shieks' and 'shimmy-shaking she-bas' are written to the music of so-called jazz?" Opinions varied: Mrs. Margaret Curran, dean of women, stated, "I do not think that the youth of today is any different from the youth of twenty years ago; if one looks for the best in people, they will get the best in return. The changing times have been accompanied by the ability of this generation to more readily take care of itself." Karl M. Arnt, an administrator in the College of Commerce, begged to differ, complaining, "The trouble with most young people today is that they have no homes—if we mean by homes centers of religious, educational, social and economic direction." The administrators enforcing social policy sided with Arnt's view, periodically providing new guidelines for a student body they felt needed direction. Thus, in a 1929 "welcome back" letter, the dean of men warned that he would not tolerate "unsportsmanlike conduct" at athletic events, unauthorized signs on University billboards, or smoking on campus, "nor on California street from 24th to 27th, nor on 25th street from California to Cass." In 1935, new dance regulations limited them to Fridays, Saturdays, or days before a school holiday, and they had to end at 12:30 A.M. Moreover, fraternities could not "hold dances or mixed (male and female) house parties in fraternity houses." Subsequently, in 1940 Fr. President Zuercher, demonstrating the impact of the wars raging in Asia and Europe, ordered the exercise of economy "during these times of uncertainty and stress." Specifically, he mandated that fraternities and other organizations holding dances "limit the fee for the orchestra to $150.00." In response, the ticket price for the junior-senior prom fell to $2, its lowest level in nineteen years (previously $3 to $5).[37]

In the interwar social scene, according to an anonymous author, "Beanery Dwellers" composed "the clubbiest and most exclusive fraternity on campus." The Beanery meant St. John's Hall men's dormitory, which granted residents one "night out" per week, allowing them to return as late as 11:00 P.M. In increasing its "parental" control of student life, in 1924 the administration standardized dorm hours with those applied to off-campus housing, establishing midnight as check-in time every day of the week. The following year, St. John's dining hall became the University Cafeteria, a "filling station" that could serve "a variety of victuals at the lowest possible prices" to an average of two hundred students per hour. While the cafeteria became a campus gathering-place, dorm life developed a distinct culture:

> Insurance companies will raise your premium if you live in the place. The risk one takes is too dangerous. If one does not kill himself fulfilling election bets [loser paid by performing some humiliating service to the winner], or wear himself out playing pinochle, or get his nerves all unstrung listening to "Blue Sky" [amateur musicians usually struck two correct notes out of five] or catch pneumonia on account of taking informal shower baths [at times, water mysteriously cascaded from the transoms above room doors], he still runs the chance of being hit by other flying objects, much harder than water—for instance, shoes, tennis rackets, soap and books, . . . when one room declares war upon another, and starts an invasion.[38]

Other cultural distinctions arose to flavor student life during the interwar era. Law students demonstrated a proclivity for politics, on occasion receiving an election-day holiday to work for their slate of candidates. Within the college, politics

consisted of hotly contested campaigns among fraternity-sponsored candidates. In
1927, in a unique occurrence, Joseph D. Fogarty, independent, "upset all political
precedents in the law school by winning the presidency of the junior class over a candidate backed by a coalition of the two fraternities." On the frivolous side, law seniors
adopted the elitist 1930s affectation of using walking canes; "Even Miss Agnes Kil-
lian, the only girl student in the class, has been seen nonchalantly tapping her way
through the venerable corridors." In an equally light-hearted vein, three law freshmen "originated the novel idea of presenting a derby to the freshman law student
making the 'dumbest crack' in class during the week." The *Creightonian* published the
name of the student and the question asked; mysteriously, the rotating "trophy" disappeared after one semester of use.[39]

In comparison to the short-lived law derby, controversy over a hat for undergraduate freshman lasted over a decade. In 1924, the SBG ironically chose a red and green
beanie, and stipulated that freshman wear it 8:00 A.M. to 5:00 P.M., Monday through
Saturday. Paddle-wielding sophomores enforced the regulation and insisted on added
subservience in the form of "buttoning"; on demand, the freshman had to "place his
forefinger on the button of his cap." In 1927, in an effort to abolish increasing hazing,
administrators induced the SBG to abolish the class-designating headgear. However,
the red skullcap with a green visor (or vise versa) reappeared the next year; then, in 1930,
a student referendum produced a vote ratio of 14-1 in favor of its retention. In 1931, the
SBG changed the cap colors to the more logical blue and white, sold them to freshmen
for $1 at registration, and established a committee composed of the presidents of the
freshman classes in the arts, commerce, and pharmacy colleges to impose compliance.
Seemingly, the controversy, the hazing, and the rate of observance atrophied during the
remainder of the decade; however, as late as 1937, wearing the beanie guaranteed free
entrance to the freshman frolics, a student vaudeville show.[40]

The lingering patriotism from World War I contributed another distinctive element to student life during the interwar era. Flag Day originated on April 17, 1917,
but moved to May and became an annual all-University affair at Creighton. At various times, the event included indoor student lectures on the significance of the flag,
poems in honor of the flag, en masse recitation of the Pledge of Allegiance, and patriotic musical selections from the ROTC band. Weather permitting, the ceremony
took place on the north lawn around the flagpole adjacent to the Observatory. In
1929, the area became the site of an additional ritual in the annual flag ceremony. The
graduating classes of all the schools collected money to purchase a new flag they
donated as a token of "their loyalty to Creighton and to their country." The evening
of the baccalaureate exercise, the presidents of the senior classes took the flag to St.
John's Church to have it blessed. Graduation morning began with a procession from
the church to the north-lawn flagpole for the official raising of the new flag before
proceeding to the gymnasium for the commencement program. Old flags subsequently flew on other campus flagpoles as long as they remained in good condition
(i.e., at the stadium) and money collected in excess of the cost of the flag went to the
Agnew Loan Fund.[41]

In comparison to the flourishing Flag Day, the attempt to make Dad's Day a tradition fell victim to the Great Depression. The inaugural event, in 1933, included a tour of campus, a luncheon, an afternoon football game, and a concluding banquet. About three hundred fathers participated the first year, fewer the second, and a third year did not materialize. Hard times, however, did not thwart the popularity of what the arts college called "fun day," the commerce college called "bum day," the Journalism College called "scoop day," and all schools alternately referred to as "sneak" or "skip day." Both the pharmacy and the dental schools claimed credit for originating the practice in 1923. Adding to the controversy, the SBG proclaimed itself the progenitor since it staged the first annual all-University picnic at Krug Park on May 22, 1923. Despite the name, the occasion did not involved "sneaking," and Fr. President Grace deserves some credit as a forefather of the outings. In 1926, he added his blessing, declaring May 6 as his feast day, stipulating he wanted no traditional ceremony, and proclaiming a holiday from classes for the arts and commerce colleges and the high school. Subsequently, the professional schools and the SBG coordinated their picnic schedules with the undergraduate schools, and a new tradition replaced the historic Jesuit holiday of President's Feast Day.[42]

On the other hand, another tradition—intercollegiate athletics—reasserted its dominance of extracurricular activities during the interwar era. In December 1919, the fifteen-member pre-war Alumni Athletic Board reorganized with Fr. Corboy returning as "faculty director." The board immediately pushed for the construction of a new six-thousand-seat grandstand on a realigned football field at a total cost of $125,000. Lacking the funds, the administration built new west bleachers to match the existing ones on the east side of the gridiron and cut an alley through to 24th Street on the south side of the gymnasium, paving it for automobile use to "relieve the congestion after games." In 1920, Edward Mulholland, M.D., coached the football team to a 2–6 season; the board swiftly replaced him with "an Omaha boy," Malcolm "Mac" Baldridge, who played tackle for Yale for two years before serving as an artillery captain in France during World War I. He obtained two assistant coaches and his first Creighton team, which weighed on average 167 pounds, racked up an 8–1 season record. The basketball team started the decade with two winning seasons (16–4 and 16–6); in each year, it took an eastern road trip playing ten games in ten nights.[43]

In 1922, Fr. President McCormick hired Arthur A. Schabinger as athletic director and basketball and baseball coach. Schabinger (A.B., College of Emporia, Kansas, 1913; Bachelor of Physical Education, International YMCA College, Springfield, Massachusetts, 1915) had played football, basketball, baseball, and track and had seven years of coaching experience. Besides coaching and overseeing intramural and intercollegiate sports, he served on a reconfigured athletic board, which consisted of chairman Fr. Corboy, four faculty members, two alumni and two students appointed by the SBG. The old alumni athletic board admitted that on occasion, "its actions were misunderstood"; as it disbanded, it issued a "new policy" promising to "certify both to the scholastic and amateur standing of its men," as well as to abide by the "three year rule prohibiting Freshmen from the Varsity team." The mea culpa signified that some

Creighton athletes had not qualified as traditional students seeking a college education (e.g., "the same man played the same tackle position for eight years," or "men played who did not know the location of a single class room," or a basketball "star who played a full college career before coming to Creighton"). The following June, the new board established football, basketball, baseball, and track as Creighton's "major sports," and gymnastics, wrestling, tennis, swimming, golf, and boxing as its "minor sports." In 1922, Homecoming began its association with football (it was previously celebrated with Commencement), and that year the returning alumni enjoyed a 9-0 victory over the Michigan [State] Aggies. The second Homecoming welcomed over one thousand alumni, one of whom dropped a football on the field from "an aeroplane" at the start of the game against the Haskell Indians, a losing effort, 0–26. Nonetheless, with the new arrangements in place, Fr. Corboy effused, "My dream of thorough athletic training for all and not the few is to be realized . . . and under the leadership of Mr. Schabinger, who has signed a five year contract as Athletic Director, we will have the best organized athletics in the west, and hope to turn out teams that Omaha will be proud of."[44]

Unfortunately, on most levels, Fr. Corboy's vision dissolved into a fantasy. He championed intramural sport as providing the opportunity for athletic participation to the majority of students and a *Chronicle* editorial ballyhooed the idea of an intramural baseball league as a unity devise for the University. "Too long has the spirit of localism dominated our sports and socials, and the fruit of this too-prominent stay-in-your-own-class spirit has reached a mellowness that should mean a quick fall and a certain dissolution." The baseball league, however, did not materialize, the student publications paid scant attention to intramural competitions, and the school-basis for fraternities and clubs and their activities remained the norm. Essentially, coeds followed the same pattern; the affiliated schools—the College of Saint Mary, St. Catherine's Nursing Unit, and St. Joseph's Nursing Unit—for several years during the 1920s organized basketball teams that occasionally played each other or a team from the YWCA or the Jewish Community Center. Subsequently, however, they emulated Duchesne and fielded intramural teams exclusively. In 1933, Lucille Kendall, secretary of the commerce college, organized the first "girl's gymnasium class," held on Mondays evenings, in which "every girl in the university [was] eligible to attend and will have the use of the swimming pool, the indoor track and the basketball floor." Thus, intramural sports scarcely affected on-campus coeds and it played a significant role in the student life of only a small minority of the men. Intramural leagues, with the relative exception of men's basketball, remained small and did not serve as a unity device for the University. The scant coverage of intramural sports in the yearbook attested to their declining stature in student life. While some male students enjoyed extracurricular athletics, intramurals did not attain Fr. Corboy's lofty goals of universality or unity.[45]

Before World War I, the stature of the vigorous intramural program at Creighton had begun to suffer from competition with intercollegiate sports. The 1920s witnessed the culmination of the transformation of the majority of students from participant to spectator and the expenditure of vast sums of money on athletic training for the few. The athletic board, however, did not realize the objectives of its "new policy" for an elite program of intercollegiate athletics. Its "minor sports" program rarely went beyond pronouncements due to the lack of funding. The University failed to organize gymnastics, tennis, wrestling, or boxing teams, although ad hoc wrestling and boxing matches continued to provide entertainment at fraternity and club smokers. In May 1923, the Creighton golf team, consisting of one law and three medical students, played its first and only match of the season at the Omaha Country Club against a foursome from the University of Nebraska. The *Creightonian* did not publish the results of the contest and the paper's only other reference to a golf team came in 1925, alluding to the fact the illness of the coach temporarily prevented organizing a team. Similarly, a swim team held a meet at the Creighton pool in March 1923, but the only other references to a team appeared as a single article in 1930, and two in 1931 (significantly, the latter team lost two swimmers because of academic ineligibility). More disappointment ensued in 1930, as the University announced the creation of a tennis team, but it did not take to the court.[46]

Unplanned, rifle became the prominent "minor sport" of the interwar era, because all undergraduate males had to join the ROTC and the United States Army assumed the minimal costs associated with the teams. ROTC officers served as coaches and the military provided the rifles. On occasion, they avoided travel costs by conducting matches telegraphically, comparing individual and team scores fired separately at each school's range. For unexplained reasons, the intercollegiate team disbanded in 1929, but reorganized in 1931, and remained quite popular for the remainder of the decade (over one hundred men competed for positions on the squad in 1936). Moreover, the sport produced the first women's team sponsored by the University (although the affiliated women's colleges had fielded teams in basketball). In 1932, commerce junior Marcella Lindberg captained the first Creighton women's rifle team, which allowed Duchesne girls to participate in the school's last year of affiliation. In 1934, the team made a road trip to Lincoln to shoot against the University of Nebraska and the following year interest peaked at such a level that the coaches announced that they would cut all coeds who did not practice at least two hours per week. Inexplicably, the University disbanded the team in 1938, although it allowed women to shoot noncompetitively at the range. It reorganized the team in 1940, and the next year the SBG allotted $50 to the coed rifle team as a "pump primer" to defray the cost of a trip to Booneville, Missouri, for a match and to encourage the University to support the team in the future. The onset of war, however, established a new priority for the use of rifles.[47]

The "major sports" experienced similar lack-of-funds problems during the interwar era. The athletic board rendered lip service to its "four-sports policy," but did not field a baseball team because of the high costs involved. The *Creightonian* editorialized in the sport's favor, and in 1925 the SBG presented the athletic board with a petition signed by approximately eleven hundred students, which advocated creating a Creighton squad. The athletic board studied the situation, but its answer "to disappointed baseball candidates" stated, "TURN OUT FOR TRACK" (emphasis in the original). The first track team appeared in 1921, and rose quickly in stature as indoor runners, hosting home meets in the gymnasium. The team won consecutive North Central Conference indoor championships in 1924 and 1925. Thereafter, as competition moved outdoors to the stadium, but with the addition of field events, the team did not fare as well. The University abandoned the sport in 1934, tried to revivify it in 1937, but ceased after one year.[48]

On the other hand, basketball enjoyed admirable success as one of two continuous "major sports" of the Creighton program during the interwar era. As part of the "new policy," Creighton participated in the creation of the North Central Intercollegiate Conference (NCC) in the spring of 1922, and coach "Mac" Baldridge became the league's first president. Charter members also included the College of St. Thomas, Des Moines University (absorbed by Drake University), Morningside College, Nebraska Wesleyan, North Dakota (State) Agricultural College, the University of North Dakota, the University of South Dakota, and South Dakota State College (Marquette and Michigan [State] Agriculture and Mining College declined invitations). The freshman-ineligibility rule resulted in the creation of freshman squads; the 1925–26 team included the first African-American basketball player in Creighton history, William Waldon Solomon, who switched to football as a sophomore, but did not graduate from the arts college. In 1925, Coach Schabinger instituted spring practice for the basketball team, which established an outstanding record, winning consecutive league championships from 1923 through 1926. The administration constructed an outside concrete stairway on the east side of the gymnasium, leading up to court level to "provide a better way in and out of the gym for part of the large basketball crowds that watch the games in the winter."[49]

In 1927, Creighton announced it would not schedule the required number of league games to compete for the NCC title. The following year, it achieved a decade-long goal by becoming a member of a reorganized Missouri Valley Conference (MVC), which had been decimated by the withdrawal of the "rebellious Big Six" (Iowa State, Kansas, Kansas State, Missouri, Nebraska, and Oklahoma). The revamped circuit included Drake, "one of the leading track centers in the country," Oklahoma (State) A&M, "chiefly known, nationally, as a leader in wrestling," Grinnell, "one of the oldest colleges in the middle west," and Washington University of St. Louis, "a stranger to Creighton athletics." Between 1928 and 1941, Creighton won six MVC championships and finished second four times. Coach Schabinger (1922–35) compiled an overall record of 163-66, a .712 winning percentage. His successor, Edgar S. "Eddie" Hickey, continued the stellar performance. The winning tradition usually filled the five-thousand-seat gymnasium; at times, about one half of the crowd included paid admissions. Throughout the 1930s, main-floor and balcony reserved seats sold for $1, while general admission went for $.40. Season tickets, thirteen reserved seats for $7.15, first appeared in 1939–40 (since attendance remained strong, their introduction at this time probably indicated an attempt to gain guaranteed income from the non-student fans). The basketball team completed the last season of the interwar era in the spring of 1941 with an 18-7 record, winning the MVC championship and two games in the NCAA post-season tournament.[50]

Basketball, however, could not satiate the tastes of the fans of Creighton athletics; football remained the king of sports and it determined athletic policy. In 1922, the four thousand seats available on the wood bleachers did not accommodate the large crowd that turned out for the Marquette game. Moreover, the plan for the four new buildings south of California Street (only law and dentistry actually built) encroached on the existing gridiron, necessitating its realignment parallel to Burt Street. The time seemed propitious to construct a suitable stadium:

> In the consideration of the necessity of the new stadium for Creighton, several points command the attention of Omaha businessmen. Within a reasonably short space of time, Creighton will undoubtedly be admitted to the Missouri Valley Conference, with the result that the largest and best known football teams of the entire Missouri Valley—in fact of the Middle West—will play annually on the Creighton field. This will ensure a better brand of football at Creighton and will guarantee a number of the best games in the West being played in Omaha. Businessmen undoubtedly will support Creighton athletics and the new Creighton stadium, not only because of pride in Omaha and Omaha institutions, but also for business reasons, because each big-calibered football game played on the Creighton field will bring to Omaha thousands of visitors.[51]

Unfortunately, virtually all of the administration's assumptions proved fallacious. It took six years to gain entrance to the MVC, which by then had lost stature because of the defection of the big state-school football powerhouses. The stadium fund drive failed, saddling the University and the athletic program with a large debt. In the inaugural game on October 3, 1925, a small crowd watched Creighton battle the South Dakota (State) Aggies to a 0-0 tie in drizzling rain. Poor attendance remained a problem, since Creighton's football schedule attracted few "big-caliber" games; yearbook photos revealed meager crowds, which exacerbated financial concerns. In 1929, the addition of lights for night games temporarily increased attendance, but the novelty soon dissipated. Omaha businessmen had not supported the stadium fund drive and did not lavish attention or money on the lightly regarded football team. Moreover, the stadium caused further anguish because it sat too close to Burt Street. Administrators believed verbal permission from a city commissioner gave them the authority to build within eight feet of the curb. Property owners across the street, including the University's night watchman and a former student, disagreed and sued after the edifice overwhelmed their southern exposure. Following a two-year struggle, the city government absolved the University, since the structure did not obstruct sidewalk or street traffic, and the administration settled out of court with the property owners, offering a minimal compensation for "damages."[52]

Stadium construction, however, sparked a brief period of enthusiasm from the students. At the behest of the athletic board and the Alumni Association, the *Omaha Bee* newspaper coordinated a contest to select a mascot for the Creighton teams. University publications had always referred to the teams by the school colors, the "White and Blue," or vice versa. Local newspapers, because of the school's location atop a bluff, occasionally designated the teams the "Hilltoppers," but the University did not adopt the appellation. The contest attracted approximately two hundred entries, from which the athletic board chose "Bluejays." At first, an ornithologically correct rendition of the bird, chosen because of its colors and scrappiness, became a decoration on team uniforms. In 1941, however, alumnus Joseph P. Murphy (BSC, 1931) designed the first version of the anthropomorphic "Billy Bluejay."[53]

The "stadium spirit" also induced arts junior Gordon X. Richmond to write the words to "The White and the Blue," which became the official school song. Other musical numbers supplemented Richmond's song during the interwar era. In 1928, Dan Desdunes, leader of a regionally popular African-American band that played regularly at Creighton football games, composed a march, "Rah, Rah, Bluejay," which the group performed during half-time ceremonies. Two years later, head cheerleader Cecil Muller (freshman, dentistry) obtained permission from the composer and the producer of the theme song for the popular college movie *Sweetie* to substitute the word "Creighton" for the movie and song title, and use the piece at athletic events. Subsequently, in 1933, arts students Dean Kovar and John Rebuck contributed the Creighton Victory March, and Journalism students Keith Wilson and Henry Mendelson composed a new pep song, giving the University a compendium of musical selections.[54]

Additionally, the swelling school spirit included expanding athletic booster activity. In 1922, for example, the newly formed Student Union used its weekly assemblies during the fall semester to practice cheers and songs in preparation for half-time activities at upcoming football games. Separate rallies occurred at the medical and pharmacy colleges in downtown Omaha. On November 3, 1924, the constantly reorganized Booster Club (because of the graduation of student leaders) orchestrated a massive parade of students and automobiles from the train depot to the campus to honor the football team returning from Milwaukee following its "unexpected victory" over archrival Marquette. Two years later, "Displaying real school spirit, the students . . . put over two of the biggest pep stunts in the history of athletic endeavors on the hilltop," which included a huge bonfire rally and a parade with "a dozen or more floats, seventy-five cars, the university band, 'Ike' Bauder's Collegian orchestra, twenty-five trick [truck?] Fords, a large delegation of alumni, and a thousand students on foot."[55]

Maintaining spirit also necessitated raucous cheering at games. Ad hoc pep groups had come and gone seasonally; but as late as 1924, the *Creightonian* complained, "If there is anything lacking at Creighton it is organized cheering." Purportedly, students supported cheerleaders in a "half-hearted manner." Thus, beginning with the basketball game against the University of Nebraska in February, a section reserved for students "who are dyed in the wool rooters" emerged on the north side of the gymnasium. That fall, the Bluejay Club added its name to the list of supporters that tried to establish a tradition of an "effective cheering body"; subsequent groups included the Blue Loons and the Knights of the Bluejay. Starting in 1928, women from the hospital nursing units raised spirits, and attendance according to some commentators, by supplementing or supplanting ROTC cadets as ushers at football and basketball games. In 1937, the coed presence became more prominent as Olive Odorisio (Journalism, 1941), the first female cheerleader at Creighton, joined four men from the schools of law, dentistry, pharmacy, and journalism on the squad.[56]

The stadium-induced spurt in spirit, however, soon atrophied. In 1923, as part of the "new policy" designed to develop "a 'big time' system for athletics," the administration hired Chester "Chet" Wynne, "one of the most illustrious grid figures in the annals of the game at Notre Dame," to coach football and track. He introduced the "floating pass, a modified system of the Notre Dame shift," a special diet for athletes, and spring football practice. His teams remained small in number (60 to 70) and continued to include students from the professional schools, especially law, since during the interwar era most of them did not spend four years in undergraduate school. The *Creightonian* interpreted the relatively low football participation rate ("a turnout of less than one-thirtieth of the male students") in terms of sagging spirit, but it also highlighted the demise of Fr. Corboy's dream of universal athletic training, replaced by extravagant expenditures for a minority of elite sportsmen.[57]

Coach Wynne produced a 5-5 season in 1923, and then established a winning tradition in three out of the next four years (6-1-2, 6-3-1, 4-4-1, and 6-1-1). Beating small-college teams failed to impress most Omahans and they did not adopt the team, which contested most games in a "stadium less than half filled." Commencing in 1922, football's inability to generate significant revenue created a red bottom line for the athletic department, which reached critical proportions with the failure of the stadium fund drive. To stem the tide, on October 2, 1928, "one thousand students from Creighton University [attempted] to sell $60,000 worth of season tickets for the four home games on the toughest schedule the Blue and White team ever has faced." Thus, for Creighton football, the concept of season tickets originated as a response to low football attendance and lack of revenue. Ultimately, the students enjoyed a holiday from classes, but only sold about five thousand ticket packages, netting $20,000. Although they collected only one third of the projected sum, administrators claimed success since the figure surpassed the total receipts of the previous year.[58]

Wynne's winning ways, however, convinced the administration that football fame lay just around the corner. In 1927, Kansas State Agricultural College offered him a $6,500 contract, so Creighton bumped his salary by $1,500 to retain his services. The decision proved unwise; he suffered two losing seasons (3-5-1 and 2-6) and subsequently left to coach Alabama Polytech (Auburn University) at a salary of $12,000, which the administration had refused to match. The downturn in the fortunes of the football team contributed to a general malaise that struck the student body before the onset of the Great Depression. In October 1929 before the stock market crash, the editors of *Shadows* conducted a conversation with the "campus critical lights," who revealed that "they found the Creighton spirit mostly apathetic, and not only unenthusiastic in extra-curricular intellectual pursuits, but equally as sterile in following the athletic interests of the campus." A few months later, the *Creightonian* chimed in, "The Knights of the Bluejay, in their section at the last basketball game resembled an array of Knights who had just come from a particularly deadly battle." While a small contingent of students from the various schools supported intercollegiate athletics, for a host of reasons a significant segment of the student body had not converted to sports-spectator status. The University possessed small undergraduate schools; it had a full compliment of professional students not necessarily interested in sports or too busy to attend games, or who had attended other undergraduate colleges and had no attachment to Creighton teams; plus it had a high percentage of students who held jobs and could not attend events.[59]

The Great Depression contributed to a continued downslide in Creighton's athletic fortunes, with the exception of the winning tradition in basketball that failed to salve the wounds of disillusioned football fans. In 1930, the administration chose Arthur R. Stark from among fifty applicants to become the new head football coach. Over the next four years, he compiled a record of 13-18-1, with only one winning season. In 1932, his squad consisted of only thirty-six players and a Hollywood film shot in Omaha, *Strange as it Seems,* included scenes of "the sheep in Creighton stadium as they went about their all-summer task of keeping the grass clipped and in good condition." That year, the administration reduced the cost of the season-ticket packet by 20 percent and the single-admission ticket by 25 percent "to keep in line with the times." The following year, the team lost its two-year starting fullback who "received a job which [helped] him finish his law course so that he was forced to withdraw from his athletic career." Moreover, "in keeping with the 'New Deal' spirit," general admission ticket prices bottomed out at 55 cents, and because of the price decrease, the University ceased radio broadcasts of the home games. In 1934, Eddie Hickey (LL.B., 1926) became the first alum head coach, but he and his staff of four assistants could only muster a 2-7 season on the gridiron (in 1935, Hickey switched to basketball and compiled a stellar record).[60]

The dismal football record instigated an alumni revolt. On December 12, 1933, Fr. President Mahan told the alumni assembled for the annual football banquet, "True, we did not win all our games this year and I am thankful for that. Why? Because the mania for winning every game is at the root of all that is wrong with the athletic situation in America today. . . . Creighton is, first and always, an educational institution of the highest order. It will never agree to exploit its students for four years on the athletic field for the entertainment of the public, and then send them into the world totally unfit for life." The following spring the alumni responded with a public opinion poll that revealed that a meager 28 percent of the general public and 31 percent of the alumni (only 10 percent participated in the survey) were satisfied with the "athletic department as it is now conducted." Most respondents registered complaints against the weak schedule and the pitiable won-loss record of the football team, and demanded a new athletic director, football coach, and de-emphasis of basketball in favor of the gridiron team.[61]

Father President Mahan lamented, "Why were athletics, the least educational feature of an educational institution, singled out from all these student activities for alumni comment?" He bristled at the suggestion that Creighton play "bigger" opponents in football. He dismissed "Big Time" football as a "disgrace . . . unworthy of a University and harmful to student character" because it recruited high-school athletes, paid its players, and maintained "standards of scholarship for the regulars . . . unworthy of a Seat of Learning." He concluded, "If you sit in at a crooked game, you must be crooked if you expect to win. Creighton is not going to be crooked. 'Big Time Football' is crooked." Despite his caustic interpretation, he relented and Creighton again sought entrance into "Big Time" football and the "entertainment industry." On Thanksgiving Day 1934, Creighton ended its "dismal" season with a home-field loss to Idaho University, 0-13. In January 1935, the NCAA adopted a "code of ethics" designed to "help solve the vexing problems of recruiting and subsidizing athletes," although members voted down making the nine-article code an actual set of regulations and creating an enforcement procedure. Notwithstanding the milquetoast NCAA policy, Fr. President Mahan accepted the resignation of Fr. Corboy (chairman of the athletic board since 1914) due to "ill health," although he remained "dean of men, moderator of the Student Union, faculty moderator of the Pan-Hellenic council and director of the Agnew Loan Fund." Father President Mahan appointed a temporary study committee of four Jesuit administrators to manage athletics; it immediately issued a statement declaring, "We want to do the best thing for athletics at Creighton and we do not intend to de-emphasize football at the university."[62]

The committee proposed a "New Deal" for Creighton athletics. At the end of the 1934-35 basketball season, Schabinger stepped down as coach and athletic director "to take charge of elimination tournaments to select the U. S. basketball entries to the 1936 Olympics" (in 1961, he entered the national Basketball Hall of Fame). Shortly thereafter, "The Hilltop athletic bombshell, long awaited by Creighton alumni everywhere, burst . . . with the announcement that Marchmont 'Marchy' Schwartz, who won national gridiron renown as a two-time all-American halfback for Notre Dame, and Charles F. Bongardt, professor of law on the Creighton faculty, had been appointed head coach of football and athletic director, respectively." When school reopened in the fall of 1935, Fr. President Mahan appointed a new athletic board, chaired by the Reverend B. J. Quinn, S.J., former president of Campion College and a person "experienced in athletic administration," who had also chaired the temporary study committee. New to Creighton, he seems to have influenced Fr. Mahan's change of heart concerning "Big Time" football. The new board also included two other faculty representatives, two alumni chosen for the first time from a list of five candidates submitted by the Alumni Council and the president of the SBG as a nonvoting member. Subsequently, Eddie Hickey became business manager of athletics, replacing Bongardt, who the law school had "loaned" to the athletic department for one year. To complete the "New Deal" for sports, the Alumni Council established a goal of $20,000 for the Loyalty Fund to "rehabilitate Creighton's athletic department, particularly football, and to enable your university to take its rightful place among the leaders of the Middle West." The drive actually raised $6,000, which paid for the construction of a practice football field at 25th and Burt streets and for some new football equipment.[63]

The athletic "New Deal" included a one-year reintroduction of golf and track, but Creighton's love affair with Notre Dame all-Americans again failed to produce the desired football glory. Schwartz introduced a "regulation football game at the conclusion of spring practice," and upgraded the schedule minimally, but had only one winning season in his five-year tenure, leaving with an over-all record of 19-22-2. In 1940, Maurice "Skip" Palrang ascended to the head-coach position. For the previous six years, he had served as "head coach of athletics" for Creighton (Prep) High School and had coached the Omaha McDevitts to the 1939 national title in American Legion Junior baseball. He enjoyed brief success, but then witnessed the demise of the Creighton football program during World War II.[64]

The entry of the United States into the Second World War culminated an era sandwiched between global conflicts. During the interlude, Creighton administrators and students reestablished historic extracurricular groups and activities. They also created new engines of student performance, such as the Student Union, the ROTC, the *Creightonian, Shadows* and the *Bluejay*. Social activities mushroomed with the burgeoning array of fraternities and sororities, while at the same time, spirituality increased its presence among the student body in terms of sodality membership, religious practices, charitable enterprises, and volunteer service. Intercollegiate sports, while they may have induced a "college spirit" among some, also bred controversy, budget shortfalls, and significant debt. With few exceptions, the extracurricular activities that helped define student life during the interwar era suffered because of financial constraints. The limited budgets during the otherwise prosperous "roaring Twenties" reined in the dreams of the administration and the SBG, while the ravages of the Great Depression exacerbated the negative economic pressures. Nonetheless, despite the atrophy of some programs, the unfulfilled wishes for others, and the mediocre football record, with limited finances the administration and students constructed a lively "extra-curriculum" that helped define the Creighton experience during the interwar era.

CHAPTER 8

World War II Decade

The exigencies of fighting a thirty-nine-month, two-front global war transformed American life. While the territorial United States suffered virtually no damage during World War II, the demands of total war enlisted the support of all citizens and institutions. For the second time during the first half of the twentieth century, for all practical purposes, Creighton University became a military camp. All its schools operated year-round accelerated programs designed to speed graduation and they reoriented their curriculums to meet the needs of soldier-students. Traditional extracurricular activities, including intercollegiate athletics, ceased for the duration of the conflict. With victory gained in 1945, the University once again undertook the process of converting itself back to a civilian entity. The military flavor, however, persisted until 1950, as the sizeable cohort of ex-servicemen contributed a distinctive ambience to the campus. By the end of the war decade, however, Creighton reemerged as a traditional university, with a new vision and a new president, signaling the end of one era and the beginning of another.

Rapidly, during the World War II era, Creighton University acquired a martial environment. With war rampant in Europe and Asia, in September 1940, Congress passed the first peacetime conscription law in United States history. The following spring, all thirty-five Creighton seniors who completed the four-year ROTC program immediately reported for active duty (not the reserves) upon graduation. The ritual persisted for the next two years, until the army's manpower needs eliminated Advanced ROTC because few eligible males could continue their traditional college education. Basic ROTC remained for un-drafted undergraduates, but special army training schools replaced the cadet's summer-camp experience. In November 1942, Congress lowered the draft age from twenty-one to eighteen and the pool of male civilians able to attend college plummeted; thus, in 1943 the number of Basic ROTC cadets fell from 572 the previous year to only 125. Three Creighton alumni now oversaw the diminished program, including Captain Robert J. Swanson (A.B., 1937; LL.B., 1940), at age thirty-one, the youngest professor of military science in the school's history. For the duration of the war, the program continued to limp along with approximately one hundred students per semester.[1]

While the significance of ROTC receded, male reservists came to dominate the campus. Four months after Pearl Harbor, the army and the navy established personnel programs that allowed college students to enlist in the reserves, receive inactive status, and continue their studies as long as they maintained good standing at their schools. Educators encouraged students to enlist, arguing it would allow them to study until graduating and prepare them to enter an officer candidate school. On April 15, 1942, the navy advertised its "newest plan" in *Creightonian*. It made a pitch to sophomores, aged seventeen through nineteen. It asked them to enlist in the Naval Reserve and to pursue the regular college course, but to emphasize mathematics, physics, and physical training. After a year and a half, they could take the examination for naval officer school. If they passed, they could leave college and begin training as an aviation officer, or they could remain in school until graduation as preparation for further education to become a deck or engineering officer.[2]

Three weeks later, the army advertised a "New Deferred Service Plan," for its Army Air Corps. It contained three options: (1) freshmen, sophomores, and juniors, aged eighteen to twenty-six, could enlist in the Army Air Force Enlisted Reserve (a separate, independent air force was not created until 1947); (2) any college student could enlist in the Army Air Force (unassigned) and serve until a place opened for aviation cadet training; or (3) all college students could enlist in the Army Air Force Enlisted Reserve and stay in school until ordered to report for aviation cadet training. The Reverend Henry Linn, S.J., became faculty advisor to the Army Air Corps and explained that undergraduates would receive deferments until graduation, $75 per month plus housing, medical care, uniforms, equipment, a $1 per diem for subsistence, and a $10,000 life insurance policy. When school opened in September 1942, approximately 85 percent of the male students had enlisted in one of the military reserves, including 223 of 230 medical and all 102 dental students. Upperclassmen from the schools of arts, commerce, journalism, pharmacy, and University College included 121 in the Army Enlisted Reserve, 83 in ROTC, 38 in the Naval Reserve, 26 in the Army Air Corps, 12 in the Marine Corps, 34 in the Army Medical Administrative Corps, and 12 in the Naval Medical Corps, the latter two open to pre-med and pre-dent students. In a "bite-my-tongue" statement, Fr. Linn announced no fear of a call-up for the reservists.[3]

However, later that month manpower shortages caused the army to call most of its enlisted reserves to active duty, and in November Congress lowered the draft age to eighteen, threatening the extinction of college education for the duration. The navy did not activate it reserves (it did establish new grade guidelines, mandating a "C" average), but that provided little solace for many schools, including Creighton. In February 1943, all aviation cadets and Army Enlisted Reserve Corps (unassigned) received their activation notices. By the end of the spring term, those remaining at Creighton included 59 Army Air Corps Reserves, 112 Army Enlisted Reserve Corps (pre-med and pre-dent), 29 Marine Reserves, 56 Navy V(olunteer)-1 Reserves (freshmen and sophomores), 10 Navy V-5 (naval aviation), 28 V-7 (juniors and seniors), 27 in Advanced ROTC, and 54 in Basic ROTC, and all were scheduled for active duty.[4]

The services realized they needed educated enlisted men and officers. Thus, the army and the navy worked with the presidents of prestigious universities to shape required training programs. On December 17, 1942, the military announced the creation of the Army Specialized Training Program (ASTP) and the Navy V-12 program (which absorbed the earlier V-1, V-5, and V-7 reserve programs). The former sent approximately 200,000 soldiers to 227 colleges and universities to study engineering, medicine, dentistry, personnel psychology, and thirty-four foreign languages. The latter sent approximately 125,000 sailors and marines to 131 schools to study engineering, medicine, and dentistry. The military selected the colleges based on their ability to provide housing, dining facilities, and classroom space. Men already in the service and those not yet drafted, ages eighteen to twenty-two, could enlist in the new programs. On April 2, 1943, approximately 315,000 eligible males took exams nationwide, including any student at Creighton who wished to continue his studies, and specifically all the army enlisted reservists (navy reservists excused because they had previously received orders for special training). The services and the College Entrance Examination Board designed and administered the exams, but those given at army camps lacked the stringency of standard college entrance tests and qualified many students not ready for college work. Therefore, to correct the situation, the army created Specialized Training Assignment and Reclassification (STAR) units, where men spent one to thirty days being retested before they could enter college. About two thirds of the ASTP enrollees came from men already in the army or Army Air Corp in early 1943, while far fewer V-12s came "from the fleet."[5]

The ASTP and the Navy V-12 sent students to the Creighton medical and dental schools, and undergraduates came from the separately administered Army Air Force College Training Program. The situation posed problems because, in comparison to the navy, the army downplayed the liberal arts in favor of specialized training "involving little or no general education and designed to produce technicians." Moreover, "men in the training detachments were 'at' the university but not 'in' it in the traditional sense." That is, they studied a specially designed curriculum, dressed in uniform, resided in "barracks," and attended to military duties during nonclass time. "All ASTP and V-12 men were under the strictest military discipline, wore regulation army, navy and marine uniforms; observed military protocol and stood basic formations; were subject to regular inspections of person and quarters; were generally required to march to courses and meals; and were expected always to behave as future officers and gentlemen." While V-12 men could, those in the ASTP could not attend classes with civilians. Thus, the undergraduate schools at Creighton became bifurcated institutions, populated mostly with soldier students, while maintaining a minimal distinct civilian student body.[6]

The 89th College Training Detachment of the Army Air Forces College Training Program (89th CTD or air cadets) arrived on campus on February 27, 1943, and began course work on March 1. To accommodate the influx of soldier-students, Fr. President Zuercher issued a "sudden and disturbing order" to the residents of Dowling and Wareham dormitories to vacate the premises. In a note of thanks published in *Creightonian*, he also expressed his confidence "that the entire student body on the Hilltop will accept with the same grace and cooperation the inconvenience and hardship occasioned by the closing of the cafeteria . . . for the duration." The cafeteria and kitchen of Wareham Hall became "sleeping bays" equipped with "double-decker beds." Moreover, the School of Journalism moved out of its quarters on the first floor of the law building and relocated in the basement of Dowling Hall; the University converted the former journalism rooms into classrooms for the air cadets.[7]

The 89th CTD came and went in units designated squadrons and/or flights; the air cadets carried the rank of private and studied at Creighton for three to five months. The administration rearranged the schedule of classes to meet the needs of the cadet's curriculum, which included a few academic subjects, plus military courses and physical training. The program consisted of over seven hundred hours of study; Creighton faculty taught classes in mathematics (arithmetic through plane and solid trigonometry), a general survey of physics, geography (map-making, map reading, and economic geography), current history (World War I to 1942), civil air regulations, English, and physical training. Air force officers oversaw the military training, which included "infantry drill, ceremonies and inspections, and customs and courtesies of the service." Local health officials conducted mandatory evening classes in first aid. Overall, the cadet's schedule consisted of the equivalent of twenty semester-hours per week, purposely designed to test their mettle and weed out those who lacked the capabilities for flight training. If they satisfactorily completed the curriculum, they moved on to command classification centers for aircrew training, and if they passed that muster, on to training as pilots, bombardiers, or navigators.[8]

The hectic schedule did include some free time; Saturdays and Sundays were designated "open post" days, which gave the cadets the opportunity to leave campus and to enjoy the various entertainment venues in Omaha and environs. On campus, the physical training department organized intramural activities that emphasized aquatics, "combatives," gymnastics, the obstacle course, and team sports. On the other hand, Secretary of War Henry Stimson banned ASTP participation in intercollegiate sports (the navy allowed V-12 involvement). On September 24, 1943, with the help of three "charming coeds" on the staff of the *Creightonian*, the airmen began to publish "The Bluejay Cadet" as an insert to the student weekly. Their logo consisted of Billy Bluejay in uniform, grasping books and floating on clouds numbered "89th." On November 19, they renamed the insert "Slip Stream"; by then, it had expanded from one to four pages. They published articles about local social activities, stories about other units around the country, regular columns such as "Administrative Ack-Acks," and syndicated features obtained from the Camp Newspaper Service.[9]

On February 18, 1944, Army Chief of Staff George C. Marshall proclaimed the existence of a troop shortage and issued an order that terminated the undergraduate ASTP. The directive excluded 35,000 students in advance training in medicine, dentistry, and engineering, but called to active duty 110,000 collegians studying at 222 schools across the country. Thus, the V-12 program, which dominated the Creighton health sciences schools "sailed on untouched," but the last squadron of air cadets that populated the undergrad schools left campus on June 30, 1944. While the latter program functioned, the number of cadets on campus remained classified military information and the officers admonished civilian students not to "at any time discuss the number of men here in training." Subsequent data revealed that 2,128 cadets partook of the program during its sixteen months at Creighton. Despite the altered and limited curriculum, the program provided employment for undergraduate faculty who otherwise would have lost their jobs and it allowed the undergraduate colleges to remain open to educate the limited number of civilians able to attend college during those desperate times (seventeen-year-olds, militarily medically unfit men, and women).[10]

Once again, it looked as if the undergraduate colleges might have to close. Relief arrived shortly after D-Day 1944, in the form of the Army Specialized Training Reserve Program. The army designed the program to entice seventeen-year-olds by providing them with "scholarships" to attend college until drafted. Enlistees received instruction, room and board, and medical services, but no pay or allowances. They took the same curriculum as the defunct ASTP; thus, undergraduate professors picked up where they left off without disruption. Six platoons of twenty-five cadets each of the Army Air Corps Enlisted Reserves (Acers) occupied Wareham Hall and, as teens, received an extra dose of military discipline—study hall 7:00–9:00 nightly, with bed check at 10:00 P.M. The last forty-three Acers left campus in early May 1945, largely demilitarizing the undergraduate colleges—only the small Basic ROTC remained active.[11]

Actually, while uniformed students largely disappeared from the undergraduate schools, the "military" ambience continued. In June 1944, Congress passed the Servicemen's Readjustment Act, more commonly referred to as the G.I. Bill of Rights. Its benefits included support to attend college; at Creighton, commerce dean Floyd Walsh assumed administrative responsibilities as the Director of Veterans' Service. The public relations office crafted a pamphlet, "When You March Home," which it mailed to fifteen thousand men and women alumni and service personnel. Walsh also held public forums to answer questions about benefits and, in conjunction with the Omaha American Legion Post No. 1, the University sponsored a series of radio programs, "My Career," which informed veterans about "occupations and careers open to them." The first contingent of thirty-four discharged veterans entered Creighton in the fall of 1944, well before the cessation of hostilities in Europe or Asia. They immediately formed the 1-C Club, named after their draft classification (discharged veteran). Subsequently, vets on the G.I. Bill became a majority of the professional and the undergraduate student population at Creighton, and the 1-C Club became a major force on campus.[12]

The military presence in the medical school lingered until the summer of 1946; soldiers and sailors accounted for virtually every enrollee during the duration of the war. In 1940, as recommended by the AMA, Creighton had begun requiring three years (ninety semester hours) of college for entrance into its medical school. Because of the demand for physicians for the military and the U.S. Public Health Service, as well as for civilian needs, during the war the requirement reverted to the previous standard of two years of preparatory undergraduate work. The same necessity also sparked an accelerated schedule, which allowed quarterly registration and graduation (September, January, March, July) and completion of the degree in three years of year-round study. Creighton began the program in June 1942. By then, student draft deferments had ended and all males accepted to the medical school received reserve commissions as second lieutenants in the army or as ensigns in the navy. The following year, the ASTP and V-12 units garnered all the male medical students and paid for their education in return for their impending military service (medical and dental students received an extra housing allowance because Creighton did not have "barracks" for them). Besides the color of the uniform, the only other significant difference in the two programs resulted from the army requirement for drill. On occasion, some navy medical students sat in the bleachers of the stadium on Saturday mornings to mock their army cohorts parading on the field.[13]

The medical school wartime curriculum included five new courses; the physiological principles of aviation medicine, the physiological principles of chemical warfare casualties, the treatment of casualties due to chemical warfare (various forms of gas warfare had been used in World War I), tropical medicine (due to the fighting in the Pacific islands), and first aid. Sophomore and junior students served in a "disaster squad," trained to assist in evacuations, rescues, and first aid and emergency medical care. The Missouri River flood of 1943 presented a real emergency that pressed the students into service and gave them actual experience to supplement the scheduled mock drills. Moreover, the war produced a shortage of microscopes and the school had to appeal to alums to donate them, if they had extras. As faculty physicians went into the service, a teacher shortage also developed. The school recruited local physicians, especially alums too old for military service, to fill the void.[14]

Medical school enrollment increased from about 225 in 1941 to about 250 in 1945; the military, however, maintained strict standards and, according to a faculty recollection, a significant number of students failed courses and immediately received activation orders. The all-University Commencement also became a war casualty; the first accelerated medical school class graduated in March 1943, with civilian coed Agnes Jennings becoming the first woman to win the Adolph Sachs Award, given to the senior with the highest four-year scholastic average. Subsequently, on September 22, 1944, the pharmacy, dental, and medical schools held a joint commencement at the Joslyn Art Museum, "the first group to take their entire professional training under the accelerated program." By that time, the medical school also introduced refresher courses, covered by the G.I. Bill, for physicians returning to civilian practice. At the same time, the administration reactivated its long-deferred building plan, appealing to alumni to finance a library, an undergraduate classroom building, a student union, and a combined dental-pharmacy building. The first priority, however, remained a new medical school, a need it designated as "most urgent, in fact, imperative." In that state, the school received the news that the V-12 program would end December 19, 1945, but that ASTP students would continue until the end of the fiscal year and resume civilian status on June 30, 1946. The medical school emerged from World War II and resumed its prewar schedule facing serious challenges.[15]

The dental school followed the same accelerated schedule and experienced a similar small increase in enrollment (from about seventy-five in 1941 to about one hundred in 1944), with virtually all the students enlisted in the ASTP or the Navy V-5 program. Women remained an exception in dental education; even with the demands of war, only Elizabeth Galaska graduated in 1944, and Patricia Kelley the next year. In September 1944, seemingly because it met its quota for dentists, the army discontinued its ASTP dental training. The following spring, with a total of only sixty-one students and a mere three freshmen registered for the fall semester, the University announced plans to close the dental school. Father President Thomas Bowdern (December 1943–December 1945) explained the lack of "prospective students during the time that the present Selective Service Act is in force and the difficulty of maintaining an adequate number of full-time professors on the teaching staff prompted the board of trustees to make the decision." As World War II wound down, the dental school seemed poised to become one its casualties.[16]

The war also deeply affected the School of Nursing as the shortage of practitioners mounted. Scholarships and job opportunities pushed enrollments up; between 1941 and 1945, the St. Catherine's unit rose from 83 to 108 and the St. Joseph's unit from 126 to 163. The Bolton Act of June 1943, sought to increase rapidly the number of graduate nurses through the creation of the Cadet Nurse Corps. Enlistees received tuition, books, uniforms, and a stipend to study a thirty-month accelerated course. In return, the cadet pledged "her services to essential nursing—either civilian or military, as she chooses—for the duration of the war" (note the gender assumption of the era). The Creighton nursing units returned to twice-a-year admissions and graduations and, because of soldier-related problems, added new mental health classes and increased the psych rotation from four to twelve weeks. By 1945, all students admitted to the nursing units joined the Corps, with a two-year-total of 238 trained under the program.[17]

Besides training soldiers, sailors, airmen, and military nurses, Creighton's contribution to the war effort included the role played by its alumni. The *Creightonian* initiated a column, "Battling Bluejays," to report on their exploits and Fr. Linn sponsored a Parents' Service Club (spouses and siblings welcome) to provide support—it held meetings and published a newsletter. By December 1942, 1,127 Creighton alumni wore military uniforms and 75 percent of them served as officers. By war's end, approximately 2,700 alums had answered their country's call and 150 made the ultimate sacrifice. First Lieutenant Kenneth Wilson (arts), killed in action in the Philippines, in the spring of 1942, became Creighton's first fatality; Ensign John J. Parle (BSC, 1942), killed July 17, 1943, off Licata, Sicily, received the highest decoration. Parle discovered a fire on a landing craft laden with explosives; he used a fire extinguisher and a water hose to try to douse the smoke pot that fueled the fire. When those tactics failed, he picked up the pot and threw it overboard. He died in a field hospital in Tunisia from pneumonia contracted through excessive smoke inhalation. His heroic action prevented an explosion that would have damaged the troop ship and killed numerous soldiers and sailors, as well as revealed the imminent surprise attack on the island. Posthumously, he received the Congressional Medal of Honor and had a destroyer escort, the U.S.S. *Parle,* named in his honor.[18]

Andrew Jackson Higgins became Creighton's most illustrious wartime alumni. One of ten fatherless children from Columbus, Nebraska, he attended the arts college (1900–03), studying for three years under the historic-seven-year *Ratio Studiorum*. He remembered that he "played rather indifferent football" and that he once put "a blow-up solution in the inkwell in Fr. Rigge's classroom." In comparison, the role he played in the war effort contributed immensely to the Allied victory. The United States and its allies had to assault its enemies in North Africa, Europe, and Asia by means of new methods of amphibious warfare. Higgins invented and manufactured the troop and supply-carrying landing craft with the swing-down front ramp that made seaborne landings on contested beaches possible. In May 1943, Creighton demonstrated its admiration by presenting him with an honorary degree. In turn, on March 21, 1945, the United States government honored Creighton University for its contribution to the war effort by launching the S.S. *Creighton Victory*, a cargo vessel that saw service in the central and Western Pacific and circumnavigated the globe, from San Francisco to Wilmington, Delaware, October 27, 1945, to March 20, 1946. After decommissioning, it became part of the United Nations Relief and Rehabilitation program for war-ravage Europe.[19]

While the contingents of soldiers, sailors, and marines dominated the campus during World War II, a limited number of underage and/or un-draftable males and a significant number of coeds struggled to preserve the civilian traditions at Creighton University. In comparison to the other health sciences, the war made few demands upon the pharmacy school. It received no special military program (freshmen and sophomore males had to join ROTC) and became one of the last colleges of Creighton University to join the accelerated schedule in May 1943, and its enrollment dropped from eighty-four in 1940 to thirty-five in 1944. To help attract students, ten individuals and businesses each donated a $200 scholarship in 1943 that covered "practically all expenses of the first-year work in pharmacy." The number of credit hours for graduation increased from 128 to 135 (a few science classes went from three to four credit hours each) and the State of Nebraska mandated that each student gain a practical experience in a retail pharmacy or a hospital, which did not "run concurrently with the school or college of pharmacy work." While requirements increased, the pharmacy school struggled to maintain a viable enrollment without wartime inducements.[20]

Similarly, the graduate and law schools barely survived, as graduate enrollment nationwide dropped 69 percent and many law colleges closed for the duration. The graduate school offered few classes; five or fewer students received their degrees annually during the war and about half were women. In 1943, law joined pharmacy as one of the last schools to initiate an accelerated schedule. The law school began a year-round trimester calendar commencing that summer, which led to a degree in two years. Moreover, despite backtracking to a two-years-of-college entrance requirement, its enrollment continued to plunge from eighty-eight in 1940 to thirteen in 1944. The few women law students began to play a more significant role; in 1942, the nine law seniors elected Elaine Dodson president (first woman to hold that

office) and Araminta Boger vice president of their class. That year, the total enrollment stood at nineteen, demonstrating the impact of the draft on a school with no
military-deferment program. However, the school remained open because the few
full-time law professors also employed their talents in the undergraduate military
programs and/or other university projects.[21]

Moreover, civilian undergraduate education immediately experienced the exigencies of total war. According to one commentator, "Cooperation with the government
in total war requires that the colleges and universities accept the situation, shorten
their courses, and develop those courses which have a direct bearing on the military
and allied efforts." The basic criteria for traditional undergraduate study became
acceleration, compression, and vocational training. Faculty workloads increased as
their ranks shrank due to conscription and voluntary enlistments, and those remaining did double duty teaching military and civilian classes (Dean Walsh even mowed
campus lawns and did building repairs because of the staff shortage). A week after
Pearl Harbor, as the fall semester neared conclusion, Creighton held a "Bill of Rights
Assembly," at which Fr. President Zuercher advised the students to "wait until Uncle
Sam calls you, then give it your all." At the beginning of the spring semester, he
announced that "snapping into line with the nation's 'speedup' program" meant that
the arts, commerce, journalism, and university colleges would begin an accelerated
year-round schedule, consisting of two twenty-week semesters and an eight-week
summer session that would lead to a degree in three years.[22]

The "Wartime Plan for College Training," the title of the combined bulletins for
the undergraduate schools, included a reduction in the range of courses (e.g., among
others, the Czech language and library science were eliminated) and in the number
of courses taught by individual departments. Part-time students could attend regular classes, Monday through Friday, 8:00 A.M. to 3:00 P.M., but the colleges also
offered classes in the late afternoon and early evening, as well as on Saturdays, 8:00
A.M. to noon. A new attendance policy necessitated "a million volt, eight ply, Victory
excuse" for missing a class; male students with an unexcused absence had to perform
two hours of work or of physical exercise for each class missed, while coeds paid a $1
fine. Civilian male undergraduate students also had to perform calisthenics twice a
week to promote "progressive physical hardening." At first, the exercises took place
outdoors even during winter, except during extreme weather conditions. The year-
long schedule concluded with an "obstacle race," which included "hurdles, fences,
walls, ditches, tunnels and ladders." The military built the 400-yard-long course running north to south between the law school and the stadium. In 1943, the requirement became less martial, including only ten minutes of calisthenics, followed by
gym-class team sports. Attendance remained mandatory and "over cutting" provided
"a quicker way of leaving school than being called into active service by a reserve."[23]

Civilian enrollment figures present a problem during the war years, because of the
quarterly registrations and graduations and the frequent changes in the military status of the male undergraduate students. Generally, the undergraduate schools suffered a significant decline due to the absence of male students despite the rejuvena-

tion of the depression-era alumni-recruiting program. Between December 1941 and October 1944, the total enrollment in the arts college plummeted from 394 to 123, the commerce college dwindled from 248 to 50, and the Journalism College fell from 40 to 25 (somewhat buoyed by the high percentage of coeds). The summer school increased to 464 students in 1942 because of the inception of the year-round schedule, but then decreased to only 150 civilians in 1944. During the war, University College jumped from 70 to 120, as more women, given the circumstances, sought career opportunities. Relatively, coeds became a significant proportion of the civilian undergraduate population. In comparison, non-Catholic enrollment slipped slightly with opening of the new public University of Omaha campus. Moreover, World War II reinforced the local nature of the undergraduate population. Before the Great Depression about one third of the student body came from the Omaha-Council Bluffs area, one third from the states of Nebraska and Iowa, and one third from everywhere else. As of 1944, the proportions stood at one half from Omaha-Council Bluffs, one fourth from Nebraska and Iowa, and one fourth from elsewhere.[24]

The number of undergraduate degrees awarded annually decreased significantly during the war years, and because it lacked universal recognition, the arts and journalism colleges eliminated the Ph.B. degree. The pomp and circumstance of commencement decreased because of the frequent number of midterm graduation exercises and the fewer participants in the traditional June pageant. In 1942, however, the commencement booklet began to include the war-induced "Credo of Creighton." It decried foreign dictators who sought "to perpetuate their shackles through 'youth movements,'" and the spurious doctrine of "academic freedom" used "to teach systems which destroy all freedom." Creighton promised to educate according to the following creed:

> We believe in God
> We believe in the personal dignity of man
> We believe that man has certain rights which come from God and not from the State
> We therefore are opposed to all forms of dictatorship holding that the "total man" (totalitarianism) belongs to the State [a reference to fascism and the Soviet Union]
> We believe in the sanctity of the home—the basic unit of society
> We believe in the natural right of private property, but likewise that private property has its social obligations
> We believe that Labor has not only rights but obligations
> We believe that Capital has not only rights but obligations
> We are vigorously opposed to all forms of "racism"—persecution or intolerance because of race
> We believe that liberty is a sacred thing, but the law, which regulates liberty, is a sacred obligation
> We believe in inculcating all the essentials of American Democracy and take open and frank issue with all brands of spurious "democracy."

After the war, the Credo also began to appear in all the various editions of the Creighton University Bulletin.[25]

Another wartime addition included the Creighton University Rural Life Institute, directed by the Reverend John C. Rawe, S.J, a leader in the Catholic Rural Life Conference and the author of "numerous articles and several books dealing with rural sociology." William J. Coad (Arts, 1899, and member of the Lay Board of Regents) donated the use of a 220-acre farm, complete with a dairy herd of forty registered Guernsey cows, in Elkhorn, Nebraska, fifteen miles to the west of campus. The institute sought to "build up the ideal of 'stewardship farming' . . . necessary to enable the farmer to work with the biological balance on each farm—growing a variety of crops and caring for a variety of animals on each farm." The program followed the "biodynamic" principles of Ehrenfried Pfeiffer, a Swiss scientist who came to the United States with the outbreak of war in Europe, and who started a 700-acre demonstration farm near Phoenixville, Pennsylvania.

Father Rawe had "no desire to see the institute grow beyond instructing ten to fifteen students a year," who would live in the farmhouse for one year while studying rural sociology and gaining on-the-farm experience. The "outline of courses" included various classes in "The Rural Family and the Way-of-Life on the Land," "Soil Biology," "Stability—Permanent Farms" (as opposed to "Destructive Farm Systems"), "Family Farm Organization," and "The Farm Animals" (feeding, breeding, care, judging, and management of various breeds). Students paid $100 tuition and received a certificate, but no college credit, for the one-year experience. No records exist for the experiment; considering the shortage of farm laborers and the scarcity of young un-draftable males, seemingly the project did not go beyond the elaborate announcement.[26]

As if the war did not disrupt the normal routine enough, on May 12, 1943, the Administration Building suffered its third major fire. The fire broke out about 1:15 P.M. in the area between the ceiling of the arts library and the third floor of the main building. It quickly raced between the walls up to the attic, but remained a small blaze with lots of smoke. Air cadets and civilian CCAS and high school students formed a "volunteer chain gang," which removed four thousand reference books and the filing system from the threatened area in about five minutes. Thus, while the three floors in the affected area suffered extensive water damage, the collection absorbed minor harm. Luckily, because of insurance coverage, the conflagration did not cause financial problems and at the end of the year, Fr. President Zuercher announced that the administration had "steadily whittled" its debt down "close to $200,000.00." Two decades of stadium-debt, compounded by depression and war, necessitated fiscal restraint, but the University remained solvent. Moreover, after years of meager fundraising (in 1942, the Alumni Loyalty Fund set a goal of $20,000, subsequently lowered it to $10,000, and actually raised $5,640 from a mere 646 donors—less than 10 percent of the alums), in 1943, the Loyalty Fund beat its goal by collecting $21,395.50. The University had also just received a $100,000 bequest from Walter P. Murphy, a non-alum railroad-supply executive who died in Los Angeles in December 1942. William Jeffers, president of the Union Pacific Railroad and a member of the Lay Board of Regents, arranged for the grant from the $20 million dollar estate. A second gift came from shipbuilding alum Andrew Jackson Higgins, who donated $5,000 to initiate a student loan fund named in honor of his favorite professor, Fr. Francis X. Reilly, S.J.[27]

Furthermore, while the war proceeded, planning for its aftermath began. As part of a national movement, the Creighton Alumni Association sponsored a series of postwar planning seminars at the Joslyn Art Museum every third Sunday evening during October and November of 1943. Radio station KIOL transcribed the forums and rebroadcast them on the subsequent Monday evenings. The following February, *Fortune* magazine began sponsoring a course of study on postwar planning for women's clubs, and the "Creighton University of the Air" radio program, broadcast twice weekly over station WOW, borrowed the topics and featured the analysis of University faculty members. Simultaneously, the city of Omaha began designing a new long-range plan for urban development that would rejuvenate the city after almost two decades of stagnation due to depression and war. Creighton joined the process, working with the Leo A. Daly architecture firm and devised a scheme of perpendicular malls that addressed the problem of blight east of the campus. The city dubbed the area between the University and 16th Street as "Omaha's twilight area"; Creighton's plan replaced the deteriorated structures with an east-west mall running from 15th to 20th streets, between Dodge and Davenport, and a north-south mall stretching from Dodge to Cuming, between 22nd and 24th streets. Landscaped parkways would become the home for modern civic and educational facilities, replacing dilapidated houses, apartment buildings, and warehouses. The arrangement included allowing the University to expand east to 22nd Street, between California and Cuming, and tying Central High School, the Joslyn Art Museum, and Creighton University together in a cultural complex that would mark the western edge of the downtown district. Administration spokesmen argued that the plan might take fifty years to complete; the timetable proved correct, although Creighton's expansion to the east during the last quarter of the twentieth century took a very different form.[28]

Although the war continued at a hellish pace in both the European and Pacific theaters during 1944, the year witnessed a transition to prewar scheduling at Creighton. Well into the following year, the draft continued to remove from classes eligible male civilian students who turned eighteen, and many administrators feared Congress would revise the draft classification system to conscript 4-Fs, which might force the closure of the undergraduate schools. Yet, simultaneously the administration claimed that "Space for off-the-street parking [was] now essential," despite reduced faculty numbers, minimal civilian enrollment and gas rationing. One commentator, however, nostalgically recalled the prewar situation with "cars parked so thick around Creighton that late students could not find a parking space." Looking to the future, the administration purchased land for parking, north of California and east of 24th streets. The fear of an expanded draft did not materialize, however; six weeks before D-Day, June 6, 1944, the University announced the end of the accelerated program and that it would return to its prewar schedule of starting classes in mid-September and ending the school year on June 1. It also planned to eliminate the four-week intersession in May-June, which preceded the start of the summer session. Furthermore, it increased the number of semester hours required for an undergraduate degree from 120 to 128.[29]

The anticipated departure of the air cadets led to plans to convert the dorms back to civilian use, although the administration opted to keep the bunk beds, believing students would prefer the savings entailed in sharing a room. It did not expect the total undergraduate enrollment to increase much beyond the existing three hundred students, but did look ahead to "a larger number of seventeen-year-old boys . . . to enroll to take advantage of the pre-induction courses." Actually, the unexpected arrival of ASTRP cadets postponed the transition; male civilian students did not begin to occupy rooms in Dowling Hall until the spring semester of 1945. At the same time, "repeated requests by the students" led to the elimination of the "work off cuts" policy. The administration allowed undergraduate students "to assume fuller responsibility for class attendance," but required that they file an absentee card with the dean of the appropriate college, who retained the right to dismiss a student from a course for "disinterest" (no specific maximum number of cuts prescribed). Moreover, a new letter-grading system replaced the previous percentage designations, but grade-point averages remained on a 3.0 scale. Finally, the conversion also witnessed the reintroduction of the freshmen-orientation program, which entailed a one semester, one-credit-hour class that introduced students to study skills, campus facilities, and social activities.[30]

Social activities, however, remained circumscribed due to reduced civilian enrollment and the impact of rationing. While the controls on items such as paper clips, rubber bands, and pencils with erasers affected schoolwork, shortages of cigarettes reduced the number of frequently scheduled smokers. Besides making the sacrifices asked of all citizens, the civilian students also participated in patriotic pursuits. For example, Beaux Arts, the commerce college literary club, "collected 3,000 pounds of paper for national defense within two weeks after the declaration of war." Similarly, the *Creightonian*, with support from Alpha Sigma Nu, organized a scrap drive consisting of "100 minutemen" who volunteered to spend all day Saturday, October 10, 1942, at their assigned task. That year, the SBG established the purchase of a 25-cent war stamp as the admission price for the Homecoming dance. On December 7, Creighton commemorated the first anniversary of Pearl Harbor with an all-University assembly. Then, following the arrival of the air cadets in 1943, the coeds aided the USO in sponsoring a dance for the soldiers in the gymnasium. Furthermore, the *Creightonian* spearheaded the collection of books, magazines, and games to provide leisure activities for the men in uniform.[31]

On the other hand, the wartime demands on the reduced number of faculty and the small number of civilian students forced "Creighton University of the Air" to cease broadcasting from its studio in the tower on the fifth floor of the Administration Building. Moreover, the junior-senior prom, Homecoming, and the Student Union became war casualties. On April 21, 1943, the day before Easter vacation, the

SBG voted to close the union rooms because "practically all the students will be in the armed services next year and it would be useless to attempt to keep the corporation active for the duration." One week later, it resolved "to make the union inactive until such time as it is capable of again functioning, probably after the war." It decided to invest the $2,500 in its treasury in war bonds.[32]

Equally disheartening, intercollegiate athletics disappeared because of the ASTP ban and the insufficient number of civilians to fill team rosters. Unlike the navy, the army argued that training for intercollegiate sports would demand too much time and would distract from the purpose of its specialized training programs. Colleges with sizeable navy units continued to field teams, but when the V-5 and V-12 programs replaced the naval reserve program at the end of 1942, the navy no longer maintained undergraduate programs at Creighton. Due to the loss of coaches and civilian male students to the draft and enlistments, the University curtailed intercollegiate athletics during the 1943–44 and 1944–45 seasons. Before the ultimate abandonment of intercollegiate athletics, the war already had stifled the revival of several dormant "major sport" teams. Three days after Pearl Harbor, Coach J. V. "Duce" Belford announced his intent to reorganize a swim team to represent Creighton, which was selected to host the MVC meet the following spring. Unfortunately, he failed to field a team and the competition had to find another pool. Similarly, in the spring of 1942 Belford undertook to form a track squad for the Drake relays, but it did not take to the cinders. However, by the time of the MVC finals in St. Louis on May 20, he did send eight runners, who amassed four points to finish a distant last—the school's last track venture. Finally, Belford also sought to field the first baseball squad since before World War I. He produced a squad in 1942, but it only played a few games against local sandlot teams (since it did not entail the regular college practice schedule, the air cadets also had a team in the Omaha Community League). Duce Belford joined the Army Air Corps in April 1943, resulting in the elimination of the above sports and the intramural program he directed for civilian students which was replaced by calisthenics.[33]

The post–Pearl Harbor basketball teams briefly maintained their success; in 1941–42, the Bluejay hoopsters compiled an 18-5 record, going 9-1 in the conference and sharing the MVC title, while winning two games in the National Invitational Tournament (NIT) before elimination. The following year, the team went 16-1, 10-0 in the conference, to gain the MVC championship, but lost its first game in the NIT. In March 1943, athletic director the Reverend David Shyne, S.J., announced the suspension of intercollegiate athletics at Creighton for the duration; in May, Coach Eddie Hickey joined the navy. Father Shyne probably breathed a sigh of relief in regards to the football program, the major culprit in producing a $50,000 deficit in the athletic budget, accumulated since 1937. The war deeply affected college football; between 1941 and 1943, the number of intercollegiate teams dropped from 650 to 167, and Catholic colleges contributed more than their fair share to the diminution. Coach Maurice "Skip" Palrang directed the last team to a 5-4 record and nine thousand fans witnessed the last football game in Creighton history on November 21,

1942, in the stadium against Tulsa. Creighton entered the fourth quarter tied 19-19 against a team that later played in the Sugar Bowl, but eventually lost 19-33.[34]

The transition year 1944 witnessed a "homecoming" in which rodeo replaced football. The occasion took place from Wednesday, September 13, through Sunday, September 17, in the stadium. Purses totaling $5,000 attracted a "stream of cowboys and cowgirls en route east to participate in the Madison Square Garden show in October." Events included bronco riding, calf roping, Brahma steer riding, and bulldogging, and "an entire Sioux Indian village was established at one end of the stadium." The rodeo netted a $10,000 profit earmarked for stadium improvements. That same fall, Duce Belford returned and reintroduced a civilian intramural program, consisting of touch football, basketball, volleyball, and handball. To accommodate the new program the University remodeled the fourth floor of the gymnasium into a basketball court, which helped alleviate the conflicts between intramurals, the wartime mandatory physical education classes, and practice time for the high school teams. The "upper gym" did not relieve all the congestion and a new field house joined the University's wish list. During the spring semester of 1945, the MVC pressured Creighton to reintroduce its athletic program, beginning with football in the fall. Father Shyne's succinct retort stated, "No intercollegiate athletics until the Japs are defeated." The war ended in Europe in May, leading the MVC to authorize a full sports schedule; Creighton stood alone as the only conference member not to announce a football and basketball schedule for that fall.[35]

While intercollegiate sports ceased and most of the undergraduate clubs atrophied, the Sodalities in all the colleges maintained a vibrant presence among the civilian students. They continued their charity work, such as sponsoring the distribution of Christmas baskets to "underprivileged Negro families" in the St. Benedict parish, as well as sponsoring the annual Marion Night celebration in honor of the Blessed Virgin Mary. While undergraduate fraternities disbanded, those in the professional schools remained vital, along with the undergraduate and professional sororities. Weekly, the *Creightonian* documented their crowded social calendar, including the annual inter-fraternity ball, which since 1939 included electing a "Helen of Troy."[36]

The war also affected the lives of the coeds and gave them special opportunities in all the undergraduate extracurricular activities. The first African-American coed appeared on campus, and in June 1943, Melba Fawcett received her Ph.B., becoming the first black woman to graduate from Creighton University (starting in 1951, she served her alma mater briefly as an assistant librarian). While the *Creightonian* regularly ran stories and pictures of women students who got engaged or married, it also ballyhooed their efforts in behalf of the war, such as the one hundred coeds who attended classes on first aid and home nursing to help with Civilian Defense. Moreover, the National Association for Physical Education of College Women cosponsored, with the United States Office on Education, a seven-day seminar on "Victory Through Fitness." Creighton had no women's athletic program, women's coaches, or female physical education instructors; therefore, a group of coeds took it upon themselves to create a fitness-training club that sponsored athletic activities. It sought "to get every coed interested in athletics to make herself fit for whatever duties wartime may demand." Furthermore, women contributed virtually the entire editorial staff of the *Creightonian* in 1943–44 and 1944–45, and in June 1944 Marilyn Dugdale, president of the senior class of University College, became the first coed to make the flag presentation during Commencement. Previously, in November 1943, undergraduate female students played a key role in organizing the Creighton Coop, a student cooperative society that opened a cafeteria in the "Arts Cottage," a home across California Street from the Administration Building, where students could socialize. The following year, the University rented the space for housing and the Coop moved into the former Student Union rooms in the gymnasium, allowing women equal access to them for the first time.[37]

The war-induced prominence of women at Creighton University quickly diminished during the immediate postwar era. Peacetime produced conditions that rapidly altered the gender balance as enrollment surged, especially in terms of ex-servicemen taking advantage of the G.I. Bill. In September 1945, with the war over, the University nearly matched its prewar enrollment high, registering 1,914 students, with only 133 vets on the roster. In January 1946, another 652 ex-servicemen enrolled (historically, only 25 to 30 students entered at mid-term). The administration created a special spring session, which ran from April 1 to June 1, for returning soldiers who missed the January registration. The special session allowed another 102 vets to earn nine credit hours in history, mathematics, and English before the start of the summer school. The following fall, 2,944 registrants (1,820 veterans) crushed the previous total enrollment record for the University; the CCAS mushroomed to 1,005 students, a 400 percent increase. Administrators purchased "60 double-decker beds from surplus military supplies" to increase the capacity of Dowling and Wareham halls, and enlisted the aid of alumni and the 1-C Club to find housing throughout the city. In September 1947, enrollment peaked at 3,000; ex-servicemen contributed 1,956 to the total. Thereafter, enrollment began to decline as "the inrush of veterans" began to diminish. However, as late as the spring semester 1950, veterans contributed 1,505 of the total 2,774 students registered and they remained a majority in every school of the University, except Nursing and University College. For three years, Creighton had given ex-servicemen a preference and had turned away non-veteran applicants, which it could not accommodate because of the limitations of faculty and facilities. Coeds had received a low admission priority and enrollment in University College had fallen from 197 in 1945 to 129 in 1948, before rebounding to 174 in 1949. By the later year, the administration viewed women students in a more favorable light, and with declining undergraduate enrollment, the University returned to its alumni student-recruiting campaign.[38]

The exploding enrollment necessitated larger classes and more course offerings during the late afternoon and evenings. The lack of sufficient classrooms forced the use of the Auditorium to hold large lecture classes, as well as the purchase of three surplus barracks from Ft. Crook, located in nearby Bellevue, Nebraska. The Federal Works Administration oversaw the disassembling, transporting, and reconstructing of the buildings on campus, situating them between the auditorium and the law college. "The Huts," as the students referred to them, provided five thousand square feet of space; the east and the west barracks each held two classrooms capable of holding fifty students, while the central building contained one such classroom, a lounge, and restroom facilities. They opened in time to provide sites for semester examinations in January 1947, and subsequently also housed the radio and speech studios. In addition, in the shuffle of spaces, the bookstore moved out of the Administration Building. Dowling Hall (dormitory rooms on top two floors; offices on first floor and in the basement) now stretched along the entire east side of 25th Street, California to Cass streets. To accommodate the military during World War II, the University had erected a connector with the commerce college annex. The construction created a block-long, three-building complex; with the troops gone, the administration redesigned the connector portion to house the bookstore and a snack bar.[39]

Furthermore, the burgeoning enrollment led to the acceptance of the latest technology—computers. In August 1946, Jack Williams (B.S., 1940), who had worked as a special agent for the Federal Bureau of Investigation in Washington, D.C., became registrar; former registrar Claire McDermott accepted reassignment as assistant registrar. By the end of the academic year, Williams introduced the use of International Business Machine (IBM) punch cards to tabulate grades, supplanting the offices of the various deans, which had previously generated student grade reports. Creighton staff sorted and prepared the cards, while the IBM Company in downtown Omaha, which owned and operated the machines, processed them on a service-contract basis. In the fall of 1947, Williams applied the same procedure to class registration; shortly thereafter, a picture appeared in the *Creighton Alumnus* of students seated at tables in the gymnasium with a caption reading, "Registration, 1949 style—with coffee, donuts and only half of the number of forms to be filled." Students unaware of the past, filling out "all those cards" and going through a score of validating stations before completing registration, usually on blisteringly hot days in the un-air-conditioned gymnasium, probably scoffed at the so-called efficiency. In 1950, Williams added another innovation; he designed a new diploma for the undergraduate schools, a seven-by-nine-inch, blue and white document enclosed in blue leather.[40]

Burgeoning enrollment had demanded an enlarged faculty and administration. Quickly surpassing prewar levels, by 1950 the faculty of the arts college increased to twenty-eight Jesuits, plus sixty-two lay teachers; of that total, twenty-three held the Ph.D. degree. Women reappeared on the faculty roster in small but significant numbers (ten in 1950, three with their Ph.D.). In 1944, Mrs. Charles W. (Maureen) Hamilton (M.A., 1939) became one of the first female faculty members of the postwar era, teaching education and sociology classes in the summer school. In 1946, she added the role of "women's counselor," a position subsequently enhanced in responsibilities and retitled dean of women. She joined assistant registrar Claire McDermott, librarian Mary Hunt, and bursar Gretchen Golliglee (in 1943, Isabelle Keyser, former bursar and manager of the bookstore, retired after twenty-seven years) as the small coterie of lay, female staff members. Jesuits continued to occupy the position of dean of the CCAS on the traditional three- to six-year rotation, although in 1946 the expanding demands of the bloated student population created the need for the first assistant dean in the school's history. Moreover, to handle the escalating administrative demands, the University reordered the structure of its standing committees to include ones to advise on policy and procedures concerning admissions, undergraduate studies, education policies, student counseling, student financial aid, library, rank and tenure, graduation, and veterans services.[41]

In November 1945, the administration announced that it had attained a debt-free status and that it would begin fundraising for a specific long-range development plan previously publicized as its "wish list." The proposal included $2,000,000 for bricks and mortar—a new medical school, a student-activities building that included an auditorium, an undergraduate library, an arts college building, a dormitory with a capacity for 125 students—and $5,000,000 for the endowment. The first step required the reorganization and reactivization of the Lay Board of Regents, which had atrophied during World War II and had only four serving members due to death and illness. By 1950, the administration enlarged the board to nine members by attracting the services of prominent Omaha businessmen. The second step entailed the appointment of a new rector-president. Father Thomas Bowdern had come to Creighton in 1931, had received his Ph.D. in education at St. Louis University in 1936, had served as dean of the graduate school and University College, and had become president of the University in 1943. He resigned that position in December 1945 (the first Jesuit allowed to take such an action in the United States), claiming he could not handle the fundraising chore.[42]

On Christmas Day 1945, the Reverend William H. McCabe, S.J., who had attended the arts college, 1909–11, became the eighteenth president of Creighton University. He had received a Ph.D. in English Literature from Cambridge University in 1929, and recently had served as president of Rockhurst College. He emphasized planning, established a budget system, hired a comptroller, instituted a retirement system for faculty and staff, and, in keeping with tradition and symmetrical nomenclature, temporarily renamed the arts college, Creighton College, to balance the "women's school," University College. Moreover, Fr. McCabe emphasized the Catholic nature of Creighton, although during his tenure the non-Catholic proportion of students recovered from the competition from the University of Omaha and rose to approximately 25 percent. The new president also completed the final step necessary for the development campaign. The Lay Regents argued that the job of the president consisted of establishing good public relations with the Omaha community; therefore, he needed assistants, including a layperson. Thus, Fr. President McCabe secured the services of Wendell A. Dwyer (A.B. and M.A. Creighton, Ph.D. University of Nebraska), formerly associate professor of mathematics and since 1945 manager of the Industrial Division of the Omaha Chamber of Commerce. Simultaneously, Fr. McCabe appointed Fr. Henry Linn to act as his executive secretary.[43]

Fr. Linn had come to Creighton in 1937 as an instructor in classics and in 1944 became dean of the graduate school and University College. In January 1945, he initiated the Creighton Institute on Industrial Relations, which held ten-week seminar sessions that cost students a nominal $2 registration fee. Adult workers in the "Labor School" and managers in the "Employers' Conference" earned a certificate upon completion of a session, geared to bring "better understanding between labor and management." Subsequently, the Reverend Austin E. Miller, S.J., from the sociology department, assumed the position of director of the institute and shepherded it through the remainder of the decade, as Fr. Linn had assumed his new position of executive secretary on March 31, 1946. The Reverend Henry W. Casper, S.J., instructor of history, replaced him as graduate school dean and the Reverend Gerald FitzGibbon, dean of Creighton College, accepted the added responsibilities of dean of University College.[44]

In conjunction with the impending development campaign, the Alumni Association rejuvenated efforts to organize and energize former students. In December 1945, it reinstituted dues of $2 and its first direct-mail appeal garnered 1,728 members. Then it began to organize events to vitalize the membership by building a sense of belonging to a Creighton community, possessed of a Creighton spirit. On July 28, 1947, it hosted the first annual Alumni Picnic at Peony Park, which included games, prizes, swimming, refreshments, an evening barbeque, and a culminating dance "under the stars in the Royal Grove." Other events included the annual Easter and "Hard Times" dances; the latter reprised a student ball of the depression era and required attendees to dress like hobos.[45]

Moreover, the Association directed the efforts of the alumni student-recruiting program and assumed responsibility for the reorganized student-employment service, which provided leads for local part-time jobs. Regarding employment, the war years witnessed the printing of bare-bones bulletins, which eliminated many of the policy statements previously incorporated, including the guidelines on student employment. In 1945, the administration reintroduced its principle in reference to "Opportunities for Self-support." It stated, "Work which prevents a student from carrying his college studies profitably should not be undertaken and will not be considered as a satisfactory excuse for delinquency in any course." The policy related directly to the development drive; an enlarged endowment would help defray the actual cost of educating a student and help keep tuition rates low. Lower costs, in an era before federally guaranteed student loans, could obviate the need for students working excessive hours. Scholarships and loans could provide needed assistance, but the University possessed minimal resources in that area. The Murphy and the McBride scholarships, and the Agnew, Webster, Woodbury, Reilly, and Sutherland loan funds all operated on $1,000 or $2,000 bequests, only able to make small grants to a few students. In the meantime, tuition in the undergraduate schools rose from $6 per hour ($96 for sixteen semester hours) in 1945 to $150 per semester in 1949. In its statement on financial aid, the administration acknowledged, "The Creighton University does not have enough available scholarships, and therefore tries when possible to help students who are especially deserving, by grants covering part of the tuition fee in the Colleges of Liberal Arts [CCAS and University College], College of Pharmacy, College of Commerce, and School of Journalism." Increasing the endowment presented a difficult challenge, but it remained a priority.[46]

In the spring of 1946 of Fr. McCabe revealed a new five-year development plan, which still included a new medical school, but now called for a new college of business (it recently surfaced as an accreditation requirement), a new high school, a new science building, and new dorms. Alumni teams, "organized along military lines," had solicited $450,000 in pledges by the end of the year, a woefully inadequate sum. At that time, due to the "present unsettled economic conditions" (postwar deregulation, inflation, and strikes), the Lay Regents decided against establishing a date for a spring civic drive, but vowing to start "the moment conditions become favorable." In February 1947, however, the Lay Board again decided, "now is not the time," arguing that the existence of competing drives presented unwanted competition and that Creighton had to "stake out a claim." While the drive fizzled locally, Fr. President McCabe's assistants, Fr. Linn and Dr. Dwyer, became codirectors of a national campaign that emphasized solicitations from alumni physicians. Preemptively, Louis D. McGuire (M.D., 1917), clinical professor of surgery, had spontaneously initiated a drive for the medical school in December 1945. By June 30, 1947, he and thirty-eight other Omaha physicians, paying their own travel expenses, had crisscrossed the country to secure $594,614.34, the vast majority of pledges in the total of $731,806.84 raised by University's development-campaign. That sum did not include the $100,000 bequest from John T. Smith (Arts, 1899); at the time of his death, he served as general counsel for General Motors.[47]

During 1948, Fr. Linn further promoted the campaign, visiting thirty-three states, traveling 80,000 miles by automobile and another 15,000 by train. He persuaded 1,113 alums to subscribe to the five-year development plan; his efforts raised the pledge total to $1,123,933.34, which included $410,082.42 in actual payments. Finally, in January 1949, Lay Regent Otto Swanson accepted the position of campaign chair and the long-delayed local phase of the drive began. By the time fundraising actually occurred, the development program "took a backseat," while Swanson conducted a newly fashioned "General Funds Campaign." For the first time in history, the University sought "funds for operational purposes." Swanson and the Lay Regents established a goal to collect $750,000 in three years. Archbishop Gerald T. Bergan, Omaha Mayor Glenn Cunningham, and Council Bluffs Mayor George Sparks served as honorary chairmen. Creighton revealed it had an endowment of $2,500,000 that did not generate sufficient revenue annually to cover expenses; it reiterated its standard fundraising homily, "Creighton is not wealthy," and cited "the many economic, cultural and spiritual benefits" it brought to Omaha and its environs. Nebraska Governor Val Peterson proclaimed May 15–21, Creighton Week, mayors Cunningham and Sparks duplicated the gesture for their cities, and Archbishop Bergan issued a pastoral letter urging Catholics to support the drive.[48]

The campaign opened on Sunday, May 22, with an "all-star radio program" broadcast over "all local radio stations." The program, "This Nation Under God," argued in behalf of the "place of God in education and the needs of private universities, specifically Creighton University." It featured contemporary radio and movie stars Pat O'Brien, Dennis Day, Ann Blythe, Jimmy Durante, and Fibber McGee and Mollie. Subsequently, thirty-three Creighton students, mostly World War II vets, served as a speakers' bureau to business and social clubs, and daily radio announcements and newspaper articles promoted the drive. By July 1949, the University reported $400,000 in pledges and that the Council Bluffs and "outside Omaha" phases had started to "gear up"; however, no subsequent reports for the "general funds campaign" came forward. In August 1949, the administration announced that Fr. Linn would "go on the road" to the Northwest and spend two months soliciting. Father President McCabe's heart attack postponed the trip and short-circuited the renewed development campaign. Father Linn had to assume administrative duties, aiding acting president the Reverend Everett J. Morgan, S.J., who had served as the superintendent of grounds and buildings. To help with the campaigns, Fr. Morgan appointed George A. Hey, instructor of English, assistant to the president in charge of public relations. He initiated a bequests campaign, "A Will is a Way," providing instructions and a form printed regularly in the *Creighton Alumnus.* George Hey left in April 1950, replaced by the Reverend William J. Kelley, S.J., who also held a Ph.D. degree and joined the education department. While the administration continued to report progress, at the end of Fr. McCabe's presidency, the development drive had obtained $1,213,660 in pledges—much better than previous efforts, but still acutely short of its goals.[49]

While the development campaign brought in much-needed revenue, it did not enlarge the endowment and did not underwrite the construction of a single building on the wish list. In 1949, without fanfare, the University opened the Chemistry Building, a "T" shaped, wood-frame structure that contained offices and research labs for faculty, and labs and classrooms for four hundred students. However, chemistry students continued to carry out some forms of lab work in the dental school, adjacent to the north. Obviously a stopgap facility, a larger fully-equipped science building remained on the wish list. Similarly, the medical school had to make due with its aged facility in downtown Omaha, which suffered unwelcomed major damage to its roof during a violent windstorm in early March 1950 (to the west, on campus, buildings lost windows and chimneys, the stadium had seven light towers toppled, and all campus meetings were cancelled the night of the storm). Although it lacked state-of-the-art accommodations, the medical school continued to attract record enrollment, increased from 247 in 1945–46 (last year of the military programs) to 289 in 1949–50. As of 1948, applicants took the Medical College Aptitude Test (MCAT) as the required entrance examination for the Creighton School of Medicine. Veterans remained a healthy majority of the medical student body (60 percent in 1949–50) and women continued to attend in small but significant numbers (about five in each class). In 1949, Alice Hickey (M.D., 1948) organized nineteen medical coeds into the Alpha Zeta chapter of Alpha Epsilon Iota national medical sorority. Those students of the immediate postwar era witnessed the elimination of the $100 tuition reduc-

tion granted to Creighton undergraduates and an increase in tuition from $400 to
$500 per year in 1947, before it fell back to $350 in 1949. In the latter year, the administration issued a new directive on student employment, stating, "The curriculum of
the School of Medicine requires the full time and energy of all medical students and
since it is believed that outside work greatly interferes with medical education it is
not approved."[50]

The ongoing attempt by the Jesuits to bring uniformity to the curriculum in its
schools received renewed stimulus in 1945, with the establishment of the Jesuit Education Association (JEA). It began its work with the creation of the Commission on
Professional Education, which met with the Jesuit regents of dental schools (1945),
law schools (1947), and medical schools (1948; only five Catholic medical schools at
the time). The JEA also held institutes (ten-day workshops for deans), which dealt
with such issues as curriculum and accreditation (e.g., in 1945, the Association of
American Universities placed only Boston College, Creighton, Fordham, Georgetown, Holy Cross, Marquette, and St. Louis University on its "approved" list).
Finally, the JEA held an annual convention in conjunction with the National
Catholic Education Association, which brought together presidents, deans, and
high-school principals. The JEA, however, lacked enforcement power; thus, the
"National Office met opposition, or at least passive resistance, when it attempted—
even with the blessing of the provincials—to influence the curriculum, invade the
departments, oppose new degree programs, or challenge the prerogatives of an individual president."[51]

Therefore, for the most part, curriculum changes at the Creighton Medical
School (and all the other schools of the University) came in response to national
developments and local needs and concerns. Thus, in medicine, the immediate postwar era witnessed the advent of a new technology and a reorganization of clinical
clerkships and residencies. In the spring 1947, for only the third time in the United
States and the first time west of the Missouri River, television cameras in the surgical
pavilion of St. Joseph's Hospital telecast a surgical operation; members of the
Creighton medical staff viewed the procedure "on receivers in the Nursing School
auditorium half a block away." The following year, the hospital constructed a five-
story, 135-bed psychiatric unit called "Our Lady of Victory Unit," which added to the
clinical facilities available to Creighton medical and nursing students. Earlier, in 1946,
the medical school had initiated a new Child Guidance Clinic, which helped Omaha
deal with its juvenile-delinquency problem, but stressed training in medical knowledge in reference to childhood mental and physical health. Shortly thereafter, the
medical school established new clinical clerkships for third-year students (who
rotated through the various hospitals serving in surgery, medicine, pediatrics, psychiatry, and neurology) and fourth-year students (who rotated through the various hospitals serving in medicine, surgery, obstetrics, gynecology, pediatrics, "and the various
specialties"). Moreover, in conjunction with graduate education, the medical school
began to offer three-year residencies in the departments of Obstetrics and gynecology, internal medicine, pathology, and radiology. The "curricula of the various clini-

cal departments [were] drawn up so as to meet the general requirements of each of the boards in the various fields of specialization" and study led "to a Master's degree in the respective specialty."[52]

The graduate degrees related to an amplified postwar emphasis on medical research. For example, between 1945 and 1955, the United States Public Health Service increased the amount of money granted to non–National Institutes of Health research facilities from a mere $150,000 to a substantial $70,000,000. As federal and foundation grants expanded, the significance of research by medical faculty followed suit. In 1948, in order to promote research among the Creighton medical faculty, Dean Charles M. Wilhelmj resigned and assumed the new position of director of research. Two years later, James M. Severens, Ph.D., head of the department of bacteriology, and Sydney Bausor, Ph.D., assistant professor of biology, each "developed a patentable matter." Their success prompted the Board of Trustees to announce that Creighton would begin to follow the "common practice of universities requiring the assignment of the patent to the university, with an agreement as to the inventor's share in the profits if any." The board determined that the percentage "should not be excessive," and that it should be calculated in terms "of net profits, not gross profits."[53]

The Creighton medical faculty remained largely "home-grown"; it expanded in conjunction with the rising enrollment and the availability of funds. Full-time faculty remained the minority—in 1949, they numbered sixteen, eight of whom held Creighton M.D.s. There were seventy-three clinical professors (forty-three with a Creighton M.D.), as well as fifty-four instructors (twenty-nine with a Creighton M.D.), thirty assistants (twenty-two with a Creighton M.D.), twenty-six acting assistants (eighteen with a Creighton M.D.), and seven lecturers (two with a Creighton M..D.). Retired Brigadier General Percy J. Carroll, Chief Surgeon of the United States Forces in the Southwest Pacific Theater during World War II and then-professor of preventive medicine and chief of staff of St. Joseph's Hospital, became dean of the medical school. Shortly thereafter, in keeping with the expansion of administrative chores in the postwar era, he hired the school's first assistant dean, Thomas D. Fitzgerald, M.D.[54]

While the medical school dreamed of a new facility, the dental school rose like a phoenix. At the opening of the twentieth century, fifty-seven dental schools existed, forty-four of them privately owned; by mid-century, the number dropped to forty and all but one had an association with a university. As World War II concluded, Fr. President Bowdern proposed lowering the number of dental schools in the United States by one, but "intensive work" on the part of a committee of the Omaha District Dental Society reversed his decision. The Creighton Alumni Council sparked the action, passing a unanimous resolution expressing its "deep regret" concerning the announced closing. The Nebraska Dental Association, local social-service agencies, the Omaha Chamber of Commerce, and "other groups" rallied to the cause, pledging "substantial support toward the continuance of dental education and clinic services at Creighton." Affected professionals, including those who relied upon the dental clinic for low-cost or free services for their clients, received a first-hand illustration of Creighton's historic fundraising message—the significance of the University's contributions to the community. Father Bowdern recognized the consequences of the occasion; years later, he recalled that the episode produced beneficial publicity and mobilized alumni.[55]

Dental alums quickly raised approximately $7,000 to meet the expenses of hiring additional faculty and improving facilities, which the ADA demanded for continued accreditation. The dental school, however, also failed to meet ADA financial requirements, which stipulated that a program deriving "more than 34 percent of its revenue from tuition and clinic fees is not considered to have a stable income." With alumni and community support, the University put the school's finances in order, hired two additional full-time and twenty-two part-time faculty, and renovated and expanded the dental facility, adding new administrative offices, faculty meeting room and lounge, enlarging the library, and buying new X-ray equipment. By 1950, the faculty numbered fifty-one, of which thirty-four possessed a D.D.S. (twenty-seven obtained at Creighton). By that time, the school experimented with closed-circuit TV lectures and demonstrations. In fact, in 1948, Dr. Lawrence Donahoe "performed the first televised dental operation in the United States . . . and approximately 450 educators from twelve states witnessed the history making event."[56]

Before the announced closing of the dental school, Dean Frank J. Viner had announced his retirement. To oversee the rebirth of the school, the administration appointed Herbert E. King, D.D.S., professor of prosthetic surgery, a member of the faculty for over thirty years, and a vice-president of the American Dental Association, as the new dean. He oversaw an ADA-mandated curriculum revision that had dental students take their science classes with medical students and required seniors to gain practical experience in oral surgery through clerkships in local hospitals. As part of their training, juniors and seniors also spent many hundreds of hours in the Creighton Dental Clinic; in 1950, despite opposition from the dean and some of the full-time faculty, Fr. President McCabe insisted that the school return to the World War II schedule and open the clinic during the summer. Finally, the revisions included a new grading format; letter grades, A to F, replaced the percentage system. It used the standard 4.0 numerical conversion (2.0 average needed to maintain non-probationary status) for determining grade-point averages, but added a class-weighting feature—e.g., grade in diagnosis weighted 4, in operative dentistry weighted 30.[57]

Enrollment in the reborn dental school recovered remarkably due to the influx of veterans. In September 1945, only four freshmen had registered, and the administration established a mid-year registration for vets released from the service too late to meet the deadline. Eight ex-servicemen enrolled in January, and with summer school, they attained sophomore status on schedule. The total dental enrollment for 1945–46 numbered only 61, but for 1949–50 it soared to 156. Women continued to avoid dentistry (only two women graduated between 1945–1950), but veterans contributed 142 of the student total for the last year of the decade. Those students paid a steeply increased tuition, which rose from $140 per semester in 1945 to $250 in 1948.

Despite the rise, the administration for the first time issued a dental-student employment guideline that sought to discourage work, stipulating, "The faculty reserves the right to order discontinued any work which interferes with the satisfactory prosecution of the prescribed course." The dental school ended the decade on solid footing, but it had to absorb two institutional shocks—in 1948, after forty-five years on the faculty, Dr. Charles Woodbury retired, and on May 11, 1950, Dean King died of a heart attack. The dental school would have to start the new decade minus over eighty years of institutional memory and leadership.[58]

In comparison to dentistry, which had to recover from the ill effects of conversion from soldier to civilian students, the pharmacy school had to rebound from the lack of World War II military support. The absence of an army or navy specialized training program in pharmacy had caused the enrollment to dip to only 35 in 1944. Returning servicemen pushed the number to 145 in 1949, and at that time, they remained a majority of the cohort. The curriculum continued largely unchanged, but starting in 1946, applicants had to take the Creighton undergraduate entrance exam. Although the Bulletin listed seventy faculty members, the college-specific faculty remained few—Dean William Jarrett, the Reverend Regent Harry Cummins, S.J., who lectured in philosophy, one assistant professor, one instructor, and three "assistants," one of whom was Ann Langley Czerwinski (M.A., Pharmacology), the first woman faculty member at the school (1948). As with the other schools, in the era of postwar inflation, tuition rose rapidly from $106 per semester in 1945 to $200 three years later.[59]

The immediate postwar period brought dramatic changes in nursing education. The first all-civilian class registered at the St. Joseph's and St. Catherine's hospital units in 1946, although the last group of World War II cadet enrollees graduated from St. Catherine's in October 1949. Following the war, both units suffered significant drops in enrollment—between 1945 and 1948, the number of students at the St. Joseph's unit fell from 177 to 121, while St. Catherine's unit declined form 131 to 100. By the latter date, a growing nursing shortage spurred renewed interest in the field and the units experienced increases of forty and twenty students, respectively. Some nurses who returned from the Armed Services took advantage of the G.I. Bill, and as late as spring 1950, ex-servicewomen composed seven of the fifty-seven BSN students. Nursing educators intensified their recommendation of university training for nurses; while the number of BSN students rose, they remained a small minority in the profession during the immediate postwar years. The nursing shortage actually promoted less education, which came in the form of the two-year Practical Nurse program. In 1948, in response to recommendations from the National Association of Practical Nurses Education and the Nebraska State Director of the Education Registration for Nurses, St. Joseph's Hospital established a successful but short-lived PN program (in 1953, it shifted to Omaha Technical High School).[60]

In 1947, the hospital units began to issue a consolidated School of Nursing Bulletin, which presented a standardized curriculum for the three-year graduate nurse and the five-year BSN degrees. While the academic courses remained largely unchanged from the prewar era, the hospital reliance on students to provide primary patient care began to ebb. Modeling medical education, the "Three-Year Basic Curriculum in Nursing" began to prescribe weeks of service in clinical experience. The total of 146 weeks, distributed among the major fields of nursing, related to credit hours earned in specific courses (e.g., surgical nursing, twenty-six hours, correlated with Nursing 120 and 130). Students in the Graduate Nurse Program registered at the hospital unit of their choice and paid an admission fee of $300 for the three years, which included tuition, books, uniforms, and laundering of uniforms. All references to work for tuition, hours of service, and dress code disappeared from the Bulletin. BSN candidates registered as freshmen on campus (tuition, $150 per semester) and spent their first and fifth years studying the core courses in the humanities and the sciences required by the CCAS and University College.[61]

The wartime enrollment increase had induced St. Catherine's unit to construct a new dormitory adjacent to the hospital, O'Connor Hall (1946), which contained offices, classrooms, and a library. Two years later, the hospital added a four-story wing to the north end, which provided space for forty beds, a kitchen, a laundry, a new west entrance and lobby, offices, a staff dining room, and reception rooms for patients and visitors. Eighteen hospital nurses participated on the instructional staff; all but three graduated from St. Catherine's unit, twelve were nuns and seven had earned a BSN. St. Joseph's Hospital continued to maintain a slightly larger program. Twenty-two of its nurses provided instruction, only nine of whom obtained their three-year degree from the unit, and the total included only six nuns. Just over 50 percent of the nurse-instructors (twelve) held the BSN degree (all but two of the total of nineteen BSNs at the two units had received that degree from Creighton University since 1939). Obviously, the BSN degree began to enhance the status of nursing educators, a professional prerequisite that went beyond job experience and seniority. Finally, in another act of coordinating the separate units, in 1948, the University created the office of Administrative Dean of the School of Nursing and Fr. Gerald FitzGibbon assumed the position. In 1950, Archbishop Gerald Bergan gave Fr. FitzGibbon additional responsibilities, appointing him spiritual director of the newly established Omaha Council of Catholic Nurses.[62]

Compared to the nursing school, during the immediate postwar era, the College of Law returned from near extinction. Some returning veterans used the G.I. Bill to resume their legal education, while others availed themselves of the benefits to initiate their study. The law freshmen profited from two wartime holdovers—the reduced two-years-of-college entrance requirement and the accelerated schedule, which produced a degree in two years. The school subsequently discontinued the year-round program in the fall 1947; those registered could complete the plan, but thereafter law students could only use summer school classes to reduce their course loads during the regular semesters, and would have to spend six semesters in residence to obtain their degree. Enrollment skyrocketed from 81 in the fall 1945 to 228 (178 veterans) in the fall 1949. At first, the local housing shortage curtailed a more rapid increase, as married veterans, especially, could not enroll because they could not find accommodations for their families. An Omaha student unaffected by the housing shortage, Elizabeth Davis (Pittman) (A.B., 1944; LL.B., 1948), became the first black woman graduate, and eventually established other "firsts" as a deputy county attorney (1964) and judge (1973). Despite the jump in enrollment, the full-time faculty numbered only seven, although the cohort lost its "home grown" quality, as only one had received their degree from Creighton. The most significant staff changes occurred with the retirement of Dean Louis TePoel in 1947 (forty years of teaching, twenty-seven as dean) and the death of Professor Hugh Gillespie in 1948 (thirty-eight years on the faculty). James A. Doyle became the new dean; he had earned a Ph.B. at Creighton in 1924, a LL.B. from the University of Nebraska in 1933, and a LL.M. from Harvard in 1938. In one of his first official acts, he employed Mary Ruth Booth as the first professional librarian to assume administration of the law library.[63]

The graduate school also experienced significant professionalization during the immediate postwar period. Father Henry Casper, author of the three-volume *The History of the Catholic Church in Nebraska*, became dean in 1946. He inherited a rising enrollment—59 in 1945 to 117 (35 veterans) in 1949. He oversaw the adoption of the Graduate Record Examination as an entrance requirement, supplanting a qualifying exam in the major administered by the department at Creighton. Moreover, an accepted student remained an "applicant" until advanced to the status of "candidate" after successfully completing approximately one half of the course work and giving "evidence of satisfactory ability to meet the remaining requirements." Highly qualified full-time students could now compete for fellowships, which carried stipends ranging from $250 to $750 (depending on teaching load), plus tuition remission. In 1948, the graduate school refined the program to include teaching assistants, who received a stipend and tuition remission for non-teaching services; teaching fellows, who gained the benefits for teaching six hours; and medical school research fellows, who earned $100 per month.[64]

The summer school also grew by leaps and bounds during the immediate postwar era, as many students, especially ex-servicemen, sought to speed their program. In 1945, the administration (the dean of the CCAS directed the summer programs) began to allow undergraduates to register for nine hours and graduate students for eight (tuition $10 per hour for both levels of study). In 1946, approximately 80 percent of the regularly enrolled students continued their study during the summer (1,325, triple the prewar norm). Obviously, veterans treated the summer session like a third semester; in 1947, they contributed 824 of 1,257 that attended, and the percentage persisted for the remainder of the decade. Goal oriented and eager "to make up for lost time and more mature than their non-veteran counterparts, the Vets brought a new note of seriousness" to their studies; a summer vacation seemed superfluous. As dedicated traditional full-time undergraduates followed their example, the veterans' voluntary year-round schedule changed the nature of Creighton's summer school—from an adjunct session aimed at religious women, teachers, and part-time students to a "third semester" for full-time students, making up needed classes, taking courses to lighten their load during the fall and/or spring semesters, or earning extra credits toward an early graduation. However, "special opportunities" courses for nuns and teachers also helped keep the summer enrollment at its peak. Moreover, through two-day subject-area institutes for teachers, and Sunday conferences on religious topics, the summer school provided a valuable community service and fully employed campus resources.[65]

The College of Commerce also catered to veterans and established record high enrollments during the immediate postwar period. It returned to its prewar schedule and curriculum, which demanded 128 semester hours for graduation, with majors in accounting, commerce, economics, finance, and marketing (all maintained the senior thesis requirement). The commerce college also established a two-year degree specifically aimed at ex-servicemen, which consisted of a "condensed four-semester terminal curricula" in accounting, secretarial science, and statistics. Enrollment rose rapidly to about 340 in 1945 and mushroomed to 712 the next year, before sliding back to 541 (with 249 veterans) in the fall 1949. For unexplained reasons (no records from the Creighton Veterans' Services administrator exist), the spring 1950 semester garnered 457 veteran registrants (600 total), whereas, historically, enrollment declined for the second semester of the academic year.[66]

The commerce-exclusive faculty expanded to handled the burgeoning student population, ending the decade with eleven laymen (five held a Ph.D.) and two Jesuits, plus one woman who taught the secretarial science classes (two in typing and three in shorthand). In 1947, the school added a major in management and changed the marketing major to marketing and merchandising, which included two classes in advertising. The following year, it began to offer yet another major, "general business." In 1949, the American Association of Collegiate Schools of Business issued a statement defining a core curriculum, which included classes in accounting, business law, economics, finance, industrial management (e.g., management of production, personnel, and planning), marketing, and statistics. Creighton adopted the recommendation, but also maintained a "prescribed freshman-sophomore commerce program," which included twelve hours in accounting, twelve hours in economics, twelve hours in English, eight hours of religion (philosophy of life for non-Catholics), six hours of mathematics, six hours of political science "or other lower-division non-commerce elective approved by the Dean," six hours of management or speech, and four hours of Basic ROTC. The curriculum satisfied the American Association, which granted "provisional associate membership" for three years to allow for the correction of "'relative deficiencies' preliminary to obtaining full membership." The inadequacies of the aging commerce college building, however, delayed full accreditation for over a decade.[67]

On the other hand, the CCAS had received its full accreditation in the early twentieth century and maintained it despite its space problems. It experienced the most rapid enrollment increase—from 460 in the fall 1945 to 1,075 in the fall 1947. Subsequently, however, it decreased to 980 in the fall 1948, and to 840 in the fall 1949. Once again, veterans remained a sizeable majority during the immediate postwar era and their fluctuating registration significantly affected CCAS enrollment. Thus, 525 nonvets and only 323 veterans enrolled in the arts college in the fall 1949 (848 total, which mirrored the commerce situation), but 451 nonvets and 477 veterans registered for the spring semester 1950 (reestablishing their majority position and boosting total enroll-ment by 79). During that half-decade, CCAS students followed a new schedule for entrance exams, administered on each of five Saturdays before registration, instead of during Freshman Week. The three-day student retreats again became part of the Jan-uary between-semesters recess and, starting in 1945, attendance at "Chapel Exercises" at 9:00 A.M. each Friday became mandatory for all Catholic undergraduates. At midterm, in January 1948, for the first time in over a decade (from 1932 to 1936, Creighton had held mid-year commencements), the University conferred sixty-two degrees, but conducted no formal commencement (graduates could attend the June ceremony). Moreover, they ended the decade with a new grading scheme and an opportunity to use the Observatory. In the spring semester 1949, the administration switched to the current 4.0 grade-point system (arts, commerce, University, and phar-macy colleges). Following the death of Fr. Rigge, "the observatory became more of a landmark than a place of study." However, the Reverend Raymond Strange, S.J., who had come to Creighton in 1941, rejuvenated its use; in the spring 1950, he moderated a twelve-student study group that gathered to use the historic structure weekly.[68]

The arts college offered its post–World War II students an expanded curriculum that responded to contemporary developments. The war ended, but the emphasis on physical fitness did not. In September 1945, the University dismantled the obstacle course, "which in its wartime use skinned many a knee and smeared many a face. Now growing over that scene of bloodshed just south of the stadium is a beautiful lawn with shrubs presenting a tempting carpet on which to bask, a far cry from the former wicker cages and high obstacles that made C.U. boys wince." Although the military could no longer enforce physical training upon civilian students, the admin-istration subscribed to the vigorous ethos and mandated a no-credit, three-hour course in physical education, "consisting of calisthenics and supervised intramural sports," for all men except the "physically exempt" for all four years. In 1946, it reduced the requirement to the freshman and sophomore years and excused veterans. Moreover, the physical education department established a program accepted as an academic minor, enabling it to prepare students "to assume full responsibility for the over-all direction of athletic programs in high schools."[69]

While the CCAS eliminated its combined undergraduate-professional degrees (e.g., B.S. Med) in 1945, it created a number of "Special Programs of Study," which catered to "the needs of war veterans whose interests and time limitations make it necessary for them to complete educational programs in the shortest time possible." One option offered two-year terminal courses, "not exclusively vocational," but which aimed "to secure the benefits of a period of intellectual work in college while prepar-ing for a definite position in civilian life." Obviously, the two-year programs in "Chemical Analysis, Education, Languages, Medical Technology, Public Health, Radio Speech and [the] Social Sciences" allowed both the veteran and the University to profit from the G.I. Bill. The other two-year option came in the form of pre-professional programs. The medical, dental, and law schools maintained the war-induced reduction of two years of undergraduate study for entrance. In response, the arts college fashioned a prescribed freshman-sophomore curriculum to satisfy the requirements for entrance to the Creighton professional schools. In 1947, it reintroduced the 3-3 undergraduate-law program that resulted in "the appropriate Bachelor's degree" upon the successful completion of the freshman year in the law school. That same year, it also added three other new programs; one a pre–engineering program, which counseled the student to "consult the bulletin of the school to which he intends to transfer" to guarantee that he met any distinct requirements (note the gender assumption). Second, for students "who wish to enter a graduate school of Social Work or wish to apply for employment in Public Welfare in the State of Nebraska" it designed a pre-social work program, consisting of "a minimum of forty hours in social and biological sciences." Third, it inaugurated a B.S. in Medical Technology to compliment a three-year certificate program coordinated with St. Joseph's Hospital. That new degree responded to the rapid growth of hospital laboratories and their need for trained assistants to help "the clinician in the diagnosis and treatment of the patient." The four-year course included two years of undergraduate study in the humanities and the sciences, a third year studying lab techniques at the medical school and St. Joseph's Hospital, and a fourth year of supervised work in the labs of St. Joseph's Hospital.[70]

In another curricular change of the immediate postwar era, journalism made its final transition from an independent school to a department in the CCAS in January 1948. It followed a national "trend away from the small school" concept, and the opinion of a "majority of professional and radio men [who] agree that a degree from a liberal arts college is preferable." The twenty-five classes offered by the department included seven in radio, one in television, one in photography, and three in advertising and commercial art. Although "Creighton University of the Air" had ceased broadcasting in early 1944, the formation of the Radio Guild in November 1945 reestablished radio as a mainstay of the journalism department in post–World War II. The Reverend Roswell C. Williams, S.J., served as Guild director and Edwin Puls acted as the faculty consultant. Its one hundred members received training in all aspects of radio broadcast and produced public-service programs and other finished products offered to local stations. The Guild directors also began to hold annual two-day institutes, which emphasized the use of radio in teaching; the third annual seminar attracted five hundred teachers and school administrators from eleven states. In 1947, Omaha station KBON (Paul Fry, Journalism, 1939, general manager) initiated a scholarship for the senior year for the student "who shows the greatest promise of being an asset to the radio industry." Students received better on-air training with the reintroduction of "Creighton University of the Air" (1:30–2:00 P.M. every Saturday over WOW) and the creation of station KOCU in 1947. At first, KOCU broadcasted from one of "the Huts," using a loudspeaker mounted on the roof, and via the tunnels of the underground steam system, which any radio "within 200 yards of a steam pipe on campus" could pick up without any direct connection. While KOCU continued loudspeaker broadcasts between classes, the following year, it added a carrier-current transmitter, which allowed all radios on campus to listen to it "at 640 on the dial." Reflecting the meager finances of the department, the station solicited alumni to donate records it could play during its limited noon hour and two-hour late-afternoon programs. As a sign of the times, it made a special request for "boogie-woogie" music.[71]

While it reestablished its radio program, Creighton simultaneously became a local and national leader in the development of the new medium of television. According to Fr. Williams, "That Creighton was the first university in the United States to have complete television equipment on its own campus has never been questioned." In December 1946, John J. Gillin, president and general manager of radio station WOW (A.B., 1927; LL.B. 1931), brought $40,000 worth of equipment to campus to do "experimental work in the field." The first programming included televising Radio Guild programs and high school football games played at the stadium by "coaxial cable to receivers in the auditorium and classrooms." By 1948, demonstration broadcasts to various public groups complimented the telecasts from the medical and dental schools. WOW constructed a tower to relay the programs to Lincoln, Nebraska, locating it near Gretna, Nebraska, at the highest point between the two cities. Then, in August 1949, WOW moved its equipment to its new building at 35th and Farnam streets, and "went on the air." Creighton did not have the money to purchase television equipment; therefore, the broadcasts from the various schools ceased. The journalism department, however, continued to teach television; the carpenter shop constructed tripods and dollies and a wooden facsimile of a camera box with a viewfinder in it, which allowed the students "to go through the motions of television production." Father Williams demonstrated the faux equipment at national conferences and sold the blueprints to several other large state universities. Obviously, Creighton University did not stand alone at the "cutting edge," but sadly lacked the resources to leap forward. In 1949, the University teamed with WOW-TV to produce "Creighton University Presents," in which each of its nine schools took turns presenting a telecast every other Thursday at 4:05 P.M. That same year, the educational division of the Radio Corporation of America (RCA) published an eighteen-page booklet, "The Modern School Looks at Television," which highlighted the programs at only two universities—Creighton and Iowa State. For a brief time, Creighton established a national reputation as a television pioneer.[72]

While it tried to keep pace with the latest developments in education, the University also maintained its historic commitment to the ROTC. Returning veterans possessed an advantage in the program—six months of active duty equaled one year of ROTC, and a full year of active duty replaced the two-year Basic ROTC requirement; thus, a veteran with one year of service could obtain a commission in just two years. The administration planned to revive Advanced ROTC with the start of the spring semester, January 1946. A month later, it discarded the plans; the *Creightonian* headlined the reasons for the decision, "Students Tired of Military Life; Interest is Lacking." The following fall, however, 23 students reactivated Advanced ROTC;

the prominence of veterans on campus manifested itself in the fact that Basic ROTC, required of all civilian undergraduate males, totaled only 198. Those cadets shifted from the World War II uniforms of "browns and pinks" to the new "Army Green" and began the process of reinstituting prewar activities. The rifle team, deactivated in 1942, regrouped in January 1946, but had a difficult time regaining its previous championship stature. In March of that year, it placed tenth in the Seventh Service Command match, and at the end of the decade, suffered losses to teams from the Union Pacific Railroad and Omaha high schools. In 1947, the Military Ball reappeared, and a year later, the "honorary colonel" resumed her exalted status at the annual gala. In 1949, after an eight-year hiatus, the ROTC again began to sponsor a University band. Non-military students could join, and it played at special events and athletic contests, not just at military functions. Finally, once again, summer camp became a required event, and in 1949, the location switched to Camp McCoy, Wisconsin.[73]

Reinvigorating ROTC merely entailed a snafu (World War II acronym: situation normal, all "fouled" up) or two; in comparison, reimplementing the intercollegiate athletic program caused travail and heartache. In late September 1945, one month after the surrender of Japan, the administration announced that since "almost all the coaching and playing talent at Creighton have left for distant parts," the University would not participate in the MVC and would conduct sports "on an intramural basis." Student and alumni polls supported the immediate resumption of intercollegiate competition, especially in football. Gridiron proponents recognized the "nationwide controversy concerning the buying of football and basketball talent through athletic scholarships usually, and even by less subtle means as outright payment at times." In fact, at the time, the Nebraska Legislature, dismayed by the loss of home-state football all-American Nile Kinnick to the University of Iowa, considered a bill "to appropriate funds to keep outstanding high school talent" playing for colleges in the state. In such a climate, supporters knew that Creighton and other small schools that had to discontinue their programs during the war stood at a considerable disadvantage when trying to reactivate competitive sports programs. They rested their hopes on protest and "action, of a prohibitive nature, taken by conference officials."[74]

Their hopes faded quickly; on February 8, 1946, the *Creightonian* printed Fr. President McCabe's announcement that the University would not resume intercollegiate football. He based his decision on the "reasonable unwillingness to accept the scholastic and financial hardships unfortunately involved in intercollegiate football competition in our day." One week later, the student newspaper revealed a plan promoted by the 1-C Club for the resumption of intercollegiate football "on a purely amateur basis." A "former Bluejay gridder, who later played professional," offered his services "gratis" and players promised to participate "not on the principle of subsidization." Promoters claimed that reestablishing a $10 student activity fee would finance the venture, but the proposal proceeded no further. Subsequently, because it lacked a football team, Creighton withdrew from the MVC in June 1948.[75]

While football ceased, the much less expensive to maintain basketball team hit the hardwood during the fall 1945, "strictly on an amateur basis . . . in an era when professionalism has penetrated into the ranks of intercollegiate sports." That is, the administration refused to allow athletic scholarships, although athletes could secure loans to cover tuition and expenses and jobs to earn money to repay the debt. Coach Duce Belford directed the reassembled team to a 9-12 season, which included two losses to the semi-professional Phillips 66ers and a 3-7 conference record, for sixth place in the Valley. Eddie Hickey returned from the navy and resumed his coaching position in the fall 1946, guiding the team to a 19-8 record, which included a lackluster 7-5 in the MVC, for fourth place. In 1947, Hickey left to coach St. Louis University and Belford returned to the head-coach position; he lead the Bluejay team for the remainder of the decade, but did not put together a winning season. In 1948, the team went 4-6 in the conference, to finish fourth in its last season in the MVC, and in 1950 Belford posted his best performance, with thirteen wins and thirteen losses.[76]

Several other intercollegiate sports organized, but received little notoriety in the yearbook or student newspaper. In December 1946, the *Creightonian* announced the creation of an intramural and intercollegiate boxing team. If either actually formed, it resulted from the popularity of the sport in the military and the influence of veterans on campus. However, no other records exist to document its history; the same situation exists for isolated references to intercollegiate golf, tennis, and track teams during the late 1940s. The student newspaper did not feature stories about their exploits and the *Bluejay* did not contain pictures or articles to give them recognition among graduates. Possibly, they operated as "club" sports sanctioned by the University, but receiving little or no financial support, as well as meager student recognition. Baseball floundered in similar circumstances; seemingly, in 1947, a Bluejay team played to a 5-3 season against local, not-necessarily collegiate opponents. Duce Belford resumed coaching responsibilities for the team in 1949, and the following spring he fielded a team, incorrectly recognized as the first official intercollegiate baseball team in Creighton history (as noted previously, the College had sponsored teams prior to World War I). The athletic reorganization ignored coeds; in 1950, suggestions for improvements for women included providing athletic facilities and creating opportunities for them in sports such as rifle, swimming, and basketball.[77]

Other student institutions suffered similar difficulties in reinventing themselves. The Coop experienced an unceremonious demise, and the former SBG clubrooms and snack bar it operated received new management and relocation. In October 1945, the board of the Coop (three coeds, one male) met to discuss the impending ramifications from the opening of the remodeled Beanery, which had served as a barracks for the air cadets during World War II. The Coop board decided to close its snack bar, but hoped the clubrooms would remain an "attraction of general lounging." The reopened Beanery contained new chrome furniture, a restaurant, a snack bar, a private dining room, and a jukebox. During the spring semester 1946, the snack bar expanded its menu to included sandwiches and fountain drinks, and extended its closing time of 7:00 P.M. to 11:00 P.M., to give students a "late night" place to go, such as after basketball games at the gymnasium. However, the rapidly increasing enrollment necessitated larger cafeteria facilities; therefore, the snack bar moved from the

Beanery to the bookstore. The new location provided a seating capacity of one hundred, established 9:00 A.M. to 9:00 P.M. hours of operation, and produced a place for parties and club meetings on a reservation basis. Moreover, students had a beloved "greasy-spoon" option, Walt Beal's Café that had opened on the southeast corner of 24th and California streets in 1939. After World War II, it became a Creighton institution, as Walt became a premier backer of Bluejay sports, frequently providing a team with a "free turkey or steak dinner . . . whether they were a winning outfit or not," and by providing employment for droves of Creighton students over the years.[78]

The Coop also lost control of the clubrooms in the gymnasium. Coeds, who had organized and dominated the management of the Coop during World War II, rapidly became a minority of the student population following the outbreak of peace. According to Mary Gregor (A.B., 1949), coeds of the era earned the appellation DARs ("damned average raisers") reputedly because they were dedicated students and there were so few of them. The new gender imbalance quickly manifested itself to the disadvantage of coeds; without any mention of the dissolution of the student Cooperative Corporation, the 1-C Club assumed management responsibilities for the clubrooms at the beginning of the spring semester 1946. It operated the "R&R space" (rest and recreation), 11:00 A.M. to 3:00 P.M. daily, and banned women from the premises. The Commerce Cottage, however, unoccupied during the war, had undergone some renovation and reopened as a coed study and relaxation center. Nonetheless, at the end of May, following months of protest, the 1-C Club relented, promising to open the clubrooms to women. The veteran's club, however, also experienced an abrupt demise; it did not reorganize for the fall semester, which resulted in the closing of the clubrooms. Some students attributed the situation to a lack of school spirit on the part of the ex-servicemen; others, however, argued that demise of the 1-C Club demonstrated that "the average veteran does not feel the need for such an organization and his transition to scholastic and social affairs is complete." The club had attracted only about one hundred active members, hardly a significant percentage of the over two thousand veteran-students; the low number signaled a lack of interest in the club from its origin and it did not provide a healthy base to sustain longevity. In its absence, in November 1946, the athletic department reopened the clubrooms, but operated them for only one and one-half years. In September 1948, the administration closed the rooms and transferred the space to the ROTC to use as classrooms for it burgeoning enrollment (due to the rapid increase in male non-veteran undergraduate students). While the students lost indoor recreation space, many also joked about the lack of green space for leisure: "I was sitting on campus yesterday, but someone else came and wanted to sit on it so I had to leave."[79]

The SBG played no role in the quest for places for leisure or in the disposition of its former clubrooms, because it exhausted its energy in a long struggle to reorganize. The Reverend Charles K. Hayden, S.J., dean of men and moderator of the Student Union, convened a meeting in November 1945 "to discuss possibilities of reactivating the organization." Participants decided to postpone action until the end of the academic year because key events such as Homecoming and the freshman frolic had taken place, and a new board could not coalesce in time to plan the junior-senior prom. Therefore, a union board with thirteen representatives appointed by the deans of the various schools did not meet until December 16, 1946. The temporary group began planning for a junior-senior prom at Peony Park to be held February 7, and for May elections. Unfortunately, February 7 became primary-election day and the prom shifted until after Lent. Once again, the procedure for the nomination and election of princes and princesses and the king and queen promoted spirited debate. A month before the general election, coeds circulated a petition demanding membership in the union. It made no impact and coeds ended the decade with yet another petition asking for University College representation on the SBG. The subsequent fall semester, on November 13, 1947, the newly elected SBG reacted to "criticisms of the homecoming dance" by "suspending all activities until a definite understanding" could be reached with the administration. Its action included relinquishing management of the Agnew Student Loan Fund. The argument concerned the planning procedures and the cost of the event, which the *Creightonian* labeled "a farce" and "Friday's flop." The paper aired student complaints against the SBG for poor planning, and competing SBG laments about "outside interference" from the administration. The next year, the reconstituted SBG appealed for "greater freedom in determining the amount allowed for the hiring of a band." The board of deans and regents refused the request, maintaining a limit of $250. The SBG chaffed, but resumed sponsoring its traditional events, finishing the decade without further heated controversy. In 1948, Homecoming, always co-sponsored with the Alumni Association, which held events for returning alums, moved to a weekend in December to coincide with a home game for the basketball team.[80]

Another time-honored student entertainment that survived the war, Skip Day, almost suffered extinction at the hands of postwar excess. Well into the spring semester 1948, no student organization, including the SBG, accepted the challenge of organizing the all-University fun day because of the "drinking and wanton destruction of property" that occurred the previous year. The administration had set the date as May 11, refused to change it, and only the last-minute heroics of an ad hoc student committee saved the tradition. The University banned the "use of intoxicants in the public parks" and established an honor code, which asked the students to avoid property damage and to clean their trash after the picnic. Subsequently, it prohibited alcohol at all school events, although widespread abuse continued on and off campus. However, the previous ban on the use of tobacco products on and around campus ceased. Administrators probably realized the futility of trying to enforce it among the huge contingent of veterans (most had received a daily ration of cigarettes during the war); instead, they redecorated a room on the ground floor of the Administration Building and designated it a smoking parlor. Similarly, the SBG attempt to reintroduce the freshman beanie tradition withered in the hostile environment.[81]

The burgeoning civilian student population of the postwar era also reinvigorated the Greek fraternal system. "Hell Week" again became an annual ritual and the *Creightonian* devoted at least two pages of coverage to the activities and antics of the fraternities and sororities. Most of the Greek-letter societies remained college or discipline-based, but they emphasized social activities. Old fraternities that languished during the war regrouped and new ones formed (e.g., Phi Sigma Chi Pharmacy social fraternity, 1946). Sororities had maintained their organization during the war and then expanded in the postwar era. In 1948, Kappa Zeta Kappa local sorority affiliated with Kappa Beta Gamma and became the first national social sorority on campus, closely followed by Chi Mu Kappa's affiliation with Pi Lambda Sigma, a national social sorority for Catholic women. Other distinctive social organizations of the era included the Cana Club for married students (a function of the large veteran student population and the tumbling average age of marriage) and the Hui O Hawaii Club (a culmination of the two-decade old connection with the islands). The Hawaii Club organized officially on October 1, 1948, with about fifty members, although a shipping strike in 1949 temporarily lowered the number. The club held regular meetings and social events; its only meeting rule required members to wear the latest "Aloha" shirt they received from home. In March 1950, the group, which now included its first coed member, had the honor of entertaining the University of Hawaii basketball team that came to the Hilltop to lose a hard-fought game to the Bluejays, 74-67.[82]

Moreover, traditional student academic and cultural organizations reactivated on a limited scale, compared with the flourishing 1920s or even the constrained 1930s. Business, math, science, and journalism groups reemerged first. The International Relations Club, moderated by P. Raymond Nielson, Ph.D., of the history department, and sponsored by the Carnegie Endowment for Peace, provided literature and held regional conferences, and became a postwar success. The University hired music directors for male and female choruses, but the instrumental music program continued to languish. The Sodalities flourished, the Creighton Little Theater resumed performances, and Creighton garnered awards annually in the reinstituted Missouri Province English Contest, but debate did not regain its prewar organization and stature. Surprisingly, Alpha Sigma Nu went moribund, 1946–48, then reorganized the following year and inducted nineteen into the national Jesuit honor society.[83]

Furthermore, traditional literary institutions also reemerged from wartime constraints on the use of paper. The *Creighton Alumnus* magazine, which had ceased publication in 1944 and had become a monthly insert in the *Creightonian,* reappeared as an independent periodical in October 1945. The *Creightonian* had maintained its run with a largely coed staff; in 1947, its offices moved to the first floor of the Administration Building, and by the end of the decade, the coed presence had retreated to a scant minority. In the late 1940s, women remained prominent in two news features—engagement and wedding announcements for coeds and women alums, and in cigarette advertisements (Camel, Lucky Strikes, Chesterfields, and Philip Morris placed ads regularly, and a large percentage portrayed women smoking). In comparison, the *Bluejay* had ceased in 1941, and the SBG struggled against veteran unwillingness to reestablish the yearbook. It mounted a failed subscription drive in the fall 1948; the administration granted a fifteen-day extension, but it culminated with only a 31 percent subscription rate (not a single school of the University met its quota). In December, administrators gave "the project the go-ahead signal," providing a $3,500 subsidy to print one thousand copies (918 subscriptions) of the two-hundred-page *Bluejay 1949*. The yearbook contained no advertisements, "due to the comparatively small difference between ad rates and the cost of the additional pages." The problem of low subscriptions persisted for the remainder of the decade. Therefore, in 1950, the Board of Trustees "reluctantly" agreed to assess a $5 fee from all students in the University to subsidize the yearbook.[84]

Additionally, on occasion Creighton students manifested the concerns of their times. In 1946, of the students responding to a poll, 56 percent voted in favor of banning the Communist party in the United States because it did not accept "democratic principles." Similarly, in 1949, Alpha Sigma Nu distributed a petition at all Jesuit colleges and universities denouncing Hungarian and Bulgarian court activity against Cardinal Mindszenty and other clergymen. More dramatically, some Creighton students became active in the nascent local civil rights movement, stimulated by the Double V campaign of World War II: victory over the racist Nazis abroad and victory over racism at home. On November 3, 1947, Denny Holland, arts junior, organized a meeting for all Creighton students "interested in promoting interracial justice." At a second meeting, the students choose the Reverend John P. Markoe, S.J., as moderator and named their organization the De Porres Club, in honor the Blessed Martin de Porres (canonized 1962), a Negro Jesuit missionary, who had worked among the poor in Peru. Father Markoe, a graduate of West Point, had commanded African-American troops at the time of the skirmishes along the Mexican border during the era of the Mexican Revolution. In 1917, he had entered the Society of Jesus, had taught astronomy at Creighton in 1930, and returned in 1946 after championing civil rights at St. Louis University. The De Porres Club was not a sanctioned University organization, and it moved its meetings off campus due to controversy. However, concerned Creighton students participated in the marches, picketing, boycotts, and other activities of the group during the late 1940s and early 1950s. Through its persistence, the University hired it first African American in a non-menial position, Mrs. Albertine Chandler as a secretary to Dean Fr. Casper of the graduate school in 1949.[85]

Thus, in myriad ways, World War II deeply affected the operation of virtually all institutions in the United States during the entire decade of the 1940s. For the second time during the first half of the twentieth century, Creighton University converted itself into a military camp, and then reconverted itself into a civilian institution. It was not déjà vu; history does not repeat itself, except in broad generalized comparisons. For example, the ASTP did not reprise the experience of the SATC of World War I. Moreover, the G.I. Bill of 1944 created a vastly different postwar student body (compared to the 1920s), composed of a majority of veterans, which significantly influenced the pace and the nature of the reconversion. During World War II, the military programs kept the University from closing for the duration; the United States government provided the financing and the soldiers, sailors, marines, and nursing cadets gave the un-drafted faculty the opportunity to teach, albeit in significantly restructured, accelerated programs. Because few civilian males attended college during the war, the small number of coeds experienced a brief period of heightened opportunity and status. During the immediate postwar era, their roles diminished rapidly as the G.I. Bill fostered record enrollments and the gender imbalance became severe. Burgeoning enrollments following twenty-five years of limited growth (due to the failed fundraising campaigns of the 1920s, the economic constraints of the 1930s, and the exigencies of war during the 1940s) unleashed pent up hopes for a campus replete with new edifices and a healthy endowment able to support top-notch educational programs. While the development drive of the late 1940s succeeded beyond previous efforts, it fell far short of its goals. Creighton University continued to "mark time"; it had a balanced budget and it produced successful graduates from nine schools, but it failed to create "The New Creighton University" envisioned by its leaders. In 1950, however, a new leader would take it into a new era.

PART THREE
The American Dream Accomplished

In 1950, the Reverend Carl Reinert, S.J., assumed the presidency of the University and initiated its structural assimilation into the Omaha community. The process consisted of the "University's" desire for inclusion and the acceptance of the "University" by the leaders of the dominant institutions of Omaha, and then, by extension, of the "Heartland" region and of the United States. Father Reinert enticed the elite of Omaha businessmen, non-Catholics included, to serve on the Lay Board of Regents and they spearheaded successful development campaigns that provided the wherewithal to build new facilities and to expand undergraduate and professional programs. The integration deepened as the fundraising success positioned the institution to compete for state and federal grants and for awards from local, regional, and national foundations. In 1968, the structural assimilation culminated with a Lay Board of Directors assuming ownership of the University. The new articles of incorporation guaranteed the continuation of the Jesuit presence and the Catholic tradition.

After surviving "the sixties" and the significant changes that came in the wake of the student, the women's, and the civil rights movements, Creighton University accomplished the American Dream of personal success and material comfort. It fashioned an aesthetic campus filled with new dormitories, libraries, buildings for the undergraduate and professional schools, and recreation facilities. National publications extolled Creighton's merits, its intercollegiate athletic teams acquitted themselves admirably, students garnered notice for their academic achievements and their role in service to social justice, and faculty (while emphasizing their teaching role) produced substantially more significant research. Having attained the Dream, the "Creighton 2000" plan sought to push the University into the upper echelon of American society; while progress continued, financial problems forestalled the ultimate goal. The new millennium saw the objective restated in an obtainable manner in the "Project 125" strategic plan: "Creighton University will be a national leader in preparing students in a faith-based setting for responsible leadership, professional distinction, and committed citizenship."

CHAPTER 9

Happy Days, 1950–63

The popular 1970s television sitcom *Happy Days* provided a lasting appellation for the 1950s. The program ignored the tribulations of the era (the Cold War, the nuclear arms race, the Korean "conflict," McCarthyism, labor strife, and more) to present a nostalgic view of middle-class adolescence. Similarly, despite lingering problems that plagued several schools of the University, the fifties produced much joy at Creighton. A contemporary dynamic duo, Frs. Carl Reinert and Henry Linn nurtured the desired (and necessary) structural assimilation of the institution into the Omaha community and transformed the "campus" (a few buildings interspersed among homes and businesses on California and several intersecting streets) into an interminable construction zone. Under their leadership, the federal government provided loans, private foundations bestowed grants, and non-Catholic Omaha businessmen helped conduct successful development drives. The increased funds allowed the Administration to cease "marking time." Big plans—some particulars over thirty years old—finally came to fruition. By 1963, the University acquired two sizeable dormitories, an undergraduate library, a student center, a modern College of Business Administration, and a new medical school. Moreover, the new campus gained a distinct collegiate ambience, as the girl's high school and Creighton Prep moved to other locations. As Creighton University embarked upon the modern era, with vigorous leadership, it completed its assimilation into American society; it began the construction of an autonomous campus and, with record enrollments, it fully integrated minorities and women into its programs. Although problems persisted in particular schools, in general, the era seemed to correspond to the "happy days" designation.

In September 1950, Fr. President McCabe left to teach English at Marquette University and Fr. Carl Reinert redeployed from the principal's office at Campion High School in Prairie du Chien, Wisconsin, to Omaha to take command of Creighton University. He had an inkling of the situation; as a scholastic, he had taught at Creighton Prep from 1938 to 1941. The second oldest of six brothers (James and Paul also joined the Society of Jesus) from Boulder, Colorado, at age thirty-seven, he became the University's second youngest chief executive (Fr. Dowling had been thirty-four at the commencement of his first term). During his first year, he admitted to a "strong dependence" upon his brother Paul, then president of St. Louis University. Quickly, however, he matured in the position, acquiring the soubriquet, "The Builder." On Founders' Day, December 4, 1950, he appointed Fr. Linn as his executive assistant. In their various positions of leadership, each spent the rest of their life promoting a "Creighton Renaissance."[1]

According to Walter Jahn, a contemporary commerce college graduate and eventual vice president of finance, Fr. Reinert inherited "a small tired university." Another observer from the period described the University as "at a stand still" and that the continuation of the medical and dental schools stood in doubt. The administration explained its budget woes as a "two-horned dilemma posed by the universal drop in interest rates on Creighton's endowment and much greater costs in overhead." It expected the problem to worsen for several years because of a drop in enrollment in the "non-professional schools and the law school." By 1950, the surge of veterans using the G.I. Bill to finance their undergraduate education had ebbed and the baby boom generation had not reached adolescence. Postwar inflation had left its mark and the so-called United Nations Police Action in Korea began to crimp federal government outlays for education. As late as 1954, the University described its situation by citing a *Business Week* article with the headline, "Our Colleges and Universities Face Grave Financial Problems." The critique found the "financial squeeze" was "particularly destructive" for private colleges and universities because their endowments suffered depletion from a new round of inflation induced by the Korean War and because income and estate taxes "greatly reduced" donations from the wealthy.[2]

Despite the anxiety, Fr. President Reinert developed an agenda to modernize Creighton. In an October 1950 speech, he reiterated a list of long-desired "needs," which included a library, a dormitory, a new medical-school building, space for student recreation, and a student lounge. To fulfill those needs, he reorganized the development program. In 1951, he informed the Board of Trustees of "a plan now being put into effect for contacting the heads of corporations in this territory with a request for annual donations to the University to help tide us over the difficult period of low enrollments and high costs." Shortly thereafter, he proposed that the Trustees allow the Lay Board of Regents to view the budget, arguing it would not only enlighten them, "but would liven their interest in the University, and give them a feeling of greater security when asked by outsiders where the University stands financially." Obviously, during the post–World War I era, the myth of an enormously wealthy institution (based on the bequest of John A. Creighton) and the confidential nature of the budget had stifled fundraising efforts. Apparently, the budgets twice published in conjunction with development campaigns failed to dispel the financial fable or to convince the business community of the dire straights of a noteworthy Omaha institution.[3]

Moreover, Fr. Reinert understood that the Lay Board of Regents did not represent a cross section of the Omaha economic elite; he describe the existing board as "five or six elderly men," who admitted to serving as "window dressing." Therefore, he spent his first few years in the city ingratiating himself to the business community. According to Walter Jahn, "Prior to that time, Creighton University and particularly the Jesuit Community, had little, if anything to do with the downtown business men. Creighton was rather like an island in Omaha, Nebraska." The detached arrangement began to diminish, especially through the efforts of alumni architect Leo A. Daly, Sr., who introduced Fr. Reinert to the chief executives of local corporations, including many non-Catholics. The integrating process of assimilating structurally began in earnest. In 1954, the Trustees announced a plan to increase the Lay Regents by three a year until they numbered fifteen. Furthermore, they created the President's Council, consisting of past members of the lay board and appointees from "the main Alumni geographic areas." Council member Daniel J. Gross (LL.B., 1916, past chairman of the Lay Board of Regents) organized the Gifts and Bequests Committee, and upon his death in 1958, "he left Creighton its largest single gift (in the form of insurance stocks) since the Creighton endowment." At the end of the decade, the Lay Board of Regents reached its full quota and structured itself into three working committees: financial consulting, chaired by W. B. Millard, Jr., president of the Omaha National Bank; campus planning and development, chaired by Leo A. Daly, Sr.; and university relations, chaired by A. F. Jacobson, president of the Northwestern Bell Telephone Co. Starting in the late 1950s, Northwestern Bell "assigned" two men to the University to facilitate budgeting and planning. Completing the integrative process, Omaha institutions began to seek Creighton involvement. Father Reinert exemplified the modern Jesuit university president, participating in civic affairs; he served on the boards of the Joslyn Art Museum, the Omaha Industrial Foundation, the Chamber of Commerce, and the Mayor's Bi-Racial Education Committee.[4]

Father Linn also played a key role in Creighton's integration into Omaha and in the successful development campaigns. He served as secretary on the lay board and interacted admirably with the Lay Regents. Moreover, he continued to perform as the liaison with the alumni. With many of his contemporaries, he believed "that one of the chief means of support counted on by schools in the past [a large endowment], now has gone down a victim to the internal revenue axe." He affirmed annual giving as the "only effective answer," calling it a "living endowment." He received stellar support in promoting the idea from Robert Reilly, who assumed the duties of public relations director and alumni secretary in October 1950. Reilly had attended Creighton from 1941 to 1943, then served in the United States Army in Europe in 1943–45. After World War II, he gained a degree in advertising and business from Suffolk University in Boston. Returning to his prewar alma mater, he took up office space in the former Clayton Café, two doors south of California Street on the west side of 24th Street, in a building recently purchased by the University. He worked to increase alumni support, including enticements such as changing the date for Homecoming to accommodate alums who stated their December calendars were too crowded to include travel for the occasion. While continuing the new post–World War II tradition of a home-court basketball game as a centerpiece, in 1953, the event moved to a date in February. However, the dead-of-winter schedule did not promote travel either; therefore, in 1955, it switched back to the first week of December. Event scheduling remained difficult and received unwelcome competition from new entertainment technology; one advertisement in 1954 included a picture of a television set with the caption, "Leave it Off . . . And Come to the Big Creighton Alumni Picnic,

Peony Park, July 26." Apparently, the new medium had instantaneously created the "couch potato."[5]

Administration for development and for alumni relations continued to evolve during the Reinert-Linn era. In 1956, a new fundraising campaign precipitated the creation of the Greater Creighton Committee, which consisted of over 250 invited alums nationwide that convened on campus to discuss a wide range of educational and planning issues. Logistics for the committee and the campaign demonstrated a need for staff enlargement and reorganization. Thus, in 1957, Fr. Linn assumed the position of vice president of university relations, which would oversee three separate but conjoined offices—public relations, headed by Robert Reilly; alumni relations, headed by Bernard Conway; and a director of development, Clayton D. Nielson (BSBA, 1935). Subsequently, in 1962, as part of a new fifteen-year plan, Robert Reilly assumed the distinctive development post of director of special resources. He reported directly to Fr. Reinert and became "responsible for work with foundations, national corporations and federal agencies." In his first year, he visited twenty-one foundations and submitted twenty-six proposals, receiving seven rejections, eight "indefinite continuations," nine "pending," and two gifts. Harry A. Dolphin, a member of the journalism department for eleven years, made the transition to public relations director. Obviously, during the decade, the University had identified novel twentieth-century funding sources, and in order to take advantage of them, development contributed a fair share to the burgeoning administrative bureaucracy of the modern institution of higher learning. As revealed by the names above, laymen filled most of those positions. Thus, in 1950, the Trustees instituted a staff-recognition ceremony as part of Founders' Day, honoring Pauline Cranny, executive secretary to the medical dean, 1918–50; Margaret Curran, administrative clerk in the commerce college, 1924–50; and Margaret Claire McDermott, assistant registrar, 1920–50, for twenty-five years of service (note, all had surpassed the requirement).[6]

Father Linn described the origin of the post–World War II development program as a drowning man "clutching at a straw." He dubbed it a "Survival Program," with the closing of the professional schools a "very real possibility." By the mid-1950s, however, "the most voracious of the financial wolves" had been "chased from the door." In 1953, Fr. Reinert used the University's 75th anniversary jubilee celebration to launch a fresh phase of development. The administration, once again, released an economic impact statement designed to demonstrate why Creighton deserved the support of the local community. After all, its out-of-town students and their families spent $5.5 million in the area the previous year, and the University purchased $2.2 million in goods and services for its operation. Furthermore, it provided prodigious charity health services and its professional schools produced 45 percent of the practicing attorneys, 70 percent of the dentists, 44 percent of the physicians, and 57 percent of the registered pharmacists in the Omaha-Council Bluffs area. The jubilee served as a commemoration and a public relations device. The week of festivities began on Sunday, April 12, with a solemn Pontifical Mass at St. John's Church celebrated by Omaha Archbishop Gerald T. Bergan. That afternoon, entertainers Bing

Crosby, Bob Hope, Jimmy Durante, Ann Blythe, and Ruth Hussey presented a special thirty-minute radio broadcast over twenty stations in the Midwest. On Monday, more than two thousand students purchased "comic blue derbies" to wear for the week. Inclement weather postponed a Wednesday "jubilee parade," but the evening dance in the gymnasium went on as scheduled. On Thursday, with midday classes canceled, grand marshal Col. A. J. Beck, Commanding Officer of the Strategic Air Command, led a procession of twenty-three floats, about fifty decorated cars, and the marching units from Creighton's ROTC and the Offutt Air Force Base through the streets of downtown Omaha. That evening, Samuel Cardinal Stritch of Chicago spoke at the banquet at the Fontenelle Hotel. Jubilee week concluded with a Saturday-night dinner-dance in the gymnasium, attended by over twelve hundred students, faculty and alumni, which included entertainment by Hollywood luminaries Frankie Fey, Irene Ryan, and MacDonald Carey.[7]

As the public-relations promotion intensified in behalf of the embryonic development campaign, concurrently the University acquired the property necessary to accommodate its plans. The purchases included residences along California Street and the intersecting streets 25th to 27th. The Administration removed some houses along California Street to create open space, while it retained those on the periphery as rental units. In 1957, in an effort to "green up" the emerging campus, the University acquired the skills of John J. Mulhall, who held a degree in botany from the National Botanical Gardens in Dublin, Ireland. In Dublin, he had worked for the United States Embassy, where Creighton alum Francis P. Matthews (A.B., 1910; A.M., 1911; LL.B., 1913) served as ambassador. The connection resulted in the migration of Mulhall and his wife Margaret to Omaha in 1953. After a short stint with the Omaha Parks Department, he assumed the chore of landscaping the budding campus (subsequently, he formed his own horticultural business, which continues to provide landscaping service to the University).[8]

The campus expansion reached a milestone in 1962, when a "42-year land acquisition project" culminated with the purchase of a home near the law school; Creighton now owned all the property on California Street 24th to 27th streets. In addition, two government programs asserted significant influence. The University continued to support the various urban renewal proposals put forth by the city, especially those related to the redevelopment of the area bounded by 20th to 24th, Cass to Burt streets (in 1951, the administration banned students from living east of 24th between Dodge and Cuming streets). Father Reinert argued that the renewal plans would give Creighton "more pleasant surroundings" and allow it "to purchase land at a fairly appraised value, for future growth." He revealed to the Downtown Rotary Club that he "speculated on this area as a site for our proposed medical center"; however, Omaha voters rejected all urban-renewal initiates that appeared on the ballots in the late 1950s and early 1960s. On the other hand, interstate-highway construction proceeded without a referendum; Fr. Reinert supported the construction of I-480 through an area adjacent to Creighton because it would "prevent neighborhood deterioration which was occurring to the south of the university." Moreover, he felt it "put the university in an advantageous focal position in the middle of a high-speed highway in four directions, which makes the campus more accessible to towns in Northwest Iowa and Nebraska" (he thought it would increase the number of commuter students).[9]

In addition, for the first time in Creighton's history, those students would enter a collegiate campus devoid of high-school students. By 1952, the Building Fund of Prep Fathers' and Mothers' Club had raised about $80,000 for a new site. The Jesuits negotiated with another Catholic order for a plat on the east side of 72nd near Dodge Street. According to Walter Jahn, University Treasurer, the Reverend Thomas Murphy, S.J., "very wisely thought it was better not to purchase the land from the Sisters of Mercy because we would lose no matter what the price was. We would either pay them too much or too little. If we paid them too little, we'd be criticized by the other Catholic organizations in the city (and possibly the Chancery office) for taking advantage of the poor nuns. If we paid too much, we were not using the university funds wisely." Thus, the following year, for $40,000 the University bought a thirty-five-acre tract at the western edge of the city, situated at 72nd and Western streets, which had "an unobstructed view westward to Boystown [*sic*] and eastward to downtown Omaha." Yet, the administration understood that it "may be sometime before sufficient money is obtained to initiate a building program." In 1955, as Prep prepared to depart, St. John's High School for girls merged with St. Mary's High School and evacuated the Creighton campus; the amalgam produced Mercy High, located in a new building at 48th Street and Woolworth Avenue.[10]

Moreover, the success of the new development program foreshortened Prep's interval of anxiety. On June 30, 1956, dignitaries broke ground for the separate high school at a separate site, eliminating the last vestige of the *Ratio Studiorum*. The physical separation occurred at the opening of the 1958 school year; the $1,550,000 structure accepted 700 students (100 more than the previous year in its "cramped" location; it could accommodated a total of 1,100). The Omaha Jesuit House divided; an independent Jesuit community took control of Prep, with the Reverend John J. Foley, S.J., as rector and the Reverend Joseph J. Labaj, S.J., as principal—the latter replaced the Reverend Henry L. Sullivan, S.J., who had served as principal for twenty-nine years. The flagpole followed the students to the new school grounds. With the all-University Commencement moved from the gymnasium to the Music Hall in the new Omaha Civic Auditorium in 1955, the flag ceremony ceased and the pole, surrounded by trees in a spot between the Sacred Heart statue and the Observatory, fell into disuse. Cost overruns on the new building, however, caused problems of a more serious nature. If the Prep owed the University money (projected total debt of $400,000), it could not borrow funds to erect a Jesuit residence. The Omaha Jesuit communities arranged a settlement in which Prep became an independent corporation free of debt, but with no further claims on the University's endowment. The Reverend Provincial Joseph P. Fisher, S.J., of the Wisconsin Province accepted the agreement (in 1954, for "the increased spiritual welfare of its members and better economy and efficiency," Iowa, Minnesota, Nebraska, North Dakota, South Dakota and Wisconsin had become a new vice-province).[11]

The Prep emigration from the north wing of the Administration Building allowed the CCAS to gain a "Silk purse from a sow's ear." At one-eighth the cost of a new arts college facility, the University renovated the space into eighteen "sorely-needed classrooms and office space . . . for the largest enrollment in more than a decade." The office shuffle included providing a headquarters for the expanding list of administrators; in 1958, Fr. William F. Kelley assumed the position of academic vice president (AVP), appointed to assist the president "in furthering academic unification (Fr. Linn served as vice president of university relations and Fr. Murphy as vice president of finance). Furthermore, the education department moved to the first floor, and speech, sociology, journalism, and the newsroom to the third floor. The prior first-floor newsroom became a faculty lounge, while the remodeled high-school biology room emerged as two offices and an examining room for the nursing-student health service, and the old Prep library easily converted to use as a lecture hall that sat 170. Furthermore, craftsmen sandblasted and tuck-pointed the exterior, replaced outdated wood-casement windows with "steel, projected-type [swing up and out]," lowered ceilings, and installed "modern fluorescent lighting."[12]

The north-wing renovation stood as just one of several major elements of the restructuring of the campus during the Reinert-Linn era. The "Creighton Renaissance" included a host of new buildings, recalling the John A. Creighton-financed expansion at the dawn of the twentieth century and giving currency to the historical "rebirth" analogy. New federal government programs and a new attitude toward federal aid helped finance the resurgence. Before the 1930s, Catholic educators had opposed government education programs as a threat to their autonomy. However, New Deal student-aid packages supported enrollment at Catholic schools and World War II government contracts to train military personnel provided another positive experience that led to a revised viewpoint. Subsequently, most Catholic institutions of higher learning aggressively sought federal funds, arguing that "service to the public rather than public control" should serve as the standard for aid.[13]

Creighton followed the above model. In 1950, Congress passed a new federal loan law for faculty and student housing, but President Harry Truman delayed its implementation because of the outbreak of the Korean War. Nonetheless, the Board of Trustees decided to initiate the planning for a new dorm to be ready when funds became available. The following year, Truman "unfroze" $40 million and the administration applied for a grant to build a dormitory at California Street and Lincoln Boulevard, west of the dental school, so that students could "live cheaper" than in other rental units. The application did not succeed; the University made do with the purchase of the south half of the Graystone Apartments (the College of Commerce occupied the north half), converting the complex into a men's residence, Agnew Hall. Subsequently, in 1955, the Trustees hired Cumerford, Inc. of Kansas City, Kansas, to conduct a survey, "on the possibility of a public campaign for capital funds." They also employed Leo A. Daly, Sr., to draw up a blueprint for the campus; the planning contract used a sliding fee schedule, whereby his payment depended upon the amount of architectural-design business his company received (no charge, if $2 million or more). In March 1955, the Trustees specifically engaged Daly to design a "Dormitory and Feeding Unit."[14]

Actually, beginning that year, Morris Jacobs, cofounder of the city's largest advertising firm, chaired an Omaha-area development drive that surpassed its $1.8 million goal. Clarence Landon, president of the Securities Acceptance Corporation, headed the "pattern gifts," which totaled $1,280,627; Leo A. Daly, Sr., the "large gifts," which garnered $481,790; and W. L. Shomaker, vice president of the Northern Natural Gas Company, the "general division," which raised $253,434, for a total of $2,015,851. The non-alumni, religiously diverse group of the Omaha business elite that led the successful drive attested to the University's nascent integration into the local community. In conjunction with the local drive, the Trustees authorized Fr. Reinert to seek a forty-year, $750,000 federal loan; this time the application received a favorable review, and on July 30, 1955, they authorized him to sign the loan agreement. Following the open-bidding process, they accepted Peter Kiewet as the general contractor to build a new dorm, with an attached cafeteria and student lounge.[15]

By the time the University obtained the money, the location for the dorm changed to the west side of 24th Street, south of California. Demolition crews eliminated a student parking lot, two University-owned houses and an apartment complex; the latter housed four families, who rented apartments on the second floor, and the public-relations, alumni, student-job-placement, and varsity-press offices. To expedite the start of construction in September 1955, no formal groundbreaking ceremony ensued. Instead, Fr. Reinert drove a bulldozer partially across the site. He quipped, "Conservatively speaking, I would estimate that it would take 1,500 college presidents two weeks to dig this much dirt at a formal dedication." However, on December 2, during Homecoming, a standard formal rite accompanied laying the cornerstone. Completion of the project missed the target date of the opening of school in September 1957; anxious administrators notified students of a one-week delay and then "all hands pitched in" helping with "finishing touches and final cleaning." The five-story unit accommodated 194 men (Agnew Hall became a female residence, 1957–61), and the firms of Morris Jacobs and Clarence Landon provided donations to have common rooms in the new facility named in their honor. The dorm bears the name of the "beloved Student Counselor," the Reverend Francis Deglmen, S.J. After twenty-seven years at Creighton as spiritual counselor, sodality director, sponsor of the Marion Night rite, and teacher of theology, he had died of a heart attack at St. Joseph's Hospital on February 9, 1955.[16]

Simultaneously, the Kiewit Company erected a two-story cafeteria–student lounge attached to Deglman Hall, stretching westward from its south façade. As early as 1952, Crei-Vets, a recently organized World War II and Korean War faculty-student veterans' organization, resurrected the long-dormant drive to fund a Student Union building. The SBG voted unanimously to support the effort and Fr. Reinert pledged that the University would match the student fund "dollar for dollar." The SBG held fundraising events such as a dance in which the $2.50 ticket cost went into the building fund. Two years later, however, the fund held only $12,000. At that point, the SBG presented a novel plan approved by Fr. Reinert and the Board of Trustees. Beginning spring semester 1955, and continuing subsequent spring semesters, full-time students would pay an extra $5 in their activity fee, with the money earmarked for a union building. Again, Fr. Reinert promise a 100 percent match; thus, the arrangement would produce $17,000 per year (1,700 full-time students, times $5, times two) and result in a facility by 1960. In a referendum, 64 percent of the student body voted, and 71 percent of those that cast a ballot supported the proposal. The federal loan for the dorm and the successful Omaha development campaign foreshortened the process, and the SBG began seeking student input regarding the design of the structure, promising to "select the sound and more logical ideas" to submit to the administration.[17]

On September 30, 1956, Archbishop Bergan and over one hundred local priests conducted a civic dedication for the unfinished Deglman Hall and the attached Loyola Student Center. Over 1,400 people witnessed the blessing of the two-story dining and leisure facility (students in the professional schools could not live in the dorm, but could eat in the cafeteria a la carte or by purchasing a board plan). The upper floor of the student center consisted of a five-hundred-seat cafeteria (regularly converted into a public lecture hall) and a faculty dining room that sat seventy-two. The lower level included a snack bar, student and faculty lounges, and an office for the dean of men. The Beanery, which had obtained a television set in 1951, but had prohibited card playing because "space is at a premium," closed, and public relations and alumni relations moved from the commerce annex into the remodeled space. At the dedication ceremony, the SBG presented Fr. Reinert with a check for $25,000 that "represented the student contribution for furnishing the center." The Loyola Center design included plans for enlargement as soon as possible. The SBG maintained the $5 assessment, earmarking it for expansion, but by 1959, inflation pushed the projected cost from $328,000 to $442,000. In 1962, Fr. Reinert explained that crowded conditions and an expected record enrollment prompted him to suggest the doubling of the special fee. He warned, however, that it would likely take at least three years to get the building fund up to the $250,000 needed to allow construction. However, shortly thereafter, he announced that imminent groundbreaking would ensue, due to an anonymous gift of $50,000 from a "generous friend," if the students voted in favor of the fee increase. They approved the measure 456-232; the election committee did not reveal results by school, but anecdotal conversation suggested that only the CCAS and the commerce college heartily affirmed the proposition.[18]

Mary Rodgers Brandeis surfaced as the "generous friend" and the name of the student center changed in her honor; her gift and the student contribution allowed the expansion to begin October 15, 1962. The 18,000-square-foot, three-story addition, extending sixty feet west of the original building and matching it in design, opened with the start of classes in September 1963. New lounges and the bookstore occupied the lower level. The second story consisted of three private dining rooms that opened to the Deglman cafeteria (which enlarged the lecture hall area when needed), as well as offices for yet another vice president (student personnel), the dean of women, and

their assistants. The third floor provided a multipurpose conference room and offices
for public relations, alumni relations, and student publications. At that time, Mrs. Jack
(Eileen) Lieben, who had received a B.A. at Manhattenville College of the Sacred
Heart, an M.A. in English at Creighton (1962), and spent a year as assistant to Dean
of Women Hamilton, traded positions with her mentor, who remained in a part-time
advisory position for another two years. Concurrently, Col. Urban E. Rohr retired as
commandant of the ROTC unit and became the first lay dean of men at Creighton.
The SBG converted its building assessment into an activity fee and began issuing
activity cards at registration (as in the pre–World War II era, good for free admission
to University cultural and sporting events). It also announced it would "appraise existing activities to determine how they could be bolstered financially and then recommend what amount of the money should be used per activity."[19]

In addition to leisure space, housing for women became an issue of special concern during the 1950s. Shortly before Fr. Reinert's arrival, the Board of Trustees
decided to purchase a large home on California Street and renovate it into a freshman
girl's dorm, but resolved that it should be "separately administered" and "all thought
Mrs. Hamilton should be put in charge." That transaction failed. Subsequently, Dean
Hamilton argued that eventual success ensued because Fr. Reinert proved "brave
enough" to establish dorms for women. During his tenure, the University purchased
several houses, including the above-mentioned residence at 2611 California in 1959
(most subsequently lost to interstate highway construction), and outfitted them as
female student dwellings. In September 1951, Mary Hall, a two-story white frame
house at 520 North 26th Street, between Dodge and Cass streets, established the
model, as it became home for twenty-two out-of-town freshmen women. Dean
Hamilton and "a small board of a non-profit corporation" managed the complex; a
resident "house mother" supervised operations, the roomers had to eat their meals at
Deglman cafeteria, but they did have a "special study room and a recreation room"
in their residence.[20]

The administration of women's dorms changed with the merger of University
College and Creighton College, which eliminated the artifice that had allowed
women to attend classes in the arts college. Father General Ledochowski, who had
vigorously opposed the Society's teaching of women, died in 1942. Because war
enveloped the world, no congregation could meet in Rome until 1946, to elect a new
superior general. At that international gathering of Jesuits, Creighton philosophy
professor the Reverend Herbert C. "Butch" Noonan, S.J., served as one of the two
elected representatives of the Missouri Province; he joined the group advocating the
teaching of women, arguing, "*non contra, sed praeter, Constitutiones*" (not against, but
simply beyond, the *Constitutions*). Eventually, the women's advocates won the day; in
July 1950, the Board of Trustees reported the receipt of a letter from the Very Reverend General John Baptist Janssens, S.J., which gave permission "to drop the title
'University College' and incorporate the coeds into the Liberal Arts College." Fru-
gally, since they had just reordered a batch of registration cards, administrators
decided to eliminate the name after they used the supply.[21]

In 1956, Fr. Reinert announced the second phase of the long-range plan that encompassed ten years and $14 million, and included a University-owned women's dorm to rival Deglman Hall (the men's dorm and the student center had completed phase one). Phase 2 acknowledged the significance of Creighton coeds in other ways; the campaign included the first annual convocation of the nationwide Greater Creighton Committee, which incorporated many women, including nuns, among the five hundred invited representatives of alumni and business leaders. For the next few years, the committee met to "review the university's building and long range development plans and other phases of the university's activities." Moreover, each year the SBG chose nine representatives to serve "in equal capacity" with the alums and civic leaders, one from each school (six at that time) and one each from three major organizations—the SBG, and the Inter-Fraternity and Pan-Hellenic councils.[22]

The lack of space for women had worsened during the decade as their numbers increased and they lost their lounge, the Commerce Cottage, first to the varsity press and then, to a wrecking ball to provide added parking. In 1958, the Trustees recognized a crisis: no upper-class coeds were housed in a University dorm and overall the "quality and quantity of housing are below the standards we would desire." Furthermore, the conversion of Dowling or Wareham halls for women remained "impossibly expensive." Thus, without the resources to purchase more homes or to use as collateral to support a federal loan request, they decided "not to press for recruitment of out-of-town girls." Happily, Phase 2 fundraising succeeded; the University applied for another $750,000 federal housing loan in July 1959, for a dorm for coeds, and signed the agreement the following March. At the time, women composed 29 percent of the student body (the highest in history, and rising annually); out-of-town female students lived in six University-owned homes, housing as few as eleven and as many as forty-four, while the remainder lived in forty-one off-campus dwellings, most of which did not include cooking privileges. Ironically, the new dorm did not alleviate the problem of housing out-of-town coeds. In order to avoid the cost of pilings in "spongy land," the University built it "well to the east of the original plan." That site, at 27th Street, south across California from the dental school, demanded the razing of three coed house-dorms, as well as the loss of rental income from them (plus, Agnew Hall reverted to a men's residence). The new dorm copied the style of Deglman Hall and housed 214 women, two to a room. An unrestricted gift from Benjamin Gallagher of "slightly over $100,000.00" provided most of the collateral for the federal loan, and with his and his brother Paul's permission, the dorm became a memorial to their father (who had been a partner in the successor firm to John A. Creighton's wholesale business, renamed the Paxton-Gallagher Company).[23]

While dormitory space remained scarce during the 1950s, the University maintained its historic guiding principle of nondiscrimination. At the time, few students of Asian or African-American decent attended Creighton's six schools, but photographs in the yearbook reveal that men's and women's house dorms operated on an egalitarian basis. In 1958, Creighton's existing standard received resounding support from the administrative board of the National Catholic Welfare Conference that issued a declaration in the name of the Bishops of the United States. It condemned "discrimination based on the accidental fact of race or color" because it could not be "reconciled with the truth that God has created all men with equal rights and equal dignity." As an affirmation of that proclamation, and as an extension of the standard the Creighton leadership had applied to itself, in December 1963, the Trustees unanimously adopted a resolution "vigorously" opposing "all forms" of racism, which made "open occupancy a law for owners or occupiers of property listed on the approved housing roster." Thus, before the open-housing civil rights law of 1968, the University began to insist that private home and/or apartment owners desiring to rent to Creighton students do so regardless of race.[24]

As the administration worked to solve the student-housing crisis, it also sought to replace a library that Fr. Reinert said "had more books in inaccessible storage than on the shelves" (some "in attics where the heat of the sun almost set them on fire"). Fortunately, the rapid success of Phase 1 of the development campaign "advanced the entire building program by three years." Thus, in 1956, the twenty-year-old discussion about a library became earnest; a group of alums from Nebraska and Iowa met to plan a $1 million drive and Morris Jacobs agreed to serve as general chairman. At the 1958 Commencement, Fr. Reinert announced that due to the "tireless" effort of Stephen A. Mitchell (A.B., 1926), former Democratic National Chairman, the canvass had reached its goal in subscriptions, but that construction would not begin until he received a majority of the money in hand. Already, in preparation for that joyful day, student thespians had performed *Brigadoon*, May 2–4, 1958, and the demolition crew arrived on campus that summer to remove the Auditorium from the future site of the Alumni Memorial Library, named in honor of the donors.[25]

A year later, the University had received over half the funds and broke ground on June 2, 1959. It also had to remove the World War II "Huts" from the site; they were bisected, loaded on truck beds, and reassemble adjacent to the Chemistry Building. A year later, the administration lamented, "The income on pledges has not been as ample as expected." The tight money supply slowed the pace of the concurrent renovation of the north wing of the Administration Building and of fundraising for the women's dorm. However, anxiety soon turned to contentment (temporarily) as the necessary donations materialized, financing the projects and providing the collateral for the federal loans, and the renovated north wing, women's dorm, and library added luster to the burgeoning campus. Moving the collection from the old space (it became offices for the registrar, the CCAS, and the purchasing department) entailed the public display of two of the major symbols of college life. Beginning June 3, 1961, "a continuous line of flat bed carts piled high with cardboard beer cases traveled from the Administration Building to the new Alumni Memorial Library approximately one block away." The Falstaff Brewery donated the use of the boxes that workers filled with books, not liquid refreshment, at twenty-eight cartons per cart and transferred the 125,000 volumes to a building designed to hold twice that number. The facility "opened for business" on June 15, under the direction of the Reverend James P. Kramper, S.J. Students immediately complained because it closed on Sundays

(hours: Monday–Thursday, 7:45 A.M.–9:00 P.M.; Friday, 7:45 A.M.–6:00 P.M.; Saturday, 7:45 A.M.–4:00 P.M.). They hoped to extend the schedule, at least during semester exams; the administration explained that with all the expansion, because of
staffing cost, it could not afford to lengthen the hours of operation. More to the students delight, in 1963, the Alumni Library acquired a Thermofax Photo-Copy
machine. At ten cents per copy, an attendant usually provided the duplication(s)
within one day of the request (one of the most significant inventions of office equipment in the twentieth century, copy machines became commonplace by the 1980s).[26]

The building boom that began in the mid-1950s buoyed the morale of the students and the faculty. When Fr. Reinert assumed the presidency of Creighton University, a decline in enrollment presented him with an unpleasant welcome. From a
post–World War II high of 3,000 students University-wide in 1947, the number of
registrations fell to a postwar low of 2,350 in 1953, although the professional schools
maintained "capacity enrollments." Veterans had accounted for 65 percent of the students in the fall semester 1947, but for only 37 percent in the fall of 1950; by then, most
of them had completed their undergraduate education. The administration
responded with the creation of a Student Promotion Committee that would call on
high schools; about fifty faculty volunteered to make the visitations. For several years,
the committee also sponsored Hi-C Night, a dance for high-school seniors, featur-
ing prominent local bands, in the gymnasium. It also began holding informational
meetings for prospective students and their parents, as well as distributing a special
twelve-page edition of the *Creightonian* to Omaha-area high schools, and two
twelve-page pictorial booklets, "The Creighton Story" and "Television and the
Creighton University," to high schools and colleges nationwide. Moreover, the
Creighton Alumnus revived a depression-era expedient, providing its readers with
forms to submit names of potential students, arguing, "We not only want them—we
need them." The recruitment program quickly produced another administrator (eventually expanding into a sizeable office), "a full-time student promotion man in order
to have regular and more frequent contact with the many high schools in the surrounding territory."[27]

The recruitment program became acute in 1951, as enrollment plummeted
another 10 percent, while Fr. Linn anticipated a further 40 percent decline because
"the current 'police action' in Korea chops off another sizeable segment of male
enrollment" due to the expected draft. Father Reinert visited with then Secretary of
the Navy Francis P. Matthews aboard his yacht *Sequoia* on the Potomac River, in
anticipation of World War II-type college programs. While the SS *Creighton* came
out of mothballs and "played an important part in the evacuation of troops and
ammunition during the early months of the Korean campaign when the United
Nations forces had their backs to the sea," the reinstituted draft only had ancillary
effects on the University. The victory ship continued to haul supplies from Japan to
Korea for the duration, but conscription touched few Creighton students. As early
as November 1950 (the North Korean invasion began in June), Fr. Reinert appointed
a committee to advise students on their draft status. It hired James J. Broderick,

assistant professor of education, as a full-time counselor. Some "panicky enlistments by students who feared they would lose their power of choice if they did not enlist immediately" ensued (e.g., drafted by the army, when service in the navy was preferred). However, according to Registrar Jack Williams, Creighton students showed "less tendency to succumb to the mass hysteria concerning the draft." By January 1951, only thirty students left campus, mostly reservists reactivated, plus a few who volunteered for the air force.[28]

By that time, the University experienced its first Korean War fatality, John H. Shramek (B.S., journalism, 1949), a World War II marine veteran, who reenlisted, participated in the Inchon landing, suffered a mortal wound near Seoul on September 21, 1950, and received a Silver Star posthumously. The vast majority of students, however, escaped the draft. The fear of conscription did encourage a regimen of regular class attendance; faculty had to report each absence immediately and students had to explain their absence in writing to a committee of arts and commerce faculty that meet each second Friday. Obviously, "the Deans of the various colleges cannot honestly request academic deferments from local draft boards for students who have greatly absented themselves from several classes." Moreover, with "Mars in the atmosphere," Advanced ROTC enrollment skyrocketed to a near-record level in the fall 1951. Yet, for most undergraduate males, the Korean War simply occasioned another exam, the Selective Service College Qualifying Test (professional-school students remained exempt from the draft as long as they "maintained the required standards of the school"). Undergraduate students had to score 70 percent to gain a deferment or could receive one through class rank—sophomores in the upper one half, juniors in the highest two thirds, seniors in the top three fourths (no scale for freshmen because most had not attained draft age). The draft and the test survived the war, as did military recruitment on campus; all of the services began regular visits to campus to entice enlistments from the men and the coeds.[29]

In 1953, for the first time in six years, enrollment rose, not as a result of the end of the Korean War, but from the "increase in the number of potential students felt at all levels of American education . . . [and] the herculean effort of the Creighton student promotion committee." The CCAS garnered the largest gain (142 more freshmen), the number of coeds jumped by 74 to a record level, and Korean War veterans did make their presence known by establishing the Crei-vets club. With over forty members, it became a coed organization in 1955, adding the membership of a WAVES and a WAC. The group, which lasted until the end of the decade, performed service activity such as sponsoring a Christmas party for children at the Creche Home. Despite the presence of the vets, according to the yearbook, a new kind of student predominated: "Through the winter the tenseness of the Russian instigated cold war continued, but everyone was learning to live with it. Eighteen and nineteen year olds were unburdened by lightened draft quotas causing the student body as a whole to become natural again with younger more spirited freshmen and sophomores." By 1961, the University surpassed the previous record enrollment, registering 3,169 students, with the CCAS reaping 1,877. During the era, in all schools a very small number of blacks matriculated and the few foreign students largely entered in the professional schools.[30]

Those "happy days" students became the first cohort to experience rapidly inflating tuition rates that began to double by the decade; in their case, from $10 per hour or $150 per semester for full-time students in 1950, to $20 per hour or $325 per semester in 1961. Despite the swift advance, the tuition remained relatively low for private schools, as Creighton ranked eighth out of ten in the region. Notwithstanding, in that economic environment, loans and scholarships became more significant; programs from the era of the Great Depression had atrophied during World War II, and in the immediate postwar era, the G.I. Bill had financed the education of the vast majority of Creighton students. During the 1950s, the University slowly expanded its financial aid programs; for example, in 1952, it awarded twenty $600 scholarships earned through competitive exams it administered for incoming freshmen. In 1954, it reactivated the long-dormant Agnew Loan Fund, which would advance any full-time student up to $150.[31]

Despite a meager financial-aid program, undergraduate matriculation swelled during the decade as need for college-educated professionals (e.g., teachers to instruct in schools inundated with the baby boom generation) prompted increasing percentages of high-school graduates to pursue additional education. The revolution in financial aid came in 1958, with the passage of the National Defense Education Act. Among its features, it provided a generous matching fund for student loans for public and private schools. Creighton joined the program spring semester 1959, contributing $10,000 to receive $90,000 from the federal government, which established a loan fund of $100,000 available to students in all its schools. In 1958, only 113 students borrowed $14,597 from the few existing University-operated programs; in 1962, by comparison, 394 students borrowed $206,059. Moreover, the *1961–1963 Creighton University Bulletin* needed four pages to list its "student financial aids" for undergraduate education. For the first time, admission required submission of American College Test (ACT) scores, which then became the criterion for the twenty competitive freshmen scholarships. Notably, as another demonstration of Creighton's integration into Omaha, the catalogue also listed the Ak-Sar-Ben, the Arthur Brandeis, the Omaha Advertising Club, the Omaha Press Club, and the Associated Nebraska Industrial Editors scholarships.[32]

While financial-aid packages ballooned, part-time and summer employment remained important (as did jobs during holiday recesses; in 1960, the Board of Trustees extended the Christmas break to match that of Omaha University to allow students to compete for employment). A federal grant to state employment agencies allowed them to lend personnel to universities that desired the help; on December 15, 1961, a staff member of the Nebraska State Employment Service opened an office at Creighton and worked full-time to place students and graduates. As a sign of the times (era of the "feminine mystique"), in 1961 the Alumni Association directed a survey of undergraduate summer employment, revealing that 414 of 500 students polled held jobs. However, coeds contributed only 3 percent of those jobholders, finding fewer opportunities for employment; those that did, worked as "typists, store clerks, hospital or recreational aides." The job office became another of the variety of "student services" offered by the University. In 1957, as those services multiplied and gained significance in recruiting undergraduates, the *Creighton University Bulletin* began to list them under a separate heading. In 1963, the roster expanded to include a Student Counseling Center, "not a clinic, but a help to aid students in making wise educational and vocational decisions," which "supplements the Jesuit counselor present on campus for many years." In addition, by that year, the array of offerings demanded administrative reorganization, with the Reverend John J. Halloran, S.J., appointed the first vice president for student affairs (subsequently, renamed student services).[33]

While an expanded bureaucracy added expenses, primarily the University needed to escalate the tuition rates to gain "non-traditional" income (as opposed to endowment and gifts) to compensate a burgeoning, poorly paid, undergraduate, lay faculty. Walter Jahn described the salary scale of 1950 as "ridiculously low" and fringe benefits as virtually nonexistent (actually, the situation plagued most Catholic schools at all levels). The University retirement fund disbursed $40 per month, regardless of salary level, and the Trustees recommended lowering it because of the cost of contributions to the federal Social Security program. The pharmacy clinic gave a small discount on drugs and head pharmacist Subby Pirrucello dispensed vitamins to faculty members free of charge.[34]

The circumstances began to improve in 1956 with the receipt of a Ford Foundation grant, $500 million nationally to private colleges, universities, and hospitals, of which Creighton's share was $517,100. The gift had to become part of an income-producing endowment for a minimum of ten years and be earmarked for faculty development; thereafter, it could be used for "any academic needs." At a 4 percent return, Creighton's award would generate about $20,000 annually. The administration designated the interest income from approximately $250,000 of the grant to St. Joseph's Hospital, $108,000 to St. Catherine's Hospital, and $160,000 to the CCAS and the commerce college; the latter two used it to increase faculty salaries. Yet, in 1959, AVP Fr. William F. Kelley, "cited the irony in American education where beginning grade school teachers with a Bachelor's Degree [in great demand because of the baby boom generation] begin at a higher salary in our city systems than many of their own young instructors in college were making." He also explained the necessity for tuition increases, contending, "For too long faculty members themselves [through low pay] have been, as it were, subsidizing too much of the cost of our children's education." Therefore, students had to understand their "opportunity to share in bettering the economic position of their professors." The Trustees remained "acutely aware of the problems associated with an increased salary scale of professors," but lamented, "We cannot give what we don't have." Thus, while the University became more competitive with entry salaries, despite increases well above the national average in the early 1960s, Creighton still lagged "behind schools our size in salaries paid to teachers at the level of full professor and associate professor." Obviously, the disparity in the range of salaries between medical, dental, law, business, science, nursing, and human-ities faculty (as well as staff) substantially affected the above generalizations by the Trustees. Additionally, the administration understood that to maintain quality faculty and staff it had to provide reasonable fringe benefits; thus, it initiated new insurance and retirement programs (adopting TIAA-CREF in 1961), and gradually expanded the coverage and benefits.[35]

The Trustees had to worry about more than salaries; mushrooming enrollments necessitated the hiring of more lay faculty, including many non-Catholics, in the arts college. The number of Jesuit priests and seminarians in the United States rose from 5,006 in 1945 to a peak of 7,677 in 1964 (since then, a sharp decline has halved the Order). At Creighton, their presence remained strong. In 1951, University workmen constructed an addition above the Jesuit kitchen to serve as their new library, while the former Jesuit library in the west addition to the Administration Building was ren-ovated into individual rooms, "solving some of the housing problems for the Jesuits." However, the number of Jesuits in the classroom remained stagnant between 1950 (31) and 1960 (32), while the number of lay faculty (excluding ROTC military personnel) in the CCAS proliferated from 90 to 121 and the number of assistant professors (new full-time hires) more than doubled. The number of lay part-time adjuncts also grew; in 1951, they included Whitney Young, head of the Omaha Urban League and even-tual national director of that civil rights organization, who became the first "Negro" to teach at Creighton—a sociology class for the adult education program.[36]

In 1955, with the permission of Fr. General Janssens, the Jesuit Education Asso-ciation (JEA) published new "General Policies and Procedures," which established the goal for American Jesuits to educate as many students as they could afford. The objective meant recruiting more lay faculty, and created potential competition and conflict with other Catholic educators (who also needed students and teachers), as well as with bishops, who worried about laymen teaching philosophy and theology and the innovative courses they added to the curriculum. The JEA held workshops and institutes to establish guidelines (AVP Fr. William F. Kelley directed the 1961 meeting at Gonzaga University). The teaching of theology produced little concern at Creighton during the period; in 1955, students dedicated the *Bluejay* to the Reverend Henri Renard, S.J., because, "Practically all C.U. students have used one or more of his textbooks at some time or other. He is held in high repute by all philosophers and is one of the outstanding Thomists in this country." Yet, in 1956, some undisclosed predicament plagued the administration, as it revealed, "The 'black out' which has existed concerning Creighton University news in the local Catholic paper, the *True Voice*, has been lifted. This condition has held for some eleven months."[37]

The teach-all-you-can objective caused internal concerns as well. With increased lay participation, Jesuit leaders feared the loss of denominational control, as had hap-pened at many Protestant colleges in the late-nineteenth and early-twentieth cen-turies. In an article in *Commonweal*, Oscar W. Perlmutter, vice president of St. Xavier College in Chicago, depicted the position of lay teachers at Catholic colleges as "unwanted, unpaid, uncared for and unpersoned." Edward P. J. Corbett, Ph.D., associate professor of English, and Dean of Women Hamilton, replied with rebuttal letters published in the magazine, declaring that Creighton did not match the scathing portrayal. In 1958, Fr. General Janssens appointed four *Inspectores* to "report to him directly on how well these universities [American] are achieving the aims of Jesuit education; what are the obstacles to the achievement of their aims; what means can be employed so as to be of greater use to the Church." The Reverend Leo D. Sullivan, S.J., "inspected" Creighton. Following the reports, Fr. Janssens initiated a discussion on the role of lay faculty and administrators in colleges of arts and sciences; he worried about lay power over Jesuits in the historic home of the *Ratio Studiorum* (in the other schools of the Jesuit universities, lay faculty and administrators always predominated). Heeding the call, the Creighton Trustees stressed to the deans the need to employ "competent Catholics" and to "ascertain the marital background" on non-Catholics, not hiring those "involved in bad marriages." In 1959, the concern reached students; the Trustees incorporated a "marital status" line to admission forms that included the statement, "Persons who are invalidly married, or divorced, and invalidly remarried, will not be admitted nor retained."[38]

Furthermore, the debate about faculty swirled around the related issues of academic freedom and Catholic intellectualism. In 1955, Msgr. John Tracy Ellis, professor of Church History at Catholic University, secretary of the American Catholic Historical Association, and managing editor of the *Catholic Historical Review*, presented an address, "American Catholics and the Intellectual Life," at the annual conference of the Catholic Commission on Intellectual and Cultural Affairs. He indicted Catholic higher education for its failure "to produce national leaders and to exercise commanding influence in intellectual circles." In part, the problem stemmed from the recent assimilation of Catholics in the United States; however, in the middle of the twentieth century, he argued, Catholic universities spread themselves too widely, covering all areas of education, retarding support for research. He also complained of "the absence of a sense of dedication to an intellectual apostolate." Subsequently, he published a compendium of responses to his analysis, almost all of which supported his conclusions.[39]

The address sparked a national debate. The JEA responded with the creation of the Jesuit Research Council of America, which included AVP William F. Kelley on its board of trustees. The Council functioned as a service organization assisting Jesuit universities in finding foundation support for research. Creighton proclaimed, "instruction is and will always be the primary activity," but "within the limits of modest resources," it concerned itself "with the search for new knowledge." Most research at Creighton revolved around the professional schools, especially the health sciences. Few undergraduate faculty members published and the number of Jesuits on campus with the Ph.D. degree declined (in 1950, nine of thirty-one; in 1960, seven of thirty-two). Thus, in 1958, Charles Wilhelmj, M.D., head of the existing Medical School Research Committee, became the chairman of a new Creighton University Research Committee, which would act as a "clearing house" for grant seeking and as the "agent in general research grants." Unfortunately, "Studies completed in the 1950s clearly show that Catholic students, while shunning the rewards of academic applause in the pursuit of pure science in the graduate schools, were over represented [*sic*] in law and medicine. They preferred the community prestige and the financial remuneration associated with those professions." Thus, the number of Catholic researchers and intellectuals would grow slowly until attitudes toward an academic life changed. Finally, the faculty debate included the American Association of University Professors (AAUP) 1940 "Statement of Principles on Academic Freedom and Tenure." It concerned the ancient conflict between doctrine and free inquiry, and the authority relationship between lay faculty and administrators vis-à-vis the Jesuits. Regarding both subjects, significant antipathy existed during the 1950s, but by the 1970s, most Catholic universities accepted the paradigm (generally free inquiry and laymen could supervise clerics).[40]

While those debates raged, the number of students and faculty, and the quantity and variety of classes in the CCAS all increased dramatically. The "degrees and requirements for graduation" in the arts college experienced few substantive changes during the "happy days" era. Historically significant, however, beginning in 1959, students could earn an A.B. without taking Latin. The CCAS created the "Classical A.B." for those who studied Latin, as well as four semesters of another foreign language, but the ancient tongue and the degree languished. The installation, in 1961, of "the most modern language laboratory in the area," containing forty soundproof booths and located in Wareham Hall, met with a more resounding acceptance. Similarly, the reviled senior comprehensive exams (minimum of four hours written and one-half hour oral, plus the philosophy segment of the Graduate Record Exam) began to atrophy. The early 1960s witnessed "some new approaches"; for example, speech majors could do a project instead, and the English department instituted a tutorial, one hour per week for one-hour credit to prepare for the exam.[41]

While curricular requirements experienced minimal alteration, novelty appeared in programs and departmental organization. In 1950, the CCAS bundled its array of classes in journalism (print), advertising, radio, and television into a well-promoted Communication Arts Program. In 1952, returning Korean War vets convinced the English department to launch an honors program. By the end of the era, it consisted of five sections of special classes for sophomores through seniors, and laid plans for expansion (although the department also conducted three sections of remedial English). Moreover, in 1963, Arthur Umscheid, Ph.D., left the history department to become the first lay dean of the graduate school. The departure presented the opportunity to divide disciplines; Allan M. Schleich, Ph.D., who had taught the required introductory Western civilization class to several generations of freshmen, became chair of the reorganized history department, and Rene Beauchesne assumed the chair of an independent political science department. Beauchesne organized the Political Research Center, an outgrowth of directing student research pertaining to Omaha's home rule charter (1954). The group consisted of over forty students with varied majors who did "research in the field of government for anyone." In addition, in 1962, President John F. Kennedy appointed the Reverend Edward Conway, S.J.,

Ph.D., associate professor of political science, as a member of the General Advisory Committee of the United States Arms Control and Disarmament Agency. His stature brought "gifts from friends and a $10,000.00 grant from Cardinal Cushing," which led to the creation of the Center for Peace Research. The Center operated out of remodeled space on the fourth floor of the Administration Building that included two offices and a seminar room that contained library stacks and periodical racks. Subsequently an appendage of the political science department, the Center consisted of Fr. Conway, director, and the Reverend Thomas C. Donohue, S.J., Ph.D. (philosophy), project director, and the Reverend M. Joseph Costelloe, S.J., Ph. D. (classical languages), the Reverend John Ginsterblum, S.J., Ph.D. (theology), the Reverend Robert Shanahan, S.J., Ph.D. (history), and assistant professor Beauchesne as associates.[42]

The sciences kept pace. At the behest of the Creighton Prep Astronomer's Club, the Observatory, "for three decades just a dome-shaped, dusty-windowed building in the northeast corner of campus," received new equipment and necessary repairs. The students installed an exhibit in honor of Fr. William Rigge, and in 1954 opened the facility to any high school or college science class in the region. However, the view was "somewhat handicapped by the reflected glare of city lights, by the increased smoke and dust of the city [coal still the primary heating fuel], and the growth of trees during the 30 years of inactivity." In 1955, psychology, which had originated as a few classes in the theology department, joined the list of social science majors, although the education department administered the discipline for the next ten years. Concurrently, undergraduate health-science programs expanded to include a B.S. in radiological technology and pre-professional studies in dietetics, physical therapy, and occupational therapy.[43]

In 1957, the Soviet Union rocketed the first satellite into orbit, and the United States responded with a space race and a demand for more intensive math and science training. As part of that trend, in 1962, Creighton received a $23,500 grant from the Atomic Energy Commission to purchase equipment necessary to introduce the first undergraduate classes in nuclear science in the region. The following year, approximately two hundred students from eastern Nebraska and western Iowa participated in the University's first Math Field Day. While Jesuit education had always required math and science, it "traditionally maintained that no area should be emphasized to the point of weakening the others." Thus, in response to the post-Sputnik call for an increased stress on the natural sciences, the presidents of the Jesuit universities in the United States issued a statement in favor of a balanced curriculum: "The astonishing conquest of matter, energy and space gives rise to a spiritual bewilderment in which man can lose his sense of purpose. To maintain equilibrium, the school must guard the integrity of the philosophical and humanistic disciplines which make a student aware of his spiritual origin and destiny. . . . The development of a human person at once morally mature and intellectually accomplished is the unchanging aim of Jesuit education."[44]

Those principles also applied to the commerce college, which continued its traditional course of study that required about 40 percent of its classes come from the liberal arts. The curriculum remained virtually unchanged during the era, with the exception of adding a training program in 1950, designed to prepare graduates to teach commercial courses in high school. The tuition matched that of the CCAS, and commerce shared in much of the generally undergraduate financial aide. It did generate several business-designated grants, such as the Nebraska C.P.A., Omaha Advertising Club, Omaha Sales Executives' Club, and the Women's Division–Omaha Chamber of Commerce scholarships. However, very few women and no African Americans graduated from the College of Commerce during the era. In fact, with a deteriorating building and only a "provisional associate membership" in the American Association of Collegiate Schools of Business (AACSB) until it corrected "relative deficiencies," the school suffered a sharp decline in enrollment in the late 1950s. In such circumstances, the number of faculty remained stable, but the makeup changed to meet accreditation standards. In 1950, two assistants, one associate, and four full professors taught with eight part-time instructors and lecturers. In 1960, six assistants (necessary full-time hires), three associates, and three full professors taught with five part-timers. In the meantime, in 1956, opting to follow other institutions using the "more inclusive name," the Board of Trustees adopted the name College of Business Administration (CoBA) and re-titled the degree to Bachelor of Science in Business Administration (BSBA).[45]

For CoBA, "happy days" began in 1959 when Fr. Reinert began "private conversations" with members of the Eppley Foundation board. On July 27, he announced a $1 million grant for a new business-school building. Because of the "cramped campus conditions," and following a suggestion put forward from the last Greater Creighton Committee, the administration decided to raze the south stand of the stadium and use the space for a new CoBA, which would then abut the rising Alumni Library. The old commerce college became the Student Activities Building and gave office space to student organizations, and the remainder of the stadium, with $14,000 in repairs, continued to host intramurals, intercollegiate track, and to serve as "home field for several Omaha high school football teams." For the CoBA, architect Leo Daly, Sr., presented a design of buff brick and glass that fit with his white stone and glass library building. A plaza would emerge in the open area of the "U" configuration of the dental school and the law school (with its north entrance), the Alumni Library (with its entrance facing west), and the CoBA (with south entrances) that would form "the central mall of the campus." The 50,000-square-foot, four-and-one-half-story Eppley Building contained twenty-eight offices, eighteen classrooms, additional study and seminar rooms, a faculty lounge, a student lounge, a three-hundred-seat lecture hall and "other related rooms." The University dedicated the edifice on October 4, 1961; the previous year, the AACSB had accepted the CoBA into full membership.[46]

The new facility included designated research space and prompted the establishment of a Bureau of Business Research, intended to "promote a closer relationship between the faculty and the business interests in the Omaha area, to the benefit of both." By the time the new structure opened, Delta Sigma Pi and Alpha Kappa Psi business fraternities had held four Booster Days "to promote friendship, understanding and cooperation between Creighton University and the businessmen in the Omaha area." The events included a symposium, panel discussions, exhibits in the new student center, and a banquet. Both efforts encouraged the ongoing integration of the University and the modern buildings provided premier resources to extend a snowballing effect to the process. For example, in 1962, Automation, Inc., leased space in the Eppley Building and brought the first computers to campus; the administration admitted it "could not finance such a set-up for about eight years." With the "latest IBM and related computer installations," the firm fulfilled all the University's data processing needs (with a 10 percent discount), hired Creighton students as part-time employees, and provided "qualified business administration and liberal arts students with a laboratory for specialized training in the field of business data processing." That same year, CoBA initiated the first Masters in Business Administration (MBA) program in the state (simultaneously with the University of Nebraska). With those crowning achievements, in 1963, after thirty-seven years as dean, Floyd E. Walsh stepped down. The reorganization in the late 1950s, which had created the administrative vice presidents, had eliminated the office of regent in the professional schools. Jesuit counselors replaced them; each served on the faculty, the executive and the admissions committees, and were "entrusted with the spiritual and personal well-being of the students, faculty, and staff of his particular college." As Walsh departed, the Reverend Neil Cahill, S.J., began a four-decade tenure as counselor to the CoBA.[47]

The summer school also benefited from the new facilities, as it shifted its non-science classes to the CoBA and the Alumni Library because both possessed all-building air conditioning. In the meantime, Mother Nature could make summer classes an "unhappy" experience (the temperature hit 105 degrees Fahrenheit on opening day, 1953); yet, enrollment continued to climb, ending the era hovering around one thousand students. In 1951, fearing a Korean War draft, the school offered an eleven-week session "to permit students in the seventeen-to-twenty year-old group to complete the maximum amount of collegiate work before possible summons to military service." In addition, that year Creighton became one of eight sites to host the Summer School of Catholic Action, directed by one of its former presidents, Fr. Thomas Bowdern, which attracted about three hundred people per day from June 18 to 23. The fear-of-the-draft schedule ended the next year with the return to the traditional eight-week session. The summer sessions attracted students from all colleges, but undergraduate pre-meds cramming in a full year of a science classes, teachers gaining certificates or accumulating graduate hours, and nuns seeking teacher certification dominated the student body. In 1957, for example, over 250 sisters from forty motherhouses in fifteen states attended. As late as 1961, an editorialist described the ambience: "The nun's arrival on campus each summer [all still in their habits] transforms the Hilltop into a heterogeneous Motherhouse." The University continued to provide them with dorm rooms, and as it acquired houses for coeds, it began to require lay out-of-town single women students to live in them while they attended the summer school.[48]

Another venue for nontraditional students, and another tool for integration into Omaha, reappeared in 1950 with the formation of a new School of Adult Education, directed by Fr. Austin Miller. "Creighton owes it to the city of Omaha," Fr. Reinert effused. The "revitalized program" offered over thirty classes, two hours per night for eight weeks, costing $10 per class. The program had no entrance requirements and gave no academic credit; it supplemented the traditional classes taught in the evening division. A distinct for-credit plan began in 1951 with an arrangement through the Information and Education division of the Strategic Air Command; air force personnel could take class at Creighton in the evening and Creighton faculty began to offer classes at the Offutt Air Base.[49]

Subsequently, those airmen joined the host of part-time and summer-session students (mostly lay and religious teachers) that sustained the graduate school. In 1951, the prominence of coeds prompted the creation of the Pi chapter of Phi Delta Gamma, a national social sorority for female graduate students and professional women. However, the number of full-time day students studying for a master's degree in education, English, history, one of the natural sciences, or in medical sciences remained few. Most departments maintained their programs by double dipping their services, offering 500-level courses open to undergraduate and graduate students. Expansion of the program proceeded slowly as the CCAS, CoBA, and the health sciences acquired credentialed faculty. In 1951, the M.S. in Medicine program added pediatrics, and in 1953, psychiatry-neurology. In the later year, the school introduced M.A. degrees in pharmacology (in conjunction with the existing discipline of physiology) and in religion. In 1955, it initiated a non-thesis "Plan B," which expanded the areas of study for the "minor" in the program to virtually every discipline in the CCAS. The upsurge in graduate education finally came during the early 1960s as the quantity of fellowships financed through federal and foundation grants and by the University surged. Traditional departments, with an increased staff of Ph.D.s, gained full-time day graduate-student teaching assistants to help teach introductory courses to the proliferating freshmen population. Furthermore, the MBA program, as well as the additional disciplines of biology, economics, and guidance attracted a new cohort of graduate students. With the vast increase in support, between 1961 and 1963, enrollment in the graduate school ballooned from 194 to 365.[50]

Similarly, Dean James A. Doyle and the law school had to struggle through the so-called "happy days." In 1951, Dean Doyle forecasted "gloomy things" for the school "unless more students enrolled." Unfortunately, while tuition doubled from $20 per hour or $200 per semester for ten hours or more in 1950, to $40 per hour or $400 per semester in 1963, enrollment fell by one half from its peak of 199 in 1947. More stringent admission standards abetted the declining numbers, largely associated with the conclusion of the first G.I. Bill, in 1952. The school returned to the three-years-of-college entrance requirement, and in 1961, began to require applicants to include scores on the Law School Admissions Test (LSAT). Minorities and women con-

tributed very few entrants. The law curriculum remained traditional, although in 1951
Dean Doyle proclaimed that the "courses have been carefully revised, studied and
broadened, with emphasis on public law, to adequately equip the law graduate." By
the end of the period, the school shuffled some of the core courses among the three
years of study and added required classes in estate planning, federal income tax, and
appellate procedures. For continuing education, in 1957 the school began the practice of hosting periodic law institutes, which allowed practicing attorneys from the
region to interact with nationally prominent legal experts. Moreover, notwithstanding budgetary woes, in order to maintain accreditation Doyle increased the number
of full-time faculty from six in 1950 to ten in 1960. While the prolific author and
speaker William Sternberg retired after forty years in 1958, the potential for research
at the law school increased as half the new hires possessed the LL.M. degree. Finally,
continued accreditation necessitated constant library improvement. Doyle reduced
expenditures for the materials on English law "in order to expand the American periodical collection." In 1959, the holdings were catalogued and, in a demoralizing contradiction of Jesuit and legal education, the Board of Trustees announced, "Owing
to a rather serious loss of books in the law library, where no effective means of control has been available, a sum of $500 has been expended to prepare a check point."[51]

More in line with Jesuit values, in 1951 the University constructed a new law
school entrance on 26th Street and renovated part of the basement to serve as the
new Omaha Legal Aid Clinic. Creighton donated the space and the furniture, and
the Omaha Bar Association contributed $600 for operating expenses. The venture
aimed to give law seniors "actual practice in dispensing legal advice, and at the same
time help people in the Omaha area who need and cannot afford to consult a lawyer."
All seniors had to participate, but received no class credit; a lottery system determined the order of service and local volunteer attorneys supervised the process. The
clinic accepted criminal cases, but tried to stress civil law. Ironically, considering
Catholic dogma, the first case handled concerned a divorce. In 1960, Dean Doyle and
the faculty recommended, and the Trustees approved, the closing of the clinic. At
that time, they argued that the part-time undertaking proved "inadequate," and that
"most cities as large as Omaha operate a full-time legal aid clinic as part of public
welfare projects."[52]

During the 1950s, the law students also displayed sound Jesuit values and superior
legal skills in some of their activities. "Working with their own funds, they remodeled
one large room on the west side [of the law school] to serve as an attractive, comfortable lounge." The Student Bar Association (SBA, formed in 1949) energized its
cohorts (all law students in good standing) and in 1951 began publishing a weekly,
"Assault and Flattery," to "present all the events, plans and activities." That same year,
it created the Pleiad Club to emphasize the "speaking requirements likely to be
encountered by a lawyer." It also helped establish a library service, whereby lawyers in
small towns in the area could access information from the Creighton Law Library. In
1953, the American Law Student Association named the Creighton Student Bar
Association the "most outstanding" in the United States. An article in the *Student*

Lawyer proclaimed, "Although it had only 84 members, the organization conducted an astonishing number of intra-school, professional, public service, and social activities while actively participating in the regional and national work of the American Law Association." Thus, although enrollment shrunk during the era, exceptional student leaders abounded. The special leadership also manifested in the formation of Phi Alpha Delta (1950), "the only non-restrictive law fraternity as regards racial and religious affiliations of its members." The nondiscrimination values persisted; in 1960, the Creighton chapter of Delta Theta Phi attempted to amend that fraternity's national constitution to eliminate the "White-Christian" membership prerequisite. It failed and disaffiliated, reorganizing as a local group (in 1966, the national voided the race restriction and reactivated the chapter at Creighton).[53]

Analogously, the health-science schools experienced the era's variegated pattern of troubles and triumphs. For instance, enrollment in the pharmacy college went on a roller coaster ride. After the initial decrease in the early 1950s, it climbed in the mid-1950s to over 140. New admission standards cut the total to less than 90 students in 1960, but thereafter it shot up to over 120 by 1963. Coeds (lay and religious) continued to supply between 15 and 20 percent of the cohort, while minorities remained quite scarce. As an undergraduate program (registrants came directly from high school), out-of-town pharmacy freshmen had to live in University housing. For most of the decade, the curriculum remained static, except that juniors and seniors added a pharmacy clinic requirement and gained the right to choose an elective each year. Annually, those upperclassmen made weeklong visits to pharmaceutical manufacturing plants. They also began to reintegrate into national organizations. In 1953, Phi Sigma Chi, a local fraternity, became Phi Chapter of Phi Delta Chi national pharmaceutical fraternity at "formal reactivation ceremonies at the Blackstone Hotel." Moreover, in 1956 the Creighton University Pharmaceutical Association reorganized as a chapter of the American Pharmaceutical Association, with a faculty and student branch, each of which would participate in the annual national meeting.[54]

However, 1957 marked a major shift in pharmacy instruction. In order to maintain an "A" rating, the American Council of Pharmaceutical Education mandated five years of training. The administration rejected proposals for a five-year professional school and the one-year undergrad plus four years pharmacy employed in other states. In 1955, the Board of Trustees approved a plan for two years of liberal arts and three years of pharmacy if the University of Nebraska followed suit (it was discussing the idea and state symmetry seemed logical). The following year, the Trustees changed the name from the College of Pharmacy to the School of Pharmacy to indicate its new "graduate" professional status, which began the next year. Pharmacy classes remained the same, but the School eliminated the liberal arts requirements, which became part of a two-year pre-pharmacy program that prescribed thirty hours in the sciences, math, and English. The embryonic program received a shock when Dean William A. Jarrett, who had held the office for twenty-two years, died on January 26, 1958. Assistant Dean Salvatore J. Greco, Ph.D., assumed the position and oversaw a modification to the program. The precipitous drop in enrollment and the desire to "prepare graduates for certification in the maximum number of states," encouraged the administration to add a one-four option. That is, students could chose to acquire one year of liberal arts classes in the CCAS and then apply for four years of training in the School of Pharmacy. The alternative concerned the state of California especially, because it required four years of pharmacy courses for board examinations. Finally, to facilitate the mandates, the pharmacy school had to employ more full-time faculty. In 1951, the dean was the only professor; there were no associate professors and only one assistant professor holding a B.S. in pharmacy degree. A decade later, the staff included the new dean at the professor level, two associates, and three assistants, all of the latter holding the Ph.D.[55]

The other undergraduate health-science program, nursing, experienced a similar dramatic shift. In 1952, Barbara Edwards became the first black to graduate from, and the following year Lois Turner the first black to teach at, a Creighton hospital unit—both at St. Joseph's. While the three-year hospital-unit training remained popular, professionals intensified their criticism of apprenticeship plans. In 1950, the Board of Trustees, following a recommendation of the JEA, established a committee to study the feasibility of creating a nursing department in University College. Four years later, Fr. President Reinert informed the heads of the hospital units that the University would terminate its affiliations. He explained that the new concept in nursing education had students matriculating in a university and going out to hospitals for clinical work, much like physician education. In 1955, the hospital units became independent diploma schools training RNs. However, the Mercy, St. Catherine's, and St. Joseph's hospital programs, as "associates" not "affiliates," continued to send their students to the CCAS for their humanities and science classes until their termination in the early 1970s. The University did not publicize the new arrangement and at first, as Fr. Reinert informed the Trustees, little changed: "Although the decision is a serious one, it would be well for you to know that, practically speaking, we are doing little more than changing a few titles and names."[56]

In 1955, nursing became a department in the CCAS, ending the problematic situation of multiple schools, multiple faculties, and multiple boards of directors that had presented sticky administrative issues. Actually, it took three years to establish the new curriculum. State nursing regulations presented one problem; existing policies outlined five-year BSN curriculums (three-year hospital diploma plus two additional years for the baccalaureate), which included thirty hours per week clinical and one month of afternoon and evening experience (the traditional on-the-job training). Creighton surveyed twenty nationally accredited schools and presented the data to the Nebraska board, calling for twenty hours per week clinical with no afternoons or evenings. Ultimately, the University and the state compromised on twenty-four hours per week and five weeks of afternoons and evenings. In 1958, Creighton inaugurated its "Basic-Collegiate Program for the degree of Bachelor of Science in Nursing." The course of study consisted of 52 core hours of liberal arts classes, 28 hours of nursing-support (i.e., the social and natural sciences), and 67 hours of nursing (classes and clinical experience), for a total of 147 hours. Full-time students could complete the degree in four years, including two summer sessions. It sought "to produce girls who will be more widely read; able to make better judgments; more adaptable; have more maturity and poise, and as a result be better nurses [i.e., professionals]."[57]

Recruiting credentialed faculty also slowed the development of the nursing department. In 1955, the University hired Dorothy Vossen as chair; she became one of four women on the entire Creighton faculty, and the only female head of a department for the next decade and a half. She received her RN from St. Mary's Hospital in Rochester, Minnesota, her BSN from Marquette, and her M.A. from the University of Minnesota, and she had teaching experience in diploma (hospital) and accredited basic-collegiate programs. Vossen stated that she came to Creighton because new programs allowed innovation and because an article by Fr. Gerald FitzGibbon, "Spiritual Needs of Patients," published in *Nursing World* (April 1955) "attracted her attention." The program began with a small number of nursing classes taught once a year by part-time faculty, many from the other health-science schools of the University. In 1960, the department acquired a second credentialed nurse, Betty Patterson (RN St. Joseph's Hospital, BSN Creighton, and M.A. Catholic University), to teach clinical classes to sophomores. With no graduate nursing programs in the area and without the resources to attract graduates from out of the area, the department had to encourage Creighton BSNs to go elsewhere for an M.A. or MSN and return to teach at their alma mater. With a low student-faculty ratio, especially in clinicals, nursing became the most expensive department in the CCAS, maintained through a subsidy from the College. Fortunately for the program, faculty in other CCAS departments taught over one half of the required hours. The state accredited the program in 1962.[58]

Although the University "changed to a [nursing] department to stimulate interest in the profession," enrollment lagged. About half the first freshman class (fifteen) dropped out by the end of the year. The hospital diplomas remained prevalent, and during the era Mercy sent on average 25 students to the CCAS, St. Catherine's 100, and St. Joseph's 150, annually. The University maintained a "Supplementary Program," the traditional hospital RN plus two collegiate years, so a few of the diploma students continued at Creighton for two-years to complete the BSN. In 1962, the first "Basic" graduating class produced only seven of the fourteen BSNs awarded (others from the "Supplementary"). Students in both the Basic Collegiate and the Supplementary could join the Army Student Nurse Program (1956) at the end of their second or third year, respectively. They would receive private first class pay and allowance and, upon graduation and licensure, would receive a second lieutenant commission and owe service equal to the number of years they received the educational subsidy. In 1963, three Creighton nursing students received their commissions, then granted six months before graduation.[59]

Many faculty members remained confused concerning the nursing programs. While the new department attracted only a small number of students, the cohort did fashion the distinctive elements for the program—its uniform, pin, and "square-crowned cap with a 'CU' emblazoned on its cuff." At first, the faculty resisted a capping ceremony because no other department provided a ritual upon acceptance of a major. The SBG, however, supported the rite, arguing it would provide necessary publicity. The CCAS acquiesced, and in 1961 students planned the formal conventions for the event held at St. John's Church, with a reception for family afterward. Moreover, undergraduate Rosemary Neville helped initiate the creation of a Student Health Center adjacent to the nursing department in the Administration Building, staffed by a part-time physician, subsequently complemented with a full-time nurse. Before 1958, students had to go to the Creighton Clinic on 14th and Davenport streets, or to the emergency room at St. Catherine's or St. Joseph's hospitals at even greater distances. In 1956, Creighton had begun offering students a health-insurance policy, $6.60 per nine-month period, to cover "serious illness or injury requiring hospital treatment or surgery not covered under existing University health services." It also encouraged students to obtain the Salk polio-immunization shots, and chest X-rays from the Omaha-Douglas County mobile van (the contemporary fear was tuberculosis, not lung cancer; cigarette advertisements and promotions in the *Creightonian* and on KOCU remained prominent well into the 1960s).[60]

While the nursing department struggled to find its niche, the future of the dental school remained tentative. Administrative supervision in the dental school during the era broke the pattern of long-serving deans in the health-science schools. In 1950, Dr. James H. Pence, D.D.S., retired Colonel in the Army Dental Corps and subsequent Director of the Division of Oral Hygiene in the North Dakota State Department of Public Health, assumed the position. Four years later, the Board of Trustees voted unanimously to ask for his resignation because of "dissatisfaction" with his administration. A majority of the faculty had resigned or did not renew their contracts. Committed to maintaining the school, the Trustees chose one of its faculty members, Benjamin Lynch, D.D.S, who succeeded in hiring the necessary complement of instructors. An ADA team visited and decided to continue accreditation (repeat visits every spring thereafter until 1960). However, the number of full-time dental faculty remained small; the school continued to rely on part-time instructors to teach in their area of procedural expertise. In 1955, the alumni magazine touted the inception of contributed-service teaching, whereby seventeen dental alums, one alumni lawyer (William Lindsay, who taught a "special course"), and four non-alums served as part-time instructors gratis. That same year, the army called the "youthful" dean to service. Robert Schemel, D.D.S., professor of diagnosis, became acting dean until Lynch's return in 1957. In 1961, Lynch "relinquished the position to devote more time to private practice." Galen Quinn (Creighton D.D.S., 1952) officially served for six months, commuting for periodic visits from Duke University, while John Butkus, D.D.S., handled the daily chores. In February 1962, Raymond Shaddy (Creighton D.D.S., 1953) assumed the position. The dental school ended the era seeking administrative stability and a new facility.[61]

As the Trustees sought macro solutions, the dental students reflected the gender patterns of the times. While the nursing program attracted all women, the dental school consisted almost exclusively of white males—between 1950 and 1963, zero women, two Asians, one Native American, and three African American males grad-uated. However, the religious diversity (30 percent non-Catholic) impelled the Board of Trustees to recommend that admission "policy be clarified, and efforts made to gain more Catholic candidates." The "clarification" did not affect the total enroll-ment, which varied little, averaging 180 students per year, admitted from a strong applicant pool. Its effect on the composition of the classes remains unspecified, since public registrar records do not identify students by religious denomination and the Trustees did not revisit the subject. Regardless of their faith, students not only dealt with the steady boosts in tuition (from $300 per semester in 1950 to $475 in 1962), but with steep price increases for books and instruments (the four-year cost for books rose from $236 to $419; instruments form $1,015 to $1,395). At times, the students proved exceptional; in 1960, the graduates ranked first in the national board exams and the sophomores finished second in their tests (obviously, the dedicated faculty taught well).[62]

During the era, the prescribed dental curriculum followed the established model, with adjustments in hours and/or credit for particular subjects in the year in which they were studied. Obviously, the content of particular classes evolved as individual faculty members kept abreast of advancements in their field and employed them in their teaching. A profound shift in methodology began, in Dean Lynch's terminol-ogy, from the approach of a "mouth mechanic" to the concept of a "physician of the oral cavity." It required, beyond learning the necessary techniques of dentistry, an emphasis on the basic sciences and the medical aspects of the profession. The detec-tion of cancer of the mouth, for example, received increased attention. In 1951, Dr. Lynch, then associate professor of oral surgery, became director of the United States Public Health Service Cancer Teaching Program. That same year, representatives from the medical and the dental schools attended a national meeting concerning the topic, and at Creighton, students met weekly at the "tumor clinic to [study] cancer detection." Subsequently, Dean Lynch expanded the emphasis on medical training through lectures and internships. In 1958, the dental school established an "extern" program at the Douglas County Hospital, whereby seniors, for ten days, lived at the institution to learn hospital (especially emergency room) procedures and study gen-eral medicine and surgery related to the mouth. Then, in 1961, the total credit hours required in the course of study rose dramatically, from 150 to 174. For example, required semester hours for freshmen increased by ten through additions in operative dental materials, prosthetic dental materials, crown and bridge, and operative labora-tory—areas of significant technological advance.[63]

The following year, with a grant from the United States Public Health Service, the dental school inaugurated a program "designed to train senior students in the uti-lization of dental assistants." According to Dr. Shaddy, then program director, com-petition from areas such as engineering spread the "top students more thinly among the professions. Unless graduating dentists can be trained to care for more patients without lowering the quality of their care, Americans may find themselves in a long waiting line for dental services in the future." His analysis highlighted the desire for, and the ability to pay for, dental services, which continued to increase with the baby-boom generation and the general prosperity of the era. Yet many patients continued to use the Creighton Dental Clinic, which by 1948 consumed the entire third floor of the building. The general operative area possessed forty-five chairs, while the prosthetic area had seven chairs and an adjacent laboratory for instruction and the processing of denture work. Crown and bridge maintained a distinct lab, diagnosis and X-ray its own room, and pedodontics and orthodontics a separate area for children. The oral surgery unit was on the second floor and the cancer-detection teaching lab on the first floor. In 1957, after a five-year hiatus due to the faculty shortage, the clinic opened during the summer—forty-eight seniors and twenty-eight juniors participated, handling 1,708 appointments.[64]

The need for new facilities also produced anxiety, not happiness, for the medical school during the 1950s. It began and ended the decade on "confidential probation" (1951–54 and 1959–65). In 1951, Percy Carroll, M.D., retired as dean and Frederick G. Gillick, M.D., former national director of the Bureau of Venereal Disease and former Senior Surgeon of the National Heart Institute, replaced him. In 1959, he stepped down and Richard L. Egan (Creighton M.D., 1940), associate professor of medicine, acquired the position. Before World War II, the deans were part-time administrators with teaching responsibilities; during the 1950s, the full-time deans received aid from an assistant dean, another manifestation of the evolving "big business" nature of modern American education. Budget woes plagued the health-science administrators. In 1951, the deans of the dental and medical schools "stressed the financial problem." For the medical school, it translated into exploding overhead; between 1945 and 1955, the annual cost of operating the medical school climbed from $178,000 to $641,277. Student tuition, which escalated from $400 per semester in 1950 to $575 in 1962, covered only about one third of the expense. In 1959, the Board of Trustees anguished over the lack of funds to wire the old buildings for closed circuit television, acknowledging that the dental and medical schools remained "behind other schools in use of this new medium." Besides aging, barely adequate facilities, the medical school struggled to augment the number of full-time faculty and remained dependent on loyal part-time adjuncts. The administration debated but rejected the idea of closing some or all of the professional schools. The supporters argued that the thirty-seven existing dental schools and seventy medical schools could not "supply the demand" for health practitioners and that the elimination of any professional school would "diminish the registration of pre-professional students" in the CCAS. Moreover, the advocates claimed that professional-school graduates provided the "most important contribution" the University made to the Omaha area. A 1960 survey showed that "73 percent of the dentist, 58 percent of the registered pharmacists, 47 percent of the certified public accountants and 45 percent each of the lawyers and physicians" in the area graduated from a Creighton professional school. Thus, professional education, especially in the health sciences, continued to assert its historic pre-eminence at the University.[65]

While the low number of full-time faculty worried accrediting boards, the

National Foundation for Infantile Paralysis gave its stamp of approval in 1954, award-ing the medical school a five-year, $114,436 grant "to start a program for teaching the 'team' concept of polio rehabilitation." Harold N. Nue, M.D., director of the depart-ment of medicine and director of the Creighton Polio Rehabilitation Center at St. Joseph's Hospital (one of ten in the United States), would instruct medical students in rehabilitation techniques in classes in pediatrics, psychiatry, neurology, and oto-laryngology. Following the distribution of the Salk vaccine in 1955, the number of new cases of polio plummeted, but the Center continued to receive grants devoted to the care of the "most severely involved patients," with 85 percent of those treated dur-ing the 1950s "paralyzed in all extremities." Moreover, in 1957, the Nebraska Heart Association established the first research professorship in the state (at the time, the sixth such chair in the United States) at Creighton. The holder, Alfred W. Brody, M.D., professor of medicine, conducted research on the mechanics of breathing. Yet another scourge of the 1950s, the Cold War, generated another grant that affected the medical curriculum. Creighton became one of forty-five schools contracted for Med-ical Education for National Defense (MEND), which sought to train medical per-sonnel for mass emergencies, "especially a nuclear attack."[66]

The grants that provided revenue to pay faculty salaries stimulated a vigorous debate concerning their practicality—what happened when a grant ceased? was the University liable to maintain the position? Father President Reinert settled the ques-tion in the affirmative; he also affirmed the University's commitment to maintain the medical school. Fortuitously, the decisions coincided with the federal government's perception of a physician shortage, resulting in a policy to help establish new medical schools and to preserve existing ones. Thus, federal and private grants (Kellogg Foundation five-year, $486,765 award for faculty development) provided the funds to enlarge the full-time faculty from twenty-three in 1958 to seventy-seven in 1965. Research grants followed a similar tract—in 1954, they totaled $72,000 and in 1964, $629,000. The support included the largest grant in medical school history, $534,000 to Robert P. Heaney, M.D., and his coresearcher, Thomas Skillman, M.D., to study bone metabolism. The increased assistance contributed to the resuscitation of the medical school in terms of the number of full-time faculty and the amount of research they performed.[67]

The accreditation problems of the era did not affect the enrollment, which remained relatively stable (309 in 1954, and 292 in 1963). A new admission guideline in 1953, however, temporarily diminished the number (a low of 270 in 1959); it stated that while three years of undergraduate work remained the standard, the School would give preference to those with a bachelor's degree. Moreover, the Reverend Regent Harry B. Cummins, S.J., announced another preference, this one in favor of applicants from west of the Missouri River, because Idaho, Montana, Wyoming, Nevada, New Mexico, and Arizona had no medical schools, and North Dakota and South Dakota only had a two-year pre-clinical program. Yet another preference resulted from "sev-eral objections heard by the President by outside contacts" about the number of non-Catholics in the dental and medical schools. Analysis of the medical student body, however, revealed that it was "almost entirely Catholic, with an up-trend in proportion in each succeeding freshman class." Father President Reinert also aired concerns heard about the proportion of CCAS students admitted to the dental and medical schools. In 1951, the admissions board reported that it was "careful to accept every student from Creighton College whose record made him qualify for admission." The author of the account not only used the "him" in the accepted literary fashion of the time, but as a relatively accurate descriptive pronoun. The medical graduating class of 1950 included seven women; thereafter the number decreased dramatically, with the classes of 1960 through 1963 each including only one female physician. Finally, the cohort of medical students rarely included a non-white. The low percentage of African-American population in the region and the lack of targeted programs and scholarships kept their enrollment miniscule in all schools of the University. However, highlighting the University's historic policy of nondiscrimination, the Eta Chapter of the medical fraternity Phi Rho Sigma accepted a black pledge in 1952.[68]

The curriculum for medical students underwent a significant restructuring at the end of the 1950s. The required classes essentially remained the same, but were rearranged. The first two years stressed the basic sciences, with year one constituting those related to "normal human biology" (e.g., physiology) and the second year emphasizing "abnormal human biology" (e.g., pathology). The third and fourth years became "the clinical years," whereby the students learned "by participating with the physician in the care of the sick." In addition, the junior and senior years included an elective course of study to allow the student "to engage in a learning experience in depth within one of the departments [a basic science or a clinical discipline] of the medical school." During the era, the vast majority of the graduates went into general practice; in 1962 Creighton tied for second in the nation in terms of the number of graduates entering general practice. Regardless of the nature of the graduate's practice, the 1950s witnessed the establishment of additional training before it could begin. Boards regulating practice in the various medical fields began demanding residency programs to gain proficiency. In 1957, to help Creighton graduates meet the new standard, the medical school established the "Door Opener" program. Following the suggestion of J. R. Sullivan, M.D. (Creighton, 1932), medical alumni in forty cities across the country volunteered to act as liaisons for graduates seeking residencies in institutions in their area.[69]

Ultimately, the era ended on a "happy" note for the medical school, as it began to alleviate its remaining full-accreditation obstacle, modern facilities. In 1955, the Board of Trustees established a committee "to institute discussion and planning relevant to renovation or relocation of the School of Medicine, and the means to implement it." While it cautioned the members not to publicize the project, it also engaged an architect willing "to risk drawing tentative plans without assurance of reimbursement." The University began purchasing property in downtown Omaha in the neighborhood of the medical school in anticipation of building a new complex. As part of the overall plan, and responding to the national trend toward unified health-sciences libraries, it obtained the former Warner Brothers Pictures Distributing Corporation

Building at 1401 Davenport Street. The structure provided four times the storage space for the 27,000 volumes of the formerly separate medical and pharmacy libraries, as well as twice the study space. The one-story edifice required little renovation, was well-lighted and air-conditioned, and included separate rooms for periodicals and rare books, as well as four offices and seven fireproof storage vaults.[70]

Elatedly, in 1961, the Lay Board of Regents announced receipt of a $4 million gift from Mrs. Mabel Criss, in honor of her physician husband (Clair C. Criss, Creighton M.D., 1912, founder of the United Benefit Life and the Mutual of Omaha insurance companies), to fund a new medical complex. By that time, proposed plans for I-480 construction included the elimination of the medical and pharmacy schools on Davenport Street. The administration rejected a proposal from the chancellor of the Nebraska system to construct the new research building close to the University of Nebraska Medical Center to enable sharing basic facilities. Instead, the University decided to eliminate the remaining north stands of the stadium and the playing field, and to build the new medical complex on campus. In addition to the Criss donation, the medical school received a $617,000 matching grant from the National Institutes of Health, allowing the groundbreaking to occur in 1962. The 37,370-square-foot, six-story research building opened in August 1963; with eighty-six labs, the facility tripled the previous research area. The Criss grant, "by far the largest ever made" to the University, exceeded "the original three-million-dollar endowment made by the Creightons." To honor the contribution, the Jesuits name Mabel Criss a "foundress" of Creighton University and of the Wisconsin Province (over the next seventeen years, she contributed to virtually every building in the health-science complex; her ground-breaking shovel came to hold six medallions).[71]

The rapidly expanding campus exacerbated parking and safety problems. In 1952, the administration created a faculty committee on student life; its initial achievement consisted of standardizing and publishing parking regulations. Subsequently, while the streets in the vicinity remained first-come, first-served (with the city enforcing timed-parking rules), on February 23, 1956, the University parking sticker appeared. The following fall, because automobiles in the student lots "resemble the loose pieces in a well-organized jigsaw puzzle—scattered, unable to fit, troublesome," the University hired its first "campus uniformed policeman" to enforce parking policies. Students in all schools of the main campus had to purchase a sticker to park in a University lot; violations cost $1 per offense, $2 if not paid by the first Monday following the infraction, $4 by the second Monday, and "possible" suspension from classes by the third Monday. The first year, 862 students obtained decals, but the four student lots accommodated only 246 vehicles (127 spaces in the one faculty lot, where 144 were needed). Thus, in 1959, in an attempt to alleviate the problem by limiting the number of cars, the University required freshmen in dormitories to petition for the right to have a vehicle on campus (which did not include the "unique privilege" of a parking slot), and in 1961 it extended the regulation to include sophomores. The new dorms promoted a more cohesive student life, but produced other unintended consequences. The concentration of cars and people increased theft and safety concerns, and by 1963 the administration acquired the services of the Burns Detective Agency to patrol the campus by car and on foot.[72]

Other areas of student life evolved with campus expansion, as well as manifesting the nostalgic theme of "happy days." For example, freshmen beanies reappeared. Initiated and implemented by the sophomore class, offenders paid a 25-cent fine, which went into the Student Union building fund. However, by 1956 the "beanies until Christmas rule" disappeared because upperclassmen did not enforce it, particularly since men could not wear them indoors and rarely donned them when returning outdoors. Contemporary Church and military conventions required women to cover their heads during Mass and allowed them to wear hats indoors, but forbade noncleric men to wear hats inside churches and public buildings. Sporadic attempts by the SBG to revive the beanie as a "morale booster" during the 1960s failed for lack of "direct supervision." Also in step with tradition, the annual Mother's Day celebration metamorphosed into Parent's Weekend, though the festivities continued to climax with the crowning of the statue of Our Lady. Moreover, students continued to participate in the various writing and language contests sponsored by the University and/or the Wisconsin Province, but the dramatically increasing size of the CCAS made it difficult to promote the discipline-based events (more students in a greater variety of classes, with a more numerous faculty, the events lost their all-class, all-school nature). In 1956, only five Creighton students participated in a four-province (Chicago, Missouri, Ohio, Wisconsin) Latin contest; subsequently, elimination of the Latin requirement doomed this event. A new form of winning distinction, the Pace-Setters (subsequently "Who's Who at CU"), began in 1954; over the years, various forms of committees composed of students, faculty and administrators selected twenty-four juniors and seniors who had made a significant contribution to the University (ballyhooed in the *Creightonian* and pictured annually in the *Bluejay*). Moreover, two Rhodes Scholars, Donald Bruckner (1955) and David Lutzer (1963), set a distinguished pace for the University, as did the September 29, 1963, College Bowl team. Unfortunately, the squad (Rosemary Quinn, Morris Pongratz, James Guss, and Terry Tilford, all from the CCAS) lost the quiz competition to Fairfield, but argued, "Our team as a group felt confident that we knew more than the opponents, but we seemed to freeze on television."[73]

Ironically, during the era Creighton maintained its reputation as a pioneer in television, promoted its communications program, and received kudos for its public television and radio agenda. In 1951, *Higher Education,* the semi-monthly of the United States Office of Education, commended the University for having presented on television "some of the best science programs of the nation." In 1959, thanks to gifts of Videcon equipment by Leo Pieper, who had attended the law school, Creighton resumed "experimentation in the closed circuit system," including noncredit history and English classes broadcast by direct cable to a TV monitor in the student center. Similarly, in 1955 the University received the George Washington medal awarded by Freedoms Foundation at Valley Forge, Pennsylvania, for "an outstanding achievement in helping bring about a better understanding of the American Way of Life." The honor recognized a series of history-related radio programs written by Robert Reilly, director of public relations, and in conjunction with the Omaha Junior League, broadcast over stations KOIL and WOW. Moreover, the campus station, KOCU, which used student "musicians, vocalists, actresses, actors and announcers in Hut 3," produced weekday programs of recorded music, news, religious themes, and student talent. In 1957, for the fourth consecutive year, the station won a College Radio Corporation award in the category of best newscast (University of North Dakota, 1st; Creighton, 2nd; St. Lawrence, 3rd; University of Minnesota, 4th; MIT, 5th).[74]

The *Creightonian* also continued to thrive, but musical groups virtually ceased to exist (except for the ROTC band), creative-writing opportunities languished, and the theatrical troupe ended the era in search of a new venue. After a brief post–World War II hiatus, coeds again began to garner editor positions on the student newspaper, and in 1954 the first African-American reporter joined the staff (pictured, but not identified in the yearbook). In 1956, under the leadership of managing editor Carleen Hess and faculty advisor David Haberman, the Associated College Press awarded the paper all-American status. The variety and amount of coverage of world events during the era depended upon the inclination of the editors, but generally, an assortment of anticommunist editorials and Cold War stories appeared, as did a "society page" that featured pictures and articles pertaining to the engagements and weddings of coeds and alumna. Between 1950 and 1956, at the beginning of the spring semester the weekly printed a multipage supplement of student short stories, essays, and poems, dubbed the Annual Literary Edition. The insert lapsed, and in 1959 the SBG unsuccessfully began appropriating money to create a new literary magazine, the *Phoenix*. Various financial and editorial problems prevented it from rising, but in 1963, after a lapse of twenty-two years, the administration approved the rebirth of *Shadows* as a semiannual publication sponsored by the SBG and under the direction of Pi Delta Epsilon, the national journalism society (CCAS senior Jeanette Wortman, editor). While the literary tradition experienced a renaissance, the theater program ended the era in a decades-long search for an adequate home. With the loss of the Auditorium to the library project, one of the huts served as the "Portmanteau Playhouse" until the aptly named "Little Theater" opened in the basement of the Eppley Building. Similarly, in 1959, when the Brandeis Theater closed, Edward F. Pettis, member of the Lay Board of Regents and secretary-treasurer of J. L. Brandeis & Sons Co., donated $10,000 worth of movie-projection equipment, including lens for wide projection and "cinemascope." The administration set it up in the moot court room of the law school "to await the day when the University is able to build a new auditorium."[75]

Religious activities also evolved during the "happy days" era. All students of the University had to attend the Mass of the Holy Ghost, but because of the increased enrollment, by 1959 it was celebrated simultaneously at St. John's Church and at the Cathedral. Similarly, the President's Convocation (mandatory student attendance), held in the afternoon of the same day, moved from the gymnasium to the Music Hall of the Omaha Civic Auditorium. Furthermore, all Catholic students had to attend one morning Mass per week and had to make an annual retreat, which, starting in 1950, occurred on numerous weekends during the fall semester to provide "a more effective" small-group experience. Undergraduate coeds and non-Catholics (men and women) each attended retreats scheduled for them in particular; in 1959, while the administration promised to attempt "to make it more attractive," non-Catholics were "invited," not "required" to attend their retreat. A large number of students continued to belong to the gender-specific sodalities, while the all-University Sodality Union included coed representatives. The sodalities continued to perform significant service projects with ongoing annual commitments, as well as responding to special needs. In 1956, for example, the Creighton sodalities established a drive to support the American Red Cross Relief Fund to aid refugees from the Hungarian revolt against their Soviet overlords.[76]

A disaster in the Midwest had prompted a similar outpouring of concern from the Creighton community starting on Easter Sunday 1952. To battle what proved to be the last major flood in the Omaha area (the dam system of the Missouri River Basin Project subsequently eliminated the periodic inundations), the University appealed over the radio for students to return early from the holiday and suspended classes for the four following days. Over one thousand students and faculty "reported *en masse* for levee duty," including Fr. Linn, who drove a truck, and the Reverend Raymond Strange, S.J., physics teacher at Creighton Prep and amateur radio aficionado, who established a ham-radio network to provide vital communication. The SBG postponed the prom to allow students to fill sandbags in two eight-hour shifts per day. Medical and pharmacy students sandbagged around their complex, fearing the primary dike might give way. Nursing students provided infant care for the destitute at the Salvation Army and the Creighton Gymnasium became a Red Cross "evacuation center," with the basketball floor outfitted with two hundred cots for victims in need of shelter. In a moment of humor amidst the strenuous effort, one worker mused that the Red Cross "must not have much confidence" that the levees are going to hold, "They're giving swimming lessons" at the Creighton pool. Actually, the dike held and Omaha suffered minimal flood damage.[77]

Creighton students did not wait for disasters to demonstrate ongoing commitment to service. In 1952, Creighton inaugurated a chapter of Gamma Pi Epsilon, the women's Jesuit honorary founded at Marquette in 1925. Thereafter, each spring semester members would recommend candidates to the dean of women, who would make appointments with the approval of the president, of outstanding coeds, based on grades, loyalty, and service. Alpha Sigma Nu, the Jesuit men's honorary, also emphasized service to the University and to the community. Of note, it hosted an annual public lecture—in 1962, it enticed former president Harry Truman to give an address at the Joslyn Memorial lecture hall, and Creighton used the occasion to award him a Doctor of Laws, *honoris causa*. Paradoxically, a decade earlier the Young Republicans, with members from six Creighton schools, had organized as the first post–World War II political club, in part to campaign to put Dwight Eisenhower in the White House (surprisingly, given the institution's Irish-Catholic heritage, the

Young Democrats did not organize until 1955). To celebrate one of Ike's legacies, in 1959 the Hui O'Hawaii club sponsored a party to celebrate statehood that included imported hula dancers.[78]

The non-honorary Greek-letter organizations also maintained annual service projects. However, their supplemental social nature remained problematic during the period. Before the Great Depression, "social" Greek-lettered groups emerged at Creighton and the professional fraternities and sororities acted as social, not honorary, organizations. In 1950, among the groups, University publications listed Kappa Beta Gamma and Pi Lambda Sigma as "national social" sororities, and Pi Lambda Phi as a national and Phi Sigma Chi as a local social fraternity. The following year, Alpha Phi Omega, a national service fraternity "open to all college and university men who are or have been affiliated with the Boy Scouts of America," organized as the first undergraduate interracial fraternity on campus. It had two undergraduate black members in 1954, but became all white because of the few minority students enrolled during the era, although historically the Greek system at the University had included students of Asian descent. During the 1950s, the number of sororities increased to four (all "national social"), but none had an African-American member. In 1956, the Creighton Chi chapter of Theta Phi Alpha won the sororities national President's Cup for "service to its school, quality of membership and contribution to the national group." Then, social in nature, in 1957 the Pan-Hellenic Council announced it would adopt the fraternal royalty tradition by selecting a "Ulysses" for its annual ball. Incongruously, in 1963 the Inter-Fraternity Council (IFC) eliminated its Helen of Troy competition, not for feminist reasons, but because the professional fraternities no longer wanted to attend the annual ball and assessing them for the event became unrealistic. Without the gala, the IFC no longer had a social function; it decided to become "a disciplinary group which will work with the fraternities in solving their difficulties."[79]

Curiously, given the variety and nature of the Greek-letter activity, in 1958 the committee on student life ignored a request to create a social fraternity specifically in the CCAS. That same year, unaware of the pre–World War II precedent and presumably bolstered by the historic Catholic argument against American-style undergraduate fraternities, Fr. President Reinert took the opportunity of his induction as an honorary member of Alpha Kappa Psi, "professional business fraternity" (established 1955), to speak out against "purely social" Greek organizations. He claimed they were "really nothing more than a dignified excuse for giving in to the gregarious tendencies of the adolescent" and they did not contribute to achieving "maturity" while in college. On the other hand, he felt that professional frats and sororities had proven "conducive to higher academic standards" and that he considered the undergraduate social sororities "service groups because of their contributions to university life." Following Fr. Reinert's remarks, in a cosmopolitan, "professional," gesture, Alpha Kappa Psi elected CCAS junior Jean Abraham its first "sweetie." Moreover, the following semester the University placed three "professional medical fraternities" on "social probation." The distinction between professional, service, and social Greek-letter organizations at Creighton seemed blurred. By 1960, all fifteen frats and sororities "rushed" and then accepted pledges, held numerous social events, and undertook service projects, but only two maintained houses.[80]

Besides the Greek system, the ROTC continued to provide a distinctive aura to the campus. All undergraduate males participated in two years of Basic ROTC and, because of skyrocketing enrollments, the Creighton unit, following a slight dip at the end of the Korean hostilities, posted record numbers, reaching seven hundred in 1963. As the increase made its impact, in 1956, in order to allow more cadet officers "to gain practical experience in commanding and performing staff duties," the army reorganized the cohort into a regiment consisting of two battalions of two companies each (in 1958, it dropped the battalion and regiment terminology, and arranged the four companies as a "battle group"). The unit brought honor to Creighton by sponsoring the annual convention of Phalanx at the Fontenelle Hotel in downtown Omaha in 1951; the delegates adopted a revised constitution written by three Creighton cadets and voted to move the national headquarters to the University.[81]

Moreover, in 1950 the ROTC officers organized the first band since before World War II. It played at basketball games and most other University events. Non-ROTC students could join the group and all the musicians received class credit for participation. In 1955 two commerce freshmen, Rosemary McCaffrey and Betty Murray, made the ensemble of fifty-five, coed. Additionally, in 1952 the ROTC formed a drill team to give public performances, and two years later created the "Jayettes" coed drill team, with eleven members from the CCAS, commerce, and pharmacy schools. The group, with CCAS junior Roberta Kane as president and CCAS sophomore Grace Schoofs as commander, wore white and blue uniforms, marched in Homecoming parades, and in conjunction with Phalanx, undertook service projects.[82]

Despite the contributions, the compulsory nature of the ROTC prompted a negative editorial in the *Creightonian* as early as 1955, and others followed intermittently thereafter. Yet, emblematic of the period, in the early 1960s "the windowless part of the student center's lower level and the basements of Gallagher Hall, the Eppley Building and the library" received supplies and equipment to serve as Civil Defense fallout shelters. Then protests against mandatory ROTC at the universities of California and Wisconsin reverberated across the Creighton campus. Thus, as the Cold War turned exceedingly frosty, with the Berlin and Cuba crises, the military presence in academe became more challenging. In order to maintain its strength, the army refined its program. In 1958 it started allowing post-graduate deferments for academic study (in 1962, it limited them to law and medicine). Then, in a direct reaction to the anti-ROTC groundswell on campuses, in 1960 it began to change the curriculum. It responded to the criticism that ROTC classes lacked academic content by allowing the substitution of up to forty-five hours of college courses in lieu of military instruction. It also increased the monthly pay, as well as the compensation for attending summer camp. Subsequently, the Vietnam War intensified the debate dramatically.[83]

While the ROTC touched the lives of virtually every male undergraduate, student governance finally expanded to encompass all enrolled at Creighton. Activities by and for the coeds displayed the contemporary combination of the "feminine mystique" and feminism. On one hand, the Administration encouraged a conventional sense of unity by hosting an annual Women's Tea. All the women of the University, in semiformal dress, assembled on a Sunday afternoon shortly after the start of classes in the fall for a program, style show, and refreshments designed "to give the new girls an opportunity to get acquainted with the deans, faculty and women students at Creighton." Similarly, the Faculty Wives and Women's Club, and the wives clubs of the various professional schools, promoted another traditional sense of unity in support of their distinct position as wives and in their aid to their husbands and their particular schools. In 1951, on the other hand, women of all the schools came together to form the Coed Club to foster unity in the promotion gender issues. That year, coeds gained suffrage, voting for the first time for class officers in the arts and commerce colleges. No women sought office in the commerce college and the CCAS produced only three female candidates for twenty-four positions (six officers per class). Yet the coeds cast 23 percent of the ballots ("light turnout" but "Coeds Out in Force") and helped elect the first women's arts college class officers—Terri Aldera and Nancy Fogarty, secretary-treasurer for the seniors and the juniors, respectively. Throughout most of the 1950s, the undergraduate students offered "party slates" of candidates; for example, in 1958, the Alfred E. Newman (poster boy for the popular *MAD Magazine*) slate, with the slogan, "What! Me Worry?" swept the freshman class-officer election. On a more serious note, in 1960 the CCAS class officers created the arts council to promote unity in the College and elected senior Dick Harvey president. In class governance during the era, despite their increasing proportion of the electorate and their stronger participation at the polls, the coeds produced few candidates and fewer officers.[84]

However, in April 1951, Fr. President Reinert announced at the pre-prom dinner "next year would see women represented on the board of governors [SBG] for the first time." He suggested that representatives from the law, dental, and medical schools "should always be men," because women in those schools "never constitute more than a small minority." He also argued that nurses should receive no representatives since they enrolled in affiliated hospital units, but that women in the CCAS, commerce and pharmacy schools should vote and gain election. Within a week of his remarks, with "significant input" from the administration, the necessary two thirds of those present and voting at the SBG annual meeting accepted five constitutional amendments, which included coed suffrage and the right to hold office for the women in the pharmacy, commerce, and arts colleges. The traditional argument that the Student Union existed as a corporation for males succumbed to the democratic proposition that women paid tuition, supported organizations, and demonstrated "school spirit" at events and athletic contests. Three women sought office the first year, but none survived the May 1951 primary in their particular school. Subsequently, in October 1954, the president of the Coed Club gained appointment to fill a position opened by resignation, and in 1956 women in the law, medical, and dental schools became eligible to hold office. By that time, nursing students also participated as a department in the CCAS, but only arts coeds Roberta Eckerman (1961) and Jean Markhofer (1963) won spots on the SBG.[85]

In 1961, a coed complained in a letter to the editor of the student newspaper that women could not gain election to the SBG because, despite being 29 percent of the student body, women did not vote as a bloc. Several attempts to amend the union constitution to provide for female representatives had failed. In a related effort to give women a voice, the SBG and the committee on student life jointly sponsored the Coed Caucus. Proposed to ameliorate the fears of coeds "unwilling to appear singly before the board to present their suggestions or grievances," it presented a means of group participation. About eighty coeds attended the first meeting; however, a second did not occur because Fr. Reinert found it "divisive" (should a Non-Catholic Caucus meet?). He understood the reasoning, but argued that coed "representation in student government should be accomplished in some other way than through mass meetings." The era ended with two significant "firsts" in union history—in 1962, John Clay Smith became the first African American elected as a representative, and in 1963, SBG president Mike McGill appointed the first coed officer, Mary K. Green, recording secretary.[86]

While very few served on the SBG, as in the past, women continued to provide the union with its most contentious issue—voting regulations for princesses and queens (Homecoming and prom). At virtually every annual meeting the representatives tussled with the subject, and on several occasions tinkered with the system to establish guaranteed candidates from each school, preferential primaries, proportional and weighted voting, and other features to try to instill fairness while establishing an all-University spirit. The number of queens proliferated during the 1950s, as a host of male organizations and fraternities elected female standard-bearers. Moreover, the popularity of public beauty pageants during the era led the Trustees to include a statement in the *Student Handbook*: "In keeping with its views on the dignity of the human person, Creighton University declares its women students ineligible to participate in public skill or beauty contests, in which they are required to appear or be photographed in a bathing suit or inappropriate attire." By the time it appeared in print in 1959, the Trustees had employed the criteria for a decade and had denied permission to participate about forty times.[87]

Besides voting procedures for royalty, the SBG frequently discussed alcohol regulations. In 1951, the administration presented the SBG "a dictum" of no alcoholic beverages at Creighton dances. Students of the legal drinking age (mostly, undergrad seniors and professional students over the age of twenty-one) chaffed at the rule and at the reputed "arbitrary" penalties imposed on organizations "after liquor discoveries," which "destroyed the feeling of brotherhood and sociability in the group itself." That SBG lament probably referred to the medical fraternities put on "social probation" in 1959, but the administration justified the action in terms of protecting underage students, especially women, who gained invitation to the events. That year, the SBG also engaged the administration by banning corsages at the prom, proclaiming,

"Most Creighton males resent the social mores which require flowers for their date when attending a formal event," when the money could be used to rent a tuxedo, elevating the "formalness" of the occasion. The social chairman of the event, however, revealed a different agenda—if you eliminated the cost of flowers, you could charge more for the tickets, providing enough money to hire big-name bands (the SBG had hired the Tommy Dorsey Band at a cost of $1,500).[88]

While trying to out maneuver the administration, the SBG also responded to several other issues created by the era. In 1959, for example, with television quiz-show and college-sports cheating scandals providing national headlines, twenty-one campus organizations published a proclamation on the front page of the *Creightonian* (above the fold), stating that although only "a limited minority" of Creighton students cheated, the signatories asked each student to do their part to eliminate the problem. Furthermore, the explosion in undergraduate enrollment distorted the Student Union representation scheme. By 1963, the 2,078 students in the CCAS had four representatives (one per 519), while the 116 law students elected two representatives (one per 58). A two-pronged apathy, however, prevented correction; barely over one third of the CCAS students voted in elections and the SBG annual meeting began having trouble encouraging fifty students to attend, so decisions on revisions could not ensue for lack of a quorum. Ostensibly, only the Greek-letter groups could muster enough support to produce the needed quorums, on occasion, to defeat amendments presented by "independents" to limit the number of representatives from fraternities (apparently, sororities did not organize bloc votes to elect their members, but frats organized their nonfeminist "sisters" to vote for their candidates). Significantly, the SBG did energize the creation of the Student Leadership Conference (SLC) to meet annually in conjunction with the Greater Creighton Committee established by the administration to improve its development efforts. SBG delegates joined representatives elected by other campus organizations to discuss all issues related to the University and to submit recommendations. The administration evaluated scores of proposals, publicly reported their evaluation of the suggestions, implemented many of them (e.g., establish a lecture series; give lay faculty a voice in rank and tenure decisions) and rejected others (e.g., make individuals not organizations responsible for alcohol violations; allow students to wear Bermuda shorts on campus).[89]

Finally, in the minds of many administrators and students, athletics provided a vital element of student life. However, supporters of intercollegiate athletics began and ended the decade with efforts to promote spirit and interest. In 1951, cheerleader Pierre Keitges and class president Donald Goodwin, both CCAS freshmen, made "concerted efforts to organize a better school spirit for the remaining seven [basketball] games of the season." They distributed papers in the dorms and in freshmen English classes, asking students to pledge cooperation, and hoping to receive sufficient backing to form a pep club. Why did not upperclassmen lead that effort? In part, because of the transition from the G.I. Bill-dominated late 1940s, but also because of the historic tradition of minimal student support, especially without football. That same year, the SBG revived the Homecoming parade, consisting of "enough floats to extend 20 full blocks," producing a spectacle "memorable for both its newness and its spirit." The Homecoming parade flourished during the 1950s because the fraternities, sororities, and other clubs, consisting of the organized activists among the students, gave it wholehearted support. On the other hand, they could not produce a large group of rambunctious fans. In 1952, the newly organized "PEP club" attracted only sixty members and men (possibly because of stereotypic gender roles of the era) began to avoid cheerleading; between 1958 and 1963, no males participated with the Creighton cheer squad (temporarily renamed the "yell-belles").[90]

Moreover, upon assuming the presidency of the University, Fr. Reinert immediately dashed the hopes of the football fans, categorizing its revival "out of the question." The desire lingered, but in 1956 a committee of the Greater Creighton Convocation "unanimously recommended" against its restoration, advising that "it was more practical to employ one major intercollegiate sports program, namely basketball, and back it all the way." In December 1958, in another attempt to "spark a fading ember of enthusiasm for college athletics," the all-University intramural football team, Irma's Knights, coached by food-service worker Irma Trumbauer, coalesced as a "new sports service fraternity," Iota Kappa Epsilon. Illuminating the confusion of the era, the IKEs promised that its "service aspect is definitely not being used to conceal a social function," and that its members would "assist the athletic department in maintaining the track, promoting sports events, and performing other services." Then, in 1960 the decade ended with the SLC presenting to the administration a set of proposals "to increase students' interest in athletics" (better half-time entertainment), and the reorganization of the Creighton University Honorary Letterman's Association (CUHLA), a "service" group dedicated to building interest and spirit in athletics (selling improved programs at basketball games).[91]

Obviously, the budget woes and the priority of the building campaign of the era inhibited building the level of spirit desired by sports enthusiasts. The University could not afford to reinstitute football and the few athletic scholarships went exclusively to basketball players. In 1962, from "University General Current Funds," twenty-two athletes received $7,367 in aid, an average of $335 per student (in comparison, 163 received academic scholarships worth $14,305 or $90 per student). Therefore, the "minor sports" of golf, tennis, track, and swimming limped along with "walk-ons," intermittently fielding a team for a year or two, and playing few contests (e.g., in 1953, the tennis and golf teams each played five matches). Only the ROTC-sponsored rifle team established consistency, and in 1954 hosted the prestigious 34th annual William Randolph Hearst Club championships in the gymnasium. That year it failed to place, but in 1958 members garnered first and third in trophy matches, and the following year the team shot its way to its third consecutive Inter-City League championship. In comparison, track and swimming began in 1957, but by 1961 the track team had been "swallowed up in the muck of new construction" (demolition of the stadium) and "the swimming team went down for the last time." Their demise served as an unwelcome epitaph to athletic director Duce Belford, who died that year from chronic heart disease at age fifty-nine. He had been "Mr. Everything," from athlete to coach to athletic director (since 1952) to originator of the idea of an athletic hall of fame, and "probably made more friends in the athletic world for his university (BCS, 1925) during his lifetime than any other individual in the history of the Hilltop."[92]

In 1950, Belford had helped reestablish baseball as a sanctioned sport, which scheduled two games each against five opponents (5–4, with one rainout). In 1952, the club joined the Midwestern League of the National Association of Intercollegiate Athletics (NAIA), which included Dana, Concordia, Midland, and Nebraska Wesleyan colleges. It added nonconference opponents such as Omaha University to build up to a fifteen-game season and established a winning tradition (yet, in 1957, a rally in the stadium had "more basketball players and coaches than students"). The mid-decade teams enjoyed the play of outfielder-pitcher Bob Gibson, future National Baseball Hall of Fame inductee and actually recruited to play basketball, the first black athlete of the modern era at Creighton. In 1958, Bill Fitch (future college and professional basketball head coach) guided the team to a league championship and a trip to the NAIA tournament (1-2, for fourth place). Thereafter, Fitch left and frequent coaching changes ensued, as well as losing seasons.[93]

Basketball, the only "major" sport at the University, contradicted the "happy days" theme by opening the era with six losing seasons in a row—two for Duce Belford and all three during Sebastian "Subby" Salerno's tenure. Salerno had garnered "four cage letters, served as co-captain of the all-freshman team in 1945," and captained the 1948–49 varsity team his senior year. After graduation, he remained at his alma mater to coach baseball before moving to the head spot in basketball compiling a 30–45 career record from 1952 through 1955 (the former year, Fr. Reinert instituted the annual priests' dinner and game, denoting that "we are mindful of the important part the clergy of this area play in providing students for Creighton"). Theron "Tommy" Thomsen followed. The first coach allowed to issue athletic scholarships (tuition, books, room, and board), he opened his four-year stint with an 11-12 record, which included winning the "consolation round in the NAIA Tip-Off Tournament," an inaugural event at the new Omaha Civic Auditorium. He rebounded with two winning campaigns in the next three seasons (overall, 49-39). During most of the decade, although no longer a member, Creighton followed the MVC standard that allowed freshmen to play varsity (1951–58). The University maintained a "B" team, which did well, but fans complained that both teams played mediocre competition. In 1950, in Albany, New York, a group of eastern teams had announced the formation of the National Catholic Intercollegiate Association, which included the midwestern schools Loras College of Dubuque, Iowa, and Creighton University. However, the conference had no discernible impact on the University's basketball program, except that the 1962-63 team came in third in its only visit to the National Catholic Invitation Tournament. That trip, however, demonstrated a "return to 'big-time' basketball" initiated by John J. "Red" McManus, who became head coach in 1959. He succeeded in scheduling "tough" opponents (Creighton no longer "regarded as a small school with even a smaller basketball team"). He guided the 1961–62 (21–5 overall, powered by rebounding wizard Paul Silas) and 1963–64 (22–7 overall) teams to the NCAA Tournament, winning two games and one game, respectively. With the improved schedule and the resumption of the winning tradition, the team began to play all its home games at the Civic Auditorium in 1961; it provided a larger venue and bolstered the University's integration into Omaha.[94]

Intramural sports also suffered through a dispirited decade. In 1951, the *Creightonian* described a program "falling to pieces" because of interference from "a lot of non-athletic things and indifference on the part of the students." Although five independent and twelve fraternity teams registered for the touch football league, frequent postponements and forfeitures disrupted the schedule. In basketball, teams from the professional schools suffered disqualification on occasion for violating the rule that excluded players who had lettered as undergrads (an attempt to level the court for CCAS and CoBA teams). In 1953, the *Bluejay* sports editor claimed intramurals "attained a position of prominence and interest" with "practically the entire student body" participating. Yet three years later, student sports columnist Chuck Maxwell complained, "Everybody knows that the interest in intramural athletics at Creighton is anything but spirited." The Reverend Norbert Lemke, S.J., who replaced Fr. Shyne (1938–54) as "faculty moderator of athletics," met with Maxwell and three other interested students, subsequently appointing them to head a Student Board of Intramural Athletics (one representative from each school and one from the *Creightonian*). The following year, the yearbook editor effused about "the best intramural program ever," but in 1960 the *Creightonian* labeled it "appalling to think that the university spends money each year for an intramural football program and that a large share of this money is wasted," because half the teams forfeited each week. Maintaining vigorous student volunteer leadership remained problematic. In 1962, the new faculty moderator of athletics, the Reverend Bernard Hasbrouck, S.J., hired recent graduate and basketball standout Herb Millard as supervisor of intramurals. The "sport" of pushball (soft, air-filled, six-foot in diameter) gave the new overseers a rude awakening to their posts:

> So furiously fought was the annual pushball game that the officials halted hostilities and called it a draw. But not before one referee was trampled and had to be carried unconscious from the field. Tempers flared at the outset when the two teams bombarded each other with water balloons and eggs. With the preliminaries done with, the freshmen and sophomores settled down to earnest brutality. All in all, the 12th annual pushball game was a real dilly—even if there was little ball pushing.[95]

Father Shyne, and then Fr. Hasbrouck, also inherited the struggle to provide recreation for the coeds. In 1950, women became eligible to take two gym classes, modern dance and swimming (seven and forty-one registered, respectively). The following year, however, the coed rifle team disbanded because "little interest was shown by the girls." For the same reason, the University budgeted no money for women's intramurals. In 1956, the Greater Creighton Committee recommended that because "women accounted for 28 percent of the student body, physical education for women

Father Carl Reinert poses with ROTC cadets in 1953. During the Korean War, most college students were able to escape the draft, provided that they attended classes and received adequate grades.

This aerial view of Creighton from 1956 shows the University situated in a largely residential neighborhood. The area underwent massive change when many of the houses to the north and west were demolished for the construction of the interstates in 1965.

Creighton Bluejays

Creighton Hall of Famer Paul Silas (front row, center) poses with the rest of the 1962 Blue Jay basketball team. That year, Silas had thirty-eight rebounds in one game alone. He went on to play and coach in the NBA.

Father Linn:

The Wise President

As president, Father Linn met all of the presidential contendors in 1968. He presented the then unannounced candidate Richard Nixon a plaque in December, 1967.

Philip M. Klutznick, JD'30, is a Director of Creighton University. He is chairman of the board of the Urban Investment and Development Co., Chicago.

By Philip M. Klutznick

I was already an alumnus when I first met Father Linn. We had common concern with at least two causes: Creighton, to which we had recently come and to which I owed my loyalty as an alumnus; and a genuine commitment to the concept of brotherhood. It was this latter interest that brought us together in a day long in advance of ecumenism and the late Pope John XXIII. I vividly recall that Father Linn played his role as a Catholic with Protestants and Jews in an era of brotherhood pioneering. By one of those strange oddities of human experience one of the last visits I had with the late president of Creighton was a great dinner held in his and Father Carl M. Reinert's honor in Omaha on May 25, 1969 and given by the National Conference of Christians and Jews.

I recall that at the dinner I quoted words from Alan Paton's eulogy of the Negro leader Chief Albert Luthali: "If you win in life you are a successful man. If you lose, you are an unsuccessful man, but if you go on whether you win or lose then you have something more than success or failure — you keep your own soul." Indeed Father Linn was a man who kept his own soul—this was his great success.

Father Linn presents a plaque commemorating a Creighton visit to Presidential candidate Richard Nixon in December 1967.

Creighton makes an unlikely shot in a 1967 game against the University of Houston.

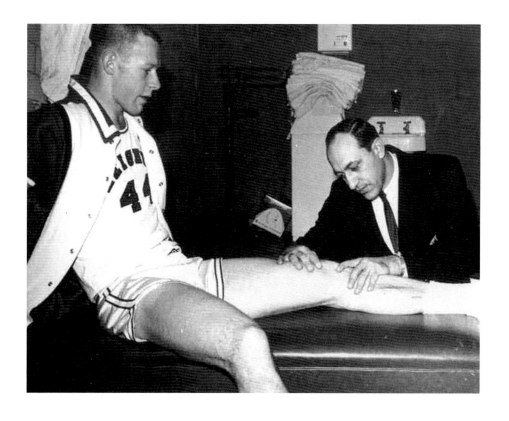

A player receives care from one of the basketball team's athletic trainers in 1968.

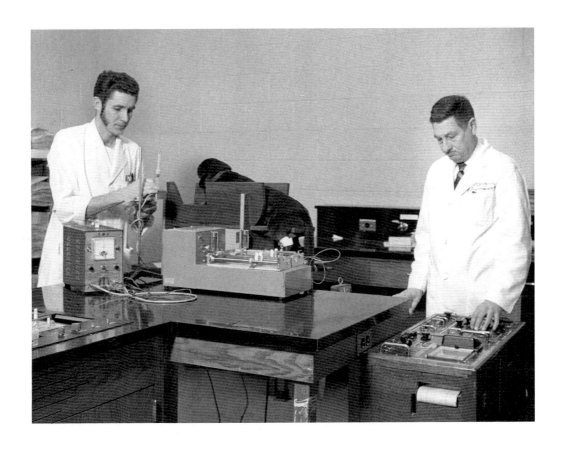

Members of the student body and faculty conduct experiments in the Criss Laboratory in 1970. The facility opened in 1963 and was dedicated to Dr. Clair C. Criss, founder of the United Benefit Life and the Mutual of Omaha insurance companies.

open dorms

A student urges others to let it known what they want.

Students felt the only reason the open dorm proposal did not pass was because outside pressures would hurt the Centennial fund drive.

Freshmen Kim Ferris, Bonnie Pancrazio and Ramona Hobart bundle up for the concert.

It was a very cold night for an outdoor rock concert, but the students still came. The combos played in the Quadrangle until 4 a.m.

One protestor encourages others to make their voices heard during a 1970 demonstration in favor of instituting an open dorm policy. Many students accused the administration of not passing their open dorm proposal because of fears that the new policy would hurt the Centennial fundraising campaign.

Member of the YAF, Jewel Lapesade and John Scully, explain their views against the protest.

Surrounded by flags and marchers, Tim Richter shows his disapproval of American involvement in Laos.

Marchers proceed from the campus to the Federal Building for a formal protest of U.S. activity in Southeast Asia.

Like many other college campuses in the 1960s and early 70s, Creighton witnessed its share of rallies and demonstrations. Here Tim Richter carries a flag of peace to protest against American military involvement in Laos. He and other demonstrators marched from the Creighton campus to the Federal Building in 1971.

"Her story" was told to Creighton men and women by journalist Gloria Steinem and attorney Florence Kennedy.

Student reporter Mary Arouni and Student Board representative Ann Hild greet Miss Kennedy as she arrives in Omaha.

Waiting for the press conference to begin, Misses Steinem and Kennedy look over the day's schedule.

Prominent radical feminists Gloria Steinem and Florence Kennedy discuss issues of gender and racial equality at the 1971 Student Leadership Conference.

Creighton welcomes the new Billy the Blue Jay mascot.

Top: Construction crews lift the new spire onto St. John's Church in 1976.

Bottom: St. John's Church and the Administration Building overlook the rest of campus.

St. John's Church serves as the spiritual center of Creighton University.

Creighton promotes community growth

By Katrina Moerles

"Creighton University came to be at the request of the Omaha community, and that relationship is just as vivid and bright today as it was in the very beginning," said the Rev. Matthew E. Creighton, S.J., president of Creighton University.

Fr. Creighton said the community has functions in, and duties to, the community, while the community is involved likewise with Creighton.

"We all chip in to solve problems and that's what a community should be about," Fr. Creighton said.

Creighton University was founded as a private institution of higher learning in 1878 by pioneer brothers John and Edward Creighton and their wives Sarah Emily and Mary Lucretia.

In the past 100 years the university has graduated 29,303 men and women. The city of Omaha is home for 3,829 Creighton alumni, and an additional 3,000 Creighton alumni live in the surrounding metropolitan area.

Leadership Provided

Creighton provides leadership in a host of professions, supplying Omaha with a large percentage of graduates who are community leaders, according to the Rev. Carl M. Reinert, S.J., vice president for university relations.

The university has educated 50 percent of

Interstate-75 divides the Medical Center from the main campus as the Woodmen Tower rises in the distance from the Omaha downtown in 1979.

Rev. Michael Morrison, S.J., Creighton University President from 1981 until 2000

Rev. John P. Schlegel, S.J., Creighton University President from 2000 through the present

should be provided." However, as late as spring 1959 an attempt to establish a coed sports club failed for lack of support. The few who attended the meeting complained that "girls can get credit for gym without ever donning a gym suit." They could simply sign in and go to the student center because they had a male coach who was "too busy to bother with them." The following fall, women's intramurals finally began with the formation of the Women's Recreation Association, CCAS senior Patricia Baxter president. It gained exclusive use of the "main gym" and the pool on Tuesdays for two hours in the evening and Thursdays for two hours midday. It organized basketball and volleyball competitions, bowling at nearby lanes, archery, and in the spring a softball league (dorm and sorority teams). Besides open swimming, it provided instruction in "water ballet." In 1962, "a mermaid in the freshman class," Judy Jackson, organized a synchronized swimming team. The administration, however, "stipulated that coeds could not present an exhibition clad only in bathing suits before a mixed audience in Creighton's pool." Somehow, the "coed swimming team was awarded two trophies at the Amateur Athletic Union synchronized swimming meet in Columbus, Nebraska." The group tried using 1920s style suits, but could not swim routines in them and thus disbanded. Subsequently, Fr. Hasbrouck coached a successful group of "naiads" (young daughters of faculty) for about three decades, even after a stroke in 1969 paralyzed his left side and confined him to a wheelchair.[96]

Thus, by the end of the "happy days" era, women (and the few African-American students that attended at the time) had integrated into the University, which in turn had integrated into Omaha. Although progress proceeded unevenly, the dynamic duo of Frs. Reinert and Linn transformed the Lay Board of Regents into an effective promoter of University development. Successful fundraising drives, sizeable personal and foundation gifts, and federal grants and loans gave Creighton the wherewithal to build dorms, a student center, a library, a College of Business Administration, a medical research facility, and to provide scholarships and loans to its students. The faculty and the administrative bureaucracy expanded to provide instruction and a myriad of services to a record number of undergraduates. With a new campus in place, in 1962, for unspecified reasons, the Reverend Provincial John J. Foley, S.J., former member of Creighton's Board of Trustees and former rector at Creighton Prep, declined to extend Fr. Reinert's tenure. On March 6, 1962, Fr. Reinert "explained the Jesuit system of tenure and the reasons for the change" to the lay board, and he and Fr. Linn exchanged administrative positions. Simultaneously, "a subdivision of responsibility" occurred. The Reverend Albert C. Zuercher, S.J., brother of the former Creighton president, became "religious superior" of the Creighton Jesuit community, serving "directly under" Fr. President Lynn. Father Reinert became head of the newly formed Creighton University Development Foundation and the reorganized team quickly announced a fifteen-year, $45 million expansion program. Lay Regent A. F. Jacobson presented the plan, which entailed "the biggest program of civic building in Omaha's 100-year history." Based on recent success, the administration looked forward to smooth sailing; neither it nor the United States envisioned the turmoil of the approaching Vietnam War generation.[97]

CHAPTER 10

The Era of Confrontation, 1969–79

In terms of historical eras, the so-called sixties stretched beyond the decade to include the early 1970s. The anomaly in terminology occurred because of the duration of the Vietnam War, which became the vital center of the political debate. While the law of continuity governed the lives of most individuals during the period, for some facets of history, "revolution" seemingly replaced the slow pace of evolution as a myriad of "movements" demanded instantaneous transformations. Historians continue to ponder which events serve as bookends for the period and the short chronological perspective clouds their ability to interpret the nature of the "radical" changes that ensued. While the long-term effects of the changes attributed to the sixties remain debatable, the nature and the intensity of the activism of the era provided it with a distinctive historical aura. At Creighton University, the "era of confrontation" began in 1964 with the escalation of American involvement in Vietnam, and closed in 1973 with its withdrawal virtually complete. In between, the antiwar movement, the youth movement, the women's movement, and the civil rights crusade deeply affected the campus. While the administration continued to address issues derived from the 1950s—to maintain its building program, to develop a modern managerial bureaucracy, to enhance its professional schools, to integrate laymen into the Jesuit system—it did so in a cacophonous milieu of faculty and student demands for changes in curriculum, governance, and the protocol for manners and morals.

Father Linn's elevation to the presidency of the University came as "a real shock to him." The "cigar chomping dynamo," who "hated strife of any sort," worried that having to succeed one of the University's "most dynamic and popular leaders" might have a negative effect on the development program. Thus, "his ascension to the presidency was ringed with doubts—his own and those of others. It was not the unequivocal joyous occasion that he deserved." Essentially, the transition proceeded smoothly, buttressed by the retention of the services of Fr. Reinert, who remained on the Board of Trustees and the Lay Board of Regents, and continued to contribute his immense skills in fundraising as the head of the Creighton University Development Foundation. In addition, Rosemary Reeves, who had become Fr. Linn's secretary in 1950, continued to ensure efficient staff support (she retired in 1986, having served five presidents). Yet Fr. Linn could not avoid strife as the confrontational student movement arose and engulfed him. The stress of the situation may have contributed to his ill health in 1968, and ultimately, his death on November 1, 1969, at age sixty-five. While Fr. Reinert acquired renown as "the Builder," the inscription on Fr. Linn's funeral program described his role and provided his lasting sobriquet; "Blessed are the Peacemakers."[1]

Father Linn assumed a relatively sovereign presidency, the beneficiary of a lengthy struggle to revise the constitution of the Jesuit Education Association. In 1958, the presidents of the Jesuit colleges and universities in the United States met for the first time as a conference within the organization. Most symbolized "the new president" of the 1950s, "academically trained, financially oriented, politically sophisticated and sensitive to the importance of public relations," especially in relation to obtaining federal grants. In 1964, the revised JEA constitution gave the presidents the freedom of action they desired. It became a "watershed in the history of Jesuit higher education in the United States" as the presidents obtained "the tacit permission of the provincials to expand their colleges and universities with very little reference to 'higher superiors.'" Father Reinert promoted the transformation; Fr. Linn participated in the culmination and acquired the autonomy. With provincials no longer in control of the institutions, the JEA (administered by a board composed of provincials) became superfluous. In 1970, it disbanded; in its place arose the Association of Jesuit Colleges and Universities (AJCU), with a board of directors composed of the presidents, which elected its officers.[2]

Moreover, Fr. Linn's presidency coincided with the Second Ecumenical Vatican Council (1962–65), which emphasized collaboration with the laity, and with the Thirty-first Congregation of the Society of Jesus that elected the Very Reverend Peter J. Arrupe, S.J., as Superior-General, in May 1965. That congregation also gave sanction to the inclusion of laymen on the boards of directors of its institutions of higher learning. The American doctrine of separation of church and state had spawned numerous court cases attempting to block state and federal grants to parochial schools at every level of education. In 1966, in response to a successful suit in Maryland that blocked state aid to three church-affiliated schools (two Catholic and one Protestant; the United States Supreme Court refused to hear an appeal), the Creighton Trustees began to discuss the inclusion of laymen on their board. Saint Louis University initiated the process, and in May 1967 the Reverend Richard Harrington, S.J., and Fr. Robert Shanahan met with its administrators to scrutinize the new governance system. At a joint meeting of the Creighton Board of Trustees and the House Consultors, Frs. Harrington and Shanahan stressed the importance that the remainder of the Jesuit Community "understand thoroughly the nature and purpose of these changes and therefore, a thorough internal public relations job remains to be done."[3]

The Jesuits serving as Trustees and Consultors recognized "that some of our men, unless they are thoroughly acquainted with the implications, might feel insecure in a situation that relegates the Community to a kind of service organization for the University." The group appointed a committee to establish "guidelines and principles for identifying and separating University-Community assets and liabilities." Father Linn's suggestion that a committee from the Lay Board of Regents help devise a plan for a new mixed lay-Jesuit board of directors met with "universal hesitation," as the

Trustees and Consultors argued that the Community should devise the "preliminary drafts" to present to the Lay Regents. Nine months later, on February 3, 1968, for two and one-half hours, the Trustees and Consultors discussed the draft proposals. Then, on April 17, Fr. Linn presented the plan to the Lay Board of Regents. It called for an enlarged board consisting of thirteen laymen and eight Jesuits, which "would assume the obligations of policy making[,] with the Jesuit community forming a separate corporation." It included new articles of incorporation, but since "Creighton has operated for nearly ninety years as a Catholic institution with Christian traditions and philosophy, the new by-laws and board structure would in no way alter its basic tenets." It guaranteed that "the president of the University would always be a Jesuit" and that two of the Jesuits on the proposed board could come from other communities. Father Linn outlined "some of the reasons" for the transformation:

> The University has become so large and complicated that five Jesuits can no longer be expert in the many areas of responsibility.
> The University needs a policy making body independent of the managerial and capable of evaluating the managerial function.
> The University needs outside help and it's the trend in private education.
> There will be less chance for loss of prospective federal and state grants with laymen on the board.
> There is no plan for any basic changes in the University but we will have the added expertise to further strengthen the institution.[4]

The existing Board of Trustees unanimously accepted the new Articles of Incorporation, which deleted "The" from Creighton University's name, and elected the new directors under the slightly revised by-laws. Ten of the twenty-five sitting Lay Regents (three years earlier, it had enlarged its membership by seven, including five from outside Omaha, who were required to attend at least one meeting per year) became directors. The new board, with an altered Internal Revenue Service (IRS) 501(C)3 status (educational not religious institution, which lessened the legal problems associated with obtaining federal grants), elected A. F. Jacobson, president of the Northwestern Bell Telephone Company, chairman. The board established four working committees: academic, business and finance, development and community relations, and student affairs, as well as an executive committee composed of the president, the chairman, two lay and two Jesuit directors. In 1972, Jacobson agreed to serve another term, but asked for the assistance of a vice chairman; the board created the position and elected Leo A. Daly, Sr. The following year, however, Daly and Peter Kiewit resigned their directorships to adhere to a new federal regulation forbidding "the direct participation in government-sponsored building projects of architects and contractors who also hold positions on the participating institution's Board of Directors." Moreover, now that the University and the Jesuit Community stood as separate corporations, Fr. General Arrupe separated the formerly united positions of leadership, rector-president, appointing Fr. Robert Shanahan rector (January 1969). Father Shanahan assumed the functions of the recently created "religious superior," but now, as the head of the Jesuit Corporation, he reported to the provincial, not to Fr. President Linn (who reported to the Board of Directors, which controlled the University).[5]

The board inherited an adjusted long-range development plan announced in 1962. The administration realized that the University still lacked "the large number of affluent alumni" possessed by the "elite" schools and that alumni giving had dropped the last three years in succession (probably a result of the outpouring in behalf of the library). However, responsive alumni giving primed the pump of corporate and foundation donations. Therefore, Creighton undertook "a series of pilot personal solicitation programs in Omaha and several other key cities having concentrations of alumni" to supplement the "national mail appeal." Subsequently, it hired the Cosgriff Organization, Inc., to organize and manage an all-encompassing fund drive. The initial phase of the revised fifteen-year development program kicked off in January 1963, with James B. Moore, vice president of administration at Northwestern Bell, as general chairman, Leo Daly, Sr., in charge of "primary gifts," and Richard W. Walker, head of the Byron Reed Company, leading the "major gifts" segment. A "resurgence" in bequests buoyed the opening stage, with the announcement of fifty-one gifts totaling in excess of $1 million and at least another $2 million "written into wills wherein Creighton is the primary beneficiary." In 1966, to hone the process, the administration partitioned the development office into two positions—director for annual resources and director for special resources. The following year, the former reported a "rapid growth of [the] annual appeal" due to "personal solicitation, personalized mail appeals and a more thorough information program." Moreover, the graduating seniors Pioneer Pledge program had more than doubled in four years, from $18,000 to $47,707.[6]

In 1969, the directors authorized another contract with the Cosgriff company to organize a new $75 million campaign dubbed Centennial Thrust (reconfigured from the fifteen-year New Goals plan). They approved adjusted campus boundaries that stretched westward to 30th Street and emphasized that the "Preliminary Gifts Phase" had to proceed on a "quiet personal basis" because any projection that included "land not currently owned would cause prices to skyrocket." The eight-year "thrust," which sought equal thirds from government, from loans, and from "all other sources," went public at the beginning of 1970. Three years later, Leo Daly, Sr., then a board consultant, chaired a committee (that included personnel from his firm) that spent ten-months evaluating the operation of the Creighton Development Foundation. He reported (absent monetary data) that the development program, "though it has not progressed along the exact line predicted, due to the changing nature of resources, is sound." However, to succeed in the future, it had to "redefine and clarify" objectives, "agree on a sound academic blueprint," and "establish realistic priorities." The University community had to complete those tasks "with due haste, since no real planning for the 'Centennial Thrust' Phase II effort in the fall of 1974 could move forward without it."[7]

Beyond fundraising, board members and their companies provided other valuable services. In 1971, for example, experts for Northwestern Bell contributed service to study the University's personnel procedures and made suggestions, including the need for "specific job descriptions." The rapid growth of administrative positions, with the necessary support staff, had created some confusion. In 1966, for example, the Trustees had created a Vice President of Student Personnel to replace the dean of student affairs; he had jurisdiction over the placement director, who became a University employee for the first time, but not religious affairs, which became the bailiwick the director of spirituality. That same year, Fr. Treasurer Murphy died and Fr. President Linn wanted Walter Jahn to replace him. However, laymen could not serve as Trustees (Jesuits); therefore, the Reverend David Meier, S.J., became treasurer and Jahn received the new title of vice president of financial affairs. The following year, Fr. William Kelly, who had left Creighton to serve as president of Marquette University (1962–65), returned to become an aide to Fr. Linn, acting as "liaison for government programs and federal grants." By then, student health services had added a staff psychologist, although undergraduates frequently and mistakenly associated psychological help with the Counseling Center, which was "designed to help in career choice and planning" (although, by 1974, the latter did metamorphose into what students had assumed by the name, employing four "licensed counseling psychologists"). In addition, in 1967, Theodore J. Kalamaja, chief engineer for the Omaha building division of the Peter Kiewit Company, a licensed architect with forty-one years experience in the construction business, became the "first fulltime director of campus planning." Thus, systematic reorganization of administrative offices became necessary and routine.[8]

Kalamaja assumed the position amidst the ongoing building boom and the welcomed disruption caused by the construction of I-480 and the North Freeway. In 1963, the University purchased a duplex that then gave it ownership of all the properties on both sides of 25th Street, California to Cass streets. Since 25th Street would dead end against I-480, the administration convinced the city to vacate it; then, along that right of way, it "crammed" a new ten-story dorm between Dowling and Wareham halls. The maneuver allowed the University to provide residence during the period of construction. A $300,000 gift from the Swanson family (originator of the frozen TV dinner) provided the collateral for a $3.4 million federal loan, as well as a name for the facility, which housed 704 men. The first two levels of Swanson Hall connected to the Brandeis Student Center addition, and the below-ground floor afforded space for the bookstore (in 1957, it had abandoned the retrieval system to operate like a modern grocery store, with self-serve shelves and cashier check-out stations).[9]

In 1965, as dignitaries laid the cornerstone for Swanson Hall, they also ceremoniously broke ground for a twin structure for women. Interstate preparation work south and west of campus led to the closing of 26th Street and, with property purchases, provided the site for the mirror-image dorm. The previous year, to house the increasing number of coeds, while awaiting completion of the structure, the University rented rooms for over one hundred female sophomores at the Commodore Hotel at 24th and Dodge streets. Creighton reserved the entire second floor, engineering the elevator to bypass it, and provided two housemothers and a separate entrance.

Then, in the fall 1965, as men vacated Deglman and occupied Swanson, women began to inhabit the former. With the men accommodated, the administration razed Dowling and most of Wareham, preserving the latter's west wing to contain faculty offices and KOCU. A $350,000 grant from the Kiewit Foundation in honor of Anna Kiewit, the mother of the company's president, Peter, secured a second $3.4 million federal loan to finance construction of the ten-story dorm, which became home to 506 women. Construction of Kiewit Hall included a two-story dining wing that attached to Gallagher Hall. The Charles and Winifred Becker Hall resulted from a donation of "10% of the cost of this facility including furnishings, a gift which will amount to no less than $80,000.00." In 1967, the University failed to obtain a third federal loan for yet another dorm, and due to "poor construction and bad condition of the building," it rejected an offer to acquire the Palms Apartments. That same year, it also abandoned a plan to provided individual phones in dorm rooms, because of the increased cost that would become part of the dorm fees that already stood "in the top category of schools our size." The following year, the administration alleviated some of the housing pressure by acquiring a five-year lease on Matthews Hall from Duchesne Academy, which had just abandoned its college status. Ninety men from four fraternities (one per floor) resided in the building until 1970, when a fire produced extensive damage. By that time, it held only fifty-seven students, who then partially filled the one hundred vacancies in Swanson. The number of freshmen and fraternity membership both had tumbled; thus, the University sought to sub-lease the structure for the remaining three-year obligation.[10]

While work on the dorms proceeded, the need for a science building mounted. According to Fr. Reinert, "Our physics department had hit the rock bottom of inadequacy. We could not recruit faculty. In varying degrees this was true of chemistry, mathematics and biology." As early 1960, the Trustees had relished the "very firm possibility" of a large forthcoming gift that would allow significant savings with the conjoined construction of the Eppley Building and a science facility. The donation failed to materialize and biology continued to meet in the dental school, chemistry in the wooden building with attached huts, and physics in the Administration Building. In 1966, a change in regulations allowed federal grants and loans to secure 75 percent of the total cost of a building. Three "downtown Omaha banks" agreed to loan "$1 million based on outstanding New Goals Pledges," and groundbreaking for a new science building occurred on May 29. The $3.4 million complex attached westward to the Eppley Building and united the natural sciences in one facility; after a "fight," it also included space for psychology (historically in theology, recently in the education department, it had to "prove" it was a science). With new equipment for all departments, it also provided desperately need classroom and research space; the biology labs "put teeth in the honors degree program" started four years earlier through a grant from the National Science Foundation. Then, when "the undergraduate Science Department heads and their faculties" deadlocked in the choice of a name for the structure, the Board of Directors broke the stalemate, choosing to honor Fr. William F. Rigge.[11]

The construction of I-480 eliminated north-south intersecting streets and the North Freeway terminated California as a through street just west of campus. To enable that construction, in 1966, the University sold the old commerce college (at the time, serving as the Student Activities Building, a workplace for *Shadows* and other groups) and Agnew Hall to the State of Nebraska, which razed them. The sale included a 100-car parking lot (plus students lost about 250 on-street spots). Simultaneously, the University acquired and demolished the only remaining house west of the dental school on 27th Street. It then constructed a private, half-circle, Periphery Road (on the south, old Cass Street, 24th to 27th; on the west, old 27th Street, Cass to Burt). Adjacent to the north-south arc, on the west edge of the campus, it built new student parking lots to hold 500 cars. Moreover, the I-480 and North Freeway construction eliminated thirty-four blocks of housing from St. John's Parish, reducing its grade school to a mere ninety students. While a few voices argued it could remain viable and do a great service by busing underprivileged children to the facility (the civil rights movement in full swing), the Archdiocese closed it and transferred the properties to the University. The convent that housed the teaching nuns became Smith Hall, home to the thirty-four-member English department; the St. John's Grade School became Bergan Hall, occupied by the education department and the staff of the ever-increasing office of University Relations.[12]

Except for 24th Street, I-480 truncated the north-south streets between 20th and 30th streets, and the North Freeway created a barrier just beyond the western edge of the campus. Thus, in 1965, the University energetically supported another unsuccessful urban-renewal referendum that held the promise of redevelopment east of 24th Street. Despite its defeat, with the new topographical situation, the University began purchasing additional property to the east, and the following year, students received another parking lot at 23rd and Webster streets. Then, in 1969, the board's development committee expanded the zone of property acquisition to include the area 20th Street to the North Freeway, I-480 to Cuming, "except the Cuming Street commercial frontage that is not available at a fair market price." By that time, the "era of confrontation" had dawned and students complained about the impact Creighton's expansion had, uprooting poor people from their low-rent neighborhood. Their objections may have helped cajole the administration into appointing a "relocation officer" to work with the displaced in finding affordable housing.[13]

The building program responded to a desire for enhanced quality, as well as a need to replace outdated facilities and to keep pace with the burgeoning undergraduate enrollment. The CCAS led the way, increasing from almost 1,700 full-time students in 1964 to almost 2,200 in 1968 (having become a majority of the University's total enrollment at mid-decade). At the time, a cooperative agreement to "better utilize facilities and faculties" by allowing Omaha University, Duchesne, and the College of Saint Mary students to take classes at Creighton, and vice versa, failed as Omaha University joined the University of Nebraska system and Duchesne abandoned the collegiate level. On the other hand, the Oblates of Mary Immaculate contributed to the record registration as the Order established a program whereby it would send about fifty juniors and seniors to study while they contemplated the decision to take vows. In 1968, they occupied the College Terrace Apartments on the southeast corner of 23rd and California streets, purchased dorm board plans, and participated in extracurricular activities. In 1971, they moved to Creighton Hall at 2104 Davenport Street, a well-appointed three-story apartment house built and subsidized through a bequest from John A. Creighton, which had served as a low-rent home for working girls. By that time, single women moving to Omaha to find employment no longer wanted to live under strict supervision; revenue from the twenty-two occupants (built to house ninety-five) did not cover the cost of operation. Therefore, its board of trustees transferred the endowment and the property to the University.[14]

In addition, in 1968, coeds became a majority by one in the arts college (supported by the transfers due to the closing of Duchesne College) and African Americans made their presence felt. While the number of undergraduate minorities increased significantly, it remained a single-digit percentage, and until 1974 only one or two graduated annually from the entire University (at the time, the registrar categorized students by gender, not by religion or race, thus the lack of specific data). A subsequently a retreat followed the record; beginning in 1969, CCAS enrollment declined annually, bottoming out at approximately 1,700 in 1973. Cuts in the federal student-loan program, coupled with increasing tuition, a drop in the number of transfers (due especially to the one-time spike from Duchesne), fewer Oblates, and a "national trend toward decreasing college enrollment," especially the "dropping private school enrollments around the country," all contributed to the downturn. Yet, the vast majority of the sharp decline in the arts college resulted from an administrative reorganization. In 1972, the department of nursing became a separate college.[15]

In 1966, the University had separated the positions of director of admissions and the registrar. Three years later, at the onset of the undergraduate enrollment decline, the administration provided an "emergency expenditure" of $30,000 to add personnel and to increase advertising for the recruitment program. Then, in 1970 admissions director Howard Bachman initiated a summer freshman preregistration procedure (by mail) and, the following year, the "student admissions assistants" program, whereby scores of undergrads could earn the minimum wage enticing their high-school contemporaries to matriculate. The downward spiral spawned another concern. In 1973, the Reverend John Cuddigan, S.J., surveyed CCAS and CoBA drop outs (well above the national average), but found "no clear cut and simple pattern," although he did highlight one major problem—disillusioned pre-med students, especially with the termination of the draft, who saw no reason to change programs and remain in school. Since the dropout rate affected the number of upperclassmen, and thus the budget in terms of the number of advanced classes offered and the faculty to teach them, "retention" entered the Administration's vocabulary. To compete with the growing community college and technical-school movements in attracting and retaining freshmen, Creighton instituted a "new, more personal advising system" and began to offer "skills courses" (e.g., reading, writing, math) for those who needed them.[16]

The operating budget reflected the enrollment roller coaster. Servicing and maintaining the many new structures, as well as financing the additional faculty and staff (virtually all of whom were laymen) to provide the instruction and new services to the mushrooming student body, presented budgetary distress. In April 1964, the budget for the coming fiscal year, projected at $6.8 million, represented a doubling of the figure in a mere five years. In 1966, once again Northwestern Bell personnel assisted in the "compilation, evaluation and presentation" of a five-year plan, which foresaw "the accrued deficit of more than $1 million by 1971." Fortunately, at the end of 1967, Vice President of Finance (VPF) Jahn "reported that the financial picture isn't bright but that the University should end the fiscal year about $20,000.00 in the black" due to increased enrollment plus higher tuition. While the annual operating budget skyrocketed to $14.9 million for 1969–70, then to $23 million for 1974–75 (onset of the energy crisis the previous year, with the creation of an all-University energy conservation committee), annual deficits managed to remain well below the projection, partially offset by rapidly escalating tuition. For full-time undergraduates, it doubled to $775 between 1964 and 1969, and increased another 40 percent by 1974. Equally portentous, in 1949–50, tuition had supplied 49 percent of the revenue for the University; by 1974–75, it had risen to 64 percent.[17]

The financial-aid program helped students contend with the rising costs of a collegiate education. In 1964, the Economic Opportunity Act included the work-study program, whereby the federal government subsidized the part-time employment of undergraduates at their institution of higher learning. In the 1965–66 academic year, the University provided over $1 million in financial aid—scholarships, grants, tuition remissions, loans, and work-study jobs (a ten-fold increase since 1957–58). By that time, Creighton had become "one of the twelve leading universities in processing student loans." In order to generate more money for the University's program, "thanks to" Leroy Galles, Creighton became "the first school to sell guaranteed student loans to Sallie [*sic*] Mae [Student Loan Marketing Association] at no discount." During the 1960s, it continued "to be the association's busiest customer, having sold six portfolios amounting to $5.3 million." Once again, demonstrating the significance of Creighton's integration into Omaha and of the new lay board, John Becker, partner in the accounting and consulting firm Peat, Marwick, Mitchell & Company, convinced downtown banks to advance the University "the annual amount of funds" needed to finance the student-loan programs "on an intermediate basis" until it could sell the loans. In 1966, the size and complexity of the financial aids resulted in a consolidation of the various programs into a single office.[18]

The following year, Fr. President Linn initiated the long, exhausting process of trying to acquire state aid. Representatives of Nebraska's private colleges met in the office of Leo Daly, Sr., to plan the organization of a commission that would lobby for a tuition-grant program (at the time, seventeen states provided students with grants that could apply toward tuition at state or private institutions). The effort failed to convince the state legislators, while in 1970 Richard Nixon's administration slashed federal funding for student aid (it "accounted for 89 percent of the total student loan program" at Creighton). The board "discussed certain problems" associated with "adequate funding" of undergrad scholarships and voted to add $30,000 for partial-assistant scholarships for the "top students in our primary feeder high schools in the Midwest region." The struggle for funds persisted; by 1973, "nearly 80 percent of the University's full-time enrollment took advantage of one or more of the financial-assistance plans available." That proportion gave the board pause: "Questions were raised as to whether we may be giving too much assistance if in fact we are doing nearly twice as much in terms of grants and loans as comparable institutions." Father Linn assured the board that the "problem is being carefully analyzed."[19]

Careful analysis of resource allocation also related to the number of faculty and to salaries. In 1965, the Lay Regents voiced "some concern over the loss of incumbent teachers due to insufficient raises in salary." While applications for positions remained sufficient, in the next two years the administration tried to make the appointments more attractive by adopting the TIAA-CREF retirement program, a "larger and better health service program," and a more "lenient program of sabbatical leaves," lessening the service period from five to three years, and reducing the eligible rank from associate to assistant professor. However, it budgeted only $10,000 for sabbaticals (a semester at full pay or half pay for a year, University wide competition). Moreover, in 1966, in "light of recent Ecumenical Council pronouncements regarding freedom of individual conscience and in as much as we have had to bypass some rather highly qualified teachers," Fr. President Linn proposed a restatement of the marriage requirements for faculty that would "still safe guard all moral aspects and avoid all danger of scandal." Thus, the University would continue to shun "invalidly married" Catholics, but concerning non-Catholics who had divorced and remarried, "each situation will be judged on its own merits with great care being exercised to establish that the second marriage is in good faith and that no serious public scandal will result if the candidate is hired."[20]

In 1969, another study of faculty compensation revealed "that even with the projected raises we find ourselves 22nd of the twenty-eight Jesuit colleges and universities. Taking into account geographical differences in the cost of living, it may well be that we are still low." While faculty recompense remained below average, it included several other nuances. Grants helped to supplement the salaries of some, especially in the professional schools, but the research presented a new compensation concern. In 1967, Creighton established a policy applicable to "all full and part-time members of the faculty, staff, students, and all other employees," whereby it owned "discoveries and inventions resulting from research conducted under University auspices or through the use of University facilities," while the inventor would receive 20 percent of any net return. Moreover, the Jesuits, after the 1968 corporate separation, supplied a different type of grant, annually returning part of their salaries (a "living endowment") in a joint gift to the University. Then, in 1971 the national economy put a straight jacket on the University's budget. The administration prescribed across-the-board cost-of-living raises, but did not have to disburse them because of the federal wage-and-price freeze aimed at curbing the inception of rampant inflation. In spite of the restriction, the CCAS notified thirteen faculty members that due to decreased enrollment in particular departments, they would not receive contracts for the following year (ultimately, five were retained).[21]

In 1970, the full-time arts faculty consisted of 118 men (22 Jesuits) and 25 women. The administration explained that it had to "compete for relatively few qualified women," and that improving the gender gap remained difficult because females concentrated in a few disciples, notably in history, speech, English, and foreign languages. Minority employment presented a similar challenge. In 1966, the chemistry department hired an African-American instructor and the sociology department followed suit the next year (each taught one year). Additionally noteworthy, two laymen joined the theology department; both possessed a master's degree, and one of them, Susan R. Hoffman, became the first female theologian at Creighton. Moreover, in 1971, a layman (a laicized priest), Michael Lawler, became chairman of the theology department. This was the first lay chair of a Jesuit theology department. Those appointments highlighted the evolution of the Jesuits in the CCAS from monopoly to majority to minority status. The situation beleaguered the Order in America and fostered a continuing debate on the nature of, and the preservation of, Jesuit education. With mounting lay participation, the enduring question became how to provide a "Jesuit presence," which preserved the objectives of a "Jesuit education."[22]

On the other hand, the concerns of the increasing number of laymen in the CCAS precipitated the creation of a chapter of the American Association of University Professors (AAUP). In March 1966, the members (open to all in the University, but the vast majority of the forty-five from arts) elected Lloyd Hubenbka, Ph.D., English department, president, and Ross Horning, Ph.D., history department, vice president. The AAUP defended "academic freedom" and the Creighton chapter sprung to life just as the Catholic colleges in the United States began to acknowledge the concept; the need to meet accreditation standards and guidelines for federal grants facilitated its acceptance. The AAUP chapter at Creighton emerged simultaneously with the appearance of new structures of faculty governance. Also in the spring 1966, the Reverend Dean Thomas McKenney, S.J. agreed to the creation of an arts faculty advisory committee, consisting of seven elected members, five lay Ph.D.s—Jack Angus (sociology), Lloyd Hubenka (English), James Karabotsos (English), Daniel Murphy (psychology), Thomas Zepf (physics)—and Fr. John Ginsterblum (theology) and the Reverend Leland Lubbers, S.J, (fine arts). The subsequent staffing problems in the arts college, however, undercut the progression of lay inclusion and exacerbated the feelings of powerlessness and unappreciation. In 1973, acting dean Fr. Robert Shanahan stressed that the new dean and the academic vice president had to "turn around a certain faculty attitude, valid or not, reflecting a belief that budgetary concerns destroy academic plans and make them an exercise in futility." Many of the faculty members in the CCAS harbored the historic complaint that although the liberal arts stood as the core of the institution, the professional schools commanded priority.[23]

The activities in the CCAS meshed with the desire for a faculty voice in University affairs. In 1964, AVP Fr. Richard Harrington established an "academic senate," consisting of himself and the deans, and "not conceived of as representing any particular school or college." It may have aided "the need for communication" among proliferating administrators, but it did not provide a conduit for faculty input. The administration recognized the "desire on the part of faculty members today to have more of a voice in school policy," as long as it remained "on the advisory level." The Lay Regents strongly recommended "that great caution be exerted in forming such a council lest the faculty attempt to take over administrative duties." Father President Linn gave permission "for internal organizational meetings which were attended by some of the Jesuits" that led to the formation of the AAUP; simultaneously, the Reverend Virgil Roach, S.J., investigated the option of a faculty council. The administration understood that some Jesuit institutions encountered "serious difficulties with their lay faculties," and even though Creighton was not "experiencing much pressure along these lines," it "should anticipate the problem and seek more lay faculty participation in an organized way." A planning committee of two representatives per school prepared a constitution accepted by the faculty and, following elections in December 1967, an all-University Faculty Council (one representative per fifteen faculty members, twenty-three members on the first council) met and elected Dr. Ross Horning chairman. The faculty chairman also served as a voting member on the newly established executive council of the Board of Directors, which would "operate as a consultative committee at the managerial level rather than as a deliberative committee." However, matters requiring a vote by directors would be "processed by the board at a separate meeting and at a different time."[24]

Unfortunately, in 1969, the death of Fr. President Linn presented an unexpected emergency for the new Board of Directors and the recently organized faculty. The previous year, Fr. Linn had chosen the Reverend Clement Schneider, S.J., acting chairman of the sociology department, to serve as academic vice president; he now became acting president, the last administrator chosen without a formal search. While he performed the duties of caretaker, eight board members (four lay, four Jesuits, Richard W. Walker, president of the Byron Reed Co., chairman) served as the presidential search committee. It chose five finalists, all external candidates. It became "evident that pressure had been brought to bear" to keep the top two candidates in the positions they already held and no consensus could be reached concerning the other three, and a new search ensued. Following "a period of negotiation," a revised committee structure emerged consisting of six faculty members, four students, four alumni, and eight directors. Faculty president Horning and SBG president John Green expressed reservations because their constituencies did not get to meet all the candidates, but on August 6, 1970, the directors approved the appointment of the Reverend Joseph J. Labaj, S.J., as the twenty-fourth president of Creighton University. The forty-nine-year-old Fr. Labaj had served as principal of Creighton Prep as it moved to its separate campus and, most recently, as superintendent of education of the Pine Ridge Indian Reservation. Father Schneider, "Clem" as he insisted on being called (Ph.D., Cornell 1964), returned to the academic vice president position, but died suddenly because of post-operative problems in October 1972, at age forty-four. During his brief administrative career, because of his empathetic positions concerning student and faculty rights, he became "one of the most controversial figures in Creighton history."[25]

The first attempt at a University-wide faculty-participation governance system proved wanting. In 1970, Robert Heaney, M.D., chaired a committee that proposed the abolition of the Faculty Council, replacing it with an "academic senate for all-University affairs." The committee criticized the existing administrative structure and the "widespread ignorance" of goals and operations of the various departments and schools by their faculties and administrators. The directors offered "many reservations" concerning the restructuring and admitted "confusion exists regarding academic governance and general University governance." Despite some qualms, the board approved the reorganization and in the fall 1971, ignoring a plea for a postponement by some faculty members, the Academic Senate came into existence by a presidential decree issued by Fr. Labaj. Three years later, he consented to the creation of the Staff Advisory Council to "give the staff a voice in University administration." In the mean time, the administration enlarged the financial affairs committee to include four faculty members elected at-large and deferred writing a policy statement concerning faculty participation in public demonstrations. The board followed the advice of Vice President of Student Personnel Thomas Burke, who "felt no written policy was needed at this time because by and large we do not have militant and radical teachers who would in anyway encourage violence on campus."[26]

Actually, the only act of violence during the "era of confrontation" came three weeks after the above board meeting, but seemingly, unknown outsiders perpetrated the deed. On Saturday evening, November 9, 1970, between 10:30 P.M. and 1:00 A.M., a series of 22-caliber rifle shots fired from the North Freeway broke windows on the fifth and eighth floors of Kiewit Hall. Luckily, the rooms were unoccupied at the time; then, two days later, students reported hearing gunshots, but no damage occurred. Moreover, during the same semester, "at least seven bomb threats" led to evacuations; in one other case, the administration determined the threat a hoax and did not vacate the building. During the rash of intimidation, the 911 emergency system received one of the warnings and traced the call to a forty-two-year-old graduated student, who was arrested, fined $300 and served twenty-four days in jail before his release after pleading no contest (he gave no motive). The incidents prompted the directors to empower the president, between board meetings, to take legal action protecting University property from disruption of its functions or harm to its officials, faculty, or students.[27]

While Creighton avoided the violence that plagued many other campuses, students did confront the administration in a "disrespectful," adversarial manner, demanding "their rights" as adults. They attacked the historic principle of in loco parentis, whereby college administrators acted as the patriarchal surrogate parent, prescribing strict regulations governing virtually every aspect of student life. To press their case, students demanded a voice in University governance; concurrently, they struggled to get their own house in order. In 1964, the SBG appointed the first of several study committees empowered to make recommendations to reform the Student Union governmental structure. Prime issues included increasing the activity fee "to meet the rising cost of quality entertainment" and "to stay independent of university handouts," reapportioning representation to reflect enrollment in the various schools, thwarting secession by the professional schools that had little interest in big-budget events like the prom, and looking into "areas of school life which students do not now but could possibly govern." Finally, in spring 1968, yet another study committee presented eight by-law amendments; at a poorly attended annual meeting, by a vote of 129-21, the few interested students voted to revise the operation of their corporation. The revisions created a twenty-four-person SBG, which elected its paid executives (president, $1,500, the others $1,000). Reapportionment distributed ten representatives to the CCAS, six to CoBA, and two each to the professional schools, which still "want[ed] out" of the union (they shared few interests with the undergrads; among them, the basketball games, and the dances, if they dated a young coed). The board of Directors approved and the students voted 1219-595 in favor of hiking the activity fee to $35, providing the wherewithal, among other things, to pay salaries to the executives. However, the conundrum remained, deciding which events were all-University and how much money to spend on them, before "kicking back" the remaining funds to the individual schools.[28]

The SBG continued to tinker with its structure and in 1969, it introduced the election of officers by popular vote. Unfortunately, a "last-minute" disqualification of a candidate (for violating the fair election practices by-law) "marred" the first popular vote. More regrettably, the annual meetings of the corporation continued to draw poor turnouts and, on several occasions during the early 1970s, the officers had to adjourn the sessions due to lack of the fifty-student quorum. During the 1972–73 academic year, the resignation of four SBG members led to another restructuring. After scouring the campus to find a quorum, by a vote of 48-6-1, the "student union" rearranged its officer structure to resemble the historic commission form of government, with a president, and vice presidents with specific tasks (e.g., events, finance). Those officers gained election at-large; arts, law, and CoBA each elected a vice president; and nursing, pharmacy, dentistry, and medicine elected one to represent the health sciences. In the spring 1973, Joseph P. "Sonny" Foster, for two years the leader of the African-American student group, won the presidency by a vote of 504–344. He stated, "The low turnout helped a lot. We were also worried that a lot of students would turn out to vote against a black student. That never developed. I was somewhat pleasantly surprised." Sadly, the apathy toward the SBG continued and two attempts to hold the required annual meeting of the corporation the following March failed for lack of a quorum.[29]

Despite the general student apathy, a few activist voices produced a very disturbing noise. The Student Leadership Conference (SLC), established by the SBG to serve as the student component of the annual meeting of the Greater Creighton Convocation and created by the development office in the 1950s, demonstrated the process. The *Creightonian* headline in the October 2, 1964, edition illuminated the new student attitude: "120 Air Gripes at Seventh SLC." The gripers represented 58 percent of the students invited to attend, and presented recommendations to the SBG, which evaluated them and advanced those deemed favorable to the administration. In 1966, a change in development strategy terminated the Greater Creighton Convocation, which forced the activists to establish new gatherings, such as the Student Symposium and the Creighton Forum of Organizations. That year, organizers publicized widely, including 1,700 "personal invitations to dorm students," but only eighty attended the meeting. In 1968, the Student Freedom League organized to "shake this university from its complacency and mediocrity" and to "correct injustices inflicted, intentionally or not, by the administration on the students." No one felt the vibrations, but the SBG continued to organize an annual symposium, in 1969 shifting its attention from a local to a national focus. It received initial commitments from nationally prominent activist, but they subsequently cancelled, producing a frantic scramble for speakers. The faltering symposium caused a summer meeting, at which it created the Community Policy Committee to reverse the "trend toward isolationism by involving students in civic matters," but only fifty attended the first meeting. In the spring 1971, by referendum, students rejected an SBG request for authorization to join the National Student Association; nonetheless, president Joseph Warin attended the national conference as an "official observer." By 1973, the SLC had downsized to a Sunday evening retreat to "talk over mutual problems between students, faculty and the administration and have a renewal of interests."[30]

Despite the exasperatingly low number of participants, SBG officers pushed the issues and the administration responded. In the spring of 1966, they demanded representation on the all-University committees of student life and spiritual life. Reportedly, the administration seemed to acquiesce, but faculty opposition stymied the prospect. The following fall, however, students joined faculty, gaining an advisory voice in University governance, with membership on four committees—student life, publications, spiritual life, and the nascent student alumni–public relations committee. As student activism intensified at Jesuit institutions, in 1968 the JEA issued a statement on student rights, which included the right to participate in making campus policy, the protection of student records, the freedom of the student press, and the freedom to participate in off-campus activities without fear of discipline if university interests were not directly affected. The administration expected immediate SBG pleas for "more involvement" in governance, but it did not materialize for several years. In the meantime, some directors worried that "perhaps some changes [in student regulations] in the direction of permissiveness were made from expediency rather than from real conviction." In April 1970, acting president Fr. Schneider explained the "present policy of the University in working *with* student government, not to achieve peace at any price, but to avoid by all means at hand any form of violence." He cited "the unhappy situation at Detroit University where without sufficient provocation the administration called for police action only to discover that the courts acquitted the students since it could not be shown conclusively that they had disrupted normal business affairs." Subsequently, Fr. President Labaj assured the board that the administration had "not followed the path of permissiveness." He felt the administration was "frequently misunderstood" and that it was "very important that good communications regarding change be established between University officials and the board." He advocated frequent meetings with individual directors "to improve communications in this regard." He vowed that "his primary objective over the next few months" would be "a clarification of the relationship between the board and the administration."[31]

In 1971, the awaited demand for "more involvement" came. The SBG exhibited unhappiness with the proportion of student representation on committees and its president threatened protests that would make previous demonstrations "look like a Girl Scout picnic" (no campus feminist chastised him for his sexist analogy). Father President Labaj responded by pointing out the "vast difference" between student and faculty proposals, which defied compromise; thus, he announced the creation of an Academic Council with twenty-three faculty, ten administrators, and seven students, as well as authorizing the committee chaired by Dr. Heaney to analyze once again the governance issue. With the "principle of faculty and student participation in decision making" established, for the next two years, the Board of Directors explored ways to implement it. In 1972, an ad hoc committee for achieving better board-student communication proposed creating a joint conference committee; "vigorous discussion" concluded that the plan would spawn similar committees for faculty and alumni. After more study, in 1973 the board approved a nine-member joint conference, consisting of three directors, three faculty, and three students that would "meet on an extremely informal basis at convenient intervals," but that had to "avoid any semblance of being a legislative body or a grievance committee." The first meeting convened on May 8. The subsequent report to the board gave no mention of the topics discussed, but Fr. Labaj said, "student reaction to the first meeting was enthusiastic; faculty reaction a little less than enthusiastic." The joint committee held a few meetings and dissolved as the "era of confrontation" ended; the board avoided student and faculty membership, but the principle of students and faculty participating in governance through advisory committees became a standard feature of the Creighton system.[32]

While the board and the administration resolved the political issue in a manner they could accept (advisory participation), both had to contend with a host of other portentous policy positions. First amendment concerns beset them as strident student publications and radical lecturers threatened to "infect" young minds. During 1963, virtually no national news appeared in the *Creightonian*, although numerous editorials dealt with political and racial issues. Beginning in the spring 1964, a presidential election year, national issues became prominent. In 1965, with the escalation of the Vietnam War and the onset of student protest, the paper gave significant coverage to those events. By 1969, the editors eliminated the society page, "so that more news of campus-wide interest can be printed." They now published wedding and engagement announcements and Greek news only every fourth Friday; the following fall, Greek news moved to an as-needed basis and the coed marital feature disappeared. By that time, the weekly had attained the all-American rating from the Associated Collegiate Press ten out of the last eleven semesters, while the editors chronically circulated "cries of censorship and managing of the news." Others held similar feelings and organized to present their views. In the spring 1967, some students in Swanson Hall published *Quaff* (alternately titled *Quadrangle Forum)*, which "the Directors seem to agree that it was not at all representative and that its very existence needs to be questioned. The makeup is poor. The articles are badly written and the general tone is negative, rude and frequently inaccurate." It was one of five short-lived unconventional student publications. The *Bag*, an "independent literary-opinion" magazine, began as a joint publication of students from Creighton, the College of Saint Mary, Duchesne, and the University of Omaha. The Administration denied the group the use of University facilities for on-campus sales, but it survived into the fall, when it announced a second edition that would shed its "rebel image." In 1969, the SBG "found it necessary to supplement" The *Creightonian* with its own weekly newsletter in order to get its message out. That same year, a group of disgruntled students announced the creation of an "underground newspaper," *Headliner*, which would give more coverage to issues before the student life committee and to black student concerns (subsequently, African-American students established a newsletter). All the alternative sheets succumbed to lack of funds, staff, and readers.[33]

Movies and speakers generated analogous controversy. In 1967, unspecified individuals raised questions "about foreign films shown." The administration responded that the policy "will continue to [*sic*] carefully screen such movies," consulting the Legion of Decency ratings. It would not allow the viewing of "a condemned movie on this campus except in the rare situation where one might be shown to a very limited advanced class again for purposes of exposure to reality of such movies, and the reason for their being considered salacious or immoral." In comparison, no policy existed concerning outside speakers on campus. The appearance of Loretta Young, a Catholic actress praised for her charity work, as the first female speaker at an annual public Alpha Sigma Nu lecture, obviously caused no stir. However, the administration, aware of problems elsewhere, feared its lack of preparation. Thus, it combined the best features from the policy statements of Saint Peter's College and St. Louis University. Creighton's policy emphasized the "extracurricular promotion of honest inquiry" and the "balanced investigation of controversial issues." It created two classifications: "open forum lectures," open to the public, which "must be cleared through the President"; and "closed forum lectures," open to a particular school or department, which "must be cleared by the respective Dean." For students to independently sponsor a speaker, the process began with a "request for approval" form obtained from the vice president of student personnel.[34]

Critics, however, complained about two defects: Procedures omitted the "possibility of committee action," thus "the responsible administrator would in a negative situation have to assume total blame," and they found the policy "not sufficiently specific." They questioned, "Would the University permit a known communist, atheist, Black Muslim to speak in that specific capacity on our campus?" The board replied that, "the University might in certain circumstances and with proper screening invite or permit such an outside speaker to address a limited and specific University audience in order that the position they hold might be better understood. Faculty members who moderate discussion and offer balancing opinions would be present. Such an event would be advertised with dignity and not in such a manner as to attract a radical group among students." Furthermore, the University reserved "the right to exclude speakers whose formal presentation on campus might create the impression of giving public endorsement to a person or to a position contrary to her published credo."[35]

The board created an all-University committee on lectures, films, and concerts, chaired by the dean of students and including five faculty and three student members, to advise the respective deans concerning "closed forum lectures," and the academic vice president and the president regarding "open forums." The committee tinkered with the policy, but it did not protect the definitive "responsible administrator" from censure; Fr. President Labaj "spoke of problems he experiences with public reaction to speakers on campus." Moreover, "several members of the board were very concerned about the type of speakers who were being permitted to appear" and "pointed out that it is difficult to raise funds and keep the good will of the public when radical speakers are invited to campus." Yet other Directors voiced precautions "lest academic freedom be interfered with and subjective judgments passed which could be questioned by faculty and students." In March 1972, Fr. Labaj rejected a request for an appearance by lawyer William Kunstler and Yippie! leader Jerry Rubin. The decision produced a "lively discussion" at the subsequent board meeting, where all agreed on the significance of academic freedom, but "opinions seemed to differ on its definition." The SBG had a similar discussion at a six-hour special session that voted down all proposals for defiance of the ruling. The activists accepted the outcome with "disappointment and discouragement."[36]

The escalation of the civil rights movement caused equal consternation for the directors, the administration, and even the SBG, all of whom assumed they displayed proper awareness to minority concerns. In contour with the contemporary civil rights movement, in 1964 the Lay Regents advised a "crash program of grants-in-aid to qualified Negro students, pinpointed" by the minority community (black became the popular self-designation after 1967). However, they advised against University sponsorship of a forum on civil rights, arguing that it should remain "in the action end" of the problem. Furthermore, the Jesuit Trustees feared that the loss of low-rent housing to interstate highway construction would pose a problem for its few "negro students"; therefore, they authorized sending remaining landlords on the list of approved housing a letter reminding them of Creighton's open-occupancy standard. By 1965, because of the regulation, the University "lost almost 25% of previously available housing facilities." At the end of the decade, the new Lay Directors, on recommendation from their legal counsel, amended the by-laws to put into print a policy the Jesuits had followed since founding the institution. It added the clause, "Creighton University's admissions policy shall be to accept all scholastically qualified students which its facilities and resources will allow regardless of race, color or religion."[37]

In the same vein, in 1964, at age seventy-three with "no good" legs and "a bum heart," civil rights stalwart Fr. John Markoe participated in three demonstrations sponsored by the Citizens Coordinating Committee for Civil Liberties (4CL). The following year, the "current affairs lecture series" included journalist and historian Lerone Bennett, who spoke on "The Negro's Role in American History." In addition, professor of education Donald Cannon, Ph.D., devised a program in which junior education majors acted as teachers aides and seniors did practice teaching, with one semester required in an inner-city school to learn about "cultural differences." As well, Fr. Austin Miller, who had headed the Creighton Institute of Labor Relations for eighteen years, established the Institute of Social Order (1963), which gave all students the opportunity "to serve the public in the areas of industrial, racial and government relations." Its primary objective became the formation of "a student group for the study and application of the principles necessary for Christian inter-human relations." The Society for Social Justice emerged, which placed "some 50 Hilltoppers" as tutors for the disadvantaged and encouraged students to participate in the Great Society's war on poverty through Omaha Volunteer Auxiliary Leaders (OVAL) and Volunteer-Community Action Program (V-CAP) projects. In 1969, the myriad of opportunities prompted students to establish the Community Services Center, which the student life committee gave official sanction.[38]

Furthermore, in 1968 the University established the Martin Luther King scholarships, which granted partial tuition remission to "qualified Negro students from Greater Omaha" (fifteen were awarded the first year). That spring, Creighton refused to allow presidential candidate George Wallace to speak on campus, because as "an alleged racist, [he] would probably alienate the predominantly Negro North Side [Omaha's "ghetto"], without sufficient educational benefit returning to the school" (subsequently, the publications board refused to accept a "youth for Wallace" advertisement in the *Creightonian*). His supporters, including his local campaign manager, an assistant professor in the dental school, arranged for Wallace to speak at the Omaha Civic Auditorium. Approximately two hundred students and faculty joined an anti-Wallace rally at that venue, which degenerated into a melee, with five Creighton students injured and two priests arrested. With anxiety rising, shortly before the end of the semester the Faculty Council organized a committee to study allegations of racial discrimination at the University. In addition, in the fall 1968 the CCAS introduced a black studies program with three classes: Thomas Kuhlman, Ph.D., "Minority Literature in America"; Fr. Robert Shanahan, "The History of the Negro in America"; and the Reverend Theodore Cunningham, S.J., "Afro-American Art and Culture." The following year, students could study for a minor in the disciple, with eight humanities and social-science departments offering a course(s) relating to the African-American experience. Completing the measures taken in 1968, the committee on student life policy approved the establishment of the Black Coalition, an interracial student group formed "to bridge the gap between ethnic groups through understanding and communication." The creation of a supposed "black power organization . . . shocked many students"; actually, white students and faculty contributed a majority of the membership, variously reported as sixty or seventy-five. The misnomer obviously caused confusion, which produced its name change to United Power.[39]

The 1969 school year opened with mixed signals. The CCAS freshman class elected African American David Pearl vice president and United Power presented Soul Week, "a concentrated effort to offer the students on this campus maximum exposure to what it means to be black in this country." However, in tandem, letters to the editor published in the *Creightonian* complained about "uneducated" behavior and outright racial animosity. The epistles prompted a subsequent front-page response from Fr. President Linn condemning "incidents of an abusive and inflammatory nature ["verbal abuse, non-acceptance and ostracism"] on the part of some students and even on the part of a few teachers in the classroom." The disquiet and the increase in black undergraduates resulting from the recruiting and financial aid programs contributed to the decision to hire an African-American counselor for the Counseling Center. He also oversaw the Black Aesthetic Program, which cosponsored with the residence halls and United Power, the Black Faculty in Residence Program that "brought young black artists and educators to live with students for several days." In 1970, to encompass the legal aspects, the directors appointed Ted Kalamaja as the Civil Rights Compliance Director to "make sure that the 1964 Equal Opportunities Act is fully enforced at Creighton and among those companies with which Creighton deals."[40]

In the spring 1970, a significant change in attitude surfaced with a cry for SBG reforms and a black culture center. An ad hoc group claiming to represent blacks at Creighton demanded a separate college, five black representatives on the SBG, and that each black student ballot count as one hundred votes. The SBG rejected those proposals, but did create a black student affairs committee, consisting of "at least six students, a majority of which shall be black," appointed by the SBG executive committee "to investigate the issues important to black students." Additionally, the SBG established an exchange program with "an unspecified black southern university." In the fall 1971, for a semester exchange, two Grambling University students came to Creighton, which sent a female sophomore in return. The following year, no white Creighton students applied for the exchange, and Grambling refused to accept the two black students that did, because their race negated the purpose of the program. The SBG attempted to rescue the project by seeking other schools, but its efforts fizzled due to "apathy." Moreover, the perennial problem of campus entertainment received an added nuance as black students grumbled that it was "white oriented."[41]

Concurrently, Fr. President Labaj accepted the "precautionary advice" from "not enthusiastic" directors and promised to "investigate the situation [a black culture center] very carefully." Jerry Lewis, director of the Creighton Upward Bound program, argued that the "nearly 90" black students on campus needed their own place for "self-pride and identity." The "separate" issue remained contentious in editorials and letters to the editor of the *Creightonian*. Ultimately, Fr. Labaj insisted that the place exist on campus in order that it could be "adequately controlled." On Sunday, February 21, 1971, a two-story house on the corner of 26th and California streets, which had housed the Campus Ministry (office moved to the basement of St. John's Church), opened as the Linn Center, dedicated in honor of the recently deceased president of the University. The student-operated "coffee house" that had opened in the basement of the building in 1970 remained temporarily, but closed the next year because of "little use." The Creighton University Afro-American Student Association (CUASA), an outgrowth of the ad hoc group, which "reorganized" United Power without white members, operated the center and hoped to develop a library, to overcome the "awful lot of ignorance on this campus," and to bring in speakers "who could talk to groups about what being black is all about."[42]

In the spring semester of 1971, the CUASA began a two-year period of intense confrontation, demanding a black editorial page editor; the *Creightonian* acquiesced, elevating reporter Ken Watts to the position. The next fall, the organization petitioned the SBG for funds, which would allow it to assume publication of *Black Realities*, a newsletter created by United Methodist Services (UMS). It withdrew its request, claiming that the SBG bowed to "racist elements on campus." With UMS funds and help from the staff at Wesley House, the CUASA succeeded in attracting a sufficient number of black students to publish the monthly for three years. Additionally, the group communicated through its choir, which began as an "informal group of students gathered around the piano in Kiewit Hall." It sang at Masses, in the dorms, and at Black History Week programs in local schools. While "founders" Marlee Davis and Michael Piondexter were Protestant, "most of the students in the choir are Catholic and they had never sung gospel music before." The choir had sixty members in 1972, which represented a majority of the African Americans on campus; thus, its denominational make revealed that Creighton had some success recruiting from the small black Catholic population in the region.[43]

However, while the dorms provided a venue for cultural exchange, they also presented a problem. In the spring semester 1971, the CUASA announced an investigation into the "discriminatory" hiring practices of dormitory residence advisors (RA). In the fall, it ceased investigating without comment; nonetheless, the SBG announced that thenceforth the RA selection committee would include a black representative. That same year, the association became embroiled in a cheerleader controversy that briefly acquired national media coverage. In 1964, Creighton had returned to its 1950s model of all women cheerleaders; until 1970, in the stands, men could "raise crowd spirit," but could not "do formal cheers from the floor as the women do." Then, in fall 1971 a race and gender integrated squad took the floor, and at the December 1 basketball game, the four black cheerleaders knelt, while the white cheerleaders stood, for the national anthem. Before the December 3rd and 6th games, the entire squad left the floor during the playing of the anthem; the stunt attracted media attention, "triggering [a] strong reaction of Creighton alumni." White cheerleaders stated it was not a black issue, but acknowledged ringleader African American Sharon Watson had performed similar gestures as a high-school cheerleader. On December 8, the administration issued an ultimatum that cheerleaders must follow expected patriotic procedure; the next day the squad resigned. After the Christmas recess, all but two members returned, with a promise to comply. However, at the January 29, 1972, game, four white cheerleaders stood for the anthem, while the four black members of the squad sat in the stands in uniform. Two days later, the administration disbanded the unit; the following fall, Vice President of Student Personnel the Reverend Michael Sheridan, S.J., announced that after he "discussed the matter with many students and athletic staff members," he "came to the conclusion that too few care enough about having cheerleaders to risk provoking more controversy." Thus, there was no squad for the 1972–73 season; "fans will take care of providing spirit." A second fallout from the episode emerged as the CUASA called for the firing of the director of the black aesthetics program, because he challenged the comment that black faculty and staff supported the actions of the black cheerleaders. For unspecified reasons, the administration did not renew his contract.[44]

While Creighton continued to sponsor an Upward Bound program, in 1971 it also became "responsible for the educational component of the City of Omaha's Concentrated Employment Program." The war-on-poverty effort was dubbed New Careers, "a two-year work-study program designed to qualify individuals for para-professional careers in human service agencies." Nonetheless, in 1972, the CUASA labeled Creighton "racist" and issued a demand for more black scholarships, faculty, administrators, directors, and coaches. It gave Fr. President Labaj one week to respond before it would contact the United States Department of Justice. Neither side responded, and the following March, the association complained that it had no money, that the black aesthetic program was defunct, and that it had sponsored no events for Black History Week. Yet, somehow, it raised the funds to create another controversy, inviting Black Power advocate Stokely Carmichael to speak at the Linn Black Culture Center and banning white-student attendance (despite the name, its by-laws stipulated that all students regardless of race had access to the Center). For several weeks before and after the event, "I said" versus "he said" letters filled the editorial page of the *Creightonian,* arguing the legality and the appropriateness of the occasion. However, soon thereafter the confrontational attitude melted away. In the spring 1973, CUASA president "Sonny" Foster became SBG president (he found the job "semi-rewarding, semi-disheartening"; number one student issue—lack of funds to engage big-name music groups). Ultimately, helping to cap the period on a heartening note, in 1973 the Creighton University Black Administrators and Faculty group established the Minority Senior Awards program, and in accord with the Equal

Employment Opportunity Act of 1972, the administration appointed the Reverend Leroy Endres, S.J., the first affirmative-action director.[45]

The affirmative-action efforts included women. Early on, the women's liberation movement made little headway on campus; "many coeds" found the national organizations "silly" or "disagreed with the radical concerns of abortion, lesbianism and female draft eligibility." Nonetheless, Creighton coeds benefited from the accruing alterations in the status and roles of women in the United States. In 1964, the *Creightonian* announced the arrival of the women's movement with an article reviewing Betty Friedan's *Feminine Mystic*; the opening statement of the piece declared, "Ladies, [the author had not grasped the new feminist terminology] look to the future. Women in the 20th century have their choice between a career, marriage or both." During the 1960s, Creighton women did not organize to push an agenda and few significant changes occurred. However, fashion trends produced an administrative paroxysm. Following complaints from some students and faculty, Dean of Women Lieben and the Women's Dorm Council "launched a campaign against 'creeping' hem lines." Finding it impossible to eliminate the mini skirt, they shifted "to the idea of sitting properly," posting signs with instructions in Alumni Library. Sitting became less hazardous on October 28, 1969, when it became acceptable for coeds to wear slacks anytime and anywhere, except to class (previously, "Culottes, shorts, slacks, jeans, bathing suits, etc. in the yard or anyplace in the campus area, even under a coat," [*Student Handbook* emphasis] were strictly forbidden). More in line with feminist goals, in 1965 the SBG elected its first coed executive, arts junior Sharon Williams as corresponding secretary. In 1973, arts senior Mary Higgins gained the secretarial post, becoming the first woman elected under the new system of direct election of officers.[46]

Actually, in 1970, the first mention on the term "women's liberation" in the *Creightonian* came in the form of a satirical editorial about fashion that compared Paris designers to American draft boards, urging the coeds to resist the call to wear "midis" and to march in protest wearing their "minis." Shortly thereafter, in the spring 1971, Dean Lieben, with a $2,000 grant from the S&H Foundation, brought genuine liberationists Gloria Steinem and Florence Kennedy to campus as speakers at the Student Leadership Conference. The following fall, a small coterie of coeds (about twenty-five) formed Adam's Rib (a sarcastic reference to *Genesis*) and issued a declaration of goals, including a statement in favor of abortion, which brought an immediate antiabortion rejoinder from Fr. President Labaj. While the abortion issue remained a hot topic for letters to the editor, Adam's Rib faded quickly, as did an ephemeral successor, the Feminine Alliance Towards Equality (FATE). The latter hosted seminars that stressed the "lack of childcare facilities and biased professors, especially in the professional schools."[47]

While feminist organizations failed to gain a foothold, the student body absorbed national trends. In 1971, members of Adam's Rib presented a resolution to the SBG, which advocated abolition of the Homecoming queen. Mary Arouni, assistant managing editor of the *Creightonian* responded with an editorial, "God Save the Queen," which asked the group to focus on important women's issues. The fraternities and sororities had already transformed Homecoming; in 1968, DZ and SAE "traded a planned $600 homecoming float for a joint project designed to raise money for the Nebraska Heart Association." The next year, the Homecoming parade ceased, and in 1973, due to lack of interest, students eliminated the queen. Similarly, the divisions between the undergraduate colleges and the professional schools transformed the prom; in 1972, because it had lost "its meaning for a great number of students," the SBG eliminated the fifty-year-old tradition, which had given so many the chance to become princes, princesses, queens, and kings. Similarly, in 1971, for "financial reasons," the ROTC eliminated the election of an "honorary colonel" for its military ball. Moreover, in 1973 the editors of the *Creightonian* announced they would no longer use "Miss or Mrs." before women's names.[48]

While students adopted social conventions, the administration incorporated national laws and norms. In 1971, it created a committee on the status of women, chaired by Kay Saline. The following year, the Counseling Center hired Caroline Sedlacek, Ph.D., the Campus Ministry chose Marilyn Maxwell to head its liturgical committee, and Eileen Lieben became associate dean of students, as the concept of gendered deans departed. Moreover, Mary Alice Rollman, the first woman member of the athletic board, became the first woman to graduate with a major in physical education (program begun in 1971). In synch with the times, in 1973 Dean Lieben began a program, "Women and the World of Work," to acquaint coeds "with the wide range of occupational options open to them." That same year, Creighton hosted the national conference of Alpha Sigma Nu, which culminated a five-year discussion by voting to merge with Gamma Pi Epsilon, creating a single Jesuit honor society. The Board of Directors supplemented the trend toward gender equality by recognizing the need for "improved recreational facilities for girls" and by amending the admissions by-law to read "regardless of race, color, religion or sex." In 1974, it welcomed its first woman director, Madeline Jacobson, owner of an insurance business. Finally, the board also had to contend with the latest movement of the era—gay rights. In 1973, an "off-campus group" tried to establish a chapter of the national Catholic organization Dignity, but could not find a priest to serve as the sponsor or to obtain University sanction. While editorials and letters to the editor kept the issue current, the directors dismissed it because, "Rumor has it that no more than ten are involved, and it's conjecture that they may not be true homosexuals, but rather young people seeking attention by being atypical."[49]

Beyond gender and racial cohorts, larger segments of the student population pressed issues of the day. Large numbers of students attacked the "stifling" and "childish" regulations of in loco parentis, which included "properly chaperoned" social events, parietal hours, and the separation of the sexes. In 1964, Deglman Hall proctor the Reverend Norbert Loehr, S.J., abolished the 11:30 lights out rule, but established quiet rooms after 8:00 for study. Without seeing the contradiction, he explained, "these men are old enough to regulate their own schedule" (as of fall 1966, dorm directors did not have to be Jesuits). In Gallagher Hall, hours for freshmen coeds stood at:

DAY	BE IN ROOM	ROOM CHECK	LIGHTS OUT
M–Th	8:00 P.M.	8:00 & 10:15 P.M.	Midnight
F–S	1:00 A.M.	1:00 A.M.	1:30 A.M.
Sun.	10:15 P.M.	10:15 P.M.	Midnight

FOR UPPER-CLASS WOMEN:

DAY	BE IN ROOM	ROOM CHECK	LIGHTS OUT
M–Th	10:30 P.M.	10:30 P.M.	Midnight
F–S	1:30 A.M.	1:30 A.M.	2:00 A.M.
Sun.	11:00 P.M.	11:00 P.M.	Midnight

Men could visit in the front lounge 1:00 to 8:00 P.M. on weekdays and as late as 10:00 P.M. on weekends, "but to no other part of the dorm" and "boys never [*Handbook* emphasis] come in after dates or dances." Furthermore, the administration banned public displays of affection (the infamous PDA!): "Anyone found kissing and/or embracing around the buildings will be severely campused." Rules violations resulted in demerits; when they totaled five, the dean of women would "campus" a coed—that is, she had to return to the dorm by 7:00 P.M., remain there and report in on the hour until retiring at 11:00 P.M. ("severe campusing" must have consisted of several such pleasant evenings). In February 1966, upper-class coeds moved into Kiewit Hall and gained the privilege of creating a dorm council "having disciplinary as well as social powers." Weeknight be-in-room hours for juniors and seniors moved to midnight and room checks became weekly. In 1968, senior women garnered a "no hours" system; in the spring 1971, the system slid down class standing, as hour limitations for second-semester freshmen coeds vanished because second-semester frosh men had no parietal restrictions. Finally, in the fall 1971, the administration established maximums for returning to the dorms (if off campus longer than twenty-four hours, a student had to sign a leave permit) of midnight for weekdays and 2:00 A.M. for weekends. Each wing of each quad (Deglman-Swanson for men, Gallagher-Kiewit for women) would vote to set hours within the University guidelines—all voted to establish the maximum. The 26th Amendment the United States Constitution (1971, eighteen-year-old majority) directed the administration's decisions on this and other related issues.[50]

Strict visitation rules also began to bend. On Sunday, February 26, 1967, between 3:00 to 6:00 P.M., the women's dorms "drew hundreds of students and faculty. Hootenanies were held in both dorms, and a go-go girl performed in Kiewit's sixth floor lobby." The Trustees viewed the open house as "experimental," and "not meant to establish a precedent." Their "present thinking" preferred an annual occasion "in that parents and faculty members are invited and each floor makes special preparation in terms of cleaning the rooms." The men's dorms held a similar event for the women, and in the subsequent fall the SBG called for "coed quadrangle housing," which would gender integrate the dining facilities. Becker Dining Hall had opened in February 1966 and the University devised a punch-card system that allowed students to use either dining room, but convenience (short, indoor walk from your dorm room) trumped socializing with the opposite sex. In February 1968, the committee on student life policy endorsed the quadrangle plan, but the following semester, a petition signed by about four hundred students radically altered the scheme by proposing that coeds occupy the eighth and ninth floors of Swanson Hall ("A preliminary check of the petition Thursday showed a majority of male signatures"). According to the SBG, the administration responded with a policy of "active non-co-operation." Acting president Fr. Schneider rejected the proposals "based on the obvious realities of a new fund drive and difficulties that the dormitory structures pose to the open dorm policy." Five hundred students gathered in the east quad to listen a plan of action. SBG president Robert Hobbins asked them to turn on all the water faucets and electrical fixtures on campus, and to flood the switchboard office with calls to the development office. Water overflowed in Swanson Hall flooding the game room, but it suffered only $50 worth of damage. Moreover, "About 20 students stayed overnight in coeducational tents in the East Quadrangle and several hundred students attended a noisy rock concert which lasted until 4 A.M. Over 200 students spent a night in the Swanson Hall lobby participating in a 'get-it-together.'" The SBG passed a resolution "to commit students to a campaign to educate the 'sadly misinformed' public about the real meaning of the policy. Hobbins was given editorial space in the *Omaha World-Herald* and time on KETV." In April 1970, a committee of three students and two administrators drew up revised visitation regulations: Friday-Saturday, 7:00–11:30 P.M., Sunday 1:00–6:00 P.M., "Rooms must be unlocked and subject to inspection when guests are present." Each wing could vote on the rules and any student in variance with the wing policy could transfer. Subsequently, in 1974, a University task force sanctioned coed dorms composed of two floors for women.[51]

Another dorm regulation caused unrest; in 1965, with Swanson Hall erected, all undergraduate males had to live on campus (professional students "cordially invited to take advantage of the conveniences offered"). In 1969, with both quads complete and one hundred vacancies because of the downturn in enrollment, the University began to enforce the policy in earnest. Only undergrads twenty-four years or older, those obtaining housing as part of employment, those in financial distress, or those with parental permission to live with "immediate relatives" could live off campus. Obtaining that right became a featured topic on the editorial page of the *Creightonian*. Finally, in spring 1974, a University task force recommended that undergraduate seniors have the privilege of living off campus. The administration acquiesced, but reserved the right to require enough students to live in the dorms "to assure that the hall's federal debt retirement is kept on schedule."[52]

Changes in cultural attitudes and in state law also affected the dormitories. The illegal use of drugs became common among white middle-class youth during the 1960s. Thus, in February 1968 the committee on student life policy mandated an addition to Chapter 4 of the *Student Handbook*, which made the "possession and use" of illegal drugs, on or off campus, "grounds for disciplinary action and dismissal." Gauging the extent of use remains problematic. Not until 1974 did the administration undertake a public display of enforcement. Yet, in February of that year, after room searches led to the arrest of four students for the possession of marijuana, the dean of students eliminated RA room searches because they did not want them testifying against students ("It can destroy their relationship with the rest of the people on their floor").[53]

Certainly, for the majority, the drug of choice remained alcohol. In February 1967, a discussion group of two hundred students reached the conclusion that a "Rathskeller" or "beer bar" on campus made sense for twenty-one-year olds, who also deserved to host "21 only parties." The Trustees felt, "There is little danger that drinking will be permitted on campus or for that matter at official Creighton functions, because of the obvious problems." Yet during the summer, they revised the regulations to allow alcohol at events attended by students "mostly of adult age" (subsequently interpreted as 60 to 70 percent of the crowd). In 1969, Nebraska lowered the drinking age to twenty; within a week, the SBG recommended that legally aged students should have the right to drink in the dorms. The administration demurred, but did grant the privilege of an open bar at prom and, in spring 1971, on-campus "beer blasts." Subsequently, in September, the committee on student life voted unanimously to repeal the ban on alcohol. The Nebraska legislature had just lowered the drinking age to nineteen, but the state liquor commission had refused to waive the law banning the sale of spirits within three hundred feet of an educational institution. Thus, Creighton became the twenty-fourth Jesuit school to permit alcohol in the dorms, since approximately 80 percent of the residents had attained the legal age of consumption. In 1972 and 1974, the legislature rejected Creighton-sponsored bills granting permission to establish a Rathskeller; for many years, the Brandeis Student Center contained a dimly-lit room with wood booths, using the name, but without beer, thus mocking its German namesake.[54]

On a more sober note, the reaction against the Vietnam War brought an equally momentous policy change—the abandonment of mandatory participation in the ROTC by male undergraduates. En route to that decision, eight months before the Gulf of Tonkin Resolution in August 1964, which signaled the escalation of United States troop involvement in Vietnam, the army introduced counter-insurgency lectures (four years later, actual training in techniques) and bayonet drill into the ROTC regimen. At the end of the year, the Reserve Officer Training Corps Utilization Act required cadets to enlist in the reserves at the beginning of the Advanced Course (no longer could they refuse a commission, and were drafted if they dropped out). As the need for officers intensified, the army added inducements: in 1965, two-year full-tuition scholarships and a program to gain a commission in two years, avoiding Basic ROTC; in 1967, a four-year "full-ride" (tuition, books, lab fees, $50 per month stipend) and a flight instruction program for seniors.[55]

With the rapid intensification of the Vietnam conflict, by 1966 mounting conscription again became a timely topic (college deferments were still based on the selective service test and semester grades). At first, the ROTC benefited from the draft; enrollment in the Advanced Course spurted, as more students sought to gain commissions, which enabled them to enter the service as an officer. The University held a military information night, and on December 1, 1967, the Reverend Richard

Spillane, S.J., made a presentation on the ethics of "draft-dodgers." The 1968 draft law eliminated many exemptions, including deferments for graduate training outside the medical fields. That September, the number of applications for Advanced ROTC increased 35 percent, including more graduate students and eleven from the law school. Associate professors of physiology in the medical school, Donal Magee, Ph.D., and Henry Gale, Ph.D., aided the draft counseling service offered by the American Friends Service Committee (a Quaker organization, Omaha chapter established by Gale's wife, Kira); 75 percent of the calls came from students. In 1969, the draft shifted to a lottery system based on birthdays. On September 14, 1970 (symbolically, the first birthday to receive a "Greetings" letter from Uncle Sam), a branch of the Omaha Draft Information Service opened in the Brandeis Student Center (located on a private-school campus to avoid state restrictions) and remained there until the creation of the all-volunteer armed forces in 1973.[56]

Despite the looming possibility of conscription, the Creighton community contributed minimal support to the antiwar movement. Largely Catholic Cold Warriors, most faculty and students apparently empathized with the co-congregant leaders of South Vietnam, and viewed the hostilities as a crusade against communism (no scientific poll data available). Additionally, the majority of students came from the Midwest and a high percentage of them held their parent's conservative political values. Also of significance, dedicated careerists committed to their academic program, in a professional school or striving to enter one, composed a sizeable cohort of the student body. The characteristics produced a miniscule antiwar movement, equally counteracted by activity in support of United States policy. Thus, in October 1965 about thirty students attended an antiwar "teach-in," and in December, a "disappointing" eighty-one turned out for a faculty forum. In the meantime, the Young Republicans counter-protested, and in November, approximately 1,600 students signed a petition supporting the Vietnam War. A year later, an "informal poll" indicated that "nine out of ten" students approved of American involvement in the struggle. During 1967, several individual war protestors devised stunts and a few letters to the editor condemned the fighting because of the resulting civilian casualties. In April, simultaneous counter demonstrations occurred—antiwar with six to eight marchers, "Back Our Boys in Vietnam" with thirty to forty. The 1967–68 academic year produced more of the same: "On several occasions students and faculty—mostly from the burgeoning fine arts department—bearing placards and distributing literature, silently protested U.S. involvement in the war." In rebuttal, William Ramsay, director of public relations, formed an anti-anti-Vietnam support group. Additionally, some students organized a "pray-in" in honor of the four Creighton alumni killed in the conflict to that date and in support of the troops, and the coed sodalities and sororities started "Operation Cheer-Up," writing letters to G.I.s in Vietnam (three hundred in the first batch). Hubert Humphrey, Robert F. Kennedy, and Eugene McCarthy brought competing messages to campus during the presidential campaign, all to well-behaved crowds.[57]

In 1969, neither marches nor moratoriums attracted much support. In April, on a Saturday afternoon, about one hundred students paraded from the University to the Douglas County Courthouse (only five from Creighton). As the event began, about fifty Creighton students "dressed for baseball and sunbathing, stood across the street, well back from the curb, staring at them curiously." The following October, by a vote of 15–6–5, the SBG voted to participate in the Vietnam Moratorium. Father President Linn announced classes as usual, but no "cuts" given. While seven students went to Washington, D.C., for the national march, the *Creightonian* covered the event with a page 3 story: seemingly, classes went on normally, the two-day fast did not materialize, satirist Allan Sherman spoke on campus, and a "small group of Creighton students and professors participated in Saturday's candlelight march from Elmwood Park to Memorial Park." Moreover, the International Relations Club, in conjunction with several other schools, cancelled the Midwest Student Symposium on United States Foreign Policy due to insufficient participants. In comparison, in May 1970, twenty-five students staged a sit-in at the ROTC office and an outpouring of five hundred students attended a Mass in the East Quad "to show concern over United States policy in Cambodia and four dead students at Kent State University." Thereafter, students returned to their minimal support for antiwar protest activity, until the cessation of hostilities in 1973. The lack of interest carried over to the Vietnam amnesty issue, despite the attempts of the Reverend Darrell Rupiper, OMI, who struggled to form a campus-based chapter of a statewide group.[58]

Only the abolition of mandatory ROTC mustered significant student support. In April 1967, an ROTC instructor commented in the *Creightonian* about the "open hostility to the Department" on campus. The following spring, well over 850 students and faculty members signed a remonstration critical of mandatory ROTC, emphasizing the intellectual inferiority of the courses. The military conducted a counter attack; the Creighton corps handed out newly created awards to three administrators, recognizing their support for the cadets, and the regional headquarters awarded Fr. President Linn the Department of the Army Certificate of Appreciation for Patriotic Civilian Service. Concurrently, the commandant of the Creighton cadets warned that if volunteerism led to a reduced corps, the army might have to abandon the post. During the fall semester 1968, some undergrads protested by refusing to attend class and accepting the promise of an AF grade (absence failure). Furthermore, a boycott of drill produced a 30 percent cut rate. The success spurred the SBG to support the goals of the protestors, resolving "to rid the academic community of the arbitrary and Non-academic personal appearance and grooming code prescribed by the Military Department for undergraduate freshmen and sophomore men in ROTC." Again, only a minority opposed the battalion because of its alleged complicity in the Vietnam War; instead, as the contemporary play stated, it was all about *Hair*. On December 6, 1968, another consideration became preeminent; at Creighton Prep, a major feeder school, 69 of 221 seniors signed an epistle to the University's director of admission warning that if ROTC remained compulsory, they would consider attending another college. Nonetheless, not intimidated, the curriculum committee delayed action on a proposal, arguing they had not studied the issue fully.[59]

Continued pressure, however, impelled a speedy resolution of the issue during the spring semester. By that time, Creighton remained one of only eleven schools, of the forty-nine institutions in the Fifth Army District, to retain mandatory participation. Undergrad critics encouraged the student-rights committee of the Creighton AAUP chapter to investigate the practical, financial, and moral concerns associated with ending the commitment. Kenneth Wise, Ph.D. (political science), chaired the ad hoc working group, which led to an AAUP resolution in favor of volunteerism. To obtain a broader understanding of faculty sentiments, the Faculty Council polled the full-time teachers of the University: none in the law school returned the questionnaire and only 44 percent from the medical school did; all other schools returned at a rate of 59 percent or higher. The arts and pharmacy faculty supported curtailing compulsion, CoBA split evenly on the issue, and Medicine and Dentistry voted to retain the obligation (as did twenty-four of thirty-four Jesuits). Following the wishes of the substantial majority of the undergraduate faculty, Dr. Ross Horning, chairman of the Faculty Council, wrote a resolution in favor of voluntary ROTC. He stressed the fact that most Catholic and Jesuit institutions in the region had already converted to that position, and that for admissions counselors, "there is no question more often asked by high school seniors than the question of mandatory R.O.T.C. at Creighton." On February 6, 1969, the twenty-three-member Faculty Council voted 15–5–1 (two from law did note participate in the decision) to recommend that the administration make the program voluntary beginning the following September and Fr. President Linn accepted the proposal.[60]

The "60s look" sprouted immediately, as "the absence of mandatory ROTC for the freshmen and sophomore undergraduate men left them free of restriction as to the length of hair, beards, moustaches and sideburns." Moreover, the Creighton expectation that students "dress in good taste at all times," which excluded wearing Bermuda shorts and T-shirts to class, church, dining halls, lectures, and formal events succumbed to the contemporary emphasis on "casualness." Only forty-eight freshmen signed up for ROTC in the fall 1969; the drill team, the band, the military ball, and the bestowing of commissions at Commencement immediately faded away. Enrollment continued to drop as selective service quotas fell with President Richard Nixon's strategy of troop withdrawal from Vietnam and the eventual abolition of the draft in 1973. That year, the number of cadets bottomed out at about sixty; thereafter, incentives such as more numerous scholarships, higher pay, and the enrollment of women began to attract more recruits (freshmen Linda Iseman, Gwendolyn Jones, and Letitia McCarthy became Creighton's first coed cadets).[61]

Faculty evaluation developed into the only other issue to exercise the interest of a sizeable segment of the undergraduate student body. The week before final exams, in December 1966, responding to a national trend, AVP Fr. Harrington distributed an evaluation questionnaire for use by ninety participating faculty members in the CCAS and the CoBA (six refused, four deferred to spring semester). The Lay Regents feared that the experiment, "if uncontrolled, can cause faculty unrest"; therefore, Fr. Harrington resisted the student plea to publish the results. The SBG, smart-

ing from the failure to circumvent administrative control of book sales through the
establishment of a book exchange (doomed because of chicanery and pilferage), took
up the cause of student evaluation of faculty and classes. After devising a form, the
SBG asked the faculty for ten minutes of class time on November 17, 1969; the
response was "almost 100% unfavorable." Therefore, in December, it distributed the
questionnaire in the dorms, realizing about a 45 percent return, planning to distribute
the tabulations at fall registration. Faculty critics complained that the evaluation "falls
short of its dual purpose" to inform students and "to point out to instructors areas in
their classes needing improvement or revision," because of insufficient participation
and "ambiguity of choices of answers." In 1970, the SBG tried to sketch a positive
public image for evaluation by creating the Robert F. Kennedy Award to honor faculty achievement. From eleven finalists, it chose Richard Shugrue, Ph.D., chairman
of the political science department, as the first recipient.[62]

The SBG persisted and the academic affairs committee relented, allowing class
time for filling out the evaluation forms. The results distributed in November 1971
produced anxiety; many undergrad faculty felt the process provided an "instrument
for the students to take 'potshots' at the instructors." It became "a sore spot" in the
sociology department; "ringleaders" assistant professor James T. Ault III and Dr. Jack
Angus proposed "several new designs." For the next three years, the *Creightonian*
published the results of the survey, which aimed to measure the characteristics of the
instructor, the course components, exams, and the professor's expectations. The com-
posite produced a "teaching effectiveness" grade, with the majority of the courses
falling in the "C" or "D" range. Continued reform of the process aspired "to take an
instrument perceived as a threat to faculty and ignored by students and make it useful for both groups." In 1974, the CCAS established a committee on faculty evaluation and the student-sponsored program ceased; the process had evolved into an
accepted administrative tool to judge faculty performance and to spur faculty development (but with never-ending disputation concerning the instrument). While students no longer read the results of the class evaluations in their newspaper, they
gained a voice in rank and tenure deliberations. In 1973, the CCAS had devised the
initial form of a system in which the SBG would choose four students from at least
two different classes taught by a faculty member up for review, and ask them to submit a letter of recommendation.[63]

With virtually no confrontation, students also experienced significant changes in
their religious obligations. Effective February 3, 1964, adhering to "the Vatican Council's emphasis on Christian freedom and personal responsibility," the University abolished obligatory attendance at a weekday student Mass. Creighton followed the lead
of other Jesuit universities that had experienced large increases in enrollment, producing scheduling and monitoring headaches. Father President Linn preferred to offer "a
positive incentive to a more active participation in the Holy Sacrifice," but insisted
volunteerism would not extend to retreats "because they are an integral part of the
Jesuit education system." However, scheduling and staffing the variety of on-campus
Christian Renewal Weekends and off-campus retreats posed problems. In an era of

shrinking numbers of priests, it became especially difficult to find ones who could give "the type of Vatican II" experience desired by the youth of the day. Thus, starting in 1965, the new director of the University Christian Life and Action (UNCLA) program, the Reverend Joseph Egan, S.J., began to move away from "mass production" events "to meet changing interests and attitudes as well as manpower shortages." One option became a series of "closed retreats" for thirty to forty students; scheduling became year-round at a pastoral off-campus site, following the gift from Laurence O'Donnell (BSC, 1927) and his wife, Kathryn, for the purchase of an eight-acre site with two house-cabins at Hummel Park at the northern boundary of Omaha.[64]

Then, in March 1969 the SBG voted unanimously to request the abolition of mandatory retreats and to replace them with "a positive program of Christian life." The following fall, the administration changed the composition of the religious welfare committee from eleven Jesuits to seven, two faculty to seven, and two students to seven, Fr. Eagan remaining chairman. The reconfigured group decided to recommend "that all retreat requirements be removed for all students, both professional and undergraduate, in order to provide a more profitable Christian Life program to meet the diverse needs of the students." UNCLA changed its name to Campus Ministry, which consisted of "a team of clergy and laity who serve the human religious needs of the total university community." The sodalities ceased. In their place arose the Christian Life Community for students "who want to develop themselves completely as persons and learn leadership in helping others." In an uneven transition, during the first year, two officers of the new organization resigned "because of a lack of response and cooperation from the members" (part of the widespread complaints about "the general apathy of the organizations on campus"). Nonetheless, Creighton "posted the highest number of retreatants of any of the twenty-eight Jesuit colleges and universities in the United States." Moreover, beginning in 1968, under the inspiration of the Reverend Don Doll, S.J., Saturday midnight Mass at St. John's Church became popular. Finally, ecumenically for non-Catholics, since 1963 the Reverend Leonard Barry had served as chaplain for Creighton's approximately six hundred Protestant students.[65]

In addition, the mind-set of the sixties had a fleeting influence on the Greek-letter system. Except for an embarrassing "rash of raids" of off-campus parties, during spring semester 1967 fraternities and sororities continued to flourish. The administration denied responsibility for the actions of the police, and city councilman Robert Cunningham alleged the council gave "no direct order" for the concentrated effort, but pointed to "a need to crack down on all cases of liquor law violations" (subsequently, the lowering of the drinking age temporarily shifted the focus to high-school students). Despite the loss of the ROTC troop, Phalanx (1967), the number of undergraduate frats increased to six, with the addition of two local groups. Significantly, the system became officially "social." According to Creighton's problematic taxonomy, in 1965, the forty-four members of the local "service fraternity" Alpha Phi Omega switched affiliation to become the Beta Chapter of Phi Kappa Psi, alternately (and mistakenly) billed as "the University's first social fraternity" or "the first national social fraternity at Creighton since 1951" (the *Creightonian* provided no explanation for its use of the date. In 1967 Delta Chi Delta organized (national charter, 1970), and in 1968 the IKEs (busted in an alcohol raid the previous year and disciplined) made the euphemistic transition from service organization to social fraternity, affiliating with Sigma Alpha Epsilon. The Phi Psi and SAE chapters at Creighton were the first at Catholic institutions in the United States. Also in 1968, Phi Kappa Psi received University sanction to lease the first undergraduate "Greek lodge house," a "non-resident facility" for use "as a meeting place, informal gatherings, studying—a place for its members to identify with." The professional frats also thrived; for example, Phi Chi (Medicine) purchased a "mansion" and Phi Alpha Delta (law) attracted sixty pledges in 1968. Sororities experienced the same popularity. In the fall 1966, "nearly 300 coeds rushed for 85 openings in the four existing chapters (79 accepted)." The following spring, the low acceptance ratio prompted the administration to authorize the formation of Kappa Beta Chi, with an out-of-sequence spring-semester "open rush cake party."[66]

However, in the fall 1968, leaders of the sororities expressed "disappointment," as only about 200 registered for rush and a mere 112 attended the last event (the *Creightonian* had eliminated the Greek page). The following year, the Greek system was "labeled racist"; the sororities responded with "Sensitivity Sunday" and the fraternities held a "symposium" to discuss "differences with blacks." Only three African Americans attended, one answered the question of why they do not rush, positing two reasons: "The black student doesn't want to become a display piece for the fraternity system," and in 1964 "a popular black student was 'balled' when he went through pledging." Crossing the racial divide remained extremely rare; fraternities remained all-white organizations, but, in the early 1970s, Theta Phi Alpha and Delta Zeta sororities each admitted a single black member. Pledge classes for both genders, however, dwindled briefly and activities atrophied because of financial problems. In 1971, Alpha Sigma Alpha sorority relinquished its charter and reorganized as a local chapter, Alpha Sigma Gamma, which eliminated the "strain" of national dues and cut pledge fees in half. The following year, Sigma Sigma Sigma sorority and Alpha Kappa Psi folded. Nevertheless, in 1973, the Inter-Fraternity Council (IFC) reorganized to settle disputes between fraternities, to represent them to the administration, and to establish rush procedures. That same year, in a rapid turnaround, the *Bluejay* proclaimed, "more students pledged than ever before"; in 1974, about 160 undergraduate women belonged to four sororities and about 200 men belonged to five fraternities. They represented a small percentage of the enrollment, but as organized cohorts, they continued to have an influence well beyond their number.[67]

The athletic program experienced analogous trials and tribulations, while the era's historical forces induced changes in its structure. It survived the cheerleader episode, doing without a squad during the 1972–73 season, but, "subject to some new regulations," the University assembled a new group in September 1973. It also weathered NCAA regulations governing the status of Division I schools and the demands of the feminist movement by fielding a series of poorly supported, non-scholarship "minor" sports. During the 1960s, the tennis team compiled a winning record with part-time faculty or student player-coaches. Interestingly, in 1964, coach the Reverend Anthony Weber, S.J. (speech department), welcomed a freshman coed to the varsity team ("proved she could hit the ball over the net as well as most of her male counterparts"); her career at Creighton and her pioneering example proved transitory. In 1971, a newly appointed coach announced the demise of the team, due to a "lack of interest and insufficient talent." However, the following year he succeeded in reestablishing a team. Contemporaneously, golfers competed in two seasons in one academic year, allowing the University to comply with the NCAA rule that stipulated the fielding of four teams each semester. Thus, during the mid-1960s, athletic director and head basketball coach "Red" McManus also directed the duffers until abandoning the assignment to the athletic business manager/sports publicist (positions created in 1962, combined in 1966; the post of Jesuit faculty moderator of athletics eliminated). Over the next three years, Stu Erickson handled his administrative chores as well as coaching the golfers to a 43-12-2 dual-meet record against mostly midwestern teams, ending the decade with "the winningest record of the varsity." In comparison, the record of the rifle team drifted into oblivion as it became "the lost son of Creighton sports." The team "met varsity teams from other schools, received a 'C' and represented Creighton at the meets," but did not collect official "varsity letters because the university considered the sport an intramural activity."[68]

In limbo also lay Creighton's second fleeting venture with soccer. Foreign students and faculty provided the majority of players and fans. CoBA freshman Eduardo Iragorri organized the club in 1963 and recruited Gerald Hutchinson, Ph.D., chairman of the math department, as player-coach (club sports received no University funds). The team folded after two years when Iragorri and the equipment did not return to school. In 1966, interested students and faculty reorganized a team and played a fall and spring schedule. The University elevated the club to varsity status in 1967, and for the next three years, the team played fall and spring games. Then, without fanfare, in 1970 cross-country replaced it as a varsity sport; soccer survived one more year as an intramural activity and then faded from the scene. Similar attempts to resurrect football (1968), and to sustain rugby (1972) and hockey (Creighton Icebirds, 1973, 1974) as club sports, endured brief flings.[69]

Even baseball, the ostensible second "major" sport, subsisted with walk-on players and part-time coaches (who handled more than one sport, or graduate assistants). The team had to vie with high school and recreational teams for reservations for a diamond at city parks for practice time (or use the gymnasium) and home games. Nonetheless, it maintained a winning record against local schools. Then in 1969, "A funny thing happened to the Creighton Bluejay on his way to an expanded baseball program. He lost twice as many games as he won." That is, former player and graduate-assistant coach Thomas Tvrdik increased the number of games from about twenty to over thirty, and added a "southern road trip" (Missouri and Arkansas) during Nebraska's cold spring weather, but had a disappointing season. In 1970, Creighton committed the program to Division I status as an independent; it hired a full-time coach, Larry

Cochell, with an assistant, David Baker (the first African-American coach at the University). They posted a 25-7 record their initial season, then strengthened the schedule and slipped to 24-21 the following year (another dramatic jump in games played, but scholarship support continued to lag). Baker became head coach in 1972, and continued the winning ways. He gained a home field in an arrangement with the City of Omaha and the College World Series (CWS). Both provided money and assistance to the University to prepare and manage a tract of land at 24th and Martha streets (leased from the Salvation Army for $1, subsequently named Booth Field) as a baseball diamond for exclusive use by Creighton from September 1 through June 1, and the CWS during its two weeks of play (summer play for city leagues).[70]

Despite the minimal effort, red ink showed brightly on the bottom line of the athletic department's budget. All the sports discussed above produced no revenue and basketball income did not cover expenses. The University budgeted a "conservative amount of money" for scholarships and recruiting, yet annual deficits of about $70,000 per year accrued during the early 1970s (first available financial reports). Basketball remained the only sport with a fan base at Creighton, but even that began to erode as McManus posted a 60–65 record from 1964–65 through 1968–69. The record 86,856 supporters that witnessed the thirteen home games during a 22-win season in 1963–64, plummeted by one half within two years and no radio sponsor stepped forward to broadcast the 1967-68 schedule. That spring, the administration renewed McManus's contract as athletic director and head coach for one year, while it purportedly prepared to separate the positions. McManus resigned the following spring, citing ten years as enough and recent media denigration ("I wanted to get out of coaching before my kids were old enough to read the papers"). He only obliquely referred to administration pressure, while friends breathed a sigh of relief, fearing his fiery temper and courtside antics might lead to a heart attack. He summed up his accomplishments, stating, he "moved the program up from playing a chump schedule to playing the best in the nation." In 1968, he also oversaw the fruition of Duce Belford's dream of an athletic hall of fame (first inductee, Robert Gibson, A.B., 1957). Furthermore, he nurtured the program's relationship with Dr. Lee Bevilaqua (Creighton M.D., 1961), who would spend four decades as the volunteer physician to the team and as mentor and housefather to many of the players.[71]

In 1969, from a list of fifty-four applicants, Creighton hired Edward "Eddie" Sutton as athletic director and head basketball coach. He retained Thomas Apke, captain of the Creighton team (1963–65), who had served as assistant coach since his graduation. In 1971, Sutton acquired additional support, hiring Thomas Brosnihan (A.B., 1958), the head coach at Creighton Prep, as a second assistant. As a ramification of the cheerleader incident, the sagging turnouts, and the voluntary ROTC, the team instituted a "modified" hair policy, with the "key words" of "neat and well-groomed." The staff explained, "The fact that Creighton has such a small student body and must depend on the Omaha public for most of its attendance," it had "to stay away from extreme hair styles." Sutton quickly reestablished the winning tradition, but had little impact on the historically weak student spirit. The *Creightonian* argued he had "no student support," because "no one ever sees the head basketball coach anywhere except the home games at the Civic Auditorium." Before departing, he concluded his five-year tenure with a 23–7 season and a return to the NCAA tournament (2–1) for the first time in a decade. This time, during the spring 1974 the University conducted a local search; "At least eight coaches called and applied for the job, but it wasn't open to others besides our two men." The position went to Apke, age thirty-one; Brosinhan, age thirty-eight, remained as his assistant, noting with his usual good humor, "I can't go back to south Omaha, because the packing houses are closing down." Daniel Offenburger, chairman of the physical education department since 1969 and sports information director since 1970, completed the reorganization by assuming the role of assistant athletic director.[72]

Offenburger also played a significant role in promoting women's participation in sports. The Women's Recreation Association reinstituted rifle as an intramural sport in 1964, and it participated at the intercollegiate level again in 1967 and 1968 ("received letters"). Moreover, the WRA sponsored sporadic intercollegiate events, the coed equivalent to club sports. For example, in 1966, "The Web, Creighton's coed [intramural] basketball team, defeated Peru State College [Nebraska] Sunday at the Creighton gym 44-34." That same year, the "first coed intramural swimming meet" occurred, followed the next year by the inaugural "mixed swimming program," made possible by "a complete remodeling of locker and shower facilities." The progression culminated in April 1968, as ten coeds swam in a meet at Kearney State College (Nebraska). The University supported the progress by hiring Marilyn Raupe as director of women's intramurals (1967). Her short-term, part-time position contributed to alleviating a "lack of communication between the Administration and the coed." In 1968–69, "coed intramurals got a big boost from the Athletic Department and IM director Dan Offenburger," garnering opportunities in basketball, volleyball, bowling, pool, and swimming.[73]

Demands for an official women's intercollegiate sports program reached a crescendo during the spring 1973 (aided by the passage, the previous year, of the Title IX amendment to the education articles of the civil rights laws). At the instigation of CCAS senior and SBG secretary Mary Higgins, "the student sub-committee of the Committee on the Status of Women initiated the organization of a woman's softball team." Higgins, Dean Eileen Lieben, and Dan Offenburger presented the proposal to the administration. Offenburger then "found emergency funding" of several hundred dollars and coached the team to a 4-6 record. The next fall, the University hired Meta Johnson to organize women's intramurals and to coach the new women's intercollegiate teams in volleyball (first season, 5-12) and swimming (2-2). It also employed Eddye McClure to teach physical education and to coach the "Lady Jays" basketball (9-5) and softball (4-7) teams (proposed programs in track and field, and in tennis did not emerge). The evolution of the coed's athletic program reached a milestone in the spring 1974, as women officiated the intramural women's softball tournament in order to avoid the frequent complaints from the previous year of "male chauvinism" hurled at the men umpires.[74]

As with sport, the historical forces of the "era of confrontation" changed the nature of the student body and the curriculum of virtually every school and college of the University. Responding to student desires, in 1963 the administration reinstituted the mid-year graduation ceremony, but then abandoned it and summer Commencement a decade later. Additionally, it moved the May Commencement from the Music Hall to the Arena portion of the Civic Auditorium (1966) and changed the time of the ceremony from Monday to Saturday morning (1970) to take advantage of better parking at the venue. Similarly, in 1967 it eliminated Saturday morning classes for undergraduates and allowed student attendance at the school-opening all-University convocation to become voluntary; by 1971, a mere 250 students participated. The next fall, the administration abolished the historic event, replacing it with an evening convocation (day classes held) for faculty, staff, and administrators, at which it distributed twenty-five-year and distinguished-service awards, followed by a cocktail party. Moreover, in the undergraduate colleges it revised the absence policy (1964, each instructor to enforce attendance); added the C+ (1965) and the Pass-Fail grades (1969) and eradicated quarterly exams (1967, maintained mid-semester "progress reports"), mandatory senior comprehensives, and the second "unrelated" minor (1968); and revised the calendar to begin the fall semester in August and end it in December, spring semester to run January to May (1971). The schedule change, debated for nearly a decade, eliminated extra travel costs for the Christmas observance, had students return in time to support the basketball team in January, and gave students an advantage in gaining summer employment.[75]

Even the Alumni Library responded to the winds of change. In 1966, it became the last library in the area to begin the transition from the Dewey decimal system to the Library of Congress cataloguing system. It hoped to realize advantages from central cataloguing and purchasing, but "based on the assumption that expenditures will be conservative," it sought grants and work-study students to facilitate the process. The discontinuance of the *Index* in 1966 posed a different problem; previously, following Catholic policy, it shelved books on the *Index* in a locked room and students had to present a permission slip signed by a faculty member to use them. Now the staff moved them to the open stacks and formulated a plan to "purchase complete works of several of the formerly banned authors." In 1967, a federal grant for book purchases helped the situation, allowing the University to shift funds to staff lines and to extend library hours to 11:00 P.M. on weekdays. Moreover, in 1968 the collection expanded through the acquisition of microfilm and microfiche materials and readers. The staff also began to study the concept of a computerized card catalogue (actually realized two decades later). The University did continue its evolution into the computer age with a 1966 National Science Foundation grant; the $33,900 was used to purchased equipment for a teaching-and-research center, directed by the Reverend Edward Sharp, S.J. (mathematics). Tangentially, in 1974 the physics department benefited from a federal surplus project, which donated a $234,000 former Minuteman-missile computer; honor students reprogrammed it from military to educational software.[76]

Specifically regarding classes, as early as 1964 the SLC petitioned the administration in favor of fine arts classes. That same year, the SBG voted to contribute $1,000 for instruments and another $500 toward the salary of a musical director, but the nascent band lasted only one year (all instrumental music venues ceased with the demise of the ROTC band in 1969). Similarly, the CCAS introduced ballet as a physical education elective in 1964, but the Board of Directors rejected appeals to create a dance program because of "space deficiencies" and the lack of information regarding what effect implementation would have, "particularly with reference to our relationship with other institutions." Furthermore, in 1972, after a decade with several all-American awards, the SBG withdrew its funding from *Shadows*, which began a second unsolicited hiatus. In comparison, in 1970 the Reverend Bernard Portz, S.J. (math department), who held an undergraduate music degree, reestablished a choral group on campus. Additionally, an art program under the direction of Fr. Lubbers, with the volunteer help of local artists, succeeded during the 1960s. First located in the remains of Wareham Hall and then in part of the downtown medical school, with a sculpture lab in a converted handball court in the gymnasium, it became a CCAS major in 1967 (a truck parked adjacent to Wareham became the "mobile art gallery"). It immediately caused a controversy with the use of the "undraped female figure," which it "considered necessary for the advanced course in life drawing." It restricted "young beginners" from the class and only used "paid professional models." It survived the flap, and in 1973 moved into the vacated dental school at California Street and Periphery Road.[77]

Simultaneously, the demand for "relevant courses" influenced the curriculum in the CCAS. In 1964, for example, the Reverend Eugene F. Gallagher, S.J., introduced "Education and Urban Renewal" (two decades later he gained notoriety for the "domestication" of campus squirrels that he fed with his hand extended through the window of his ground-floor office in the Hitchcock Building). By 1967, the "experimental university" or "X-U" made its debut, offering courses on "today's happenings," with "no tuition, no papers, no tests." It quickly morphed into the Campus Ministry's "living-room seminars," all but two of the thirty-three conducted by faculty, "primarily in [their] homes." That format also faded rapidly, replaced by the longer-lasting Creighton Extension Curriculum (CEC, 1973), which offered undergrads "a unique opportunity to participate for a semester in a non-traditional educational experience," combining "independent study projects with community living and a special interdisciplinary seminar." Father John Cuddigan, assistant dean of the CCAS, directed the program and resided with the students (about twenty per semester) at a duplex east of campus. In part, administrators viewed CEC as an "attempt to cut the disturbing dropout rate."[78]

Additional curricular changes in the CCAS sometimes worked at cross purposes, and other times featured various contending alignments of administrators, faculty, and students. For example, the administration promoted interdisciplinary programs (American Studies and Black Studies, 1968) to encourage breadth of learning; however, it also consented to the expansion of disciplinary requirements (e.g., eighteen hours for a psych major in 1955, up to twenty-one in 1967, increased to twenty-seven in 1973, and thirty in 1975), which promoted specialization. Moreover, the process of curricular revision generated acrimony; one faculty member decried "a certain meanness about the whole period" and that "timidity and yielding to the pressure of a bunch of agitators" permeated it. In 1966, Robert Apostol, Ph.D. (philosophy), organized a student panel "to discuss the role of Catholic colleges in the total picture of higher education"; the dialogue "helped place existing frustrations into sharper focus and prompted the Student Board of Governors to spearhead a curriculum revision drive." Father President Linn stated that in a world "changing so fast, we do not intend to confront the future in a spirit of reaction and disinclination." He intended "to make our educational process keep in tone with the changes which are happening all around us." Thus, he appointed an eighteen-member committee, chaired by Michael Sundermeier, assistant professor of English, which consisted of the undergraduate deans, one member each from student personnel and the counseling center, three students selected by the SBG, eight faculty appointed by the Faculty Council, plus one chosen by AVP Fr. Schneider. In addition to regular coverage in the *Creightonian*, chairman Sundermeier announced that he would place committee material in the Alumni Library for perusal by any interested party. However, the seemingly open process produced animosity. According to Dr. Allan Schleich, chairman of the history department, in February 1969 AVP Schneider called a general faculty meeting, showed a film, and gave a talk "about the new generation of students who had to be listened to and treated differently." Some faculty viewed his support for curriculum revision as an "authoritarian and divisive approach" and "some irate professors reacted quite negatively." Dr. Schleich interpreted the circumstance thusly: "What really happened here for about three and one half years was a situation where you found the higher elements of the administration almost in collusion with the members of the Student Board of Governors to try and make the faculty the enemy—which caused a tremendous amount of resentment by the faculty."[79]

The interpretation (correct or not) revealed the tense atmosphere in which students concentrated their criticism on the mandatory philosophy and theology classes. In the fall 1969, while the special curriculum committee labored, the administration restructured the requirements, lowering philosophy from fifteen to twelve hours and changing theology from four two-hour classes to three of three-hours. The program included electives instead of the Thomist sequence, which followed the trend at Catholic institutions in the United States. Nonetheless, replacing the two-generational Fr. Renard series engendered additional controversy at Creighton. Furthermore, by spring 1970 individual departments began to announce modifications in their programs; for example, the compulsory twelve-hour literature/rhetoric sequence of the English department shifted to a semi-elective scheme that allowed students to choose one class each from four groups, and the history department introduced team teaching to its required "civilization" course. Then the evaluation committee presented its ninety-page report to Fr. President Labaj in the fall 1970. One recommendation led to the creation of the CCAS curriculum committee, chaired by the Reverend Leonard Waters, S.J., and consisting of ten elected faculty and two students. Ultimately, according to Fr. Waters, that committee shaped recommendations for a "very conservative restructuring of the curriculum," which it explained at three open meetings with faculty and students.[80]

The administration approved the new CCAS curriculum in May 1971. That fall, lower-division students began fulfilling degree requirements that included a twenty-four-hour core, consisting of six hours each in English, history, philosophy, and theology (cultural studies for non-Catholics). Students could choose the additional thirty-six required hours from four "divisions": (A) humanities, (B) social sciences, (C) natural sciences, or (D) fine arts, foreign languages, speech, and journalism. Each student had to "complete a total of twelve courses distributed over at least six subjects, exclusive of the courses in the student's major subject and the core courses." The concept of a minor gave way to a novel format called "supporting courses," whereby each department advised its majors concerning twelve hours of acceptable relevant classes. A major concern remained, in that students could devise a course of study that avoided foreign languages (departments could require one), speech, mathematics, and the natural sciences. Proponents, however, "preferred to stress the positive, the intelligent choice under wise guidance and expect the basic result will be a better climate for teaching and learning." Students seemed pleased because of the diminished emphasis on philosophy, theology, and foreign languages; however, in part, faculty response divided along lines created by inclusion or exclusion in the core, which significantly influenced the size and stability of a department (e.g., a formerly required discipline placed in an elective division, worried about its ability to attract students).[81]

Anxiety continued to mount in 1973, as Fr. President Labaj, at the request of the Board of Directors, appointed a task force, chaired by Anne Scheerer, Ph.D. (Dean of the summer school and Special Programs, 1968), to study the undergraduate curriculum (a "self evaluation"). Father Labaj felt "it should be operating with a narrower focus," instead of the "19 relatively autonomous departments," with each "somewhat unwilling to relate to the modern trend toward interdisciplinary education." In comparison to the previous evaluation committee, "to avoid political pressure," the work of the committee would "not be publicized." That fall, about seventy-five of the two hundred CCAS faculty met and formulated a "Working Paper" as a rejoinder to the board mandate. It requested interdisciplinary classes, terminating some graduate programs, eliminating teaching assistants, and "reemphasizing the Jesuit foundation of this institution." The group argued the proposal would address the problems of stagnant enrollment and budget deficits in the CCAS. The paper, which did not reveal the author's name (Fr. Labaj wrote the preface), generated instant controversy. About twenty department chairs wrote letters to the AVP criticizing the "working paper." According to Dr. Kenneth Wise, many of the faculty "took it as a slap in the face" because it "seemed to imply that the faculty were responsible for the declining enrollment." He and Dr. Schleich complained that it "had a very unhealthy effect on faculty morale," which the summer school further depleted when it announced 30 to 35 percent salary reductions and that it would list twenty fewer classes. With input from students and faculty, new AVP the Reverend Donald MacLean, S.J., reworked the paper; it proposed new and revised programs to address contemporary social issues, more interdisciplinary courses, strengthening of advising, and improved retention (Creighton rate of freshmen graduating stood at 50 percent, national average 70 percent, important in relation to declining enrollment). Generally, the faculty reacted favorably, but fear of downsizing lingered. Two immediate innovations appeared—an honors seminar (a literature class taught by Nancy Fogarty, Ph.D.) and the Freshman Seminar Program (a one-hour class, with a faculty advisor and two student aides).[82]

The transitory summer school predicament resulted from a downturn in enrollment (peaked in 1971) due to the lowered draft calls (then the end of conscription in 1973). Moreover, Dean Scheerer argued that most students no longer felt "the same pressures for accelerating or completing their work because of uncertainty of demand in the job market." Also of significance, the number of nuns attending the summer school declined to about two hundred by the end of the 1960s, and practically all of them sought graduate degrees. Most graduate students attended part time and during summers; in 1968, the graduate school enrolled 81 full-time and 273 part-time students (with the decline of the number of nuns, men now contributed the majority) and they provided the largest cohort to the summer school (CCAS, 434; CoBA, 75; pharmacy, 16; graduate, 477). In 1969, the summer school began scheduling two concurrent sessions, one running six weeks (six hours maximum credit) and the other running eight weeks (nine-hour maximum). In 1971, it initiated offerings in law and pharmacy, and opened Swanson Hall as a coed facility ("not trying to construct a new life style here," but making it easier to clean other dorms for the fall, by concentrating summer students). The following year, it revamped the schedule to supplement the eight-week session with two five-week terms (six-hour maximum per term). Finally, in 1973 it allowed undergraduates to enroll in the four-year-old, foundation-supported, "mini semester for women," originally aimed at adults, formalizing it as a three-hour-credit, three-week "pre-session."[83]

During the period, Creighton graduated the first MBAs in Nebraska (twenty-six in January 1965) and expanded the graduate school offerings to include a non-thesis, no-foreign-language Plan B. Additionally, it installed an M.S. in Education and an M.A in International Relations and in Teaching (1968), as well as an M.S. in Guidance (1971) and an M.A. in Divinity (at the behest of the Omaha Senate of Priests, which wanted credit for continuing education, 1973). However, "limited library facilities precluded" Ph.D. programs in the humanities and social sciences. The natural sciences associated with the health sciences fared better; in 1966, the Trustees recommended establishing Ph.D. programs in biochemistry, physiology, anatomy, and radiology when it became "clearly feasible financially." Two years later, they rearranged the recommendation, declining to grant a request to add biology to the group, "because of certain changes at [the] Veterans Hospital and certain projections regarding federal subsidy." They proceeded with the reoriented plans, and in April 1969, the North Central Association accredited programs in anatomy, biochemistry, physiology-pharmacology, and microbiology. The new

Criss medical buildings facilitated those programs, but the NCA refused to sanction a program in "specialist in education" due to a "lack of sufficient planning." The abolition of draft deferments in 1968 and reduced federal support beginning the following year (tuition tripled between 1963 and 1975) pushed down the number of men enrolled in the graduate school (1967: 83 full-time, 212 part-time; 1968: 55 and 192). Unfortunately, due to the problems caused by declining federal subsidies, the graduate school closed the period on a sour note. In 1974, a survey of faculty, used to gain input regarding the "use of scarce resources" (85 percent return rate), encouraged a meeting of graduate students that "turned into a gripe session." They "felt left out," labeled the meeting a "token gesture," and humanities candidates complained about a perceived penchant for the sciences. Their views mirrored those of many of their arts faculty, who saw themselves as occupying "a subservient position and [merely providing] a service function in relation to the professional segments" of the University. Doctor Unscheid retired and Fr. Robert Shanahan became acting dean.[84]

The CoBA experienced similar era-ending turmoil. While it did not attract students likely to "man the barricades," the school could not escape the influence of contemporary historical forces. Its total enrollment continued to climb steadily from about 390 to approximately 480. However, whereas coeds in the 1920s had used the commerce college as a "backdoor" to the arts college, during the mid-1960s, the CoBA began to graduate five to ten women per year (arrival of the career woman). In 1966, the coed cohort established a professional sorority, Phi Gamma Nu, with twenty-two charter members, including Juanita Perry, the first known African American to attend the school. At the same time, the business undergraduates established a council to "encourage development of student responsibility" and to "serve as a communication link between the students and the administration." Obviously, they wanted a voice in curriculum design; Dean Irvin Heckman, Jr. (1963–68), subscribed to a University of Michigan survey of business executives who argued that "a combination of liberal arts and business education [would] make their successors the most effective." During his tenure, he consolidated the five existing departments into three—management-marketing, economics-finance, and accounting—while maintaining a curriculum that prescribed about 40 percent liberal arts classes and allowed only six hours of electives. Heckman acquired an associate dean, established a Center for Continuing Education for Business, and hired five new faculty members (all with the Ph.D. or in the final stage of obtaining it). He helped initiate an M.S. in Institutional Administration, which combined courses in religion and business for those interested in employment with non-profit organizations (operational after his departure). In 1968, Heckman left for more lucrative employment and the CoBA conducted its first professional search that included a committee with faculty and student members. The administration accepted the recommendation to hire George Hardbeck, Ph.D., formerly the school's first associate dean and Creighton's first non-Catholic dean. He started a program in industrial relations that combined CoBA and CCAS classes and, following an evaluation of the curriculum, he guided revisions that reduced requirements and increased electives to sixteen hours. Hardbeck continued to support the liberal arts component, and a 1971 adjustment realigned it into four groups of disciplines with required classes, but many elective opportunities.[85]

Hardbeck left after three productive years, and on February 1, 1972, William D. Litzinger began a short, controversial tenure as dean. On his watch, the Sloan Foundation provided funds for another computer, which had the capability of analyzing masses of business data, allowing "real world courses" (otherwise, students "work on problems too small to be realistic"). Moreover, in 1973 the University established its first endowed chair, in honor of John Begley, in Accounting (his fiftieth year at Creighton; in 1966, Pope Paul VI had made him a Knight of St. Gregory for "exceptional accounting work for the Archdiocese of Omaha). Dean Litzinger also established the Council of Business Executives as "a sounding board for proposed plans and policies," as well as stressing his intention to communicate with students. Unfortunately, the dialogue that ensued became quite acrimonious. Members of the faculty claimed the dean "arbitrarily" established a new curriculum, "a matrix management system," which eliminated departments and created three "generic functional areas": environment analysis, process function, and systems. In addition, the scheme included "temporary task groups and innovative-experimental projects," as well as team teaching, mini-courses, modular scheduling, and smaller classes made possible by faculty teaching twelve hours. One faculty member resigned and the others met and voted 12-2 to ask the AVP to evaluate the situation. He did, and in July 1974, the dean resigned and the curriculum reverted to its pre-matrix design.[86]

In comparison, the law school struggled early and ended the period on a high note. Legal education expanded astronomically in response to the demands of the 1960s; law school enrollment (Law School Admission Test required, 1961) exploded from approximately 150 in 1964 (5 women) to over 500 in 1975 (89 women). In 1968, students published the first *Law Review*, edited by senior Ronald Volkmer (subsequently a professor of law at his alma mater). Indicative of the increasing significance of women in law, in 1970 Maureen McGrath became the first female editor of the journal, and in 1974 women gained election to three of the four offices of the Student Bar Association. In the latter year, the SBA sponsored an honor code, but in a referendum, the budding barristers rejected it, fearing that it would create "Big Brother" and "inspire jealousy and a suspicious climate." The school's growth prompted the administration to establish more stringent admission guidelines and to limit the number of freshmen because the old building could not accommodate more students (212 freshmen in 1970, limited to 175 in 1971, which precipitated the instigation of summer classes). In 1972, the law school launched the advisory Faculty-Student Governance Committee to "consider anything pertaining to the law school community." That same year, some members of the Board of Directors opposed a $150 raise in law tuition (approved 8-4-1), but the new assistant for admissions had difficulty keeping up with the 200 percent increase in applications (1970 to 1974, the ABA began to try to control the production of attorneys). In admissions, the law school gave preference to two groups: (1) geographically, the states of the Great Plains, because the University drew its support from the area and the school "feels an obligation to support it," and (2) Creighton undergraduates.[87]

The upsurge in enrollment eventually garnered additional full-time faculty. The number remained at ten all during the 1960s, the decade closed with a 40:1 student-faculty ratio. In 1971, James A. Doyle stepped down and Steven Frankino became the fifth dean of the Creighton law school. The University granted him the wherewithal to double the size of the full-time faculty, which included the first woman, Frances Ryan (1973). Cramped quarters, however, had five new hires occupying office space in truck trailers parked adjacent to the building. Additionally, Frankino appointed an associate and an assistant dean, because accrediting teams had criticized "the lack of administrative adequacy." The staff enhancements provided the resources to add "depth to the program" and to introduce an elective curriculum (seminars with a 15:1 ratio). In 1965, Creighton had adopted the new degree designation *Juris Doctor* (J.D.), which reflected the post–World War II graduate status of a law degree (the LL.B. signified a baccalaureate in legal letters). Then-dean Doyle argued that the role of the attorney had become "more than a technician and a scrivener," and that an expanded curriculum needed to provide the law student with "more intensive training in the planning functions of a lawyer." Beginning in 1972, the program of study continued to prescribe freshman core requirements, but the second and third years consisted of electives from designated groups of classes. The senior year also encouraged clinical experience, emulating the direction of "professional education" in the health sciences. The student acquired "real-life" on-the-job training at agencies such as the Omaha Legal Aid Society, spearheaded by Colleen Buckley (J.D., 1962), with assistance from the Omaha Bar Association, the United Community Services, and the Junior League, and supplemental funds from the Office of Economic Opportunity. Students also participated in the Omaha Pre-Trial Release Program, interviewing those arrested for misdemeanors and advising a judge on their likelihood to appear in court if released until trial, and in a rural-aid program funded through a $134,583 grant from the Law Enforcement Assistance Administration. As part of the Creighton Legal information Center, juniors and seniors (with a faculty advisor) researched cases for attorneys and judges practicing in areas without adequate legal libraries.[88]

Then, in 1974, the enrollment rose 14 percent as the law school obtained a new facility. Dean Doyle had pressed for a new building all during the 1960s, as he had to schedule classes in the Rigge and Eppley buildings. In 1969, the Board of Directors "firmly reiterated their commitment to include a new law school in the goals and objectives of the forthcoming campaign" and selected a site between 21st and 22nd streets, California to Cass. In 1972, Philip Klutznick (LL.B., 1930) arranged for a $1.68 million loan from the Aetna Life Insurance Company at 8.8 percent interest. Creighton would pay 3 percent and a federal subsidy covered the remainder of the interest. The following year, William Ahmanson, in behalf of the family foundation, presented "a gift of approximately $2 million in Home Savings and Loan stock." In 1974, the University dedicated the new law school named in honor of Hayden W. Ahmanson (LL.B., 1923); the family donated another $280,000 to pay for the purchase of the "full square block across California Street" to the north, and to clear it "for both practical and aesthetic reasons" (it became a well-landscaped parking lot).[89]

The health science schools also celebrated the opening of new facilities. In 1964, the medical school broke ground for Criss II, a five-story 70,000-square-foot structure, fronting Periphery Road, which contained administrative offices, classrooms, and laboratories for first and second-year medical students. Floors three through five had walkway connections to Criss I and a 6,600-square-foot deck topped the building to house research animals. Its completion in 1966, enabled a systematic abandonment of the complex at 14th and Davenport Streets, purchased by the Nebraska Department of Roads for the extension of I-480 eastward through downtown Omaha. Creighton had to vacate the north building by July 1, 1968, and the south structure by July 1, 1969. The clinic moved to the former nurse's dorm at St. Catherine's Hospital. In 1972, a $5.87 million federal grant contributed the majority financing for Criss III, a mirror image attached to the east side of Criss II, but a fire, a strike, and material shortages delayed occupancy until August 1975.[90]

During the same timeframe, the administration dreamed of a new hospital neighboring its new on-campus medical complex. To maintain accreditation for the medical school, "eventually" the University had to "own and operate its own teaching hospital." As early as 1965, the Trustees and the Lay Regents began discussions with the Sisters of St. Francis regarding the relationship between the medical school and St. Joseph's Hospital. Simultaneously, some Lay Regents, then lay directors, questioned "large" medical school deficits and spent time "seriously discussing the survival" of the institution. However, the board's health affairs committee, headed by James B. Moore, vice president of Northwestern Bell, "turned things around." Subsequently, following years of painful discussion (management, ownership, location), in 1973, after 102 years of proprietorship, the Sisters transferred the hospital to a lay group, the Creighton Omaha Regional Health Care Corporation, organized by "nine prominent [University affiliated] Omahans as a non-profit organization." They guided the University through the largest building project in its history, which included a plan to connect the hospital and the Criss complex with a pedestrian walkway/parking platform that would straddle the North Freeway. Inflation and the costs of negotiating the "maze of planning and government approvals" for the four-hundred-bed hospital, with adjacent doctor's office building, pushed the proposal $10 million over budget, to $64 million. Funds from the Centennial Thrust campaign, a $50 million federally guaranteed loan, and $1 million from the Eppley Foundation underwrote the construction (completed in 1978), minus the over-the-freeway parking structure. More encouraging, thanks to the good offices of Leo Daly, Sr., the development expanded, as the Boys Town Institute for Hearing and Speech Disorders decided to build a hospital attached to the new St. Joseph's Hospital.[91]

While Creighton upgraded the medical bricks and mortar, it had to manage a budget that correlated enrollment, tuition, financial aid, and the number of faculty, with all profoundly affected by the amount of federal sustenance. During the 1960s, federal support for medical education increased to underwrite the training of more physicians and "auxiliary health personnel." In 1967, the number of freshmen in the medical school increased for the first time in fifteen years, though only slightly, from seventy-six to eighty-two. Tuition doubled between 1964 and 1970, while the actual costs of educating a medical student rose more dramatically (in 1970, tuition reached $2,400 per year, while the costs to educate a physician soared to over $8,000 per year). The University augmented its financial-aid packages; in 1964, it instituted a series of long-term loans, payable after graduation, as well as expanding scholarships. In 1966, a gift of $100,000, and then a bequest of $1 million, both from Neil Criss (M.D., 1912), bankrolled medical scholarships, as well as salaries for faculty and staff. He recalled that at graduation time, he and his brother C.C. owed Creighton $125; the administration trusted them to pay the debt and allowed them to receive diplomas with their class.[92]

Inflation, induced by the Vietnam War and the subsequent oil crisis, and federal spending cutbacks instigated by the Nixon administration (anti-Great Society) pushed the medical school to seek funds for its operating budget through tuition increases and enlarged freshmen classes (82 in 1970 to 110 in 1973), which boosted total enrollment from 320 in 1969 to 439 in 1974. Cognizant of the rapid growth, "several board members urged that the University continue to give preference to local and alumni-related applicants where there was evidence of ability to perform well in school." Despite the upsurge in undergraduate women and minorities, their presence in the medical school during the period remained infinitesimal, although their recruitment emerged as a priority. Demonstrating a sensibility to the civil rights movement, in 1967 Drs. Donal Magee, Henry Gale, Robert Heaney, and William Niemer organized "Saturdays for Science," a five-week program for black high school students. In 1971, African-American faculty member Claude Organ, M.D. (Creighton, 1952), headed a drive to establish "a program of remote preparation, recruitment and admissions"; the "concentrated effort" attracted six minority applicants to the medical school. In April 1972, it sponsored a Health Careers Opportunity Conference, attended by seventy-five minority students from area high schools. However, successful recruitment depended on "substantially increased amounts of financial aid"; in 1972, the Robert Wood Johnson Foundation donated $72,295 to provide scholarships and loans over the next four years to rural students, women, and minorities. To enhance the recruiting and retention efforts, in 1974 the University established an Office of Minority Affairs for the Health Sciences.[93]

Beyond the composition and size of the student body, the University had to contend with restructuring the medical school administration and the need for "massive funding" to lower the faculty-student ratio. In 1970, Richard Egan resigned and Joseph M. Holthaus, M.D. (Creighton, 1947), became dean. He oversaw a restructuring of the school's governance system to include participation by elected full-time and clinical faculty, as well as the presidents of the sophomore and senior classes, on the standing committees. The new "democratic" governance also inaugurated regular faculty meetings, and the subsequent pursuit of support resulted in the creation of the Medical Alumni Advisory Council. The reorganization included administration.

Alert to national trends, Dr. Robert Heaney formulated a proposal for the creation of a vice president of health sciences (VPHS) to coordinated the oversight of the programs of the related schools. The Board of Directors approved the plan in 1970 and, following a search, hired Heaney for the position with Egan as assistant VPHS. The medical school also obtained the needed faculty: In 1970, 89 men and 6 women taught full-time, 207 men and 8 women taught part-time; by 1973, the full-time faculty increased to 134, with women remaining marginal. Contributed-service part-time faculty continued to supply a crucial element toward meeting the budget, as did a revised practice plan for full-time faculty. The latter allowed them to generate revenue that increased their salaries and supported the school's operating budget, in turn facilitating more hires. Moreover, the new VPHS sought savings in joint ventures. In 1971, the Board of Directors approved the formation of the Creighton-Nebraska Universities Health Foundation to bring the two institutions together in "certain interrelated cooperative academic programs." Furthermore, the following year, Creighton and St. Joseph's Hospital established a formal affiliation with Rosary Hospital in Corning, Iowa, whereby the latter would send patients to specialists at Creighton; in turn, the medical school would send specialists to Corning to conduct continuing education. In another venture, seventy-three hospitals in the region had the option to send their EKGs via telephone lines for analysis by Creighton cardiologists. Creighton had teamed with Northwestern Bell to "pioneer" the service, and in 1973 a new device expanded the program by allowing long-distance monitoring of batteries in pacemakers.[94]

As national trends and historical forces of the era influenced the evolution of the medical school faculty and administration, they also manifested themselves among the students. In 1967, Creighton's medical students abandoned two "rather weak" and out-of-touch organizations and formed a new Student Health Organization, which gained student representation on the education policy committee and began to publish the *Beat*, a monthly magazine designed to improve student-faculty communication. It also enlisted students from the other health-science schools to promote the "right to health." To fulfill that goal, Henry H. Herrera (M.D., 1970) organized the efforts that culminated in the creation of the Willis Avenue Project. It obtained supplies from the Omaha-Douglas County Health Department and converted a "sparsely furnished house within Omaha's rotting north side" (donated by a Jesuit) into the Willis Avenue Clinic, open on Wednesday evenings. Additionally, in 1972 the Reverend Ernesto Travieso, S.J., chaplain to the schools of medicine and pharmacy, established the Institute for Latin American Concern (ILAC), which sent teams of students from the health science schools to the interior of the Dominican Republic for eight weeks. Locally, the civil rights movement brought attention to the race-based problem of sickle-cell anemia; in 1974, Matilda McIntire, M.D., began a screening program in conjunction with the Omaha Public School District.[95]

During the same period, the medical students initiated an examination honor code (1966), gained the right to offer faculty evaluations (1967), established the independent Creighton Medical Student Government (1968), and inaugurated a public ceremony at which seniors received their "Doctorate Hood" (regarded by many students as more important than Commencement). The Medical Student Government negotiated an agreement with the SBG for a "kickback" from the student fees in order that it could fund events more amenable to the desires and schedules of its constituents. It also clamored to make the curriculum "more responsive to the actual needs of the student" and to "stimulate student interest not only in medicine, but in the people of the community they serve." The faculty and administration believed in similar goals and sought to revise the curriculum toward a "team approach to health care" that integrated the health sciences. VPHS Heaney appointed a study committee "to prepare recommendations to reduce the time students must spend in established programs, increase academic mobility with curricula, and more fully integrate minority groups into the health sciences." In 1972, Heaney announced the establishment of the Criss Institute of Health, but attempts to secure federal funding grants failed. Nonetheless, curriculum reform proceeded with the introduction of the all-elective senior year and allowance of sophomores to gain some clinical experience.[96]

Moreover, reacting to the trends of the time, the medical school established Family Practice as a division of the department of preventative medicine to try to alleviate the shortage of general practitioners (in 1940, 80 percent of physicians were GPs; by the 1960s, 80 percent were specialists). It opened a Family Practice Clinic on 13th Street in a densely populated area of historic South Omaha. In the areas of specialization, in 1973 the AMA approved and Creighton inaugurated a three-year residency in psychiatry, using the St. Joseph's and Douglas County hospitals. On the other hand, cancer detection and the training of medical, dental and nursing students in preventative techniques suffered from the cessation of federal funds. Henry Lynch, M.D., headed a cancer-detection unit (a mobile home outfitted with the necessary equipment) that lost grant funding in 1973, becoming "immobile." Finally, in evaluating medical education at Creighton during an era that presented enormous challenges, in 1970 an article on medical schools in the *Washington Post* disparaged Creighton's school. The *Omaha World-Herald* printed a rejoinder and the Board of Directors reached a consensus that the criticism had not "hurt too seriously and that the report might actually have helped us in our fundraising efforts." In 1971, the students answered the critics emphatically; in the National Board Examinations, they scored in the upper twenty-fifth percentile of the seventy-seven medical schools in the United States, ranking first in surgery, ninth in obstetrics, and fifteenth in internal medicine (some schools chose their twenty-five best students to take the tests, at Creighton all seniors participated).[97]

Similar to the experience of the medical school, pharmacy struggled through the 1960s, but by the end of the era it recouped its vigor and played a major role in completing the Criss complex. In 1966, the Trustees rejected a request to establish a graduate program, arguing that the school was "not ready" because of a "lack of faculty, proper facilities, library, etc." It considered putting the dental school in the proposed Criss III Building with Medicine, and then allowing the CCAS and pharmacy share the old dental building. It deemed a new facility too costly "when it is obvious that the future of pharmacy is somewhat shaky." Enrollment fluctuated near 130 until 1969, and then began a significant and steady ascent for the next decade. Women continued to constitute about 20 percent of each class, but minority students remained rare; however, in 1974 African American Cedric Jones gained election as national president of the 13,000-member Student American Pharmaceutical Association.[98]

With the loss of the 14th Street building, the pharmacy school established offices in a duplex on California Street and students attended classes in Rigge, Eppley, and the Criss II buildings. The number of full-time faculty expanded from nine to thirteen to serve the increasing enrollment, and personnel from the hospital and the other health-science schools taught part-time. In January 1971, Dr. Greco resigned to return to full-time teaching and Ann Czerwinski served as acting dean; on June 14, she received the heartening news that the Department of Health, Education, and Welfare approved the grant for Criss III "only after Creighton proved . . . that the schools of medicine and pharmacy planned an imaginative team effort." Pharmacy gained a new home and an enhanced stature, and completed the design of a new curriculum to meet the team-education goals. During the late sixties, it had shifted courses, revised their content, and emphasized "more experience in drug therapy" by observing the administration of anesthesia and by making rounds with physicians, cataloguing "the effects of the drugs they are called upon to dispense." In 1972, new dean Robert Gerraughty, Ph.D., oversaw the introduction of a revised three-year professional program (two years undergraduate study and a passing score on the Pharmacy College Admission Test, PCAT, necessary for admission). The modified program of study included a "modular approach," which allowed a student to "learn at their own speed" and emphasized the "health team" concept. It eliminated "most senior laboratory work" in order to schedule "nearly 800 hours gaining practical experience," which entailed "clinical studies" in community and hospital pharmacies, and a drug information service. Since the late 1960s, pharmacy students had volunteered to provide drug information by going to schools to talk about drug abuse. In 1972, Creighton became one of five schools nationwide to participate in Project Speed (Student Professionals Engaged in Education on Drugs), which trained teams of students from the health sciences and law to visit high schools to talk about drug problems.[99]

Nursing followed an analogous path of status augmentation as it joined the health-science team. In 1964, the National League of Nursing accredited the baccalaureate program (but not the "supplemental") for six years, and returned in 1970, to grant an eight-year extension. During the interim, the department struggled to find adequate teaching space, especially to employ "sophisticated equipment," at times relying on empty rooms in Gallagher Dormitory. Subsequently, with the opening of the Rigge Science Building in 1968, nursing gained the use of fourth-floor labs, but the faculty retained their offices on the second floor of the Administration Building. By that time, the Mercy (1966) and St. Catherine's (1967) hospital programs had ceased, eliminating many part-time students. The enrollment in the baccalaureate program fluctuated considerably during the era, graduating a low of twenty-six BSNs in 1966 and 1967, and a high of fifty-six in 1973 (minorities and men were extremely scarce). Providing clinical experience caused problems as the students had to find transportation to hospitals distant from campus. Psychiatry training made students psychoactive; until the St. Joseph's Mental Health Unit opened in 1971 (on South 10th Street, adjacent to the hospital), they had to arrange carpools to the Regional Health Center in Lincoln, Nebraska. Ultimately, enrollment jumped when the Health Manpower Act of 1968 provided a scholarship program for nurses. Within a few years, Creighton experienced an "unusual growth in applications," which pushed the number of freshman to over one hundred in 1973.[100]

Those freshmen entered the newly established Creighton College of Nursing. VPHS Heaney included nursing in the health-science team concept. In March 1971, department chair Abby Heydman (after fifteen years at the helm, in 1970 Dorothy Vossen returned to teaching) submitted a request for college status. In April, the Board of Directors "expressed reluctance" and asked for further study; the analysis dispelled its disinclination, and in October it approved the creation of Creighton's eighth component. The report pointed out that many confused the Creighton and St. Joseph's Hospital programs, and that only three universities in the United States with a medical school had nursing as a department, and none resided in an arts college. Heydman argued that a college could better address the "needs and problems" of nursing education, and VPHS Heaney supported the change as "necessary for the nursing program to maintain equality with the other health care schools." Probably most important for the board, it "would not cause any increase in cost" and it "would make it easier for us to obtain federal funding."[101]

Controversy marred the inception of the nascent College of Nursing. Saint Joseph's Hospital merged its program into the school, Heydman became acting dean, and a nationwide search acquired Eleanor Repps, BSN, MSN, Ph.D., and professor of clinical nursing at the University of Kentucky, as the first dean, effective July 1, 1972. She complained that "nursing has been surprisingly lacking in power," saw "the whole women's lib program as benefiting nursing tremendously," and thought the "nursing profession could actually help solve the maldistribution of physician health care" by assuming "a range of functions that have been traditionally thought of as medical." The ideas meshed with the team approach, but internal administrative problems led to her quick departure. The dean had to break two tie votes concerning curriculum committee recommendations with regard to the time allotted to maternity and children's nursing versus psychiatric nursing. The psych-nursing faculty protested that, with the proposed trimester schedule, the Thanksgiving and Christmas holidays would disrupt their course outlines. VPHS Heaney and Fr. President Labaj supported the dean and all four involved faculty members resigned. Shortly thereafter, in late March 1974, approximately 115 students gathered (faculty and administrators barred) to discuss the new trimester system. In August, "for personal reasons," Repps resigned and Creighton faculty nurse Sheila Ryan became acting dean. Not an auspicious beginning, but, subsequently, the college hired replacement faculty and Ryan became its second dean.[102]

The dental school survived its own shuffling of deans during the early 1960s, and then entered a period of significant growth as federal funds flowed to confront the perception of a looming shortage of dentists. Indirectly, other federal grants supported specific projects such as the formation of an oral cytology center or targeted research and teaching about specific diseases, such as cancer. In 1967, for the first time in sixteen years, the school enlarged its freshman class from forty-six to fifty-one; administrators admitted the increase would "tax our physical facility to an absolute limit of capacity." In 1970, they added the new ADA requirement of three years (ninety semester hours) of undergraduate work for admission (passing the Dental Admission Test was mandatory since 1966). Neither qualification slowed the climb in enrollment, which mushroomed from 200 in 1969 to 267 in 1974 (while tuition doubled to about $1,700 per semester). The school welcomed its first woman since 1949, when Cheri Lewis enrolled in 1972 (four had been accepted). Moreover, modeling the efforts in the other schools, in 1969 Frank Dowd, student president of Alpha Sigma Nu (subsequently, professor and chair of pharmacology at his alma mater), and member Donald Chase organized a Dental Career Day for minority students at nearby Omaha Technical High School. The following year, a "concentrated effort" recruited three African-American students, but the administration realized, as with its efforts in the other colleges, it had "to provide substantially increased amounts of financial aid" to reap further success.[103]

The dental faculty expanded to meet the burgeoning teaching demands. In 1968, a Public Health Service "Special Improvement Grant" provided a very welcome $1.9 million "primarily for recruitment of additional faculty, new equipment in all clinical areas, and alteration of existing physical plant facilities." A major refurbishing of the dental clinic ensued, including the replacement of chairs that enabled students to adapt to the new sitting position to perform dental work. Moreover, within four years, the number of full-time faculty soared from thirty to forty-five, and included its first woman, Mary K. Dunn, Ph.D., assistant professor of preventative and community dentistry. The faculty played a key role in the local acceptance (1969) of a novel (but controversial) dental technology, the fluoridation of water. Additionally, the number of administrators multiplied to oversee grant requirements and student services, as well as to coordinate faculty functions. In 1962, Dean Shaddy obtained the first assistant dean in the school, Dr. John Butkus. By the end of the decade, the latter became associate dean and two new assistant deans, Theodore Urban, Ph.D., and the Reverend John Holbrook, S.J., aided with the mounting administrative tasks, and the Alumni Advisory Board (1968) provided professional input. In 1971, Dr. Shaddy became associate vice president for health science and Robert Vining, D.D.S., succeeded to the deanship. In 1974, Vining established a new format for the operation of the dental school. He signed contracts (negotiable annually) with seven surrounding states (Wyoming, New Mexico, Kansas, North Dakota, South Dakota, Idaho, and Utah) to accept an agreed-upon number of their residents in the freshman dental class. In the first year, forty of seventy freshmen seats could go to contract states if the applicants met requirements and gained the approval of the admissions committee.

The contracts would "keep the budget healthy" by generating about $300,000 in revenue per year. At the same time, the dental school promised to maintain the policy favoring qualified Creighton undergrads and scions of alumni.[104]

During the period, the dental curriculum continued "shifting from a technical orientation to a medical and basic science orientation with sociological implications." The description revealed the concerns of the 1960s, but also delineated the health-sciences proclivity toward specialization and the team approach. The school established programs in oral biology (combined biochemistry, microbiology, physiology, pharmacology, and nutrition) and in preventative and community dentistry, as well as appointing Dr. Benjamin Lynch as Coordinator of Graduate Studies and Continuing Education (1967). The latter struggled due to a lack of resources, finally issuing forth with a Master of Science in Dentistry, with a major in periodontology, after several false starts. That same year, the school established a relationship with St. Joseph's Hospital, which had students rotate through "the various departments of the hospital" to "fulfill a long-standing need that this school has had for greater involvement in hospital dentistry." Significantly, the school resisted a trend toward shortening dental education to three years and, like the other health-science schools, continued to place the emphasis of training on clinical experiences.[105]

For the dental school, the happiest note sounded at the Commencement of 1964, with the announcement that Harry N. Boyne (D.D.S., 1913; M.D., 1930) and his wife, Maude, had named Creighton the sole beneficiary of their estate. He had just retired after thirty-eight years of teaching in the dental school, having funded a full-tuition scholarship, established the department of dental surgery, and "almost fully equipped the four-chair oral surgery department." Immediately, his name went up on the existing dental building and the bequest provided seed money for a new school. In 1970, through the good offices of George Blue Spruce (D.D.S., 1956), the first full-blooded Native American dentist in the United States and then administrator in the Public Health Services, that agency approved a $6.55 million grant toward the new $10 million facility. The University used $3.4 million in marketable securities it possessed and $1 million from the Boyne estate to meet the 2:1 match. In fall 1970, crews began clearing twenty-four houses on 28th Street from Burt to Webster (west of the North Freeway) and the groundbreaking ceremony followed on July 16, 1971. The era ended with occupation of the new facility during the summer of 1973.[106]

Beforehand, on January 9, 1973, the Board of Directors voted to raise tuition in all schools to gain income "to produce an average five per cent increase in salaries and a three per cent increase in non-salaried items as well as sufficient moneys for anticipated new faculty positions and a small increase in our budgeting reserve." The public announcement prompted an SBG protest and the presentation of a list of demands that the administration had to meet before students would agree to higher tuition. The SBG proclaimed a tuition-withholding scheme to bludgeon acceptance and 380 students signed refusal pledges. Father President Labaj consented to initiate studies of certain areas of concern, such as food service, but refused prior agreement to any demand requiring expenditures. In response, the SBG extended the withholding plan to include the annual Senior (Pioneer) Pledge campaign. In March, approximately one thousand students attended a forum at which Fr. Labaj and VPF Walt Jahn explained the budget. The school year ended and so did the protest (senior pledges topped the goal); the sound and the fury collapsed in a whimper and signaled the end of the "era of confrontation." In chorus, alleged student apathy led to the closing of the Community Service Center and the *Bluejay* asked, "What happened to all the controversial issues? Most had been dulled by either change or simply the passage of time." Moreover, "student dress, once confined to blue jeans and army jackets, blossomed out into checkered flares, and the skirt returned to the classroom." Actually, a state of "undress" heralded that "the times, they were a' changing": at 9:00 A.M., thirty-five coconspirators blocked the aisles and ensured the escape route of a "streaker," who ran through the biology class of Allen Schlesinger, Ph.D., in Rigge 120, giving a new connotation to the phrase "naked as a Jaybird."[107]

At Creighton, continuity and evolution governed developments during the "era of confrontation," 1964–73. However, confrontation, mild and non-violent, did produce a foreshortening of the process of change in certain social and cultural areas. None of the eight schools and colleges escaped influence from the antiwar, civil rights, women's, and youth movements of the period. The confrontational attitude contributed to a distinct aura and the persistence of the student demands helped to terminate in loco parentis and compulsory ROTC, induced more "elective" curriculums, attempted to integrate women and minorities, and incorporated students (and faculty) into an advisory governance structure. While the development of the bricks-and-mortar aspect of the University continued its spectacular evolution, the social-cultural facets of a Creighton education experienced a noisy, but peaceful, revolution.

CHAPTER 11

Attaining the American Dream, 1979–92

By the early 1970s, Creighton University had fully assimilated into the region. Culturally, an American curriculum had long replaced the *Ratio Studiorum*, and structurally, Frs. Reinert and Linn had finally guided the Jesuit institution into the Omaha and Midwestern mainstream. During the 1980s, the University attained the American Dream: "a life of personal success and material comfort" (*Random House Webster's College Dictionary*, 1991). The personal success derived from innovative programs, an expanding enrollment inclusive of women and minorities, award-winning student activities, and national publications that began to tout the excellence of a Creighton education, especially lauding the teaching prowess of its faculty. Renovated buildings and sizeable expansions of the Alumni Library and the gymnasium improved existing venues. Additionally, new facilities—dormitories, a physical fitness center, a student center, a hospital, a health-sciences learning resource center; and the development of the California Street Mall—added substantial material comfort. During the era from 1974 to 1992, Creighton University climbed the American social ladder, eventually attaining solid middle-class status.

In 1974, the Board of Directors labeled Creighton's financial picture "precarious" (that year the University began paper recycling "to attempt to conserve what has become an expensive product"). The directors had "relied rather heavily on the now encumbered United Benefit stock [Criss gift]" to secure financing for the new St. Joseph's Hospital and needed almost $1 million to complete the new central utilities structure (1976). It had become "apparent that a very vigorous effort" had to ensue to raise money to cover operational and capital expenditures. Ballooning inflation, reaching double-digit annual rates, and an energy crisis resulting from an embargo by the Organization of Petroleum Exporting Countries (OPEC) accentuated their apprehension. The University relied on a "gas/oil system" and Fr. President Labaj revealed his lack of optimism "in terms of an assured supply of natural gas for future regular operations, much less for future buildings," as well as the mounting costs for oil that "depend on the world situation." Thus, in conjunction with the Boys Town Institute and St. Joseph's Hospital, he initiated "a board-level committee to pursue the energy problem." The administration of President Jimmy Carter established an energy policy that created use priorities (dorms high, classrooms low on the list) and that encouraged (could even mandate) conversion to coal-fired boiler systems. Understanding that state of affairs, the conclusion of the fourth study in ten years "showed that for cost reasons as well as seven or eight other reasons, e.g., availability of fuel, reliability of service, ability to furnish chilled water regardless of outside temperature, and ability to effectively address technological changes in the next twenty years, the University should contract with Energy Systems." The board approved a contract, as well as an expenditure of $2 million, to construct a pipeline system from 24th and Dodge streets to connect existing lines of Energy Systems (plant at 21st and Howard streets) with the Creighton utility plant at 25th and Burt Streets. In 1978, four pipelines of various sizes began to carry steam (building heat) and chilled water (drinking fountains) to the campus, the hospital, and the Boys Town Institute. The arrangement produced a combined system, whereby if a problem occurred in either power plant, the other could provide backup service. It relieved the forty-six other downtown Omaha customers of having to build a second unit; thus, in a physical and economic manner, it further incorporated the University into the business community.[1]

Many of those businessmen served on the Board of Directors, helping to pilot the University through the "precarious" times. They guided successful fund drives, which included their personal gifts, as well as those made in behalf of their companies, and the bankers among them facilitated necessary loans. While raising funds remained an agonizing process, and while anxious interludes accompanied several projects, the University garnered the resources to attain the American Dream. Phase I of the Centennial Thrust Campaign surpassed the $75 million goal by over $30 million. Phase II sought $100 million, of which $34 million would provide matching funds for 2:1 grants from the federal government and foundations. At least one board member, harkening to the historic squabble over the apportionment of resources, pleaded for "a definite concern for making sure that the undergraduate divisions received their fair share and a proper proportion of the emphasis in the fund raising effort." While the distribution of funds remained contentious, despite inflation the cost of soliciting dropped "partly because of lessons learned and more experienced personnel." Moreover, the Creative Improvement Program, directed by Jack Nenemen, which encouraged employee input regarding operating efficiencies, won a $10,000 cost-control award. Residually, Fr. Reinert said the award generated "at least one million dollars in pledges that he otherwise would not have received."[2]

Yet, proportionally, giving declined; rising enrollment and tuition increases beyond the cost-of-living index had become the engine generating small budget surpluses, which allowed the transfer of some revenue to maintenance and capital projects, and to a reserve fund. In 1976, the Reverend Michael G. Morrison, S.J., Ph.D., who had taught at Creighton Prep (1967–70), at age thirty-nine became academic vice president. The following year, Fr. Labaj announced he planned to retire. On July 1, 1978, the Reverend Matthew E. Creighton, S.J., became the "centennial" president. In December, the new leaders presented the board with an "annual update of the five-year planning"; Fr. President Creighton noted that the North Central accrediting agency looked askant at gift and endowment earnings that "dwindled considerably." He contended that the University had to raise an additional $3 million annually for the next five years. Furthermore, AVP Morrison divulged the disconcerting fact that despite the tuition increases, undergraduate faculty salaries, especially in the CCAS, remained below average, and that the number of eighteen-year-olds would decline over the next few years. Thus, to maintain undergraduate enrollment (and balanced budgets), the University had to strengthen financial aid and had to address the "absolute need for expanding and modernizing" Alumni Library.[3]

The above report concluded the centennial year on an anxious note, and only a minimal celebration had taken place. A planning committee of administrators, faculty, and students had organized the yearlong fête only ten months before; obviously, the "precarious" financial situation and the search for a new president, constricted the funds and effort devoted to organizing festivities. There was one memorable event, however. Using a ladder and metal detector, workers located the 1878 time capsule in a stone at the second level of the east entrance of the Administration Building, the original entrance to Creighton College. The ceremony to open the copper box produced the headline, "Treasure box seals 100-year old debris;" the cornerstone layers had not sealed it correctly and most of the contents had deteriorated. In a more fulfilling rite, at Commencement, the University awarded Irma Trumbauer, the undisputed "Queen of Bluejays," the title "Centennial Sweetheart." The SAE's Golden Daughter of Minerva, the "food service employee, counselor to students, darling of faculty, fraternities and athletes," eventually retired in 1991 after thirty-nine years, and lower Becker Hall was renamed in her honor.[4]

The post-centennial year opened with the announcement of the "Challenge for Century II Drive" (without a formal cessation to Centennial Thrust II) "to raise operational and capital dollars over the next five years." The board again employed the Cosgriff Company and established a goal of $25 million ($20 local, $5 national), matched by $35 million from other sources. To enable Fr. President Creighton "to solicit monies for endowed chairs, etc.," the board created another office, the vice president of administration. It was expecting financial savings, as well as reacting to a North Central review that "pointed toward the need for additional administrative assistance for the president." The directors chose pharmacy dean Robert Gerraughty and instructed him to work at institutional efficiency—"grass roots cost-saving ideas; governmental relations, and the continuing efforts to fight the effects of inflation[, which] need more attention than the president and current vice presidents can afford to devote." Abruptly, at the August 3, 1981, meeting of the board, Fr. President Creighton tendered his resignation, effective August 16, "in order to take a new assignment in Washington, D.C." The directors appointed Fr. Morrison acting president; then, on December 7, 1981, they accepted the recommendation of the search committee and appointed him president.[5]

As Fr. Morrison settled into the office, the directors empowered the nominating committee, since it annually presented the slate of officers to the board, to initiate an annual evaluation of the president. A "general feeling" existed "that this review process should be more formalized." In addition, they deemed it necessary to increase their number to as many as thirty (more business and foundation connections, more fund raisers), maintaining the ratio of one-third Jesuits, stating specifically that no issue to date had divided the board in terms of lay versus Jesuit (a circumstance that would create a constitutional crisis). Concurrently, in 1982 the board changed the fiscal year from commencing on June 1 to July 1, in order "to better conform" with like institutions. Coincidently, it created the position of internal auditor to monitor the University's fiscal performance, especially regarding loans and grants. In 1979, three auditors from the federal Department of Health, Education, and Welfare (HEW) "spent eight months at Creighton reviewing every contract we had with the government over the last eight years." Astoundingly, they billed the University $500,000 for their efforts; VPF Jahn negotiated a greatly reduced final settlement of $8,000. In the meantime, Arthur Anderson audited the University to provide certified reports to creditors, the city and the state audited regarding "related financial interests," and the federal Department of Housing and Urban Development (HUD) reviewed "grants related to dormitories and dining operations." Understandably, the government agencies and the foundations demanded accountability for their grants and donations; their resources provided the funds for growth, but their regulations (all those strings attached) spawned a large bureaucracy to ensure compliance.[6]

In 1983, in order to improve on its solicitation in the evolving environment, the University restructured the fundraising system. Vice President of University Relations the Reverend James Hoff, S.J., announced a three-pronged organization, including capital campaigns, annual giving, and "an organized, formal planned giving program." The office employed individual directors to lead each effort, and despite previous yearly appeals, in 1984, the administration declared that, "for the first time in its history Creighton is initiating an Annual Fund to supplement tuition revenues in meeting the university's yearly operating expenses." Moreover, another "first" occurred as the capital campaigns would no longer include St. Joseph's Hospital, which established a separate development office. Subsequently, in 1987 the president acquired another assistant, and two years later the purchasing, inventory, accounts-payable, and check-disbursement departments moved out of the Administration Building to new sites, to free space for the development office, "whose staff has been and will continue to expand."[7]

The stock market plunge on "Black Monday," October 19, 1987, temporarily hindered their efforts, as well as decreased the value of the endowment by "approximately 11% to 12% which was considered a mild decline when compared to the Dow and S & P." It did, however, defeat the "University's goal to reach a total endowment principal balance equal to the University's general educational operating budget by May 31, 1990." Nonetheless, by that time, Creighton had weathered the storms. It reached the landmark of $100 million annual budgets, the budget remained balanced throughout the era, no school in the University was in financial trouble, no major deferred maintenance project lingered, enrollment had rebounded to the second highest in history, and gift income for the 1980s totaled $89.6 million. However, distinguishing the amounts attributed to the various campaigns of the period (Centennial Thrust II, Campaign for Creighton, Century Two) remains problematic; they overlapped each other, as well as the new annual appeal and planned giving, and they need "a more thorough study" to "satisfactorily cover those campaigns."[8]

Supplementing the federal programs and gift income, a new source of revenue appeared. The State Legislature created the Nebraska Education Facilities Authority (NEFA, 1981) for the "purpose of issuing tax-exempt bonds to provide funds for financing and refinancing of projects of private higher education institutions." Thus, in 1991, the University obtained a $10.7 million loan to renovate existing buildings and to "recapture expenditures made in equipment and land, [and the] purchase of hardware and software for the financial system [i.e., mainframe computers and the necessary programs]." In the meantime, Creighton continued as a leader in the Nebraska Association of Independent Colleges that toiled "to pass a constitutional amendment to permit the state to aid students who attend private colleges and universities as well as to legalize contractual relationships between state agencies and private educational agencies." In 1976, the legislature passed such a provision by a healthy margin (35-8), but in the subsequent required referendum, the voters rejected it. Two years later, a similar proposition succeeded, but provided "minimal" funding, and lawsuits blocked any appropriations. In 1981, the Nebraska Supreme Court ruled the funding amendment constitutional, but a "budget squeeze" precluded an appropriation. Eventually, in 1988, the administration received notice that, "Based on the federal funding ratio of allocating 82% of the funds to public schools and 18% to private schools, Creighton will receive approximately $29,000 of the $750,000 that was approved" (i.e., state funds matching the grant given to it under the federal State Student Incentive Grant).[9]

Unfortunately, the state contribution did little to augment financial aid, which buttressed enrollment, which in turn provided the tuition revenue that remained a mainstay of the operational budget. The baby-boom population bubble steadily pushed full-time undergraduate enrollment up, from 2,334 in the fall of 1973 to 3,503 in the fall of 1981. Then the bubble began to deflate and full-time undergraduate enrollment steadily declined to 2,954 in the fall of 1987. Significantly, in 1981 the number of full-time male undergraduates "decreased slightly," and that year's enrollment increase resulted "exclusively among female students." Subsequently, as total enrollment contracted, the number of women (reared on "liberation" ideology) enrolling rose dramatically (25 percent); thus, by 1987 women accounted for 50 percent of the full-time undergraduate students (percent per individual school differed dramatically). With successful recruiting, full-time undergraduate enrollment began to rebound with the shift to a new decade, reaching 3,260 in 1992 (approximately 60 percent female).[10]

On the other hand, African-American enrollment began to wane well before the bubble burst (seventy black freshmen in 1973, only twenty-seven in 1978) and the variegated pattern of race relations persisted. One administrator proclaimed "a 99 percent improvement" during the decade, while other observers claimed that blacks and whites segregated themselves. Those same commentators claimed that the CUASA became "more social than political" and did not complain about minimal office space in "trailers" behind the old law school, although some students gave it "a bad connotation" because of its exclusively black membership. The University maintained its

Upward Bound program and the Special Services office, which assisted "disadvantaged students in graduating from Creighton's undergraduate divisions" (both created by the Higher Education Act of 1965 and temporarily curtailed by federal budget cuts in 1976). Moreover, following federal guidelines, in 1976–77 on three occasions the directors amended the nondiscrimination policy to eventually read, "regardless of race, color, national or ethnic origin, sex, handicap or religion." Despite policy, "insensitivity" could cause problems. In 1978, at a fraternity-sponsored show, which parodied the outrageous television amateur-performance program "The Gong Show," a group performed a black-face routine, "Gene-Gene the Dancing Machine." It provoked forty African-American students, with placards denouncing the action, to march across campus and elicited several weeks of comments and apologies in the *Creightonian*. Though chastened, the SAE fraternity continued to hold annual Gong Shows to raise money for local charities.[11]

In 1982, the expanded office of Educational Opportunities Activities moved into the former College Terrace Apartments at 23rd and California streets, renamed Markoe Hall in honor of the Jesuit civil rights icon. Further strengthening the University's commitment, in 1987 Fr. President Morrison reported that he and "some of the vice presidents" met with "Omaha's Black Forum to improve the enrollment of minority students at Creighton and the recruitment of Black faculty." That year, African American John Pierce (J.D., 1981) became Creighton's affirmative-action director. Moreover, complaints from concerned faculty and students prompted administrative support for a formal celebration of the new national holiday in honor of Martin Luther King, Jr. Classes remained in session, but special observances occurred in various venues (the University did not close on federal holidays). Seeking to fulfill "the Dream," in 1990 the administration hired a former African-American student-athlete, Reggie Morris, as minority affairs counselor. Yet, in 1992 the head of the Urban League of Nebraska claimed that racial tension ran "rampant" on campus. Once again, the charges condemned "insensitivity," such as aiming programming exclusively to white tastes and the alleged perception among whites that all black males on campus played on a sports team. Ultimately, bridging cultural divides became more complex, as Creighton began special recruiting programs geared toward Native American and Hispanic students. In 1991, the University initiated an annual "Day of Diversity," which allowed groups to "display diversity" on campus. The score of participants included the new Native American and Latino student associations. However, because of the low number of all minorities in the immediate locale, the administration recognized "a growing need to recruit Catholic, minority students outside the Omaha area," and that to do so required "endowed financial aid to compete with more affluent schools." Actually, it most successfully recruited minority students in the census category "Asian or Pacific Islander," which included the historic contingent of Hawaiians, and foreign and American students of that ethnicity. For example, in the CCAS that cohort advanced from 68 in 1977 to 150 in 1992, doubling the number of registered "black non-Hispanics," and tripling the Hispanic contingent.[12]

Improving the method of recruiting all undergraduates occupied the attention of the directors even during the enrollment boom (generally, the professional schools chose a limited number of students from a surplus of applicants). With the downturn, the discussion became urgent. In 1983, the administration hired an admissions consultant, who provided twenty-five recommendations, including the consolidation of management and the development of a research program. The University had initiated a Student Outcomes Survey for seniors in 1978; the following year, a poll of freshmen asked the question, "Why attend Creighton?" The top four answers revealed: (1) academic reputation, (2) preferential admissions policy to its professional schools, (3) small size, and (4) Jesuit Catholic identity. In 1987, a new research office introduce a broader freshmen survey, and four years hence, graduating seniors could repeat the exercise and provide longitudinal data that could chart student progress, as well as provide a comparison with other schools.[13]

Moreover, in 1974, the University had begun to chart the "dropout" situation and had devised an undergraduate leave of absence policy (LOAP) to give students "time off" before returning to finish their studies. Interviews with departing students exploded a prevalent myth: dropouts were not "frustrated professional-school hopefuls who found the competition too tough." Actually, most fit the "undecided" category, they did not have a specific career goal. When the decline began, the Survival Strategies program ensued to offer bewildered students psychological, social, and academic advice. In 1985, Howard Bachman, admissions director since 1971, assumed the newly created position of assistant vice president of enrollment management. In 1987, the survival coordinator became the first director of retention in the expanding Office of Enrollment Management. A subsequent retention study discovered that the undergraduate dropout rate matched the average for comparable schools. For freshman, fall semester to fall semester, it was 18 percent, an "acceptable" figure, but the administration desired improvement. The graduation rate, which stood well above average at "about 65% after six years," provided greater satisfaction.[14]

Those undergraduate students paid a tuition that doubled during the 1970s and again during the 1980s; the cost of room and board followed a similar trajectory. The rate increases continued to relate directly to faculty salaries and the overall operations budget. Between 1983 and 1990, the University offered a Tuition Stabilization Plan targeted "to middle and higher income families who are being excluded from federal loan and grant programs." It "locked in" the undergraduate tuition by allowing the family to prepay the going rate for the arts, business, nursing, or pharmacy colleges for two to four years. The ability to deduct the interest on a loan from federal income taxes may have benefited certain families, but it did not gain wide acceptance and it did not generate the desired revenue source. In the mid-1980s, the academic affairs committee reported that a review of comparative data revealed that the University's "faculty salary level is not competitive and runs as much as 20% below the average in some fields." Father President Morrison proposed a plan for "gradual tuition increases to bring Creighton's tuition more in line with its competition." The additional revenue would fund increases in faculty salaries and financial aid, as well as "needed improvements" in programs. The SBG supported the plan, expressing "the concern that potential students may perceive that the University's lower tuition may reflect a lower quality of education." By the end of the decade Fr. Morrison explained, "So we have done two things at once: the price value concept establishing a lower level than the competition, but pushing the prices up as much as we could in order to have the financial aid to attract students." Moreover, in 1991 the University hired a consultant to "conduct an independent review of its compensation and benefits program, with particular emphasis on determining the competitiveness of the current package." Based on the review, the board approved an increase in retirement benefits and improvements in medical coverage. Thus, the tuition increases supported Creighton's endeavor to maintain competitive aid packages to attract highly qualified faculty and students. *Changing Times* magazine put its stamp of approval on the price-value strategy; in 1977, it began to list Creighton as one of its "bargain-priced colleges," pointing out that a high "price isn't necessarily a guide to excellence."[15]

Student aid, the other strategic element of enrollment management, also contributed to the budget concerns of the 1980s. It had fared well during the 1970s. VPF Jahn attributed the "success in recruiting and retaining students [to] the fine loan program that our directors from the banks so graciously provided." Actually, in 1977 the size of the program brought close government scrutiny because of the number of loans "currently in the grace period," which shortly would move into "the payment stages." Creighton had maintained below average delinquency and default rates, while providing aid "to three out of four students." Finding no fault, the regulators did ask the University to improve in two areas: "to tighten up its collection procedures and to study its high-risk student borrower." However, beginning in 1982 a severe contraction in financial aid followed the coincidental downturn in enrollment (less revenue for operations and financial aid) and the federal budget reductions (that included education grant and loan programs) initiated by the administration of President Ronald Reagan. That year, in response to the diminution of government funds, the board called for a $500,000 budget reduction (actual shortfall $749,000; but it expected to cover the variance through increased revenue, keeping the budget in balance). The cuts constrained future budgets (the lost tuition from each student times four years), contributed pressure for tuition increases, and provoked novel approaches. For example, the administration cancelled its outside custodial service and hired students "in order to provide them with job employment and financial aid" (a short-lived experiment). As part of the budget triangle, the diminished resources for financial-aid contributed to the declining enrollment. A 1987 study demonstrated a "steady decline" in yield "from 57% ten years ago to 39% last year" (e.g., applications versus registrations); those who did not enroll listed "better financial aid elsewhere" as their primary reason (withdrawing students reiterated the same cause). Unfortunately, in 1991 Fr. Morrison lamented that "inadequate financial aid" in a "buyer's market" had students going to schools "giving better scholarships and financial aid packages."[16]

Despite the problem, enrollment did rebound, but did not reach the optimal level. Simultaneously, capital expenditures inflamed anxiety, but the University methodically developed a substantial campus. In 1974, the Kresge Foundation granted $50,000 toward the renovation of the old law school for offices and classrooms for the departments of journalism, foreign languages, and English and speech, as well as for the *Creightonian* and the *Bluejay*, and KOCU and the instructional television studios. The following year, the Hitchcock Foundation provided the "substantial portion" of the $250,000 needed to complete the overhaul and the building became the Hitchcock Communication Arts Building. Concurrently, with the dental school resituated in its new facility, the fine arts department gained a consolidated campus location. Then, in 1980, the University acquired the triangle of property at 30th and Burt and Cuming streets, which added parking for dental students. The site also included an Omaha Parks and Recreation storage Quonset hut; three years later, the refurbished facility became home to the theater program. It included faculty offices, classrooms for acting and dance, costume and scenery shops, rehearsal space, and a two-hundred-seat theater (first play, "Indians").[17]

Moreover, Creighton achieved another goal of Centennial Thrust Phase II with the acquisition of a new recreation facility. Unannounced, Peter Kiewit visited campus and picked a site; he then met with VPF Jahn and told him to arrange interim seven-year financing. In 1974, the campus planning committee changed the location of the desired structure from north of the new law school to between Swanson and Kiewit dorms, "where it will be visible and easily accessible to students." In April 1975, the board learned of an "anonymous donor" for a new $4 million physical education and recreation building; on May 5, Peter and Evelyn Kiewit stepped forward as the patrons. In the fall 1975, construction ensued. The project included razing Wareham and Smith halls, the Black Culture Center, and two private residences, as well as the loss of the tennis courts and two parking lots. Only Bergan Hall remained to house the University Relations, the Alumni, and the Development offices (education moved to Hitchcock and the Counseling Center to the third floor of the Brandeis Student Center). The Kiewit Fitness Center (KFC) opened in 1976, containing offices for coaches and the physical education department, five multipurpose courts (circled by a track), a swimming pool with adjacent sundeck and coed whirlpool, four racquetball courts, a weight-training area, and men's and women's locker areas with saunas. In 1978, for his service and generosity, the Society of Jesus named Peter Kiewit a founder of Creighton University.[18]

The KFC opened space in the gymnasium (now Old Gym); the ROTC staff moved into the former athletic offices and the pool area became central receiving. Plans for further immediate renovation (for example, a theater on the lower level) endured a decade-long funding drought. Eventually, in 1986 the renovated first floor became the Computer Center (removed from its double classroom location on the fourth floor of the Administration Building) and the remainder of the remodeled front (west) upper three floors provided new offices and classrooms for the math and computer science department. The renovation included the removal of the elevated running track and conversion of the main athletic area into a practice area for men's and women's teams, which included new batting cages and training and weight rooms.

In 1990, a Criss Foundation grant funded a $2.4 million, 15,000-square-foot addition to the Old Gym, named in honor of Joseph J. Vinardi (B.A. Phil., 1930; LL.B., 1932), a founder and charter officer of the Jaybackers Club. The appendage matched the original architecture and extended east to 24th Street. It contained two athletic floors and the lower level consisted of twenty-two offices for athletic staff (who vacated the KFC), an enlarged weight room, and updated locker rooms for all teams.[19]

The Computer Center, and the revolution it symbolized, also demanded frequent enlargement and upgrading. It received its first Univac 1100/60 C1 in April 1980, and shortly thereafter added a second mainframe (a room in the first-floor entry of the Old Gym housed about fifteen terminals for student use and faculty research). In 1983, the hardware allowed the registrar to abandon a twenty-year relationship with Automation, Inc., and to produce grades and the student directory in-house. The next year, the early registration system debuted, an eleven-day process in which a small group of students met with a computer operator at one of many stations, signaling the demise of the historic bane of waiting in long lines. In 1987, the Health Sciences Library and Learning Resource Center computerized its card catalogue, purchasing the Public Access Library System (PALS) software, and the other libraries followed shortly thereafter. The next year, a Hitchcock Foundation grant "established a computerized [journalism] writing lab and a computerized newsroom," and in 1991 the English department inaugurated its own lab (twenty-six computers, six software packages) to teach expository and business writing and advanced composition. The planning for the seemingly endless technological onslaught convinced the directors that "if computers are to be given the necessary emphasis in the immediate future, the person in charge should be at the vice presidential level." In 1991 they chose Leon "Benny" Benschoter, former director of Bio-Med Communications, as the first vice president for information systems. Those systems included linking together all buildings on campus with fiber-optic cable to create one integrated communications network for faculty and students that would hook into regional, national, and international systems (the emergent internet).[20]

Technology also factored into the projected expansion of the Alumni Library. In 1978, the North Central accreditation team criticized the space as "overcrowded" and the administration realized that the collection remained "pitifully small." In April 1981, as undergraduate enrollment peaked, lacking a major donor but based on collections from the Century II fund drive and "the dire need for book and study space," the board authorized library construction. In 1979, it had already resolved to add Fr. Reinert's name to the proposed expanded facility. The previous year, physicians had detected heart disease. He underwent heart surgery on September 6, 1979, Fr. Reinert fell into a coma for six weeks, and never fully recovered. He died August 13, 1980; construction to extend the renamed Reinert Alumni Library (RAL) to the west and to the north, on three levels abutting the Eppley Building (intended to augment shelf capacity from 252,360 to 400,000 and seating from 524 to 900), began in May 1981. A $500,000 cost-projection error engendered a fiscal crisis, and in August 1982 Fr. Morrison announced, "with deep regret that the decision was made that the University cannot, at the present time, construct phases 1b [lower level] and 2 [renovation of existing structure] of the library." The Hawkins Construction Company "began the transition work to complete phase 1a," to enable students to gain access to the building by October. The board authorized seeking a loan from NEFA, and the following year board member and founder of Godfathers' Pizza William "Willie" Theisen donated $350,000, which provided the funds to complete the project. The Theisen Instructional Technology Center, in the lower level of the RAL addition, provided the non-health-sciences schools with audio-visual service, television production (studio and movie-theater classroom), photography, graphics, and with "mediated instruction and an instructional media laboratory." In 1984, Instructional Technology moved from Hitchcock to RAL, and at the end of the 1986 school year, the remodeling of the original library area (new lights, carpeting, furniture, and enlarged rare book room) "neared completion." Shortly thereafter, ten Creighton librarians began working on an unusual project—helping to identify the thousands of rare books and manuscripts pilfered over several decades by Stephen Blumberg of Ottumwa, Iowa. In 1993, the FBI donated over "3,000 of these unclaimed treasures" (e.g., a first edition of Milton's *Paradise Lost*) to the University, because of the librarians' "dedication to the project."[21]

"Overcrowded" also described the housing situation. Despite the senior off-campus option, in 1974 the University had to confront "the problem of overbooked dorms." The number of undergraduates had begun to rise and many seniors decided to stay on campus. Among the reasons—dramatically rising gasoline prices, loss of nearby housing due to interstate construction, sleep more because of the proximity of the dorms and the classrooms, no need for cooking or expensive eating out, close to the KFC, the new coed dorms, and, as a sign of the times, "less emphasis on nonconformity among the students." In August 1978, for $700,000 the University purchased the Guest House, a motel at 24th and Dodge streets. Renamed in honor of Fr. Michael Sheridan, the recently deceased vice president of student personnel, it housed 135 upper-class males (sold in 1981 and vacated 1984). Furthermore, in 1979 Creighton arranged a lease-purchase agreement for the fifteen-story Palms Apartments at 20th and Chicago streets, and the following year arranged a similar contract for the Central Towers, an eighty-four-apartment complex at 22nd and Davenport streets. On its third try, the University obtained a $3.5 million low-interest loan (3 percent versus a possible 12 percent in the open market) from the Department of Education (independent cabinet post, 1979) for the purchase of the two buildings. VPF Jahn successfully negotiated the novel deal—one loan, two buildings—as the "Twin Towers Project," since the same brothers owned both structures. For the first time in a decade, professional and graduate students could live in a dorm, and for the first time ever, married students acquired the opportunity. Then the enrollment dip in the mid-1980s eased the housing pressure, but changes in student attitudes presented new challenges: students wanted apartment style living. In 1988, for the existing older dorms the University accepted the recommendation of RAs and initiated "a house system," a mixture of classes on floors with a common area, to build "community activities" as a way "of reacting to problems in large residence halls." In 1989, envisioning the future, students presented their concerns to a Board of Directors committee, arguing that high-rises did not satisfy contemporary lifestyles and that Creighton needed low-rise apartment complexes closer to the medical and dental schools. In the meantime, the administration had undertaken an enormous renovation project that encompassed renewal of twenty-one buildings erected before 1970, and in 1991 it spent $2.5 million to modernize the Palms, including enclosing its balconies to make those apartments more spacious for double occupancy.[22]

Higher enrollment and more dorms exacerbated the parking problem and posed related security issues of vandalism, car theft, and illegal entry into residence halls. To address the former, the University expanded existing lots and, in 1983, after successfully contesting a fraudulent bid, it purchased the Metropolitan Area Transit (MAT) car barn, a property that stretched from 25th to 27th streets, between Burt and Cuming, eliminating the structure (except for the office, occupied by the ROTC) and creating a large parking area. Regarding the safety concerns, in 1977 it added two security guards and employed seventy students to check identification cards and patrol dorm floors. In 1979, the board approved "an in-house security system" and hired James R. Russell to establish the Public Safety department, which would employ seventeen officers that would also work with students and staff on "awareness and crime prevention." The expansion of the campus escalated personal-security concerns and the Public Safety budget mushroomed as a few rented patrolmen transitioned into a sizeable twenty-four-hour staff. Electronic surveillance replaced the student dorm patrol (1981), but volunteers established the "buddy system" escort service to walk coeds to their destination in the evening (1982), and "blue-light" emergency-phone stations dotted the campus expanse (1989).[23]

As the campus expanded, the University retained the Leo A. Daly Company as campus planners; in 1976, the board renewed the 1955 "formal agreement." It had begun to assemble data to present to city officials "to show how we will develop California Street into a mall while at the same time we carefully provide for fire access and exit." The Reverend Richard Hauser, S.J. (theology), and the Reverend Donald Doll, S.J. (fine arts), worked with the Daly Co., to produce a model of a plaza in front of St. John's Church. In 1976, Fr. Doll chaired a campus planning task force that presented the concept of a California Street Mall stretching from 24th to 27th streets, with the church "piazza" as the centerpiece, and "a large kidney-shaped pond, approximately half the size of a football field and crossed by a pedestrian bridge" as the anchor on the west end. Obviously, the "rate of completion [would] depend on attracting private gifts." In 1977, the city vacated California Street (now truncated by the North Freeway), 24th to Periphery Road, and the University expanded the parking lot east of 24th to compensate for the loss of on-street spots. In addition, the plaza concept received an unexpected gift; during the summer, a second steeple (east tower) finally came to don St. John's Church. In July 1977, strong winds for several days delayed its positioning, but the 60-foot spire eventually came to rest on the original, long-unoccupied platform. The gift honored John Gardiner (M.D., 1922) and his wife, Bonnie Marie. Mister and Mrs. Kenneth J. Hawkins donated a carillon, and support from Col. and Mrs. Hardin Sweeney, Dr. and Mrs. G. O. Austria, and Maureen Hamilton allowed the purchase of the movements for the three clocks (historically timeless) embedded in the church towers.[24]

Concurrently, at the June meeting of the Board of Directors, chairman Jack A. MacAllister, CEO of Northwestern Bell Telephone, suggested to Terry Moore, president of the Omaha Central Labor Union, that he get workers to donate time for the construction of a fountain in front of St. John's Church. A centennial project ensued as the first element of a mall. Bergan Hall came down to create better "green space" around the proposed fountain with a planned crown of a sculpture depicting "the Jesuit spirit of education." Groundbreaking took place on June 24, 1978, with most labor and supplies obtained gratis, including 27,000 reclaimed street-paving bricks, and the fountain spurted water, minus the sculpture, on Labor Day. Various grant requests to fund the proposed "tree of knowledge" sculpture that would have water dripping down its branches failed to gain support. Finally, in 1989 CCAS alumni John and Anna Lou Micek contracted with sculptor Grant Kenner to create and "extended crescenta form," symbolic of an "eternal flame," in which water would move up and through the rotating piece. Installed August 13, 1993, the new motif caused some controversy and, unfortunately, did not operate as planned.[25]

In the meantime, the campus beautification program moved eastward. In 1980, Lloyd Skinner (A.B., 1936) chairman of the Skinner Macaroni Company, made an unrestricted gift of $1 million. The University used the funds to extend the plaza to 24th Street, and in 1983 named the "central campus mall" in honor of Lloyd E. and Kathryn G. Skinner. Plans to make 24th Street into a two-way boulevard and reroute it to "provide a better buffer zone at the edge of campus" failed because of rapidly escalating costs and "a dispute within the city bureaus." However, the southeast corner of 24th and California gained embellishment. In 1986, Howard Fiedler (Walt Beal's son-in-law) retired; he and his wife, Bernice (Walt's daughter), sold the property to Creighton. The University razed the café and an anonymous donation financed landscaping of the area into a small green space. That same year, the University acquired the Schaeffer Building on the northeast corner of 23rd and California streets, which had housed a medical facility for a union. Renovated, it became home to the public relations, personnel, and payroll departments. On February 5, 1989, as apart of Founders' Week, Fr. Morrison dedicated the renamed building in honor of the Wareham sisters (former Wareham Hall had been lost to dorm and KFC construction). The Alumni office switched places on the first floor of the Administration Building, moving to the former PR space, and the Development Office expanded once again into the vacated area. By that time, the administration had announced plans to lengthen the mall to the law school, as well as to build a softball-baseball complex bordering Burt Street between 22nd and 23rd streets. The city agreed to vacate 23rd Street between Burt and California streets, which then became part of the east parking lot. Creighton agreed to participate in the widening of 24th Street into a four-lane, two-way street, aiding the project by buying a car wash at 24th and Cuming streets, because the city did not have an easement necessary for the widening. Moreover, the University purchased the remaining houses west of the law school and announced that it would raze them and Markoe Hall to use the block to build a new fine and performing arts center. Except for a house and a couple of apartment units (whose owners unwilling to sell) surrounded by a two-block long and two-block wide asphalt parking lot, the campus now included an east segment, Cass to Burt, 22nd the 24th, with a landscaped California Street Mall bisecting it.[26]

The mall also elongated westward. In 1983, crews stripped the asphalt from California Street west of St. John's Church to Periphery Road, exposing the historic brick roadway and its trolley tracks, as well as planting trees and shrubs to create a park-like effect. Moreover, as an indication of the burgeoning size, the campus planning committee arranged for the placement of outdoor maps at six locations, and in 1984, the board approved planning for a new student center. An SBG task force asked the planning committee to consider two preeminent criteria for site selection—placement in student "traffic ways," and no alteration to the green spaces currently found within the central campus. The site chosen lay west of the KFC, where the steep hill allowed a multilevel facility in a small space in the center of the main campus and a significant amount of the building underground meant subsequent energy savings. Groundbreaking for the $5 million (funded through the Campaign for Creighton), three-story center attached to the KFC occurred on July 21, 1986, and it opened for student use at the start of the following school year. The underground first floor contained a large reception room that divided into eight smaller spaces, a game room, two dining venues (fast-food "C-Jays," and "Jebbies Restaurant"), and a fireplace common area. Wide steps, inviting students to congregate on them, led to the second floor consisting of a television area, offices, and meeting rooms, with adjoining terraces. The aboveground third floor had an entrance to the KFC, offices, meeting rooms, and commercial space. Its opening prompted another office shuffle: The bookstore, owned and operated by the Follett Company, moved into the old student center snack bar, the admissions office acquired the old bookstore in lower Swanson, and financial aid absorbed the area vacated by admissions in the Brandeis Building. Simultaneously, the University purchased the Thacker Building on Cuming Street, completing the main campus development, and shifted the maintenance department out of the old power plant adjacent to the Old Gym. That structure, remodeled for office and athletic use, became the new Markoe Hall, and the parking lot that ran from it up between RAL and St. John's Church received landscaping to broaden the mall area northward.[27]

As the campus gained a scenic unity, the faculty also shaped a new concord. In December 1976, they unveiled a novel "legislative body," a rejuvenated "University Faculty," which would elect a president who would serve on the Academic Council and chair its committee on committees. Additionally, the person would head the Faculty Caucus, composed of all the faculty members of the Academic Council, who would function as the "official voice" of the faculty at large. The previous Faculty Senate had atrophied due to "lack of interest," but "recent court decisions" induced an updating of the University statutes "promulgated" in 1971 and the Faculty Handbook published in 1972. The directors acknowledged that, "since faculty are also legally bound by these documents, they are actively involved in the revision." In March 1977, Theodore Clements, professor of law, gained election as the first president of the faculty. The administration hoped the new system would operate efficiently and would thwart an attempt at collective bargaining, which had originated in the medical school, due to fiscal problems. The AAUP chapter took up the cause and sought to gain the sanction of the National Labor Relations Board for an election to decide the issue. Regulations required that the entire University faculty participate as a single bargaining unit; the law school's belief that it had to act as a separate unit derailed the effort, moderately supported in the CCAS and the health-science area.[28]

While it stifled unionization, the University continued to encourage research by its faculty. In 1976, it established the Creighton Institute for Business, Law, and Social Research, which would promote research and consulting by arts, CoBA, and law faculty, who lagged behind the medical school in research. After three years, it abandoned that format (too narrow, presentist, and pragmatic), and replaced it with two new ventures: summer Faculty research fellowships and the Office of Research Assistance (professional grant-seeking aid), both offered through the graduate school.[29]

The University also focused on the composition of its faculty. In 1978, because of passage of amendments to the Age Discrimination in Employment Act, the board modified the Creighton retirement plan, eliminating the mandatory retirement age. Additionally, the lack of minority teachers (seven full-time, six part-time out of a total of five hundred) became "a big concern." In 1990, Fr. Morrison alerted the deans that, "a new position will be created for every new minority faculty member they hire." He argued they would provide the "supportive environment" necessary to recruit more minority students. Research revealed "the demographic curve starts back up in 1993, but the increase is almost entirely in minority students." In response, in 1991 the University diversified the faculty, hiring eight African Americans, seven Hispanics, and two Native Americans.[30]

Moreover, the Jesuits undertook an evaluation of their role. In the mid-1970s, the American provincials mandated that each community associated with an institution of higher learning devise a "rationale statement, which should not remain theoretical but include a concrete plan of action." As an outgrowth of that planning, in 1988, as part of the work on the new Collaborative Ministry Office, the directors established the Jesuit Identity Committee to keep it informed "on significant developments in Jesuit education and to assist the board in establishing the Jesuit identity at Creighton." Keeping "the Jesuit influence strong as the number of Jesuits actively involved in administrative and teaching roles decreases" became the primary goal. With the hope of attracting "younger Jesuits to the University," the Creighton Community constructed a new residence apartment, Ignatius House, built into the terrace west of the North Lawn/Jesuit Garden. The ability to recruit Jesuits became more significant in the 1990s, as the Order established the principle of national placement, minimizing the preference for assignment in one's province. Ultimately, however, to preserve the Jesuit identity of the institution, the lay faculty and administrators had to enter into a symbiotic relationship with the Jesuit community. Therefore, the committee recognized that "of the ten strategic issues, the two which will be emphasized are hiring and promotion." It had to "work toward instilling the spirit (harmony) which goes along with the mission of Creighton into our present personnel and those who are being hired." Equally significant, in 1985, the presidents of Jesuit colleges and universities from around the world met in Rome to discuss the "Proposed Schema for a Pontifical Document on Catholic Universities," drafted by the Vatican's Congregation for Catholic Higher Education. The document covered "norms" and included "a requirement that church authorities approve anyone who teaches theology in Catholic institutions." Father Morrison appreciated the discussion, but worried that the document denied academic freedom, "and we're not American universities if we don't have academic freedom." Thus, three traditions—Jesuit, Catholic, and American—interacted in a manner to cause deep concern.[31]

Jesuit and lay faculty also had to deal with the problems of grade inflation and cheating. In 1975, responding to a growing public apprehension, Registrar Jack Williams studied undergraduate grade trends and compared them to a twenty-year-old study of Creighton grading practices. Earlier, an ad hoc committee had recommended a bell-curve "distribution in all courses" of 7 percent, A; 23 percent, B; 50 percent, C; 15 percent, D; and 5 percent, F. Actually, final grades in the CCAS for the fall 1974, inventoried at 30.2 percent, A; 32.1 percent, B; 28.8 percent, C or C+; 3.9 percent, D; 1.6 percent, F; 3 percent, Incomplete. Although the Creighton onslaught lagged behind other prominent institutions (concurrently, Dartmouth had 41 percent, A), between 1963 and 1974, the number of "A" grades doubled and the percent of "superior grades" (A and B) rose from 46.2 percent to 62.3 percent. An *Omaha World Herald* editorial attributed the grade explosion to the "creeping deterioration of standards, discipline and sense of responsibility which is detectable in the academic world as well as other aspects of American life" (i.e., negative values of the "sixties" counterculture). Registrar Williams argued that the inflation cycle began with professors reluctant to give low grades that would push students into the draft during the Vietnam era, and then continued with those disinclined to impair their chance of getting into a professional school. Others pointed to the embellishing impact of "+" grades, the pass/no pass option, the extended period to drop a class, and the incomplete grade. In comparison, pharmacy dean Robert Garraughty attributed the phenomenon to higher admissions standards that resulted in better students, to programs for slow learners, and to stronger student motivation and better career counseling. Dean Jean Carrica "could only guess" that the slower 7 percent grade-inflation rate during the same period in the CoBA resulted from the school's older faculty who held the line. Less gratifying, in 1980 an alleged incidence of cheating in the CoBA induced a demand that each school write a policy-and-procedures statement. At first, the administration contended that each unit required "a distinct way of handling it." The CCAS defined "it" in terms of "academic honesty," and established flexible disciplinary measures administered by the instructor (e.g., "F" for the work or the class) and/or the dean (e.g., expulsion). Nonetheless, in 1983 an all-University cheating committee toiled to standardize guidelines, because "some of the present policies are not too well defined." The next year, the University lost a court case involving an instance of cheating in the medical school, because the judge said it "did not follow its own handbook." Attacking the problem at its source, the Academic Council resolved that students in each of the schools and colleges take a course in moral reasoning as a graduation requirement.[32]

By that time, the CCAS met the requirement with six prescribed hours of study in Division I, "Values Consciousness," of its new General Education Curriculum (GEC), which replaced the core-division scheme in 1977. Division II, "Humanistic Tradition," included six hours each in theology, philosophy, history, and literature. Division III, "scientific Inquiry," entailed six hours each in social and natural sciences, and an additional six hours of elective science study. Division IV, "Modes of Expression," necessitated choosing six hours from an array of courses in reading, math, speech, composition, journalism, foreign languages, and fine arts. The GEC met the goal of preserving liberal arts education, while protecting departments by providing most of them with a slice of the mandatory core (physical education disappointed with exclusion, due to "terminology and details of implementation") that consumed almost half (60) the total hours needed for graduation (128). Some departments realigned. For example, speech lost its independence and joined the English department, while drama left English to coalesce into a new department of fine and performing arts, which then offered a theater major (1975). Foreign languages, absent a specific requirement (as in the previous core-division), continued to atrophy and moved out of Hitchcock into the renamed Fine Arts Building (old dental school), and became part of the reconfigured classic and modern language department (1977). Concurrently, theology expanded to include a course about the Jewish people and their writings, taught by Rabbi emeritus Meyer S. Kripke of Beth El Synagogue in Omaha. The Jewish Chautauqua Society endowed his services. Subsequently, a $1 million gift established the Philip M. and Ethel Klutznick Chair in Jewish Civilization (1987), which entailed teaching and community service to promote interreligious understanding; Menachem Mor, University of Haifa historian, initiated the chair.[33]

Furthermore, new disciplines and programs emerged. Business communications, an intercollege major consisting of twelve hours of English and speech and nine hours of business classes, emphasized the application of the materials "as an organizational skill" (1977). Two years later, CoBA accreditation concerns (it had to administer anything with "business" in its name) resulted in a morphed moniker for the program—it became "organizational communications." In 1980, an anonymous $300,000 gift (the University sought an additional $500,000) endowed the first chair in the CCAS, the A. F. Jacobson Chair in Communications (open to all departments), so named in honor of the former head of the Northwestern Bell Telephone Company and the first chairman of the reincorporated Board of Directors, 1968–76. Additionally, in 1980 a request from the Global Weather Command at the Offutt Air

Force Base resulted in the establishment of a meteorology program that within two years expanded to a major in atmospheric science. Following the same timeline, administrators drew together existing classes to formulate a computer science program that became a major within the math department, which also added a major in statistics (1985). Then a disconnect in the sociology department led to the creation of a separate social work department (1991)—the former wanted to develop an autonomous community outreach effort and the latter had accrediting needs that clashed with course requirements for a sociology major.[34]

With the new GEC, the arts college took a year to develop a program "to assure competency in reading, writing and mathematics." Students with less than 15 on the ACT had to take skills tests and, if deficient in any area, had to take development classes in the area(s). They could earn one to nine hours credit as they improved their skills and "tested out" of the course(s). On the other hand, Program 101 did not survive within the new GEC; it had originated in "the need to bridge a perceived gap between liberal education and professional school career preparation." An $18,000 Danforth Educational Challenge Grant supported a summer workshop that devised a program that instantly provoked substantial controversy. Initially, the "alternative structure" for the freshman year relied on "two key ideas," interdisciplinary problem solving and team teaching. The initial student cohort (which would become part of the 101st graduating class, thus the name) and one of the seven-member faculty team lived as a group in Swanson Hall (providing an example of a coed residence), where they studied individually, as a group, and in small seminars with a professor. The board approved Program 101 as an "updating [of] our liberal arts program in order to attract and retain more undergraduate students." While it existed the enrollment in the CCAS increased from 1,999 to 2,548. Unfortunately, Program 101 annually attracted less than half the planned freshman allotment of 120 students. Moreover, faculty in the program could not teach their regularly scheduled classes, weakening their departments and presenting the added expense of hiring part-time instructors to fill the slots. As well, some students had problems making the transition to a conventional schedule in their sophomore year. A poll of the faculty displayed "a negative tone"; in November 1978, with new dean William F. Cunningham, Ph.D., remaining neutral, the Executive Committee of the CCAS voted, 20-11-2, to allow the experiment to expire at the end of the academic year.[35]

As Program 101 ended, the "Japanese program" began; the latter mitigated but could not impede the downturn in enrollment in the CCAS, a steady decline from 2,599 in 1980 to 2,005 in 1987, but thence upward to 2,211 in 1992. The Ueno-Juku Foundation, or Institute for Educational Development (IED), a Japanese family educational entity, in 1977 approached the University seeking a "contractual relationship," whereby it would send thirty students per year to study in the arts college, and then, hopefully, in the medical, dental, or pharmacy school. The SBG recommended rejection of the arrangement, fearing an adverse impact on the number of Creighton undergrads admitted to the health-science schools. The Jesuit members of the board had to make "a sincere effort to resolve their difference of opinion on the subject[,] with a view to doing what is best for the institution in this somewhat sensitive situation." Ultimately, based on the financial and cultural advantages for Creighton, the full board approved the contract with only one "nay." It appointed Dr. Raymond Shaddy director of the Institute for International Programs. The students underwent one year of intensive English-language training in Japan, followed by a three-month "familiarization program" at Creighton, before enrolling in the CCAS. The health-science schools "would make additional seats available" for them, thereby not infringing on existing preference guidelines for traditional arts college graduates.[36]

Regrettably, the program experienced fiscal and educational problems from its launch. John Herman, who had served as associate director of the Japanese Program and in 1984 succeeded as director of the Office of International Programs, listed several factors for its limited success. Moreover, he argued, "Common to all of these was a lack of understanding of the depth of the cultural differences between Japan and the United States, and their implications for the program. The language barrier was underestimated, and the expectations of Japanese parents were not well understood." In due course, however, the IED did not fulfill its fiscal obligation. In October 1986, Creighton terminated the contract "because of a drop in the number of students recruited and because of financial mismanagement" in Japan.[37]

The demise of the Japanese program (and the declining undergraduate enrollment) energized the office of International Programs to search for students elsewhere. All during the twentieth century, Creighton had attracted a few foreign students, especially to the health-science schools. In 1968, thirty-three foreign and American students organized the International Student Organization to help the foreign students "feel more at home" and to promote "better understanding between foreign and American students." As late as 1975, after it "experienced an influx," the University enrolled only ninety-one foreign students. However, in 1979 the University had to create an English Language Program for the Japanese students, which provided the opportunity to market itself to other foreign students. In 1980, approximately 250 foreign students from forty countries reorganized the International Student Organization. Active recruiting kept the foreign-student enrollment near that number during the entire decade; in 1985, International Programs also began offering study-abroad programs at Richmond College (London), the Loyola Rome Center, and Sogang University (Seoul). In 1986 it added Northwest University in Xian, China, and in 1992, in conjunction with ILAC, a semester in the Dominican Republic became an option.[38]

At the same time, the CCAS incorporated several other significant changes. For example, Jesuits in training provided it with another distinctive group of students. In the late 1960s, the Wisconsin Province had eliminated the humanities portion of the curriculum for seminarians. By 1978, however, its administrators felt that some who had completed their two-year novitiate, "just weren't ready to begin the intensive study required in the philosophy sector of their training." Thus, they created the Jesuit Humanities Program, located it at Creighton, appointed the Reverend Thomas Shanahan, S.J., director, and purchased an apartment building at 19th and California streets as a residence for the participants. The ten or more novitiates interacted with lay undergraduates in standard classes and in special seminars that humanities faculty devised for the program (faculty submitted topic proposals and students made registration requests to the director). Then, in another return to the humanistic tradition, and in an attempt to reverse an "alarming national trend," in 1982, the GEC began to require students to choose six hours in a foreign language or math/computer science (85 percent of the colleges and universities in the United States required the study of a foreign language in 1915, dropped to 34 percent in 1966, dropping further to 8 percent in 1981). On the other hand, acceding to student desires, in 1988 the CCAS sanctioned the concepts of a co-major (minimum of twenty-four hours in the discipline) and a double major (with the anomalous "support area" instead of a minor, some students pressed for methods to enhance their degrees). Plus the next year, they received a new calendar, which provided a weeklong fall break, reestablished a December graduation exercise and established Easter Monday as a holiday (each semester, classes would begin a week earlier on a Wednesday to maintain the appropriate number of school days).[39]

The new calendar applied to all the undergraduate students, including those in the CoBA. In 1976, the directors found the "lack of growth" in the school "particularly disturbing" since it defied the upward national trend (full-time enrollment for the year remained stagnant at about 450). The following year, the apprehension eased as the number began a steady ascent to 757 in 1982; much of the increase resulted from an over 100 percent jump in female registrations, 270 of the latter year's total. However, replicating the CCAS pattern, the number of African-American CoBA graduates dropped from eight in 1976 to one in 1980. While the total-enrollment problem eased, a lack of accreditation plagued the new dean, Jean Carrica (A.B. and J.D., 1961). The recently reorganized and renamed American Assembly of Collegiate Schools of Business (AACSB) lumped the accreditation of BSBA and MBA programs, and the latter degree necessitated higher percentages of faculty with the Ph.D. At first a lack of funds prevented hiring additional faculty, and a gift from retired Dean Walsh of a 360-acre farm, valued in excess of $300,000, income from which would go into the CoBA general fund, did not alleviate the shortage (the lecture hall in the Eppley Building was named in honor of Dr. Floyd E. and Berneice C. Walsh). Eventually, the University strategy of tuition increases in the period of burgeoning enrollment subsidized the restructuring of the school's faculty from ten of twenty-two full-time teachers with the Ph.D. in 1970, to twenty-two of twenty-nine in 1981. In the latter year, the school received two announcements of good news: an anonymous gift of $300,000 established the Robert B. Daugherty Chair in Management (founder of Valmont Industries, Inc.) and the AACSB granted accreditation. Increased admission standards and faculty research as well as a revised curriculum contributed to garnering the stamp of approval. The revamped "general education requirements" maintained a substantial liberal arts segment (fifty-two hours), the "general business requirements" added another forty-two hours, and the "field of concentration" necessitated eighteen more, leaving a maximum of nineteen hours of electives.[40]

Some CoBA faculty members believed that Dean Carrica had a mandate from Fr. President Labaj and the directors to gain the accreditation, and that it led the dean to attempt to fire long-serving teachers who lacked the Ph.D. degree and/or a record of publication. He succeeded in eliminating two "targets," but threatened lawsuits forced him to retreat in least two other cases. In 1981, the ongoing turmoil prompted an ad hoc meeting of tenured faculty that produced a vote of "no confidence," which a group the dean dubbed the "dirty seven," conveyed to the president's office. A year later, Dean Carrica resigned, saying he felt "intimidated" by the administration; Fr. Morrison denied the accusation, but revealed that he had no plans "to extend or renew" the dean's contract due to the ten-year rule. A recent addition to the *Faculty Handbook*, the regulation aimed at preventing the lifetime deanships that had dominated the professional schools; the article read, "Ordinarily, a dean should not serve more than 10 years."[41]

A slight dip in enrollment (1983 and 1984) greeted the new dean, but then the climb resumed to a peak of 851 in 1989, before down-sliding drastically to 662 (299 women, 32 African Americans) in 1992. On the other hand, shortly after his arrival, Dean Guy Banville, Ph.D., received the good news that under a new program the accounting department became the eighteenth granted a special accreditation by the AACSB. He announced his intension to reestablish the certificate program for CCAS students and to have the business school respond to two major forces—computers and communications technology, and globalization. In 1983, the CoBA initiated a master's in computer systems management, a program tailored to part-time students, which sought to train managers, not technicians. In 1986, Jeanne McManus Wade, widow of Le Roy L. Wade (BSC, 1941), donated $250,000 that funded a computer center in the Eppley Building, named in their honor. Unhappily, however, in 1989 a "non-scientific" survey of two hundred CoBA seniors conducted by the student affairs committee revealed that 56 percent of them would not recommend the school to others. Their major grievances included the loss of faculty, the high number of night classes and the significant number of required liberal arts classes. A review of the curriculum, aimed at devising one for the 1990s, ensued, and in 1992 a significant addition to the faculty resulted from a $1 million gift, which endowed the Jack MacAllister Chair in Regional Economics; Dr. Ernest P. Goss, Ph.D., filled the position.[42]

The CoBA student complaints about night classes erupted as the school got "caught up in the efforts to support" University College, the culmination of Creighton's renewed commitment to continuing education. In 1974, the administration hired a full-time coordinator, with the goal of enlarging offerings, including those at "Creighton West, the evening adult education program at Boys Town." In 1982, a task force studied "the possibility of inaugurating degree programs for part-time students," which would entail night and weekend classes. With enrollment dropping in the CCAS, the board approved the start-up of University College (UC), convoyed with "an extensive advertising campaign," including billboards, radio, and newspapers. The Eppley Little Theater closed and its renovated space became administrative offices and a student-staff lounge. Dr. Wesley Wolfe, Ed.D., associate dean of the CCAS, became dean of the school, which offered eight degree and four certificate majors. Virtually all departments offered courses necessary to fulfill core requirements, and UC offered on-campus childcare during evening and Saturday class hours. In October 1983, the 834 UC students (50 audits, 552 women) pushed Creighton to record enrollment, although both CCAS and CoBA numbers fell that year. However, the UC figure plummeted to 509 in 1991, before improving to 572 the next year, which included 387 women and 29 listed as "black non-Hispanic" (government and foundation application and reporting requirements, responding to law and to social expectations, called for sophisticated enrollment data; Creighton now had four distinct minority categories).[43]

Enrollment in the UC and the other colleges affected the summer school; thus, its enrollment resumed an upward scramble in the mid-1970s, reaching 1,513 in 1981, and then retreated as the number of undergraduates declined. The inception of UC produced a one-year spike to 1,672 in 1984, but enrollment fell to the low 1,400s for the remainder of the decade, before regaining momentum in 1990. The number of graduate students attending the summer school matched the registration from the arts college: 650 and 680 respectively in 1981, bottoming out at 500 and 465 in 1989, then, bouncing back to 556 and 603 in 1991. A summer graduate program in Christian Spirituality commenced in 1974. A $10,000 grant from DeRance, Inc., subsidized the expansion of the related library collection. The program sought to "equip the students to give spiritual direction and to direct retreats," but soon reacted to a "strong demand for courses that include preparation for other apostolates which have to do with spiritual renewal." By 1977, Christian Spirituality, directed by the Reverend John Sheets, S.J., chairman of the theology department, became the largest summer graduate program. On the other hand, the number enrolled in the graduate school during the academic year fell precipitously following the 1975 decision to cease tuition remission for graduate education in order to have a consistent policy covering all professional schools. Graduate enrollment and "higher attrition than in previous years" became a board concern in 1978 (the total had dropped to 351 from 514 in 1974). The launch of UC resulted in a jump of part-time students registering for a graduate classes, resulting in a return to over 500 students in the graduate school between 1984 and 1990. At the same time, master's degrees in atmospheric science (1979), professional accountancy (1982–88), computer systems management, and nursing (1988), and a Ph.D. in pharmacology buoyed the total. The suspension of the master's program in English (1990) and abolition of those in history and biology (1992) had little effect on the total for the latter year: 87 men and 47 women full-time; 205 men and 212 women part-time (11 black non-Hispanic). In the meantime, the North Central accreditation team vented "criticism" of the few existing Ph.D. programs, necessitating a four-year initiative "for strengthening interest and increasing enrollment," before making a decision "about their continuation."[44]

Continuation did not worry the law school. After a slump in applications in the mid-1970s, the administration reported in 1978 that "despite the oversupply of lawyers in the country," the clamor for admission to the school remained passionate. Except for an aberration of 488 full-time students in 1984, enrollment persisted at well over 500, causing the board, in search of "qualitative improvement," to consider limiting the freshmen of 1991 to "approximately 180." While the total remained fairly constant, the nature of the cohort changed. The number of women skyrocketed from 89 (16 percent) in 1975 to 235 (40 percent) in 1992. A decade earlier, the increase generated the formation of the Women's Legal Resource Center to "provide seminars on legal issues as they relate to women in a changing society and to address the concerns and interests of women as legal professionals." The receipt of its first Professional Opportunities Grant (1978), which provided scholarships and stipends, allowed the law school to significantly improve its recruitment of women, but the number of minority students only edged up "little by little." After years of virtually no African-American graduates, in 1975 a sufficient cohort emerged to establish an affiliate of the Black American Law School Association (BALSA), which sponsored an annual civil rights lecture and a minority admissions workshop. In 1983, Creighton formulated a Minority Assistance Program that annually would grant five three-year scholarships to blacks, Hispanics, and Native Americans. In 1992, sixteen "black non-Hispanic," sixteen Hispanic (Hispanic Law Student Association, 1983), but no Native American students studied law at Creighton.[45]

The locale of the law school improved as a third grant from the Ahmanson Foundation furnished funds to "help purchase and raze old buildings in the three blocks surrounding and immediately adjacent" to the facility. The following year, Rodney Shkolnick, who had served as associate dean while maintaining teaching duties, succeeded to the position of dean. His tenure began auspiciously as Creighton's recently established Legislative Research and Drafting Service, "designed to give students an opportunity to acquire research and writing experience and improve interview and persuasion skills," became the ABA's ninth "national showcase" project. In 1978, seniors William G. Schiffenbauer, Michael Krochmalny, and Gary Garrison and law alumni Kevin Hare authored a pamphlet, "Guide to Legislative Research," and Schiffenbauer became national director of the student project.[46]

Dean Shkolnick also witnessed the completion of the revision of the curriculum that provided a "shift back to building block types of courses," prescribing all freshman classes and twenty hours of the second year. Up to one half the students expressed opposition to the alterations, fearing they would hinder their ability to work as clerks, as well as objecting to roll call in second year class (deemed necessary because required classes commanded a record of 80 percent attendance). In 1979, their education obtained a unique enhancement; for the first time, the Nebraska Supreme Court sat outside the Capitol courtroom, hearing five cases at the law school. Subsequently, the administration established two new formats: an MBA-JD combined program (1981) and a part-time program (1985). In the former, the law school would accept nine hours from the MBA toward a law degree and the graduate school would accept six hours from law toward the MBA. The part-time program did not involve a night school. The ABA-approved scheme stemmed from the increase in nontraditional, reentry students and established a six-year timeline, which entailed attending classes with full-time students, but carrying half the load.[47]

Completing his decade as dean, Shkolnick returned to teaching, and in 1988 the law school hired Lawrence Raful, associate dean of the Southern California Law Center in Los Angeles, as his successor. Upon his arrival, an accreditation committee reported concerns about the under-funding of the law library. To remedy the situation, the directors agreed to enhance the law library's budget $50,000 in 1989–90 and another $100,000 in 1990–1991. Raful also inherited ongoing tinkering with the recently revised curriculum. The basic design remained in place, but in 1989, required freshmen hours dropped from thirty-six to thirty-two. Afterward, attempts to refine the delivery of the material engendered occasional shifts in the hours mandated for specific courses and the year in which they appeared in the sequence of required classes. Upperclassmen could take up to "six hours in courses in other divisions of Creighton University or other fully accredited institutions," which would qualify as electives, but the classes had to relate "to the study of law and must not be available in the law school curriculum." Supporting the new design, in 1991 the law school received its first endowed chair, the A. A. and Ethel Yossem Chair in Legal Ethics. Additional recognition arrived the following year, as the Phi Delta Phi international legal fraternity (over 160 chapters and more than 144,000 members) cited the local group as International Inn of the Year because of its "academic excellence, community service projects, school service and other Creighton chapter activities."[48]

In comparison to law's surplus applications for admission, nursing enrollment continued its roller coaster ride, which related to the changing nature of the profession and to job opportunities, as well as corresponding to national demographics. In 1975, a shortage sparked the creation of an accelerated nursing program; a $98,846 HEW grant funded the implementation for two years. Elizabeth Ann Furlong (M.S., University of Colorado) assumed direction of the program, which encouraged applications by "men, minority students, individuals over thirty years of age, and those who plan to work in areas of health-care shortage." Students studied fifty-eight hours of nursing (same as the BSN) in three terms, completed in one year. The first class consisted of seven men and five women, and eleven of them graduated. During the entire period, due to tuition differentials and the fact that an RN degree provided a quicker route to employment, the number of African Americans seeking the BSN from Creighton did not rise above a single digit. For the later degree, enrollment increased with the continuance of the baby boom generation, and then began to decline uniformly. Technically, Nursing "lost" over one hundred students in 1978, when Creighton followed a national trend, fashioning the three-year School of Nursing (symbolically, the change established a standardization of names in the health sciences). Pedagogically, the reorganization gave students a freshman year of study before committing to the professional study of nursing. In the past, a significant amount of transferring between the CCAS and Nursing, and vice versa, had occurred. The number of three-year students hovered around 330 until 1983, and then in conjunction with the ebbing of the baby boom (and the success of feminism which opened other professions to women) began a precipitous waning to 222 in 1985, remaining in the mid-200s until the end of the decade (the total included between 15 to 30 men annually).[49]

The School of Nursing also joined the health-science "team" on site. With the completion of Criss III, medical personnel vacated space in Criss II. Moreover, the medical school Library moved from the first floor of Criss II into the new $4.7 million Bio-Medical Library-Learning Resource Center, adjacent to the east of the Boyne Dental School. The two-story, 57,000-square-foot facility combined the holdings of all the health-science schools (90,000 volumes, plus about 1,200 journals and magazines), provided audio-visual services, and had computers tied in to the National Library of Medicine in Bethesda, Maryland, and the libraries of other medical schools. It became the second facility on the "West Campus," and a shuttle service began between it and the RAL. A $650,000 HEW grant covered 75 percent of the costs to renovate the first and second floors of Criss II into the long-sought home of the School of Nursing. It completed the move in the spring 1977, and began to enjoy the revamped space, which included administrative and faculty offices and classrooms—a one-hundred-seat lecture hall, five seminar rooms, a learning lab, and five patient units, with hospital equipment and simulators for demonstration and practice.[50]

To gain practice and to provide a service to dorm students, in 1974 students began volunteering as "campus nurses." The Nursing School and the RAs "realized that students needed medical treatment between 4:30 P.M. [when the Student Health Office closed] and 8:00 A.M." As an alternative to immediately going to an emergency room, students could call public safety, which would relay the information to one of the student nurses on duty, who would visit the ill student to assess the situation. Additionally, in 1975 the Skills Learning Lab began to provide all student nurses opportunities to practice, on average ten hours per week for nine weeks (i.e., giving shots to objects before patients). The lab represented "new trends in teaching technology as well as the determination to have all nurses be at ease with the physical tasks nurses are called upon to do." It also aimed to overcome the perception that diploma nurses (trained in hospital units) have better patient skills, while degree nurses have better book knowledge.[51]

Moreover, in 1974 the Nebraska Legislature mandated a study to develop "a statewide comprehensive plan for nursing education that focused on the career ladder concept, improvement of instruction and continuing education." Dean Ryan responded by initiating a curriculum study and by establishing an Office of Continuing Education that, among other things, devised a six-week "Nursing Update" course for nurses that had left the workplace and sought reentry. An $84,418 HEW grant funded the curriculum study and the 1977 *Bulletin* announced that "[a]reas of new knowledge and patient care skills [were] added: assessment of physical and mental health, personal and family crisis, gerontology, cultural attitudes that influence health and health care, chemical dependency conditions and administrative principles." However, "before committing time and monies" to create a graduate program, the administration "wished to have more precise information." Thus, in 1977, it commissioned Betty Jo Hadley, Ph.D., to conduct a feasibility study, which pointed out the need for qualified faculty (presently, none held a Ph.D.) and the requisite for flexible scheduling, since most potential students would attend part-time while remaining employed. Dean Ryan left to acquire the Ph.D. in 1977, and returned with it in 1980. In the interim, one short-term dean and two acting deans filled the position. Thereafter, a three-year $225,000 HEW grant provided the funds to begin an MSN program with qualified faculty in two graduate majors, "family nurse clinician and gerontological nurse clinician with their corollaries in management and education." The "non-traditional program" began in 1981, offering classes in the evening, on weekends, and during the summer, which attracted mostly older students from outside Omaha.[52]

The graduate majors highlighted emerging areas of nursing research (little done before 1980), which demonstrated concern "about patient care, quality of life, and the prevention of illness," as opposed to medical research that focused on diseases and their cures. Furthermore, the majors reacted to the demands for preventive care and reduced medical costs that pushed health care out of hospitals, as well as to organizations arguing that "nurses need more college level training so that nursing can become a true and respected profession in the eyes of the American public, which sometimes tends to view nurses as nothing more than physicians handmaidens." Thus, in 1980 senior nursing students began clinical training in community health at the Family Practice Clinics of the medical school. Eugene Barone, M.D., chairman of the department of family practice and director of the Ames Avenue Clinic stated that the home-visit program gave affordable care, provided nurses with an expanded role and responsibilities, and allowed them to work as a team with a physician (he asserted that the old "captain leads the ship" philosophy no longer applied). Within two years, the project evolved into the Creighton Home Health Care Agency, which received state certification and the ability to collect fees for service from Medicare and Medicaid. In 1983, the School of Nursing became one of eleven recipients of a four-year $500,000 grant from the Robert Wood Johnson Foundation "to improve the quality of nursing-home care and to expedite the return of nursing-home patients to more economical levels of care, hopefully to their own homes." Barbara Braden (BSN, Creighton, 1973; M.S., University of California at San Francisco, 1975) directed the project in conjunction with the Mercy Care Center in Omaha and the University of Nebraska School of Nursing and the Madonna Professional Care Center in Lincoln. Subsequently, with Braden as the primary researcher (Ph.D., University of Texas at Austin, 1988), a $205,000 grant funded the study of "etiological factors that predispose development of pressure sores." A second grant for $59,000 supported further education in gerontology for three faculty members.[53]

Despite the new programs, enrollment continued to fall. In 1986, in a "move designed to increase enrollment and retention," nursing returned to a four-year curriculum and the status of a college. Secondarily, the reorganization followed a swiftly reoriented national trend, which reflected lower employment at hospitals and the shift to home health care and community care. That same year, enrollment received a boost as Sheila Ciciulla (M.Ed., Creighton, 1977) played a "major role" in arranging for a "satellite baccalaureate program" at Mary Lanning Hospital in Hastings, Nebraska, which decided to discontinue its diploma program. Concomitantly, in September 1986, Ciciulla became acting dean for a second time, as Dean Ryan left to go to the University of Rochester. Following a national search, Dr. Shirley Dooling, Ph.D., succeeded to the position in August 1987. Fortuitously, she inherited a sorting out of the job market that resulted in a shortage of nurses by the end of the decade. Hospitals began offering higher pay, sign-up bonuses, flexible hours, free day care, and assistance for the pursuit of a master's degree. Enrollment began to increase in 1989, and by 1991 the problem of recruiting nursing faculty returned. Suddenly the Creighton pay scale became "very low" because of the abrupt shift to a seller's market, and the board allocated an extra $47,000 to the salary pool for the College of Nursing.[54]

The School of Pharmacy also experienced enrollment problems. Although it increased from about 170 in 1974 to over 200 in 1978, it fell back into the 190s from 1979-1982. Subsequently, the school retained "a full-time recruiter and student ombudsman," and thereafter enrollment steadily increased to 290 in 1992. During the mid-1980s, the number of women gained parity with men and coeds ended the period at 60 percent. In comparison, the number of African Americans dwindled from a high of fourteen in 1986, to only five in 1992. However, as with the other health-science schools except for Nursing, a large increase occurred in the number of "Asian or Pacific Islander" students (beyond the historic group from the Hawaiian Islands), from five in 1977 to forty-six in 1992. Those students of that era participated in a revolution in pharmacy education. By that time, pharmaceutical companies mass-produced virtually all medicine. With little "compounding" necessary, more training became necessary in pharmacology in order to give advice to physicians on the effects of drugs. In 1974, the pharmacy school received a $100,000 HEW grant to introduce a "modular system," a series of self-study packages that allowed students to work at their own pace and to test out by passing a standardized exam on the material. The first-in-the-country curriculum, also encouraged students to interact with faculty responsible for each module and to deal with "specific pharmacy questions and problems intelligently and individually." Moreover, as a symbol of the emerging role of pharmacy in the "health care team structure," in 1975 the school established the Pharmacy Drug Information Service, staffed by two seniors on two-week clinical rotations who would provide advice on "adverse drug reactions, side effects and drug interactions."[55]

During this period, the pharmacy school developed in several other directions. In 1977 it "entered into a contract with the United States Government for educational affiliation services for the Academy of Health Sciences, U. S. Army, Fort Sam Houston, Texas, to include the awarding of college credit to enlisted students" for courses in the Pharmacy Specialist Program and the Sterile Products Program. The arrangement ended in 1984 as the Academy "terminated all undergraduate agreements with nonmilitary educational institutions" (it established its own community college to award the credits). At the same time, in 1976 Creighton became one of thirteen schools to offer a "doctorate in pharmacy." The one-calendar-year program limited enrollment to eighteen, the maximum that the clinic facilities could accommodate. At first, the *Bulletin* stated that the "Pharm.D." was "not designed to replace" the B.S. in pharmacy degree. However, by the late 1980s, the former had evolved into a competitive three-year degree with few distinctive classes (the transition in nomenclature mimicked the change from LL.B. to J.D.). Besides stature, another indication of the changes in the profession, in 1984 a class in "computer applications" became a requirement: "The little flickering light spots racing across screens have replaced mortar and pestle."[56]

Furthermore, in 1982 the reorganized School of Pharmacy and Allied Health Professions emerged. The frequently changing array of baccalaureate programs had moved from the CCAS to become the Allied Health Division of the medical school in 1977. Students would take three years in the CCAS, and then apply to the Division to complete the degree with a one-year internship at St. Joseph's Hospital. Programs included radiological technology and audiology/speech pathology, and expanded in 1980 with the addition of respiratory therapy and nurse anesthetist. Then the allied-health programs administratively shifted to the pharmacy school, and in 1985 Creighton introduced the first bachelor-degree program in occupational therapy in Nebraska, because a strong need existed and would "continue to grow in direct proportion to the growth in senior citizen population." The enrollment in allied heath grew progressively from 10 in 1977, to 115 in 1992 (20 men, 95 women, 5 black non-Hispanic). By the end date, AT&T provided eighteen computers to establish a lab, open twenty-four hours a day, for pharmacy and allied health students.[57]

Similarly, enrollment in the dental school continued upward during the 1970s, leveling at around 315 in the mid-1980s. That student body maintained its volunteer effort at the Indian-Chicano Clinic in historic South Omaha, and in 1980 the American Student Dental Association awarded them with the Preventive Dentistry Award in recognition of nearly 10,000 treatment hours at the facility the previous year. Those students studied at the new Boyne Building, constructed to incorporate color televisions in most rooms and labs (like elsewhere, VHS began to eliminate the slide projector, but the facility's TV production studio did not generate much use). Creighton benefited from the absence of dental schools in many western states. In 1976, Nevada became the seventh state to contract with the University to train dentists. That same year, Cheri Lewis became the first woman to graduate from the dental school since 1949; thereafter, the number of women enrolled rose rapidly, fourteen in 1975, to forty-four in 1992, but proportionally remained the smallest coed cohort in the professional schools. During the period, the number of African Americans remained a single numeral, while the number of Asian/Pacific Islanders quintupled from six to thirty-one. Moreover, alone among the health-science schools, the number of foreign students jumped significantly from five in 1985, to twenty-three in 1990. Also of note, dental students of the era had to follow a dress code initiated in 1984 by new dean Gerald Brundo (D.D.S., 1969), who argued that the profession involved "not only practicing competent dentistry, but also manner of dress, character and activity."[58]

However, the dental school maintained its enrollment from a shrinking pool of applicants. In 1981, Creighton received only 1.2 applications per place available. Meanwhile, the costs of dental education were "skyrocketing," producing a national "crisis." During the 1970s, the federal government had provided the dental school with more than $1 million annually; as of the fall 1981, nothing. Factors such as the end of the baby boom and fluoridation reversed the trend, and the contemporary fear became a surfeit of dentists (between 1975 and 1986, applications to dental schools fell by over 60 percent). In 1981, Creighton subscribed with a national application service to supplement its own recruiting, which doubled the number of applicants to 750, ensuring an entry class of "77 qualified students." The contracts with Idaho and Utah also affected the freshman class, as revision allowed students from those states (nineteen of them) to spend their first year at a home-state university and then transfer to Creighton for the remaining three years. While some dental schools closed, Creighton weathered another transition in the profession, "from tooth repair and replacement" to "care involving aesthetic and cosmetic reconstruction, and emphasis on prevention and early control of dental problems." The transformation required a reorientation in the clinic in order to reduce costs. It sought to preserve student-patient contact hours, while reducing the number of hours of full-time faculty. Their Creighton salary diminished while they were allowed to expand their private practices. Despite maintaining a faculty-student ratio above the national average (5.9:1 versus 4:1), Creighton students continued to perform well on regional and national tests. Eventually, the situation returned closer to equilibrium and the turbulence subsided in 1991, with a 20 percent increase in applications to a dental school "unique in that a comprehensive dental education is provided, with no specialty training," and whose costs remained "among the lowest in the nation."[59]

A similarly rocky situation existed in the medical school, but because it received more and larger federal grants, the diminution of federal funds produced a proportionally more sever budgetary crisis. With a surfeit of applicants (despite a temporary decline during the 1980s), maintaining enrollment did not present a problem. Between 1974 and 1992, the annual total enrollment ranged between 440–480. In 1974, a contract with the State of Wyoming (no medical school) assured acceptance of up to twenty students per year and the IED program promised thirty additional places to Japanese students, although for the latter, six became the highest number to matriculate in any year of the short-lived arrangement. At times, the "Creighton preference" could become awkward if too high a percentage of those admitted chose to go elsewhere because of costs (the professional schools needed competitive scholarships and financial aid to garner the best of Creighton's undergraduate scholars). The number of women grew spectacularly, from 48 in 1975 to 144 in 1992 (30 percent of the total); but the peak of 19 African-American students in 1977 dwindled during the 1980s, until recovering to 23 in 1991. The Office of Minority Affairs for the Health Sciences worked to overcome the debilitating effects of the cuts in federal grant and loan programs (as tuition escalated). In 1974, it gained a full-time director, John Pierce, to recruit and retain minority students. Moreover, in 1975 John Elder, Ph.D., professor of pharmacology in the medical school, became director of the federally funded Health Care Opportunities Program that worked "to correct deficiencies" in English, math, and the sciences of minority applicants. It established a 77 percent admissions rate for students that completed the one-year of intensive supplementary training. As in all the other schools, the number of Hispanics remained small but stable during the era, while the size of the Asian/Pacific Islander contingent almost quadrupled (ten in 1977, thirty-eight in 1992).[60]

The medical students of the period garnered the advantage of doing clinical work in the new St. Joseph's Hospital; nursing students finally gained clinical opportunities at a nearby facility, and Creighton faculty and students staffed the hospital pharmacy. While the hospital provided all the health-science schools with a state-of-the-art facility, it exacerbated a fiscal crisis. As hospital construction began, the Nixon Administration announced a constriction in capitation grants, "matching money allotted to the health science schools on a per capita basis for students enrolled." While also fighting inflation (the University budget increased 13 percent in the 1975–76 fiscal year), the federal reduction caused a cash-flow problem for the Creighton Omaha Regional Health Care Corporation (the hospital) and the University, which would "require a lot of money not available at the present." To balance the budget for the year, the "entire $800,000 in additional general current funds [needed to make up for the loss of capitation grants] came from tuition increases in Dentistry and Medicine, price increases in the clinic area, and from additional state contract funds." For the following year, however, a balanced budget demanded operational reductions: ten to thirteen positions in the health sciences would remain vacant due to retirements, and projections called for the elimination of 15.8 faculty lines and nineteen staff lines by June 1977 due to the loss of about $3 million from federal programs. The forecast prompted a brief attempt at organizing a collective-bargaining unit.[61]

Moreover, the University contributed $31.7 million to the $120 Regional Health Care Corporation project (it obtained a $5.5 million HEW grant and a $22 million low-interest, subsidized loan; donated the land valued at $2.3 million and the heating and air conditioning costing $1.9 million). Creighton's directors affirmed the use of University funds for the venture as "prudent," and realized "that though the corporations are separate, our problems are mutual." Two problems loomed: a "surplus [of] hospital beds in Omaha" and the "rather dim" prospect of getting Douglas County to pay for indigent patients "now coming to St. Joseph's in great number." Creighton's board supported the idea of a "community-wide effort to develop a bed-need plan for our metropolitan area," but did not want to take the issue public, preferring to deal with it on a board-member to board-member basis. In such circumstances, on December 17, 1977, United States Army and Air Force personnel combined "forces with city departments and the staff of the hospital to move from 10th and Martha streets to the Creighton West Campus" (all but the mental-health services). The

Boys Town Institute, which had functioned out of the old hospital since its founding in 1972, also made the move to its new building attached to the hospital to the south (which began to include girls in its program). The Omaha Public Power District constructed a new substation on the northwest corner of 24th and Burt streets to provide the increased demand for electrical power on the West Campus. In 1979, a group of investors from Madison, Wisconsin, purchased the old St. Joseph's Hospital and the University leased back all its remaining medical operations at the site.[62]

The administration had to contend with continued government cutbacks in grants and loans, and the loss of state contracts on into the 1980s. VPHS Heaney had to promote savings and generate more income; besides gifts, that could include additional research grants (indirect costs support the operational budget), expanded clinic operations, attracting a higher number of patients to the clinics and to St. Joseph Hospital, better management, and effective billing (a suggestion from alumni to initiate a school of podiatry was studied but rejected). The stress of the novel situation entailed "a significant morale problem because an entire generation of health professions educators had had no experience other than with a 'cost-plus' or 'the sky is the limit' approach to program management." Moreover, regrettably, the death of Mabel Criss in 1982 yielded supplemental stress, as a four-way, five-year tussle ensued, finally mediated by the Nebraska Supreme Court, which arranged for Creighton to receive "two thirds of the annual income from the corpus of the trust [then valued at approximately $25 million]." In the meantime, with a federal grant, Creighton physicians studied but rejected creating a Health Maintenance Organization (HMO) in 1976, arguing it would cost families more than "prevailing coverage in a normal insurance program." Subsequently, however, in 1983 medical school faculty (full-time and contributed service), in conjunction with St. Joseph's Hospital, created a Preferred Provider Organization (PPO) to encourage University employees to use the system, which would "waive the $100 deductible as well as the 20% coinsurance."[63]

For the hospital and clinics, the situation seemingly improved in 1982 as the Nebraska Supreme Court "clarified the obligations that counties have for the sick poor." Yet, in 1982 Creighton and St. Joseph's Hospital "provided 9 million dollars of free care to the indigent sick." VPHS Heaney argued that if "the Hospital were to continue accepting the majority of cases of the indigent sick in the Douglas-Sarpy County area, the Hospital could face bankruptcy in the near future." The Creighton-Nebraska Universities Health Foundation (1971) identified "a great need for the Foundation and the two universities to work jointly for adequate public payment of indigent health care." They also sought cost-savings in joint education ventures, such as orthopedic and pediatric residency programs, as well as several others. In this period of anxiety and innovation, American Medical International (AMI), an investor-owned health management firm headquartered in Beverly Hills, California, which operated 111 hospitals in the United States, sought to add St. Joseph's to its chain. The hospital and health affairs committee of Creighton's board assessed the situation thusly: "Weaknesses include declining census at St. Joseph, loss of contributing service faculty, medical staff morale, Hospital/University relationship, financial position due in part to the large debt service, competitive environment (excess of hospital beds in Omaha and a second medical school), and lack of planning for the future."[64]

Some directors worried about philosophical differences, because AMI was for profit and was not Catholic. However, a report noted that nothing in the proposal would prevent St. Joseph's "from continuing as Catholic and as a teaching hospital." The board assessment stated that the hospital medical staff supported the sale, the nonmedical employees were "very concerned," the health-science faculty approved or had "no particular strong feelings about it," and the Omaha medical community seemed "curious but supportive of the sale." On the other hand, Right to Life organizations and a "small minority" of CCAS and health-science faculty objected, while some priests in the Omaha Archdiocese wondered if St. Joseph's should be called Catholic. Yet, the directors felt that the "broad-based faculty support" resulted from "frequent and detailed communications." Furthermore, the Reverend Ned Cassem, S.J., M.D., a native of Omaha, a member of Creighton's board and member of the faculty of the Harvard Medical School, became a symbolic spokesman, arguing that the merger with AMI would help control costs while maintaining service.[65]

In 1984, "an unprecedented merger of academe and free enterprise" transformed St. Joseph's Hospital into "a model—or flagship—academic health center for AMI's system." The sale price of about $100 million would pay off the $62-million construction debt and the net proceeds would create an endowment for the newly established Health Future Foundation (HFF). The interest income from the approximately $40 million endowment would fund grants "earmarked for the encouragement of research, teaching capital improvements, faculty development and the establishment of new programs at the Creighton Health Science schools." The proceeds from the sale and funding from AMI would also found a Center for the Study of Health Policy and Ethics. Saint Joseph's Hospital would remain Catholic and would continue to provide care to the poor, but would not perform abortions. AMI brought "the proven expertise in such areas as financial management, purchasing and marketing" (e.g., cost reduction resulting from the economy of scale in purchasing). Furthermore, AMI "agreed to resolve the problem posed by the need for a Catholic Center for Mental Health at an appropriate location to be determined" (the unit at the old hospital was no longer adequate).[66]

The HFF operated as expected. Notable among its annual disbursements, a $3.9 million grant, which funded the development of Centers of Excellence in "areas such as hypertension, nuclear medicine, diabetes, hard tissue research and cancer research." However, the problem of indigent care continued as an area of concern. In 1985, the Center for Applied Urban Research at University of Nebraska at Omaha (UNO) embarked upon a study of the health-care needs of the poor, seeking "identification of alternative funding" and providing "the basic data and information needed to proceed with our plan [Creighton Directors] to transfer indigent care to the county." Concomitantly, the HFF participated in attempts to pass "appropriate legislation in the [Nebraska] Unicameral to develop appropriate funding." The efforts came to naught and strained the relationship between AMI, St. Joseph's Hospital, and the University. Historically, the hospital had "remitted to Creighton funds to reimburse for the cost of teaching residents in training" and "for a number of years" Creighton remitted funds to the hospital for indigent care. After the sale to AMI, the question of who paid how much to whom became contentious; in 1986, St. Joseph's informed the University of its "plans to cancel and renegotiate the contract for resident teaching cost." Subsequently, the University agreed to pay the hospital $1 million for the "future care of indigent patients at the rate of $200,000 a year commencing in 1987–88 and continuing through 1991–92."[67]

While the institutions attended to the issue of reciprocal payments, the Creighton board became anxious over rumors that AMI sought to sell St. Joseph's; in October 1986, company officers assured the Directors that the firm was "doing well financially and has not indicated they are considering selling the hospital." However, six months later, the administration complained that AMI had not changed "the reimbursement of faculty teaching in the hospital" for five years and that it refused to expend promised money in "support of our teaching mission." Moreover, "AMI had six CEOs at St. Joseph's in the last six years." The administration proclaimed that "an adversarial relationship" had developed. In response, the directors passed a resolution imploring the boards of St. Joseph's Hospital and the St. Joseph Center for Mental Health to urge AMI to live up to the acquisition agreement by fully reimbursing the University for the costs of teaching and to develop parking, as well as to build a new psychiatric facility. In May 1990, the unrequited plea led the board to file suit, asking the court "to order AMI to take all actions necessary for funding, implementation and completion of approximately $12.8 million in capital improvements to St. Joseph Hospital budgeted for fiscal 1990." Attempts at a negotiated settlement placed the suit on hold, but the discourse "broke down" at a meeting in April 1992, and Creighton reinstituted the legal action.[68]

While the business arrangements concerning the new St. Joseph's Hospital produced consternation, the education of physicians continued amidst the din. In 1975, a four-year residency in orthopedic surgery began, and during that summer Kiewit Hall became home for twenty-seven Vietnamese physicians and their families as they participated in an English language and American acculturation program. Simultaneously, they studied medicine at the University of Nebraska Medical Center with the aim of passing United States license exams and practicing in small towns in Nebraska. With traditional students in mind, in 1977 the medical school obtained a Kellogg Foundation grant to study its curriculum, intending "to develop new systems which could eliminate duplication, strengthen areas that may be weak, and make available health-related programs to a broader spectrum of students" (e.g., interdisciplinary courses available to all four members of the health-science team now in proximity in the Criss and Boyne buildings). That same year witnessed the fruition of two National Endowment for the Humanities grants ($30,000 in 1974 for planning; $200,000 for three years for implementation) to introduce humanistic perspectives to the study of the health sciences. The Reverend James Quinn, S.J., became the director of Humanities in the Health Sciences (HHS) program, in which CCAS professors taught mini-courses to students in all four of the health sciences, which put medical issues in the perspective of their discipline. Some medical-school faculty and students complained, arguing that the classes belonged in undergraduate education; however, with various modifications over the following decade, the HHS program persisted.[69]

Additionally, in 1977, *Social Forces* magazine published a report based on a 30 percent response to a questionnaire sent to physicians and scientists, which ranked the medical school ninety-first out of ninety-four evaluated. The authors explained that "medical schools vary significantly in terms of their visibility to others within the medical school community," and that research and geographic location played a key role in that visibility. John Herman, then executive assistant to the dean of the School of Medicine, admitted that research production needed improvement, but doubted that the ranking would affect the number or quality of students and faculty recruited to the school. Furthermore, he asserted that Creighton's mission consisted of "educating physicians not scientists." Demonstrating that mission, that same year, Thomas W. Hilgers, M.D., established the Natural Family Planning Education and Research Center, and the next year, the medical school became the first to offer a certificate of Instruction in Natural Family Planning. Also that year, ILAC adopted the "team approach," sending six teams of medical, dental, nursing, and pharmacy students to "remote villages or 'campos'" in the Dominican Republic for eight weeks during the summer (a pilot program to "humanize" health-science students). The pilot worked well, and in 1989 the seven-building complex (church, kitchen, dining room, one-hundred-bed dorm, administration building, and library), the Creighton Center of Health Education, opened near Santiago. It served as the headquarters for ILAC and as a "training site providing rural Dominicans with basic health skills and information." A $200,000 gift from the Wisconsin Province to the Campaign for Creighton helped finance the project.[70]

In the meantime, in 1980, VPHS Heaney and then AVP Fr. Michael Morrison issued a letter reminding chairs of the nine-year rule and deans of the ten-year rule. In a matter of weeks, Medical Dean Joseph Holthaus resigned; approximately one hundred faculty members signed a letter opposing his removal. The standard also affected a significant number of chairmen, but despite the opposition, the administration applied the rule. After a two-year search, Richard L. O'Brien, M.D., became dean; subsequently, he honored the ten-year rule and resigned as dean in 1992. In the interim, he had added the position of vice president of the health sciences (1985), as Dr. Heaney relinquished the position to become the John A. Creighton Professor—the first University professorship—which functioned outside the department structure of the medical school. The transition and an accreditation review occurred simultaneously. As the "only serious concern," the assessors mentioned the "lack of sufficient research." While research has a relationship to teaching, the teaching remained good, as attested to by the fact that 75 percent of the medical students received a residency offer from one of their first three choices, and that Creighton never had anyone unmatched on Match Day. In 1991, a donation from alums Gilbert A. (M.D., 1945) and the late Clinton G. Beirne (M.D., 1948) addressed the research deficiency by providing the primary source of funding for a five-story tower, with 15,000 square feet of lab and office space, attached to the Criss I research building, itself undergoing a $3.4 million renovation partly funded by a $2 million federal grant. Ten years before, the Beirne brothers each made "sizeable gifts" in honor of their parents, Arthur and Marie, to construct an amphitheater in the Criss complex.[71]

Research potential also improved in 1987 when Dr. Arthur E. Prevedel (M.D., 1943) pledged $500,000 to establish the first endowed professorship in the medical school in surgery. Two years later, a $3.8 million National Institutes of Health (NIH) grant funded the establishment of the Osteoporosis Center, "operated by Creighton's internationally renowned team of osteoporosis researchers, [which] provides physician evaluations, identification of high risk patients, nutrition counseling, prevention information and disease management advice." Also in 1989, the board approved construction of a $7 million, three-story medical building on the west side of 30th Street, between Webster and Burt streets, to accommodate increased faculty and programs, as well as outpatient services and clinical research in cardiology, nephrology, pediatrics, radiology, and pathology. The directors expected the "building will pay for itself." Within a year of completion, the building lost "the largest dialysis facility in the state" (due to reduced government funding) and the pediatrics section, and converted solely to cardiac care because the patient load in that area had doubled in a decade. Two other clinics designed to generate revenue and, if necessary, patients for St. Joseph's Hospital located themselves in the Omaha Housing Authority Burt Towers (Creighton Comprehensive Gerontology Medical Clinic, 1984) and the Florence Care Center (a nursing home, 1991). Additionally, in 1990 Creighton opened its Center for Metabolic Imaging at the old St. Joseph's Hospital site; it became only the third center in the United States to have a positron emission tomography (PET) scanner for use by practicing physicians.[72]

Furthermore, in 1983, the health sciences had entered the era of "artificial intelligence" with the creation of the Creighton On-line Multiple Modular Expert System (COMMES). An outcome of the $890,000 Kellogg Foundation curriculum study grant, Steve Evans, director of Creighton's Instructional Science Research Division, designed "the elaborate computer program that helps 'teach' health sciences personnel at locations in Nebraska and elsewhere." It consisted of "a series of expert learning systems for health care education," which acted as "tutors" by providing "carefully tailored" study materials related to "specific medical topics on request." COMMES supplied five programs, each using the terminology specific to the disciple: a "program consultant" for the M.D., the medical technologist, nurses, audio-visual materials, and test writing. In addition, it contained a "programmed approach to learning and can give a test (generated entirely by the computer) [hence, artificial intelligence] which, when sent to Creighton, is graded and can result in CEU (continuing education units) credit." The Kellogg Foundation presented a second grant ($47,745) to disseminate awareness "through publications, professional conferences, and specific presentations, information about the COMMES artificial intelligence system and its data base."[73]

The dramatic changes in professional education since the 1950s, which consisted of increased hours of study and more time in clinical work, as well as the fact that contemporary law, dental, and medical students had graduated from college, separated them in age and temperament from the undergraduate cohort. In comparison, nursing remained an undergraduate program and pharmacy partially so, and many students in those programs lived in the dorms on campus (graduate students remained tangential, as most attended part-time at night). Thus, despite a geographically unified campus, the law, medical, and dental students enjoyed new buildings with their own lounges and did not need to encounter undergraduates in the student center (significantly, the law and dental buildings stood separately at the east and west edges of the University). In addition, with the explosion in the number of undergrads, no longer could the combination of those professional schools claim majority status in the student body. The situation boded ill for the SBG; in 1974, officers complained that no dental or medical representatives attended meetings. Students in those schools complained about the amount of the rebates to their schools and about the nature of the programs (older and/or married professionals did not want to attend "keggers" with "teeny boppers"). As late as 1985, dire predictions of the demise of the SBG floated around campus.[74]

Actually, the Student Union survived a tumultuous period and women began to play an increasing role in the SBG. In March 1975, Mary Bradley, arts senior-to-be, won a three-way election (against two coed candidates) to become its first female president. The following year, she struggled with the perennial jockeying for professional-school rebates and subsidies for the myriad of student groups. Subsequently, attempts to generate interest in student governance and to reform the structure of the SBG manifested the historic undergraduate protests of fraternity domination and of "railroading" the passage of self-interest issues. Additionally, the 1980s witnessed the return of cancelled annual corporation meetings because of a lack of a quorum. In the 1981–82 academic year, the union tumbled to a nadir of sorts, with "over a half dozen resignations, two executives recalled, and three investigations, [which included] two presidents, four vice presidents of student services, [and] three vice presidents of finance." The resignations and recalls (the president and the vice president of finance) continued the following year. Law students Steve Maril and Colleen Parsely cochaired a committee to revise the by-laws, necessitated by the controversy and recalls. The 1984 corporation meeting lacked a quorum; however, a previous meeting had given the SBG the power to amend the by-laws at its regular meetings. As it continue to work toward a major revision, it raised the number of representatives to thirty, giving the CCAS, CoBA, and Allied Health each one more, based on enrollment. Unfortunately, the changes did not overcome the divisions within the student body or the general apathy toward student government. In 1986, the SBG president found it "really frustrating" that only thirteen students attended the annual corporation meeting; by then, there were thirty-three representatives and only one had asked to be excused. Obviously, in this atmosphere of indifference (which included elected representatives), the Creighton Board of Directors deflected another SBG request for a seat (1991). While the joint conference of the 1970s had atrophied, "for several years" the SBG president had attended the meetings of the board's student affairs committee, and the directors felt that provided an "appropriate means of communication."[75]

With the student government and other activities, the Greek system afforded unity for its members, but could produce discord among independents that viewed it as a juggernaut. Actually, the mid-1970s witnessed a decline in vitality. In 1974, sorority Kappa Beta Chi disbanded because of insufficient pledges and "Creighton Capers," a talent-show competition, met its demise because of a lack of Greek support. Subsequently, in 1976 the fraternities abandoned the "Miss Cutie and Mr. Ugly" contest that for two decades had consisted of competitive skits, signs, and other efforts to support the female and male candidates who amassed the largest list of blood donors. During its stint, the gala pushed blood donations at Creighton to twice the number at similar-sized schools. The first post-cutie-ugly year garnered six hundred donors, still above the average, but a drop of two hundred from the last year of the contest.[76]

In comparison, the 1980s engendered rejuvenation. In 1981, after a lengthy zoning dispute with neighbors who feared disturbances, Pi Kappa Alpha became the first undergraduate fraternity to gain approval for an off-campus house. Phi Kappa Psi followed suit in 1984, the year that Delta Chi successfully reactivated (had tried in 1981) and Sigma Alpha Epsilon garnered another disciplinary action. The administration had just reinstated the fraternity in the spring, when a "couple of incidents" that remained "confidential" resulted in a second suspension. Numerous community service projects shortened the penalty and it gained reinstatement in January 1985. By the end of that year, Sigma Phi Epsilon became the seventh national undergraduate social fraternity at Creighton, and in 1990 the black fraternity Kappa Alpha Psi reactivated its chapter, temporarily becoming the eighth. It had originated on campus in 1927, but lasted only briefly; in the post–World War II era, occasionally African-American students reorganized a chapter in conjunction with UNO, trying to keep it functioning in Omaha. While the white fraternities now accepted blacks, they did not recruit them successfully. With the renewed vigor during the 1980s, the Board of Directors, which estimated that 30 percent of the student body participated in fraternity/sorority activities, began an on-going discussion of the creation of a fraternity row adjacent to the campus.[77]

Sororities followed a similar path. The number of women rushing tripled in the first half of the 1980s. Enigmatically, Sigma Sigma Sigma, which had activated in 1978, disbanded in 1984, but Gamma Phi Beta replaced it as the fourth undergraduate sorority. The following year, the local group Alpha Sigma Gamma joined Alpha Gamma Delta; thereby, all four of the undergraduate sororities claimed national affiliation. In 1985, Delta Zeta became the first sorority at Creighton to obtain a house. The Greek women ended the decade with a fifth sorority, Alpha Phi, and the number of coeds rushing had gone up every year (the rise reflected the gender enrollment pattern).[78]

Father President Labaj demonstrated the new status of women at Creighton by canceling class at 1:00 P.M. on Wednesday, October 29, 1975, so that students could attend a special mass and educational programs in recognition of the International Women's Year. Creighton coeds "wanted to take a positive approach instead of the negative aspects of a strike or some of the other activities that are being planned nationally." Subsequently, supporters claimed "attendance was good" (seminars attracted twenty to forty, including a few men at each), but those "closely involved would have liked more." The SBG absorbed the message. In 1976, it recognized and funded a Women's Resource Center, with a part-time volunteer faculty director, Patricia Fleming (philosophy). In 1981, the University hired a director, but the center closed at the end of the decade "because of low funding and the office's lack of activities on campus." During the interim, the committee on the status of women provided an advocacy venue and promoted recognition. In 1980, it created the Mary Lucretia Creighton Award, given to "a person associated with Creighton who has created an environment supportive of women, has encouraged women faculty, administrators, staff or students in the development and utilization of their talents or has served as a role model of accomplishment for women." Dean Eileen Lieben and Fr. Labaj became the charter recipients.[79]

Moreover, the elevating status of women manifested itself in 1981 with the "promulgation" of a sexual harassment policy "to meet federal guidelines" (federal courts had held corporations without a policy liable for the actions of their employees). It included establishing a committee to review complaints in accordance with rules formulated by the United States Office of Civil Rights. By 1984, the number of complaints had "steadily increased" to six for the fall semester. However, all but one complaint dissolved through the early informal stages of conflict resolution. The University also acknowledged the significance of women by opening a Child Care Center in 1982; it became only the second employer in Omaha to offer such a facility. It consisted of three portable-classroom units purchased from the Omaha Public School District, situated on a lot at 22nd and California streets, and it charged competitive rates for children of employees and students, and three and four-year-olds participated in a formal pre-school program. In 1983, Rose Marie Greco Wilson (B.S. Pharmacy, 1958) contributed another example of feminine prominence, gaining election as the first female president of the Alumni Council. The decade ended with a momentous indicator, as Creighton became one of fourteen schools to share a $3 million endowment, a bequest from Clare Booth Luce, playwright, war correspondent, diplomat, and widow of publisher Henry R. Luce. In 1948, while she served as Ambassador to Italy, she had delivered the Commencement speech and received an honorary doctor of laws from Creighton. It marked her first appearance on television, as WOW-TV broadcast the address closed circuit in one of its pioneer experiments in conjunction with the University. Her will instructed the schools to "fund scholarships, fellowships and professorships for women teaching science and engineering." In 1990, the University hired Holly Ann Harris, Ph.D. (chemistry), to become the first Clare Booth Luce Chair holder and funded one graduate and five undergraduate scholarships to women majoring in a science.[80]

Additionally, women enhanced their position in the ROTC. In 1975, the University signed an agreement that incorporated the College of Saint Mary into the Creighton program, becoming the first women's college with Army ROTC in the Fourth Region. That same year, Janice Stallman, a pre-pharmacy freshman, received the first four-year ROTC scholarship given to a coed at Creighton. Thereafter, in 1979, Lt. Col. Richard Terry explained that he simply chose "the most qualified individual," when he appointed Cheryl A. Linscott, senior biology major, as Cadet Lt. Col., the first woman to command the Creighton battalion (110 men, 35 women). Although the *Blue-jay* eliminated the ROTC section in 1974, that year witnessed the first increase in participation since the program went voluntary. It continued to rise because of intensive recruiting, and the handful of students that protested against devices such as "Army Awareness Day" could not stem the tide. The battalion benefited from agreements that added UNO (1975) and Metropolitan Community College (1981), and from a "more positive attitude toward military service [despite negative editorials and letters to the editor of the *Creightonian*] and [a] generous scholarship program." Enrollment reached 227 cadets, 27 of them women, by the latter date. In 1985, the unit changed its name to the "Blackwolves Battalion," in honor of the symbol on the coat-of-arms of St. Ignatius. Scholarships for nursing students had attracted some of the women to the battalion, but the number jumped appreciably in 1986 based on the Army's projected need for nurses. The number of nursing scholarships multiplied ten-fold in the following three years, buoying enrollment in the ROTC and the Nursing School (fourteen freshmen awarded nursing scholarships in 1989). Subsequently, the battalion celebrated its seventy-fifth anniversary (1994) commanded by Lt. Col. Joan Sisco, a nineteen-year Army veteran beginning her third ROTC tour, and by the end of the decade, women would comprise over 50 percent of the unit.[81]

Three other institutions that had floundered during the "era of confrontation" revitalized. In 1975, the SBG and the administration agreed to split the $1,200 cost to publish *Shadows*. The proclamation proved premature, as "interest in 'Shadows' did not merit the costs"; a creative writing contest in honor of Leo Jacks, open to all undergraduates in Nebraska, served as a replacement. Subsequently, in 1978, after a four-year hiatus, *Shadows* returned. By 1990, it garnered its second consecutive medal from the Columbia Scholastic Press Association (the stalwart student publication, the *Creightonian*, received a first-place ranking). Second, the Reverend Marion Sitzman, OSB, revived a slumbering debate team and transformed it once again into a trophy-winning powerhouse that attained a "top ten" reputation nationally. Third, Homecoming returned. Without the floats, the parade, or the royalty, it had become an alumni affair (for students, it had morphed into the "Winterfest" carnival). Returning to tradition, in 1983 the SBG sponsored the highly successful "Winter Formal," a dance at a downtown hotel. Sensing the new mood, in 1986, Alumni Director Michael Leighton (A.B., 1970) "joined forces with Student Services to plan this weekend's homecoming activities" to include the "student body." Plans embraced the return of royalty, and by 1989 the student referendum on a king and queen commanded a two-page spread in the *Creightonian*.[82]

Two other student institutions highlighted a technological transformation. In 1971, radio station KOCU had celebrated its twenty-fifth anniversary with a staff of forty-seven disc jockeys and seven news reporters, who broadcast eighty-four hours per week; programming consisted mostly music and news, as television had rendered listening to live dramas passé. It did not make it to its fiftieth birthday; as of the summer of 1989, it went silent, the victim of lost interest. The faculty no longer used the facility to train broadcast students, and the few non-major volunteers did not always handle the equipment correctly, causing frequent breakdowns. A $55,000 gift from the family of Frank E. Pellegrin (BSC, 1931, nationally prominent radio and TV broadcaster and owner-investor) funded the remodeling of the space into two "fully equipped audio studios," which opened in the fall of 1990. Students would "learn broadcast journalism on state-of-the-art equipment," but "minus the signal."[83]

While radio faded, cable and satellite TV emerged. In 1980, cable television entered the Omaha market. The Cox Cable Company won the bidding, and as part of its community service, it donated equipment to Creighton for use in its studio to produce cable-access programming. On November 2, 1981, "Creighton Close-Up," a thirty-minute, weekly "magazine program" debuted. Journalism students received training with on-camera interviewing and reporting. Simultaneously, Fr. Leland Lubbers brought satellite communications to campus; he and a team of students built "three homemade spherical antennae on the roof of the sculpture lab at 2102 Burt St." The Creighton Satellite Network began receiving signals in December 1981, but transmitting them to other buildings on campus remained "technically impractical." Shortly thereafter, the team relocated the dishes to an area north of the RAL; from there, they created a cable network, relaying educational programming, wired to campus buildings through the heating and air conditioning tunnels (as part of a private university, it could not use public utility poles). Concurrently, Fr. Lubbers organized and became president of the international consortium Satellite Communications for Learning Association (SCOLA), which aimed to "make available the widespread use of satellite communications technology in teaching." For his efforts, the French Government bestowed the rank of Chevalier in the *Order des Palmes Academiques*, founded by Napoleon in 1808, to "reward outstanding achievements in teaching." In 1991, Fr. Lubbers and the administration clashed over costs, services (did not include the Palms and the Towers), and the mushrooming size of the antennae "farm." The following year, trucks and helicopters moved most of the satellite dishes and transmitters to a new home in Iowa. Their removal freed space for parking, although SCOLA agreed to "leave behind a few reception antennas to provide on-campus service to the Jesuit Community and the University dormitories."[84]

In the meantime, the historic institution St. John's Church transformed itself with a reoriented student-centered mission. Beginning in the 1970s with the drastic loss of parishioners due to construction of I-480 and the North Freeway, Pastor John J. Lynch, S.J., encouraged the integration of the church with the Campus Ministry.

The priests moved from the rectory into the Jesuit residence in the Administration Building, freeing space for Campus Ministry personnel, and in 1973 other campus groups gained access to space in the remodeled church basement. It became the "marryingest" house of worship in Omaha, averaging about one hundred nuptials per year. Concurrently, the other Order on campus, the Oblates (who fought the image of "baby Jesuits"), reactivated the Community Service Center (CSC), which became a project of Campus Ministry. The Oblates operated a storefront senior center that offered food and recreation, which the SBG helped to subsidize and that attracted student volunteers. The CSC also funneled volunteers to Sienna House (1974, emergency shelter for women and children) and to the St. Francis House (1978, served breakfast and dinner to men), both founded by the Catholic Worker organization. In 1982, the SBG contributed $1,500 to support the CSC, which included an Appalachian-region service trip during spring break. In 1988, the United Methodist Community Service organization presented the CSC with an award for its placing of forty student volunteers on a North Omaha housing-renovation project. By 1991, the service trips occurred during the Christmas and spring recesses, and included projects on the Sioux Rosebud Reservation, in Appalachia, at a homeless shelter in the nation's capital, and at an environmental-education center in rural New England. Back in Omaha, projects expanded to include tutoring in North Omaha and building a house for Habitat for Humanity.[85]

Peace and justice issues also attracted student adherents. In 1974, at Fr. President Labaj's suggestion, a committee drafted a revision of the "Creighton Credo" that incorporated the spirit of Vatican II and emphasized justice and spiritual values. Students exhibited those ideals in numerous ways. For example, in 1974, the SBG supported World Hunger Week activities, which included a one-day fast. The next year, 380 students signed up for the Third World Hunger Plan, whereby once a week the student would eat an inexpensive "third world meal" and donate the regular meal-plan money to a world hunger organization. While the efforts to combat hunger proliferated, faculty leaders also gained support for specific causes. One exemplar, Fr. Richard Hauser, in 1975 organized a campus lettuce boycott in support of Cesar Chavez and the United Farm Workers that cut lettuce consumption 70 percent in the Brandeis dining Hall and 55 percent in Becker. Similarly, in 1979 the Reverend James Datko, OMI, local leader of the nationwide boycott of Nestle Company products (because of problems associated with the use of its baby formula in the Third World), received SBG support, which resulted in the removal of all its products from the campus store and the vending machines. Father Datko also directed the Oblate Office of Peace and Justice, which interested students in events such as the 1982 Nuclear Freeze Week (the Cold War had intensified during the first term of the Reagan administration). In May 1989, the shrinking number of Oblates (fourteen) left Creighton for St. Louis; the vacated Oblate House, the former John A. Creighton Home for Working Girls, became the home of the CEC. The administration renamed the program Creighton House because of its location, but retained the distinct curriculum.[86]

Concurrently, Fr. Richard Spillane had succeeded to the directorship of the Creighton Peace and Justice Center (1965) and preserved its mission. Following his death (1982), the Campus Ministry maintained its heritage. It added a "Soup with Substance" lecture series that focused on contemporary concerns and it continued to seek student participation in community projects related to social justice. Furthermore, in 1990, with funding from the Wisconsin Province and a gift from Philip Maschka (D.D.S., 1953), the University launched the (Fr. Francis) Deglman Center for Ignatian Spirituality "for the promotion of spirituality focused on the *Spiritual Exercises* of St. Ignatius." The Board of Directors already had established the Manresa Medal (1974), named for the village and cave in Spain where Ignatius had formulated his *Spiritual Exercises*. The award recognized "inspirational leadership and enduring achievements in the tradition of St. Ignatius of Loyola and of John and Edward Creighton, founders of the University." Leo A. Daly, Sr., received the first medal.[87]

Instilling inspirational leadership remained a principle of Jesuit education, but John Cernich, Ph.D., vice president of student services, revealed that the administration worried that students lacked preparation for such leadership. Therefore, in 1986, student services administrator Martha Brown chaired a taskforce to study the concern. The review resulted in the reestablishment of a student leadership conference and the organization of a circle of Omicron Delta Kappa (ODK), a Greek-letter society formed in 1914, which initiated juniors with a 2.5 GPA who "exhibited leadership qualities." The leadership taskforce chose twenty-nine charter members from seventy-seven applicants and the official induction ceremony ensued at St. John's Church on May 1, 1988. The following year, a grant from the Coca-Cola Bottling Company of Omaha funded the creation of the Freshman Leadership Apprentice Program, which established mentoring relationships and conducted seminars for the thirty to forty enrollees. Moreover, the new ODK circle began to sponsor annual leadership conferences for high-school students. Then, in 1989 the administration initiated the Student Leadership Recognition Day, presenting five students with an award named in honor of the Reverend Thomas N. Schloemer, S.J., former assistant to the president and the driving force behind leadership awareness.[88]

Alcohol and drug use remained an area yearning for student leadership. The administration continued to demand that sponsors of "keggers" enforce a strict no-minors policy and employ an efficient carding system (for years, the SBG sponsored the most popular gathering on campus, the Friday Afternoon Club). In 1977, the University initiated an alcohol awareness program aimed at curbing excessive drinking; ironically, the story on the new effort appeared on page 8 of the *Creightonian*, surrounded by beer and tavern advertisements. In 1980, the endeavor became more nuanced as the Nebraska Legislature raised the legal drinking age to twenty. Enforcement in the dorms became a dreadful chore and fines jumped from $5 to $25 as a "deterrent," but the Counseling Center and the conduct committee maintained a busy schedule dealing with alcohol-related problems. Moreover, Iowa's legal age remained at nineteen; thus, student groups held their "keggers' at near-by Carter

Lake, Iowa (on occasion, the SBG subsidized buses to the venue). Iowa bars also had a later closing time, resulting in a late-night parade of student-laden cars across bridges over the Missouri River. In the meantime, the SBG continued to petition (unsuccessfully) the Omaha City Council for support before the Nebraska Liquor Commission for a license to operate a rathskeller in the Brandeis Student Center.[89]

In 1982, Creighton hired David J. Clark to fill the new position of director of Survival Strategies. While he addressed issues of "mental health: helping people develop a positive self-image, decision-making and communication skills, and problem-solving" associated with retention, he emphasized assistance with alcohol and drug problems. As of January 1, 1985, the legal drinking age in Nebraska stepped up to twenty-one (Iowa remained at nineteen). The University policy stated that students of the legal age could possess alcohol in "confined spaces such as their room or at student group events where Public Safety" checked for identification. Purportedly, fraternity and sorority rushes became dry events, but the administration continued to receive complaints from neighbors regarding "massive parties" that included "drunk and disorderly conduct."[90]

Surprisingly, the first in a series of articles in the *Creightonian* examining drug use at Creighton did not appear until March 22, 1985; none of the reports contained any data on drug use (the Family Educational Rights and Privacy Act of 1974, prevented the release of information from a student's file without their consent). An Omaha police spokesman simply stated that it "does not appear any more prevalent than on any other campus." In 1987, student services conducted an "on-campus survey" in which 17 to 20 percent (seven to eight students per floor) polled said they tried marijuana and 4 to 5 percent (one to two per floor) considered "themselves regular users." Only 6 percent of the students felt pressured to use drugs, while 38 percent sensed harassment concerning alcohol. In response, the administration replaced the "survival strategist" with a more specific drug and alcohol educator, who acquired "Call Suzie," a computerized service with automated answers to frequently asked questions (funded by a local businessman), and initiated the Addictive Compulsive Support Group. Moreover, in 1989 Congress passed the Drug Free Schools and Campuses Act, which required Creighton "to provide enrolled students with various pieces of information [laws, penalties, health effects] regarding the unlawful use of drugs or alcohol on University property or at any University-sponsored event." One distinctive alcohol-free event of note, which delighted students during the era, came in the form of the annual fall visit of the Royal Liechtenstein Circus, "a big-sounding name for a little show," performed outdoors on one of the grass knolls on campus (changed over the years due to construction). The Reverend Nick Weber, S.J., with degrees in theology and theater and based at the Jesuit novitiate at the University of Santa Barbara, organized the small troupe that visited campuses in over thirty states.[91]

Other federal regulations affected the University considerably. Title IX, in conjunction with the machinations of the NCAA, continued to shape the dimensions of Creighton's intercollegiate athletic program. The NCAA established the guidelines for maintaining "big school" Division I status (e.g., number of teams, number of games played, status of the opponents, and much more) and Title IX demanded equality for women. The Creighton Board of Directors believed that intercollegiate athletics served a strategic public relations purpose, particularly for fundraising and student recruitment ("especially with out-of-town alums who hear little else about Creighton on a regular basis"); therefore, the requisite number of teams had to compete in Division I. The decisions meant dramatic increases in an athletic budget that produced equally dramatic increases in red bottom lines. Men's basketball remained the only sport that generated significant revenue, but not nearly enough to cover the costs of the expanding number of teams and the demands placed on each team. Expenditures for athletics soared from approximately $220,000 in 1974 to almost $3.8 million in 1992 (the latter year, the athletic department sought approval to sell pull-tab "pickles"; although it might raise $500,000 annually, the directors disdained the idea of associating the University with gambling).[92]

Intramural activity for men and women increased substantially with the opening of the KFC, directed by Michael Leighton, who had worked in admissions and as athletic business manger, and the second athletic facility presented new costs. Moreover, the growth of women's sports demanded additional expenditures (modest at first). In 1976, Lady Jay basketball, volleyball, and softball gained individual coaches (but no assistants) and a twelve-passenger van for travel to away games. In the past, they had to car pool. Basketball coach Gaye Kinnett quipped that the men's team had earned the nickname, the "travelin' Jays," but the "longest road trip for the women is to Des Moines, Ia." In 1977, the women's athletic program awarded its first scholarships, six to freshmen and one to a junior college transfer; three of the seven went to two-sport athletes because "they could help the overall women's program more quickly." In 1979, basketball and volleyball also gained an assistant coach each. During the second half of the decade, the basketball team established a moderate winning record, but the exploits of the volleyball squad (eliminated) and the lightly regarded tennis and golf teams ("hit-and-miss proposition") did not garner media guides to preserve their histories. In comparison, Coach Mary Higgins (promoted from women's intramural director) developed the softball team into a small-school powerhouse, winning back-to-back small college state championships in 1978 and 1979 and, during the latter year, secured an on-campus home field at 21st and California streets. In 1980, the squad (46-18) made its first appearance in an expanded world series sponsored by the Association for Intercollegiate Athletics for Women (AIAW).[93]

Men's athletics suffered similar growing pains. In club sports, hockey melted away in 1976 due to a rules violation. The team did not win a single game during the first half of the Omaha Amateur Hockey League season; then, after league officials assigned five non-Creighton skaters, it went on to win the championship. The extracurricular athletes violated the guideline for SBG funding, which decreed that only those registered at Creighton could suit up on a team. On the other hand, in 1977, in its first year of competition in the new KFC pool, the swim club posted a 16-6 season overall and a "second place in the Midwest Swim League with a 15-3 record." Equally impressive, the martial arts club placed second and third in national tournaments. In addition, in 1976, "Fr. John Schlagel, S.J. [*sic*]," new assistant professor of political science, "who had spent the past six years in England" (thus, the reporter failed to spell the name of the University's future president correctly), thought "its time Creighton has a crew." Within four years, "nearly 60 men and women participated in the 1980–81 Crew Club (its first year)."[94]

Yet, in tandem, "representatives of the golf and tennis intercollegiate teams pleaded with the [athletic board] subcommittee [evaluating sports policy] not to let their programs die from a lack of funding." In 1979, the administration decided to eliminate the golf program (because of the few students involved, it made "no impact on the rest of the university") and elevated the successful men's soccer club (1975) to varsity status. The players saluted attorney Robert Murray as the "Bobfather," in tribute to his role in that elevation, and subsequently the 1993 team presented him with a plaque with the inscription, "The Father of Creighton Soccer." The team continued its winning ways against regional schools, 25-12-3 under Coach Mark Schmechel in 1979 and 1980, playing their home games at Dodge Park and Rosenblatt Stadium ("field was narrower than most and took some getting used to"). Creighton's other two (no records on tennis) Division I sports, baseball and basketball, rejoined the Missouri Valley Conference in 1977, as well as reestablished the crowd-drawing (i.e., revenue) contests against the University of Nebraska. That year, Assistant Athletic Director Dan Offenburger announced the imminent construction of an athletic field at 21st and Webster streets; however, the baseball team had to wait another decade for its facility. The team did not play a conference schedule, only in the post-season MVC tournament, and suffered losing seasons against largely local teams. On the other hand, Tom Apke coached the basketball team to a 130-64 record from 1974 to 1981, including one appearance in the NIT and three in the NCAA tournaments, but without a victory in the post season.[95]

The following decade entailed extensive turmoil amidst the occasional cause for celebration. In 1981, Lady Jay volleyballers expressed "disappointment and despair" after learning that the athletic department canceled the season. Acting President Fr. Morrison explained that the decision to terminate the coach's contract and to abandon the schedule resulted from "a lack of recruiting of student athletes [only eight players returning] and because of a lack of scheduling adequate opponents." The following year, the administration had to contend with a new NCAA regulation, which stipulated that universities in Division I sponsor eight men's varsity teams. The requirement did not include women's teams, and facing the task of adding four men's sports, women's volleyball ceased. Creighton reintroduced golf and inserted swimming, cross country, and rifle into its inventory of men's intercollegiate sports, obviously minimal costs dictated the choices. Then, in 1984 the NCAA incorporated women within its jurisdiction, and ruled that by 1986, Division I schools had to maintain six separate teams for each gender. The administration decided to drop men's rifle and soccer (not an MVC sport, no Division I teams nearby, no field under the team's control, and a $90,000 budget) and field complementary gendered teams in the remaining sports.[96]

It had problems doing so. In 1988, the NCAA placed the athletic program in a "restricted category" for one year (no post-season play for any team and no voting right at the annual meeting), because it failed "to meet participation requirements in men's and women's swimming and women's golf during the fall 1987 and spring 1988 seasons." The Board of Directors established a committee "to overlook the athletic program" and, despite a statement from the SBG arguing against an increased emphasis on sports, approved a plan recommended by Fr. President Morrison that would add one hundred partial minor-sport scholarships. Father Morrison hoped the scholarships would attract students who would not have come to Creighton otherwise, thus enhancing total enrollment. The design included reinstating men's soccer, with a matching women's team possessing an equal number of scholarships. The relatively massive infusion of money still left Creighton with "the lowest budgeted athletic department in the Missouri Valley and the High Country Athletic [women's softball] conferences. Yet, in 1990, due to a "lack of finances, inadequate facilities [KFC pool not of regulation length and the diving area too shallow to allow use of the three-meter board], and a lack of student participation," the University eliminated the swim teams. The next year, the NCAA increased the number of men's and women's teams required for Division I status to seven (a decrease in scholarships for other sports helped reduce the cost of the additions). The administration announced it would reactivate women's volleyball in the fall 1992, "but there is some uncertainty as to what the seventh men's sport will be" (think inexpensive).[97]

In the meantime, athletics (contrary to its purported strategic function) produced a public relations nightmare. In 1978, Creighton admitted Kevin Ross "as a special permission student" who would receive "special help and skills courses," while playing on the basketball team. Ross had a reading problem, but did not follow the tutoring regimen established for him; however, he maintained his eligibility for four years. Subsequently, his academic prospects at Creighton seemed dim. Thus, to continue to assist his development, during the spring and summer 1982, administrators made four trips to Chicago to investigate Westside Preparatory School operated by Marva Collins. The University arranged to pay tuition and expenses for Ross to enter the school. On September 14, 1982, the *Chicago Sun-Times* broke what became the "Kevin Ross Story," dredged up for the next two decades every time the media needed an example of a "star" athlete exploited by a university and abandon as soon as his eligibility expired. The distortion of the "story" defamed Creighton's attempts to help Ross and the national media attention yielded a public relations disaster. In 1990, Federal District Judge John A. Nordberg dismissed a case of "educational malpractice" brought by Ross. However, a three-judge panel of the United States Court of Appeals in Chicago reinstated the breach-of-contract charge, which claimed that Creighton failed to provide him with an adequate opportunity to gain an education. In 1992, Creighton General Council Greg Jahn negotiated a settlement that paid Ross $30,000, "prudent in light of the estimated legal costs" and the fact that juries generally backed plaintiffs in cases against large companies and institutions.[98]

While the Ross affair played itself out, the men's basketball program seesawed between feast and famine. In April 1981, Tom Apke resigned to accept the head-coaching position at the University of Colorado. Within weeks, new Athletic Director Dan Offenberger (positions had finally separated) announced that former National Basketball Association standout Willis Reed would become the new head basketball coach. He suffered through 7-20 and 8-19 seasons before turning things around with 17-14 and 20-12 (9-7 in the MVC, tied for fourth place) campaigns. Following his best year, on May 1, 1985, with two years remaining on his contract, Reed resigned effective immediately, explaining, "Most of my reasons are personal ones. But college recruiting and the legality aspects are tough problems today." Offenberger also resigned. During the summer, the University hired Don Leahy as his replacement and Tony Barone as head basketball coach. Barone later stated that "at first glance" the position did not interest him, that the program had a "stigma attached," and that, "[t]here was a perception that the basketball team was not representative of Creighton or of the students." On August 26, 1985, Leahy and CCAS Dean Cunningham announced the appointment of Rosemary Gross (A.B., 1957), adjunct instructor in the math and computer science department, as academic advisor to athletics. She charted the progress of student-athletes in their classes and held counseling sessions and study halls. The next fall, the University instituted mandatory, random, noninvasive drug testing of student-athletes.[99]

Barone's teams struggled to reach the .500 mark (12-16, 9-19, 16-16), but then put together three 20-win seasons in a row: 1988–89, 20-11, lost in the first round of the NCAA tournament; 1989–90, 21-12, lost in the first round of the NIT; 1990–91, 24-8, beat New Mexico State, lost to Seton Hall in the NCAA. As with several coaches in the past, Barone's success led to a more lucrative position elsewhere. "In the middle of the night Sunday [April 14, 1991, one week after Barone's departure, assistant coach Rick] Johnson received a phone call from the athletic department telling him to be in the office at 6:00 A.M. the following morning. There, Johnson found out he had been chosen to be the thirteenth head coach in seventy-four years of CU basketball." Unfortunately, Johnson toiled through three consecutive losing seasons, compiling an overall record of 24-59.[100]

The other men's round-ball teams rode similar seesaws (minor sports received virtually no publicity). The baseball team began competing in an MVC schedule in 1981, but while compiling overall winning seasons, they played well under .500 ball in the Valley. After three years, Dave Underwood resigned as head baseball coach under circumstances that neither he nor the players would discuss publicly. Jim Hendry became coach in 1985, and in 1988, he posted the first winning season in the conference (12-8). The following fall the team acquired the long-awaited home diamond (included three intramural fields), adjacent to the Lady Jay field, west of 21st Street between Webster and California streets. At the dedication, the University sought to enter the Guinness Book of Records with the longest sub sandwich (1,600 feet). Rob Kirk, owner of the "Submarine Sandwich" shop, donated the fixings ($12,000), but wind blew ingredients to the ground as an estimated four hundred student "submariners" toiled to construct the sandwich; they settled for a Nebraska record of

1,000 feet (500 feet of which eventually went to local charities). In 1990, the 48-22 baseball team went 2-2 in the NCAA Regionals, and the 1991 squad finished 51-22, 4-0 in the NCAA Regionals, and 2-2 in the College World Series. Not uncommonly, Creighton reached a pinnacle of sports success and then lost its coach; subsequently, Todd Wenberg coached two winning seasons, but without post-season invitations.[101]

Coach Bob Warming instantly established a winning tradition for the revivified men's soccer team. The MVC initiated play in 1991, and Creighton finished second in the standings. Then, in 1992, with a 14-3-1 overall record, the Jays captured the Valley crown (4-0-1). The success of all three round-ball teams attracted attention; in January 1992, the administration announced that the Midwestern Cities Conference offered Creighton membership. The University organized a meeting of the presidents of the MVC schools "for the purpose of discussing Creighton's disenchantment with the Conference, and what the Missouri Valley Conference might do to appease our concerns, especially in the area of costs." Ultimately, the idea of the reallocation received "a serious blow by the withdrawal from the conference [MCC] of Dayton [University]." Unsure of the stability of the MCC, Creighton decided to remain in the MVC.[102]

The Lady Jay softball and basketball teams joined the men's teams in the Valley when the University decided to remain in the conference. Previously, they had competed in the High Country Athletic Conference (HCAC, 1987–88 through 1989–90) and then two years in the Western Athletic Conference (WAC). In women's hoops, new head coach Bruce Rasmussen (1980) started with two losing season, but then strung together six winning campaigns (114-55), and subsequently endured two years significantly below the break-even mark. He ended his coaching career on the upswing in 1991–92, going 28-4 overall, and 11-1 in the WAC. During his tenure, as part of the historic 1988 athletic department budget, the team received an added $10,000 "for rent at the Civic Auditorium because major college teams are refusing to play in the Old Gym." In association, coach Higgins propelled the softball team to even greater heights, with twelve consecutive winning seasons (1980–91) that included ten with thirty or more victories, a fifth-place finish in the 1986 Women's College World Series, and three consecutive second places at the NCAA Regionals, 1988–90. The 1991 team has the distinction of playing in the longest softball game in NCAA history, a 1-0 victory over the University of Utah in thirty-one innings (unfortunately, they lost the second and final tournament game to Utah in twenty-five innings, having played softball continuously from 6:00 P.M. to 6:00 A.M.). Finally, coach Ray Leone kicked off the women's soccer program with three consecutive ten-win seasons (out of seventeen games) before failing to reach the .500 level in 1992. Thus, given the overall records of the men and women's teams, by the end of the period Creighton intercollegiate athletics reclaimed a positive image and may have provided the strategic public-relations role the administration and the directors desired. Yet, only 165 students bothered to answer a survey on athletics placed at voting booths for SBG elections in March 1992; the limited result manifested the historic "lack of spirit," as the few respondents displayed ignorance of and lack of support for sporting events.[103]

In 1971, the *Insiders Guide to Colleges* published by the *Yale Daily News* maintained the stuffy, elitists, pseudo-intellectual attitude of proto–Henry Menckens in rating Creighton as "Something less than excellent-but-restless liberal arts college." The editors "heavily criticized" the University for "its lack of privacy and conservatism," which translated to the issue of men visiting with women in the dorms, and to the fact that those coeds were "generally virgins" and the men "not much more promiscuous." The mind-set of the editors of the 1985–86 edition had not improved; they questioned if Jesuit teaching was inferior. They also described the relaxed academic atmosphere at Creighton, where women attended to "snag a doctor or lawyer in the making." SBG president Catherine Moore fired off a letter to the editors chastising their "comically inaccurate" evaluation. The droll, sophomoric assessments served as a reminder of the low esteem garnered by Catholic education in Protestant America until the 1960s, and the manner in which it lingered in the uninformed and/or prejudiced mind. With John Fitzgerald Kennedy as president of the United States, the ultimate symbol of assimilation, Catholics confirmed their integration into the American mainstream. Creighton University had demonstrated the process of cultural and structural assimilation, and appraisals by *U.S. News & World Report* announced its attainment of the American Dream. In 1987, the publication polled college presidents, who ranked Creighton fifth best among 137 comprehensive universities in the western half of the United States. In 1989, the magazine changed its configuration, rating universities in the Midwest; thereafter, Creighton consistently ranked in the top seven. Moreover, Creighton continued to make *Money* magazine's "100 best buys in private education," *Barron's 300 Best Buys in College Education*, and *Seventeen* magazine's "Overlooked-Underrated" colleges.[104]

The last weekend in May 1987, thirty alums from around the country met on campus "to plan the formation of a national alumni organization and to revitalize Creighton's alumni group." The conference led to the creation of the National Alumni Board (NAB) to supplant the Omaha-based Alumni Council. The first NAB was appointed, but subsequently consisted of elected representatives from thirteen regions. It would assume a more significant role in nationwide capital campaigns, as well as have input in strategic planning. Concomitantly, the Board of Directors restructured the planning process. Several members argued that the board should have a role; otherwise, "if only internal University deans and administrators work on planning, each person will want to perpetuate his own area." Therefore, it authorized the hiring of Walter Blackburn as assistant to the president for planning, who organized the University faculty and administrators into twenty-four subcommittees. Three and a half years later, on October 5, 1992, the board unanimously approved the first fully integrated long-term plan, a living document that would evolve as circumstances changed. The "Creighton 2000" plan established the goal "to become the outstanding comprehensive Jesuit university in the United States by the end of the current decade." The University had achieved the American dream. It had a unified campus with modern structures. It had recognition as a prominent educator. It now sought to amplify the Dream, to join the elite.[105]

CHAPTER 12

Extending the American Dream, 1992–2003

The Creighton 2000 plan established the idealistic goal "to become the outstanding comprehensive Jesuit university in the United States by the end of the current decade." Creighton University seemed to have attained the American Dream, but the objective remained elusive, demanding an incessant pursuit for more. Having achieved an impressive regional stature, the administration and the directors set their sights on an elite status. Whatever criteria they employed—number and reputation of professional schools and Ph.D. programs, quantity and quality of research, admissions selectivity, historical reputation—they would not go unchallenged by the other Jesuit institutions that believed they deserved that appellation. Despite the colossal strides made in the post–World War II era, they posited an exceedingly short timetable to accomplish an enormous task. While striving to finance a substantial qualitative advance, evolving circumstances intervened, necessitating immediate responses, which usually imposed hefty financial burdens. For example, demographic trends strained efforts to recruit and retain students to support a tuition-driven budget, which experienced a mid-decade crisis that doomed the goal. Moreover, the endowment soared with the stock-market technology bubble, but diminished with the end-of-the-decade bust. During the interim, the shifting demands of middle-class students rendered existing dormitories obsolete, established new priorities, and diverted attention from program goals. The University did continue to grow, and grew impressively, but financing that growth remained an arduous task that could not meet the goal of reducing the rate of tuition increases. The new millennium brought a new president, and subsequently a new strategic plan, Project 125, with a modified "vision statement": "Creighton University will be a national leader in preparing students in a faith-based setting for responsible leadership, professional distinction, and committed citizenship."[1]

In 1993, in anticipation of a new fund drive in "support of needs as identified in the Creighton 2000 Strategic Plan," the board increased its membership to thirty-three, but again denied a request for a seat from the SBG. It approved a $100 million campaign to run from September 24, 1994, to June 30, 1998, to include $54 million for endowment, $23.5 million for capital construction, and $2.5 million for technology. Three years into the drive, the administration announced that because of "unanticipated expenses which necessitated spending campaign funds it is important that we not only reach the goal of $100 million, but that we exceed that goal by at least $10 million so needs which have been identified since the campaign began can be covered." Fortunately, the solicitors garnered 30,000 total donations (compared to 11,000 in the last campaign), including those from 17,000 alumni (previously 8,000), although corporate and foundation giving "remained flat." They surpassed the amended goal, raising $127 million in "gifts, pledges and irrevocable deferred gifts." In 1997, the Council for the Advancement and Support of Education changed its accounting guidelines to allow the tabulation, at face value, of certain deferred gifts for a current canvass, since otherwise they never got counted. The Creighton 2000 drive also realized more money because it cost only 9.6 cents to collect each dollar, well under the average of 17 cents.[2]

On the eve of and during the solicitation, the University experienced budget difficulties. The 1992–93 fiscal year ended a string of twenty-five years of annual balanced operations budgets; "The problems surfaced about midyear, and the reaction was not as fast as it could and should have been." Primarily, a decline in clinical revenues caused the deficit. The administration projected a balanced budget for the following year that included a continued reduction in clinical revenue, which it would monitor monthly for adjustments. The 1993–94 fiscal year concluded in the black, even though clinical income missed its projection by $2.5 million (e.g., shifts to HMO and PPO coverage; impact of insurance and Medicare/Medicaid reimbursement guidelines—what is covered and how much paid—affected income). Reductions in clinical expenses and an increase in medical school revenue provided the favorable variance. Subsequently, in October 1995, Registrar John Krecek presented the final fall count, revealing that seventy-nine fewer students registered than had been budgeted for, creating a shortfall of $1,166,000. The administration asked each school to reduce its budget 1 percent and the reserve account contributed the difference to balance the budget. Spring 1997 witnessed a similar scenario caused by a medical school deficit.[3]

The administration attacked the fiscal problem by borrowing from the business world. It sought to control costs by restructuring and reengineering, with the goal of eliminating the substantial annual tuition increases. The Consumer Price Index rose 53 percent between 1984 and 1996; Creighton tuition increased 159 percent during the same time frame. To cushion the impact on students, between 1989 and 1993, the University augmented its scholarship money by $5.1 million, or 73 percent, and the Creighton 2000 fund drive designated $25.3 million to scholarships, creating 162 new ones in 1998. However, in 1996 the NCA accreditors worried about the "burden of indebtedness being assumed by students ($40 million the last year)," in terms of loans to pay tuition. Father President Morrison researched the operations of other universities seeking the methodology to rein in the escalating costs, reporting that the exploration had "not been fruitful," a lot of discussion, but little action. Following a "brain-storming session" by the vice presidents and deans, in 1996 the University contracted with the KPMG Peat Marwick Company to study restructuring in all areas except academics. The ten-month effort, dubbed the "Process Redesign Project," produced 149 recommendations projected to cut $7.5 to $12.5 million from the operations budget. Father Morrison argued, "the biggest change to be made is a cultural one. Creighton administrators must do business differently." Therefore, in 1997 the University continued the services of KPGM Peat Marwick to act "as a kind of conscience," to keep administrators "focused on confronting the issues" and from "avoiding the tough decisions." The "biggest recommendation" involved budgeting. The University hired Arthur Andersen to help it shift to a "process similar to zero based budgeting or activity-based budgeting, or flex-based budgeting." Meanwhile, the vice presidents implemented sixty suggestions deemed "either easy, or critical." A year into the process, Fr. Morrison "voiced some disappointment over the fact that not as much money had been saved as was originally anticipated." The battle to balance the operations budget continued and the onset of the volatile stock market in 1999 (endowment earnings fluctuate) produced added anxiety.[4]

Volatile enrollment figures added to the discomfort (the significance of tuition revenue in the budget and the ability to project the numbers per school or college correctly). Total enrollment in the University in the fall 1993 set a record, and that of the fall 1994 topped it further, at 6,424. However, as of the latter year the number of undergraduates, based on a decline in the number freshmen, began to wane (the CCAS, CoBA, and Nursing each attracted fewer new students). Moreover, the yield (applicants vs. registrants) fell from 32 percent to 27 percent. Thus, between fall 1993 and fall 1995, the number of undergraduate freshmen tumbled from 945 to 840. The "serious concern" (the impact of each annual decline rolls through the budget for four years) resulted in a "full court press": that is, establishing an 800 telephone number, creating a web page, providing e-mail correspondence, hiring a recruiter to concentrate on the state of California, and having faculty call applicants. Moreover, a 60/40 percentage, female-male gender imbalance in the arts college led to "stronger recruiting at male-attended Jesuit high schools" and a review of "marketing material in order to ascertain if it is attractive to males." The administration sought "to eliminate an imbalance greater than 55/45 in either direction" (it did not succeed). The recruiting coup de grace came with the announcement in November 1995 of a guaranteed-admission program "designed to reward Creighton's best and brightest" and to "help position Creighton in a highly competitive undergraduate market." Accordingly, CCAS graduates with a 3.5 GPA and in the top 30 percent on the LSAT, those with a 3.5 GPA and 16 or better on the DSAT, and those with a 3.5 GPA and no MCAT necessary gained automatic acceptance to the respective professional school.[5]

The administration noted that the "program for the medical school [Freudian slip?] seems to be a spur for securing students." In point of fact, it did not affect applications to the other professional schools, nor did it curtail the downward slide in the CoBA or the Nursing School, and even the CCAS numbers varied as MCAT scores and an interview crept back into the admissions process (1995—627; 1997—729; 1999—685; 2000—716; 2001—600; 2003—714). While it lasted (1996–2000), the guaranteed-admission program contributed to the volatility in the size of the CCAS freshman class and generated significant controversy. Some faculty and students worried that it subverted the service mission by attracting single-mined pre-med students, while others feared that CCAS undergraduates would take all 110 freshman slots, undermining the diversity goals and threatening the reputation of the medical school. The VPHS reported that it discouraged outside applicants, who perceived an unfair advantage in favor of Creighton undergraduates. Ultimately, the program caused more problems than it solved, and Fr. Morrison "agreed to discontinue" it as one of his final acts as president. In the meantime, a dramatic improvement in the attrition rate of freshmen (20.2 percent in 1994, 12.5 percent in 2003) and sophomores (14.8 percent to 9.0 percent) softened the blow of declining numbers (the administration credited Director of Retention Mary Higgins, the freshman seminar program, and the Career and Academic Planning Center, the last created in 1994). However, in 2001, freshmen enrollment plummeted by 141, and resulted in the creation of a new position, the associate vice president for enrollment management, to oversee and coordinate admissions, financial aid and retention.[6]

Inadvertently, the guaranteed-admission program distorted the Campaign 2000 diversity objective, which established the goal of 20 percent minority enrollment, excluding foreign students, by the end of the decade. Some board members questioned the wisdom of such an "aggressive goal," but the proponents planned to "draw from California, Hawaii [Creighton's eighth largest feeder state], the southwest United States, Chicago, St. Louis and Omaha itself." By 1996 it became obvious, considering the low minority population in the area adjacent to Creighton and the stiff competition from other private (several Jesuit) and public institutions in the region, the University could not meet its target. Thereafter, however, with the guaranteed-admissions program, minority students composed 21 percent of the fall 1997 freshman class, "the bulk of them Asian Americans," largely of Indian and Pakistani descent, matriculating because they were "the children of immigrant doctors and other professionals." In 1998, the newly organized Indian Culture Society held its first banquet, joining the international students, the Africans, the African Americans, the Hispanics, and the Native Americans in hosting an annual event to promote appreciation of their distinct cultures. Moreover, in part because of minority recruitment and the unforeseen effects of the guaranteed-admission program, the cohort of Catholics among the freshmen dropped from 75 percent in 1987 to 59 percent in 1996. Minority enrollment peaked at 17.3 percent in 2000, and then declined slightly to 16.5 percent in 2003. Asian Americans outnumbered all other minorities combined, as the number of both African-American and Hispanic students fell during the 1990s to below 3 percent. Thus, the administration came close to attaining its Campaign 2000 diversity goal in terms of percentage of the student body, but not in terms of the composition of the minority student population. The ratio of the originally targeted minorities actually declined; the overall total resulted serendipitously from the "law of unintended consequences." Furthermore, two disheartening events distorted the diversity objective. In 1999, an accounting scandal in the Upward Bound program obliged the University to reimburse the Department of Education over $400,000 to pay two "whistleblowers" $15,000 each and to reorganize its administrative office. With reforms and new personnel, the federal government resumed funding the program the following year. Additionally, the results of a 2001 "climate survey" revealed the persistence of "diversity tensions," confirming the necessity for the continuation of special efforts to attain diversity goals in terms of the inculcation of understanding and acceptance. Affirmative Action Administrator John Pierce was "surprised by the amount of incivility from students toward students."[7]

The enrollment and budget woes caused concern and moderated, but did not prevent, the physical expansion of the University. Creighton 2000 included a master plan for the campus, and every project reached fruition. In the first instance, the University gained more inviting entrances. First, between Burt and California streets, the city vacated 23rd Street, and it became an entry for an expanded parking lot (peculiarly, a couple of owners refused to sell their properties and for several years those residences sat surrounded by students' vehicles). Simultaneously, between May 17 and November 28, 1993, 24th Street closed while a construction crew widened it to four lanes, two in each direction. Then, at 24th and Cass streets, the University erected signage and landscaped a triangular parcel into a new "front door" for northbound drivers. Concurrently, an anonymous donor financed the construction of a new east-west entrance, which consisted of six pillars in a semi-circle on the east side of 24th Street and a walkway that included a segment of the historic brick thoroughfare, extending the California Street Mall to the law school.[8]

The master plan also called for the relocation to the periphery "facilities not directly related to the educational process." In 1996, the University wanted to buy and renovate the OHA Burt Tower on 21st Street, but it did not come on the market. Thus, the administration decided to construct a "strip-mall" building on the northeast corner of 23rd and Burt streets to house the day-care center, public relations, and human relations. It abandoned the portable education units and, once again, razed a building dedicated to the Wareham sisters (the former Schaffer Building), but named the new strip mall in their honor. Public Safety moved out of the Old Gym to the Walter Jahn Building directly east of the new facility (named in honor of the former vice president of finance, who retired 1989; originally inhabited by finance offices). In 1997, in the "biggest real estate transaction in the modern history" of the institution, Creighton purchased five buildings belonging to the Epsen-Hilmer Graphics Company; the "owner went out of his way to be a good neighbor." The firm leased back the main plant building, while administrative offices occupied the other renovated structures east of 20th Street, the Linn, the Labaj, and the Murphy buildings (legal counsel and various finance offices moved to those locations). Moreover, in 1990, maintenance moved to a Burt Street building named in honor of Brother Frank Jelinek, S.J., who had come to Creighton as a student in 1945, left for two years of study at the Jesuit Seminary at Florissant, Missouri, and returned to his alma mater to oversee the refectory. In 1961, he became superintendent of buildings and grounds, which he managed in a "tyrannical" fashion until a few years before his death in 1995, at age seventy-five. Actually, those who knew him well described him as a "gruff marshmallow," arguing he adopted the brusque exterior "over the years as the work load pressed beyond human capabilities." Brother Jelinek and his crews had aided the physical expansion of the University, including moving his and many other non-educational offices to the periphery.[9]

The land purchases and the shuffle of offices related to two other Creighton 2000 goals—modifying the Administration and Brandeis buildings for improved administrative office space, and acquiring additional parking. Both structures received overhauls; of note, the first and second floors of the north wing of the Administration Building, which included sizeable new space for the Office of the President (consisted of an expanding number of administrators and support staff) and the correlated offices of development and of alumni relations. The offices on the periphery obtained adjacent parking and the main campus acquired more spaces with the purchasing and razing of the Canfield properties along Cuming Street, west of 24th Street, which created a large, three-block-long lot. Furthermore, in 1995, in anticipation of a new facility, the University the razed the Interim Theater located on the Burt-Cuming-30th streets triangle and paved the area for more parking for the west campus. The SBG had opposed the demolition, wanting to acquire the Quonset for a party center (buy it for $1, but then pay all maintenance), but the administration refused, explaining that several parts of the building were unsafe. Additionally, in order to influence decisions concerning its vicinity, the University began to purchase available properties between 16th and 33rd streets, between I-480 and Cuming Street. It had sought the properties west of 30th Street, along California, during the late 1970s for parking for the hospital complex. However, Kathryn Thomas, Ph.D., classics, headed a neighborhood group (her parents owned one of the homes, in which Creighton students over the years had rented rooms) that convinced the Omaha City Council to change its plans to designate the area "blighted," which would have allowed it to acquire the properties by eminent domain and turn them over to a private developer (in this case, the Creighton-Omaha Regional Health Care Corporation). Twenty years later, as the properties became available, the University began to secure them. It cooperated with other public and private institutions that hired the architectural-engineering firm HDR to draw up a master plan for the area between 24th Street and Saddle Creek Road on the west, and Cuming to Center Street on the south. Creighton participated to ensure that the design, "Destination Midtown," fit with its master plan and that students would benefit from the redevelopment.[10]

Simultaneously, the University fulfilled another two Creighton 2000 objects: obtaining a new education center for the arts and creating "academic neighborhoods" on campus to coordinate related disciplines. In 1993, the Lied Foundation matched a $5 million Kiewit Foundation grant to build the 71,000-square-foot Lied Education Center for the Arts. Construction began in spring 1994, and the project quickly presented cost overruns of $900,000 because the "plans were more complex than anyone knew." Both foundations added to their pledges, but upon completion in November 1995, part of the building lacked the expensive stone façade. Built into the hill that sloped steeply upward, north to south, between California and Cass streets, immediately west of the law school, the facility contained spaces for theater (including a 350-seat performance hall and an acting studio/black box), dance, music, photography, and art (including a gallery) programs. As the fine arts faculty abandoned the old dental School building, the CCAS accomplished the creation of another "academic neighborhood." The structure received its third name—the Humanities Build-ing—as the departments of theology, philosophy, classical and Near Eastern studies, and modern languages moved into the renovated venue. After the philosophy depart-ment evacuated its "squirrel cemetery" (their decaying carcasses in the rafters left "a stench throughout the entire building"), the University leveled the duplex, which sat to the south of the Hitchcock Building (old law school), to fashion additional green space for the California Street Mall. Also in 1995, the mall received a tangent "pedes-trian route linking the central to northern and western areas of campus" with the dedication of the Conagra Plaza, which included a fountain between St. John's Church and the RAL.[11]

Beyond the master plan, the administration realized that the main-campus dor-mitories needed updating to remain a competitive housing choice for students. In 1993, it spent $1.3 million to refurbish Deglman Hall (the oldest) with new furniture and fixtures, enlarged rooms that each had a sink and washstand, renovated baths and showers, and new lounges on each floor. The remodeled dorm tripled its retention rate and included a ramp entrance and elevator to make it handicap accessible. The administrators understood the "tremendous consequences" of the Americans with Disabilities Act (ADA, 1990), in terms of access on a hilly campus with step-entry buildings, but "much more difficult are the provision of interpreters, readers, equip-ment, extra time for exams, etc., for disabled students." A worthy cause, but another drain of a "lot of time and money" on a budget already stretched to the maximum.[12]

In the dorms, the student services office desired "a 'learning environment' sup-ported by a strong Jesuit presence and experience in 'service to others.'" Moreover, the administration realized that the thirty-year-old Swanson Hall had become "anti-quated compared to what students prefer today [1995]." It housed over 700 students, but revamped into a "suite concept," the number would plunge to approximately 450. The board approved the construction of a new dorm to "decrease the overcrowding in Swanson," and to "minimize parking loss," determined the location on the northeast corner of California and the vacated 23rd Street. Some alumni approached Fr. Morrison regarding the name of the new facility. He told them to raise $1 million and they could have that right; they raised $1,145,777 and chose to honor the Reverend Richard D. McGloin, S.J., who had resided in old Dowling Hall for ten years and then in Swanson for every day of its thirty-three-year existence. Indicative of why the alumni donors selected Fr. McGlion, over the years, he and the author regularly exchanged pleasantries at about 6:45 A.M. at one of the entrances to the Administra-tion Building. Having arrived at Creighton as a student in 1927, he clarified the loca-tions and uses of the rooms in the old Prep north wing, and in one of the conversa-tions he declared, "Don't forget to write about all the good work the [Jesuit] brothers do." The dorm named in honor of this thoughtful soul consisted of five stories of "suite-style living" for approximately 270 students. When it opened in 1998, it allowed the renovation of Swanson into similar suites, accomplished one half at a time during the summers of 1998 and 1999.[13]

The KFC also now required renovation. Since it opened, enrollment had surged

40 percent. While revenue from the dorms would pay off the bonds issued to finance that work, the "students' decision to tax themselves" funded the remodeling and a 15,000-square-foot addition to the fitness facility. The weight training, martial arts, and aerobic areas demanded expansion, and the increasingly popular exercise-science program needed offices and classrooms. Thus, during the summer of 1996 construction commenced on a two-story (one below ground) structure attached to the east side of the existing building. In the meantime, in 1993 the west side of the complex received a new name, the V. J. and Angela Skutt Student Center. V. J. (LL.B., 1923), retired president of the Mutual of Omaha companies, former president of the National Alumni Association, and generous benefactor of the University, approved the dedication, but requested that the announcement come "posthumously." Delores Hope, entertainer and wife of comedian Bob Hope, member of the Mutual board of directors, came to campus for the dedication ceremony, entitled "The Feeling is Mutual," and in addition, received an honorary doctor of humane letters degree. Subsequently, in 1995 the University renamed the Palms in honor of John C. Kenefick, former chairman of the Union Pacific Railroad and long-serving former chairman of Creighton's board. Then, in 1998 the Towers changed its label to the Charles and Mary Heider Hall, recognizing the munificent benefactors. Charles (BSC, 1949), a financial counselor, served on the Board of Directors and helped pilot the HFF; in 1994, the couple had endowed the Jesuit Faculty Chair, which supported the work of prominent photographer Fr. Don Doll. The latter two buildings contributed to a spread-out nature of the expanding campus. In response, in 1994, Public Safety initiated bicycle patrols: "Response time is much quicker, every area of campus is now accessible, and more rapport is being established with people on campus." Additionally, in 1996 security concerns contributed to a new identification system as electronic cards began to serve as "keys" to the dormitories and secured buildings, as well as functioning as debit cards ("CampusFunds" administered by American Express).[14]

While the campus spread out, a revolutionary technology knitted it together. The United States Department of Defense had established an "internet" in the 1960s, and in the following decades, some universities copied its network technology. In 1991, Swiss physicists created the World Wide Web, and two years later the first "browser" appeared, allowing neophytes to "log on" and find data. In 1992, fiber-optic cable began to link campus buildings to a communications network, allowing faculty and students to utilize regional, national, and international systems. By 1994, the number of Creighton Internet accounts skyrocketed to about three thousand, and the following year the "Jaynet" became fully operational. That year, part of the $1 million gift to the Creighton 2000 campaign by US West Communications, Inc., funded the US West Academic Development and Technology Program "to help faculty members [twenty-one annual fellows] learn how to incorporate new interactive technologies into teaching."[15]

The technologies brought other opportunities and a novel threat. In 1996, the University introduced two new ventures, Web radio and the Creighton Institute for Information Technology and Management. The former presented prerecorded, nonlinear, on-line programming (listener chooses an archived broadcast) as part of a "broadband sequence" in the journalism department. The latter presented non-degree and certificate programs at a "West Campus," located in the Old Mill development north of Dodge and west of 108th streets, to persons who already had a career but sought training in the use of computers. On the main campus, technological sophistication led to the introduction of telephone-computer registration in 1997, and a year later the loss of the provider of the telephone registration service (not as profitable as hoped) "forced [the] implementation [of] on-line registration ahead of schedule." Simultaneously, however, the addition of technology at "warp speed" also involved the dreaded Year 2000 (Y2K) problem. Technicians feared that chips imbedded in personal computers, elevator controls, medical equipment, and an array of other machines would fail because they would misread the 00 of the last year (or first, depending on how you count) of the second millennium. Actually, the technical staff began work on the problem with the acquisition of a new mainframe in 1988, and continued to keep Creighton "on line or ahead of other universities" in making the necessary software and hardware adjustments. The University survived largely unscathed; the Institute for Information Technology became the major casualty, as enrollment plunged following the deflation of the Y2K craze. The University maintained the West Campus for some professional-development and certificate programs at the undergraduate and graduate level, and some of the Institute's other offerings merged into University College. Ultimately, in 1999, noting Creighton's technological advances, *Yahoo! Internet Life* magazine listed it as one of the "most wired" campuses in the United States (ninety-eighth). In the next three years, it moved up seventeen rungs, and to monitor the continued development, the directors established the board committee on information technology and information management.[16]

Likewise, religious issues contributed a novel area of apprehension. For example, in 1983, the Church had issued a new Code of Cannon Law, "some of which applied to Catholic Universities," but did not directly affect Creighton University. Then, in 1990, Pope John Paul II "issued a constitution in which he set down the relationship between the Catholic Church and universities who call themselves Catholic." *Ex Corde Ecclesiae* did include Creighton, and it ignited a ten-year discussion concerning the mandate that bishops certify teachers of theology (presidents of American Catholic universities "recognized [it] as impractical"). While the debate raged, the administration responded with the completion of a new mission statement. In 1970, Fr. Labaj had appointed the first revision committee, but issues such as race and gender had stymied the efforts to produce an acceptable draft. Eventually, a statement that emphasized the Catholic and Jesuit nature of Creighton University appeared for the first time in the 1995–97 *Bulletin*. Moreover, in 1995 spiritual matters produced another vice president (for University Ministry) to oversee the Campus Ministry, retreats, service in the community, and the ILAC. The office inherited the new Wakonda Retreat Center, located on 150 acres "of virgin timber along the Nishnabotna River" in Griswold, Iowa, about forty-five minutes from Omaha. The University sold the O'Donnell Center, and by 2000, the "Campus Ministry Retreat Program [*sic*] exploded in size and scope." Moreover, by the new millennium, the University and Archbishop Eldon F. Curtis reached a "mutually satisfactory approach to implementing" *Ex Corde* and all Creighton theologians received their *mandatum*, "attesting that they are teaching in accordance with the Catholic Church."[17]

Another religious issue, preserving the Jesuit nature of the University, highlighted in the mission statement, continued to generate significant effort. In 1994, Jesuit University Students Concerned with Empowerment (JUSTICE) began promoting Jesuit values on campus, hosting Jesuit Awareness Week, which consisted of events that gave students an opportunity to interact with Jesuits (e.g., bingo, a fireside chat, an ice cream social). By 1996, the number of Jesuits in the United States had dropped to 4,047 and only 89 novitiates had joined the Order that year. Father Morrison had initiated a policy whereby the University would hire any available Jesuit, creating a new position if no opening existed. Further illuminating the predicament, at the end of the fall 2000 semester, the Wisconsin Province abandoned the Jesuit Humanities Program: "The declining number of young Jesuits parallel[ed] the program's demise." Thus, the significance of the evolving role of lay faculty intensified. In 1975, the University began questioning non-Jesuit applicants if they understood, and could contribute to, the Jesuit mission. By the 1990s, the directors had established a task force to study "how the Catholic Jesuit identity of Creighton will be continued in the future with fewer Jesuits." The new Collaborative Ministry Office provided one answer; it offered orientation and continuing education programs to faculty and staff. In 1997, it added a staff member to expand the Jesuit-identity orientation beyond the five-minute presentation made to new hires.[18]

The maintenance of the Jesuit identity, the upsurge of software and hardware, and the abundance of brick-and-mortar projects all strove to enhance the educational ecosystem. The enterprise included incessant review of the curricular component. For instance, the concept of "assessment," in one connotation, a means besides grades by which to gauge a student's development, emerged as one of the pedagogical fashions of the 1990s (meetings filled the decade explaining, defining, and devising the models each discipline would use). In 1996, an NCA accreditation report's list of "strengths" included the "establishment of the Office of Institutional Research and Assessment" that held the "promise of a broad-based and effective implementation of assessment and the development of comparable data systems across the campus." Six years hence, as "a result of the Carnegie Project that has been on-going across the University and the evolving approach to assessment as an inextricable part of a continuing quality improvement process to enhance student learning, the Carnegie Project Steering Committee proposed the name and role of the Office for Institutional Research and Assessment be changed." It became the Office for Excellence in Teaching, Learning, and Assessment, which sought to "provide ongoing support and resources for enhancing faculty effectiveness as teachers." Among the Office's many tasks, it sought "extramural funding for program development and expansion in targeted areas of need—i.e., justice education, issues of diversity and inclusion in the classroom." Creighton had initiated multicultural retreats, diversity conferences, and, for faculty, the Diversity Project (reading groups, workshops, seminars), and wanted to expand its efforts.[19]

Previously, the CCAS had identified those targets in its 1993 curriculum revision. The existing Division I, "Values Consciousness," had mushroomed with a glut of offerings and many faculty members worried that it did not accomplish its purpose. Others argued the core required too many hours, reducing the opportunity for study in the major and for upper-division electives. The intensity of the debate delayed the introduction of "Curriculum 90"; when it appeared, the core continued to contain virtually one half of the hours needed for graduation (sixty-one). However, it had a new organization and novel pedagogical goals. Arranged into five categories, "A" required eighteen hours of theology, philosophy, and ethics; "B," eighteen hours of "culture, ideas and civilizations" (i.e., history and literature); "C," seven hours of natural science; "D," six hours of social and behavioral science; and "E," twelve to fifteen hours of "skills" (i.e., writing, math, speech/studio and performing arts, and languages). Additionally, the new core curriculum encouraged the teaching of "diversity issues" across the curriculum. It began by adding materials to existing classes and developing new courses pertaining to the goal, and eventually, it led to the creation of new multidisciplinary programs such as Women's and Gender Studies and Native American Studies. In terms of the latter, the Jesuits of the Missouri (then Wisconsin) Province had a historic relationship with the Sioux Rosebud Reservation. In 1997, Tami Buffalohead-McGill (B.A., 1989, the University switched to the modern degree title in 1971), the co-coordinator of multicultural student services, organized Creighton's first Native American Retreat, with eighty high-school students from eleven schools and agencies in a three-state area in attendance. The retreat intended "to introduce Native American high schoolers to the college environment, provide information and skills necessary to succeed in college, and promote learning as a life-long journey." With continued effort, Native American enrollment more than doubled, from twenty-five in 1993 to fifty-seven in 2002, and supplied scaffolding for the studies program.[20]

The revised CCAS curriculum also emphasized a "global perspective" to overcome the lack of knowledge about world affairs, as well as another means to understand diversity. Actually, as early as 1982, Fr. Eugene Gallagher, S.J., education, had attended a summer seminar on "Teaching Global Perspectives," but had little success in developing interdisciplinary classes that would focus on topics such as hunger, pollution, or migration. A decade later, the outlook gained acceptance and manifested itself in numerous ways: in the core requirements (e.g., a non–Western-Civilization history class), in a three-hour "international/global studies" requirement (Category B), in the encouragement to study abroad (e.g., in 1997, Dr. Terry Clark, Ph.D., introduced a Lithuanian exchange program with the Jesuit-administered University of Vilnius), and in the introduction of new programs (e.g., the African Studies co-major, 1998). The African Studies program highlighted a shift in the source of foreign students. In 1998, the Asian economic crisis began to diminish government support and parental ability to finance study in the United States. The Office of International

Programs began to recruit in Africa, and its success produced an African Student Association in 1999. While the studies program and the student association survived, the September 11, 2001, terrorist attacks severely curtailed the foreign student enrollment at Creighton (the administration avoided the burden of the rigorous security regulations).[21]

The new CCAS curriculum also stressed justice education. The responsibility of the renamed assessment office consisted of supporting increased incorporation of existing service activities into the educational environment. Predating it, in 1992 students had organized the Best Buddies program designed to "encourage friendships between students and people with mild retardation." The following year, the University had organized "Christmas Spirit," an effort to do good works as part of service to the community by student, administrator-staff, and faculty groups (that year, about one hundred projects "gave an estimated 1,500 individuals a merrier Christmas"). Ongoing ventures such as fraternity community endeavors and the spring break service trips (in 1997, 136 students worked at fifteen sites) multiplied, including the organization of a Creighton chapter of Habitat for Humanity (1998). In its first year, the home-construction group raised $51,000 in material and in-kind services, and more than 550 volunteers built a residence at 2517 Maple Street—"the house that Creighton built." Moreover, in 2003, the University received the first Champion of Greatness Award from the Nebraska Special Olympics in honor of its having hosted the Summer Games for thirty years.[22]

Another major objective, in terms of building upon Creighton's stellar record of service to the community, consisted of efforts to assimilate it into the classroom. The Board of Director's Jesuit-identity committee reported that, "there must be a way to get everyone to buy into service as part of Creighton's central message so that it is not a peripheral add-on. It should be perceived by our faculty and students as an integral part of the curriculum." In 1994, the CCAS hired Roger Bergman, lecturer in theology, to create Justice and Peace Studies, consisting of classes concerning social justice and community service. The following year, the Campus Ministry initiated a new Center for Service and Social Justice to act as a clearinghouse for classes and programs with "community-based practicums and service as an integral part of their curriculum." Then, in 1999 CCAS dean the Reverend Albert Agresti, S.J., and associate dean Patricia Fleming, Ph. D., received a $150,000 grant from the William and Flora Hewlett Foundation to train arts faculty to offer a "service-learning" feature in their classes.[23]

The 1993 CCAS curriculum revision addressed other faculty concerns. For instance, it instituted "writing across the curriculum," whereby by all courses in the core (with some exceptions in large natural-science sections) contained a required writing component. Furthermore, upper-division arts students had to complete four "writing-certified" classes; they gained certification by having a "writing intensive" agenda. Another communication skill, foreign languages, regained a mandate. Then, in 1997 the deferred "senior perspective" requirement ensued; designated a "capstone course" and team-taught to provide interdisciplinary approaches, it sought classes that stressed ethical discussion and Jesuit ideals from the perspectives of the instructors' disciplines. The CCAS did not have the funding to alleviate the strain on departmental resources that would have resulted from faculty group-teaching small seminars instead of the core courses and/or upper-division classes need by majors. However, the chairs favored the concept and the requirement remained in a scaled-down fashion (one or two faculty members teaching a class from a variety of perspectives).[24]

As the modified arts college curriculum unfolded, some individual departments experienced noteworthy expansion. The English department established a creative writing program that attracted forty majors by the end of the decade. The fine arts also grew, propelled by the new facility and the earmarked Grace Keenan scholarships. In 1994, the department established a degree program in music, which subsequently led to the creation of a wind ensemble, and gamelan and chamber orchestras. Moreover, in 2001 the theology department "answered the call for religious educators" by creating a theology-education co-major and a youth ministry program. The Creighton House program (old CEC), however, fell on hard times. Squabbles over its curricular purpose arose in 1997, but the death knell rang with the sale of its historic home as part of a three-way transaction involving Creighton University, Omaha Central High School, and the Joslyn Art Museum. The razing of the house in 2003 terminated the 1960s concept of a student living-learning community, but provided "a much-needed opportunity to revamp the program and improve such things as its level of academic standard[s] and correlation to students lives." Academic standards also caused controversy with the introduction of the "B+" grade in spring semester 1996. Some argued it promoted grade inflation (63 percent of the CCAS faculty that responded to a poll in 1998, favored a plus-minus grading structure), while some students complained about the opposite effect, claiming some professors raised the percentage needed to gain an "A" (35 percent of all grades in 1997).[25]

The natural sciences also advanced: Biology introduced a course in botany and a program in environmental sciences evolved rapidly, gaining sixty-one majors in 1997. In 1999, both departments benefited from the acquisition of a greenhouse, a gift of James and Susan Stuppy, who operated a floral supply and greenhouse manufacturing business. In addition, the Success in Science Initiative sought to establish an endowed fund for equipment repair and replacement. In 1997, Vice President of University Relations and President of the Creighton foundation Michael Leighton (in yet other positions) reported that John Gottshalk, CEO of the *Omaha World-Herald* Companies and member of the board's academic affairs committee, had received an account that described "Creighton's need to improve the condition of the undergraduate science equipment." Subsequently, the *Omaha World-Herald* Foundation pledged $500,000, which provided the wherewithal to approach the Kresge Foundation for a $400,000 challenge grant (2:1 match). Wayne Ryan (B.S., 1949; M.S., 1951), CEO of Streck Laboratories, Inc., bestowed $100,000, which supplied a major portion of the remaining challenge, and the University announced receipt of the Kresge grant in 2000.[26]

In 1993, the CoBA also adjusted its curriculum, which included a new math sequence and business-writing course, as well as a strengthened "international focus." It contained four categories: (I) effective reasoning and communication, twenty-five to twenty-six hours of writing, math, and introduction to business classes; (II) moral reasoning, twelve hours of theology and philosophy; (III) domestic and international environment of business, eighteen hours of macroeconomics, a foreign language, and economics and arts college classes pertaining to international studies; (IV) general education electives, eighteen to nineteen hours of approved CCAS classes in history, literature, fine and performing arts, and the natural and social sciences. Thus, the rearranged seventy-three to seventy-five hour core maintained a liberal-arts requirement and matched the CCAS in emphasizing values education and a global perspective. The CoBA further promoted the latter with the inclusion of an international business major; the department of economics and finance administered the program, which required six hours of a foreign language and study abroad. The concept of service learning spread to business education at the graduate level. In 1998 the CoBA initiated a "business and society" course, which teamed MBA students with North Omaha (African-American and other minorities) entrepreneurs as a "bridge for transcending race and class differences" and "promoting corporate social innovation."[27]

The CoBA also had to stay abreast of the technological innovation affecting business operations. To meet the needs of the Omaha area, it responded with an association with the National Technological University to provide classes and training from prominent universities through satellite telecommunications and computer technology to offer credit and non-credit classes in "engineering and technological topics." Additionally, it supported the creation of the briefly popular Institute for Information Technology and Management in 1996, and that same year the master's degree in computer systems morphed into the broader program of information technology management. The new department benefited from a $1 million gift from Joan and Jack McGraw (BSC, 1953) to endow a chair in their name. Of significance, in 1998 the first chair holder, Uma Gupta, Ph. D., established the Women in Technology group to create a "statewide network for women in technology fields" and to encourage "initiatives to improve science and math education for Nebraska children."[28]

The next year, technological instruction leapt forward with a $1.4 million donation from J. Joe Ricketts (B.A., 1968), founder of Ameritrade, which endowed the Joe Ricketts Center in Electronic Commerce and Database Marketing "as a focal point" for a new master's degree program in e-commerce. In spring 2000, Donald Waite (BSC, 1954), CFO of Seagate, advanced the new discipline, contributing $100,000 to establish the Seagate Technology Electronic Commerce Laboratory, consisting of twenty-four workstations equipped with telecommunications infrastructure. That fall he supplemented his beneficence with a $1.1 million donation to launch the Anna Tyler Waite Center for Leadership in honor of his wife. It would provide leadership scholarships to undergraduate and graduate business students and "support a professional development workshop series in the revised MBA program, sponsor a fall leadership symposium, and host a student leadership recognition banquet. Moreover, in 2001 Deloitte & Touche and its Enterprise Risks Services, in conjunction with the Ricketts Center, assisted "with the design and development of an Internet lab appropriately configured to simulate e-commerce traffic and the associated security risks and controls." The company also provided "hardware, software, access to firm resources and experts who will lecture on specific e-commerce security topics."[29]

The Waite scholarship program (ninety participants in 2002) helped to rejuvenate a plunging CoBA enrollment, a disturbing national trend of the era. In 1992, Fr. Morrison petitioned the board to create "a blue ribbon" committee to study the situation (a steady decline since 1989), "because this school is the one element in the enrollment report which is not improving." In 1993, the declining registrations led to a $250,000 cut in the budget for faculty appointments (affecting adjuncts), as well as cuts in staff and resources for travel. In addition, the admissions office gained a CoBA graduate to target recruitment. Yet the decline continued, with 156 freshmen in 1994 and only 123 in 1996; in the latter year, women contributed 42 percent of the students. In addition, minorities furnished 10 percent, aided by the Partners in Leadership for Tomorrow (PILOT) scholarship program in collaboration with "sponsoring business firms." At the time, the CoBA had forty full-time faculty, all but one tenured, sufficient to teach 800 students, but only 550 registered for fall classes. Father Morrison stated that the transfer of funds from the CCAS had to cease. He listed three alternatives: raise enrollment, convince some faculty to retire early, or declare financial exigency and terminate tenured faculty.[30]

The administration argued that a turnaround in enrollment would not occur without a renovation of the Eppley Building. Thus, it felt it had to take "the risk," estimated at $2.5 million, "an amount which will not break the University budget." Late in the evening of April 28, 1994, a one-inch chilled-water pipe on the third floor broke and soaked the lower floors of the building, contributing to the decision of the necessity to include new heating and cooling systems in the remodeling, which actually cost $4.5 million. In 1997, the Eppley restoration and the shift of "a number of scholarships" out of the arts college (which suffered a decline of 25 freshmen) raised the number of CoBA freshmen by 40, to 173. The student increment and "the reduction of personnel from a total of 40 to 33" (3 were rehired June 1997, because of the increase in applications) cut the school's deficit "in half by at least $1 million." The good times did not last, however, and the next year the number of freshmen fell to 137 ("disappointing and the reason unclear"). In 1998, the numbers remained dismal despite the addition of fifteen Lied Scholarships, valued at $4,500 each; the cohort returned to 173 freshmen in 2000, but then toppled to 161 and 141 during the next two years, respectively. Coincidently, an AACSB accreditation study fueled further concern with its criticism of the low percentage of faculty involved in research and publication. Nevertheless, the era ended on a high note for the CoBA, as the Waite and the Lied scholarships (sixty total, fifteen per year) contributed to a rebound that harvested 183 freshmen. Additionally, $1 million in buyouts during the previous four years retired nine non-publishing faculty (and discussion with seven more), allowing the school to "replace them with more active scholars."[31]

The third undergraduate school, Nursing, experienced a similar U curve in development. In 1993, it also reorganized its core curriculum to coordinate it with the altered categories of the CCAS. The school required fifty-four hours of "general education" classes "to ensure the students of a liberal arts background," and they took them "concurrently with nursing courses," which continued the existing professional model. Unfortunately, fewer students matriculated in the BSN program. In 1993, the administration lamented, "Nursing applications are at the level of the early 1980s—this is a cause for nervousness, as Nursing enrollment tends to run in a ten-year cycle." In the summer 1995, following a nationwide trend, the school strengthened its graduate offerings, establishing a nurse practitioner program (particular training that allowed nurses to relieve physicians of basic counseling functions; aimed to provide fundamental health care in rural areas and in inner cities) that attracted thirty-five students, fourteen of whom sought "post master's certificates." In 1997, it launched Linking Education and Practice (LEAP), designed to allow working RNs to earn a BSN. In the latter year, only forty-four freshmen registered in the traditional baccalaureate program, while the school had budgeted for sixty-four; fortunately, the accelerated program took an upswing, and forty-seven students signed up for the inaugural of LEAP (thirty-one full-time equivalent). The successful program included "specifically designed" required classes, and "individually designed" clinical requirements "completed in the work setting." It also employed interactive teleconferencing classes for students at the Hastings satellite campus and at Bryan Lincoln General Hospital in Lincoln, Nebraska.[32]

By 1999, the low enrollment for the tradition BSN degree and changes in the nursing profession (nurses leaving hospitals for new health-care venues and "burned out" nurses leaving the profession) initiated "the early stages of a potentially dangerous nursing shortage." Omaha had "more than 300 full-time nursing openings in a very competitive health care market." However, "unlike the cyclical shortages in the last two decades, the late 1990s shortage appear[ed] to be hitting harder regionally and in very specific fields such as emergency medicine, labor and delivery, intensive care and coronary care." Thus, in 1999 the Nursing School received an $817,000 federal grant to establish the first "dual track cardiac health/nurse practitioner program in the country," which would focus on recruiting and preparing nurse practitioners who are specializing in cardiac health, wellness and rehabilitation. The previous year, the University had established a "strategic alliance with St. Joseph's Hospital and the Alegent Health system, whereby participating hospitals in Omaha, Hastings, Grand Island, and Kearney, Nebraska, each provided a specific number of scholarships to students to complete the accelerated nursing program in exchange for an employment commitment (e.g., the Alegent system offered twenty-four full-tuition scholarships to recipients promising four years of service). The number of freshmen BSN students remained static around sixty (dropping to fifty-two in 2001), but then rose dramatically to eighty-six in 2003. Concurrently, the school obtained a $575,624 three-year federal grant "to help alleviate the shortage of qualified advance practice nurses in rural and underserved areas." The funds underwrote the expansion of the existing

MSN program to include a new offering, which combined the community-health and the family-nurse-practitioner curriculums. The agenda also sought to attract minority candidates; employed BSNs and the school's undergraduates provided potential applicants (in 2000, it included six Native Americans, thirteen African Americans, fourteen Asian/Pacific Islanders, and eight Hispanics, approximately 11 percent of the total). Furthermore, each student would receive a laptop computer "with video conferencing ability for activities such as community presentations and home visits," as well as "to enable students to utilize distance learning."[33]

The turn-of-the-millennium post-baccalaureate programs in new areas in Nursing and business technology helped revitalize the graduate school enrollment, which had stagnated and then suffered a decline during the 1990s. M.A. disciplines disappeared (history, 1992), others reappeared (English, 1994), and new ones materialized (liberal studies, 1996), but except for teachers and a few other occupations, the significance of a terminal M.A. declined (most graduate programs were formulated to achieve a Ph.D.). In addition, despite a newspaper and radio advertising campaign, a mid-decade sluggish MBA program (coincided with the decreasing number of business undergraduates and the moderation of corporate support for the traditional advanced degree) contributed to a decreased total enrollment that dropped below 500 in 1999. Moreover, the NCA accreditation team (1996) declined to "lift the stipulation on the introduction of new doctoral programs," arguing "all departments of the institution are not currently prepared to specifically undertake such programs." The number of M.A. candidates inched back above five hundred in 2003, with part-timers contributing at least three fourths of the students.[34]

In tandem, the law school experienced reduced enrollment, but for profession-specific reasons—a perceived surfeit of attorneys. Furthermore, the administration sought to enhance the school's reputation through more selectivity in admissions, increased expenditure per student, and a lower student-faculty ratio. Thus, from a peak of 580 students in 1992, the school reduced its existing objective of 180 freshmen annually, to a "more manageable" 150 (sum of 450). The total enrollment actually dipped to 431 in 1999, while the University's reserve fund covered "the [annual] shortfall in income" (faculty in place to teach the higher number). By that time, even without actively recruiting women, they came to compose about 40 percent of the admissions, but despite "focusing on increasing minority enrollment," their percentage began to erode. As the number of African Americans, Asian/Pacific Islanders, and Hispanics each remained at about fifteen annually, their proportion of the cohort (forty-nine or 9.8 percent) dwindled as the total enrollment steadily mounted back over five hundred by 2003. A construction project provided additional space in the Ahmanson Building, making the higher enrollment "more manageable."[35]

The strategy of enrollment reduction also related to accreditation issues and the fact that in 1995, *U.S. News & World Report* dropped the law school from a third-tier rank to fifth tier (the lowest). The magazine "informed the school that the areas of low ranking were the reputation of the school, student faculty ratio, dollars spent for students, and job placement for students upon graduation." It also criticized a discrepancy in reported LSAT scores that apparently resulted from the "omission of some minority admittees in special programs." Dean Raful admitted, "we made a mistake, and we weren't as careful with the numbers as we should have been." While cognizant of the high overall ranking given to the University, he claimed his school's low rank had "no credibility." He pointed out that 40 percent of the scoring relied on a survey of 2,000 lawyers and 176 colleges, and that only 25 percent and 70 percent responded, respectively. Father Morrison reported to the Directors that "remedial policy changes" included the already-initiated reduction in the size of the freshman class, which would "facilitate improvement in expenditures per student, reduce the number of law school alumni seeking jobs, and improve the faculty to student ratio." Moreover, "in response to the reduction in enrollment, law school faculty members [*sic*] agreed to double their publications in the next year which will help the school's reputation." Numerous improvements ensued and the school maintained the lowest tuition of the thirteen Jesuit law schools. Additionally, on average 96 percent of the law graduates passed the bar exam and 98 percent found employment within nine months of graduation. Nonetheless, the ranking of the Creighton law school continued to fluctuate between the third and fourth tier, in the magazine's restructured four-tier system.[36]

The magazine's evaluation anticipated the ABA accreditation review that occurs on a seven-year cycle. During their 1995 visit, the seven-member team observed that the school had an effective administration, and that it maintained good relations with the students and with the local bar association. However, it expressed concern that "the self study done by faculty and administrators was overly negative" and that the faculty seemed "rather insular, with few visits out and few visitors in." Moreover, "although scholarship improved since the last visit," too many publications appeared in the *Creighton Law Review*; to enhance the school's stature, "faculty members must get out and publish in other venues." The team also emphasized "skills development" and recommended "planning for a Center of Excellence." Based on the discussions, the administration decided "to postpone groundbreaking for the law school Library expansion [*sic*], to concentrate on raising additional funds [goal increased from $2.5 million to $3.5 million], and to include in the renovation plans additional space for skills development." The final 110-page report granted accreditation, but the administration recognized three major problems: the need for improvements to the building (lack of seating, especially in the library, and sound problems), to the library collection plan, and to guidance of the intern program.[37]

The University responded quickly; first, it hired Judge Lyle Strom to oversee the intern program. Then the board approved a $17 million bond issue to finance several capital projects (e.g., the Swanson renovation), including the expansion of the law school Library. The Campaign 2000 master plan (three years before the accreditation review) had identified the goal of enclosing the parking area on the east side of the building to enlarge the library and provide space for a new community law clinic. Construction began at the end of May 1997 to double the library space, with seating for 350, to increase the size of the computer lab, and to provide spaces for student meetings, study groups, and small classes. A dedication ceremony for the redesigned east side of the building occurred on October 2, 1998, with completion of final details the following January. By that time (following a one-year extension to the ten-year rule), the administration had announced the selection of the next dean Patrick Borchers, J.D., who would assume the position in July 1999. He also inherited a gift to establish a law clinic; the Lozier Foundation donated $1 million and its director, Alan Lozier, asked that it bear the name of Milton R. Abrahams (LL.B., 1927) because of his lengthy linkage "with service to education and social justice." Those values received reinforcement in 2001 with a $41,000 grant from the Nebraska Commission for Public Advocacy, which extended the reach of the social justice aspiration, funding the employment of a Spanish-speaking attorney to allow Creighton law students to expand their clinic services to the Juan Diego Center and the Latina Center in South Omaha to serve Spanish speakers.[38]

The ten-year rule also affected the School of Dentistry. In 1994, Dean Gerald Brundo, D.D.S., stepped down. Enrollment had remained constant at about 330, and the previous year he had the pleasure of initiating a major renovation of the twenty-year-old Boyne Building. Wayne Barkmeier, D.D.S., gained promotion to the position of dean of the dental school and inherited the updated facility (he had joined the Creighton faculty in 1978, left in 1982, returned as assistant dean for research in 1985, and became associate dean in 1991). The school maintained its prescribed enrollment (even when applications decreased, they far outnumbered places available in the first-year class), which included seventeen or eighteen freshmen annually from the contract states of Idaho and Utah. The number of minority students doubled to sixty-one by 2000, based on the significant increase in Asian/Pacific Islanders (the number of African Americans and Hispanics lingered in the single digits). Women, on the other hand, overwhelmed their historic avoidance of the profession. By 2003, their enrollment more than doubled and they contributed over one third of the dental cohort (221 men, 117 women). While the established curriculum persisted, the school benefited from HFF grants that funded two new research centers: one analyzed "the performance of new dental materials clinically with unparalleled accuracy," and the second, with an additional grant from the Caulk Division of Dentsply International, focused on "restorations that release fluoride and just how well the fluoride they release is absorbed into the tooth."[39]

In comparison to the established number of places in the freshman class of the dental and medical schools, the School of Pharmacy and Health Professions experienced significant growth. Despite a drop in applications in the late 1990s in each of the three fields (pharmacy and occupational and physical therapy), which "caused some concern," the school doubled its total enrollment during the era. Women continued to provide a sizeable majority of the students, and it became one of only two schools to attain the diversity goal, with approximately 26 percent minority enrollment in 2000 (resulting from an upsurge in the number of Asian/Pacific Islanders in pharmacy). Total enrollment swelled to over 950 in 2002, the year the school dropped "allied" from its name. It followed a national trend—therapists argued the term implied the programs lacked the stature of "full-fledged health care professionals, when in fact they are independent practitioners who work cooperatively with other health care professionals" (the team concept, although complaints about the attitude of physicians endure). All of the fields became doctoral programs; pharmacy abandoned the B.S. program and the freshmen of 1994 became "the first class in which all graduates" were "awarded a doctoral degree." The next year, following a suggestion from alums, the school established the Non-traditional Pharm. D. Program (part-time), expecting 20 to 30 applicants, and received 130.[40]

Similarly, in answer to a "tremendous national shortage," the University inaugurated a Doctor of Physical Therapy (DPT) program in 1992, consisting of a two-year pre-professional core in the CCAS and a four-year professional schedule in the Pharmacy and Health Professions School. Then, in the fall 1995 Creighton announced the first "professional doctorate for occupational therapy [OTD] in the U. S," but experienced "some serious problems" gaining accreditation. The NCA perceived "a lack of clarity" in the two-year (five semesters) post-baccalaureate degree and felt it needed to make a "focus visit" to "identify the appropriate degree structure as soon as possible." Ostensibly, the accreditors had reevaluated a purported mutual understanding with the University that differed between a Ph.D. degree and a Pharm.D. or DPT degree. Subsequently, Creighton reorganized the structure of the OTD degree. In 1999, it eliminated the B.S. in occupational therapy (the term "occupational represents the flow of activities that fill a person's life and that have effect on his or her health"). In place of the former programs, it established an OTD program, a four-year entry-level clinical degree that required two years of pre-professional study and equated it to the DPT. It also added a two-year post-professional OTD for degree holders seeking advanced study. However, between 1997 and 2000, applications for the OTD program plummeted from 277 to 66, reflecting a nationwide trend related "to negative Medicare reimbursements" and to the discontinuation of the B.S. degree. By that time, the school had initiated three new programs, which buoyed total enrollment: an M.S. in Pharmaceutical Sciences, a Doctor of Pharmacy/MBA, and an M.A. in Health Services Administration (in conjunction with Nursing and the CoBA), in response "to the growing demand from front-line health-care managers who are preparing for leadership challenges associated with a complex health care environment."[41]

During the era, the School of Pharmacy and Health Professions garnered a number of significant grants. In 1994, it arranged with the Haskell Indian Nations (Kansas) to develop programs to "encourage Native Americans to enter health care professions." Their number in the school jumped from one to eight in a decade; moreover, the expertise garnered in the project led to other federal grants. In 1997, it received a three-year $418,000 U.S. Department of Health and Human Services (HHS) grant "to provide physical and occupational therapy care at U.S. Public Health Services hospitals on the Omaha and Winnebago reservations [Nebraska]." Two years later, it received a second HHS grant for $454,000 to expand the care and training by including pharmacy students. The goals included developing "culturally sensitive" practitioners. The projects garnered the school the Outstanding Minority Health Community-Based Program award from the Nebraska Public Health Association in 2003. In the meantime, OTD student Jeff Crabtree, with associate professor of physical therapy Andrea Zardetto-Smith serving as principle investigator, obtained a five-year $1.3 million grant from the Science Education Drug Abuse Partnership and the National Institute of Drug Abuse to promote fairs "to help elementary school-aged children learn more about the functions of the brain and the nervous system." Finally, in 2000 Creighton and the U.S Public Health Service signed an agreement ("one of few") giving its pharmacy students "preferential entry to clinical sites."[42]

Additionally, in 2000 each pharmacy student received a laptop computer upon matriculation because compact discs and the Internet held such a vast array of information. The $1,500 cost, for a two-year lease, became part of a 16 percent increase in tuition for incoming freshmen, "in order that students can rely on financial-aid funds to help cover this cost." That same year, Walgreen Drug Stores provided $50,000 to support the creation of "a web-based degree program"; the next year, the school launched "the first online pharmacy degree program in the nation." Except for "clinical rotations, annual assessments and two lab courses, students [could] receive the four-year degree without leaving the comfort of home." A $1 million grant from the Institute for the Advancement of Community Pharmacy funded the program—"distance learning" needed software, hardware, a dedicated server, and technical staff, all quite expensive. The program attacked a growing pharmacist shortage. In 2001, HHS "estimated 10,000 pharmacist vacancies across the country." That year, the on-line program drew 112 applications, with 72 accepted; in 2003, it rose to 427 and 78, respectively. A grant from Schering-Plough Animal Health helped the school expanded the concept in 2002 by creating an online "Veterinary Therapeutic Program for Practicing Pharmacists" to train practitioners to counsel pet owners. Moreover, the school's expertise enticed a $156,000 grant from the U.S. Department of Education "to create a performance-based testing program for evaluating pharmacy curriculum" to measure the American Council on Pharmaceutical Education "recently revised accreditation standards." Finally, in 2003 an HFF grant of $850,000 created a Toxicology Center, where Dean Sidney Stohs, as primary investigator, could collaborate with Creighton's pathology department and the Poison Control Center at Children's Hospital in Omaha to study "nutrients in food, food additives, chemicals and drugs used in our everyday lives."[43]

The concept of centers and institutes, among several other factors, also affected the training of physicians; for example, the Cardiac Center or the Institute of Neurosurgery, "which cluster professionals in related fields." Moreover, as federal funds dwindled, medical schools and researchers had to find alternate sources for support. At the same time, state governments and insurance companies changed the landscape by "propelling America toward a system of managed care." In that new system, Creighton and St. Joseph's Hospital had to compete for patients for medical education and research. They also had to attract patients to generate revenue for their budgets. By the mid-1990s, about one half of the medical school budget stemmed from patient care, while competition lowered prices and income. Further complicating the transition, Medicare and managed-care organizations controlled patients' use of specialists and hospitals. Thus, during the 1990s the medical school continued to experience a fiscal crisis, which sparked rumors of its closing. In 1993 it employed a consultant "to assist in developing a systematic program which will allow the Health Sciences division to compete more effectively in a reformed healthcare environment."[44]

However, for most of the decade, the medical school produced deficits. Thomas Cinque (M.D., 1959) returned to his alma mater as dean in 1992, and the following year benefited from the largest gift bestowed on the University to that time. Frederick J. de la Vega (A.B., 1942; M.D., 1946) bequeathed a $7 million endowment for scholarships, shared by the medical school and the CCAS. Additionally, in 1993 Eugene Barone, M.D., and Michael Kavan, Ph. D., of the department of family medicine, received a three-year $733,139 grant from HHS "to develop a rural community-based curriculum in family medicine (rural areas have distinct psychological needs and medical problems, such as farm accidents). The scholarships helped attract the best applicants to the medical school and the grants helped finance educational expenditures, but it could not suitably reign in the costs of medical training or realign clinical operations to generate sufficient revenue. In May 1996 the University projected a balanced budget, but over the summer it turned into a $2.5 million shortfall, mostly because of "departments in the School of Medicine expending approximately $1 million over the non-salary budget." The administration instituted "some 'draconian' control measures" to "prevent a recurrence." Simultaneously, a Physicians at Teaching Hospitals (PATH) audit loomed on the horizon; the Office of the Inspector General had begun to audit all 126 medical schools in the United States regarding their Medicare/Medicaid coding and billing practices, especially regarding billing by physicians not present when students treated patients. Several universities had incurred fines of $10 to $30 million—a school with a distressing fiscal situation faced yet another alarming threat. In these circumstances, in the spring 1997 the University asked Dr. Cinque to resign "because the School of Medicine ran budget deficits in four of the five years he was at the helm."[45]

While the University conducted a yearlong search for a replacement, the administration continued to work with consultants to restructure the system. It struggled to standardize payment schedules among the physicians in different departments in order to make correct estimates of income and to improve the business procedures of billing. It also sought to resolve payment issues with St. Joseph's Hospital and to coordinate "twenty independent kingdoms [departments], all running their own shop," into a "single practice plan," as well as to "restructure the way physicians are paid so there is an incentive" for them to practice efficiently and generate higher revenue. The reorganization would produce "a drastic culture change," but Creighton had moved "too slowly in these areas," and physicians had to accept "that things are going to be done differently from the past." During the summer 1997, the medical school employed Arthur Anderson to assist in "a financial performance improvement initiative." It organized committees "to attack six areas to increase revenue and decrease expense: billing and collection, clinic operations and space, clinical compensation, basic science compensation, budget redesign, and organization and mission," with the hope "to realize $4.1 million improvement in revenue and expenses, annualized." While they analyzed, the school ran another deficit of approximately $3 million, forcing the use of over $1.2 million from the reserve account to balance the University's budget.[46]

However, by the summer of 1998 a turnaround ensued. Significantly, the General Counsel for the Health Care Finance Administration reviewed the ongoing PATH audits and released "an opinion stating that of the 18 medical jurisdictions, five had not issued clear instructions regarding physicians at teaching hospitals," and Creighton was located in "one of the fortunate five." While it avoided a potentially penalizing audit, the incident did prompt the University to draw up a corporate compliance plan that dealt with "the variety of health care laws and regulations that apply to billing for receipt of Medicare funds." Moreover, Arthur Anderson and the medical school committees began to make progress. HSVP O'Brien reported that contracts for clinical faculty "had resulted in some significant changes" that based compensation "relative to productivity," that clinic reorganization and consolidation resulted in "significant reductions in staff," and that Arthur Anderson handled "an accounts receivable clean-up project which resulted in approximately $2.2 million in additional revenue." That same summer, Dr. O'Brien stepped down and the University hired M. Roy Wilson, M.D., an African American, as dean of the medical school and vice president of health sciences, the first minority to hold either title at Creighton. Under his direction, the budgetary situation in the medical school continued to improve, and by spring 2002 it projected it would end the fiscal year with a surplus of over $650,000.[47]

During the excruciating restructuring of the medical school's business operations, the University also had to reorganize its relationship with St. Joseph's Hospital. In 1992, negotiations with AMI concerning its refusal to expend money generated by the Hospital "to implement the budget its board had passed," stalled. Therefore, Creighton amended and refilled its lawsuit; AMI retaliated by filing a countersuit in its home state of Texas. After two years of point-counterpoint maneuvering that continued to postpone the court date, and approximately $2 million spent by each side that "accomplished nothing for health care," Creighton and AMI reached an out-of-court settlement that established a "new health care partnership." The University repurchased 25.94 percent of the Creighton-St. Joseph Healthcare System (the hospital and the St. Joseph Center for Mental Health) for $37 million, financed with a loan from the HFF. The agreement resolved the issue of capital expenditures and devised an acceptable formula for the reimbursement of teaching costs. The University created a subsidiary, Creighton Healthcare, Inc., and successfully lobbied the Internal Revenue Service to grant it the status of a 501(C)3 corporation and to rule that its income from the hospital was tax exempt. Then, on March 1, 1995, AMI merged with National Medical Enterprises to form a new corporation, Tenet Healthcare. Relations between the University and the new firm proceeded smoothly, and the hospital operation produced more revenue than projected, allowing the University to pay down the loan "well ahead of schedule." By June 2002, it became "the debt-free owner of 26 percent of St. Joseph Hospital." However, a 1995 survey had identified it as the "area's least popular hospital." Thus, as part of a "branding" project (that is, Belin Consulting recommended "the need to better define an institutional identity"), on June 27, 2002, the facility officially changed its name to the Creighton University Medical Center. However, the Catholic litany remained to identify "St. Joseph as the patron saint of the hospital. A source of hope to the sick, a protector of the poor and a comfort to the dying."[48]

The Creighton-AMI agreement also facilitated the cooperation of faculty and hospital physicians in a managed-care system. The clinical faculty at the medical school had just established Creighton Medical Associates as a group-practice plan. Now the faculty group could "more closely align [its] interests with those of the Hospital and the Center for Mental Health" by participating in the soon-to-be-developed Physicians Hospital Organization and in an enlarged primary care network to benefit "more fully in managed care contracts." In 1996, the combined operation began "marketing itself as a single organization," Creighton Family Health Care, that combined the University's eleven clinics with the hospital's nine clinics and three emergency centers. In 1996, to expand its system, Creighton signed a ten-year agreement with Children's Hospital to "create a comprehensive pediatric primary healthcare delivery network" for the greater-Omaha area (twenty-six pediatricians at twelve locations). The alliance gave Creighton "resident physicians, medical students and students in nursing, pharmacy and allied health professions priority for rotations at Children's Hospital," as well as offered that institution's affiliated physicians the opportunity to become clinical faculty at Creighton University. The following year, it extended its rural outreach program, adding another affiliation by agreeing to provide "all specialty services" in Atkinson, Nebraska, in conjunction with West Holt Memorial Hospital.[49]

By that time, the "conventional wisdom" declared that "the Omaha community will be divided into two large healthcare-providing networks." The affiliations posed a "potential threat," and the University worked "to acquire assurances" preventing exclusion of its programs at participating hospitals. As early as 1988, competition with Bergan Mercy Hospital in Omaha had led Creighton to propose that the two entities create a Catholic Hospital Consortium. Discussions failed, and in 1996, Bergan Mercy created Alegent Healthcare, which included Immanuel Medical Center in Omaha, Mercy Hospital in Council Bluffs, Iowa, and a hospital in Corning, Iowa. Creighton board members heard rumors that the University of Nebraska Medical Center would join the system; however, it did not, and subsequently established its own system in combination with its neighbor, Clarkson Hospital. Then, "a little before Thanksgiving" 1997, Alegent approached Creighton about forming an alliance. The following January, the University signed a letter of intent, and at the end

of June signed "a definitive alliance agreement" that also included Midlands Hospital in Papillion, Nebraska, and six hospitals in small towns in the area. The alliance
created a faith-based system in which Alegent contributed a "strong primary care
base" and Creighton a "broad range of specialty care services." The system controlled
nearly 50 percent of the Omaha market and the eight-hundred-strong physician
organization could offer businesses and insurance companies competitive health-care
contracts. The system would consolidate psychiatric health, physical rehabilitation,
and home health services; Alegent would operate the St. Joseph Center for Mental
Health for one year, while the Immanuel Center completed remodeling, and then
close it. Ultimately, Creighton joined a system to gain "market strength and, in the
current evolving area of managed care, to gain access to contracts with managed care
companies that provide coverage for large numbers of patients." In this alliance,
Creighton "gained access to in excess of 120,000 lives in our region."[50]

While the medical school grappled with monumental changes in finances and
health-care delivery, its student body also experienced a revolutionary change. In
1999, for the first time in the 107-year history of the school, women outnumbered
men in the freshmen class, 57 of 113 (just three years before it had been 35 of 112).
Thus, by 2003, coeds contributed nearly 50 percent of the total enrollment of 244
men and 222 women. Like the other schools, the sizeable increase in minority enrollment came from Asian/Pacific Islanders, while the number of African-American and
Hispanic students remained constant. In 1999, the school received a $1 million HHS
grant to fund the Health Careers Opportunity Program aimed at interesting minority seventh and eighth graders in the fields and guiding them through high school
in preparing to enter college as pre-health-science students. By 2003, the project did
not have time to make a significant impact in terms of the targeted minorities; while
the medical school claimed a 30.9 percent minority cohort, it included only 19
African Americans and 12 Hispanics, with 106 Asian/Pacific Islanders. Nonetheless,
in fulfilling its mission, that same year the University received two awards for providing heath-care services to the poor and minorities, one from the Nebraska Public
Health Service and the other from the Association of American Medical Colleges.[51]

Moreover, the medical school elevated its service through increased research.
While traditional areas such as cardiac and osteoporosis continued, cancer research
gained two novel infusions of support. In 1993, a three-year effort in which Creighton
played a key role culminated with the Nebraska Legislature increasing the tax on cigarettes two cents per pack and distributing the money for cancer research. The University received over $1 million per year from the fund. In 1995, in one distinctive area
of investigation, Dr. Henry Lynch established the Hereditary Cancer Prevention
Clinic. He had studied the role of genetics in cancer development for over thirty
years; at first, the medical community doubted the significance, but eventually he
secured worldwide acclaim. Then, all biomedical research in Nebraska benefited from
the class-action prosecution of an alleged prime promoter of cancer, the tobacco
companies. Nebraska's share of the settlement stood at $16 million. Creighton, the
University of Nebraska Medical Center, and the Boys Town National Research Hos-

pital supported a bill to allocate about one third of the money to biomedical research. The bill passed and Creighton acquired a share of about $2.25 million. The medical school decided to utilize the funds in research areas likely to attract additional grants from the National Institutes of Health, as outlined in the "Healthy People 2010" initiative. Furthermore, with money from the tobacco settlement, Creighton partnered with the Nebraska Department of Health and Human Services project "Every Woman Matters" to open a clinic in the Benson area of North Omaha to provide free or low-cost examinations, dispense information and encourage North Omaha women (many of whom would be low-income and/or African Americans) to participate in research studies.[52]

Some of the research and the developments in the health sciences had a direct effect on student activities in general. For example, a wellness campaign based on the increasing importance of a healthy life style to prevent disease, encouraged by managed-care medicine, succeeded incrementally in implementing a smoking ban on campus (e.g., RAL commons area, 1994; the dorms, 2000). Furthermore, with the new mindset, the existing effort to control the illegal use of alcohol and drugs intensified. In 1996, in response to an increase in repeat offenders, the student services office studied the situation and the policy at other Jesuit universities, and decided to raise the fine for violations and to require attendance at a drug and alcohol awareness class. However, the new suite-style dormitories (more students in the area, more efficient oversight by staff) and the off-campus residences and parties (several high-profile incidents by fraternities and sororities) contributed to a continued increase in infractions. Student services lauded exemplary efforts such as the Greek Week alcohol-free events and some administrators, concerned about off-campus drinking problems, supported the revival of the concept of a pub (updated terminology) on campus.[53]

The SBG supported the smoking ban and the idea of a pub, but on most issues it realized it served an apathetic student body. The divergent concerns of the various schools and colleges, the disparate student organizations, the different representative bodies (e.g., in the residence halls or the arts senate), and the Greek system seemed to minimize its significance and to defy the nostalgic quest for unity. It lacked legislative authority and in the increasingly large and diverse University, it failed to generate interest or "union." The number of candidates and voters remained quite low. Thus, in 1997 the SBG moved its elections to the fall, allowing freshmen to run for office and providing newly elected representatives with more time to establish priorities and to work on them over the summer (previously, elected in the spring, they had no time to organize and pass resolutions before dispersing at the end of the semester). The election schedule briefly produced larger voter turnouts, but it did not solve the dilemma of unity. Therefore, in 1999, student governance restructured itself with the goal of enticing the professional schools back into a corporation that had evolved into an institution with a fundamentally undergraduate focus. It eliminated the historic SBG, but maintained the equally historic concept and name, Creighton Student Union. In an attempt at meaningfully reintegrating the professional schools,

the president of the governing body of each school or college would serve on the
board of directors of the union, while the students elected representatives and executives to make and carry out policy approved by the board. Nonetheless, apathy persisted, as a few voters generally cast ballots for candidates running unopposed, and
funding of particular organizations and by school remained problematic. Professional
education, because of age and curricular requirements, continued to become more
disassociated from undergraduate student life.[54]

For undergraduates at Creighton, the Greek life remained an attractive feature. In
1993, approximately 30 percent belonged to one of the fraternities or sororities (12
percent higher than the national average). That year, the mix of sororities changed, as
the Pan-Hellenic Council dismissed Alpha Gamma Delta's plan to reorganize and
sought bids to charter a new group; subsequently, Pi Beta Phi joined the system. In
1995, Delta Chi surrendered its charter, but 190 coeds joined one of the other five
sororities. Following a national trend, in 2000 the Greek system abandoned "rush"
and replaced it with "recruitment," a terminology that "more accurately reflects the
process and avoids the idea of anyone rushing into a decision." Then, in January 2003,
the Pan-Hellenic Council decided to forsake the guaranteed-bid system, arguing that
a new bidding system would keep pledge classes smaller and would better match
coeds with chapters. Moreover, the thirty-year-old rule, which did not apply to fraternities, seemingly demonstrated sexism; a spokeswoman proclaimed, "It is a major
step for this university to finally recognize that women are mature and emotionally
stable enough to handle open bidding." The new system did establish a maximum
pledge class per sorority; however, the small Alpha Phi (forty) did not fare well during the first recruiting effort, accepted no pledges, and voted to dissolve gradually as
members graduated. The Inter-Fraternity Council experienced similar alterations as
it added Phi Delta Theta in 1994, but lost Sigma Nu in 1998. During the decade, 110
to 135 men joined one of the five (briefly six) active chapters annually. As in the past,
few minorities participated, with the discussion revealing traditional contentions.
Many fraternal leaders asserted "that increased minority participation would be an
asset to the Greek system," but "you cannot force people to join." On the other hand,
a black fraternity member who joined because of his friends claimed the Greeks did
not "do enough in reaching [out to] minority groups."[55]

Other undergraduate activities, such as the debate (perennial national ranking,
with national titles in 1994, 1995, 2002, 2003), *Shadows* (gold medal, Columbia University Scholastic Press Association competition, 1997), and the *Creightonian* (undergraduate staff, but university-wide news reporting) promoted institutional pride and
provided a semblance of unity. However, for the sports enthusiasts, intercollegiate
athletics supplied the adhesive for *E Pluribus Unum*. Yet, the historic problem persisted—building school spirit and support. In 1996, men's soccer tried to develop a
student section "next to the goal area" (difficult since the team played at a distant city
park) and the men's basketball program created the "birdcage" (the latest of the tran-
sient student yell sections) to "increase support for the team." Unfortunately, the pep
band also continued to come and go, floating in "financial limbo, unsure whether the

Athletic Department or the music department [would] pick up the tab." Moreover, safety and fiscal concerns eliminated the traditional cheerleaders, who were replaced by the dance squad that added the cheering function. The former cheerleaders had insisted on performing pyramids and other dangerous stunts, and the athletic department worried about injuries and liability (insurance premiums had skyrocketed). In addition, determining the location of student seating remained a budgeting decision—choice seats behind the bench at center court seemed appropriate since it was a student activity, but that prime area would raise more revenue as a reserved-seat section for individuals and corporations supporting the program financially. The other "major" men's and women's teams did not experience seating problems; they advertised their home games, but received minimal support, while the other athletes (e.g., crew or cross country) largely participated in a vacuum. In 1998, with the goal of building nonstudent fan support for the teams, Athletic Director Bruce Rasmussen instituted a policy of free attendance and game-day newspaper and radio advertising (excluding men's basketball and soccer).[56]

The athletic budget needed all the help it could get because of the NCAA requirements for Division I status (must field fourteen teams) and of the Title IX gender equity prerequisite. In 1994, the obligations resulted in the addition of three intercollegiate teams, crew for men and women (elevation from club sport) and the reestablishment of women's volleyball. Creighton now sponsored eight squads for women and six for men. Nevertheless, the mid-decade self-study for NCAA Division I certification identified gender equity as the most significant problem. Creighton lacked compliance standards in funding recruiting, facilities, travel, and women coaches for women's sports. The report, due in 1997, had to establish a plan that demonstrated it would "make progress in these areas on a year-by-year basis," and solve the facilities problem by 2002. The NCAA granted certification, but emphasized "developing a specific timetable for capital improvement of women's facilities [e.g., locker room at a cost of $300,000 to $500,000] and a plan for improvement of women in head and assistant coaching positions." Additionally, the department had to improve scholarships and travel arrangements for women; men flew to some away games, while women had to drive, although both men and women stayed "in the same level hotels" and received "the same amount of meal money." By 1998, scholarships met the target, but recruiting and operating had "not met compliance" (however, "trends headed in the right direction"). By 1995, women composed 57 percent of the athletes at Creighton, but only received only 40 percent of the operating budget. The budget for the following year granted them 55 percent of the scholarships, and aimed at a 50-50 split on the operating budget. Ultimately, in 1998, another significant step toward gender equity occurred with the $1.7 million refashioning of the athletic area of the old gymnasium. The following year, a $500,000 gift from John "Jackie" Gaughan (BSC, 1946) financed the construction of a two-story facility located between the women's softball and men's baseball fields. Dedicated in his mother's honor, the Kitty Gaughan Pavilion consisted of offices, men and women's locker rooms, training rooms, a concessions room, and a laundry.[57]

The expenditures on women's teams helped to drive up the red figure in the loss column of the annual budget statement (over $3 million by 2000). Paradoxically, coed success exacerbated the situation; revenue from their trips to conference and national tournaments did not equal expenses. Moreover, all but one of the men's teams also lost money each season, including the highly successful soccer program, with its annual travel to NCAA regional and national play-off sites. Fortunately for the athletic budget, between 1994 and 1999 support from the Jaybackers Club tripled, ticket sales for men's basketball games increased dramatically (10 percent of annual revenue in 1997), and overall revenue increased by $1.2 million, as Coach Dana Altman reestablished the winning tradition. His success helped to keep the University subsidy for athletics (few collegiate programs operate without one) near the historical proportion (revenue versus expenditures), while the athletic program expanded exponentially in order to meet Division I and Title IX requirements (in the spirit of the regulation, all women's teams dropped the "sexist" Lady Jays designation in 1998).[58]

The euphemistic "title-niners" brought acclaim to the University, although rebuilding the women's volleyball program presented a difficult challenge because of its location in a very competitive recruiting region. The team played their matches at the local high-school gyms or in the KFC (not constructed for spectator sports). Coaches Ben Guiliano (25-58, 1994–96) and Howard Wallace (1997, 15-13, MVC Co-Coach of the Year; but 68-94, 1997–2002) struggled to make the teams contenders in the conference. In comparison, recruiting for the new sport (at Creighton and in terms of acceptance in the United States) of soccer proved easier because of few long-established programs in the region. Thus coach Ray Leone (1989–1993, 50-35-5), Cathy Klein, two-time college All-American (1994, 14-4-0), and former Creighton men's soccer player, Ira Philson (1995–98, 38-32-3) immediately fashioned a winning tradition. Subsequently, Coach Bruce Erickson compiled losing seasons in 1999 and 2000; however, in 2002, the team kicked their way to an MVC championship, but lost in the opening round of the NCAA tournament.[59]

In 1993, Mary Higgins stepped down as softball coach. She had amassed a 564-298 (.654) record, one of eight active coaches at the time with 500 wins, and became the first woman inducted into the Creighton Hall of Fame (1987). She became the first full-time compliance coordinator, working to ensure that each team followed the increasingly large body of stringent regulations instituted by the NCAA. Brent Vigness became the team's second head coach and continued its winning ways. He began two of his first three seasons ending with a less-than-.500 record, but then produced five consecutive 30-win seasons from 1997 to 2001. In 1998, the MVC named him Coach of the Year, as the team claimed the first of three consecutive conference championships, which included a 0-2 appearance in the NCAA regional tournament. After a year's lapse, in 2003 it again won the conference trophy and went 1-2 in the NCAA tourney. Women's basketball established an equally impressive record. Connie Yori (subsequently inducted into the Creighton Hall of Fame with her sister, softball All-American Mary, 1992) replaced Bruce Rasmussen as head coach. She had only two years with more losses than wins and compiled a career total of 170-115, .596

(1992–2002). She completed her tenure with a 24-7 season, but the team lost in the first round of the NCAA tournament. Her assistant coach for ten years, Jim Flannery, acceded to the top spot. He quickly posted consecutive 24-9 seasons and produced the first national championship team in Creighton history, winning the Women's National Invitational Tournament in 2004.[60]

The two traditional "major" men's athletic teams had to regroup during the 1990s. In 1993, John Sanders, the University of Nebraska baseball coach, accused Jim Hendry ("the only player or coach in Creighton baseball history to have his number retired") and the Creighton athletic program of NCAA rules violations (Higgins claimed her appointment as the first full-time compliance director "was in no way conceived due to allegations of rules violations by the Creighton baseball program"). Subsequently, the University's self-study uncovered thirty-three violations, none serious; for example, Dr. Lee Bevilacqua, volunteer team physician, "provided overnight lodging for sick or injured athletes, as well as student patients. This was considered less available to the general student body than it was for athletes." The program received no sanctions and it continued to serve as the host of the College World Series, because of its proximity to the championship venue, Omaha's Rosenblatt Stadium. However, financing the NCAA Division I and Title IX mandates meant that the baseball team lost some of its prominence. Two-year head coach Todd Wenberg (73-44-1) continued the winning habit, including going 1-2 in the NCAA Central Regional in 1992. Jack Dahm succeeded to the position in 1994, and suffered four losing and two .500 seasons during his ten-year tenure. However, his 283-276-2 career included trips to the NCAA regional tourney in 1999 (0-2) and 2000 (0-2).[61]

In comparison, the reestablished men's soccer team made thirteen straight appearances in the NCAA tournament starting in 1992, won the MVC regular-season championship 1992 through 1996 and in 2003, and triumphed at the MVC post-season tournament in 1992, 1993, 1994, 1995, 1997, 1998, 2000, and 2002. As the premier fall sport at the University, in 1993. Homecoming moved to coincide with an October home soccer game. In 1998, students assumed the responsibility for organizing the event and, unfortunately, in 2003 the annual ad hoc committee that formed to plan the event failed to organize. Participation had dwindled over the years, "mainly because much of the planning occurs over the summer." To save that year's event, in September the Creighton Student Union Planning Board had to rush in to arrange some festivities. While students struggled to maintain the traditional fall event (minus American football), Coach Bob Warming (a superb "football" coach in all other areas of the world) left in 1994, and his two-year assistant, Bret Simon (1995–2000, 96-26-8, .769), replaced him. His stint at Creighton included playing in the College Cup semifinals in 1996 (lost to St. John's 1-2), and in the championship game in 2000 (lost to Connecticut 0-2). Stanford University lured Simon away and Warming returned in 2001, maintaining the national reputation. Also signifying the sport's stature, in 1997 the Board of Directors discussed the idea of a public-private partnership for an indoor-outdoor soccer facility. In its championship runs, the team had to play all its tournament games away because the field at Tranquility Park (an

Omaha public facility) did not meet NCAA standards. In 2004, to correct the situation and in conjunction with its plans for eastward expansion, the University broke ground for a $12 million, five-thousand-seat "state-of-the-art soccer stadium" at 19th and California streets, a prime facility for a first-rate team, which would anchor the eastern edge of campus. Hopefully, a superior on-campus venue would draw student support and would transform soccer into a revenue-generating sport.[62]

Historically, men's basketball usually delivered enough revenue to pay its bills and to assist with other costs, helping to restrain the size of the University's athletic subvention. Unfortunately, Rick Johnson's three losing seasons as head coach (1991-93, 24-59, .289) compromised Creighton's "competitive stature" in the MVC and posed a budgetary problem. He resigned and the University "took the first step in rebuilding its men's basketball program by hiring Dana Altman as head coach." In four years he produced a remarkable turnaround, with records of 7-19, 14-15, 15-15, and 18-10, which include a trip to the NIT (lost at Marquette 68-80). Then he completed six consecutive 20-win seasons, the first five included trips to the NCAA tournament, but the teams won only two games at that level, one each in 1989 and 2002. In 2003, the 20-9 team received a bid to play in the NIT and gained the home court at their new venue, the Omaha arena-convention facility, the Quest Center (lost to Nebraska 70-71). The new domicile contained nearly double the previous capacity and, thanks to corporate and Jaybacker support, the team filled the seats, continuing its crucial fiscal contribution.[63]

In the June 1999, Fr. Morrison announced he would resign as of the following June, or sooner if the search committee found a replacement. He believed that the institution had reached the Creighton 2000 goal of becoming "the outstanding comprehensive Jesuit university in the United States." When he made his decision public that fall, for the fourth successive year, *U.S. News & World Report* had listed Creighton as the number one Midwestern Regional Comprehensive University. Father Morrison had collected the longevity record, serving just shy of nineteen years, and because of the undergraduate enrollment explosion, he had signed 44 percent of all degrees conferred in the school's 121-year history. During his tenure, the endowment grew from $20 to $200 million and the campus gained ten new buildings (the last, a home for the Center for Health Policy and Ethics at 2616 Burt Street, financed by a $700,000 HFF grant). He did not consider fundraising a "natural instinct"; his "interaction with students, however, [did] seem instinctive." He initiated the "Fireside Chat" with students during Founders' Week (in 1988, he had returned the celebration to its 1950s length) and he "habitually perched [himself] on the wall near St. John's campus church," to serve as "a familiar and approachable counselor, confidant or friend." Thus, the bench in his honor in front of the Church; moreover, current and emeritus board members contributed $1 million to endow the Michael Morrison, S.J., Scholarship, awarded to "Native American students who are members of federally recognized tribes, with preference to graduates of Red Cloud Indian School in Pine Ridge, South Dakota."[64]

Six board members served as a committee that began to "conduct a quiet search during the summer of 1999; they contacted other Jesuit universities "to procure the names of as many qualified candidates as possible." That fall a second "Presidential Nominating Committee," consisting of four board members and two from the SBG, with four representing the faculty, two the staff, and one the alumni, gathered to assist in "identifying the qualities and qualifications of potential candidates, as well as to provide the names of Jesuits who could be considered for the presidency." Among the challenges facing the next occupant of the position, Fr. Morrison advised, "Competition is intense for the best students, for gift income and for patient referrals to our clinics. Higher education must keep pace with changes in the ways people live work and learn."[65]

In the spring 2000, the University announced that the Reverend John P. Schlegel, S.J. (Ph.D., international relations, Oxford, 1976), would become Creighton's next president. He had served as a lecturer in the CCAS in 1969, then returned to become an assistant professor of political science in 1976, and gained administrative experience as assistant AVP from 1978 to 1982. Thereafter, he served as dean at Rockhurst and Marquette, as AVP at John Carroll, and since 1991 as president of the University of San Francisco. He described his choice to return to Creighton as "based, in part, on a desire to 'go home' to an institution that introduced me to higher education administration." Two of his earliest decision demonstrated his commitment to diversity. In 2001, he created a new position, vice president for institutional relations, which involved "internal communications" and "a strong role in community relations," and he appointed Patricia R. Callone, the University's first woman vice president. She had previously served as assistant, and then associate, dean for lifelong learning (1979–84), associate dean of University College (1984–90), and thereafter as assistant to the president. Then, as of July 2002, Marquette law professor Christine Wiseman became academic vice president. Moreover, Fr. Schlegel directly addressed "the hottest topic on Jesuit campuses" since the early 1990s, "the recognition of gay, lesbian and pro-choice groups." The University did not have a policy and experienced only occasional insubstantial demands to produce one (e.g., in 1994, a task force to investigate the situation; in 1999, a Sexual Orientation Issues Dialogue Week). However, in 2000 a Gay/Straight Alliance composed of undergraduate and professional students sought "official status as a Creighton student organization." A year later, Fr. Schlegel, after consultation with Archbishop Eldon Curtiss, alumni, the parents' council, the student government and the board, approved the group as a registered student organization.[66]

Father Schlegel also inherited the predicament of preserving the Jesuit identity. He comprehended the fact that the "long black line [was] getting shorter and grayer." At Creighton a "disturbing" coincidence existed, in that it sustained a population of sixty-six Jesuits and that number came "close to the average age in the community." The situation meant fewer Jesuits in the residence halls and in the classrooms; the three Jesuits in the theology department composed only 20 percent of its faculty. In addition, Fr. Schlegel predicted that the board would soon have to amend the University by-law mandating a Jesuit president. Thus, the members of the Society of

Jesus had "to entrust lay colleagues with the Jesuit mission." In 2002, the Association of Jesuit Colleges and Universities issued a statement, "The Role of the Society of Jesus in the Selection of a President for a U. S. Jesuit College or University." In essence, the local provincial would guide "a search that actively identifies individuals who can meet the needs and advance the mission of the Jesuit institution." That same year, law professor Ronald Volkmer, for the second time in a decade, chaired a committee that worked to reinforce the "Jesuit identity by relocating campus ministry," that is, "making campus ministry more visible" and "enhancing the role of St. John's as a central spiritual and liturgical center." The committee hoped "to attract students from different faiths to Creighton while 'fostering a vibrant Jesuit presence.'" Then, in 2003, an all-University committee headed by the Reverend Bert Thelen, S.J., received a $2 million grant from the Lily Endowment "to help prepare a new generation of leaders for church and society." The Cardoner Project, named "for the river where Ignatius of Loyola received profound insights about his own vocation," would include programs in which students, faculty and staff could investigate their vocation. In terms of the project, "vocation" meant, "discerning one's connection to God, whether one's career is in medicine, business, education or the church." Thus, in numerous ways the Jesuits sought to preserve their identity and to instill a sense of the Society's "apostolic work" in the lay faculty and administrators who would have to help advance it.[67]

The new administration had to confront another old problem, the competition to attract competent undergraduates. Father Schlegel stated he appreciated his predecessor's attempts to "avoid substantial tuition increases," but he felt that Creighton was "priced dangerously low which, in his opinion, could lead to some very negative repercussions." Thus, the board agreed to a 4 to 6 percent increase, plus a new freshman advance of about $1,700, which placed the University eighteenth on the list of twenty-eight Jesuit institutions of higher learning. In the spring of 2001, the board learned of a projected budget deficit due to higher costs for utilities and snow removal, and a tuition shortfall of $1 million (undergraduate freshmen enrollment had plunged by 141). Gifts from directors and their companies and a $100,000 bequest reduced the deficit to approximately $500,000. In an attempt to control the cost of utilities, the University contracted with Cogenex to design "performance energy conservation measures that would be paid for from the energy savings" (e.g., contract cost $4.27 million, the company "guaranteed energy cost savings of not less than $475,000 annually over a 15-year period"). The University also began to plan a new $200 million campaign "to grow its endowment and to underwrite its operations through gift income."[68]

However, the September 11, 2001, terrorist attacks delayed the campaign's launch and the unstable stock market fell precipitously, pushing the endowment down further; it had stood at $195 million at the end of the fiscal year, but descended to $188 million in December 2001. The board approved another round of tuition increases, 4 to 7 percent and a "new-freshmen undergraduate" boost of 9 percent. Nonetheless, freshman enrollment began an upswing: CCAS up sixty-two, Nursing up thirteen, but CoBA down twenty, for an overall recovery of fifty-six. The stock market remained in its bearish mood and the University restructured its portfolio, which then performed as well as (at times better than) the standard benchmarks (e.g., down 8.5 percent in FY 2001–02). The University ended the fiscal year with a balanced budget, which resulted from cuts in expenses, especially in the areas of "unfilled positions and other reductions in Academic Affairs and Health Sciences."[69]

The administration realized that faculty compensation stood "somewhat behind the national norm" and that some new hires had higher salaries "than some ongoing faculty"; that is, the problem of "compression," where some faculty had been hired at low salaries some years before and had received minimal annual raises, while newly hired faculty gained higher starting salaries at nationally competitive rates. Still, to control costs, the 2002–03 budget called for "no funding for general merit increase for employees—essentially freezing salaries at current levels." Yet, in October the administration foresaw a shortfall of $750,000 looming and requested reductions from all departments. That year, however, "for the first time in its history" the University had undertaken "a five-year financial plan." It paid dividends, resulting in a balanced budget for "the current year and succeeding fiscal year." Burgeoning freshman enrollment bolstered budget stability—in the fall 2003, freshmen in Nursing went up twenty, CoBA forty, and the CCAS fifty. Cautiously, as part of the extended planning, "The cuts that have been made to budgets for these two years are permanent and ongoing. Further cuts will be reviewed and analyzed as the need arises." While strategic belt-tightening proceeded, the freeze on faculty salaries did not; Fr. Schlegel's announcement of a 4 percent raise was "well received."[70]

While the administration and the board struggled to right the budget, they also continued the redesign of the campus master plan. By the end of 1997, the University had "very nearly" completed the initial phase of the Creighton 2000 plan. Father Morrison had appointed a committee to begin the "process to update and rethink elements" of the plan blueprint and to deal "with such future projects as renovation of Rigge Science and Criss II and III." By 2000, the renovation plans included the construction of a new science building; the existing facilities were "taxed to their limits due to a dramatic increase in the number of students taking science courses, the addition of new departments and advances in technology." Fifty-five percent of Creighton undergraduates majored in a science, compared to the national average of 5 percent. Additionally, the medical school lacked lab space, which hindered hiring faculty, and it needed research faculty to increase its revenue. The Nursing School contributed to the project with a $1.2 million federal grant supporting its accelerated program—the project included the classrooms and labs used by nursing students. In October, the board approved a $48 million project for the remodeling of Criss II and III and Rigge Science, and a new science building, expressing "a strong desire" to make it "more architecturally pleasing."[71]

Construction of the new complex began in 2001, and it eliminated the Eppley-Rigge parking lot. Three new student lots opened at properties purchased on Burt and Cuming streets east of campus; new, larger twenty-two-person shuttle buses transported students back and forth. The science departments moved into their new spaces during the Christmas recess in January 2003. The five-story, 82,000-square-foot structure adjoined the Criss and Rigge buildings still undergoing renovation. It included offices, multi-purpose classrooms, lecture halls, teaching and research laboratories, "shared core facilities for research equipment and instruments," and common spaces for students. On February 1, 2003, Lt. Col. Michael Anderson (M.S. in physics, 1990), who had previously served as a mission specialist on a flight of the shuttle "Discovery" in January 1998, perished with the crew of "Columbia." Subsequently, the University erected a bust of the astronaut and dedicated the plaza in front of the new complex in his honor. The new building also received a name, the Hixon-Lied Science Building, a tribute to Christina Hixson, sole trustee of the Lied Foundation, which had given generously to capital projects, and to the memory of Ernst F. Lied and his parents, Ernst M. and Ida Lied.[72]

By 1999, two new factors affected the master plan: the reconstruction of the bridges and on-off ramps of the North Freeway, and the construction of a new Omaha convention center on 10th Street between Cass and Cuming streets. With the former, the University hoped to "square off" the campus by closing Burt Street and making Cuming a two-way street. Regarding the later, in 1999 the University increased its purchase of properties east of 20th Street, and in 2001 and 2002, with Omaha voters having agreed to the bond issue for a convention center, the board approved further purchases, especially in the area now designated for a new soccer stadium. The administration also thought in terms of new housing for upperclassmen to bring them back to campus and hoped to attract student-oriented businesses to the area. The acquisitions included the OHA Burt Towers, although at this time the University did not wish to renovate the structure. Instead, on Sunday, February 2, 2003, over two thousand spectators sat in the bleachers of the baseball complex and witnessed the implosion of the forty-year-old, fifteen-story building. On the site (the southeast corner of 21st and Burt streets), Creighton constructed an apartment complex to house 250 juniors and seniors. It consisted of three connected L-shaped, three-story buildings, with an internal courtyard. The University dedicated the complex on September 2, 2004 as the Davis Square. The name honored the First National Bank and the two families that succeeded Edward Creighton and Herman Kountze as officer-owners: the family of the Omaha pioneer and subsequent director of the bank, Thomas Davis; and the family of John Lauritzen, including his son Bruce, who currently headed the bank and served on Creighton's board.[73]

As Creighton University stood poised to celebrate its 125th anniversary, it had established new boundaries that stretched from 16th Street on the east (making it part of a "North Downtown" development propelled by the Quest Center) to 33rd Street on the west (becoming part of the planning for "Destination Midtown"). It had begun as a single building on a hilltop on the western edge of a mushrooming river town, dispensing a European curriculum. To remain viable it had to assimilate, to become American. It did so culturally, as the Jesuits of the Missouri Province altered the *Ratio Studiorum* during the early twentieth century, eventually replacing it with the "American Plan" in 1920. Creighton did not adopt completely the idea of an all-elective course of study; it maintained a required "core" of the liberal arts. Although the University adopted the American culture (while preserving its basic values), in the nature of the process of assimilation, it remained outside the mainstream of Protestant-controlled institutions in the United States. Following World War II, however, Fr. Carl Reinert made the connections that facilitated the structural assimilation of the University into Omaha and the region. Thereafter, Fr. Linn oversaw its completion, with the separation of the University and the Jesuit corporations, and the creation of the lay-dominated Board of Directors. Fathers Linn and Labaj administered continued institutional growth, while addressing the militant issues of the "era of confrontation." Then, during his record-breaking tenure, Fr. Morrison guided the institution to middle-class status and issued the challenge to become "the outstanding comprehensive Jesuit university in the United States" by 2000.

When he stepped down as president, Fr. Morrison proclaimed the objective accomplished; *U.S. News & World Report* had listed Creighton as the number one comprehensive university in the Midwest four years running. His successors chose to redefine the elite goal in less contentious terms. On March 19, 2003, Fr. Schlegel released "Project 125," which launched the anniversary commemoration and provided "the guiding principles for our strategic planning and budgeting process for the next five years." Its "vision statement" declared, "Creighton University will be a national leader in preparing students in a faith-based setting for responsible leadership, professional distinction, and committed citizenship." The "mission statement" emphasized the Catholic faith, the Jesuit tradition, and the comprehensive nature of the University. Project 125 also represented "the five primary themes that will shape our collective future":

(1) Enhance Creighton's national identity and focus its dedication to mission
(2) Nurture Creighton's academic excellence
(3) Create a diverse human community of students, faculty and staff
(4) Provide a dynamic environment [services, programs, technology] for students
(5) Ensure overall financial stability for Creighton University and its schools and colleges

Creighton University had evolved from a grade school with a pretentious name to a prestigious institution. It had attained the American Dream and had a strategic plan to extend it. While of necessity, the Jesuit administrators had to forsake the *Ratio Studiorum*, they did not disavow their values. Although modern education has become extremely scientific and technological, the liberal arts remain the focal point of Jesuit undergraduate education and Project 125 proclaims the historic Ignatian objective (to prepare moral, Christian gentlemen) in modern American terms—to train moral, spiritual people to become leaders of their communities.[74]

Notes

Preface

1. Kathleen A. Mahoney, *Catholic Higher Education in Protestant America: the Jesuits and Harvard in the Age of the University* (Baltimore: The Johns Hopkins University Press, 2003), p. 2.

2. Ibid., pp. 12, 236.

3. Philip Gleason, *Contending with Modernity: Catholic Higher Education in the Twentieth Century* (New York: Oxford University Press, 1995), pp. 21–61.

Chapter One

1. Letters, John B. Creighton to Bowdern, January 15, 1937; Bowdern to William McCabe, S.J., September 30, 1944, and McCabe to Bowdern, October 30, 1944; "Creighton Arms," drawing and text document, Vertical File, Creighton University President's Office (PVF).

2. Thomas Russell Creighton, "Creighton—Its Origin As a Surname," (New Haven: privately printed manuscript, 1960), pp. 3–5; letter from D. R. H. Crichton to William H. Creighton, May 6, 1982, both in the Genealogy File, Rare Book Room, Reinert Alumni Library (RAL), Creighton University.

3. Donald M. Schlegel, "The Creighton or McCraren Family, Catholic Pioneers in Ohio and Omaha," Barquilla de la Santa Maria, Bulletin of the Catholic Record Society-diocese of Columbus, XIX (October, 1994), p. 78, and XIX (November, 1994), p. 92.

4. Ibid. XIX (October, 1994), pp. 77, 79, 81; National Archives Microfilm Publications, "Population Schedules of the Fourth Census of the United States, 1820," Belmont County, Ohio, and "Population Schedules of the Sixth Census of the United States, 1840," Licking County, Ohio. Due to the poor print quality of the microfilm of the 1830 census for the relevant Ohio counties, I was unable to find most members of the Creighton family.

5. Oral Interview of Felix McShane, April 28, 1930, Genealogy File, RAL; Schlegel, XIX (October, 1994), pp. 77–81.

6. Schlegel, XIX (October, 1994), pp. 78–81; Eugene H. Roseboom and Francis P. Weisenburger, *A History of Ohio* (Columbus: Ohio State Archaeological and Historical Society, 1961), pp. 52–54, 73.

7. Schlegel, XIX (October, 1994), pp. 81–82; William G. Wolfe, *Stories of Guernsey County, Ohio* (Cambridge, Ohio: self-published, 1943), p. 217.

8. Schlegel, XIX (November, 1994), pp. 85–86; Felix McShane Interview; P. A. Mullens, S.J., Creighton, *Biographical Sketches of Edward Creighton, John A. Creighton, Mary Lucretia Creighton, Sarah Emily Creighton* (Omaha: Creighton University, 1901), pp. 5–9. Fr. Mullens' biography is more of a hagiography. In the Preface he wrote "[the author] feels sure that he will be pardoned if occasionally he allowed a feeling of gratitude on behalf of the institution he represents to color his pages with a glow of eulogy somewhat foreign to sober history." "Population Schedules of the Fourth Census of the United States, 1820," Belmont County,

Ohio. In the James Craton household no one was recorded under the category "foreigners not naturalized." However, in the Andrew Craton household two were. Thus, he or the matriarch Bridget or one of her other two sons John and/or Michael did not obtain citizenship by 1820.

9. "Catholic Columbian," January 12, 1895, quoted in Schlegel, XIX (November, 1994), p. 86; Mullens, pp. 9–10; Joe Koller, "Edward Creighton, Singing Wire Chief," *Golden West*, I (September, 1965), p. 18. Koller claimed "Ed, an aggressive youngster managed to get through the fifth grade in school and then became a prize fighter and took part in many matches." He did not cite sources and no other biographer mentions the specific number of years Edward remained in school or that he became a pugilist.

10. Mullens, pp. 11–12; Barbara Sorensen, "A King and a Prince Among Pioneers: Edward and John A. Creighton" (unpublished M. A. Thesis, Creighton University, 1961), pp. 13–17; *Journal of the Telegraph*, vol. III (June 1, 1870) and an unidentified clipping in the scrapbook of Mrs. A. V. Kinsler, both in the notes of Fr. Henry Casper, Creighton University Archives (CUA), RAL.

11. Mullens, pp. 7, 12; Schlegel, XIX (November, 1994), p. 87; *Journal of the Telegraph*.

12. Mullens, pp. 12–13; Sorensen, p. 25; Allen Johnson and Dumas Malone, eds., *Dictionary of American Biography* (New York: Charles Scribner's Sons, 1930), p. 535; Robert Luther Thompson, Wiring a Continent: The History of the Telegraphy Industry in the United States, 1832–1866 (Princeton: Princeton University Press, 1947) pp. 289–92.

13. Ralph G. Coad, "Irish Pioneers of Nebraska," *Nebraska History Magazine*, XVII (July–September, 1936), pp. 171–72; Alfred Sorenson, *History of Omaha From the Pioneer Days to the Present Time* (Omaha: Gibson, Miller, & Richardson, Printers, 1889) p. 216; Mullens, pp. 13–14; Sorensen, pp. 26–29.

14. Mullens, p. 13; Sorensen, p. 30; J. Sterling Morton, *Illustrated History of Nebraska*, 3 vols. (Lincoln: Jacob North & Company, 1907), vol. I, p. 628; P. Raymond Nielson, "Edward Creighton and the Pacific Telegraph," *Mid-America: An Historical Review*, XXIV (January, 1942), p. 63, note 14, p. 66; *Omaha Daily Herald*, November 7, 1874, A.M., p. 2.

15. *Journal of the Telegraph*; Nielson, p. 64; Edward Creighton Clipping File, Historical Society of Douglas County (HSDC); Diane Kirkle, "Mary Lucretia Creighton: The Woman Behind the Bequest," unpublished paper, Rare Book Room, RAL.

16. Nielson, pp. 66–67; Sorensen, pp. 49–55; Edward Creighton Clipping File, HSDC. Koller (pp. 17–9) told a fanciful story of Edward being robbed of his rifle and packhorse at Dobytown outside Ft. Kearney. He supposedly chased the thieves, but his horse fell through the ice on the Platte River. He became very ill and was taken to Denver where a physician restored his health and he continued his journey in March 1861. The saga contradicts known facts and the correct time line of the journey.

17. Nielson, p. 68. He stated that Edward paid $18,000 for his shares in Pacific Telegraph. Other sources claim he paid 10 or 15 percent of face value. Sorensen, pp. 56–59; Thompson, p. 363.

18. Sorensen, pp. 55–69; Thompson, pp. 363–68; A. T. Andreas, *A History of the State of Nebraska* (Chicago: The Western Historical Company, 1882), p. 764; Charles Brown, "My Experience on the Plains in 1861 Assisting in the Construction of the First Telegraph Line Across the Continent," unpublished diary, Archives Center, National Museum of American History, Western Union Telegraph Company Records, Series 1, Box 6A, Folders 3–4, pp. 58–60. Hereafter, Brown Diary.

19. Sorenson, p. 219; James W. Savage and John T. Bell, *History of the City of Omaha, Nebraska* (New York: Munsell & Company, 1894), pp. 596–97.

20. *Journal of the Telegraph*; Nielson, pp. 73–74; Records of Holy Sepulchre Cemetery, W. Dale Clark Library, Omaha, Nebraska.

21. Thompson, p. 370; Nielson, p. 73; Sorenson, p. 218; Sorensen, pp. 98–99.

22. Mullens, pp. 22–23; Sorensen, pp. 73–78; William E. Lass, *From the Missouri to the Great Salt Lake: An Account of Overland Freighting* (Lincoln: Nebraska State Historical Society, 1972), pp. 131–32, 165, note 53, p. 281.

23. Sorensen, pp. 95–96; Lass, pp. 183–84, 243, 238–39,

24. Mullens, p. 23; Robert H. Burns, "The Laramie Plains," *The Westerner*, VIII (May, 1945), p. 38; Marianne Brinda Beel, ed., *A History of Cherry County, Nebraska* (Cherry County Centennial Committee, 1986), p. 7; Agnes Wright Spring, *Seventy Years: A Panoramic History of the Wyoming Stock Growers Association* (Gillette: Wyoming Stock Growers Association, 1942) pp. 9–15.

25. Letter from Edward Creighton to Dr. H. Latham, April 15, 1870, included in Frank J. Burkley, *The Faded Frontier* (Omaha: Burkley Envelope & Printing Co., 1935), pp. 284–86. Burkley was a Creighton University graduate, an associate of the extended Creighton family, and had the letter in his possession at the time he published this personal reminiscence of Omaha history.

26. Sorenson, pp. 182-3, 219; Sorensen, note 45, p. 145; Morton, vol. I, p. 629; Andreas, pp. 373, 535; Beel, pp. 7, 13; Edward Creighton Clipping File, HSDC; James C. Olson and Ronald C. Naugle, *History of Nebraska* (Lincoln: University of Nebraska Press, 1997), p. 189-91; Charles S. Reece, *A History of Cherry County, Nebraska* (Simeon, Nebraska, privately published, 1945) p. 21; John Bratt, *Trials of Yesterday* (Lincoln: University of Nebraska Press, [1921] 1980), p. 191; Norbert R. Mahnken, "Ogallala—Nebraska's Cowboy Capital," *Nebraska History*, XVIII (April-June, 1947) p. 89; *History of Cheyenne County, Nebraska, 1986* (Cheyenne County History Book Committee, 1987), pp. 3, 25–26.

27. *Journal of the Telegraph;* Edward Creighton Clipping File, HSDC; Beel, p. 34; Bratt, p. 145; Brown Diary, pp. 63–64; Spring, pp. 18, 21; Sorensen, pp. 137–45; Louis Pelzer, *The Cattlemen's Frontier* (Glendale, Calif.: Arthur H. Clark, 1936), p. 154, appendix, p.10; Robert G. Athearn, *Union Pacific Country* (Chicago: Rand McNally & Co., 1971) pp. 138–39; Edward Everett Dale, *The Range Cattle Industry* (Norman: University of Oklahoma Press, 1930), pp. 78, 83; Robert H. Burns, "The Famous Heart Ranch," *The Westerner*, VIII (July, 1945) pp. 17–18.

28. *Journal of the Telegraph;* Andreas, p. 764; Savage and Bell, p. 425; Neilson, pp. 67, 73–74; Sorensen, pp. 50–54, 146. Both Neilson and Sorensen point out that Mormon historians claim no records indicate the existence of the loan to Brigham Young, but the debt is listed in the "Warrant and Inventory," Estate of Edward Creighton, Filed June 16, 1875, Douglas County, County Court, Probate Division, Estate Record C, p. 130, Nebraska State Historical Society Archive (NSHSA), Lincoln, Nebraska. Also, payments to Mary Lucretia Creighton are listed in her estate, Douglas County, County Court, Probate Division, Estate Record, vol. D, p. 19, NSHSA.

29. Mullens, p. 24; Sorensen, pp. 148–51; Morton, vol. I, p. 629; Savage and Bell, p. 254.

30. Sorensen, pp. 115-26, 148–50, 168; Omaha City Directory, 1871–72 and 1872–73.

31. Mullens, pp. 23–24, 30; Sorensen, pp. 151–58; Edward Creighton Clipping File, HSDC.

32. Mullens, p. 32; Sorenson, p. 220; Morton, vol. I, p. 629; Sorensen, pp. 31–32, 131–32.

33. Savage and Bell, p. 157; Edward Creighton Clipping File, HSDC; Edwin Fry, "The Story of Creighton," in Danny Liska, *Bigfoot 7: Our Valleys, the Niobrara and Verdigris* (Bogata, Columbia: Relikasa, Ltda, 1986), p. 526; Edward Creighton File, Cowboy Hall of Fame, Oklahoma City, Oklahoma; Eileen Lieben, "Edward Creighton, Immigrant's Son to University Founder," *Treasure Chest*, 1960 (a comic book distributed to Catholic elementary schools), CUA; Zane Grey, Western Union (New York: Harper & Brothers, 1939); Elton Perky, *Perky's Nebraska Place-Names* (Lincoln: Nebraska State Historical Society, 1982), stated "One source says the town named by Mr. Bruce in honor of John A. Creighton." The source is faulty

because John Creighton had not established himself as a prominent businessman in Omaha by 1870.

34. Mullens, p. 36; Schlegel (November, 1994), p. 88, note 27, p. 90.

35. Morton, vol. I, p. 629; Michael P. Dowling, "John A. Creighton: Benefactor of Mankind," unpublished manuscript, Rare Book Room, RAL, p. 2. Hereafter, John Mss.

36. Mullens, pp. 36–37; Sorensen, p. 27; Burkley, p. 84; Morton, vol. I, p. 629.

37. Mullens, pp. 38–39; Sorensen, pp. 75–76; Morton, vol. I, p. 629.

38. Mullens, pp. 39–43; Sorensen, pp. 77–88, 136.

39. Mullens, pp. 44–45; Sorensen, pp. 131–34; Edward Creighton File, Midwest Jesuit Archives (MJA), St. Louis, Missouri. Thanks to Mary (William) Lindsay for explaining that at the time Catholics had to fast from midnight in order to receive the Eucharist.

40. Mullens, pp. 45–47; Sorensen, p. 133; Omaha City Directory, 1866 through 1876; Will of Mary L. Creighton, Vol. D, pp. 18–41, 259–60.

41. Charles Barron McIntosh, *The Nebraska Sandhills: the Human Landscape* (Lincoln: University of Nebraska Press, 1996), pp. 101, 121; Mullens, p. 47; Beel, pp. 9, 34; Mahnken, pp. 94–98; Coad, pp. 176–77; A. B. Wood, "The Coad Brothers: Panhandle Cattle Kings," Nebraska History, XIX (January–March, 1938), p. 41; Mark Coad was Long Jim Creighton's son-in-law.

42. Savage and Bell, pp. 597, 609; "Omaha Stockyards: A Century of Marketing Commemorative Book, 1884–1984," privately printed, 1984.

43. Savage and Bell, pp. 112, 286; John A. Creighton Clipping File, HSDC; Richard Orr, O & CB: Streetcars of Omaha and Council Bluffs (Omaha: Published by Richard Orr, 1996), pp. 52, 102-3, 107-11.

44. Morton, vol. I, p. 630; Dowling, John Mss, p. 3; Orr, p. 152; John A. Creighton Clipping File, HSDC; "Omaha's Magnificent Theatres," printed by the Western Heritage Museum, no date; Omaha World-Herald, October 7, 1987, Metro Extra, p. 1.

45. Mullens, p. 52; Savage and Bell, p. 112; Morton, vol. I, p. 630–31; Dowling, John Mss, pp. 11, 66–68; Charles W. Martin, "Omaha 1868–1869: Selections from Letters of Joseph Barker," *Nebraska History* 59 (Winter 1978), pp. 510–11; A *North Omaha Sun* article on March 16, 1961, claimed John participated in a lynching, but the dates are not correct and an *Omaha World-Herald* article on March 28, 1986, claimed that on October 31, 1883, the *Omaha Bee* had reported that he had kicked a waterworks engineer in the behind several times on Farnam Street. The author could not find that article and research shows that type of behavior was associated with Long Jim Creighton. The articles are in the John A. Creighton Clipping File, HSDC.

46. John A. Creighton Clipping File, HSDC; Dowling, John Mss, pp. 8, 18–26.

47. Mullens, p. 50; John A. Creighton Clipping File, HSDC; Dowling, John Mss, pp. 41–42; Poor Clares File, CUA; Steven Szmercsanyi, *History of the Catholic Church in Northeast Nebraska* (Omaha: The Catholic Voice Publishing Company, 1983), pp. 466–67.

48. Dowling, John Mss, pp. 51–81, 114–31; John A. Creighton Clipping File, HSDC; *Dictionary of American Biography*, pp. 535-6.

49. Mullens, p. 9; Sorensen, pp. 78, 67–68; Brown Diary, pp. 83, 120–21; Andreas, pp. 796, 800; Records of Holy Sepulchre Cemetery; "Population Schedules of the Eighth Census of the United States, 1860," Douglas County, Nebraska. The ages listed for the brothers at various times conflict. The 1860 census listed John as 25, although he was born in 1831. The same census listed Joseph as 30, thus born in 1830, but the Holy Sepulchre record listed him as 68 at his death in 1893. Seemingly, the census taker transposed the ages of the brothers. Also, that census listed James as 40, making him older that Edward, recorded as 38 years old in Montgomery County, Ohio, in 1860. Mary Shelby sued her father's estate over the bequest to the Bishop but the court ruled against her (NSHSA, Douglas County Court, Probate Record, vol.

71, p. 512). She also sued John A. Creighton, claiming he "swindled" her father out of "a great deal of property." She lost the case. *Historia Domas* [a somewhat daily chronicle of Creighton University, December 6, 1877, to August 31, 1888, and Summer 1911 to May 1, 1930, written by various administrators], entry for March 7, 1898.

50. Creighton Family Clipping File, HSDC; Genealogy File, CUA; Records of Holy Sepulchre Cemetery; Omaha City Directory, 1867 through 1880; "Population Schedules of the Seventh Census of the United States, 1850," Clark County, Ohio. In 1850 the census listed Francis as 34, thus born in 1816, but the Records of Holy Sepulchre Cemetery listed him as age 54 at death in 1873, while the Douglas County Death Records at the W. Dale Clark Library, Omaha, Nebraska, state that he died on August 1, 1873, at 57 years, 3 months, and 6 days from an "inflammation of bowels."

51. Creighton Family Clipping File, John D. Creighton Clipping File, and Frederick Nash Clipping File, HSDC; Genealogy File, CUA; Savage and Bell, pp. 172, 278; Omaha City Directory, 1900 through 1915.

52. Sorenson, pp. 31, 440; Savage and Bell, pp. 81, 95, 112, 215, 267, 313, 397, 495; Schlegel (October, 1994), pp. 79–80; Felix McShane interview; Morton, vol. II, note 1, p. 449; Lass, p. 99; Andreas, p. 740; Charles Creighton Clipping File and Creighton Family Clipping File, HSDC; *Creighton University Alumnews*, May, 1978; "Population Schedules of the Eighth Census of the United States, 1860," Douglas County, Nebraska.

53. Andreas, p. 782; Sorensen, pp. 8–9; Brown Diary, p. 91; *True Voice* (Omaha), December 11, 1908, p. 5.

54. Mullens, p. 19; Andreas, pp. 769, 783; John B. Furay Clipping File, HSDC; Genealogy Files, CUA; Omaha City Directory, 1867 through 1918; M. P. Dowling, *Creighton University, Reminiscences of the First Twenty-Five Years* (Omaha: Press of Burkley Printing Company, 1903), p. 180.

55. Andreas, p. 783; Sorensen, p. 7; James H. McShane Clipping File and Thomas J. McShane Clipping File, HSDC; Thomas McShane note card in Casper notes, CUA; Genealogy Files, CUA; Omaha City Directory, 1867 through 1883.

56. Andreas, p. 783; Sorensen, p. 7; Felix McShane Clipping File and Thomas S. McShane Clipping File, HSDC; Genealogy Files, CUA; Omaha City Directory, 1867 through 1920.

57. Dowling, *Reminiscences*, p. 177; Morton, vol. II, p. 451; Savage and Bell, pp. 81–82; Sorenson, pp. 324–26; John A. McShane Clipping File, HSDC; Genealogy File, CUA; "Omaha Stockyards Commemorative Book," pp. 2–5; Omaha City Directory, 1874 through 1923. Because all their living children were in Omaha when the patriarch Thomas McShane died in 1885, his body was brought from Ohio to Omaha and buried in the Creighton family plot at Holy Sepulchre Cemetery. Alice moved to Omaha and when she died in 1891 she was laid to rest next to her husband. Their names are inscribed on the north side of the Creighton obelisk.

58. Mullens, p. 55; Sorensen, pp. 28–30; letter from Kevin J. Smith, Dayton Collection Librarian, to Mrs. Peggy Troy, Philosophy Department, Creighton University, February 2, 1982 (Smith provided material on the Wareham family culled from city directories and censuses to the secretary of the philosophy department seeking information for a committee establishing an award in honor of Mary Lucretia Creighton); Marriage Certificate, Probate Court, Montgomery County, Ohio, Ohio Historical Society Archives (the date on the record is October 4, 1856, but that was a civil record and the church wedding was probably three days later); Records of Holy Sepulchre Cemetery; an inscription on St. Joseph's altar at St. John's Church dedicated to David A. Wareham provides the date of death.

59. Mullens, p. 56.

60. Mullens, pp. 59–60; Creighton Family Clipping File and Edward Creighton Clipping File, HSDC; *Omaha Daily Herald*, January 25, 1876, A.M., p. 2.

61. Alfred Sorenson, "Biographical Sketch of Edward Creighton," Nebraska History Magazine, XVII (July–September, 1936), pp. 168–69; Dowling, *Reminiscences,* pp. 45–46; Will of Mary L. Creighton, vol. D, pp. 18–41, 259–60.

62. Mullens, pp. 63–65; Marriage Records, Douglas County, HSDC; "Reminiscences of Early Omaha," *Nebraska History Magazine,* XVII (July–September, 1936), p. 205.

63. Dowling, John Mss., p. 11; *Omaha World-Herald* clippings, no dates and Memoranda: N. P. Dodge, Jr. to Alden Aust, et. al., May 9, 1962; Carl Reinert to Henry Linn, November 15, 1965, and January 13, 1965; Ralph E. Svoboda to Henry Linn, November 1, 1965, John Creighton House File, PVF.

64. Mullens, pp. 67–68; Sorensen, p. 130; John A. Creighton Clipping File, HSDC.

65. Creighton Wills File, PVF; Will of Sarah E. Creighton, Douglas County, County Court, Probate Division, Estate Record, vol. I, p. 192, NSHSA.

66. Sorensen, p. 130; Omaha City Directory, 1889 through 1908; *Creighton University Alumnews,* August, 1985; A. V. Kinsler Clipping File, HSDC; *True Voice,* October 30, 1908, p. 5. The Wareham sisters' brother Philip spent one or two years in Omaha in 1879–80 working as a stationary engineer, but the other brother, George, never left Dayton. The family's mother, Emily, also never left Dayton, not even to attend the funerals of her daughters, although they had visited her regularly.

67. Lucylle H. Evans, *The Good Samaritan of the Northwest; Anthony Ravalli, S.J., 1812–1884* (Stevensville: Montana Creative Consultants, 1981), pp. 174, 340–44; V. Rev. Victor F. O'Daniel, O.P., *The Dominican Province of Saint Joseph, Historic-Biographical Studies* (Somerset, OH: The Rosary Press, 1942), p. 290, cited by Schlegel, (November, 1994), note 26, p. 90; "Reminiscences of John B. Furay [Jr.]," unpublished paper, 1950, Creighton University President's Office.

68. Dowling, *Reminiscences,* p. 46; William J. McGucken, S.J., *The Jesuits and Education* (New York: Bruce Publishing Company, 1932), pp. 1–8; M. P. Dowling, "John A. Creighton, Founder," *Woodstock Letters,* vol. 33 (1904), p. 64.

69. Allan P. Farrell, S.J., *The Jesuit Code of Liberal Education* (Milwaukee: Bruce Publishing Company, 1938), pp. XI, 431–39; George E. Ganss, The Jesuit Educational Tradition and Saint Louis University (St. Louis: Saint Louis University Press, 1969), pp. 17–23; Edward A. Fitzpatrick, ed., *St. Ignatius and the Ratio Studiorum* (New York: McGraw-Hill, 1933), pp. 13–15, 19, 40; *The Constitutions of the Society of Jesus,* Part IV, chapter 15, number 4.

70. McGucken, pp. 4, 19–22, 28–37, 130–32, 163; Fitzpatrick, pp. 28–33; Robert Schwickerath, S.J., *Jesuit Education, Its History and Principles Viewed in the Light of Modern Educational Problems* (St. Louis: B. Herder, 1903), pp. 136–39; Edward J. Power, *Catholic Higher Education in America: A History* (New York: Appleton-Century-Crofts, 1972), pp. 144–45.

71. McGucken, pp. 82–83; Gilbert J. Garraghan, S.J., *The Jesuits of the Middle United States,* 3 vols. (New York: America Press, 1938), vol. III, p. 461; Roland Reichmuth, S.J., notes, CUA; "Historical Note," Archdiocese of Omaha Archival Collection (AOA), Chancery, Omaha, Nebraska.

Chapter Two

1. Frederick Rudolf, *The American College and University, A History* (New York: Alfred A. Knopf, 1962), pp. 3, 25–26, 34–43, 51–55, 88, 137–54, 246–49, 264–86; Richard Storr, *The Beginnings of Graduate Education in America* (New York: Arno Press and the New York Times, 1969 [1953]), p. 3.

2. George M. Marsden, *The Soul of the American University: From Protestant Establishment to Established Nonbelief* (New York: Oxford University Press, 1994), p. vii; Power, pp. 6–7, 42–54, 122.

3. Rudolph, *American College and University,* pp. 55, 88; Power, pp. 125–58, 181–86.

4. Szmrecsanyi, pp. 2-3; Henry W. Casper, S.J., *The History of the Catholic Church in Nebraska,* 3 vols. (Milwaukee: Bruce Publishing Company, 1960–66), vol. 2, pp. ix, 8–22, 32–52, 99–104, 148–52, 183–84.

5. Olson and Naugle, pp. 97–100, 256–57; Kathryn Margaret Holland, "A History of the Omaha Public School System," unpublished Master's Thesis, Creighton University, 1933, pp. 4–15, 25, 54–64.

6. Casper, vol. II, pp. 59–90, 129–37, 178–79; Omaha City Directory 1867 through 1880; Mrs. M. B. Newton, "History of Education in Omaha," Transactions and Reports of the Nebraska State Historical Society, vol. III (1892), pp. 61–62; Joseph H. Ostdiek, "Catholic Education in Omaha, Past, Present, and Future," unpublished Master's Thesis, Creighton University, 1927, pp. 4–12; Sr. Mary Edmund Croghan, R. S. M., *Sisters of Mercy of Nebraska, 1864–1910* (Washington, D.C.: Catholic University of America Press, 1942), pp. 16–19, 126; William P. Leahy, *Adapting to America: Catholics, Jesuits, and Higher Education in the Twentieth Century* (Washington, D.C.: Georgetown University Press, 1991), p. 11.

7. Olson and Naugle, pp. 98, 257–59; Robert E. Knoll, *Prairie University: A History of the University of Nebraska* (Lincoln: University of Nebraska Press, 1995), pp. 2–10.

8. Rudolph, *American College and University,* p. 486.

9. *Omaha Daily Bee,* March 22, 1877, Casper notes; Letter, James O'Connor to Thomas O'Neill, S.J., April 15, 1877, Creighton file, MJA.

10. Dowling, *Reminiscences,* p. 55; Letters, O'Neill to O'Connor, April 20, 1877, July 11, 1877, and November 11, 1877, O'Connor file, AOA; Letter, O'Connor to O'Neill, April 24, 1877, Creighton file, MJA; *Historia Domas,* December 6, 1877; unidentified newspaper clipping in Kinsler scrapbook, Casper notes; Omaha Herald, April 3, 1877, AOA; Garraghan, vol. III, pp. 464–67.

11. *Historia Domas,* December 7, 10, 16, and 19, 1877; *Omaha Daily Herald,* December 20, 1877, Creighton Clipping File, HSDC.

12. Letters, O'Neill to O'Connor, November 10, 1877, November 11, 1877, and Shaffel to O'Connor January 18, 1878, O'Connor file, AOA; Letters, O'Connor to O'Neill, November 16, 1877, and November 7, 1877, and "historical sketches," Creighton File, MJA; *Historia Domas,* December 10 and 15, 1877, and January 8, April [?], July 23, and July 31, 1878; William F. Rigge, "The First Faculty," unpublished reminiscence, 1903, PVF.

13. William Francis Rigge, "Memoirs of Creighton University, 1879–1927," (serialized in *The Creighton Alumnus* (*TCA*), December, 1937–June, 1939), January, 1938, p. 4; Fr. William F. Rigge, S.J., "Year One at Creighton," unpublished reminiscence, 1903, PVF.

14. Rigge, "Year one"; Rigge, "Memoirs," *TCA,* January, 1938, p. 2–3; Fr. John B. Furay, Jr., S.J., "Reminiscences of John B. Furay," unpublished paper, 1950, pp. 7–10, PVF.

15. Dowling, *Reminiscences,* p. 58; Furay, "Reminiscences," pp. 5–6; Rigge, "Memoirs," *TCA,* January, 1938, p. 4; letter, Shaffel to O'Connor, February 26, 1878, O'Connor file, AOA.

16. Unidentified clipping, Kinsler scrapbook, Casper notes.

17. Dowling, *Reminiscences,* pp. 54–55, quotes a letter by Higgins; Furay, "Reminiscences," pp. 14–5; interview with Fr. T. J. Smith, S.J., July 27, 1955, Casper notes.

18. Dowling, *Reminiscences,* pp. 11–12, 57–59; Garraghan, p. 467; Rigge, "First Faculty" and "Year One"; *Historia Domas,* August 6 and 22, 1878; "First faculty," Casper notes.

19. Dowling, *Reminiscences,* p. 58; Furay, "Reminiscence," p. 13; Rigge, "First Faculty" and "First Year"; "First faculty," Casper notes.

20. Dowling, *Reminiscences,* p. 58; Furay, "Reminiscence," p. 13; Omaha City Directory, 1870 through 1880.

21. *Omaha Daily Herald,* September 3, 1878, p. 8; *Historia Domas,* September 2, 1878.

22. Garraghan, p. 467; Rudolph, *American College and University*, pp. 436–37; Rigge, "Memoirs," *TCA*, April, 1938, p. 2; Furay, "Reminiscence," pp. 3–4; *Historia Domas*, August 30, September 2, October 1, and November 18, 1878, and January 6, 1879; Smith interview, Casper notes.

23. Catalogue of Creighton College, 1881–82. After 1909, the publication became the *Creighton University Bulletin* and all volumes catalogued with the latter designation. Hereafter, cited as *CUB*, with the appropriate school or college identified.

24. *Historia Domas*, October 16 and November 14, 1878, and March 25, 26, and 31, April 9 and 22, and May 27, 1879.

25. *Historia Domas*, September 6, November 28, and 29, 1878, and April 25 and 29, May 30, and November 28, 1879, and May 30, 1881; Rigge, "First Faculty"; Rev. William Rigge, S.J., "Log Book," chronicle of handwritten notes on loose sheets, September 6 and 7, 1878, and April 24, 1879; Dorothy Dustin, *Omaha & Douglas County: A Panoramic History* (Woodland Hills, Calif.: Windsor Publications, 1980), p. 55.

26. Rigge, "First Faculty"; *Historia Domas*, September 8 and 21, 1878, and September 12, 1880; "Opening of Creighton College," Casper notes.

27. Rigge, "First Faculty"; Rigge, "Log Book," November 5 and 17, 1878, January 23 and May 4, 1879, and November 3, 1881; *Historia Domas*, October 11, 1878, February 2 and November 10, 1879, and November 3, 1881; "Opening of Creighton College," Casper notes; Letters, William H. McCabe, S.J., to Henry L. Snyder, March 22 and March 28, 1947, Colors folder, PVF.

28. Dowling, *Reminiscences*, pp. 59, 197; Rigge, "First Faculty" and "First Year"; Furay, "Reminiscence," p. 10; *Historia Domas*, February 18, 1879.

29. Unidentified clipping from Kinsler scrapbook, "early days," Casper notes; *Historia Domas*, June 16 and 25, 1879.

30. Dowling, *Reminiscences*, p. 59; Savage and Bell, p. 265; *Historia Domas*, April 23 and May 22, 1880; Rigge, "Memoirs," *TCA*, February, 1938, pp. 2–3.

31. Letters, J. M. Woolworth to E. A. Higgins, S.J., July 16, 1879, Omaha-Creighton file, MJA; Higgins to O'Connor, July 8, 1879, O'Connor file, AOA.

32. Rudolph, *American College and University*, pp. 336–44; Dowling, *Reminiscences*, pp. 46–48; "Incorporation," Casper notes.

33. Dowling, *Reminiscences*, 53–55; "Incorporation," and "growth and development," Casper notes; Letters, Higgins to O'Connor, November 20, 1879, and December 4, 1879, O'Connor file, AOA; *Historia Domas*, June 23 and 30, 1880; M. P. Dowling, "John A. Creighton, Founder," *Woodstock Letters*, vol. 33, p. 66; Frederick Rudolph, *Curriculum: A History of the American Undergraduate Course of Study since 1636* (San Francisco: Jossey-Bass Publishers, 1977), pp. 146–47.

34. Dowling, *Reminiscences*, pp. 161–63; Dowling, John Mss., p. 36; Letter, Michael P. Dowling to Fr. Provincial, August 23, 1888, Omaha-Creighton University file, MJA; *Historia Domas*, January 21, 1882; CCC, 1881–82, 1882–83, 1883–84, 1884–85, 1886–87.

35. James M. Vosper, "A history of Selected Factors in the Development of Creighton University," unpublished dissertation, University of Nebraska, 1976, pp. 29–31, 80, 189–90; "Growth and development," Casper notes.

36. Dowling, *Reminiscences*, pp. 64–65, 84–85; *Historia Domas*, May 9 and November 24, 1881, and January 11 and 13, 1882; CCC, 1881-82.

37. Dowling, *Reminiscences*, p. 56; Garraghan, pp. 470–71; Letter, L. Bushart, S.J. to O'Connor, March 21, 1883, O'Connor file, AOA; *Historia Domas*, August 9, 1885.

38. Dowling, *Reminiscences*, p. 110; Rudolph, *Curriculum*, pp. 147, 218; Rigge, "Memoirs," *TCA*, February, 1938, p. 4; *Historia Domas*, June 28, 1882; CCC, 1882.

39. Dowling, *Reminiscences,* pp. 62, 109; Rudolph, *Curriculum,* pp. 181–82; Vosper, p. 30; CCC, 1883-84.

40. CCC, 1883-84; Woodstock Letters, Vol. 13, 1884, pp. 162–63.

41. Dowling, *Reminiscences,* pp. 87-8; Rudolph, *Curriculum,* p. 104–6; CCC, 1883–84.

42. Dowling, *Reminiscences,* p. 62; Rigge, "Memoirs," *TCA,* January, 1938, p. 4, and April, 1938, pp. 3–5.

43. Dowling, *Reminiscences,* pp. 61, 90–91; Rigge, "Memoirs," *TCA,* April, 1938, p. 5, and May, 1938, p. 11; CCC, 1881–82 and 1885–86; "Varia," Woodstock Letters, vol. 15, 1886, p. 338.

44. Dowling, *Reminiscences,* pp. 93–97; Vosper, p. 95; Rigge, "Memoirs," *TCA,* January, 1938, p. 4, and June, 1938, pp. 9–11; CCC, 1886–87.

45. CCC, 1886–87.

46. Dowling, *Reminiscences,* pp. 82–83; Rigge, "Memoirs," *TCA,* February, 1938, p. 5; CCC, 1881–82 and 1886–87; *Historia Domas,* December 19, 1881, January 23, February 8, March 1 and September 4, 1882, and November 2, 1886.

47. Dowling, *Reminiscences,* pp. 59, 190–91; *Historia Domas,* September 7, 1885.

48. Dowling, *Reminiscences,* p. 79; *Historia Domas,* September 20, 22, and 23, 1880, May 21 and 28, September 26, and October 1, 1881, January 18 and September 15, 1882, and November 27, 1885.

49. CCC, 1884-85 and 1885–86.

50. Dowling, *Reminiscences,* pp. 61, 74, 79–80; Rigge, "Memoirs," January, 1938, p. 4; Rigge, "Log," May 22. September 29, and October 4, 1880, and May 3, 1881; *Historia Domas,* September 9, 1880, September 29 and October 25, 1881, September 27, 1883, and May 23 and October 13, 1885. The May 29, 1925, issue of the student newspaper, *The Creightonian,* incorrectly pictured the 1897 baseball team as the first at the University.

51. Dowling, *Reminiscences,* p. 198; *Historia Domas,* March 15, 1885; CCC, 1881–82,1884–85, and 1885–86; Rigge, "Log," January 3, 1884.

52. CCC, 1885–86 and 1886–87; *Compendium of the Eleventh Census* (Washington, D.C.: Government Printing Office, 1894), Part I, p. 559.

53. Rigge, "Memoirs," *TCA,* December, 1937, pp. 1–2, and January, 1938, pp. 2–3; Rigge, "Log," August 7, September 10, and October 10 and November 3, 1884, May 5, 1885, and October 22, 1886; *Historia Domas,* November 18 and November 22, 1886.

54. Rigge, "Log," August 3 and August 20, 1885; *Historia Domas,* July 27, 1882, and August 3, 11, and 14, 1885.

55. Rigge, "Memoirs," *TCA,* January, 1938, pp. 3–4, and February, 1938, pp. 3–4; *Historia Domas,* October 4, 1885, and February 27 and March 2 and 7, 1887.

56. Rudolph, *Curriculum,* p. 3; Garraghan, vol. 3, pp. 117–8, 506; *Historia Domas,* December 16 and 30, 1886; "Circulars of the Reverend Fathers Provincial," in Committee on Studies, 1893–1920, MJA (despite the title the compilation includes circulars from 1886–88).

57. CCC, 1887-88; "Supplement to the Report of the Central Committee on Studies to Reverend Father Provincial," Reports of Committees of Studies, Missouri Province, MJA; McGucken, p. 185.

58. Leahy, p. 15; Rudolph, *Curriculum,* pp. 206–12.

59. Dowling, *Reminiscences,* p. 194; CCC, 1887–88; *Historia Domas,* September 17, 1887, September 3, 1888, and September 2 and 19, 1889.

60. Dowling, *Reminiscences,* p. 80; Rudolph, *Curriculum,* p. 122; Rigge, "Log," May 24, 1888; *Historia Domas,* February 17, March 24, September 5, 18 and 19, and October 16, 1888.

61. Rigge, "Memoirs," *TCA,* January, 1938, pp. 2–5; *Historia Domas,* June 14, 1877, and October 16, 1888, and May 6, 1890; House Consultors Minute Book, 1888–1928 (HCM), November 7, 1888, April 24, 1889, and May 5, 1890. "By the Constitution of the Society of Jesus, the

Rector of a Jesuit House is obliged to meet regularly with a board of consultors (4 Jesuits) who assist him in making decisions that affect the Community and the apostolate." At first, the Omaha house ignored the responsibility, but in 1888, the Provincial mandated that minutes be kept.

62. "Omaha-*Historia Domas*," MJA; Rigge, "Log," January 3, 1888; *Historia Domas*, November 12, 1887, April 27 and May 1, 1888, and January 25, 1889, and January 13 and 27, 1890.

63. Dowling, *Reminiscences*, pp. 162, 175; "St. John's Church," Casper notes; Rigge, "Memoirs," *TCA*, April, 1938, p. 3; *Historia Domas*, March 5 and April 2, 4, and 5, 1887; Rev. Roland J. Reichmuth, S.J., *St. John's, 1887–1987* (Omaha: Creighton University, 1987), p. 4.

64. Dowling, *Reminiscences*, pp. 105–6; Reichmuth, pp. 1-2; *Omaha DailyWorld*, June 27, 1887, Creighton Clipping File, HSDC.

65. Dowling, *Reminiscences*, p. 106; Reichmuth, p. 4; Omaha Daily World, evening edition, May 7, 1888, p. 1; *Omaha Daily Bee*, morning edition, May 7, 1888, p. 8; Clare McDermot, ed., *The Creighton University: Its Story, 1878–1937* (Omaha: Creighton University, 1937), p. 4.

66. Mullens, p. 67; Dowling, *Reminiscences*, p. 58; Reichmuth, p. 4; Rigge, "Log," February 25, 1889; HCM, September 6, 1888.

67. Rigge, "Memoirs," *TCA*, April, 1938, pp. 2–3.

68. Dowling, *Reminiscences*, pp. 81–82, 124–25; Leahy, p. 11; Casper, vol. II, pp. 153-55; Ostdiek, pp. 10-4; Holland, pp. 61-77; *CUB*, Arts, 1890-91; "Varia," *Woodstock Letters*, vol. 20, 1891, p. 473.

Chapter Three

1. Humphrey J. Desmond, *The A.P.A. Movement* (Washington: New Century Press, 1912), pp. 7-15, 29–30, 51–68; Szmrescanyi, pp. 4–7, 16–17; Wolfe's Omaha City Directory, 1886 through 1900.

2. Dowling, *Reminiscences*, p. 134; Desmond, pp. 18–19; Szmrescanyi, p. 16.

3. Thomas J. Archdeacon, Becoming American: An Ethnic History (New York: Free Press, 1983), p. 78; Casper, vol. 2, p. 328; Szmrescanyi, p. 16; Croghan, pp. 110, 114–18.

4. Dowling, *Reminiscences*, pp. 131, 137; "white caps," Casper notes; Ed. F. Morearty, *Omaha Memories: Recollections of Events, Men and Affairs in Omaha, Nebraska, from 1879 to 1917* (Omaha: Swartz Printing Co., 1917) p. 44; Croghan, p. 121.

5. Szmrescanyi, p. 17; Rigge, "Memoirs," *TCA*, February 1939, p. 13; HCM, February 5, 1889, September 26, 1892, and September 28, 1893; *Historia Domas*, March 28, 1889, and July [no day], 1899.

6. Dowling, *Reminiscences*, pp. 131–33; Desmond, pp. 46–51; Morearty, pp. 44–55; HCM, July 1, 1893.

7. Dowling, *Reminiscences*, p. 135; Garraghan, p. 474; Casper, vol. 2, p. 180; Croghan, pp. 112, 118, 120; *Historia Domas*, December 5, 1897.

8. Dowling, *Reminiscences*, pp. 165–67.

9. Ibid, pp. 164–5; HCM, February 2, 1894, and April 9, 1895.

10. Dowling, *Reminiscences*, p. 126; Casper, vol. 2, pp. 196–200; *Historia Domas*, August 28 and September 1, 1893; *CUB*, Arts, 1894–95, 1895–96, and 1896–97.

11. Rigge, "Memoirs," *TCA*, May 1938, p. 11; HCM, June 13, 1894, and December 4, 1896; *Historia Domas*, July 5, 1894, and September 22, 1897.

12. Dowling, *Reminiscences*, pp.167–68; Garraghan, pp. 475–76; HCM, November 23, 1898.

13. Dowling, *Reminiscences*, pp. 126, 172; Szmrescanyi, pp. 362–63; *CUB*, Arts, 1891–92; Leahy, p. 21; *Historia Domas*, September 11, 1897; "Varia," *Woodstock Letters*, vol. 25 (1896), p. 529.

14. Dowling, *Reminiscences*, p. 125; Power, pp. 269–70; *CUB*, Arts, 1891–92 and 1892–93.

15. "Revised Course of Study, 1893," Circulars, 1893–1920, and "Memorial," April 4, 1892, MJA; Leahy, pp. 12–13; Rudolph, *Curriculum,* pp. 232–33; John Richard Betts, "Darwinism, Evolution and American Catholic Thought, 1860–1900," *Catholic Historical Review,* 45 (July 1959), pp. 165–84.

16. CCC, 1881–82 and 1891–92; "Varia," *Woodstock Letters,* vol. 21 (1892), p. 446.

17. Dowling, *Reminiscences,* pp. 192, 194.

18. Ibid, pp. 192, 198-9; *CUB,* Arts, 1895–96.

19. Dowling, *Reminiscences,* p. 147; HCM, October 11 and November 4, 1892; Memorandum on St. John's Church, James Hoeffer, S.J., to Fr. Provincial, February 13, 1893, Omaha: Creighton University File, MJA; "Varia," *Woodstock Letters,* vol. 21 (1892), p. 145.

20. Dowling, *Reminiscences,* pp. 150–51; Reichmuth, p. 6; Hoeffer memorandum, MJA; Casper, vol. 3, pp. 201–6.

21. Dowling, *Reminiscences,* pp. 64, 151; Casper, vol. 2, pp. 160–62; Reichmuth, p. 8; Hoeffer memorandum, MJA.

22. Power, pp. 335–39; Rudolph, *American College and University,* pp. 395–96; Richard J. Storr, The Beginnings of Graduate Education in America (New York: Arno Press & New York Times, [1953] 1969), pp. 7–17, 57–58, 115, 153, note 1; *CUB,* Arts, 1881–82, 1891–92, 1892–93, and 1895–96; Thomas S. Bowdern, "The Graduate School of The Creighton University," in McDermott, pp. 63–64.

23. *CUB,* Arts, 1891–92; letter, Fr, James Hoeffer to Fr. John Fieden, April 27, 1892, Casper notes.

24. Casper, vol. 2, pp. 78, 109; Carolyn J. Boro and Beverly T. Mead, *A Century of Teaching and Healing; The First One Hundred Years of the Creighton University School of Medicine* (Omaha: Creighton University School of Medicine, 1891), pp. 35–40; Dorothy E. Vossen, *Nursing at Creighton University: A History, 1899–1985* (Omaha: Creighton University School of Nursing, 1991), p. 3.

25. Savage and Bell, pp. 353–59; Boro and Mead, pp.14–16; Knoll, pp. 52–53.

26. Rudolph, *Curriculum,* p. 8; Dowling, Reminiscences, p. 139; Boro and Mead, pp. 18–19, 43; *CUB,* Medicine, 1892.

27. *CUB,* Medicine, 1892–93 through 1899–1900; Dowling, *Reminiscences,* p. 139; Boro and Mead, pp. 44-56; Vosper, p. 209; Leahy, p. 69; Power, p. 165. On p. 219 Power states that the Creighton University Medical School established the four-year curriculum following the Georgetown University example.

28. Dowling, *Reminiscences,* pp. 139–42; Boro and Mead, pp. 56–58; HCM, February 15, 1895; "Varia," *Woodstock Letters,* vol. 24 (1895), p. 510; *Omaha World-Herald,* January 3, 1897, John Creighton Clipping File, HSDC.

29. Dudley, p. 80, note 41, p. 89; Dowling, *Reminiscences,* p. 144; James B. Haynes, *History of the Trans-Mississippi and International Exposition of 1898* (Omaha: 1910); Arvid E. Nelson, Jr., *The AK-SAR-BEN Story* (Lincoln, Nebraska: Johnson Publishing Company, 1967), pp. 40–41, 101; *Historia Domas,* March 24, 1904; *CUB,* Arts, 1903-04.

30. Dowling, *Reminiscences,* pp. 168–69.

31. Ibid, pp. 184–86; McDermott, pp. 14, 46–49; Rigge, "Memoirs," *TCA,* February 1938, p. 1 and May, 1938, p. 11; Rigge, "Log," March 21, 1902; *Historia Domas,* August 30, 1903; CCC, 1901–02.

32. Dowling, *Reminiscences,* pp. 92, 151–52; Reichmuth, pp. 8–10; Rigge, "Memoirs," *TCA,* February 1938, p. 1, and April, 1938, pp. 3–5; Rigge, "Log," April 15, 1900, and March 31, April 23, and 24, 1901, and March 21, 1902.

33. Vosper, pp. 34–35; *Historia Domas,* May 1, 1900, and October 27, 1901; "Varia," *Woodstock Letters,* vol. 31 (1902), p. 309.

34. McDermott, p. 53; Dowling, "John Mss," p. 38; *Historia Domas*, February 17, 1904; HCM, June 18 and August 22, 1904; *CUB*, Arts, 1903–04.

35. Vosper, p. 142; Knoll, pp. 50–51; Steven P. Frankino and C. Benjamin Crisman, "An Historical Look at the Creighton University of Law," *Creighton Law Review*, vol. 9, 1975, pp. 228–29; Hoeffer letter, April 27, 1892, Casper notes.

36. Vosper, p. 142; Frankino and Crisman, pp. 229–30; Rudolph, *Curriculum*, pp. 178–79; *The Creighton Brief*, Creighton Law School, 1909, CUA, pp. 9, 59, 80–82, 96, 102 ff.; Rigge, "Log," May 17, 1905; Rigge, "Memoirs," *TCA*, February 1938, p. 1; *True Voice* (Omaha Catholic newspaper), January 20, 1905, p. 5; *CUB*, Dental, 1904–05 through 1945.

37. Vosper, pp. 170-1; Charles Vacanti, "History of Dentistry," unpublished paper, Creighton University, 1983; Dowling, "John Mss.," p. 42; HCM, September and October, 1904 and March 1905 (no days recorded); Rigge, "Log," July 20, 1906; *CUB*, Dental 1905-06.

38. Vosper, pp. 176–77; HCM, June 22, 1905; CCC, Dental, 1905–06 and 1907–08.

39. Boro and Mead, pp. 56–57, 290; Howard W. Caldwell, *Education in Nebraska*, United States Bureau of Education, Circular of Information No. 3 (Washington, D.C.: Government Printing Office, 1902), p. 144; J. E. Copus, S.J., "The Edward Creighton Institute," *Woodstock Letters*, vol. 34 (1905), pp. 355–56; Rigge, "Log," December 28, 1904, and May 17, 1905. The House Consultors secretary wrote, "An application had been made, a week or two ago, by a Japanese for admission to College, and a previous application made by a Negro was recalled, for the purpose of ascertaining the views of the Consultors on similar applications. Their reception was viewed with disfavor, because of the treatment of them by our white students, though at the same time it is well understood that no direct refusal of them can be made." The Negro was probably William Gordon in the medical school. Subsequently, in 1906, John "Jap" Tamisiea enrolled in the high-school department.

40. Rigge, "Memoirs," *TCA*, December 1937, pp. 2–3, and February, 1938, p. 1; Rigge, "Log," August 31, September 7 and 20, October 2, 21, and 23, and November 20, 1905, and May 11 and 22, 1906; *Historia Domas*, August 15 and September 3, 1905, and February 15, March 9, April 23, May 11, and July 3, 1906.

41. Neil Cahill, S.J., *Creighton University College of Business Administration, the First Seventy-five Years* (Omaha: Creighton University College of Business Administration, 1996), p. 4 (he incorrectly stated that about 1908 Creighton University "repaired and joined to old apartment buildings across the street from St. John's Church and added a brick extension to the south along 25th Street—on 'a strictly temporary basis'—as a residence for male freshmen attending Creighton." Maurice William Kirby, "History of Creighton University, 1878-1926," unpublished M. A. Thesis, University of Nebraska, 1954, p. 108; McDermott, p. 52; Rigge, "Log," May 22, 1906; *Historia Domas*, May 13 and September 6, 1906; HCM, October 2, 1905, and April 2, 1906; *The Creightonian* (student newspaper), October 19, 1951, p. 6.

42. Dowling, "John Mss.," pp. 46–54; Rigge, "Memoirs," *TCA*, February 1938, p. 1; Rigge, "Log," October 15, 1906; *Historia Domas*, June 8, July 3, and October 15, 1906; *Omaha World-Herald*, January 16, 1966, Edward Creighton Clipping File, HSDC.

43. Rigge, "Memoirs," *TCA*, February, 1938, pp. 3–4; Rigge, "Log," August 6, 1907; *Historia Domas*, August 8 and October 6 and 7, 1907, and January 27, 1908; *CUB*, Arts, 1907–08.

44. Charles W. Eliot, "Recent Changes in Secondary Education," *Atlantic Monthly*, 84 (October 1899), p. 433; Herbert M. Kliebard, *The Struggle for the American Curriculum* (Boston: Routledge & Kegan Paul, 1986), pp. 10–12, 26–29; Rudolph, *American College and University*, p. 294.

45. Rudolph, *Curriculum*, p. 16; Ruth Everett, "Jesuit Educators and Modern Colleges, *The*

Arena, 23 (1900), pp. 647–52; Rev. Timothy Brosnahan, S.J., "President Eliot and Jesuit Colleges: A Defense," Sacred Heart Review, January, 1900, pp. 9–10.

46. Dowling, *Reminiscences*, pp. 111–19; CCC, 1899–1900; *Historia Domas*, June 19, 1903; Robert Schwickerath, S.J., *Jesuit Education, Its History and Principles Viewed in the Light of Modern Educational Problems* (St. Louis: B. Herder, 1903).

47. Rudolph, *Curriculum*, p. 220; Leahy, p. 23; Rev. James Howard Plough, "Catholic Colleges and the Catholic Educational Association: The Foundation and Early Years of the CEA, 1899–1919," unpublished dissertation, University of Notre Dame, 1967, pp. iii, 23; "The Conference of Catholic Colleges," *Woodstock Letters*, vol. 28 (1899), pp. 121–23.

48. Caldwell, pp. 83–84; Knoll, p. 88; Power, p. 262; Rudolph, *Curriculum*, p. 220; Rigge, "Memoirs," *TCA*, March, 1938, p. 5.

49. "The Conference of Catholic Colleges," pp. 122–23; "Ours at the Second Annual Conference of Catholic Colleges," *Woodstock Letters*, vol. 29 (1900), pp. 342–43.

50. Plough, pp. 520–23; Rigge, "Memoirs," *TCA*, April 1938, p. 2; CCC, 1900–01, 1904–05, and 1906–07; *Historia Domas*, June 23, 1899, and September 6 and 8, 1904.

51. Dowling, *Reminiscences*, pp. 224–25; Rigge, "Memoirs," *TCA*, March, 1938, pp. 4–5; CCC, 1898–99 through 1909–10.

52. *CUB* Arts,, 1906–07; HCM, September 12, 1899; Caldwell, pp. 142–43.

53. Letters, Paul L. Martin to Rev. Michael P. Dowling, January 4, 1903, and February 2, 1905, PVF.

54. Rudolph, *American College and University*, pp. 446–47; Boro and Mead, pp. 51–52; Dudley, p. 90, note 63; Rigge, "Log," August 16, 1907; *Historia Domas*, August 16, 1907; CCC, 1904–05 through 1912–13.

55. Dowling, *Reminiscences*, pp. 187, 190.

56. Ibid, pp. 188, 203, 209–13; "Varia," *Woodstock Letters*, vol. 30 (1901), pp. 154–56; Fr. M. I. Stritch, S.J., "The Creighton University in the State and Interstate Oratorical Contests," *Woodstock Letters*, vol. 31 (1902), pp. 96–100; *Historia Domas*, March 22, 1901, May 4 and 18, 1904, and February 17, 1905; *CUB*, Arts, 1898–99.

57. Dowling, *Reminiscences*, pp. 203–5; CCC, 1898–99 and 1900–01, and 1905–06; *Historia Domas*, December 22, 1898, and January 18, 1899.

58. "Varia," *Woodstock Letters*, vol. 30 (1901), p. 155; Rudolph, *American College and University*, pp. 428–29.

59. Dowling, *Reminiscences*, pp. 244–47; "Varia," *Woodstock Letters*, vol. 31 (1902), p. 482; *Historia Domas*, March 23, 1904, and November 15, 1905; *CUB*, Arts, 1903–04.

60. "Ours at the Second Annual Conference of Catholic Colleges," p. 343; Power, p. 278; Rudolph, *American College and University*, pp. 374–88; Ronald A. Smith, *The Rise of Big-Time College Athletics* (Oxford: Oxford University Press, 1988), pp. 119-38.

61. Dowling, *Reminiscences*, pp. 198-201.

62. Smith, pp. ix, 3–4; CCC, 1898–99; *Historia Domas*, October 19 and 26, 1901.

63. *Omaha World-Herald*, November 29, 1901, p. 6, and April 13, 1943, John Creighton Clipping File, HSDC; *Historia Domas*, November 28, 1901; *CUB*, Arts, 1901–02. In rugby running the ball "in-goal" got three points and the place kick after goal two points.

64. "Varia," *Woodstock Letters*, vol. 30 (1901), pp. 154–55; *Historia Domas*, May 20 and October 12, 1901.

65. Smith, pp. 148, 154; *Historia Domas*, October 25, 1902; *CUB*, Arts, 1901–02. A *TCA* article of September 1948, p. 11, identified Herbert A. Whipple as the football coach in 1900 and 1901. The register of faculty and students did not list him.

66. Dowling, "John Mss.," p. 27; *Historia Domas*, April 26, May 17, September 30, October 28 and November 6, 1906.

67. Smith, pp. 88–89, 192–208; Rudolph, *American College and University*, pp. 374–76; *Historia Domas*, May 12, September 28, October 13, and November 10, 1906; *True Voice*, October 5, 1906, p. 5.

68. Rigge, "Memoirs," *TCA*, February 1938, p. 1; Rigge, "Log," July 17 and August 15, 1907; *Historia Domas*, July 17, 1907, and March 18 and 28, and July 13, 1908; HCM, March 2, 1908; *CUB*, Arts, 1907–08; True Voice, January 17, 1908, p. 5.

69. Rigge, "Log," June 26, 1908.

70. Rudolph, *American College and University*, p. 419; Rigge, "Memoir," *TCA*, January 1938, p. 5.

71. "Father Michael P. Dowling," *Woodstock Letters*, vol. 44 (1915), pp. 228–29; Letter, M. P. Dowling to Fr. Provincial, February 29, 1908, Omaha: Creighton University file, MJA; Herman J. Muller, S.J., *The University of Detroit, 1877-1977: A Centennial History* (Detroit: University of Detroit, 1976), pp. 49–53.

72. Rigge, "Memoirs," *TCA*, December 1937, p. 4; Szmrecsanyi, pp. 407–9.

73. Typewritten obituary, M. P. Dowling file, MJA; "Father Michael P. Dowling," pp. 231–34; Letter, M. P. Dowling to Fr. Provincial, February 13, 1908, Omaha: Creighton University file, MJA.

74. Undated *Omaha World-Herald* article [1907], Edward Creighton Clipping File, HSDC; *True Voice,* July 19, 1907, p. 5; Dowling, "John Mss.," pp. 142, 152–59; letter, M. P. Dowling to Fr. Provincial, February 13, 1908, Omaha: Creighton University file, MJA; Creighton Wills File, PVF.

75. Dowling, "John Mss.," pp. 147, 162; undated *Omaha World-Herald* article [1907], Edward Creighton Clipping File, HSDC; True Voice, November 22, 1907, p. 5; HCM, March 12, 1907; *Nebraska Supreme Court Journal,* vol. 10, no. 43, July 15, 1941, pp. 1196-9.

76. Typed, undated, two-page eulogy, and letter, Fr. John C. Kelley to Rev. L. Bushart, April 23, 1908, both in Omaha: Creighton University file, MJA.

77. *Historia Domas,* January 9, 1908; *Omaha Daily News,* January 9, 1908, p. 1.

Chapter Four

1. Power, pp. 286–87; *CUB*, Arts, 1909–10 through 1919–20.

2. *Creighton Chronicle,* October 1912; *Historia Domas*, May 6, 1910, and January 12, 1913; *Creighton Courier,* August 1, 1917, p. 3; Rigge, "Memoirs," *TCA*, January 1939, p. 6, and March 1939, p. 16.

3. *Chronicle,* October 1909, pp. 39–40; October 1914, pp. 19–21; "cathedral gift," Casper notes; HCM, September 10, 1913.

4. Rigge, "Memoirs," *TCA*, March 1938, pp. 1–3; *Historia Domas*, February 23, 1905, and May 9–11, 1911.

5. *Historia Domas*, December 31, 1906, August 13, 1908, and January 5, 1909, and March 23, 1910, and May 31, 1911; HCM, September 18, 1908 and January 6, 1909.

6. Rigge, "Memoirs," *TCA*, January 1938, pp. 2–3, January 1939, pp. 4–5, and February 1939, pp. 12–13; *Historia Domas*, August 2, 1909, June 7, September 26, and October 1 and 16, 1910; HCM, September 28, 1917.

7. Rigge, "Memoirs," *TCA*, February 1938, p. 2, and February 1939, pp. 12–13; Rigge, "Log," April 21 and May 13, 1915; HCM, September 10, 1915; *Historia Domas*, April 10 and October 16, 1910, and August 7, 1911.

8. Rigge, "Log," May 22, 1913, and April 11, 1916; *Historia Domas*, May 19, 1913, and February 25 and April 11 and 14, 1916; *CUB*, Arts, 1916–17.

9. Rigge, "Memoirs," *TCA*, January 1938, p. 3, and February 1938, p. 2; Rigge, "Log," September 7 and November 17, 1917; HCM, December 22, 1912; *Historia Domas*, September 7 and November 17, 1917; *Chronicle,* October 1917, pp. 55-6; Szmrecsanyi, pp. 363-67.

10. *Chronicle*, October 1909, p. 45, and October 1913, p. 58; Rigge, "Log," June 7, 1919; *CUB*, Dentistry, 1909-10 through 1919-20; Vosper, pp. 166–71.

11. *Chronicle*, March 1913, p. 411, October 1913, p. 70, and October 1918, pp. 42, 50; *CUB*, Pharmacy, 1910–11 through 1920–21; Edward Kremers and George Urdang, *History of Pharmacy*, 2nd ed. (Philadelphia: J. B. Lippincott, 1951), pp. 298–308.

12. *CUB*, Law, 1907–08 through 1914–15; Frankino and Crisman, p. 231.

13. *CUB*, Law, 1911–12; Anson H. Bigelow, "The Model House," *Chronicle*, January 1917, p. 221.

14. Bigelow, pp. 222–27.

15. HCM, May 2, 1911, and March 9, 1912; *CUB*, Law, 1912–13; *TCA*, September 1949, p. 6.

16. *Chronicle*, October 1910, p. 34, February 1913, p. 347, March 1914, pp. 402–03 and May 1916, p. 466, October 1916, pp. 26-27, October 1918, p. 42, and October 1919, p. 49; *Courier*, January 15, 1913, p. 3; *CUB*, Law, 1911–12 through 1919–20.

17. *Historia Domas*, November 9, 1919; "Paul Martin interview," October 1, 1957, Casper notes.

18. *Chronicle*, May 1913, pp. 537, 558; Boro and Mead, p. 61; Rigge, "Memoirs," *TCA*, February 1938, p. 2; *CUB*, Medicine, 1909–10.

19. Power, pp. 219–20; Boro and Mead, pp. 65–68; *CUB*, Medicine, 1909–10 through 1917–18.

20. Boro and Mead, pp. 71–73; *Chronicle*, January 1912, p. 179, October 1918, p. 42, and October 1919, p. 49; *CUB*, Medicine, 1910–11 through 1919–20.

21. HCM, November 6, 1906; *Chronicle*, October 1909 and October 1911, p. 18.

22. *Chronicle*, April 1910, p. 26, November 1911, pp. 57–58 and March 1914, p. 406, and May 1915, p. 390; Rigge, "Log," April 29 and June 16, 1915.

23. *Chronicle*, March 1912, pp. 280–86; *Historia Domas*, August 16 and September 15, 1919.

24. *Chronicle*, December 1911, pp. 107–09; *Omaha World-Herald*, September 29, 1912.

25. *Chronicle*, April 1912, pp. 371–74, and October 1912, p. 35; *Courier*, June 1, 1912.

26. *Chronicle*, May 1912, pp. 371–74 and December 1912, p. 178.

27. *Chronicle*, December 1912, p. 179, November 1913, pp. 100–04, 118–19, 142, December 1913, pp. 189–94, 221, January 1914, p. 274, and January 1915, pp. 166–70; "Varia," *Woodstock Letters*, vol. 43, 1914, pp. 137–38.

28. *Chronicle*, April 1914, pp. 429-30, 448, May 1914, pp. 467–72, May 1916, pp. 448–50, 467, June 1917, p. 597, June 1918, p. 629, and April 1922, p. 353; *Courier*, April 1, 1914, p. 1; *Historia Domas*, May 29 and June 17, 1914, and April 17, 1915.

29. *Chronicle*, February 1913, pp. 314–5, 346, and December 1913, p. 191; *Historia Domas*, February 16, 1911.

30. *Chronicle*, October 1909, p. 41, and November 1909, p. 39; *Historia Domas*, February 24, 1909, and April 25, 1914; HCM, November 11, 1913.

31. *Chronicle*, April 1911, p. 298, April 1912, p. 340, January 1914, p. 284, and January 1915, pp. 170–71.

32. *Chronicle*, December 1909, p. 38, February 1910, pp. 47–49, and March 1918, p. 393; *Historia Domas*, October 1, 1914; HCM, October 14, 1914, and November 12, 1915; *CUB*, Arts, 1917–18.

33. *Chronicle*, October 1909, p. 41, October 1912, pp. 1–6, and November 1915, pp. 96–97; *CUB*, Arts, 1914–15 and 1915–16.

34. Casper, Vol. II, pp. 331–37; *Chronicle*, April 1913, pp. 485–88.

35. *Chronicle*, April 1913, pp. 485–87; *Historia Domas*, April 5, 1913.

36. *CUB*, Arts, 1909–10.

37. HCM, December 18 and 26, 1908 (The text refers to the Trustees, but no meeting minutes exist. At the time, the same Jesuits served as Consultors.); *Courier*, August 1, 1912, p. 4, June 1, 1913, p. 3, and December 1, 1915, p. 3; *Creighton Brief*, pp. 90–92.

38. HCM, December 26, 1908 and January 6, 1909; *Chronicle,* April 1912, p. 339, and October 1912, pp. 61, 70; Rigge, "Log," October 5 and 23, 1912; *CUB,* Arts, 1909–10; *Courier,* August 1, 1912, p. 4; Benjamin G. Rader, *American Sports* (Englewood Cliffs, NJ: Prentice-Hall, Inc., 1983), p. 127.

39. HCM, April 6, 1910; *Chronicle,* October 1911, pp. 18–20, November 1911, p. 58, December 1911, pp. 105–07 and October 1912, p. 33.

40. HCM, December [no day], 1914 and June 6 and August 28, 1915; Chronicle, November 1913, pp. 93, 143. and December 1914, pp. 109–10, 132–33.

41. Rigge, "Log," September 30, 1916; *Chronicle,* October 1915, pp. 7, 11, 46–48, and January 1916, p. 203; *Omaha World-Herald,* June 2, 1916, p. 7.

42. *Chronicle,* November 1911, pp. 72, 76, April 1912, p. 385, October 1912, p. 69, April 1913, p. 489, and February 1915, p. 215.

43. *Chronicle,* May 1911, pp. 344-5 and April 1913, p. 483; Courier, May 1, 1913, p. 3.

44. *Chronicle,* February 1911, pp. 214–15, March 1913, p. 410, April 1913, pp. 483, 561, and April 1917, p. 476.

45. *Chronicle,* March 1912, pp. 296, 338–39 and April 1915, pp. 298, 326, 355–56; Rader, p. 47.

46. *Chronicle,* May 1916, p. 465, February 1917, p. 315 and December 1917, p. 177; *CUB,* Arts, 1917-18. Compared to the 1916–17 season statistics held by the Athletic Department, the *Chronicle,* March 1917, p. 383, stated that the team also played city and Commercial League teams, while compiling a collegiate record of 9-4. The April 1917 issue, p. 474, cited the final record of 13–6.

47. Letter, Francis Xavier Wernz, Father General of the Society of Jesus, to Father Rudolph Meyer, Provincial of the Missouri Province, May 1, 1909, and Wernz to Father Alexander Burrowes, Provincial of the Missouri Province, June 17, 1914, Meyer File and Burrowes File, MJA.

48. *Chronicle,* October 1911, pp. 9–13 and January 1913, p. 270.

49. *Courier,* August 1, 1912, p. 3; *Chronicle,* October 1909, p. 42, and December 1912, p. 206; the *Brief,* p. 93; HCM, February 26, 1912.

50. *Chronicle,* November 1912, pp. 139–40, November 1913, p. 117, April 1914, p. 455, and November 1914, p. 86.

51. *Chronicle,* February 1915, p. 216, December 1916, p. 187, March 1917, p. 382, and December 1917, p. 183.

52. "Report, Committee on Studies, 1909," "Course of Studies, 1911," and "Course of Studies, 1915," MJA; McGucken, pp. 138–39, 188–89; Garraghan, pp. 508–09; Power, pp. 241–45; Rudolph, Curriculum, p. 211.

53. HCM, October 16, 1914, December 29, 1915, and February 25, 1916; *Historia Domas,* June 17, 1916; *Chronicle,* November 1911, p. 72, May 1913, p. 566, and October 1913, p. 56; *True Voice,* April 14, 1916, p. 4.

54. Rigge, "Log," September 4, 1912; McDermott, p. 5; *Chronicle,* October 1919, p. 49; Szmrecsanyi, p. 611; Albert Muntsch, S.J., "Coeducation From A Catholic Standpoint," *Catholic Education Association Bulletin,* November, 1913, pp. 358–65.

55. Power, p. 275; Croghan, p. 146, n. 61, p. 148; Sr. M. Ruth Sandifer, R. S. M., "The Construction of a Four-Year Teacher Training Curriculum for the Sisters of Mercy in the Province of Omaha," unpublished M.A. Thesis, Creighton University, 1936, pp. 37–40; *CUB,* Summer, 1913.

56. Rigge, "Log," June 23, 1913; "Martin interview," Casper notes; *Chronicle,* October 1913, pp. 58, 69–70; *CUB,* Summer, 1913, 1914.

57. *Chronicle,* October 1913, p. 58, and February 1914, p. 342, and October 1919, p. 49; *CUB,* Summer, 1917, 1919, 1920; "Martin interview," Casper notes; McDermott, p. 67.

58. Rigge, "Log," October 8, 1919; *Historia Domas*, October 19, 1919; *CUB*, Arts, 1920-21; Leahy, pp. 71–83.

59. *CUB*, Arts, 1909–10.

60. *CUB*, Arts, 1909–10 through 1919–20; *Chronicle*, April 1910, p. 35.

61. "Supplement to the Course of Study, 1911," MJA; *Chronicle*, October 1910, p. 34, October 1912, p. 62, October 1913, p. 70, November 1913, p. 143, and October 1919, p. 49.

62. HCM, May 2, 1911; Rigge, "Memoirs," *TCA*, May 1938, p. 11; *Chronicle*, October 1913, p. 42; *CUB*, Arts, 1911–12.

63. *CUB*, 1911–12 and 1912–13.

64. "Report of the General Committee on the Course of Studies, 1915," MJA.

65. Ibid; "Supplement to the Course of Studies of the Missouri Province, Report on the Committee on History," MJA; *CUB*, Arts, 1915–16.

66. *Historia Domas*, June 6, 1916; *CUB*, Arts, 1915–16; C. Joseph Nusse, "The Introduction of Sociology at the Catholic University of America," *Catholic Historical Review*, vol. LXXXVII (October 2001), pp. 643–45.

67. Rudolph, *College and University*, pp. 430–32; Power, pp. 288–89; Leahy, pp. 21–24; Rev. Timothy Brosnahan, "The Carnegie Foundation for the Advancement Of Teaching—Its Aims and Tendency," *Catholic Education Association Bulletin*, vol. 7 (August 1911), pp. 119–20, 141–45, 155.

68. Leahy, p. 20; Rudolph, *Curriculum*, pp. 220–6; *Chronicle*, April 1916, pp. 384–85, and November 1917, pp. 99–100; Lester F. Goodchild, "The Turning Point in American Jesuit Education: The Standardization Controversy Between the Jesuits and the North Central Association, 1915–1940," *History of Higher Education Annual*, vol. 6 (1986), pp. 81–85.

69. *CUB*, Arts, 1917–18, 1918–19, 1919–20.

70. Rudolph, *Curriculum*, pp. 16, 227–29; *CUB*, Arts, 1918–19.

71. McGucken, p. 187; Garraghan, vol. 3, pp. 509–10; Goodchild, pp. 89–91; Vosper, pp. 37–39; *Historia Domas*, December 12, 1917, CCAS faculty "unanimous" in favor of eliminating Greek requirement; "Report of the Committee on Studies, 1920," MJA.

72. *Chronicle*, November 1914, pp. 50–51, December 1914, pp. 92, 136 and April 1915, p. 326, and March 1916, pp. 289–94; HCM, March 27, 1917; *TCA*, "Ten Year Flashback," p. 4.

73. Rigge, "Log," April 6, 1917; HCM, May 24, 1917; *Historia Domas*, May 23, 1917; *Chronicle*, April 1916, p. 386, April 1917, p. 477, May 1917, pp. 546, 550–51, and June 1917, pp. 623–26.

74. *TCA*, October 1927, "Ten-Year Flashback," p. 4; Michael Williams, *American Catholics in the War: National Catholic War Council, 1917–1921* (New York: Macmillan, 1921), preface and pp. 1–8.

75. Rigge, "Memoirs," *TCA*, March 1938, p. 3; Rigge, "Log," February 15, 1915; *Chronicle*, March 1916, p. 277, May 1917, pp. 517–19, and June 1917, p. 621; Boro and Mead, pp. 74–76.

76. HCM, October 28 and November 30, 1917; *Historia Domas*, September 11 and October 4, 1917; *Chronicle*, October 1917, pp. 52–54, November 1917, pp. 118–19, December 1917, p. 180, February 1918, pp. 332, 391, and March 1918, pp. 390–91.

77. *Chronicle*, May 1917, pp. 517–19, October 1917, pp. 26–28, 44, 50, January 1918, pp. 222–35, February 1918, pp. 295–301, April 1918, pp. 416–57, May 1918, pp. 491–98, 593–98, and June 1918, pp. 599–601.

78. HCM, April 14, 1916; Courier, August 15, 1917, p. 2; *Chronicle*, February 1918, pp. 303–05, 339, 396, October 1918, pp. 49–50, January 1919, pp. 171, 404, and October 1919, p. 43.

79. HCM, April 5, 1918; *Historia Domas*, April 6, 1918; Rigge, "Memoirs," *TCA*, March 1938, p. 3; *Chronicle*, April 1918, p. 474, May 1918, p. 529, June 1918, pp. 624–26, and May 1920, pp. 384–90.

80. Boro and Mead, pp. 74–76; *Chronicle*, October 1918, pp. 32, 40; HCM, May 13, 1918;

Historia Domas, September 12, 1918; Rigge, "Memoirs," *TCA*, March 1938, pp. 3–4; *CUB*, Arts, 1918–19.

81. HCM, September 4, 1918; *Historia Domas*, November 2, 1918; *Chronicle*, October 1918, pp. 40–42; Courier, November 1, 1918, p. 1.

82. *Historia Domas*, November 7, 11, and 18 and December 12, 1918; Rigge, "Memoirs," *TCA*, March 1938, p. 4; *Chronicle*, December 1918, p. 141.

83. HCM, January 24 and 28, 1919; *Courier*, September 1, 1919, p. 1; *Chronicle*, January 1919, p. 180, February 1919, p. 230, March 1919, p. 298, June 1919, pp. 414–15, and November 1919, pp. 90–91, 125; Allan Millet and Peter Maslowski, *For the Common Defense* (New York: The Free Press, 1984), pp. 342, 386.

84. *Historia Domas*, June 21, 1919; "Martin interview," Casper notes; *Province News-Letter*, March 1920, p. 12, MJA; *Chronicle*, October 1919, pp. 43, 46, and November 1919, pp. 86–87.

85. Knoll, pp. 46, 65–67; *Chronicle*, November 1917, pp. 83–84; *Historia Domas*, May 2 and November 29, 1917, February 6 and 9 and November 20, 1918, and July 2, 1919.

86. Rigge, "Log," October 6, 21, and 30 and November 4 and 11, 1918; Rigge, "Memoirs," *TCA*, March 1938, p. 4; *Historia Domas*, November 7, 11, 18, and 28, 1918 and June 3, 1921; HCM, February 24 and March 18, 1919; *Chronicle*, December 1918, p. 139, and January 1919, p. 171; *Courier*, June 21, 1921, p. 1.

87. Garraghan, pp. 560–65; *Chronicle*, October 1917; *Historia Domas*, September 28 and 30, 1919, and June 5, 1920; Edward D. Reynolds, S.J., *Jesuits for the Negro* (New York: The American Press, 1949), pp. 145–48.

88. Casper, vol. II, p. 337; Croghan, pp. 147–49; *Omaha World-Herald*, January 27, 1919, evening, p. 2; *Chronicle*, June 1919, pp. 451–58; *Historia Domas*, January 6 and February 2, 1919.

89. *Historia Domas*, October 27 and 28, and November 28 and December 2, 10, and 13, 1919; *Chronicle*, November 1919, pp. 88–90, and December 1919, pp. 123, 171.

90. Alexander J. Burrowes, S.J., "Attitude of Catholics Towards Higher Education," *Catholic Education Association Bulletin*, 16 (November 1919), pp. 159–74.

Chapter Five

1. *Historia Domas*, October 27, 1921; *Chronicle*, April 1920, p. 319; *Shadows*, December 1922, back cover; *Courier*, November 1925, p. 2; *CUB*, Arts, 1927–28; *Bluejay* (yearbook), 1927, p. 33.

2. HCM, June 1, 1921, and February 27 and October 2, 1925; *Chronicle*, October 1921, p. 41; *Courier*, October 1921, p. 2, March 1922, pp. 1, 4, October 1923, p. 4, November 1925, p. 4, and May 1926, p. 2; *Creightonian*, November 7, 1924, p. 3, and October 2, 1925, p. 1; Rigge "Log," June 8, 1925; Rigge, "Memoirs," *TCA*, February 1938, p. 4; *Bluejay*, 1928, p. 24; *Alumnews*, May 1973, p. 5; *CUB*, Arts, 1919 through 1963.

3. *Courier*, October 1923, p. 2; *TCA*, October 1936, p. 3.

4. Paul A. Fitzgerald, S.J., *The Governance of Jesuit Colleges in the United States, 1920–1970* (Notre Dame: University of Notre Dame Press, 1984), pp. 4–10, 18–20, n. 9, 10, p. 236; Leahy, pp. 38–39 (on p. 94 he stated that in 1912, Fr. Thomas McCluskey, S.J., president of Fordham, asked to appoint non-clergy to his board of directors, but Fr. General denied the request. Subsequently, on p. 105 he stated that Saint Louis University created a lay board in 1909); Flaherty, pp. 215–18; *Courier*, February 1923, p. 3; BRM, 1925, PVF.

5. *Historia Domas*, August 24 and 31, 1920, March 21 and May 16, 1921, and September 9, 1925; HCM, December 5, 1920; Reichmuth, p. 12; McDermott, p. 6.

6. *Historia Domas*, November 28, 1921, and October 23, 1922; *Courier*, February 1922, p. 4, and November 1925, P. 5.

7. Rigge "Log," April 18, 1921, April 16, 1922, July 18, 1923, and May 25, 1925; HCM, February 22 and March 8, 1923, March 13, 1924, January 12, 1925, and August 11, 1926; *Historia*

Domas, April 14, 1922, July 20, and September 30, 1923, and May 28 and July 14, 1925; Rigge, "Memoir," *TCA,* December 1937, p. 4; *Courier,* April 1926, p. 3; *Creightonian,* April 23, 1926, p. 8; *Alumnews,* November 1995, p. 3.

8. *Chronicle,* March 1920, p. 230, and April 1920, p. 277, 296–97; *Courier,* April 1920, pp. 1, 4, and September 1920, p. 3.

9. *Courier,* May 1920, p. 1.

10. *Chronicle,* November 1921, pp. 82–83, and January 1922, p. 203; *Historia Domas,* September 28 and October 17, 1921.

11. *Historia Domas,* September 3, 1922; *Courier,* September 1922, p. 1, and October 1922, p. 2.

12. *Historia Domas,* October 5, 1922; *Courier,* November 1922, p. 1, and December 1922, p. 1; *Shadows,* December 1922, p. 18.

13. *Courier,* December 1922, p. 1, January 1923, p. 1, February 1923, p. 3, and March 1923, p. 2; *Shadows,* February 1923, p. 20.

14. *Historia Domas,* February 7 and March 18, 1923; *Courier,* March 1923, p. 1, and April 1923, p. 2.

15. *Historia Domas,* May 31, 1924; *Shadows,* October 1923, pp. 23–24; *Courier,* June 1923, p. 4, and December 1925, pp. 3–6; Leahy, p. 45.

16. HCM, April 25, 1921, July 3 and November 27, 1923, and January 17 and March 13 and 20, 1924; *CUB,* Arts, 1924–25.

17. *Historia Domas,* March 21 and April 22, 1925; Board of Regents Meeting Minutes, October 1, 1925, PVF; *Courier,* July 1923, p. 3, and February 1926, p. 4.

18. *Historia Domas,* September 9, 1925, and January 18, 1926; *Courier,* January 1926, p. 1.

19. HCM, September 18, 1925; *Historia Domas,* November 19–21, 1925; *Courier,* August 1920, p. 3, and November 1925, p. 4.

20. HCM, January 28, 1926, and May 31, 1927; *TCA,* October 1929, p. 5.

21. *CUB,* Arts, 1920; *Courier,* July 1922, p. 1; *Historia Domas,* October 24, 1926.

22. *Courier,* November 1926, p. 1; *TCA,* October 1927, p. 6, December 1927, pp. 3–4, and January 1928, p. 3.

23. HCM, November 16, 1926; *TCA,* November 1927, p. 8; *Creightonian,* September 28, 1926, p. 1, November 30, 1926, p. 3, May 31, 1927, p. 1, October 4, 1927, p. 1 and March 20, 1928, p. 1; Milton Abrahams, River City Roundup Interview #43, August 4, 1988, HSDC.

24. *TCA,* February 1928, p. 4, and November 1928, p. 3; *Historia Domas,* October 16–19, 1928; Golden Jubilee file, PVF.

25. *TCA,* June 1927, p. 3; HCM, September 20, October 18, and November 29, 1927, and July 23, 1928.

26. *Historia Domas,* April 25 and September 1, 1929; *TCA,* October 1928, p. 4, and October 1929, p. 3; *Creightonian,* October 2, 1930, p. 1; McDermott, p. 59.

27. *TCA,* October 1929, p. 3; McDermott, pp. 56–57; *Bluejay,* 1932, p. 11, has a picture of the Administration Building minus the cupola.

28. *CUB,* Arts, 1921–22 and 1928–29 and High School, 1921-22 and 1928-29; *TCA,* December 1928, p. 3, October 1929, p. 3, and February 1931, p. 12; McDermott, pp. 57–59; *Creightonian,* September 28, 1928, p. 2, and January 8, 1931, p. 1.

29. Szmrecsanyi, pp. 172–93; *Creightonian,* September 25, 1930, p. 1; *Omaha Chamber of Commerce Journal,* October 1930, p. 11.

30. *TCA,* March 1931, pp. 2, 8, April 1931, p. 2, May 1931 p. 4, June 1931, p. 4 and January 1933, p. 2; *Creightonian,* December 8, 1932, p. 1, and February 16, 1933, p. 1.

31. *TCA,* February 1934, p. 2, June 1934, p. 3, and January 1937, p. 1; Letter, Thomas J. Murphy, S. J, to Fr. Rector, March 25, 1948, and April 12, 1948, and William McCabe, S.J., to Fr. Provincial, April 14, 1948, Wills Folder, PVF; Szmercsanyi, pp. 141–43.

32. *TCA*, February 1933, p. 1, and May 1934, p. 4.

33. *TCA*, March 1931, p. 6, April 1933, p. 1, May 1933, p. 3, December 1934, p. 5, and October 1936, p. 4 and December 1936, p. 3 and May 1937, p. 3.

34. *TCA*, April 1933, p. 4, September 1933, p. 6, April 1934, p. 1, September 1934, p. 2, and December 1935, p. 6; *Creightonian*, March 30, 1933, p. 1, April 4, 1934, p. 1, May 23, 1934, p. 1, and September 25, 1934, p. 1; McDermott, pp. 59–60.

35. *TCA*, September 1933, p. 3, June 1937, p. 7, January 1938, p. 5; *Creightonian*, May 19, 1937, p. 1.

36. *Creightonian*, February 2, 1938, p. 1.

37. *TCA*, October 1939, p. 5, May 1940, p. 3, November 1940, p. 6, and December 1941, p. 4.

38. Leahy, pp. 34, 46.

39. Fitzgerald, pp. 10–12 and Appendix B, "Summary of Recommendations by the Commission on Higher Studies, 1931"; Leahy, pp. 37–43; *CUB*, Arts, 1920–21, 1931–32, 1932–33; 1937–38; *Creightonian*, October 2, 1935, p. 1.

40. Leahy, pp. 43–44, 95–102; Fitzgerald, pp. 21–24.

41. *TCA*, June 1927, p. 3; *Historia Domas*, July 25, 1928; *Bluejay*, 1926, 1927; *CUB*, Arts, 1926–27.

42. *CUB*, Arts, 1921–22, 1932–33, and 1938–39; *Historia Domas*, December 25, 1923, May 1, 1924, and September 29, 1929; Fitzgerald, Appendix B; Leahy, p. 112.

43. *Historia Domas*, March 30, 1925; HCM, February 27, 1925; Fitzgerald, Appendix B; *CUB*, Arts, 1920–21 and 1939–40; Paul C. Reinert, S.J., *Faculty Tenure in Colleges and Universities From 1900 to 1940* (St. Louis: St. Louis University Press, 1946), pp. 1–10.

44. *Historia Domas*, June 11, 1922, December 25, 1923, and May 1 and October 30, 1924; HCM, February 27, 1922, and October 27 and September 13, 1925; *Courier*, November 1922, p. 3, February 1923, p. 2, and December 1926, p. 2; *TCA*, November 1933, p. 12, October 1935, p. 10, November 1936, p. 9, February 1941, p. 4, and March 1941, p. 10; *Bluejay*, 1935, p. 178.

45. *Historia Domas*, December 20, 1920 and February 2, 1921; *Courier*, May 1926, p. 4; *Bluejay*, 1928; *TCA*, December 1937, p. 6, and October 1941, p. 5.

46. Rigge, Log, August 28, 1921; *Historia Domas*, April 3 and May 27, 1923; HCM, September 13, 1925; *Shadows*, May 1927, p. 7; *Creightonian*, December 14, 1927, p. 4; *Dictionary of American Biography*, vol. XV, pp. 601–02; Reynolds, pp. 146–49.

47. *CUB*, Arts, 1920–21 through 1940–41; *Courier*, February 1921, p. 2.

48. *CUB*, Arts, 1920–21 through 1940–41; Farrell, pp. 404–30.

49. *CUB*, Arts, 1920–21 through 1940–41; Leahy, p. 39.

50. *CUB*, Arts, 1920–21 through 1940–41; Leahy, p.

51. *Courier*, October 1921, p. 3; *TCA*, March 1931, p. 3; *CUB*, Arts, 1920–21 through 1940–41.

52. *CUB*, Arts, 1921–22, 1929–30, 1931–32, and 1938-39; *Shadows*, March 1924, p. 29; Rudolph, *Curriculum*, p. 248.

53. *CUB*, Arts, 1920–21 and 1929–30; *Creightonian*, March 29, 1939, p. 1; Rudolph, *American College and University*, pp. 456–60; Rudolph, *Curriculum*, p. 231.

54. *CUB*, Arts, 1925–25, 1931–32, and 1939–40, and combined issue 1940–42; *Creightonian*, October 17, 1924, p. 1, October 24, 1924, p. 1, December 5, 1924, p. 1, October 5, 1926, p. 1, November 6, 1930, p. 1, October 27, 1932, p. 1, September 23, 1936, p. 1, October 6, 1937, p. 1, and October 9, 1940, p. 1; *Courier*, October 1926, p. 2, and December 1926, p. 4.

55. HCM, September 15, 1925; *TCA*, October 1935, p. 15, and February 1940, p. 3; *Creightonian*, May 29, 1934, p. 1, and February 26, 1936, p. 1; *Chronicle*, November 1920, pp. 70–71, and December 1920, p. 139; *CUB*, Arts, 1920–21 through the combined issue 1941–43.

56. *CUB*, Arts, 1925–26 through the combined issue 1941–43.

57. *CUB*, Arts, 1924–25 and 1931–32; *Shadows*, April 1932, p. 9; *Creightonian*, February 12, 1931, p. 1, January 18, 1934, pp. 1–2, and October 30, 1935, p. 1; *TCA*, April 1937, p. 5, and February 1940, p. 4.

58. *CUB*, Arts, 1920–21, 1929–30, and 1931–32; *TCA*, January 1931, p. 12.

59. *TCA*, March 1934, p. 2, April 1937, pp. 4–5, and February 1940, p. 4; *Creightonian*, October 9, 1935, p. 1, April 15, 1936, p. 1, and September 20, 1939, p. 1.

60. Leahy, pp. 35–41; HCM, February 25, 1926; *CUB*, Arts, 1920–21 through 1940–41.

61. Knoll, p. 69; *TCA*, May 1929, p. 4, and November 1934, p. 2.

62. *TCA*, September 1933, p. 2, February 1934, p. 1, March 1934, p. 6, April 1934, p. 6, June 1935, p. 10, April 1938, p. 1, and May 1939, p. 9; *CUB*, Arts, combined issue 1941–43.

63. *TCA*, May 1934, p. 5, and March 1937, p. 5.

64. *Creightonian*, May 29, 1925, p. 8; *TCA*, February 1931, p. 12; *Bluejay*, 1924–1941; *CUB*, Arts, 1925–26 through 1940–41.

Chapter Six

1. Fitzgerald, p. 23; *TCA*, February 1935, p. 1.

2. *CUB*, Summer School, 1920 through 1932.

3. *CUB*, Summer School, combined issue 1933–34 through 1940–41; *Historia Domas*, June 25, 1922.

4. *CUB*, Arts, 1920–21 through 1939-40, containing enrollment figures for all schools; *CUB*, Summer School, 1920 through 1932, combined issue 1933–34 through 1938–39; *Courier*, August 1921, p. 1.

5. *CUB*, Summer Session Supplementary Announcement, 1919; *CUB*, Summer School, 1920 through 1940; *CUB*, Arts, 1940–42 (two-year issue); *Historia Domas*, September 30, 1923; HCM, October 9, 1925.

6. *CUB*, Arts, 1920–21; HCM, January 22, 1920; *Historia Domas*, March 8, 1920; *Courier*, March 1920, pp. 1, 3, and May 1922, p. 1; *Chronicle*, November 1920, p. 77, November 1925, p. 1, and December 1925, p. 2.

7. *CUB*, Arts, 1923–24 through 1931–32, including insert "Teachers' Course Special Bulletin, 1930"; *TCA*, November 1927, p. 3, and April 1941, p. 2.

8. *CUB*, Graduate School-University College, 1932–33 through 1940–41, *Bluejay*, 1933, p. 25; Vosper, p. 211.

9. *Historia Domas*, July 26, 1925; Leahy, p. 88, n22; T. L. Bouscaren, S.J., "The 'Corporate Colleges' Plan," *America*, January 9, 1926, pp. 307–08; *CUB*, Duchesne, 1926–27.

10. *CUB*, Duchesne, 1926–27; HCM, October 26, 1926, and December 3, 1926; *Historia Domas*, June 2, 1927; *Bluejay*, 1931, pp. 38–39; Sister Mary Mariella Bowler, *A History of Catholic Colleges for Women in the United States of America* (Washington, D.C.: The Catholic University of America, 1933), p. 70.

11. *CUB*, Duchesne, 1926–27 through 1931–32; *Creightonian*, November 2, 1926, p. 1; *TCA*, November 1929, p. 3; *Bluejay*, 1931, pp. 38–39; Bowler, p. 70; *Golden Record* (College of Saint Mary student publication), February 1930, p. 15, and October 1930, p. 5.

12. *CUB*, Duchesne, 1926–27 and 1930–31; *Courier*, April 1926, p. 3; Casper, Vol. II, pp. 337–43.

13. *Historia Domas*, April 30, 1929; *TCA*, May 1929, p. 3; *Creightonian*, May 2, 1929, p. 1; *CUB*, St. Mary, 1928–29 through 1935–36; Casper, vol. II, p. 343.

14. Vossen, pp. 4–5, 18.

15. Vossen, pp. 5–6; Boro and Mead, p. 88.

16. Vossen, pp. 5, 30; *Bluejay*, 1924; HCM, September 28, 1927.

17. Vossen, pp. 5–7, 30–31; *CUB*, St. Joseph's Nursing, 1928–29; *TCA*, March 1928, p. 3.

18. *Historia Domas*, January 17, 1929; *TCA*, February 1928, p. 3; Vossen, p. 17; Boro and Mead, pp. 82–84.

19. *Creightonian*, January 24, 1929, p. 1; Vossen, 18–21; Boro and Mead, p. 82.

20. *TCA*, September 1930, p. 5; *CUB*, Nursing, 1928–29 through 1937–39 (two-year issue); Vossen, pp. 33–35.

21. *CUB*, Nursing, 1929–30 through 1937–39, and Commencement Program insert, May 1940; Vossen, pp. 6-7, 20, 30–35.

22. *CUB*, Nursing, 1928–29 through 1939–40.

23. *CUB*, Nursing, 1928–29 through 1939–40; Vossen, pp. 13, 20.

24. *Courier*, February 1920, p. 1; *Historia Domas*, December 4, 1919; *CUB*, Commerce, 1920–21; Knoll, p. 54.

25. *CUB*, Commerce, 1920–21 through 1923–24; *Historia Domas*, September 29, 1923; The Creightonian, October 24, 1922, p. 1; Cahill, p. 6.

26. *CUB*, Commerce, 1920–21 through 1923–24; Cahill, pp. 5–6.

27. *CUB*, Commerce, 1920–21 through 1923–24; Cahill, pp. 6, 117.

28. *CUB*, Commerce, 1924–25, 1925–26, and 1934–35; *Historia Domas*, August 4, 1925; *Creightonian*, October 17, 1924, p. 1; Cahill, p. 7.

29. *CUB*, Commerce, 1924–25; *Courier*, March 1924, p. 1; *Creightonian*, October 4, 1924, p. 1, and October 28, 1960, p. 7; *Bluejay*, 1925, p. 128; Cahill, pp. 73–74.

30. *CUB*, Commerce, 1924–25 through 1939–40; *Bluejay*, 1925, p. 139; *Creightonian*, October 17, 1924, p. 3; Cahill, p. 13.

31. *CUB*, Commerce, 1924–25 through 1926–27; E. T. Grether, "The Development of the AACBSB Core Curriculum," in *The American Association of Collegiate Schools of Business, 1916–1966* (Homewood, IL: Richard D. Irwin, Inc., 1966), p. 147.

32. *CUB*, Commerce, 1927–28; *Shadows*, October 1929, p. 27; *Creightonian*, October 16, 1935, p. 1; Cahill, pp. 10–14; Vosper, 1975 interview with Walsh, pp. 134–35.

33. *CUB*, Commerce, 1935–36 and 1936–37; *TCA*, April 1929, p. 6; Cahill, pp. 14–19.

34. *CUB*, Commerce, 1924–25 through 1940–41; *TCA*, May 1940, p. 5.

35. *CUB*, Commerce, 1924–25 through 1940–41; *Courier*, March 1924, p. 1; *TCA*, May 1940, p. 1; Cahill, pp. 10, 14, 21, his enrollment figures sometimes differ from the numbers presented in the *CUB*.

36 *Creightonian*, May 3, 1927, p. 1, and May 18, 1933, p. 1; *TCA*, October 1927, p. 8, and February 1941, p. 1; *CUB*, Journalism, insert in 1933–34.

37. *CUB*, Journalism, 1933–34; *TCA*, June 1933, p. 14; McDermott, p. 15.

38. *CUB*, 1933–34; *TCA*, December 1935, p. 3, and February 1941, p. 1; *Bluejay*, 1936.

39. *CUB*, Journalism, 1933–34 through 1947–48;

40. Kremers and Urdang, p. 306; *CUB*, Pharmacy, 1920–21 through 1926–27; *Creightonian*, October 19, 1926, p. 1; *TCA*, October 1940, p. 9.

41. *CUB*, Pharmacy, 1920–21 through 1940–41; *Bluejay*, 1926; *TCA*, March 1931, p. 3, and February 1934, p. 6; *Creightonian*, September 25, 1935, p. 3.

42. *CUB*, Pharmacy, 1920–21 through 1940–41; *Bluejay*, 1926.

43. Kenneth M. Ludmerer, *Learning to Heal: The Development of American Medical Education* (New York: Basic Books, 1985), pp. 249–50, 270; HCM, April 26, 1928; *CUB*, Medicine, 1919–20 through 1932–33.

44. *Courier*, April 1920, p. 4, and November 1926, p. 3; *CUB*, Medicine, 1920–21 through 1940–41; Boro and Mead, pp. 85–89; McDermott, p. 1.

45. *CUB*, Medicine, 1920–21 through 1940–41; *TCA*, January 1929, p. 6; Boro and Mead, p. 80; Vosper, p. 160; Ludmerer, pp. 207–14; Martin Kaufman, "American Medical Education," in Ronald L. Numbers, ed., *The Education of American Physicians* (Berkeley: University of California Press, 1980), p. 22.

46. Ludmerer, p. 217; Boro and Mead, p. 85–86; HCM, April 26, 1928; *TCA*, March 1931, p. 3.

47. Boro and Mead, pp. 81, 105–08; *Creightonian*, September 21, 1933, p. 1; *TCA*, October 1932, p. 3, October 1939, p. 5, November 1940, p. 2, and December 1941, p. 6.

48. *CUB*, Medicine, 1920–21 through 1932–33; *Creightonian*, October 11, 1923, p. 1; *TCA*, May 1929, p. 3; *Bluejay*, 1936.

49. *CUB*, Medicine, 1932–33; *Courier*, April 1923, p. 1; *Creightonian*, August 30, 1931, p. 1; Boro and Mead, p. 95.

50. *CUB*, Medicine, 1932–33 through 1940–41; Boro and Mead, pp. 80–81, 94.

51. Rigge, Log, May 28 and November 23, 1920, September 23, 1921, and January 15, 1922; *Historia Domas*, November 23, 1920, and April 4 and 7 and June 28, 1921; *Chronicle*, October 1920, p. 37; *Courier*, December 1926, p. 3; *TCA*, March 1931, pp. 2–3, 8.

52. *CUB*, Dental School, 1920–21 through 1940–41; *Chronicle*, February 1921, p. 253; *Courier*, June 1922, p. 2, August 1923, p. 2, and May 1924, p. 1; *TCA*, February 1937, p. 5, and November 1939, p. 5; Vosper, pp. 171–72.

53. *CUB*, Dental School, 1920–21 through 1940–41; *Chronicle*, December 1921, pp. 146–47; *TCA*, September 1933, p. 3; *Creightonian*, September 21, 1933, p. 1, and October 16, 1935, p. 1.

54. *CUB*, Dental School, 1920–21 through 1940–41.

55. *CUB*, Dental School, 1920–21 through 1940–41, *Shadows*, February 1923, pp. 8–9, 40; *Bluejay*, 1925, p. 117; *Creightonian*, October 30, 1926, p. 2; *TCA*, October 1927, p. 8, and November 1939, p. 7.

56. Frankino and Crisman, p. 233; *Historia Domas*, October 4, 1921; *Creightonian*, December 5, 1929, p. 1.

57. *CUB*, Law, 1920–21 through 1940–41; *Courier*, May 1920, p. 1; *TCA*, June 1936, p. 7, and June 1937, p. 9; Frankino and Crisman, p. 232; Vosper, p. 145.

58. Robert Stevens, *Law School: Legal Education in America from the 1850s to the 1980s* (Chapel Hill: University of North Carolina Press, 1983), pp. 158–62; *CUB*, Law, 1919–20 through 1940–41; HCM, January 8, 1924; Frankino and Crisman, p. 233.

59. *CUB*, Law, 1920–21 through 1941–42; Chronicle, February 1921, pp. 249–50; *TCA*, June 1936, p. 14, and October 1938, p. 3.

60. *CUB*, Graduate School, 1926–27; Vosper, p. 120; Kirby, 63; McDermott, p. 67.

61. *TCA*, October 1927, p. 4 and October 1928, p. 6, and April 1941, pp. 2–3; McDermott, pp. 68–69; Goodchild, pp. 94–96.

62. *CUB*, Graduate School, 1926–27 through 1939–40; *TCA*, June 1927, p. 3.

63. *CUB*, Graduate School, 1926–27 through 1939–40; *TCA*, March 1931, p. 5; McDermott, pp. 69–70; Leahy, pp. 48–54; Fitzgerald, pp. 25–78.

64. *CUB*, Graduate School, 1926–27 through 1939–40; Vosper, p. 208.

65. Chronicle, November 1920, p. 91; *Shadows*, December 1924, pp 17–18, 29–30; *Creightonian*, February 26, 1936, p. 2.

Chapter Seven

1. *Chronicle*, January 1922, pp. 177–79 and May 1922, p. 415; *Courier*, March 1, 1922, pp. 1, 4, April 1922, pp. 1, 4, June 1922, pp. 1, 4, and December 1925, p. 2.

2. *Shadows*, March 1923, p. 23, and October 1923, p. 7; *Creightonian*, November 15, 1923, p. 2, and October 17, 1924, p. 3.

3. HCM, December 5, 1920; *Bluejay*, 1925, p. 163, and 1926, p. 150; *Creightonian*, October 30, 1925, p. 1, October 19, 1927, p. 1, September 28, 1928, p. 1, November 2, 1928, p. 1, September 19, p. 1, April 27, 1933, p. 1, and May 2, 1934, p. 1; Courier, December 1926, p. 1; *TCA*, June 1927, p. 8, and November 1932, p. 3; *Shadows*, October 1923, p. 7, January 1926, p. 40, and March 1930, pp. 14–15; *Colleagues* (Employee Newsletter), March 1997.

4. *Creightonian*, March 12, 1926, p. 1, February 28, 1928, p. 1, and September 29, 1932, p. 2; *TCA*, April 28, p. 8.

5. *Creightonian*, February 16, 1923, p. 1, February 15, 1927, p. 1, February 15, 1934, p. 2, February 22, 1934, pp. 1–2, and March 1, 1934, p. 1.

6. *Creightonian*, March 7, 1934, p. 1, April 4, 1934, p. 1, April 18, 1934, p. 1, and April 25, 1934, p. 1; *TCA*, May 1934, p. 5.

7. *Creightonian*, January 25, 1936, p. 1, February 5, 1936, p. 1, October 6, 1936, pp. 1–2, December 15, 1937, pp. 1–2, and May 4, 1938, p. 1.

8. *Creightonian*, October 24, 1924, p. 1, January 9, 1925, p. 2, March 3, 1934, p. 1, December 15, 1937, p. 2, and May 6, 1940, p. 1.

9. *Chronicle*, December 1919, title page, and April 1920, title page and p. 248; *Shadows*, December 1922, title page and p. 25.

10. *Shadows*, 1922 through 1941; *Creightonian*, September 19, 1929, p. 1, and March 3, 1942, p. 1.

11. *Creightonian*, 1922 through 1941, and October 11, 1924, p. 4; *Courier*, November 1922, p. 2; *Shadows*, May 1923, p. 19.

12. *Courier*, November 1925, p. 4; *Shadows*, April 1930, p. 19; *TCA*, April 1931, p. 12; *Creightonian*, April 27, 1933, p. 1, May 15, 1935, p. 1, May 13, 1936, p. 1, April 14, 1937, p. 1, October 1, 1941, p. 1, and January 14, 1942, p. 1.

13. *Courier*, March 1921, p. 2, and April 1921, p. 2; *Shadows*, December 1922, pp. 39–40, and May 1923, p. 19. *Creightonian*, March 30, 1930, p. 2, April 3, 1930, p. 1, October 6, 1932, p. 1, January 15, 1936, p. 1, October 21, 1936, p. 1, and September 25, 1940, p. 1.

14. *Courier*, December 1923, p. 2, and March 1924, p. 2; *Creightonian*, November 23, 1923, p. 1, December 7, 1923, p. 1, February 1, 1924, p. 1, March 13, 1924, p. 1, and May 22, 1924, p. 1; *Bluejay*, 1924.

15. *Bluejay*, 1924 through 1941; HCM, January 10, 1928; *Creightonian*, December 12, 1924, p. 1, March 19, 1925, p. 1, March 26, 1926, p. 1, September 28, 1928, p. 2, December 7, 1928, p. 1, November 17, 1932, p. 1, November 2, 1938, p. 1, and November 26, 1941, p. 1.

16. *Chronicle*, April 1922, p. 383; *Creightonian*, May 8, 1925, p. 2; HCM, September 13 and October 1, 1925; *Historia Domas*, October 21, 1925.

17. *Bluejay*, 1924 through 1941; *TCA*, March 1929, p. 5; *Creightonian*, March 5, 1941, p. 1.

18. *Chronical*, March 1920, p. 262; *Creightonian*, December 5, 1924, p. 1, December 12, 1924, p. 2, and September 25, 1934, p. 1; *TCA*, February 1928, p. 8, and May 1929, pp. 3, 8; *Shadows*, October 1929, p. 13; *Bluejay*, 1929, p. 198.

19. *Chronical*, November 1921, p. 92; *Shadows*, May 1923, p. 7; *Creightonian*, February 14, 1924, p. 1, May 8, 1924, p. 1, and May 22, 1924, p. 1; *TCA*, April 1927, p. 6; *Bluejay*, 1925, pp. 180–81, and 1926, pp. 166–72.

20. *TCA*, May 1929, p. 3, February 1931, p. 12, October 1934, p. 4, April 1937, p. 7; *Creightonian*, November 21, 1929, p. 4, March 18, 1931, p. 2, November 23, 1933, p. 1, October 2, 1935, p. 1, and October 23, 1935, p. 4; *Bluejay*, 1932, pp. 188–90, and 1939, pp. 138–39.

21. *Shadows*, May 1927, p. 28, and subsequent spring editions; *Creightonian*, March 22, 1927, p. 1, March 18, 1936, p. 1, and May 6, 1936, p. 1.

22. *Courier*, September 1921, p. 4, and November 1925, P. 7; *TCA*, December 1928, p. 7, and January 1933, p. 12; *Bluejay*, 1924 through 1941, *CUB*, Arts, 1921–22 through 1940–41, and Commerce, 1921–22 through 1940–41; Cahill, p. 12.

23. *Bluejay*, 1924 through 1941; *CUB*, Commerce, 1921–22 through 1940–41, Duchesne, 1925–26 through 1935–36, Nursing, 1928–29 through 1940–41, Saint Mary, 1929–30 through 1935–36; *Creightonian*, March 25, 1931, p. 1; Vossen, p. 20.

24. *Chronicle,* May–June, 1921, p. 424; *CUB,* each school, 1921–22 through 1940–41; HCM, September 17, 1925; *Bluejay,* 1926, p. 302.

25. HCM, November 18, 1921; *Courier,* November 1921, p. 1, and May 1926, p. 1; Rigge, Log, May [no day], 1922; *Creightonian,* December 21, 1922, p. 1, May 15, 1924, p. 1, and May 17, 1928, p. 1; *TCA,* November 1927, p. 8; *Bluejay,* 1934, pp. 180–82.

26. *Bluejay,* 1932, p. 168, 1933, pp. 158, 217 and 1934, pp. 268–69, and 1935, pp. 162–72; *Creightonian,* January 12, 1933, p. 1, May 25, 1933, p. 1, January 25, 1934, p. 1, January 30, 1934, p. 1, and October 2, 1964, p. 5; *TCA,* March 1940, pp. 5–6.

27. *Courier,* September 1919, p. 1, December 1920, p. 4, January 1920, 172–75, October 1920, pp. 35–37, November 1920, p. 5, March 1921, pp. 304–05, and June 1922, p. 4; *Historia Domas,* May 7, 1924; HCM, January 14, 1926 and December 7, 1927; *Bluejay,* 1928, p. 228–32 and 1931, p. 181–84.

28. *Courier,* November 1919, p. 3, April 1921, p. 369, and July 1922, p. 2; *Bluejay,* 1924 through 1941.

29. *Shadows,* December 1930, p. 17; *Creightonian,* March 11, 1931, p. 1, October 19, 1933, p. 4, April 11, 1934, p. 2, April 13, 1938, p. 1, and September 25, 1940, p. 1; *Bluejay,* 1931, 1933, 1935; *TCA,* June 1937, p. 9.

30. *Bluejay,* 1930, pp. 168–69, 1931, p. 183–84, 1934, p. 211 and 1935, pp. 190, 233, and 1936, pp. 202, 254.

31. Cahill, p. 88; *Creightonian,* October 4, 1922, p. 1.

32. *Creightonian,* November 6, 1925, p. 2.

33. *Shadows,* February 1923, p. 7; *Courier,* February 1926, p. 2; *Bluejay,* 1924, p. 267, 1925, pp. 308–09, and 1929, p. 299; *Creightonian,* November 2, 1922, p. 1, December 4, 1925, p. 1, and December 14, 1928, p. 1; *TCA,* October 1929, p. 3; virtually every issue of the *Chronicle* in the early 1920s had articles reviewing the social activities of the fraternities, as well as issues of the *Creightonian* during the entire interwar era.

34. *Creightonian,* October 11, 1924, p. 2, and December 18, 1925, p. 1.

35. *Chronicle,* February 1922, pp. 237–38; *Courier,* May 1922, p. 4, April 1926, p. 1, and May 1926, P. 4; *TCA,* December 1927, p. 8, April 1928, p. 6, May 1928, p. 8, April 1929, p. 3, and March 1931, pp. 8, 12; *Creightonian,* February 8, 1927, p. 1, and May 7, 1931, p. 1; *Shadows,* April 1930, pp. 14, 29; *Bluejay,* 1924 through 1941.

36. *Bluejay,* 1925, pp. 294–95, and 1929, p. 302, 1930, p. 214, 1936, p. 268, and 1941, p. 241; *Creightonian,* November 27, 1934, pp. 1, 4, December 5, 1934, p. 2, October 2, 1935, p. 1, and December 4, 1935, p. 1.

37. *Creightonian,* May 1, 1925, p. 1, October 3, 1929, p. 2, January 23, 1935, p. 1, December 18, 1940, p. 1, and January 29, 1941, p. 1.

38. *Shadows,* May 1927, pp. 26–27; *Creightonian,* April 24, 1924, p. 1, and October 2, 1925, p. 2; *Historia Domas,* March 5 and September 18, 1925; HCM, April 25, 1921, and September 18, 1925.

39. *Chronicle,* April 1921, p. 371; *TCA,* November 1927, p. 8, and May 1931, p. 12; *Creightonian,* November 24, 1932, p. 1, and February 16, 1933, p. 1.

40. *Creightonian,* October 4, 1924, pp. 1, 4, October 7, 1925, p. 1, September 27, 1927, p. 1, September 28, 1928, p. 2, September 19, 1929, p. 2, May 8, 1930, p. 2, September 18, 1930, p. 1, April 9, 1931, p. 1, September 28, 1933, p. 2, and September 29, 1937, p. 1; *TCA,* October 1927, p. 8.

41. *Historia Domas,* May 28, 1920; *Courier,* June 1922, pp. 1–2, 4; *Creightonian,* May 22, 1924, p. 1, May 14, 1931, p. 1, and May 28, 1931, p. 1.

42. *Historia Domas,* May 6, 1926; *Courier,* May 1926, p. 4; *Creightonian,* November 23, 1933, p. 1, May 23, 1936, p. 1, and May 30, 1936, p. 1.

43. *CUB*, Arts, 1920-21; *Historia Domas*, August 6, 1921, and September 30, 1922; *Courier*, January 1920, p. 2, April 1920, p. 4, and May 1920, p. 3; *Chronicle*, April 1920, p. 273, December 1920, p. 153, March 1921, p. 322, October 1921, p. 48, and December 1921, pp. 123–30.

44. *Chronicle*, November 1922, p. 77; *Historia Domas*, November 18, 1922, and November 3, 1923; *Courier*, insert between May and June 1922, September 1922, p. 3, and June 1923, p. 3; *Creightonian*, June 1, 1923, pp. 4–6, November 3, 1923 p. 8, and November 22, 1923, p. 1; *TCA*, April 1930, p. 6.

45. *Chronicle*, April 1921, pp. 352-3; *Bluejay*, 1929, p. 125, 1930, p. 140, 1931, pp. 140–44, and 1932, p. 154-60; *Creightonian*, October 5, 1933, p. 5.

46. *Creightonian*, March 9, 1923, p. 5, May 3, 1923, p. 1, May 22, 1925, p. 4, January 9, 1930, p. 3, January 23, 1930, p. 3, March 13, 1930, p. 3, and January 15, 1931, p. 3.

47. *Courier*, March 1926, p. 3; *TCA*, March 1928, p. 8, March 1931, p. 12, January 1933, p. 12, and April 1936, p. 10; *Creightonian*, March 5, 1941, p. 1; *Bluejay*, 1932, p. 148, 1933, pp. 136, 148, 211, 1934, p. 146, 1935, pp. 120, 132, 1936, pp. 139–40, 1938, p. 160, 1940, pp. 122–23, and 1941, pp. 120–21.

48. *Chronicle*, April 1920, pp. 250–51; *Courier*, April 1920, p. 2, and April 1923, p. 3; *Creightonian*, January 18, 1924, pp. 1, 2, January 25, 1924, p. 1, February 21, 1924, p. 3, January 23, 1925, p. 4, February 20, 1925, p. 4, March 4, 1925, p. 7, and February 10, 1937, p. 3.

49. Official Creighton University Varsity Basketball Records (VBR), Athletic Department; *Creightonian*, April 17, 1925, p. 7, and October 28, 1926, p. 6; *Bluejay*, 1926, p. 223, and 1927, p. 231.

50. VBR; *Creightonian*, December 6, 1927, p. 1, and October 26, 1928, p. 3; *TCA*, April 1937, p. 8.

51. *Courier*, November 1922, p. 3.

52. *Historia Domas*, October 3, 1925, and October 6, 1929; HCM, May 15 and September 13, September 17, September 30, October 1, 1925, October 12, November 14, and December 3, 1926.

53. *Courier*, March 1924, p. 4; VBR.

54. *Creightonian*, October 11, 1924, p. 2, October 17, 1924, p. 3, March 13, 1930, p. 2, and December 7, 1933, p. 1; *TCA*, December 1928, p. 8.

55. *Courier*, November 1922, p. 2, and October 1926, p. 4; *Historia Domas*, November 3, 1924.

56. *Creightonian*, February 1, 1924, p. 1, October 11, 1924, p. 2, December 14, 1933, p. 1, and January 23, 2003, p. 5; *Bluejay*, 1924 through 1941; Vossen, p. 6.

57. *Creightonian*, November 3, 1923, p. 8, April 17, 1925, p. 7, March 5, 1926, p. 4, December 20, 1926, p. 3, and March 13, 1930, p. 3; *Courier*, September 1923, p. 4.

58. *Historia Domas*, September 25 and October 30, 1926, and October 2, 1928; HCM, March 18 and June 15, 1926, March 22 and May 27, 1927, and January 17, 1928; *Omaha Chamber of Commerce Journal*, vol. 17, September 22, 1928, p. 9; *Creighton University Football Dope Book*, 1942 (FDB), p. 23.

59. HCM, December 14, 1927; *Shadows*, October 1929, p. 13; *Creightonian*, February 2, 1930, p. 2; *TCA*, April 1930, p. 2; FDB, p. 23.

60. *TCA*, May 1930, p. 6, October 1932, p. 8, November 1932, pp. 2, 9, October 1933, p. 9, February 1934, p. 10, and April 1934, p. 6; *Creightonian*, September 21, 1933, p. 5, and October 5, 1933, p. 5; FDB, p. 23.

61. *TCA*, December 1933, p. 1, and March 1934, pp. 1–2.

62. *TCA*, March 1934, p. 1, December 1934, pp. 9–10, and January 1935, pp. 8-9.

63. *TCA*, March 1935, p. 1 and May 1935, p. 1, November 1935, p. 10, January 1936, p. 1, and April 1936, p. 7; *Creightonian*, April 21, 1961, p. 8.

64. FDB; *TCA*, May 1935, p. 13, and April 1937, p. 9.

Chapter Eight

1. *TCA*, May 1941, pp. 5–6; *TCA*, March 1941, p. 10, and October 1943, p. 5; *Creightonian*, March 25, 1942, p. 1, September 30, 1942, p. 1, September 24, 1943, p. 1, and October 6, 1944, p. 4.

2. Harold W. Dodds, "Education in Uniform: The Army and Navy Programs for the Colleges," *Atlantic Monthly*, vol. 171, February 1943, p. 44; Gene M. Lyons and John W. Masland, *Education and Military Leadership* (Princeton: Princeton University Press, 1959), p. 59; *Creightonian*, April 15, 1942, p. 3.

3. *Creightonian*, May 6, 1942, p. 3, May 13, 1942, p. 1, and September 23, 1942, p. 1.

4. Lyons and Masland, pp. 60–61; Louis E. Keefer, *Scholars in Foxholes: The Story of the Army Specialized Training Program in World War II* (Jefferson, N. C.: McFarland & Co., Inc., 1988), pp. 17–22; Jennings Wagoner and Robert L. Baxter, Jr., "Higher Education Goes to War: The University of Virginia's Response to World War II," *Virginia Magazine of History and Biography*, vol. 100, 1992, p. 404; *TCA*, April 1943, p. 1; *Creightonian*, October 23, 1942, p. 1, November 6, 1942, p. 1, February 12, 1943, p. 1, February 19, 1943, p. 1, and March 26, 1943, p. 1.

5. Lyons and Masland, pp. 60–61; Louis Keefer, "Exceptional Young Americans: Soldiers and Sailors on College Campuses in World War II," *Prologue*, 1992, no. 4, pp. 375–77; Robert G. Hawley, "The Army Quits the Colleges," *Harper's*, April 1944, pp. 423–24; *Creightonian*, March 26, 1943, p. 1.

6. Dodds, p. 42; Wagoner and Baxter, pp. 414–15; Keefer, Prologue, pp. 377–78.

7. *Creightonian*, February 19, 1943, p. 1, February 26, 1943, p. 1, and December 15, 1944, p. 7; *TCA*, April 1944, p. 3.

8. *Creightonian*, February 26, 1943, p. 1, March 5, 1943, p. 1, March 19, 1943, p. 1, May 19, 1943, p. 1, and November 19, 1943, p. C (an insert); *TCA*, February 1943, p. 3, and April 1944, p. 3.

9. *Creightonian*, April 9, 1943, p. 1, September 24, 1943, p. 3, November 19, 1943, unnumbered insert, and December 3, 1943, p. A (an insert); Keefer, Prologue, p. 378.

10. Hawley, p. 419; Keefer, Prologue, pp. 379–80; *TCA*, April 1944, pp. 3, 6, and June 1944, p. 11; *Creightonian*, February 26, 1943, p. 1, and April 28, 1944, p. 8.

11. Keefer, *Scholars in Foxholes*, p. 66; *Creightonian*, October 6, 1944, pp. 1, 7, and May 4, 1945, p. 6.

12. *Creightonian*, September 22, 1944, p. 1, October 6, 1944, p. 1, October 20, 1944, p. 1, and November 3, 1944, p. 1.

13. Boro and Mead, pp. 106-12; *CUB*, Medicine, 1942–43.

14. Boro and Mead, pp. 110-13; *CUB*, Medicine, 1943–44.

15. Boro and Mead, pp. 112–15; *TCA*, February 1943, p. 6, March 1943, p. 6, April 1943, p. 5, and February 1944, p. 7; *Creightonian*, October 6, 1944, p. 1, and October 5, 1945, p. 1.

16. *CUB*, Dental, 1942–43 and multi-year edition 1944–47; *Creightonian*, September 22, 1944, p. 1, and May 4, 1945, p. 1.

17. Vossen, pp. 7-8, 22; *CUB*, Nursing, multi-year editions 1941–43 through 1945–47.

18. *Creightonian*, September 24, 1943, p. 8, October 8, 1943, p. 1, March 24, 1944, p. 1, and February 9, 1945, p. 8; *TCA*, April 1942, p. 4, December 1942, p. 8, December 1945, pp. 12, 15, and December 1947, p. 11.

19. *TCA*, June 1942, p. 7, February 1943, p. 5, June 1943, p. 1, and August 1947, p. 8; "Nebraska Heroes, Their Deeds of Valor," *Nebraska History*, vol. 25, January–March, 1944, pp. 11–13; Letter, Robert W. Horton, Director of Public Relations, U.S. Maritime Commission to Rev. J. P. Zuercher, February 12, 1945, PVF.

20. *CUB*, Pharmacy, multi-year edition 1942–46; *TCA*, June 1943, p. 6, and December 1943, p. 7.

21. Wagoner and Baxter, p. 407; *CUB*, Graduate School, 1942–43 through 1946–47; Frankino and Crisman, pp. 233–34; *CUB*, Law, 1942–43 through 1945–46; *TCA*, June 1943, p. 6; *Creightonian*, November 6, 1942, p. 1.

22. Robert F. Spiller, "Higher Education and the War," *Journal of Higher Education*, vol. 50, July–August, 1979, pp. 514–20; Wagoner and Baxter, p. 407; Cahill, p. 25; *TCA*, February 1942, pp. 1, 7; *Creightonian*, January 14, 1942, p. 1, and January 21, 1942, p. 1.

23. *Creightonian*, September 23, 1942, p. 1, October 7, 1942, p. 1, November 20, 1942, p. 1, and January 29, 1943, p. 1; *TCA*, April 1944, p. 10; *CUB*, undergraduate combined, 1942 and 1943–44.

24. Wagoner and Baxter, p. 405, n9; *TCA*, December 1941, p. 6, February 1942, p. 1, and April 1944, p. 9; *Creightonian*, March 9, 1945, p. 1; *CUB*, undergraduate combined, 1942 through 1945–46; *CUB*, Summer, 1942 through 1946.

25. *Creightonian*, January 22, 1943, p. 1, and October 6, 1944, p. 3; *CUB*, undergraduate combined, 1942 through 1946–47; Commencement insert, *CUB*, undergraduate combined, 1942.

26. *TCA*, February 1942, p. 6; "Forward on the Land," Creighton University Rural Life Institute brochure, PVF.

27. *Omaha World-Herald*, May 13, 1943, p. 4; *TCA*, June 1943, p. 6, and December 1943, p. 3.

28. *TCA*, October 1943, p. 11, and February 1944, p. 12; *Creightonian*, September 22, 1944, pp. 1–2, and October 6, 1944, p. 2.

29. *TCA*, April 1944, p. 9; *Creightonian*, April 28, 1944, p. 2, October 6, 1944, p. 2, October 20, 1944, p. 1, January 2, 1945, p. 2, and February 9, 1945, p. 8.

30. *Creightonian*, October 6, 1944, p. 1, December 1, 1944, p. 2, February 23, 1945, p. 1, and March 23, 1945, p. 1.

31. Wagoner and Baxter, p. 419; *TCA*, February 1942, p. 9; *Creightonian*, September 30, 1942, p. 1, October 23, 1942, p. 1, December 4, 1942, p. 1, March 5, 1943, p. 1, and May 19, 1943, p. 1.

32. *Creightonian*, April 16, 1943, p. 1, and May 7, 1943, p. 1; *TCA*, April 1944, p. 4.

33. *Creightonian*, December 10, 1941, p. 3, April 22, 1942, p. 3, September 23, 1942, p. 3, and April 9, 1943, p. 3.

34. Wagoner and Baxter, p. 416; Power, pp. 279–80; *Creightonian*, March 6, 1943, p. 3, and May 7, 1943, p. 5; *TCA*, October 1945, p. 4; *Window*, vol. 9, no. 2 (Winter 1992–92), pp. 15–21; VBR.

35. *Creightonian*, September 22, 1944, p. 3, October 20, 1944, p. 2, December 1, 1944, p. 7, and May 18, 1945, p. 11.

36. *TCA*, February 1942, p. 9; *CUB*, all university, 1942–43; *Creightonian*, December 3, 1943, p.1, and May 4, 1945, p. 1.

37. *Creightonian*, January 21, 1942, p. 1, October 23, 1942, p. 4, November 19, 1943, p. 2, October 6, 1944, p. 8, and November 17, 1944, p. 2; *TCA*, June 1944, p. 3, February 1946, p. 12, and October 1951, p. 3; Creighton Alumni Office records; Nancy B. Bourchier, "Let Us Take Care of Our Field: The National Association for Physical Education of College Women and World War II," *Journal of Sport History*, vol. 25, Spring 1998, p. 72.

38. *TCA*, November 1945, p. 4, February 1946, p. 5, December 1946, p. 5, August 1947, p. 11, March 1948, p. 6, September 1948, p. 7, and March 1949, p. 11; *Creightonian*, September 27, 1946, p. 1, and September 30, 1949, p. 1; G. I. Bill File, Registrar's Office; Vosper, p. 211, 1975 interview with Registrar Jack Williams.

39. *Creightonian*, September 27, 1946, p. 1, November 1, 1946, p. 1, November 8, 1946, p. 1, November 17, 1947, p. 1, February 14, 1947, p. 1, October 3, 1947, p. 1, and November 9, 1951, p. 6; *CUB*, Arts, 1947–48.

40. *TCA*, December 1946, p. 5, July 1947, p. 7, and October 1949, p. 7; *Creightonian*, February 14, 1947, p. 1, October 3, 1947, p. 1, and May 5, 1950, p. 4.

41. *CUB*, Arts, 1945–46 through 1949–50; *TCA*, December 1943, p. 5, February 1946, pp. 5, 12, December 1946, p. 4, and July 1948, p. 8; *Creightonian*, February 8, 1946, p. 1.

42. *TCA*, December 1943, p. 3, November 1945, p. 4, April 1946, p. 5, September 1947, p. 6, and July 1950, p. 5; Vosper, pp. 58–62, 1975 interview with Fr. Bowdern.

43. *TCA*, January 1946, p. 4, January 1947, p. 5, December 1947, p. 8, and January 1948, p. 3; Vosper, pp. 62–66; Board of Trustees Minutes (Jesuits), December 13, 1951, PVF (hereafter BTM); Lay Board of Regents Minutes, April 8 and 29, and November 22, 1946, and September 8, 1948, PVF (hereafter, (LBRM).

44. *TCA*, December 1945, p. 5, January 1946, p. 5, April 1946, p. 4, July 1947, p. 12, November 1947, p. 12, and October 1948, p. 8.

45. *TCA*, November 1945, back cover, April 1946, p. 8, January 1947, p. 13, and April 1948, p. 4.

46. *TCA*, November 1947, p. 12, and June 1950, back cover; *CUB*, undergraduate combined, 1945–46, and Arts, 1946–47 through 1949–50.

47. LBRM, November 22, 1946; *TCA*, May–June 1946, p. 4, December 1946, p. 4, January 1947, p. 5, April 1947, p. 4, July 1947, p. 4, December 1947, p. 8, and vol. XXVII, no. 10 (1954, new serial identification form), p. 9.

48. *TCA*, January 1948, p. 5, November 1948, p. 4, January 1949, p. 10, and May 1949, p. 4, 8; LBRM, November 1, 1948.

49. *TCA*, May 1949, pp. 8, 10, June 1949, p. 5, July 1949, p. 4, August 1949, p. 7, October 1949, p. 5, November 1949, p. 6, January 1950, p. 6, March 1950, p. 9, and October 1950, p. 8.

50. *Creightonian*, September 30, 1949, p. 1, and March 10, 1950, p. 1; *CUB*, combined undergraduate, 1945–46, and Arts, 1950–51; *CUB*, Medicine, 1949–50; *TCA*, March 1949, p. 11; G.I. Bill File; Boro and Mead, p. 119.

51. Fitzgerald, pp. 83–90, n44, p. 261.

52. *TCA*, June 1947, p. 6, and October 1948, p. 10; *Creightonian*, March 22, 1946, pp. 1–2; *CUB*, Medicine, 1945–46 through 1949–50.

53. BTM, July 6, 1950; Boro and Mead, p. 121; *TCA*, August 1948, p. 4; *CUB*, Medicine, 1949–50.

54. *TCA*, August 1948, p. 4, and November 1949, p. 8; *Creightonian*, September 17, 1948, p. 4; *CUB*, Medicine, 1949–50.

55. Herbert E. King, "Dental Education Through the Years," *TCA*, September 1949, pp. 4–5; *Creightonian*, May 18, 1945, p. 1; Vosper, pp. 58–59, 1975 interview with Fr. Bowdern.

56. *TCA*, November 1945, p. 5, and April 1946, p. 4; *Creightonian*, March 15, 1946, p. 1; *CUB*, Dentistry, 1949–50; Vacanti, p. 3.

57. *Creightonian*, May 18, 1945, p. 1; *TCA*, April 1946, p. 4; *CUB*, Dental, 1949–50; LBRM, February 2, 1950.

58. *CUB*, Dental, 1946–47 through 1949–50; *TCA*, July 1950, p. 7; G.I. Bill File.

59. *CUB*, Pharmacy, 1945–46 through 1949–50; *Creightonian*, September 30, 1949, p. 1; G.I. Bill File.

60. *TCA*, May-June 1946, p. 5, October 1949, p. 6, and January 1952, p. 10; *CUB*, undergraduate combined, 1945–46; *Creightonian*, September 30, 1949, p. 1; G.I. Bill File; Vossen, pp. 9, 36–38.

61. *CUB*, Nursing, 1947–48 and 1948–49.

62. *CUB*, Nursing, 1948-49 (no new Bulletin for 1949–50); *TCA*, October 1948, p. 10; Vossen, pp. 21, 36; *TCA*, July 1950, p. 5.

63. *CUB*, Law, 1946–47 through 1949–50; *Creightonian*, January 18, 1946, p. 1, March 14, 1947, p. 1, October 10, 1947, p. 3, and October 2, 1964, p. 5; *TCA*, September 1947, p. 7, March 1948, p. 4, and April 1948, p. 14; G.I. Bill File; Alumnews (succeeded *TCA*), May 1973, p. 2.

64. *CUB*, Graduate School, 1946–47 and 1948–49 (no 1949–50 printed); *Creightonian*, September 30, 1949, p. 1; G.I. Bill File.

65. *CUB*, Summer, 1945 through 1950; *Creightonian*, March 9, 1945, p. 1, and May 4, 1945, p. 1; *TCA*, May–June 1946, p. 5, and August 1947, p. 9; Wagoner and Baxter, p. 427.

66. *CUB*, Commerce, 1945–46; *Creightonian*, September 30, 1949, p. 1; G.I. Bill File.

67. *CUB*, Commerce, 1947–48 through 1949–50; *Creightonian*, September 30, 1949, p. 1; *TCA*, June 1949, p. 16; Grether, p. 152; Cahill, pp. 26–27.

68. *CUB*, Arts, 1945–46 through 1949–50; *TCA*, March 1934, p. 2, February 1948, p. 7, March 1949, p. 9, and June 1950, p. 10; *Creightonian*, February 3, 1937, p. 1, February 4, 1949, p. 1, and September 30, 1949, p. 1; G.I. Bill File.

69. *CUB*, Arts, 1945–46 and 1946–47; *Creightonian*, September 28, 1945, p. 1.

70. *CUB*, Arts, 1945–46 and 1947–48; *Creightonian*, October 12, 1945, p. 1; *TCA*, December 1945, p. 6.

71. *TCA*, April 1944, p. 4, December 1945, p. 4, June 1947, p. 5, December 1947, p. 7, February 1948, pp. 5, 12, August 1948, pp. 9, 10, and October 1948, p. 11; *Creightonian*, November 9, 1945, p. 1, and February 6, 1948, p. 1; *CUB*, Arts, 1948–49; *Bluejay*, 1949, p. 133.

72. *TCA*, December 1946, p. 7, January 1947, p. 9, February 1948, p. 7, October 1948, p. 12, August 1949, p. 12, and October 1949, p. 8; Rev. R. C. Williams, S.J., "C. U. and TV," *TCA*, March 1950, pp. 4–8; *Creightonian*, October 23, 1959, p. 3.

73. *TCA*, December 1945, p. 6, January 1946, p. 12, and December 1947, p. 12; *Creightonian*, November 23, 1945, p. 1, November 8, 1946, p. 1, March 22, 1946, p. 00, March 21, 1947, p. 4, September 23, 1947, p. 1, and April 14, 1950, p. ; *Bluejay*, 1950, p. 141.

74. *Creightonian*, September 28, 1945, p. 3, October 5, 1945, p. 1, December 7, 1945, p. 3, and December 21, 1945, p. 7.

75. *Creightonian*, February 8, 1946, p. 3, and February 15, 1946, p. 3; VBR.

76. *1947–48 Basketball Team: Pocket-Size Dope Book*, p. 15; VBR.

77. *Creightonian*, March 22, 1946, p. 3, December 6, 1946, p. 3, April 8, 1949, p. 5, October 21, 1949, p. 5, January 13, 1950, p. 7, March 24, 1950, p. 5, April 14, 1950, p. 5, and May 17, 1950, p. 5; Mark E. Lange, "The History of Creighton University Baseball."

78. *Creightonian*, October 26, 1945, p. 3, February 8, 1946, p. 1, October 3, 1947, p. 1, November 14, 1947, p. 1, December 19, 1947, p. 7; *TCA*, November 1945, p. 7, and March–April 1957, p. 10.

79. *TCA*, February 1946, p. 12; *Creightonian*, October 19, 1945, p. 1, February 8, 1946, p. 1, May 17, 1946, p. 2, May 22, 1946, p. 1, November 8, 1946, p. 3, September 24, 1948, p. 8, and May 4, 1984, p. 7.

80. *Creightonian*, November 30, 1945, p. 1, December 20, 1946, p. 1, January 17, 1947, p. 1, November 14, 1947, p. 1, November 21, 1947, p. 1, January 16, 1948, p. 4; *TCA*, January 1947, p. 9, April 18, 1947, p. 2, and January 13, 1950, p. 7.

81. *Creightonian*, October 5, 1945, p. 1, April 30, 1948, pp. 1, 7, May 7, 1948, pp. 1, 8, and April 28, 1950, p. 4; LBRM, January 17, 1950.

82. *Creightonian*, December 14, 1945, p. 4, November 15, 1946, p. 4, October 31, 1947, p. 7, and March 3, 1950, p. 3; *TCA*, October 1948, p. 12, and September 1949, p. 8; *Bluejay*, 1949, pp. 68, 95, 98, 103, and 1951, p. 116.

83. *CUB*, Arts, 1945–46; *Creightonian*, November 16, 1945, p. 2, and February 18, 1949, p. 1; *TCA*, November 1945, p. 7, April 1946, p. 6, April 1947, p. 12, February 1948, p. 5, October 1948, p. 12, March 1949, p. 9, and May 1950, pp. 6–7; *Bluejay*, 1949, pp. 72, 135–37.

84. *Creightonian*, December 21, 1945, p. 6, October 1, 1948, p. 1, October 15, 1948, p. 1, December 3, 1948, p. 4, February 4, 1949, p. 1, and March 3, 1950, p. 4; *TCA*, February, 1949, p. 8; *Bluejay*, 1949; BTM, July 12, 1950.

85. *Creightonian,* October 17, 1930, p. 2, December 6, 1946, p. 1, September 24, 1948, p. 2, and March 25, 1949, p. 1; Szmrecsanyi, pp. 291-3; Jeffrey Harrison Smith, "The Omaha De Porres Club," MA Thesis, Creighton University, 1967, pp. viii–ix, 20–26; *Omaha Star,* March 11, 1949, p. 1.

Chapter Nine

1. *TCA,* October 1950, p. 2, December 1950, p. 8, and October 1960, pp. 3–5; Vosper, pp. 67–68.

2. Walter Roger Jahn, *My Memories* (Omaha: privately published, n. d. [1993]), p. 47; *TCA,* June 1952, p. 8, and vol. XXVII, No. 10, p. 11 (the publication temporarily changed its form of dating issues in the mid-1950s); *Creightonian,* January 17, 1975, p. 1.

3. Article, no source citation, October 29, 1950, in the Fr. James P. Kramper, S.J., Scrapbook, CUA; BTM, October 27 and December 29, 1951.

4. BTM, August 30, 1954; LBRM, September 19, 1961; Jahn, pp. 48, 101-02; *TCA,* XXXI, No. 1, p. 2; Vosper, pp. 69–70; Kelley, pp. 45–47.

5. *TCA,* October 1950, p. 9, October 1951, p. 11, March 1952, p. 8, vol. XXVII, No. 5, p. 12, and vol. XXVII, No. 10, back cover.

6. *TCA,* December 1950, p. 7, March 1956, p. 3, December 1957, p. 3, March-April 1958, p. 3, July 1962, p. 5, and October 1964, p. 6.

7. *TCA,* April 1953, p. 11, and vol. XXVII, no. 8, pp. 3–4; *Creightonian,* April 17, 1953, p. 1; four articles with no date or source citation in the Kramper scrapbook.

8. BTM, September 7, 1950, March 10, 1953, February 14, 1957, and September 7, 1958; *Creightonian,* October 30, 1959, p. 7.

9. *Creightonian,* September 21, 1951, p. 1, January 31, 1961, p. 1, October 20, 1961, p. 2, and December 14, 1962, p. 3.

10. BTM, September 16, 1952; *TCA,* February 1953, p. 6, and August 1956, p. 5; Jahn, pp. 52–53; Reichmuth, p. 16.

11. *TCA,* vol. XXVII, No. 10, p. 7, and May–June 1955, p. 3; *Creightonian,* May 18, 1956, p. 1, November 15, 1957, p. 4, September 19, 1958, p. 3, and September 26, 1958, p. 2; BTM, March 15, November 19, 1959, and March 1, 1960.

12. *TCA,* October 1957, p. 5, and July 1958, p. 4; *Creightonian,* September 19, 1958, pp. 1, 3; BTM, July 17, 1963 (new title of Director established July 27, 1960, but minutes continue in same volume titled Trustees. To avoid confusion with the subsequent lay Board of Directors, BTM will be used to designate the Jesuit group).

13. Leahy, p. 133.

14. BTM, August 4, 1950, January 26, 1955, and March 8, 1955; *Creightonain,* February 9, 1951, p. 1, and March 11, 1966, p. 1.

15. Articles with no date or source citation in Kramper scrapbook; BTM, April 20, July 30, and September 27, 1955.

16. Article with no date or source citation in Kramper scrapbook; *TCA,* March 1955, pp. 3–5, July 1955, pp. 3–4, October 1955, p. 3, and January 1956, p. 6; *Creightonian,* February 11, 1955, p. 1, September 23, 1955, p. 1, and March 11, 1966, p. 1; Jahn, p. 51.

17. *Creightonian,* October 31, 1952, p. 2, March 27, 1953, p. 1, October 29, 1954, p. 7, January 7, 1955, p. 1, and March 18, 1955, p. 6; *TCA,* February 1955, p. 7.

18. *TCA,* March 1951, p. 7 July 1955, pp. 3–4, and September–October 1956, p. 4; *Creightonian,* September 22, 1950, p. 1, September 21, 1956, p. 1, December 7, 1956, p. 8, February 5, 1960, p. 5, January 12, 1962, p. 1, January 19, 1962, p. 1, and March 16, 1962, p. 1; BTM, March 15, 1959; *CUB,* professional Schools, 1957 through 1963.

19. *TCA*, July 1962, p. 7, September 1963, p. 6, November 1963, pp. 4–5, and July 1965, p. 11; *Creightonian*, September 21, 1962, p. 1; *Bluejay*, 1964, p. 23.

20. BTM, April 10, 1950; "Women's Folder," Reichmuth papers, CUA; *TCA*, July 1951, p. 6; *The Creightonian*, September 21, 1951, p. 7.

21. Cahill, 80–81; BTM, July 25, 1951; *Window*, Fall 1991, p. 9.

22. *TCA*, February 1956, pp. 3–4; *The Creightonian*, February 17, 1956, p. 1, and March 16, 1956, p. 1.

23. *TCA*, May 1957, p. 11, and May 1960, pp. 3-4, 8-9; BTM, November 9, 1958, July 12, 1959, March 22, 1960, and March 25, 1961; *Creightonian*, December 2, 1960, p. 5, and March 11, 1966, p. 1.

24. *Bluejay*, 1951 through 1960; John Tracy Ellis, ed., *Documents of American Catholic History, 1866 to 1966* (Wilmington, Del.: Michael Glazer, 1987), vol. 2, pp. 646–52; *Creightonian*, December 13, 1963, p. 1.

25. *Omaha World-Herald*, October 12, 1956, Kramper scrapbook; *TCA*, August 1956, p. 3, July 1958, pp. 2, 19, and May 1959, p. 3; Szmrecsanyi, p. 521.

26. *TCA*, March 1959, p. 3 and May 1959, pp. 3, 18 and November 1959, p. 7; BTM, March 15, 1959 and March 20, 1960; *Creightonian*, May 5, 1961, p. 1, October 20, 1961, p. 4, and November 8, 1963, p. 2.

27. *Creightonian*, November 10, 1950, p. 1; *TCA*, March 1951, p. 12, April–May, 1951, p. 12, July 1951, p. 8, and October 1951, p. 7; BTM, March 10, 1953.

28. *Creightonian*, November 10, 1950, p. 8, January 12, 1951, p. 1, February 9, 1951, p. 2, and November 16, 1951, p. 1; *TCA*, February 1951, p. 4, October 1951, p. 7, and January 1952, p. 18.

29. *Creightonian*, September 29, 1950, p. 2, October 6, 1950, p. 3, February 9, 1951, p. 6, February 23, 1951, p. 8, April 6, 1951, p. 3, September 21, 1951, p. 3, October 10, 1952, p. 6, October 17, 1952, p. 6, November 7, 1952, p. 6, and November 4, 1955, p. 1; *TCA*, October 1951, p. 7, and April–May 1952, p. 23.

30. *TCA*, February 1952, pp. 10–11, and vol. XXVII, No. 5, p. 3, October 1955, p. 6, September-October 1956, p. 6, October 1957, p. 3, and November 1961, p. 10; *Creightonian*, October 1, 1954, p. 4, and October 28, 1955, p. 7; *Bluejay*, 1953 and 1955, no pagination; BRM, September 20, 1963.

31. Jahn, pp. 52, 75; *Creightonian*, March 21, 1952, p. 1; *TCA*, vol. XXVII, no. 10, p. 6, and March–April 1957, p. 10; Minutes of the President's Council (PCM), February 13, 1962.

32. *TCA*, March 1961, p. 4, and November 1963, pp. 8–9; PCM, December 5, 1961.

33. BTM, April 5, 1960; PCM, February 13, 1962; *TCA*, January 1962, p. 6, September 1963, pp. 2, 6, and November 1963, pp. 8–9; *Creightonian*, September 27, 1963, p. 2.

34. Jahn, p. 47; BTM, December 13, 1951; Leahy, pp. 102–03.

35. *TCA*, January 1956, p. 3, January 1959, p. 4, September 1959, pp. 8–9, October 1964, p. 5, and October 1965, p. 18; article dated 3-29-57, but no source citation in Kramper scrapbook; BTM, July 27, 1958, April 12, 1959, November 28, 1961, and February 7, 1959.

36. Leahy, p. 106; *TCA*, July 1951, p. 7; *Creightonian*, February 23, 1951, p. 3.

37. Fitzgerald, pp. 102–06, 154-6, p. 268, n91, and p. 280, n40; *CUB*, Arts, 1950 through 1960; BTM, February 14, 1957.

38. Leahy, p. 100; Fitzgerald, pp. 149–50, p. 278, n2, p. 279, note 13; BTM, July 29, 1958, and July 26, 1959; *TCA*, July 1958, p. 7.

39. Power, p. 382; John Tracy Ellis, *American Catholics and the Intellectual Life* (Chicago: Heritage Foundation, 1956), pp. 44–45; John Tracy Ellis, "No Complacency," *America*, vol. 95, April 7, 1956, pp. 14–25.

40. Power, pp. 420–21; Fitzgerald, p. 275, n36; *CUB*, Arts, 1950 through 1960; *TCA*, November 1958, p. 6, and May 1959, pp. 10–11.

41. *Creightonian*, April 20, 1951, p. 1, May 11, 1951, p. 3, March 13, 1959, p. 1, and March 8, 1963, p. 2; *TCA*, March 1961, p. 15.

42. *CUB*, Arts, 1950 through 1963; *Creightonian*, November 16, 1962, p. 4; *TCA*, March 1963, pp. 3–4, and September 1963, p. 6; LBRM, December 11, 1962; *Bluejay*, 1963, p. 200.

43. *CUB*, Arts, 1950 through 1963; *Creightonian*, November 12, 1954, p. 3; *TCA*, February 1955, p. 8, and July 1955, p. 7.

44. *TCA*, March 1960, p. 4, and July 1963, p. 8; *Creightonian*, January 12, 1962, p. 1.

45. *CUB*, Commerce then CoBA, 1950 through 1963; BTM, March 28, 1956; *TCA*, August 1956, p. 11; *Creightonian*, September 26, 1958, p. 1; Cahill, pp. 26–28.

46. BTM, February 7 and July 12, 1959; *TCA*, September 1959, pp. 3, 14, and January 1962, pp. 3–5; *Creightonian*, February 19, 1960, p. 1, and March 11, 1966, p. 1; Cahill, pp. 26-8.

47. Cahill, pp. 28–29, 74; Vosper, pp. 136–37; *TCA*, January 1962, pp. 3–5, and March 1963, pp. 8–9; *Bluejay*, 1959, p. 36; *Creightonian*, February 10, 1961, p. 1, January 12, 1962, p. 2, and February 15, 1962, p. 1; PCM, February 13, 1962.

48. *CUB*, Summer, 1950 through 1963; *Creightonian*, March 9, 1951, p. 6, and March 7, 1952, p. 1; *TCA*, June 1951, p. 11, July 1953, p. 9, October 1957, p. 18, April 1959, pp. 3–4, and July 1961, p. 3.

49. *Creightonian*, November 17, 1950, p. 1, February 9, 1951, p. 1, and September 21, 1951, p. 4; *TCA*, December 1950, p. 8, February 1951, p. 13, October 1951, p. 7, and November 1951, p. 7.

50. *CUB*, Graduate, 1950 through 1963; *Creightonian*, March 30, 1951, p. 3, and December 6, 1963, p. 7; *TCA*, June 1951, p. 7; *Bluejay*, 1951, p. 30; Fitzgerald, pp. 131-2; Vosper, p. 123.

51. *CUB*, Law, 1950 through 1963; *TCA*, April-May 1951, p. 11, October 1957, p. 9, and July 1958, p. 5; BTM, July 6, 1950, and July 12, 1959; *Bluejay*, 1951, p. 26; Frankino and Crisman, pp. 234–35.

52. *TCA*, November 1951, p. 8; *Creightonian*, October 19, 1951, p. 1, October 26, 1951, p. 1, November 9, 1951, p. 3, and September 30, 1960, p. 6; BTM, July 27, 1960.

53. *Bluejay*, 1951, pp. 26, 94, 114, and 1953, no pagination, and 1954, p. 65; *TCA*, April–May 1952, p. 15, and vol. XXVII, No. 7, p. 8; *Creightonian*, February 8, 1952, p. 4, April 29, 1960, p. 6, March 10, 1961, p. 3, and April 1, 1966, p. 1.

54. *CUB*, Pharmacy, 1950 through 1963; registrar's enrollment data; *Creightonian*, November 9, 1951, p. 1, November 6, 1953, p. 7, and February 10, 1956, p. 7.

55. BTM, January 26, 1955, and March 28, 1956; *TCA*, June 1957, p. 5, March–April 1958, p. 4, and July 1958, p. 9; *Creightonian*, February 10, 1956, p. 1, and September 26, 1958, p. 7; *CUB*, Pharmacy, 1957 and 1958.

56. BTM, August 4, 1950, and Memo: President to Trustees, June 18, 1954; Letter from Carl M. Reinert, S.J., to Venerable Mother Mary Asella, O.S.F., July 15, 1954; *Bluejay*, 1952, p. 68, and 1953, no pagination, and 1954, p. 32; Vossen, pp. 10–11, 23–24, 39–44.

57. *CUB*, Nursing, 1950 through 1959; *Creightonian*, September 26, 1958, p. 3, and January 19, 1962, p. 5; Vossen, pp. 51–54; Vosper, p. 183.

58. Vossen, pp. 49–60.

59. Vossen, p. 55; *TCA*, July 1955, p. 7; "History," Army Nursing Corp Web site.

60. *TCA*, July 1955, p. 7, and August 1956, p. 10, March 1960, p. 5; *Creightonian*, January 20, 1956, p. 8, September 21, 1956, p. 8, November 30, 1956, p. 1, and September 26, 1958, p. 2; *Bluejay*, 1960, p. 97; Vossen, pp. 54–56.

61. *CUB*, Dental, 1950 through 1963; BTM, April 1, 1954; *TCA*, October 1950, p. 6, July 1955, p. 8, November 1955, p. 7, July 1961, p. 7, and May 1962, p. 7; interview with Dr. Benjamin Lynch, D.D.S., December 3, 2004.

62. Registrar enrollment data; BTM, October 21, 1954; *TCA*, October 1950, p. 6.

63. *CUB*, Dental, 1950 through 1963; *TCA*, November 1951, p. 8, and November 1958, p. 6; *Bluejay*, 1951, p. 24; Lynch interview.

64. *CUB*, Dental, 1953–55; *TCA*, October 1957, p. 19, and March 1962, p. 9.

65. *TCA*, April–May 1951, p. 11, October 1951, p. 6, and October 1960, p. 8; Vosper, p. 156; Boro and Mead, pp. 140, 148–50; Kirby, pp. 115–17, BTM, March 1, 1959.

66. *TCA*, vol. XXVII, No. 10, p. 5, October 1957, p. 9, May 1958, pp. 10–11 and January–February 1958, p. 11; Boro and Mead, p. 141.

67. Boro and Mead, pp. 156–57; *TCA*, November 1963, p. 3, and October 1964, p. 4.

68. *CUB*, Medicine, 1950 through 1963; BTM, September 25, 1951; Boro and Mead, pp. 129, 293, *Bluejay*, 1952, pp. 104–5.

69. *CUB*, Medicine, 1950 through 1963; *TCA*, May 1957, p. 6, Boro and Mead, pp. 118–19, 137.

70. BTM, January 26 and September 29, 1955, and March 18, 1957; *TCA*, March 1960, pp. 3–4; Boro and Mead, p. 166.

71. BTM, February 22, 1961; LBRM, September 19, 1961; *TCA*, September 1961, p. 8–9, November 1962, p. 6, September 1963, p. 3, and November 1963, pp. 4–5; *Alumnews*, April 1978, p. 2; Boro and Mead, pp. 160–61.

72. *CUB*, Arts, 1957 through 1963; *Creightonian*, March 7, 1952, p. 1, January 17, 1956, p. 4, October 5, 1956, pp. 1, 8, September 27, 1961, p. 1, March 17, 1961, p. 1, May 5, 1961, p. 2, and March 1, 1963, p. 7.

73. *Creightonian*, December 3, 1954, p. 4, January 7, 1955, p. 3, March 9, 1956, p. 1, September 21, 1956, p. 1, September 21, 1962, p. 2, May 10, 1963, p. 2, October 4, 1963, p. 5, and December 20, 1963, p. 1; *TCA*, May 1957, p. 19, September 18, 1964, p. 7, and October 1, 1965, p. 4; *Bluejay*, 1955 through 1963.

74. *Creightonian*, September 29, 1950, p. 8, October 13, 1950, p. 2, April 6, 1951, p. 8, February 25, 1955, p. 1, and November 22, 1963, p. 2; *TCA*, December 1957, p. 4.

75. *Creightonian*, May 23, 1952, p. 1, March 20, 1959, p. 2, October 16, 1959, p. 6, November 13, 1959, p. 1, March 25, 1960, p. 4, October 27, 1961, p. 5, November 17, 1961, p. 2, and February 15, 1963, p. 2; *TCA*, November 1956, p. 19, April 1959, p. 2, and November 1959, p. 15; *Bluejay*, 1951 through 1963, in particular 1954, p. 38 and 1963, p. 97.

76. *CUB*, Arts, 1950 through 1963; *Creightonian*, September 29, 1950, pp. 1, 8, Sept 28, 1951, p. 3, October 10, 1952, p. 5, December 7, 1956, pp. 1–2, January 11, 1957, p. 3, October 3, 1958, p. 4, and September 21, 1962, p. 1; *TCA*, October 1952, p. 9, and November 1958, pp. 3, 18; BTM, July 26, 1959; *Bluejay*, 1951, p. 169, and 1959, pp. 18–19.

77. *Creightonian*, April 25, 1952, pp. 1–4; *TCA*, April–May 1952, pp. 9–10; Vossen, p. 22.

78. *Creightonian*, September 21, 1951, p. 8, and May 1, 1959, p. 6; *TCA*, March 1952, p. 12; *Bluejay*, 1954, p. 60, and 1955, no pagination, and 1962, pp. 52, 228.

79. *Bluejay*, 1950 through 1963; *CUB*, Arts, 1950 through 1963; *Creightonian*, September 29, 1950, p. 7, February 23, 1951, p. 7, April 12, 1957, p. 5, November 14, 1958, p. 2, January 13, 1961, p. 5, and December 20, 1963, p. 7; *TCA*, August 1956, pp. 13–14.

80. *Creightonian*, May 18, 1956, p. 7, November 2, 1956, p. 7, February 21, 1958, pp. 1, 4, March 28, 1958, pp. 1–2, April 25, 1958, p. 2, May 16, 1958, p. 5, October 24, 1958, p. 4, February 26, 1960, p. 5, and January 11, 1963, p. 4.

81. *Creightonian*, May 18, 1951, p. 8, September 23, 1955, p. 3, February 10, 1956, p. 4, November 9, 1956, p. 8, October 4, 1957, p. 2, November 14, 1958, p. 2, and September 20, 1963, p. 2.

82. *Creightonian*, October 20, 1950, p. 5, February 1, 1952, p. 8, November 19, 1954, p. 1, and October 21, 1955, p. 6.

83. *Creightonian*, September 23, 1955, p. 2, Sept 27, 1957, p. 2, November 15, 1957, p. 4, November 13, 1959, p. 5, April 18, 1960, p. 1, October 6, 1961, p. 3, April 6, 1962, p. 2, April 27, 1962, p. 2, and December 7, 1962, p. 1; *TCA*, May 1960, p. 14; *Bluejay*, 1950, p. 146, and 1952, p. 132, and 1957, p. 105.

84. *Creightonian*, September 29, 1950, p. 7, October 12, 1951, p. 1, March 17, 1958, p. 1, and March 18, 1960, p. 2; *Bluejay*, 1952, p. 85.

85. *Creightonian*, April 20, 1951, p. 1, April 27, 1951, pp. 1, 6, May 4, 1951, p. 1, May 11, 1951, p. 1, May 18, 1951, p. 6, October 8, 1954, p. 1, April 20, 1956, p. 1, and April 21, 1961, p. 1; *TCA*, June 1951, p. 12.

86. *Creightonian*, February 10, 1961, p. 1, March 10, 1961, p. 4, April 7, 1961, p. 1, and May 17, 1963, p. 1; *Window*, Winter 1992–1993, pp. 22–25.

87. *Creightonian*, April 9, 1954, p. 1, October 29, 1954, p. 1, March 25, 1955, p. 8, April 10, 1956, p. 8, April 26, 1957, p. 1, and April 10, 1959, p. 2; BTM, July 26, 1959.

88. *Creightonian*, December 7, 1951, p. 5, March 6, 1959, pp. 1, 2, and March 20, 1959, pp. 3, 4.

89. *Creightonian*, April 13, 1956, p. 1, April 25, 1958, p. 1, October 30, 1959, p. 1, March 11, 1960, p. 4, April 1, 1960, p. 1, November 15, 1963, p. 4, October 3, 1958, p. 2, December 5, 1958, p. 2, September 25, 1959, p. 2, January 8, 1960, p. 1, September 30, 1960, p. 2, and March 2, 1962, p. 1; *TCA*, May 1960, pp. 6–7; *Bluejay*, 1960, p. 19.

90. *Bluejay*, 1950 through 1964; *Creightonian*, February 9, 1951, p. 5, September 18, 1959, p. 2, September 20, 1963, p. 1, and November 22, 1963, p. 5.

91. *Omaha World-Herald Magazine*, October 29, 1950, Kramper Scrapbook; *Bluejay*, 1951, p. 84, 1954, no pagination, 1960, p. 164, and 1961, p. 143; *Creightonian*, September 29, 1950, p. 5, October 19, 1951, p. 5, October 2, 1953, p. 5, April 13, 1956, p. 5, October 3, 1958, p. 1, February 20, 1959, p. 2, January 1, 1960, p. 1, and September 30, 1960, p. 8; *TCA*, July 1970, p. 19.

92. *Creightonian*, October 1, 1954, p. 5, October 29, 1954, p. 5, December 3, 1954, January 9, 1959, p. 8, and November 6, 1959, p. 8; *Bluejay*, 1950 through 1963 (1961, p. 145, for quote); Joseph P. Murphy, "Remembering Duce," *Window*, Spring 1989, p. 11; LBRM, March 6, 1962.

93. Mark E. Lange, "The History of Creighton University Baseball," unpublished student paper, 1979, Athletic Department records; *Bluejay*, 1952, p. 182; *Creightonian*, May 10, 1957, p. 8, and September 19, 1958, p. 8.

94. VBR, 1950 through 1963–64; *TCA*, May, 1950, p. 11, February 1952, p. 15, and April-May 1952, p. 17; *Creightonian*, April 6, 1951, p. 7, May 23, 1952, p. 5, October 9, 1959, p. 8, September 23, 1960, p. 8, and March 23, 1962, p. 8.

95. *Bluejay*, sports section, 1950 through 1963, quote in 1963, p. 306; *Creightonian*, October 19, 1951, p. 5, April 25, 1952, p. 5, September 17, 1954, p. 5, April 20, 1956, p. 5, May 4, 1956, p. 5, January 9, 1959, p. 8, November 11, 1960, p. 8, and September 21, 1962. p. 8.

96. *Creightonian*, December 15, 1950, p. 3, February 9, 1951, p. 5, September 24, 1954, p. 5, April 13, 1956, p. 1, April 10, 1959, p. 1, Sept 18, 1959, p. 5, January 8, 1960, p. 5, September 23, 1960, p. 8, October 28, 1960, p. 8, November 2, 1962, p. 8, February 15, 1963, p. 4, May 8, 1964, p. 8, February 4, 1965, p. 8, and May 7, 1971, p. 7.

97. LBRM, March 6, 1962, and February 5, 1963; *TCA*, March 1962, pp. 3–4 and May 1962, p. 3, and January 1963, pp. 3–4; *Creightonian*, March 9, 1962, p. 1; Vosper, p. 73.

Chapter Ten

1. *TCA*, January 1970, p. 7; *Creightonian*, March 21, 1986, p. 3; Vosper, p. 74–75.

2. Fitzgerald, pp. 104–14, 126–30, 169–88, 216–19.

3. Ibid., pp. 201–2, and note 11, pp. 294–95; LBRM, December 1, 1966, and April 14, 1967; BTM, September 28, 1967.

4. BTM, October 1, 1967, October 22, 1967, and February 3, 1968; LBRM, April 17, 1968.

5. BTM, August 13, 1968; LBRM, February 5, 1968; Board of Directors Minutes, October 29, 1968, January 6, 1969, November 6, 1972, and March 5, 1973, hereafter BDM plus the date; Jahn, p. 66; *Creightonian*, September 20, 1968, p. 3.

6. *TCA,* January 1962, p. 6, and January 1963, pp. 3–4; BTM, August 2, 1962, and March 24, 1966; LBRM, February 5, 1963, and January 20, 1967.

7. BDM, February 3, October 15, November 17, 1969, and April 2 and June 29, 1970; *Creightonian,* February 13, 1970, p. 1.

8. BTM, October 18, 1965 and March 16 and 24, and October 25, 1966; BDM, December 6, 1971; *TCA,* May 1966, p. 11, March 1967, p. 8, and July 1967, p. 16; *Creightonian,* January 3, 1967, p. 1, and October 27, 1967, p. 8; *Alumnews,* August 1975, p. 4.

9. *Creightonian,* February 8, 1957, p. 1, and September 27, 1963, p. 1; BTM, September 17, 1963; LBRM, March 20, 1964; *TCA,* January 1964, pp. 3–4, and May 1965, p. 12; Jahn, pp. 59–60.

10. *Creightonian,* April 17, 1964, p. 1, January 8, 1965, p. 1, September 20, 1968, p. 1, and April 10, 1970, p. 1; *TCA,* January 1965, pp. 6–7, and May 1965, p. 12; Jahn, pp. 59-60; LBRM, March 20, 1964; BTM, October 31, 1965, January 22, 1966, and January 5, 1967; BDM, March 30, 1967, and May 31, 1967.

11. Symrescanyi, p. 521; Jahn, p. 77; David, p. 2; BTM, April 5, 1960, and January 28, 1968; LBRM, January 21, 1966; *TCA,* July 1966, pp. 14–15 and April 1968, pp. 3, 9.

12. *Creightonian,* February 18, 1966, p. 1, Sept 23, 1966, p. 1, September 30, 1966, p. 1, and September 22, 1967, p. 1; *TCA,* May 1966, p. 7, and October 1968, p. 19; LBRM, April 14, 1967; BTM, May 31, 1967; Reichmuth, pp. 16, 18.

13. LBRM, March 26, 1965; BTM, November 3, 1966; BDM, February 3, 1969; *Creightonian,* October 2, 1970, p. 1.

14. *True Voice,* December 3, 1915, p. 6; Jahn, p. 70; LRBM, May 6, 1966, and January 12, 1968; *TCA,* July 1969, pp. 12–15; *Creightonian,* September 26, 1969, p. 6, and October 22, 1971, p. 5; BDM, December 6, 1971; registrar enrollment data.

15. *Bluejay,* 1964 through 1974; BDM, April 7, May 5, September 4, 1969, February 5, and March 5, 1973; registrar enrollment data.

16. BTM, March 24, 1966; *Creightonian,* September 18, 1970, p. 4, and September 1, 1972, p. 1; *Alumnews,* November 1973, p. 1; registrar enrollment data.

17. LBRM, April 17, 1964, April 13, October 28, 1966, and December 15, 1967; *TCA,* September 1970, pp. 4-5; *Creightonian,* November 30, 1973, p. 1; Jahn, pp. 91–92.

18. *Creightonian,* December 4, 1964, p. 6, and September 23, 1966, p. 6; LBRM, December 1, 1966; Jahn pp. 72–73.

19. LBRM, March 3, 1967; BDM, March 2, 1970, and November 5, 1973; *TCA,* September 1970, p. 4; *Creightonian,* October 2, 1970, p. 3; *Alumnews,* February 1973, p. 2.

20. LBRM, May 7, 1965; BTM, January 6, April 21, 1966, and May 31, 1967.

21. BDM, March 3, 1969; Jahn, p. 58; *Creightonian* August 25, 1971, p. 1, November 19, 1971, p. 3, and February 4, 1972, p. 1.

22. *Creightonian,* October 1, 1965, p. 1, September 3, 1971, p. 2, and October 13, 1972, p. 1; *Bluejay,* 1966, p. 26, and 1967, p. 68; *Alumnews,* October 1973, p. 1, and January 1976, p. 3; Fitzgerald, pp. 160–68.

23. *Creightonian,* March 11, 1966, p. 5, and April 15, 1966, p. 2; BDM, March 5, 1973; Fitzgerald, pp. 209–13; Neil G. McClusky, S.J., *The Catholic University, A Modern Appraisal* (Notre Dame: University of Notre Dame Press, 1970), Preface, pp. 1–26; William F. Kelley, S.J., *The Jesuit Order and Higher Education in the United States, 1789-1966* (Milwaukee: Wisconsin Jesuit Province, 1966), Preface, p. 10.

24. *The Creightonian,* December 4, 1964, p. 2, February 24, 1967, p. 2, and January 12, 1968, p. 1; LBRM, May 7, 1965; BTM, October 18, 1965, March 1, March 8, 1966, October 31, 1967, and January 26, 1968; *TCA,* January 1968, p. 16.

25. BDM, November 17, 1969, March 2, April 6, and August 6, 1970; *TCA,* July 1970, p. 4, and October 1970, p. 3; *Alumnews,* November 1972, p. 1; Vosper, p. 76; Jahn, pp. 67–68.

26. *Creightonian*, May 1, 1970, p. 1, and October 8, 1971, p. 2; BDM, October 19, November 23, 1970, April 19, 1971, and August 5, 1974.

27. *Creightonian*, November 13, 1970, p. 1, and November 20, 1970, p. 1; BDM November 23, 1970.

28. *Creightonian*, February 24, 1964, p. 2, April 9, 1965, p. 1, February 24, 1967, p. 1, March 3, 1967, p. 3, April 14, 1967, p. 1, October 20, 1967, p. 1, December 15, 1967, p. 1, March 22, 1968, p. 5, April 26, 1968, p. 1, May 3, 1968, p. 1, and December 5, 1969, p. 7; BDM, December 12, 1967; Dennis N. Mihelich, "Living By the Rules, *Window*, Fall 1989, p. 17.

29. *Creightonian*, March 7, 1969, p. 1 April 18, 1969, p. 1, May 2, 1969, p. 2, March 5, 1971, p. 5, March 2, 1973, p. 2, March 30, 1973, p. 2, and March 15, 1974, p. 1.; *Alumnews*, April 1973, p. 1; *Bluejay*, 1973, p. 216.

30. *Creightonian*, October 2, 1964, p. 1, October 14, 1966, pp. 1, 4, December 13, 1968, p. 2, December 13, 1968, p. 1, February 7, 1969, p. 1, October 10, 1969, p. 1, April 10, 1970, p. 2, September 3, 1971, p. 2, and February 11, 1973, p. 3.

31. *Creightonian*, April 1, 1966, p. 1, December 9, 1966, p. 1, March 1, 1968, p. 3; BDM, May 5, 1969, April 6, 1970, August 30, 1971, and April 17, 1972.

32. *Creightonian*, March 19, 1971, p. 1; BDM, October 4, 1971, April 17, 1972, November 6, 1972, February 5, 1973, and June 4, 1973.

33. BTM, April 2, 1967; *Creightonian*, April 28, 1967, p. 2, October 13, 1967, p. 7, February 14, 1969, p. 2, September 19, 1969, p. 1, and October 3, 1969, p. 2; Bluejay, 1970, p. 248.

34. BTM, January 22 and March 24, 1966, and April 2, 1967; *Creightonian*, April 15, 1966, p. 1, and November 11, 1966, p. 1.

35. BTM, April 2 and July 12, 1967.

36. BTM, July 19, 1967; *Creightonian*, December 15, 1967, p. 7, March 13, 1970, p. 7, and March 10, 1971, p. 1; BDM, November 23, 1970, March 1, 1971, and March 6 and June 5, 1972.

37. LBRM, November 1, 1963; BTM, December 5, 1963; *Creightonian*, January 8, 1965, p. 1; BDM, November 23, 1970.

38. *TCA*, September 1963, p. 6, and October 1970, pp. 14–15; *Creightonian*, November 22, 1963, p. 7, February 14, 1964, p. 2, March 6, 1964, p. 3, September 18, 1964, p. 1, October 23, 1964, p. 1, January 4, 1965, p. 2, November 12, 1965, p. 1, March 3, 1967, p. 3, December 1, 1967, p. 2, and February 7, 1969, p. 3.

39. *TCA*, January 1969, pp. 7–8; *CUB*, Arts, 1969–71; *Creightonian*, March 8, 1968, p. 1, April 26, 1968, p. 3, May 5, 1968, p. 5, May 10, 1968, p. 3, September 27, 1968, p. 1, March 28, 1969, p. 6, October 4, 1968, p. 1, and January 9, 1970, p. 1; *Bluejay*, 1969, p. 226.

40. *Creightonian*, September 26, 1969, p. 4, October 3, 1969, p. 1, October 10, 1969, pp. 1, 2, November 14, 1969, p. 1, 5, May 1, 1970, p. 2, and March 3, 1972, p. 2; *Bluejay*, 1970, p. 136; BDM, June 29, 1970.

41. *Creightonian*, February 27, 1970, p. 1, March 13, 1970, p. 1, November 6, 1970, p. 2, September 10, 1971, p. 2, November 19, 1971, pp. 1–2, February 11, 1972, p. 5, September 8, 1972, p. 4, November 17, 1972, p. 5, and December 6, 1974, p. 7.

42. BDM, October 19, 1970; *Creightonian*, February 6, 1970, p. 9, September 25, 1970, p. 1, October 2, 1970, pp. 4–5, February 19, 1971, p. 1, and September 22, 1972, p. 3; *TCA*, April 1971, p. 7.

43. *Creightonian*, March 17, 1971, p. 1, September 24, 1971, p. 3, October 22, 1971, p. 3, February 18, 1972, p. 1, October 6, 1972, p. 3, October 20, 1972, p. 5, and September 21, 1973, p. 10; *Alumnews*, November 1972, p. 2; *Bluejay*, 1974, p. 197.

44. *Creightonian*, October 9, 1964, p. 3, October 15, 1965, p. 1, December 9, 1966, p. 5, September 29, 1967, p. 5, October 24, 1969, p. 5, September 24, 1971, p. 8, December 10, 1971, p. 1, January 28, 1972, p. 2, February 4, 1972, pp. 1, 4, March 17, 1972, p. 2, and October 13, 1972, p. 6; *Alumnews*, November 1972, p. 3.

45. *CUB*, Arts, 1971–73; *Bluejay*, 1974, p. 259; *Creightonian*, May 5, 1972, p. 1, March 2, 1973, p. 3, November 2, 1973, p. 4, February 1, 1974, p. 9, and April 23, 1999, p. 4.

46. *Creightonian*, December 4, 1964, p. 5, February 26, 1965, p. 5, May 7, 1965, p. 1, February 17, 1967, p. 7, and October 31, 1969, p. 1; *Bluejay*, 1973, p. 94; Mihelich, p. 19.

47. *Creightonian*, September 25, 1970, p. 4, January 12, 1971, p. 1, September 24, 1971, p. 1, 8, October 1, 1971, p. 11, October 12, 1973, p. 2, and January 25, 1974. p. 9.

48. *Creightonian*, May 1, 1964, p. 5, December 16, 1966, p. 1, November 22, 1968, p. 5, October 1, 1971, p. 2, October 15, 1971, p. 4, March 17, 1972, p. 1, and December 7, 1973, p. 1; *TCA*, January 1971, pp. 10–11, and January 1973, p. 4; *Bluejay*, 1978, p. 163.

49. *Creightonian*, April 28, 1972, p. 2, September 15, 1972, p. 8, September 22, 1972, p. 2, November 3, 1972, p. 12, March 30, 1973, pp. 3, 12, October 19, 1973, p. 1, January 18, 1974, pp. 4–5; *Alumnews*, April 1973, p. 1; BDM, March 5, October 1, November 5, 1973, and March 4, 1974.

50. *Creightonian*, February 14, 1964, p. 1, February 18, 1966, p. 1, December 6, 1968, p. 3, February 6, 1971, p. 2, and September 3, 1971, p. 2.; BTM, March 24, 1966; Mihelich, pp. 18–19.

51. *Creightonian*, February 19, 1965, p. 5, February 4, 1966, p. 6, March 3, 1967, p. 5, October 20, 1967, p. 1, February 23, 1968, p. 3, May 2, 1969, p. 2, April 10, 1970, p. 3, and April 5, 1974, p. 1; BTM, April 2, 1967; *Bluejay*, 1970, p. 283.

52. *Creightonian*, March 26, 1965, p. 3, September 19, 1969, p. 2, and April 5, 1974, p. 1; *CUB*, Medicine, 1966–68; BDM, March 5, 1973; *Bluejay*, 1973, p. 80 *Alumnews*, May 1974, p. 2.

53. *Creightonian*, February 16, 1968, p. 3, and February 8, 1974, p. 1; *Bluejay*, 1968, p. 4.

54. BTM, April 2, 1967; *Creightonian*, February 10, 1967, p. 1, October 6, 1967, p. 4, April 18, 1969, p. 1, April 25, 1969, p. 1, November 21, 1969, p. 5, February 19, 1971, p. 5, September 22, 1971, p. 2, October 8, 1971, p. 1, November 19, 1971, p. 1, March 3, 1972, p. 2, October 6, 1972, p. 1, and March 15, 1974, p. 1; *Alumnews*, October 1972, p. 1; *Bluejay*, 1973, p. 39.

55. *Creightonian*, January 10, 1964, p. 6, February 21, 1964, p. 2, December 4, 1964, p. 2, February 26, 1965, p. 6, October 22, 1965, p. 3, February 9, 1967, p. 2, February 11, 1967, p. 3, and September 27, 1968, p. 2.

56. *Creightonian*, January 7, 1966, p. 11, February 4, 1966, p. 1, September 28, 1966, p. 2, October 27, 1967, p. 5, December 1, 1967, p. 9, May 17, 1968, p. 6, March 1, 1968, p. 1, March 22, 1968, p. 6, September 27, 1968, p. 2, February 28, 1969, p. 3, December 5, 1969, p. 1, September 25, 1970, p. 2, September 3, 1971, p. 2, and December 1, 1972, p. 2; *Bluejay*, 1971, p. 40.

57. *Creightonian*, October 29, 1965, pp. 2, 4, November 6, 1965, p. 1, October 29, 1965, p. 2, December 10, 1965, pp. 1, 4, October 28, 1966, p. 1, February 17, 1967, p. 5, March 10, 1967, p. 5, April 28, 1967, p. 7, October 13, 1967, p. 3, October 20, 1967, pp. 2, 4, November 10, 1967, p. 3, December 1, 1967, pp. 3, 5, 10, February 9, 1968, p. 3, March 1, 1968, p. 5, and May 10, 1968, p. 1; *Bluejay*, p. 4.

58. *Creightonian*, April 25, 1969, p. 6, October 3, 1969, p. 1, October 10, 1969, p. 1, November 21, 1969, pp. 3, 5, 7, May 8, 1970, pp. 1, 5, May 15, 1970, p. 1, February 12, 1971, p. 8, April 28, 1972, p. 1, and March 2, 1973, p. 8.

59. *Creightonian*, April 4, 1967, p. 7 and March 22, 1968, p. 1 and May 10, 1968, p. 9 and September 20, 1968, p. 1 and October 25, 1968, p. 3 and November 8, 1968, p. 4 and November 10, 1968, p. 1 and November 22, 1968, p. 1 and December 6, 1968, p. 4 and December 13, 1968, p. 1.

60. *Creightonian*, November 22, 1968, p. 3, January 10, 1969, p. 1, February 7, 1969, p. 1, February 21, 1969, p. 1, February 28, 1969, p. 4, and May 4, 1979, p. 4.

61. BTM, May 18, 1967; *Creightonian*, September 29, 1967, p. 4, September 26, 1969, p. 3, February 6, 1970, pp. 4, 8, March 6, 1970, p. 1, May 8, 1970, p. 1, October 22, 1971, p. 12, September 29, 1972, p. 5, December 8, 1972, p. 8, February 16, 1973, p. 12, and August 31, 1973, p. 3; *Bluejay*, 1970, p. 276, 1971, p. 38, 1972, pp. 31, 122, and 1973, p. 76; *Alumnews*, August 1973, p. 3.

62. LBRM, January 21, 1966; *Creightonian*, February 4, 1966, p. 2, February 11, 1966, p. 1, November 7, 1969, p. 2, November 14, 1969, p. 1, December 5, 1969, p. 1, January 9, 1970, p. 1, February 27, 1970, p. 3, October 9, 1970, p. 3, October 23, 1970, p. 1, and April 6, 1973, p. 1; *Bluejay*, 1970, p. 74.

63. *Creightonian*, October 1, 1970, p. 2, December 4, 1970, p. 1, May 14, 1970, p. 1, November 19, 1971, p. 10, November 2, 1973, p. 5, November 30, 1973, p. 9, March 6, 1974, p. 6, and March 22, 1974, p. 9.

64. *Creightonian*, January 10, 1964, p. 1, October 9, 1964, p. 2, and October 16, 1964, p. 4; BTM, January 4, 1967; LBRM, March 3, 1967; *TCA*, July 1969, pp. 3–5, 8–9.

65. *Bluejay*, 1968, p. 4 (contains no pictures of sodalities), and 1970 pp. 204, 264; *Creightonian*, October 11, 1968, p. 7, March 7, 1969, p. 7 September 5, 1969, p. 1, and September 19, 1969, p. 1; *TCA*, July 1970, p. 5; Reichmith, p. 18.

66. *Creightonian*, May 14, 1965, p. 1, October 8, 1965, p. 5, November 12, 1965, p. 3, September 23, 1966, p. 5, April 21, 1967, p. 5, April 28, 1967, p. 1, September 22, 1967, p. 5, March 1, 1968, p. 1, March 29, 1968, p. 1, December 6, 1968, p. 9, April 18, 1969, p. 7, and May 1, 1970, p. 3; *TCA*, January 1966, p. 2; *Bluejay*, 1968, p. 5, and 1978, p. 163.

67. *Creightonian*, October 11, 1968, p. 5, October 31, 1969, p. 5, October 30, 1970, p. 3, September 3, 1971, p. 8, September 24, 1971, p. 4, November 16, 1973, p. 3, February 1, 1974, p. 8, and March 29, 1974, p. 9; *Bluejay*, 1970, p. 211, 216, 262, 1972, p. 266, 1973, p. 264, 1974, p. 273, and 1975, p. 243.

68. *Creightonian*, November 6, 1964, p. 8, September 24, 1965, p. 8, April 1, 1966, p. 8, May 16, 1969, p. 8, March 25, 1966, p. 8, February 9, 1968, p. 8, February 23, 1968, p. 11, March 5, 1971, p. 6, March 19, 1971, p. 6, and September 21, 1973, p. 9; *Bluejay*, 1964, pp. 241, 274, 276, 1967, p. 248, and 1970, pp. 319, 324, 1971, p. 237, and 1972, p. 250; BTM, March 24, 1966.

69. *Creightonian*, May 10, 1963, p. 8, September 27, 1963, p. 8, February 21, 1964, p. 8, September 25, 1964, p. 8, November 4, 1966, p. 8, March 17, 1967, p. 7, April 14, 1967, p. 8, April 21, 1967, p. 7, March 22, 1968, p. 5, September 22, 1967, p. 8, September 20, 1968, p. 7, March 10, 1972, p. 11, and May 6, 1972, p. 11; *Bluejay*, 1964, p. 266, 1971, pp. 239, 243, 1973, p. 250, and 1974, p. 239.

70. Lange, pp. 6–11; *Creightonian*, April 18, 1969, p. 11, May 16, 1969, p. 8, and September 9, 1970, p. 3; BDM, April 17, 1972.

71. Athletic department, "Financial Reports"; *Bluejay*, 1964, p. 251; *Creightonian*, February 19, 1965, p. 8, October 27, 1967, p. 11, December 15, 1967, p. 4, February 23, 1968, p. 10, March 29, 1968, p. 2, April 5, 1968, p. 10, and February 7, 1969, p. 8; *TCA*, March 1965, pp. 4–5; LBRM, December 2, 1965; VBR, 1964–65 through 1968–69; Interview with Dr. Ross Horning, Ph.D., contemporary athletic board member, by Angelo Louisa, Ph.D., March 24, 2004.

72. VBR, 1969–70 through 1973–74; *Creightonian*, March 14, 1969, p. 8, October 2, 1970, p. 6, September 3, 1971, p. 6, September 17, 1971, p. 7, April 13, 1973, p. 1, March 15, 1974, p. 10, April 5, 1974, p. 7, and August 30, 1974, p. 7.

73. *Creightonian*, January 10, 1964, p. 8, March 18, 1966, p. 6, December 16, 1966, p. 8, September 22, 1967, p. 8, October 27, 1967, p. 11, December 1, 1967, p. 10, and April 5, 1968, pp. 7, 10; *Bluejay*, 1964, p. 278, and 1969, p. 329.

74. *Creightonian*, February 9, 1973, p. 8, February 23, 1973, p. 3,, March 23, 1973, p. 7, August 31, 1973, p. 8, September 14, 1973, p. 2, December 7, 1973, p. 10, February 1, 1974, p. 10, August 30, 1974, p. 7, and September 20, 1974, p. 11; *Bluejay*, 1974, pp. 235, 237, 247.

75. *Creightonian*, February 8, 1963, p. 1, September 18, 1964, p. 1, May 14, 1965, p. 1, March 18, 1966, p. 6, October 28, 1966, p. 1, October 6, 1967, p. 1, February 9, 1968, p. 1, April 25, 1969, p. 3, February 13, 1970, p. 6,, October 30, 1970, p. 1, March 26, 1971, p. 1, April 14, 1972, p. 1, and September 22, 1972, p. 2; BTM, March 24, September 20 and October 21, 1966; *Bluejay*, 1968, p. 4, 1972, p. 302, and 1973, p. 36; "Schedule of Classes," 1967, 1968, 1971.

76. BTM, January 6, 1966; LBRM, May 6, 1966; *TCA*, July 1966, p. 2; *Creightonian*, October 14, 1966, p. 1, September 29, 1967, p. 7, and February 23, 1968, p. 5; *Alumnews*, April 1974, p. 2.

77. *Creightonian*, January 10, 1964, p. 1, February 21, 1964, p. 2, October 30, 1964, p. 5, September 18, 1964, p. 3, May 14, 1965, p. 1, October 1, 1965, p. 3, November 19, 1965, p. 5, September 22, 1967, p. 2, November 14, 1969, p. 7, October 30, 1970, p. 8, and October 20, 1972, p. 10; BTM, April 2 and May 31, 1967; *TCA*, March 1965, pp. 10–11, March 1966, pp. 4–7, and March 1967, pp. 12–13; *Alumnews*, November 1973, p. 5.

78. *Creightonian*, September 18, 1964, p. 3, September 22, 1967, p. 7, and March 8, 1968, p. 6; *Bluejay*, 1970, p. 135 and 1974, p. 108; *Alumnews*, November 1972, p. 3, and March 1974, p. 2; *CUB*, Arts, 1973–1975.

79. Szmrecsanyi, pp. 524–25; *CUB*, Arts, 1955 through 1975; *TCA*, October 1968, p. 3, and January 1969, p. 8; *Creightonian*, February 21, 1969, p. 8.

80. *Creightonian*, March 28, 1969, p. 1, April 25, 1969, p. 1, September 19, 1969, p. 5, October 3, 1969, p. 7, May 1, 1970, p. 6, May 8, 1970, p. 3, and September 25, 1970, p. 3; *TCA*, September 1971, p. 36; *Alumnews*, January 1973, p. 1.

81. *Creightonian*, April 2, 1971, p. 1, and May 7, 1971, p. 1; *TCA*, September 1971, p. 36; *CUB*, Arts, 1971–72.

82. BDM, February 5, 1973; *Creightonian*, October 18, 1968, p. 2, October 19, 1973, p. 1, November 2, 1973, p. 3, and March 1, 1974, p. 2; *Alumnews*, May 1973, p. 3; *CUB*, Arts, 1973–75.

83. Registrar enrollment data; *CUB*, Summer School, 1963 through 1974; LBRM, May 6, 1966; BTM, October 5, 1966; *Creightonian*, March 12, 1971, p. 7, and March 26, 1971, p. 2; *TCA*, October 1969, p. 3; *Alumnews*, April 1973, p. 4; BDM, August 4, 1975.

84. *CUB*, Graduate School, 1964 through 1975; BTM, April 15, 1966, and January 26, 1968; BDM, April 7, 1969; *TCA*, March 1965, p. 10, October 1968, pp. 5–6, October 1969, pp. 10–11, and September 1971, p. 38; *Alumnews*, October 1972, p. 2, and May 1974, p. 5; *Creightonian*, March 1, 1974, p. 9; Vosper, p. 78; Boro and Mead, p. 173.

85. Registrar enrollment data; *CUB*, CoBA, 1964 through 1975; *TCA*, November 1964, p. 6, October 1968, p. 4, October 1969, p. 7, July 1970, pp. 10–11, and September 1971, p. 36; *Creightonian*, October 9, 1964, p. 7, February 19, 1965, p. 1, February 4, 1966, p. 5, and September 19, 1969, p. 5; *Bluejay*, 1966, p. 185; BTM, April 15, 1966; Cahill, pp. 33–43.

86. *Creightonian*, November 18, 1966, p. 3, November 3, 1972, p. 1, and March 16, 1973, p. 1; *Alumnews*, April 1973, p. 4, August 1973, p. 1, and May 1974, p. 2; *Bluejay*, 1973, p. 152; Cahill, pp. 45–51.

87. Registrar enrollment data; *CUB*, Law, 1965 through 1975; BTM, March 16, 1966; BDM March 1, 1971, and February 7, 1972; *Creightonian*, November 6, 1970, p. 3 and April 2, 1971, p. 3 and March 1, 1974, p. 8 October 4, 1974, p. 1; *TCA*, September 1971, p. 36; *Alumnews*, February 1974, pp. 4.

88. *CUB*, Law, 1965 through 1975; *Creightonian*, December 4, 1964, p. 2, October 2, 1970, p. 5, September 1, 1972, p. 4, and September 14, 1973, p. 8; *TCA*, September 1967, p. 12, and October 1969, pp. 12–13; *Alumnews*, March 1973, p. 2, February 1974, pp. 4–5, August 1974, p. 2, April 1975, p. 4, and November 1975, p. 4; *Bluejay*, 1968, p. 201, 1971, p. 156, and 1972, p. 212; BDM, April 7, 1969; Vosper, pp. 146–47; Jahn, p. 80.

89. BDM, December 18, 1972, March 5, 1973, and October 1, 1973; *Alumnews*, February 1973, p. 1.

90. *TCA*, November 1964, pp. 4–5; BTM, January 26, 1968; *Alumnews*, October 1972, p. 1; Boro and Mead, pp. 163–64.

91. BTM, October 18 and October 31, 1965, January 6, February 15, August 22, October 25, November 16, December 12, 1966, and January 30, 1968; LBRM, November 3, 1965, January 21,

March 4, October 28, December 1, 1966, and March 3, 1967; BDM, February 3, and March 3, 1969, January 5, 1970, and May 7, June 4, and November 5, 1973; *Alumnews*, February 1973, p. 1, and October 1973, p. 1 and August 1974, p. 1; Boro and Mead, pp. 190–95; *Creightonian*, March 22, 1974, p. 1.

92. *CUB*, Medicine, 1964 through 1975; LBRM, May 6, 1966; *TCA*, July 1966, p. 16, October 1967, p. 2, and October 1968, p. 7; Boro and Mead, p. 172.

93. Registrar enrollment data; BDM, March 1 and June 7, 1971, and January 9, 1973; *TCA*, January 1968, p. 9, and September 1971, p. 34; Boro and Mead, pp. 176, 206–8, 293–94.

94. Registrar faculty data; BDM, May 25, 1970, and March 1, 1971; *TCA*, October 1970, p. 18, and September 1971, p. 34; *Alumnews*, October 1972, p. 4, and January 1973, p. 2; *Bluejay*, 1973, p. 180; Boro and Mead, pp. 178–89, 224.

95. *Creightonian*, October 27, 1967, p. 2; *TCA*, July 1970, pp. 14–15; Boro and Mead, pp. 176, 217, 226; *Omaha World-Herald*, December 26, 2004, p. 6A.

96. *TCA*, October 1969, pp. 12–13, and September 1971, p. 34; *The Creightonian*, September 17, 1971, p. 5; *Bluejay*, 1972, p. 180, and 1973, p. 180; Boro and Mead, pp. 176–77, 188, 209–10.

97. BDM, June 29, 1970; *CUB*, Medicine, 1970–72; *Creightonian*, November 6, 1970, p. 5, and October 22, 1971, p. 5; *TCA*, October 1970, pp. 10–13; *Alumnews*, February 1973, p. 4, and March 1973, p. 2.

98. Registrar enrollment data; BDM, April 15, and September 30, 1966; *Alumnews*, January 1974, p. 3.

99. *CUB*, Pharmacy, 1969 through 1973; *TCA*, September 1967, pp. 12–13, and October 1969, pp. 16–17, and September 1971, p. 33; *Creightonian*, January 12, 1971, p. 5, and September 15, 1972, p. 5; *Bluejay*, 1972, p. 200, and 1973, pp. 161, 165; *Alumnews*, March 1973, p. 4.

100. Registrar enrollment data; *CUB*, Nursing, 1969–71; BDM, April, 19, 1971; Vossen, pp. 57–70, 99.

101. BDM, April 19 and October 4, 1971; *TCA*, September 1971, p. 34; *Creightonian*, October 15, 1971, p. 1; *Bluejay*, 1972, p. 220; Vossen, pp. 64–65.

102. *Alumnews*, October 1972, p. 2; *Creightonian*, February 18, 1972, p. 3, and March 22, 1974, p. 1, and August 21, 1974, p. 2; Vossen, p. 69–71.

103. Registrar enrollment data; *CUB*, Dental, 1963 through 1975; *TCA*, September 1967, p. 12, and September 1971, p. 34; *Creightonian*, February 21, 1969, p. 2, and September 22, 1972, p. 3.

104. Registrar faculty data; *TCA*, October 1968, p. 4; *Creightonian*, October 13, 1972, p. 1; *Alumnews*, January 1973, p. 2; BDM, August 5, 1974; Lynch interview.

105. *TCA*, September 1967, p. 11, and October 1969, pp. 8–9; *CUB*, Dental, 1972; *Bluejay*, 1972, p. 190, 1973, p. 170, and 1974, p. 179.

106. *TCA*, July 1964, p. 4; *Creightonian*, October 16, 1970, p. 2; BDM, August 6, 1970, and March 5, 1973; Jahn, p. 78.

107. BDM, January 9, 1973; *Creightonian*, January 19, 1973, p. 1, January 26, 1973, p. 1, February 2, 1973, pp. 5, 8, February 9, 1973, p. 1, March 3, 1972, p. 1, March 16, 1973, p. 1, August 31, 1973, p. 1, September 19, 1973, p. 2, April 13, 1973, p. 1, and March 15, 1974, p. 4; *Bluejay*, 1973, pp. 16, 41; *Alumnews*, February 1973, p. 1, and April 1974, p. 3.

Chapter Eleven

1. BDM, February 4 and August 5, 1974, August 1, 1977, and February 6, 1978; *Alumnews*, March 1974, p. 3, and August 1978, p. 4; Jahn, pp. 81–82.

2. BDM, August 26 and November 4, 1974, and August 4, 1975; Jahn, pp. 71–72.

3. BDM, February 2, 1976 and December 4, 1978; *Creightonian*, December 10, 1976, p. 1; *Alumnews*, August 1977, p. 1, and April 1978, p. 1.

4. *Alumnews*, February 1977, p. 1, May 1978, p. 10, and May 1991, p. 12; *Creightonian*, August 24, 1977, p. 1; *Bluejay*, 1978, pp. 112–13.

5. BDM, February 5 and April 2, 1979, and August 3 and December 7, 1981; *Alumnews*, May 1979, p. 1, August 1981, p. 1, and January 1982, p. 1.

6. BDM, December 7, 1981, and April 5 and December 6, 1982; Jahn, pp. 95–96.

7. BDM, October 3, 1983, October 5, 1987, and December 4, 1989; *Alumnews*, January 1982, p. 3, and March 1984, p. 1.

8. BDM, June 7, 1982, December 7, 1987, and October 2, 1989; Jahn, p. 96.

9. BDM, November 3, 1975, February 2, 1976, June 5, 1978, June 6, 1988, and June 3, 1991; *Alumnews*, November 1981, p. 1, and May 1983, p. 1.

10. BDM, October 5, 1981, June 3, 1985, June 1 and December 7, 1987, December 4, 1989, and March 2, 1992.

11. BDM, March 1 and September 29, 1976, August 1, 1977, and October 2, 1978; *Creightonian*, September 17, 1976, p. 2, September 16, 1977, p. 1, September 23, 1977, p. 1, February 24, 1978, p. 1, March 10, 1978, p. 4, and February 6, 1981, p. 1; Registrar enrollment data.

12. *Creightonian*, September 16, 1977, April 8, 1988, p. 1, February 7, 1986, p. 6, March 21, 1986, p. 3, February 19, 1988, pp. 1, 3, September 28, 1990, p. 8, April 10, 1992, pp. 1, 2, November 20, 1992, p. 10, November 12, 1993, p. 2, February 11, 1994, p. 2, and November 18, 1994, p. 4; *Alumnews*, March 1982, p. 3; BDM, October 5, 1987; registrar enrollment data.

13. BDM, (starting in 1975, the academic committee reported on enrollment and a discussion on recruiting ensued), February 4, 1980, and December 5, 1983; *Alumnews*, February 1992, p. 4.

14. BDM, March 7, 1988, and March 4, 1991; *Creightonian*, August 21, 1974, p. 2, and May 1, 1987, p. 7; *Window*, Summer 1985, p. 27.

15. *Alumnews*, April 1977, p. 5, October 1982, p. 4, and May 1983, p. 1; BDM March 2 and December 7, 1987, and March 6, 1989, March 4, October 7 and December 2, 1991.

16. BDM, February 2, 1976, February 7, 1977, October 6, 1980, August 3, 1981, August 2 and October 4, 1982, June 2, 1986, and March 2, 1987; *Alumnews*, March 1978, p. 12, November 1982, p. 1, and August 1991, p. 2.

17. *Alumnews*, August 1974, p. 2, January 1976, p. 5, and August 1983, p. 3; *Bluejay*, 1976, p. 192; BDM, August 4, 1980.

18. BDM, February 4, 1974, and April 7, 1975; Jahn, pp. 82–83; *Creightonian*, April 25, 1975, p. 1; *Alumnews*, May 1975, pp. 1–2, and April 1978, p. 3; *CUB*, Arts, 1977.

19. *Creightonian*, September 3, 1976, p. 1, November 5, 1976, p. 12, December 2, 1977, p. 4, January 30, 1987, p. 10, and September 14, 1990, p. 1; *Alumnews*, May 1986, p. 4, and May 1990, p. 2.

20. *Creightonian*, May 1, 1981, p. 6, October 12, 1984, p. 3, November 2, 1984, p. 1, January 30, 1987, p. 12, February 5, 1988, p. 1, January 27, 1989, p. 3, and September 13, 1991, p. 2; *Alumnews*, April 1983, p. 3,, November 1985, p. 15, August 1991, p. 2, and May 1992, p. 4; *Window*, Spring 1988, p. 27, and Winter 1988-89, pp. 20–25; BDM, June 3, 1991.

21. BDM, December 3, 1979, December 1, 1980, April 6, 1981, April 5, and August 2 and December 6, 1982; *Alumnews*, November 1979, pp. 1–2, August 1980, p. 1, May 1981, p. 5, May 1983, p. 1, and May 1993, p. 4; *Creightonian*, May 1, 1981, p. 1, September 10, 1982, p. 1, March 30, 1984, p. 9, and March 7, 1986, p. 1.

22. BDM, August 7, 1978, April 2, 1979, February 4, 1980, October 5, 1981, and October 2, 1989; *Alumnews*, September 27, 1974, p. 8, October 1974, p. 2, May 1979, p. 1, May 1980, p. 1, October 1981, p. 1, and May 1991, p. 3; *Creightonian*, August 21, 1974, p. 3, September 19, 1975, p. 6, August 25, 1976, p. 1, October 18, 1976, p. 1, February 15, 1980, p. 1, March 6, 1981, p. 2, and April 8, 1988, p. 1; Jahn, pp. 97–99.

23. *Creightonian*, August 30, 1974, p. 1, September 30, 1977, p. 1, August 31, 1979, p. 1, February 6, 1981, p. 1, October 30, 1981, p. 1, March 26, 1982, p. 3, December 9, 1983, p. 1, September 27, 1985, p. 1, and December 1, 1989, p. 5; BDM, October 2, 1978, and June 6, 1983; *Alumnews*, August 1979, p. 1; Jahn, pp. 86–87.

24. BDM, February 4, 1974, and March 1, 1976; *Alumnews*, February 1977, pp. 1–2, and August 1977, p. 1; *Creightonian*, November 11, 1976, p. 1, and September 2, 1977, p. 4, *Bluejay*, 1978, pp. 30–31; Jahn, p. 89.

25. BDM, June 5, 1978; *Alumnews*, August 1978, p. 1, January 1979, p. 1, August 1989, p. 8, and August 1993, p. 1; *Creightonian*, September 22, 1989, p. 1, and November 3, 1989, p. 1.

26. *Alumnews*, January 1980, p. 1, January 1983, p. 1, December 1986, p. 4, and May 1991, p. 3; BDM, June 7, 1982, June 2 and October 6, 1986, October 5, 1987, and June 1, 1992; *Creightonian*, October 30, 1987, p. 7, November 14, 1986, p. 1, and October 2, 1987, pp. 1, 3; Wareham Building Dedication pamphlet, PVF.

27. *Creightonian*, September 16, 1983, p. 1, May 4, 1984, p. 6, and February 19, 1988, p. 1; *Alumnews*, November 1985, p. 1, August 1986, p. 1, and May 1991, p. 3; BDM, December 3, 1984, October 5, 1987, and March 5, 1990.

28. BDM, February 7, 1977, and December 5, 1977; *Creightonian*, November 19, 1976, p. 3, February 4, 1977, p. 3, March 25, 1977, p. 1, October 28, 1977, p. 1, and November 4, 1977, p. 1; author's recollection.

29. *Alumnews*, January 1976, p. 1, and March 1978, p. 1; *Creightonian*, March 10, 1978, p. 1.

30. BDM, December 4, 1978, and December 3, 1990, and March 4 and June 3, 1991; *Alumnews*, November 1991, p. 4.

31. BDM, February 7, 1977, March 7 and October 3, 1988, March 4, 1991, March 2 and October 5, 1992; *Alumnews*, February 1986, p. 2, and February 1988, p. 5.

32. *Alumnews*, April 1975, pp. 1–2, and August 1983, p. 4; *Creightonian*, April 18, 1975, p. 2, November 7, 1975, p. 1, October 17, 1980, pp. 1, 3, March 27, 1981, p. 1, and February 18, 1983, p. 1; BDM, June 4, 1984; *CUB*, Arts, 1977.

33. *Creightonian*, January 24, 1975, p. 1, November 7, 1975, p. 2, February 6, 1976, p. 1, and September 16, 1977, p. 8; *Alumnews*, February 1975, p. 2, October 1976, p. 3, and February 1988, pp. 1–2.

34. *Creightonian*, December 9, 1977, p. 8 and October 5, 1979, p. 3, November 16, 1990, p. 1, and August 31, 1991, p. 1; BDM, October 6, 1980; *Alumnews*, November 1980, p. 1, January 1981, p. 1, August 1982, p. 4, and November 1985, p. 4.

35. BDM, August 5, 1974; *Alumnews*, August 1974, p. 3, March 1975, pp. 1–2, and April 1975, p. 5, April 1977, pp. 1, 6, and January 1979, p. 5; *CUB*, Arts, 1975-77; *Creightonian*, January 31, 1975, p. 1, May 6, 1977, p. 1, May 5, 1978, p. 1, October 27, 1978, p. 11, and November 10, 1978; Registrar enrollment data.

36. BDM, August 1, 1977, January 4, 1978, and June 6, 1983; registrar enrollment data; *Alumnews*, October 1977, p. 1, January 1978, p. 12, February 1978, p. 4, and May 1978, p. 1; *Creightonian*, February 3, 1978, p. 1, March 19, 1982, p. 1, February 3, 1984, p. 4, and September 7, 1984, p. 3.

37. BDM, October 6, 1986; *Creightonian*, February 3, 1984, p. 4; Boro and Mead, p. 214.

38. *Creightonian*, March 13, 1964, p. 7, December 6, 1968, p. 8, November 5, 1971, p. 12, May 5, 1982, p. 3, March 31, 1989, p. 5, November 9, 1990, p. 8, and March 13, 1992, p. 3; *TCA*, January 1966, p. 2; *Bluejay*, 1969, p. 225; *Alumnews*, April 1975, p. 3, April 1982, pp. 1–2, October 1983, pp. 3, 16, February 1990, p. 3, and May 1991, p. 8; *Window*, Winter 1986–87, p. 9; *CUB*, Arts, 1985–86; Kelley, p. 44.

39. *Creightonian*, September 22, 1978, p. 2, January 27, 1989, p. 1, March 3, 1989, p. 1, and

September 22, 1989, p. 1; *Alumnews*, October 1978, p. 9, November 1982, p. 1, and November 1989, p. 2; *CUB*, Undergraduate, 1988–89.

40. BDM, April 5 and September 29, 1976, and June 1, 1981; *Creightonian*, February 7, 1975, p. 9; *Alumnews*, January 1977, p. 1, March 1980, p. 4, May 1981, p. 2, and October 1981, p. 1; Registrar enrollment data; *CUB*, CoBA, 1970 through 1981.

41. Cahill, pp. 51–57; *Creightonian*, January 29, 1982, p. 1, and February 12, 1982, p. 4.

42. BDM, June 7, 1982, and March 6, 1989; registrar enrollment data; *Alumnews*, August 1982, p. 2, November 1982, p. 3, August 1983, p. 5, February 1986, p. 3, and February 1992, p. 3; Cahill, pp. 60–64.

43. *Creightonian*, August 30, 1974, p. 3, and April 29, 1983, p. 8; BDM, October 4, 1982, June 6 and October 3, 1983, and March 6, 1989; *Alumnews*, April 1983, p. 1.

44. BDM, August 4, 1975, October 2, 1978, December 1, 1986, and December 7, 1992; *CUB*, Graduate, 1974 through 1992; *Alumnews*, November 1977, p. 3; *Creightonian*, November 7, 1975, p. 3, November 21, 1975, p. 1, and February 16, 1990, p. 2; Registrar enrollment data.

45. BDM, February 7, 1977, and February 1978, and February 1, 1982, June 13, 1989,, and March 4, 1991; *Bluejay*, 1976, p. 155; *Creightonian*, December 7, 1979, p. 5; *CUB*, Law 1981 and 1983; Registrar enrollment data.

46. BDM, December 6, 1976; *Creightonian*, December 2, 1977, p. 1, December 9, 1977, p. 2, and December 8, 1978, p. 2; *Alumnews*, April 1979, p. 3.

47. *Creightonian*, April 7, 1978, p. 4, December 12, 1979, p. 1, March 29, 1985, p. 1, and October 11, 1985, p. 3; *CUB*. Law, 1979, 1981 and 1985; *Alumnews*, March 1981, p. 1, and November 1981, p. 2.

48. BDM, October 2, 1989; *CUB*, Law, 1989; *Alumnews*, February 1988, p. 3, February 1991, p. 2, and August 1992, p. 3.

49. *Creightonian*, October 11, 1974, p. 1, and April 21, 1978, p. 7; *Alumnews*, May 1978, p. 1; *CUB*, Nursing, 1975; Vossen, pp. 72–82; Registrar enrollment data; *Window*, Summer 1986, p. 5.

50. *Alumnews*, November 1975, pp. 1, 4; *Creightonian*, February 13, 1976, p. 1, February 25, 1977, p. 2, and September 16, 1977, p. 3; Vossen, pp. 78–81.

51. *Alumnews*, February 1975, p. 3; *Creightonian*, November 30, 1984, p. 6.

52. Vossen, pp. 71–84; *CUB*, Nursing, 1973 through 1977; *Alumnews*, March 1980, p. 1.

53. *The Creightonian*, October 1, 1982, p. 6; *Alumnews*, January 1983, p. 5; *Window*, Summer 1986, p. 5 and Winter 1994-95, p. 18; Vossen, pp. 83–88.

54. *Alumnews*, October 1980, p. 2; BDM March 3, 1986, and March 4, 1991; *Window*, Summer 1986, p. 9; *Creightonian*, March 7, 1986, p. 1, March 21, 1986, p. 2, September 26, 1986, p. 1, and February 24, 1989, p. 2; Vossen, p. 91.

55. BDM, August 3 and December 7, 1981; Registrar enrollment data; *Creightonian*, October 25, 1974, p. 1, and April 11, 1975, p. 2; *Alumnews*, February 1975, p. 4, and November 1975, p. 2; *Bluejay*, 1975, p. 161.

56. *CUB*, Pharmacy, 1974 through 1988; *Alumnews*, January 1976, p. 1; *Creightonian*, May 4, 1984, p. 2; *Window*, Winter, 1988–89, pp. 20–22.

57. *Alumnews*, October 1977, p. 2, and August 1982, p. 4; BDM, August 2, 1982; *Window*, Winter, 1984–85, p. 27; *Creightonian*, September 13, 1991, p. 2.

58. *Alumnews*. March 1975, p. 3, March 1976, p. 1, and January 1980, p. 2; *Creightonian*, September 28, 1984, p. 8; Registrar enrollment data; Terry M. Wilwerding, D.D.S., unpublished history paper; Lynch interview.

59. BDM, April 6 and December 7, 1981, December 6, 1982, October 3, 1983, October 3, 1988, and March 4 and June 3, 1991; *Alumnews*, April 1981, pp. 1–5; *Creightonian*, February 24, 1984, p. 1, and April 18, 1986, p. 8; *Window*, Summer 1987, pp. 21–22.

60. *Creightonian*, September 20, 1974, p. 8, and November 10, 1978, p. 3; *Alumnews*, August

1977, p. 5, November 1983, p. 6, and August 1990, p. 6; BDM, March 7, 1983, December 5, 1988, and March 4, 1991; Boro and Mead, p. 213; Registrar enrollment data.

61. BDM, August 4 and December 1, 1975, and March 1 and May 3, 1976; *Creightonian*, March 19, 1976, p. 1.

62. BDM, April 7, 1975, and August 2 and December 6, 1976; *Creightonian*, March 11, 1977, p. 3, and March 10, 1978, p. 6; *Alumnews*, November 1977, p. 4, March 1978, p. 2, and March 1979, p. 2; Vossen, p. 81; Jahn, pp. 88–89.

63. BDM, December 5, 1977, December 4, 1978, June 2 and August 4, 1980, August 3, 1981, October 4, 1982, December 5, 1983, and March 2, 1987; *Alumnews*, October 1976, p. 5.

64. BDM, April 5, 1982, December 5, 1983, March 5, 1984, March 4, 1985, and March 2, 1987; *Alumnews*, March 1984, p. 3; Boro and Mead, p. 246–47.

65. DBM, March 5 and October 1, 1984; *Alumnews*, August 1984, p. 3.

66. BDM, June 4, 1984; *Alumnews*, August 1984, pp. 1, 3; Boro and Mead, p. 247.

67. BDM, June 3, 1985, and March 3 and June 2, 1986; *Alumnews*, August 1987, p. 5, and August 1989, p. 5.

68. BDM, October 3, 1988, March 6, 1989, June 4, 1990, March 4, 1991, and March 2 and June 1, 1992; *Alumnews*, May 1990, p. 4.

69. *Creightonian*, October 11, 1974, p. 1, August 20, 1975, p. 1, and April 11, 1977, p. 10; *Alumnews*, August 1975, p. 3, August 1976, pp. 1–2, February 1977, p. 2, March 1977, p. 1, and April 1977, p. 2; *CUB*, Medicine, 1977 through 1987; Boro and Mead, p. 225.

70. Johnathon R. Cole and James A. Lipton, "The Reputation of American Medical Schools," *Social Forces*, vol. 55, no. 3, March 1977, pp. 662–71; *Alumnews*, October 1977, pp. 4–5, October 1981, p. 3, and August 1989, p. 6; *Creightonian*, April 14, 1978, p. 1; Boro and Mead, p. 224.

71. *Creightonian*, January 29, 1982, p. 1, February 5, 1982, p. 1, and March 30, 1984, p. 8; *Alumnews*, October 1981, p. 1, March 1983, p. 2, May 1991, p. 3, and November 1991, pp. 3–4; BDM, October 11, 1985; Boro and Mead, pp. 229–30.

72. *Creightonian*, December 7, 1984, p. 7; *Alumnews*, February 1988, p. 12, February 1990, p. 8, and August 1990, p. 4; BDM, December 4, 1989, and October 7, 1991; *Window*, Fall 1990, p. 5.

73. *Alumnews*, November 1983, p. 2, and January 1984, p. 2; Vossen, pp. 76–77.

74. *Creightonian*, October 11, 1974, p. 2, February 21, 1975, p. 1, October 8, 1976, p. 1, February 4, 1977, p. 1, and May 3, 1985, pp. 1, 3.

75. *Creightonian*, March 7, 1975, p. 7, October 8, 1976, p. 1, April 11, 1977, p. 3, March 2, 1979, p. 1, March 6, 1981, p. 2, November 29, 1981, p. 3, April 29, 1982, p. 1, September 3, 1982, p. 1, October 29, 1982, p. 1, October 29, 1982, p. 9, November 5, 1982, p. 1, February 18, 1983, p. 1, March 25, 1983, p. 1, March 2, 1984, p. 4, and February 28, 1986, p. 1; *Alumnews*, April 1975, p. 3; BDM, June 3, 1991.

76. *Creightonian*, November 15, 1974, p. 4, September 24, 1976, p. 1, and October 15, 1976, p. 1; *Bluejay*, 1960 through 1976.

77. September 30, 1977, p. 2, February 20, 1981, p. 5, September 25, 1981, p. 8, April 6, 1984, p. 6, Sept 14, 1984, p. 2, December 6, 1985, p. 1, February 14, 1986, p. 2, March 27, 1987, p. 2, and September 28, 1990, p. 8; BDM, October 1, 1990; *Bluejay*, Greek section, 1974 through 1992.

78. *Creightonian*, April 21, 1978, p. 9, February 3, 1984, p. 4, February 7, 1986, p. 1, February 8, 1985, p. 2, March 1, 1985, p. 9, Sept 13, 1985, pp. 1, 9, December 6, 1985, p. 1, January 31, 1986, pp. 3, 5, and January 28, 1990, p. 12.

79. *Creightonian*, October 24, 1975, p. 1, October 31, 1975, p. 1, February 22, 1980, p. 2, October 26, 1990, p. 12, and November 16, 1990, p. 2; *Alumnews*, August 1981, p. 2, and May 1985, p. 2.

80. *TCA*, February 1956, p. 19; BDM, October 5, 1981, and June 7, 1982; *Creightonian*, October 16, 1981, p. 3, and February 10, 1984, p. 7; *Alumnews*, November 1982, p. 3, April 1983, p. 4, August 1989, p. 6, and November 1990, p. 4.

81. *Creightonian*, September 6, 1974, p. 8, November 8, 1974, p. 4, February 7, 1975, p. 12, September 19, 1975, p. 1, September 26, 1975, p. 2, April 7, 1978, p. 7, April 21, 1978, p. 1, 6, April 28, 1978, p. 6, February 9, 1979, p. 5, February 16, 1979, p. 7, January 30, 1981, p. 4, February 27, 1981, p. 9, and September 23, 1994, p. 1; *Alumnews*, October 1974, p. 2, April 1979, p. 6, and November 1989, p. 5; *Bluejay*, 1974, 1975, 1976, 1977, p. 119, and 1999, p. 64; *Bluejay*, 1999, p. 65.

82. *Creightonian*, March 16, 1973, p. 4, November 20, 1973, p. 6, January 24, 1975, p. 1, November 21, 1975, p. 1, February 4, 1977, p. 5, April 11, 1977, p. 1, February 17, 1978, pp. 3, 8, February 11, 1983, p. 2, February 14, 1986, p. 2, December 5, 1986, p. 2, February 3, 1989, pp. 6–7, February 10, 1989, p. 1, February 2, 1990, p. 8, November 2, 1990, p. 3, and January 31, 1992, p. 9; *Alumnews*, November 1978, p. 4.

83. *Creightonian*, October 1, 1971, p. 12, September 8, 1989, p. 1, and November 16, 1990, p. 1; *Alumnews*, February 1991, p. 3; *Window*, Spring 1996, pp. 10–13.

84. *Creightonian*, September 5, 1980, p. 4, September 11, 1981, p. 3, November 6, 1981, p. 1, September 24, 1982, p. 6, October 4, 1991, p. 2, April 3, 1992, p. 6, and February 19, 1993, p. 1; *Alumnews*, May 1982, p. 5, and August 1989, p. 10; *Window*, Fall 1984, p. 27; BDM, December 7, 1992.

85. Reichmuth, pp. 18-22; *Creightonian*, September 20, 1974, p. 1, March 21, 1975, p. 7, May 2, 1975, p. 13, February 13, 1976, p. 3, March 23, 1979, p. 3, December 12, 1979, p. 1, May 1, 1981, p. 2, October 29, 1982, p. 10, February 17, 1984, p. 6, January 31, 1986, p. 8, April 29, 1988, p. 2, April 19, 1991, p. 3, and February 14, 1992, p. 1; *Alumnews*, November 1982, p. 3, and February 1991, p. 2.

86. *Alumnews*, January 1975, p. 1, August 1981, p. 2, August 1989, p. 5, and February 1990, pp. 2, 8; *Bluejay*, 1976, p. 105; *Creightonian*, September 7, 1984, p. 13, September 6, 1985, p. 4, March 31, 1989, p. 3, November 10, 1989, p. 4, and November 13, 1992. p. 7.

87. *Creightonian*, September 27, 1974, p. 1, November 15, 1974, p. 8, April 4, 1975, p. 3, November 14, 1975, p. 2, December 1, 1978, p. 1, February 23, 1979, p. 3, and April 27, 1979, supplement, p. 4ff., and April 23, 1982, p. 1; BDM, October 7, 1974.

88. *Creightonian*, February 28, 1986, p. 14, September 12, 1986, p. 1, November 7, 1986, p. 2, January 30, 1987, p. 3, April 24, 1987, p. 7, October 2, 1987, p. 5, March 25, 1988, p. 7, April 15, 1988, p. 3, February 17, 1989, p. 2, March 31, 1989, p. 2, and February 11, 1994, p. 2; *Alumnews*, May 1993, p. 5.

89. *Creightonian*, September 6, 1974, p. 1, September 16, 1977, p. 8, February 1, 1980, p. 1, February 15, 1980, p. 1, September 12, 1980, p. 5, November 21, 1980, p. 1, December 5, 1980, p. 1, September 5, 1980, p. 12, January 30, 1981, p. 2, February 18, 1983, p. 3, and February 15, 1983, p. 3.

90. *CUB*, Arts, 1975-1977; *Creightonian*, September 24, 1982, p. 7, February 10, 1984, p. 1, September 7, 1984, p. 3, March 20, 1985, p. 1, September 11, 1987, p. 1, and January 29, 1988, p. 1.

91. *Creightonian*, October 3, 1980, p. 7, March 22, 1985, p. 7, April 12, 1985, p. 7, March 29, 1985, p. 7, September 26, 1986, p. 8, February 10, 1989, p. 6, February 24, 1989, p. 3, and October 26, 1990, p. 11.

92. BDM, March 4, 1974, October 5, 1981, October 3 and December 5, 1988, and June 1, October 5, and December 7, 1992; Annual athletic department, Financial Report, 1974 through 1992.

93. *Creightonian*, March 26, 1976, p. 9, April 9, 1976, p. 11, August 25, 1976, p. 4, September 3, 1976, p. 6, September 17, 1976, p. 11, August 24, 1977, p. 4, September 2, 1977, p. 8, April 29, 1977, p. 14, and August 31, 1979, p. 11; *Bluejay*, 1976, p. 242, 1977, p. 268, 1978, pp. 243, 277, and 1979, p. 169; *Softball Media Guide; Women's Basketball Media Guide.*

94. *Creightonian*, March 19, 1976, p. 11, March 26, 1976, p. 9, September 17, 1976, p. 11, and April 27, 1979, p. 1; *Bluejay*, 1977, pp. 233, 276, and 1981, p. 294.

95. *Creightonian*, August 29, 1975, p. 7, March 19, 1976, pp. 1, 10, October 28, 1977, p. 16, May 6, 1977, p. 1, December 9, 1977, p. 10, April 27, 1979, p. 1, September 7, 1979, p. 7, and January 24, 1997, special supplement; *Bluejay*, 1975, p. 229, and 1981, p. 300; *Baseball Media Guide; Men's Basketball Media Guide.*

96. BDM, October 5, 1981; *Creightonian*, September 4, 1981, p. 1, March 19, 1982, p. 11, April 2, 1982, p. 8, January 28, 1983, p. 10, February 17, 1984, p. 14, December 6, 1985, pp. 1, 9, and January 31, 1986, p. 14.

97. BDM, March 7, October 3, and December 5, 1988, and June 4, 1990; *Creightonian*, September 16, 1988, p. 1, October 14, 1988, p. 8, December 9, 1988, p. 1, February 9, 1990, p. 1, April 20, 1990, p. 4, February 8, 1991, p. 18, and February 15, 1991, p. 15.

98. "The Blue News," October 6, 1986; *Chicago Tribune*, March 3, 1992; "Memorandum," from Greg Jahn, April 27, 1992, Kevin Ross File, CUA.

99. *Creightonian*, April 10, 1981, p. 7, April 24, 1981, p. 9, May 3, 1985, p. 1, September 6, 1985, p. 9, February 14, 1986, p. 15, March 20, 1987, p. 1, and November 3, 1989, p. 10; *CUM*, Fall 1985, p. 27; Michael J. Reasoner and Michael J. Marcil, "Athletes and Drugs: Testing Begins at Creighton," *Window*, Fall 1986, p. 10–11.

100. *Creightonian*, April 19, 1991, pp. 1, 9; *Men's Basketball Media Guide.*

101. *Creightonian*, April 27, 1984, p. 1, October 2, 1987, p. 1, and October 14, 1988, p. 1; *Baseball Media Guide.*

102. BDM, March 2 and December 7, 1992; *Creightonian*, January 24, 1992; *Men's Soccer Media Guide.*

103. *Creightonian*, November 21, 1980, p. 7a, October 14, 1988, p. 8, September 1, 1988, p. 14, and April 3, 1992, p. 1; *Women's Basketball Media Guide; Softball Media Guide; Women's Soccer Media Guide.*

104. *Creightonian*, February 19, 1971, p. 3, February 6, 1987, p. 1; *Alumnews*, November 1987, p. 1, November 1988, p. 8, November 1989, p. 1, November 1990, p. 2, November 1991, p. 2, and November 1992, p. 3; Power, pp. 436–53; Leahy, pp. 135–46.

105. BDM, June 1, 1987, June 13, 1989, and June 1 and October 5, 1992; *Alumnews*, February 1988, p. 4, November 1989, p. 4, and November 1992, p. 2.

Chapter Twelve

1. "Strategic Plan: Creighton University," PVF.

2. BDM, June 7, 1993, June 6 and October 3, 1994, June 2 and October 6, 1997, and December 7, 1998; *Alumnews*, August 1998, p. 2.

3. BDM, October 4, 1993, October 3, 1994, October 2, 1995, and June 2, 1997.

4. BDM, October 4, 1993, October 2, 1995, March 4, June 6, October 7, and December 2, 1996, June 2 and October 6, 1997, and June 1 and October 9, 1998; *Alumnews*, February 1993, p. 2.

5. BDM, October 3, 1994, June 5, October 2, and December 4, 1995, and October 4, 1999; *Alumnews*, November 1994, p. 2, and November 1995, p. 2; *Creightonian*, September 22, 1995, p. 1, October 13, 1995, p. 1, November 3, 1995, p. 1, and March 22, 1996, p. 3; Registrar enrollment data.

6. BDM, June 3, 1996, December 1, 1997, June 1 and December 7, 1998, March 1 and June 7, 1999, June 5, 2000, March 5 and June 4, 2001, and October 7, 2002; *Alumnews*, November 1997, p. 2; *Creightonian*, April 29, 1994, p. 2, September 13, 1996, p. 2, November 1, 1996, p. 1, October 16, 1998, pp. 1, 5, February 4, 2000, p. 1, January 25, 2002, p. 3, and May 3, 2003, pp. 1, 2; Registrar enrollment data.

7. BDM, March 1 and October 4, 1993, December 5, 1994, October 6, 1997, December 6, 1999, March 6 and June 5, 2000, and June 3, 2002; *Creightonian*, February 23, 1996, pp. 1–2, October 10, 1997, p. 1, March 27, 1998, p. 2, December 11, 1998, "Special Section," and March 16, 2001, pp. 1, 2; *Window*, Fall 1997, pp. 13–14; *Creighton University Magazine (CUM)*, Winter 2000, p. 5, and Summer 2002, p. 5; Registrar enrollment data

8. *Alumnews*, November 1992, p. 7 and May 1993, p. 2, and November 1993, p. 3; *Creightonian*, September 10, 1993, p. 3, and November 19, 1993, p. 1.

9. *Alumnews*, November 1990, p. 3, November 1992, p. 7, November 1994, p. 12, August, 1995, p. 12, and November 1996, p. 2; BDM, June 3, 1996, and March 3, 1997; *Creightonian*, April 11, 1997, p. 1.

10. *Creightonian*, April 1, 1977, p. 1, September 10, 1993, p. 3, September 29, 1995, p. 7, and January 23, 2003, p. 4; *Alumnews*, November 1992, p. 7, and November 1995, p. 3; BDM, December 7, 1998.

11. *Alumnews*, November 1992, p. 7, August 1993, p. 3, August 1995, p. 1, February 1996, p. 2, and August 1998, p. 3; BDM, March 7, December 5, 1994, and March 5, 1995; *Creightonian*, September 1, 1995, p. 6, January 26, 1996, p. 4, and October 11, 1996, p. 2.

12. BDM, October 5, 1992, and June 6, 1994; *Creightonian*, February 28, 1992, p. 1, and September 10, 1993, p. 1; *Alumnews*, May 1993, p. 3.

13. BDM, June 6, 1994, October 2 and December 4, 1995, June 6 1996, June 2 and October 6, 1997, and March 2, 1998; *Creightonian*, January 23, 1998, pp. 1, 4, and January 30, 1998, p. 3; Author's recollection.

14. BDM, March 1, 1993, June 6, 1994, October 2 and December 4, 1995, and March 2, 1998; *Alumnews*, October 1981, pp. 4–5, August 1993, p. 4, February 1996, p. 3, May 1996, p. 3, and November 1998, p. 3; *Creightonian*, September 10, 1993, p. 3, April 15, 1994, p. 1, and October 4, 1996, p. 1; *CUM*, Spring 2005, p. 40.

15. *Alumnews*, May 1992, p. 3, and August 1995, pp. 2, 5; *Creightonian*, September 16, 1994, p. 7, and February 18, 2000, p. 5; *Window*, Spring 1997, pp. 4–6.

16. BDM, December 7, 1998, and March 5 and June 4, 2001; *Creightonian*, September 26, 1997, p. 4, November 14, 1997, pp. 1, 5, January 23, 1998, pp. 1, 4, October 16, 1998, pp. 1, 5, January 22, 1999, p. 2, November 5, 1999, p. 2, September 29, 2000, p. 3, and February 1, 2002, p. 3; *Window*, Spring 1997, pp. 6, 10–11; *CUM*, Fall 2001, p. 15.

17. *Creightonian*, February 20, 1970, p. 3, February 10, 1995, p. 1, and August 18, 2000, p. 3; *Alumnews*, May 1994, p. 3, and August 1995, p. 5; BDM, October 4, 1993, June 4, 1994, March 5, 1995, March 5, 2001, and March 4, 2002.

18. BDM, March 3 and June 2, 1997, and October 9, 1998; *Creightonian*, March 1, 1996, pp. 1, 2, March 19, 1999, p. 1, and January 19, 2001, p. 3.

19. BDM, December 2, 1996; *Creightonian*, April 22, 1994, p. 1, April 7, 1995, p. 2, and March 30, 2001, p. 6; http://www.creightontoday.edu, Wednesday-Thursday, June 5–6, 2002.

20. *CUB*, Arts, 1992–94; *Alumnews*, May 1997, p. 3; *CUM*, Winter 2000, p. 9; *Creightonian*, March 2, 2001, pp., 1, 2, November 9, 2001, p. 1, and October 4, 2002, p. 5; Author's recollection.

21. *CUB*, Arts, 1992–94 through 2004–05; *Alumnews*, November 1982, p. 7; *Creightonian*, September 17, 1993, p. 3, February 21, 1997, p. 4, and March 6, 1998, pp. 1, 5, September 11, 1998, p. 3, and November 3, 2000, p. 4.

22. *Creightonian*, April 2, 1993, pp. 1, 2, March 31, 1995, p. 1, and November 21, 1997, supplement section, March 6, 1998, p. 2, and November 10, 2000, p. 4; *Alumnews*, February 1994, p. 2, February 1998, p. 6, and November 1998, p. 3; *Window*, Spring 1998, p. 27; *CUM*, Spring 2003, p. 8.

23. BDM, October 7, 1996; *Creightonian*, September 10, 1993, p. 18, and November 21, 1997,

supplement section; *Alumnews*, August 1995, p. 5; *CUM*, Winter 2000, p. 8; CCAS "Dean's Announcement," October 8, 2003.

24. *CUB*, Arts, 1992–94 through 2003–04; *Creightonian*, December 4, 1992, p. 1, and October 17, 1997, p. 1; Author's recollection.

25. *Creightonian*, January 26, 1996, p. 1, February 2, 1996, pp. 4, 8, February 28, 1997, p. 1, March 7, 1997, p. 1, March 21, 1997, p. 1, September 5, 1997, p. 9, April 24, 1998, pp. 1, 7, February 16, 2001, p. 10, August 30, 2002, p. 1; *CUM*, Winter 1999, p. 12, Spring 2000, pp. 20–21, 40–41, and Spring 2003, p. 55.

26. BDM, October 6, 1997; *Alumnews*, May 1998, p. 8; *CUM*, Fall 1999, p. 8, and Spring 2000, p. 50.

27. *CUB*, CoBA, 1992–94 through 2004–05; *Creightonian*, February 5, 1993, pp., 1, 3; *Alumnews*, August 1993, p. 4; *CUM*, Spring 2000, pp. 26–27.

28. BDM, December 4, 1995; *Alumnews*, February 1996, p. 4, and February 1998, p. 2.

29. *CUM*, Fall 1999, p. 39, Spring 2000, p. 50, Spring 2001, p. 8, and Summer 2002, p. 8; *Creightonian*, November 17, 2000, p. 1.

30. BDM, October 5, 1992, June 7, 1993, June 3, October 7, and December 2, 1996; *CUB*, CoBA, 1990–92; *Creightonian*, September 13, 1996, p. 1; *CUM*, Summer, 2002, p. 8; Registrar enrollment data.

31. BDM, December 4, 1995, March 3, June 2, and October 6, 1997, June 1 and October 9, 1998, and March 6 and October 2, 2000; *Creightonian*, August 30, 1996, p. 1, April 11, 1997, p. 1, and September 5, 1997, p. 4; *Window*, Winter 1996–97, pp. 12–13; *CUM*, Winter 2000, p. 56; Cahill, p. 67; Registrar enrollment data.

32. BDM, June 7, 1993, and October 6, 1997; *CUB*, Nursing, 1992–93 through 2004–05; *Alumnews*, November 1995, p. 5; *Creightonian*, October 2, 1998, p. 6; Registrar enrollment data.

33. *Window*, Spring 1999, pp. 4–5; *Creightonian*, September 17, 1999, p. 1, and September 7, 2000, p. 1; *CUM*, Winter 1999, p. 9, Summer 2001, p. 9, and Spring 2002, p. 9; BDM, March 5 and June 4, 2001; Registrar enrollment data.

34. *CUB*, Graduate, 1992–93 through 2003–04; BDM, December 2, 1996, and October 6, 1997; *Window*, Winter 1993–94, p. 27; *Creightonian*, February 11, 1994, p. 5; Registrar enrollment data.

35. BDM, March 7, 1994, June 5, 1995, and December 1, 1997; *Alumnews*, May 1994, p. 3; *Creightonian*, March 29, 1996, p. 3, and September 17, 1999, p. 1; Registrar enrollment data.

36. BDM, June 5, 1995, and December 1, 1997; *Creightonian*, April 7, 1995, p. 1, April 28, 1995, p. 1, March 29, 1996, p. 3, and February 27, 1998, pp. 1, 4.

37. BDM, December 4, 1995, and June 3, 1996.

38. BDM, June 3, 1996, March 3 and December 1, 1997, and March 1, 1999; *Alumnews*, May 1997, p. 2, and August 1998, p. 3; *CUM*, Fall 1999, p. 4, and Summer 2001, p. 10.

39. *Alumnews*, August 1992, p. 3, May 1993, p. 3,, and May 1994, p. 6; *Window*, Fall 1996, pp. 10–13.

40. BDM, March 1, 1993, October 2, 1995, March 2, 1998, and December 6, 1999; *CUM*, Fall 2002, p. 12; Registrar enrollment data.

41. *CUB*, Pharmacy, 1992–93 through 2003–04; BDM, June 6, 1994, December 2, 1996, March 3 and October 6, 1997, June 7, 1999, and June 5, 2000; *Alumnews*, August 1992, p. 3, November 1995, p. 5, and August 1998, p. 3; *Window*, Winter 1998–99, p. 27.

42. *Alumnews*, May 1994, p. 6, and November 1997, p. 4; *Creightonian*, December 11, 1998, pp. 1, 4; *CUM*, Winter 2000, p. 7, Fall 2001, p. 10, and Spring 2003, p. 10.

43. BDM, March 6, 2000; *Creightonian*, October 29, 1999, p. 1, September 22, 2000, p. 2, November 3, 2000, p. 3, January 26, 2001, p. 3, and November 7, 2003, p. 3; *Alumnews*, Summer 2001, p. 13; *CUM*, Spring 2001, p. 9, Spring 2002, p. 8, and Spring 2003, pp. 8–9.

44. BDM, March 1 and October 4, 1993; *Window*, Spring 1995, pp. 10–12.

45. *Alumnews*, August 1992, p. 3, November 1993, pp. 2, 4, and May 1997, p. 3; BDM, October 7, 1996, and March 3 and June 2, 1997.

46. BDM, March 3 and October 6, 1997, and March 2, 1998; *Alumnews*, February 1998, p. 5.

47. BDM, June 2, 1997, March 2 and June 1, 1998, October 2, 2000, and March 4, 2002; *Alumnews*, August 1998, p. 6.

48. BDM, March 1, 1993, December 5, 1994, March 6 and June 5, 1995, October 7, 1996, June 4, 2001, and March 4 and June 3, 2002; *CUM*, February 1995, p. 2, and Fall 2002, p. 5; *Creightonian*, March 8, 2002, pp. 1, 2.

49. BDM, March 7, 1994, and March 3 and June 2, 1997; *Alumnews*, August 1994, p. 2, and August 1996, p. 2.

50. BDM, December 5, 1988, June 3, 1996, and March 6, June 1, and October 9, 1998; *Alumnews*, February 1998, p. 2, and August 1998, p. 2.

51. Registrar enrollment data; *Creightonian*, September 17, 1999, p. 1, and October 29, 1999, p. 5; *CUM*, Spring 2003, p. 10; *Omaha World-Herald*, November 9, 2003, p. 9B.

52. *Alumnews*, August 1993, p. 4; BDM, June 1 and October 9, 1998, and March 5, 2001; *Window*, Spring 1997, p. 24; *CUM*, Spring 2001, p. 7, and Spring 2003, p. 5.

53. *Creightonian*, February 25, 1994, p. 1, September 2, 1994, p. 3, September 20, 1996, p. 3, November 1, 1996, p. 1, March 19, 1999, p. 1, February 4, 2000, p. 4, April 28, 2000, p. 2, October 13, 2000, pp. 1, 2, February 1, 2002, pp. 1, 2, and April 25, 2003, pp. 1, 4.

54. *Creightonian*, March 29, 1996, p. 1, May 3, 1996, p. 4, February 14, 1997, p. 1, April 18, 1997, pp. 1, 5, September 19, 1997, p. 1, September 24, 1999, p. 1, October 5, 2001, p. 3, October 1, 2002, p. 1, and May 2, 2003, p. 4; BDM, October 4, 1999, and October 2, 2000.

55. *Creightonian*, February 5, 1993, pp., 4, 5, September 17, 1993, p. 5, October 1, 1993, p. 1, December 9, 1994, p. 2, January 20, 1995, p. 2, February 3, 1995, p. 2, February 9, 1996, p. 5, October 25, 1996, p. 1, August 18, 2000, p. 2, January 23, 2003, p. 3, February 14, 2003, p. 1 and November 7, 2003, p. 3.

56. *Creightonian*, February 11, 1994, p. 2, April 22, 1994, pp. 1, 6, February 24, 1995, p. 1, March 24, 1995, p. 1, August 30, 1996, p. 11, September 13, 1996, p. 10, February 7, 1997, p. 4, February 14, 1997, p. 1, October 10, 1997, p. 1, March 20, 1998, p. 9, September 11, 1998, p. 11, October 9, 1998, p. 1, March 3, 2000, p. 3, May 3, 2002, p. 3, and April 25, 2003, p. 2; *Alumnews*, May 1994, p. 3; *CUM*, Fall 2002, p. 12; BDM, June 6, 1994, and June 2, 1997.

57. *Creightonian*, March 25, 1994, p. 2, and May 3, 1996, p. 10; BDM, June 6, 1994, June 5 and December 4, 1995, June 3, 1996, June 2 and October 6, 1997, and June 1 and October 9, 1998; *CUM*, Spring 2002, p. 5.

58. BDM, June 2 and December 1, 1997, and June 7 and October 4, 1999; *Creightonian*, March 20, 1998, p. 9; *Alumnews*, August 1998, p. 3; Athletic department financial reports, 1992–2000.

59. *Creightonian*, March 18, 1994, p. 6, September 1, 1995, p. 14, September 29, 2000, p. 11, and April 2, 2004, p. 11; *Media Guide, 2004–05*, for women's volleyball and soccer.

60. *Creightonian*, Sept 18, 1992, p. 10, and September 17, 1993, p. 1; *Media Guide, 2004–05*, for women's softball and basketball.

61. *Creightonian*, September 17, 1993, p. 1, and January 21, 1994, p. 1; *Baseball Media Guide*.

62. *Creightonian*, April 23, 1993, p. 1, September 10, 1993, p. 23, September 18, 1998, p. 1, February 9, 2001, p. 1, September 30, 2003, p. 3, and April 23, 2004, p. 12; BDM, March 1, 1999; *Soccer Media Guide*.

63. *Creightonian*, March 4, 1994, p. 1, April 15, 1994, p. 14, and March 20, 1998, p. 7; *Men's Basketball Media Guide, 2004-05*.

64. *Creightonian*, February 12, 1988, p. 1; *Alumnews*, November 1996, p. 2, November 1997, p. 2, and November 1998, p. 3; *CUM*, Fall 1999, pp. 5–6, and Winter 1999, pp. 7, 10, 15; BDM, June 7, 1999, and June 5, 2000.

65. BDM, June 7 and October 4, 1999; *CUM*, Fall 1999, pp. 5–6.

66. BDM, October 1991, and March 5 and June 4, 2001; *Creightonian*, November 30, 1990, pp. 1–2, January 28, 1994, p. 4, October 7, 1994, pp. 4, 5, October 14, 1994, p. 4, March 19, 1999, p. 1, November 17, 2000, p. 1, March 16, 2001, pp. 1, 2, and September 7, 2001, pp. 1, 2; *CUM*, Spring 2000, p. 6, Summer 2001, p. 8, and Spring 2002, p. 5.

67. *Creightonian*, May 3, 2002, p. 4, and November 15, 2002, pp. 4–5; *CUM*, Spring 2003, p. 5

68. BDM, December 4, 2000, and March 5 and June 4, 2001; Registrar enrollment data.

69. BDM, June 4, 2001, and June 3 and October 7, 2002; Registrar enrollment data; CCAS "Dean's Announcement," October 8, 2003.

70. BDM, December 3, 2001, October 7, 2002, and March 3, 2003; Registrar enrollment data.

71. BDM, October 6, 1997, June 7, 1999, and March 6 and October 2, 2000; *CUM*, Summer 2001, pp. 38–39; *Creightonian*, January 25, 2002, p. 4.

72. *Alumnews*, May 1997, p. 5; *Creightonian*, September 7, 2001, pp. 1, 6, January 24, 2003, p. 1, and May 2, 2003, p. 1; *CUM*, Summer 2001, pp. 38–39, and Spring 2003, p. 56.

73. BDM, June 7, 1999, March 5, 2001, and March 4, 2002; *Creightonian*, February 18, 2000, p. 1, January 31, 2003, p. 1, and September 3, 2004, p. 3; *CUM*, Spring 2003, p. 8; Davis Square dedication plaque.

74. Cover letter from John P. Schlegel, S.J., March 19, 2003, and "Project 125 Strategic Plan, March 2003."

Bibliography

Archives

Catholic Archdiocese of Omaha
  Materials pertaining to the creation of Creighton University, and Holy Family and St. John's parishes.
College of Saint Mary
  Limited materials related to the era of the corporate college.
Cowboy Hall of Fame, Oklahoma City, Okla.
  Edward Creighton file.
Creighton University
  Records and publications related to all schools from their inception.
Creighton University, President's Vertical File, President's Office
  Minute books of the Trustees, the Lay Regents, and the Board of Directors, committee reports, and biographical and events files.
Douglas County Historical Society
  Possesses biographical and institutional files on the Creighton family and the University from most of Omaha's historic newspapers, but especially the *Omaha World-Herald* clipping file, 1907–1984.
Duchesne Academy
  Limited materials related to the era of the corporate college.
Midwest Jesuit Archives, St. Louis, Missouri
  Records and publications of the Missouri Province of the Society of Jesus from its inception and continuing as the depository for the successor Detroit, Chicago, and Wisconsin provinces.
Nebraska State Historical Society
  Probate records, incorporation records, Nebraska manuscript censuses, and county histories.
Ohio Historical Society
  Birth, marriage, and death records.
The Smithsonian, Archives Center, National Museum of American History
  Charles H. Brown, "My Experiences on the Plains in 1861 in assisting in the construction of the first telegraph line across the continent." Unpublished manuscript, Western Union Telegraph Company Records.
Western Reserve Historical Society
  Ohio manuscript censuses.

Books Cited

Andreas, A. T. *History of the State of Nebraska.* Two vols. Chicago: Western Historical Company, 1882.

Archdeacon, Thomas J. *Becoming American: An Ethnic History.* New York: Free Press, 1983.

Athearn, Robert G. *Union Pacific Country.* Chicago: Rand McNally, 1971.

Boro, Carolyn J., and Mead, Beverly T. *A Century of Teaching and Healing: The First One Hundred Years of the Creighton University School of Medicine.* Omaha: Creighton University School of Medicine, 1991.

Bowdern, S.J., Thomas S. "The Graduate School of The Creighton University" and "St. John-Before-the-Latin Gate." In *The Creighton University: Its Story,* edited by Clare McDermott. Omaha: Creighton University, 1937.

Beel, Marianne Brinda, ed. *A History of Cherry County, Nebraska.* Cherry County Centennial Committee, 1986.

Bowler, Sister Mary Mariella. *A History of Catholic Colleges for Women in the United States of America.* Washington, D.C.: Catholic University of America Press, 1933.

Bratt, John. *Trails of Yesterday.* Lincoln: University of Nebraska Press, 1980.

Burkley, Frank. *The Faded Frontier.* Omaha: Burkley Envelope and Printing Co., 1935.

Cahill, S.J., Neil. *Creighton University College of Business Administration: The First Seventy-five Years.* Omaha: Creighton University College of Business Administration, 1996.

Caldwell, Howard W. *Education in Nebraska.* Washington, D.C.: Government Printing Office, 1902.

Casper, S.J., Henry W. *The History of the Catholic Church in Nebraska.* Three Vols. Milwaukee: Bruce Publishing, 1960–66.

Cheyenne County History Book Committee. *History of Cheyenne County, Nebraska.* privately published, 1987.

Creighton, Thomas Russell. *Creighton—Its Origins as a Surname.* New Haven, Conn.: privately published, 1960.

Croghan, R.S.M., Sister Mary Edmund. *Sisters of Mercy of Nebraska, 1864–1910.* Washington, D.C.: Catholic University of America Press, 1942.

Dale, Edward Everette. *Cow Country.* Norman: University of Oklahoma Press, 1942.

——. *The Range Cattle Industry.* Norman: University of Oklahoma Press, 1930.

Desmond, Humphrey J. *The A.P.A. Movement.* Washington, D.C.: New Century Press, 1912.

Dowling, S.J., Michael P. *Creighton University, Reminiscences of the First Twenty-Five Years.* Omaha: Burkley Printing, 1903.

——. *John A. Creighton: Benefactor of Mankind.* Omaha: Creighton University, unpublished manuscript, 1908.

Draper, Solomon. *Historical Sketch of Knox County, Nebraska.* Niobrara, Neb.: Pioneer Publishing House, 1876.

Dustin, Dorothy Devereux. *Omaha & Douglas County: A Panoramic History.* Woodland Hills, Calif.: Windsor Publications, 1980.

Ellis, John Tracy. ed. *Documents of American Catholic History, 1866 to 1966.* Wilmington, Del.: Michael Glazier, 1987.

——. *American Catholics and the Intellectual Life.* Chicago: Heritage Foundation, 1956.

Evans, Lucylle H. *The Good Samaritan of the Northwest, Anthony Ravalli, S.J., 1812-1884.* Stevensville, Mont.: Montana Creative Consultants, 1981.

Farrell, S.J., Ph.D., Allan P. *The Jesuit Code of Liberal Education.* Milwaukee: Bruce Publishing, 1938.

Fitzgerald, S.J., Paul A. *The Governance of Jesuit Colleges in the United States, 1920-1970*. Notre Dame: University of Notre Dame Press, 1984.

Fitzpatrick, Edward A., ed. *St. Ignatius and the Ratio Studiorum*. New York: McGraw-Hill, 1933.

Fry, Edwin. "The Story of Creighton." In Danny Liska, *Bigfoot 7: Our Valleys, the Niobrara and Verdigris*. Bogotá, Columbia: Relikasa, Ltda, 1986.

Furay, S.J., John B. *Reminiscences of John B. Furay*. Omaha: Creighton University, unpublished manuscript, 1950.

Ganss, S.J., George E. *The Jesuit Educational Tradition and Saint Louis University: Some Bearings for the University's Sesquicentennial, 1818-1968*. St. Louis: Saint Louis University, 1969.

Garraghan, S.J., Ph.D., Gilbert J. *The Jesuits of the Middle United States*. 3 vols. New York: American Press, 1938.

Gleason, Philip. *Contending with Modernity: Catholic Higher Education in the Twentieth Century*. New York: Oxford University Press, 1995.

Grether, E. T. "The Development of AACSB Core Curriculum." In *The American Association of Collegiate Schools of Business, 1916–1966*. Homewood, Ill.: Richard D. Irwin, 1966.

Haynes, James B. *History of the Trans-Mississippi and International Exposition*. Omaha, 1910.

Historia Domas. December 6, 1877, to August 31, 1883, and summer 1911 to May 1, 1930. Omaha: Creighton University, unpublished manuscript.

House Consultors Minute Book. 1888–1928. Omaha: Creighton University, Unpublished manuscript.

Holland, Kathryn Margaret. *A History of the Omaha Public School System*. Omaha: Creighton University, unpublished M.A. thesis, 1933.

Jahn, Walter Roger. *My Memories*. Omaha: Privately published, no date [1993].

Johnson, Allen, and Malone, Dumas., eds. *Dictionary of American Biography*. New York: Charles Scribner's Sons, 1930.

Kaufman, Martin. "American Medical Education." In Ronald L. Numbers, ed. *The Education of American Physicians*. Berkeley: University of California Press, 1980.

Keefer, Louis E. *Scholars in Foxholes: The Story of the Army Specialized Training Program in World War II*. Jefferson, N.C.: McFarland, 1988.

Kelley, S.J., William F. *The Jesuit Order and Higher Education in the United States, 1789–1966*. Milwaukee: Wisconsin Jesuit Province, 1966.

Kirby, Maurice William. *History of Creighton University, 1878–1926*. Omaha: Creighton University, unpublished M.A. thesis, 1954.

Kliebard, Herbert M. *The Struggle for the American Curriculum*. Boston: Routlage & Kagan Paul, 1986.

Knoll, Robert E. *Prairie University: A History of the University of Nebraska*. Lincoln: University of Nebraska Press, 1995.

Kremers, Edward, and Urdang, George. *History of Pharmacy*. 2d ed. Philadelphia: J. B. Lippincott, 1951.

Lass, William E. *From the Missouri to the Great Salt Lake: An Account of Overland Freighting*. Lincoln: Nebraska State Historical Society, 1992.

Leahy, S.J., William P. *Adapting to America: Catholics, Jesuits, and Higher Education In the Twentieth Century*. Washington, D.C.: Georgetown University Press, 1991.

Ludmerer, Kenneth M. *Learning to Heal: The Development of American Medical Education*. New York: Basic Books, 1985.

Lyons, Gene M., and Masland, John W. *Education and Military Leadership*. Princeton, N.J.: Princeton University Press, 1959.

McCluskey, S.J., Neil G. *The Catholic University, A Modern Appraisal.* Notre Dame: University of Notre Dame Press, 1970.

McDermott, Clare., ed. *The Creighton University: Its Story, 1878–1937.* Omaha: Creighton University, 1937.

McGucken, S.J., William J. *The Jesuits and Education.* New York: Bruce Publishing, 1932.

McIntosh, Charles Barron. *The Nebraska Sandhills: The Human Landscape.* Lincoln: University of Nebraska Press, 1996.

Mahoney, Kathleen A. *Catholic Higher Education in Protestant America: The Jesuits and Harvard in the Age of the University.* Baltimore: Johns Hopkins University Press, 2003.

Marsden, George M. *The Soul of the American University: From Protestant Establishment to Established Nonbelief.* New York: Oxford University Press, 1994.

Millet, Allan, and Maslowski, Peter. *For the Common Defense: A Military History of the United States.* New York: Free Press, 1984.

Miller, Mark. *The Singing Wire.* Philadelphia: John G. Winston, 1953.

Morton, J. Sterling. *Illustrated History of Nebraska.* Three vols. Lincoln: Jacob North, 1907.

Mullens, S.J., P. A. *Creighton. Biographical Sketches of Edward Creighton, John A. Creighton, Mary Lucretia Creighton, Sarah Emily Creighton.* Omaha: Creighton University, 1901.

Muller, S.J., Herman J. *The University of Detroit, 1877–1977: A Centennial History.* Detroit: University of Detroit, 1976.

Nelson, Arvid E. *The AK-SAR-BEN Story.* Lincoln, Neb.: Johnson Publishing, 1967.

Neiberg, Michael S. *Making Citizen-Soldiers.* Cambridge: Harvard University Press, 2000.

Olson, James C., and Naugle, Ronald C. *History of Nebraska.* 3d ed. Lincoln: University of Nebraska Press, 1997.

Omaha Stockyards: A Century of Marketing Commemorative Book, 1884–1984. Omaha: privately published, 1984.

Orr, Richard. *O & CB: Streetcars of Omaha and Council Bluffs.* Omaha: Richard Orr, 1996.

Ostdiek, Joseph H. *Catholic Education in Omaha, Past, Present and Future.* Omaha: Creighton University, unpublished M.A. thesis, 1927.

Pelzer, Louis. *The Cattlemen's Frontier.* Glendale, Calif.: Arthur H. Clark, 1936.

Purkey, Elton. *Perkey's Nebraska Place-Names.* Lincoln: Nebraska State Historical Society, 1982.

Plough, Rev. James Howard. *Catholic Colleges and the Catholic Education Association: The Foundation and the Early Years of the CEA, 1899–1919.* Notre Dame: University of Notre Dame, unpublished dissertation, 1967.

Power, Edward J. *Catholic Higher Education in America: A History.* New York: Appleton-Century-Crofts, 1972.

Rader, Benjamin G. *American Sports.* Englewood Cliffs, N.J.: Prentice-Hall, 1983.

Reece, Charles S. *A History of Cherry County, Nebraska.* Simeon, Neb.: privately published, 1945.

Reichmuth, S.J., Roland J. *St. John's Church, 1887–1987.* Omaha: Creighton University, 1987.

Reinert, S.J., Paul C. *Faculty Tenure in Colleges and Universities From 1900 to 1940.* St. Louis: St. Louis University Press, 1946.

Reynolds, Edward D. *Jesuits for the Negro.* New York: American Press, 1949.

Rigge, S.J., William F. *Log Book (1879–1927).* Omaha: Creighton University, unpublished manuscript.

———. *The First Faculty.* Omaha: Creighton University, unpublished manuscript, 1903.

———. *Year One at Creighton.* Omaha: Creighton University, unpublished manuscript, 1903.

Roseboom, Eugene H., and Weisenburger, Francis P. *A History of Ohio.* Columbus: Ohio State Archaeological and Historical Society, 1961.

Rudolph, Frederick. *The American College and University: A History*. New York: Alfred A. Knopf, 1962.

———. *Curriculum: A History of the American Undergraduate Course of Study Since 1636*. San Francisco: Jossey-Bass, 1977.

Sandifer, R.S.M., Sister M. Ruth. *The Construction of a Four-Year Teacher Training Curriculum for the Sisters of Mercy in the Province of Omaha*. Omaha: Creighton University, unpublished M.A. thesis, 1936.

Savage, James W., and Bell, John T. *History of the City of Omaha*. New York: Munsell & Company, 1894.

Schwickerath, S.J., Robert. *Jesuit Education, Its History and Principles Viewed in the Light of Modern Educational problems*. St. Louis: B. Herder, 1903.

Smith, Jeffrey Harrison. *The Omaha DePorres Club*. Omaha: Creighton University, unpublished M.A. thesis, 1967.

Smith, Ronald A. *The Rise of Big-Time College Athletics*. Oxford: Oxford University Press, 1988.

Sorensen, Barbara. *A King and a Prince Among Pioneers: Edward and John A. Creighton*. Omaha: Creighton University, unpublished M.A. thesis, 1961.

Sorenson, Alfred. *History of Omaha From Pioneer Days to the Present Time*. Omaha: Gibson, Miller & Richardson, Printers, 1889.

———. *The Story of Omaha From the Pioneer Days to the Present Time*. 3d ed. Omaha: National Printing Company, 1923.

Spring, Agnes Wright. *Seventy Years: A Panoramic History of the Wyoming Stock Growers Association*. Gillette, Wyo.: Wyoming Stock Growers Association, 1942.

Stevens, Robert. *Law School: Legal Education in America from the 1850s to the 1980s*. Chapel Hill: University of North Carolina Press, 1983.

Storr, Richard J. *The Beginnings of Graduate Education in America*. Reprint. New York: Arno Press & The New York Times, 1969.

Szmrecsanyi, Steven. *History of the Catholic Church in Northeast Nebraska*. Omaha: Catholic Voice Publishing, 1983.

Thompson, Robert Luther. *Wiring a Continent: The History of the Telegraph Industry in the United States, 1832-1866*. Princeton: Princeton University Press, 1947.

Thompson, Tommy R. *The History of the University of Nebraska at Omaha, 1908–1983*. Dallas: Taylor Publishing, 1983.

Vosper, James M. *A History of Selected Factors in the Development of Creighton University*. Lincoln: University of Nebraska, unpublished dissertation, 1976.

Vossen, Dorothy E. *Nursing at Creighton University: A History, 1899–1985*. Omaha: Creighton University School of Nursing, 1991.

Williams, Michael. *American Catholics in the War: National Catholic War Council, 1917-1921*. New York: Macmillan, 1921.

Wolfe, William G. *Stories of Guernsey County, Ohio*. Cambridge, Ohio: self-published, 1943.

Bluejay, 1924-1941; 1949–Present.

Creighton Alumnews, 1967–1999.

Creighton Alumnus, 1959–1964.

Creighton Chronicle, 1909–1922.

Creighton Courier, 1912–1920.

Creighton University Magazine, 1999–Present.

The Creightonian, 1922–Present.

P.S.: A Postscript to Education, 1964–1971 (continued and bound with *Alumnus*, therefore cited as *Alumnus*).

Shadows, 1922–Present

Window, 1984–1999.

Betts, John Rickard. "Darwinism, Evolution and American Catholic Thought, 1860–1900," *Catholic Historical Review*, 45 (July 1959), pp. 161–85.

Bouchier, Nancy B. "Let Us Take Care of Our Field: The National Association for Physical Education of College Women and World War II," *Journal of Sport History*, vol. 25 (Spring 1998), pp. 65–86.

Brosnahan, S.J., Timothy. "President Eliot and Jesuit Colleges: A Defense," *Sacred Heart Review* (January 1900), pp. 8–10.

———. "The Carnegie Foundation for the Advancement of Teaching—Its Aims and Tendency," Catholic Education Association *Bulletin*, 7 (August 1911), pp. 119–59.

Burns, Robert H. "The Famous Heart Ranch," *The Westerner*, VIII (July 1945), pp. 16-8.

———. "The Laramie Plains," *The Westerner*, VIII (May 1945), pp. 13, 38–40.

Burrows, S.J., Alexander J. "Attitude of Catholics Towards Higher Education," Catholic Education Association *Bulletin*, 16 (November 1919), pp. 159–74.

Coad, Ralph G. "Irish Pioneers of Nebraska," *Nebraska History Magazine*, vol. XVII (July–September 1936), pp. 171–77.

Cole, Johnathon R., and Lipton, James A. "The Reputations of American Medical Schools," *Social Forces*, vol. 55 (March 1977), pp. 662–84.

Copus, S.J., J. E. "The Edward Creighton Institute," *The Woodstock Letters*, Vol. 34, 1905, pp. 354–57.

David, Christine. "The History of the Psychology Department at Creighton University," Creighton University, unpublished student paper, no date [1989].

Dodds, Harold W. "Education in Uniform: The Army and Navy Programs for the Colleges," *Atlantic Monthly* 171 (February 1943), pp. 41–45.

Dowling, S.J., M. P. "John A. Creighton, Founder," *The Woodstock Letters*, vol. 33 (1904), pp. 64–73.

Dudley, Richard E. "Nebraska Public School Education, 1890–1910," *Nebraska History*, Vol. 54 (Spring 1973), pp. 65–90.

Eliot, Charles W. "Recent Changes in Secondary Education," *Atlantic Monthly* 84 (October 1899), pp. 433–44.

Ellis, John Tracy. "No Complacency," *America*, Vol. 95 (April 7, 1956), pp. 14–25.

Everett, Ruth. "Jesuit Educators and Modern Colleges," *The Arena*, 23 (1900), pp. 647–53.

Fogarty, Frank P. "The Story of Creighton," Souvenir Program of the Golden Jubilee, 1953.

Frankino, Steven P. and Crisman, C. Benjamin. "An Historical Look at the Creighton University School of Law," *Creighton Law Review* Vol. 9 (1975), pp. 228–35.

Goodchild, Lester F. "The Turning Point in American Jesuit Education: The Standardization Controversy Between the Jesuits and the North Central Association, 1915-1940." *History of Higher Education Annual*, 6 (1986), pp. 81–113.

Hawley, Robert G. "The Army Quits the Colleges," *Harpers*, April 1944, pp. 419–25.

Keefer, Louis. "Exceptional Young American Soldiers and Sailors on College Campuses In World War II," *Prologue*, 1992, no. 4, pp. 375–83.

Koller, Joe. "Edward Creighton, Singing Wire Chief," *Golden West*, vol. 1 (September 1965), pp. 16–19, 72–73.

Mahnken, Norbert R. "Ogallala—Nebraska's Cowboy Capital," *Nebraska History*, vol. XXVIII (April-June 1947), pp. 85–109.

Martin, Charles W. "Omaha 1868–1869: Selections from Letters of Joseph Barker." *Nebraska History*, vol. 59 (Winter 1978), pp. 501–25.

Muntsch, S.J., Albert. "Coeducation From A Catholic Standpoint," Catholic Education Association *Bulletin*, 13 (November 1916), pp. 352–66.

Newton, Mrs. M. B. "History of Education in Omaha." *Transactions and Reports of the Nebraska State Historical Society*, vol. III (1892), pp. 59–66.

Nielson, P. Raymond. "Edward Creighton and the Pacific Telegraph," *Mid-America: An Historical Review*, vol. XXIV (January 1942), pp. 61–74.

Nusse, C. Joseph. "The Introduction of Sociology at the Catholic University of America, 1895–1915," *Catholic Historical Review*, vol. LXXXVII (October 2001), pp. 643–61.

"Reminiscences of Early Omaha," *Nebraska History Magazine*, vol. 17 (July-September 1936), pp. 193–214.

Rigge, William Francis. "Memoirs of Creighton University, 1879–1927," *Creighton Alumnus*, serialized December 1937–June 1939.

Schlegel, Donald M. "The Creighton or McCraren Family, Catholic Pioneers in Ohio And Omaha." *Barquilla de la Santa Maria, Bulletin of the Catholic Record Society—Diocese of Columbus* [Ohio], vol. XIX (October 1994), pp. 77–83 and vol. XIX (November 1994), pp. 85–92.

Sorenson, Alfred. "Biographical Sketch of Edward Creighton," *Nebraska History Magazine*, vol. XVII (July-September 1936), pp. 163–69.

Spiller, Robert F. "Higher Education and the War." *Journal of Higher Education*, vol. 50 (July-August 1979), pp. 514–25.

Vacanti, Charles, J. History of Dentistry. Creighton University, unpublished paper, 1983.

Wagoner, Jennings L., and Baxter, Robert L. "Higher Education Goes to War: The University of Virginia's Response to World War II," *Virginia Magazine of History and Biography*, vol. 100 (1992), pp. 399–428.

Wood, A. B. "The Coad Brothers: Panhandle Cattle Kings," *Nebraska History*, vol. XIX (January–March 1938), pp. 28–43.

Index

Morton, J. Sterling, 7, 44
Mother's Day, 205, 296
Mount Saint Mary Academy, 37
movies, 146, 155, 324–25
Mueffels, Joseph, 72
Mulhall, John J., 267
Mulhall, Margaret, 267
Mulholland, Edward, 213
Mullaney, Eugene P., 148
Mullany, Leo H., 152
Mullen, Arthur F., 142, 204
Mullen, Carroll R., 198
Mullen, J. F., 92
Muller, Cecil, 218
Mullin, John, Mrs., 142
multidisciplinary programs, 420
Mundelein, George, Cardinal, 148
Murphy, Edward D., 196
Murphy, James, 153
Murphy, Joseph P., 218
Murphy, Kathryn O'Keefe, 185
Murphy, Thomas, 268–69, 312
Murphy, Walter P., 233
Murray, Betty, 300
Murray, Robert, 405
music programs
    in early years, 56, 59, 86, 88
    in 10s, 108–9
    in 20s and 30s, 149, 159, 201–2, 218
    in 40s, 253
    in 50s, 297
    in 60s, 345
    in 90s, 422

Nachtigall, J. M., 113
Naismith, James, 114
Naphtaline & Natural Soap Company, 19
Nash, Catherine, 173
Nash, Emma Creighton, 22
Nash, Frederick, 22
National Alumni Board, 409
National Association of Intercollegiate Athletics,
    Midwestern League, 305
National Catholic Intercollegiate Association,
    305
National Catholic War Council, 126
National Catholic Welfare Conference, 273–74
National Collegiate Athletic Association
    (NCAA), 92, 127, 406, 437
National Defense Education Act, 277
National Dental Education Council, 187
National Education Association, Committee of
    Ten, 82
National Endowment for the Humanities, 393
National Eucharistic Congress, 148
National Institutes of Health, 295, 395
National Medical Enterprises, 433
National Science Foundation, 313, 344
National Youth Administration, 162

Native Americans, 150, 359, 366, 420, 429–30,
    440
Natural Family Planning Education and
    Research Center, 394
Naval Reserve, 224
Nebraska Association of Independent Colleges,
    365
Nebraska Education Facilities Authority, 365
Nebraska Pharmaceutical Association, 182
Neihardt, John, 146
Nenemen, Jack, 362
Nestlè boycott, 401
Neville, Rosemary, 290
Newman Movement, 163
Newton, Howard, 181–82
Newton, Josephine, 202
Nielson, Clayton D., 266
Nielson, P. Raymond, 258
Niemer, William, 353
nine-year rule, 394
non-Catholic students
    in early years, 43
    in 20s and 30s, 152–53, 164–65, 206
    in 40s, 232, 240
    in 50s, 291
    in 60s, 339
nondiscrimination. *See* minorities
Noonan, Herbert C. "Butch," 272
Nordberg, John A., 406
North Central Association, 123, 170–71
North Central Intercollegiate Conference, 216
Northwestern Bell Telephone Company, 265,
    311–12, 316
Nue, Harold N., 293
nursing school
    in early years, 171–72
    in 20s and 30s, 172–75
    in 40s, 229, 247–48
    in 50s, 288–90
    in 60s, 356–57
    in 80s, 384–87
    in 90s, 425–26

Oblates of Mary Immaculate, 314, 401
O'Brien, Edward A., 42, 45
O'Brien, Pat, 243
O'Brien, Richard L., 394, 432
O'Brien, Johanna, 37
Observatory, 53, 100, 251, 282
O'Connell, Ella, 23
O'Connell, John, 23
O'Connor, Agnes, 25, 62
O'Connor, James, 29, 36–38, 40, 47, 50, 60–61,
    69–70
O'Connor, Michael J., 92
O'Connor, Michael P., 63
O'Connor, Thomas, 16
O'Connor Hall, 101, 148, 248
O'Donnell, Laurence and Kathryn, 339